A Computer Science Tapestry

Exploring Programming and Computer Science
with C++

W9-AZP-624

McGraw-Hill Series in Computer Science

Senior Consulting Editor
C. L. Liu, *National Tsing Hua University*

Consulting Editor
Allen B. Tucker, *Bowdoin College*

Fundamentals of Computing and Programming
Computer Organization and Architecture
Systems and Languages
Theoretical Foundations
Software Engineering and Databases
Artificial Intelligence
Networks, Parallel and Distributed Computing
Graphics and Visualization
The MIT Electrical and Computer Science Series

Fundamentals of Computing and Programming

*Abelson and Sussman: *Structure and Interpretation of Computer Programs*
Astrachan: *A Computer Science Tapestry: Exploring Programming and Computer Science with C++*
Bailey: *Java Elements: Principles of Programming in Java*
Bailey: *Java Structures: Data Structures in Java for the Principled Programmer*
Blank and Barnes: *The Universal Machine*
Cohoon/Davidson: *C++ Program Design*
*Cormen: *An Introduction to Algorithms*
Kamin: *An Introduction to Computer Science Using Java*
Fischer, Ross, and Eggert: *Applied Programming in C*
Sahni: *Data Structures, Algorithms and Applications in C++*
Sahni: *Data Structures, Algorithms and Applications in Java*
*Springer and Friedman: *Scheme and the Art of Programming*
Uckan: *Problem Solving Using C*
Wu: *An Introduction to Object-Oriented Programming with Java*
Wu: *An Introduction to Programming: An Object-Oriented Approach with C++*

*Co-published by the MIT Press and The McGraw-Hill Companies, Inc.

A Computer Science Tapestry

Exploring Programming and Computer Science with C++

Second Edition

Owen L. Astrachan
Duke University

Boston Burr Ridge, IL Dubuque, IA Madison, WI New York San Francisco St. Louis
Bankok Bogotá Caracas Lisbon London Madrid
Mexico City Milan New Delhi Seoul Singapore Sydney Taipei Toronto

McGraw-Hill Higher Education

A Division of The **McGraw-Hill** Companies

A COMPUTER SCIENCE TAPESTRY
EXPLORING PROGRAMMING AND COMPUTER SCIENCE WITH C++
Copyright ©2000, 1997 by The McGraw-Hill Companies, Inc. All rights reserved. Printed in the United States of America. Except as permitted under the United States Copyright Act of 1976, no part of this publication may be reproduced or distributed in any form or by any means, or stored in a data base or retrieval system, without the prior written permission of the publisher.

This book is printed on acid-free paper.

.   4 5 6 7 8 9 0 DOC/DOC   0 9 8 7 6 5 4 3 2 1

ISBN 0-07-232203-9

Vice president/Editor-in-Chief: *Kevin T. Kane*
Publisher: *Thomas Casson*
Executive editor: *Elizabeth A. Jones*
Developmental editor: *Emily J. Gray*
Marketing manager: *John T. Wannemacher*
Project manager: *Amy Hill*
Senior production supervisor: *Heather D. Burbridge*
Freelance design coordinator: *Mary Christianson*
Cover freelance designer: *Kristin A. Kalnes*
Cover image: *Gujarat 1880/Planet Art: Textiles of India*
Photo research coordinator: *Sharon Miller*
Supplement coordinator: *Rose M. Range*
Compositor: *Techsetters, Inc.*
Typeface: *10/12 Times Roman*
Printer: *R. R. Donnelley & Sons Company*

Library of Congress Cataloging-in-Publication Data

Astrachan, Owen L.
    A computer science tapestry : exploring programming and computer
science with C++ / Owen L. Astrachan. – 2nd ed.
    p. cm.
    ISBN 0-07-232203-9
    1. C++ (Computer program language)   2. Computer programming.
I. Title.
QA76.73.C153A83   2000
005.13'3–dc21   99-36139
                                                                  CIP

http://www.mhhe.com

About the Author

Owen L. Astrachan is Associate Professor of the Practice of Computer Science at Duke University and the department's Director of Undergraduate Studies for Teaching and Learning. After receiving his A. B. degree from Dartmouth College, he taught high school for seven years before returning to graduate school. He received his Ph.D. in computer science from Duke in 1992. Professor Astrachan was a member of the Duke programming team that placed fourth in the world in the ACM programming contest in 1989 and coached the third-place team in 1994. He was the chief reader for the Advanced Placement computer science exam from 1990 to 1994. Professor Astrachan has written many technical and pedagogical articles and has been the principal investigator in three NSF-sponsored educational projects: "The Applied Apprenticeship Approach: An Object-Oriented/Object-Based Framework for CS2," "CURIOUS: Center for Undergraduate Education and Research: Integration through Performance and Visualization," and "Using and Developing Design Patterns." A well-regarded teacher, Professor Astrachan received the 1995 Robert B. Cox Distinguished Teaching in Science Award.

To my teachers, colleagues, and friends, especially to those who are all three, for educating, arguing, laughing, and helping.

To Laura and Ethan

Contents

2 PROGRAM AND CLASS CONSTRUCTION: EXTENDING THE FOUNDATION

3 DESIGN, USE, AND ANALYSIS: EXTENDING THE FOUNDATION

H How to: Use the Graphics Classes in `canvas.h`   795

I How to: Cope with C++ Environments   817

List of Programs

Preface

The Tapestry Viewed from Afar

This book is designed for a first course[1] in computer science that uses C++ as the language by which programming is studied. My goal in writing the book has not been to cover the syntax of a large language like C++, but to leverage the best features of the language using sound practices of programming and pedagogy in the study of computer science and software design. My intent is that mastering the material presented here will provide:

- A strong grounding in the analysis, construction, and design of programs and programming.
- A means for honing problem-solving skills associated with the study of computer programming and a taste of both the science and engineering aspects of programming.
- An introduction to computer science that gives the student more of an idea of what the discipline is about than most introductory programming texts.

In particular, this is a book designed to teach programming using C++, not a book designed to teach C++. Nevertheless, I expect students who use this book will become reasonably adept C++ programmers. Object-oriented programming is not a programmer's panacea, although it can make some jobs much easier. To mix metaphors, learning to program is a hard task, no matter how you slice it—it takes time to master, just as bread takes time to rise.

The material here is grounded in the concept that the study of computer science should be part of the study of programming. I also want students to use classes before writing them, so a library of useful classes is integrated into the text. Students will better appreciate good design by seeing it in practice than by simply reading about it. This requires studying and using classes that actually do something and that are easy for novice programmers to use. For example, I don't use any examples about bank accounts or automated teller machines. These traditional examples work well in explaining concepts, but it's not possible to implement a real bank account class or an ATM in the first programming course. I do supply classes for calendar dates, unbounded integers, timing program segments, reading directories, random numbers, and several others. These classes can be used early (or late) in a semester, allowing students to write more interesting programs without writing more code. For example, using the Date class, students can write a three-line program to determine how many days old they are whenever they run the program, an eight-line program to find out what day Thanksgiving falls on in any year, and a forty-line program to print a calendar for any year. Using

---

[1] This first course has traditionally been called CS1 after early ACM guidelines.

the classes for reading directories makes it possible to write a twenty-line program for finding all files that are large, or were last modified yesterday, or a host of other problems.

Most importantly, this book takes the view that the study of computer science should involve hands-on activity and be fun. The study of programming must cover those areas that are acknowledged as fundamental to computer science, but the foundation that is constructed during this study must be solid enough to support continued study of a rapidly changing programming world, and the process of studying should make students want to learn more. Support for this position can be found in several places; I offer two quotes that express my sentiments quite well:

> Having surveyed the relationships of computer science with other disciplines, it remains to answer the basic questions: What is the central core of the subject? What is it that distinguishes it from the separate subjects with which it is related? What is the linking thread which gathers these disparate branches into a single discipline? My answer to these questions is simple—it is the art of programming a computer. It is the art of designing efficient and elegant methods of getting a computer to solve problems, theoretical or practical, small or large, simple or complex. It is the art of translating this design into an effective and accurate computer program. This is the art that must be mastered by a practising computer scientist; the skill that is sought by numerous advertisements in the general and technical press; the ability that must be fostered and developed by computer science courses in universities.

C. A. R. Hoare
Computer Science (reprinted in [Hoa89])

A supporting view is expressed in the following quote:

> Programming is unquestionably the central topic of computing.
>
> In addition to being important, programming is an enormously exciting intellectual activity. In its purest form, it is the systematic mastery of complexity. For some problems, the complexity is akin to that associated with designing a fine mechanical watch, i.e., discovering the best way to assemble a relatively small number of pieces into a harmonious and efficient mechanism. For other problems, the complexity is more akin to that associated with putting a man on the moon, i.e., managing a massive amount of detail.
>
> In addition to being important and intellectually challenging, programming is a great deal of fun. Programmers get to build things and see them work. What could be more satisfying?

John V. Guttag
Why Programming Is Too Hard and What to Do about It in [MGRS91]

Programming and Computer Science

This is more than a book about programming. Although its principal focus is on programming using C++, this is also a book about computer science. However, this is neither a book that adopts what some have called a breadth-first approach to computer science, nor is it a book whose only purpose is to teach object-oriented programming in the first course (although glimpses of both approaches will be evident).

Introductory courses are evolving to take advantage of new and current trends in software engineering and programming language design, specifically object-oriented design and programming. Some schools will adopt the approach that learning object-oriented design principles should be the focus of a first programming course. Although this approach certainly has some merit, students in the first course traditionally have a very difficult time with the design of loops, functions, and programs. I believe that attempting to cover object-oriented design in addition to these other design skills will not be as conducive to a successful programming experience as will using object-oriented concepts in the context of learning to program by reading and using classes before writing them. This may seem a subtle distinction, but if the focus of the course is on learning about the design and use of objects, there may be a tendency to delve too quickly and too deeply into the details of C++.

The approach taken in this book is that C++ and OOP permit students with little or no programming background to make great strides toward developing foundational knowledge and expertise in programming. In subsequent courses, students will hone the skills that are first learned in the study of the material in this book and will expand the coverage of computer science begun here. Computer science is not just programming, and students in a first course in computer science must be shown something of what the discipline is about. At the same time, programming provides a means of relating the subdisciplines that compose computer science. Many of the examples and programs in this book rely on classes, code, and libraries that are documented and supplied with the book.

A major tenet of the approach used here is that students should read, modify, and extend programs in conjunction with designing and writing from scratch. This is enabled to a large extent by using the object-oriented features of C++ whenever appropriate. I view C++ as a tool to be used rather than studied. One of the most important ideas underlying the use of classes and objects in C++, and one of the most important concepts in computer science, is the idea of *abstraction*.

> Its [computer science's] study involves development of the ability to abstract the essential features of a problem and its solution, to reason effectively in the abstract plane, without confusion by a mass of highly relevant detail. The abstraction must then be related to the detailed characteristics of computers as the design of the solution progresses; and it must culminate in a program in which all the detail has been made explicit; and at this stage, the utmost care must be exercised to ensure a very high degree of accuracy. . . . The need for abstract thought together with meticulous accuracy, the need for imaginative speculation in the search for a solution, together with a sound knowledge of the practical limitations of the tools available for its implementation, the combination of formal rigour with a clear style for its explanation to others—these are the combinations of attributes which should be inculcated and developed in a student … and which must be developed in high degree in students of computer science.

> C. A. R. Hoare (reprinted in [Hoa89])

Students and teachers of computer science are not obliged to understand the IEEE standards for floating-point numbers in order to write code that uses such numbers. Although at one time a deep understanding of machine architecture was necessary in order to write programs, this is no longer the case. Hoare exhorts the programmer to be articulate about his or her activity; this book is designed to bring the novice programmer and student of computer science and program design to a point where such behavior is possible. The use of C++ provides a mechanism for doing so in which details can be revealed if and when it is appropriate, and hidden otherwise.

Programming in C++

Although this book uses C++ as a tool to be used rather than studied, students coming out of a first course must be well prepared for subsequent courses in computer science and other disciplines. Therefore, the essential features of C++ must be used, studied, and mastered. The syntactic and semantic features of C++ sufficient for an introductory course are thoroughly covered. At Duke, we teach our first courses using C++, and then we move to Java. We have had great success with this approach. This book uses C++, not C. In particular, there is no coverage of I/O using `printf` and `scanf`, there is no coverage of C-style (char *) strings, and the coverage of C-style arrays is minimal and included only because initializing an array with several values shortens code. Instead, we use streams for I/O, the standard C++ class `string`, and a modification of the STL `vector` class called `tvector` that performs range-checking on all vector accesses.

Many thought and programming exercises are integrated in the text, particularly in the Pause to Reflect sections. These exercises are designed to make students think about what they're doing and to cover some of the messier language details in thought-provoking and interesting ways. On-line materials accessible via the World Wide Web provide supporting programming lab assignments.

A Closer View of the CS Tapestry

This book is different from most other introductory programming contexts in several ways:

- Functions are introduced very early, but in a natural way that makes programming with functions easier than without.

- Strings are used before ints or doubles, though all are introduced early in the text so that numerical examples can be mixed with text and string examples.

- Whenever possible, the computer is exploited—small programs do not necessarily equate with toy programs. The classes included in the text make this possible.

- Classes, programs, and libraries are supplied with the book. Students will use the classes first, studying only their interfaces, before delving into implementation and design issues.

- Features of C++ that simplify programming are used, but not all features of C++ are emphasized. For example, since we use string and vector classes rather than pointer-based C-style objects, there is no reason to cover copy constructors or assignment operators. These topics are covered in the text, but there's no compelling reason to cover them.

How to Use the Book

I do not cover every section of the book in my courses, and instructors who used the first edition indicated that they skip some sections as well. I'll provide an overview of how chapters can be covered, but the best recommendations will be your own after looking at the material. I'll also post sample syllabi on the book's Web site as people using the book send the syllabi to me.

The How to Sections

The How to sections are new to this second edition. One of the common complaints from users of the first edition was that it was not an ideal reference. Material on language-specific features of C++ was introduced as needed so that related material was not always found together. To address this valid concern, I have created How to sections that condense C++ specific topics into a series of appendices, making it easier to use the book as a reference as well as a textbook. The How to sections are referenced in the text by a flying carpet icon as shown to the left, with the relevant How to referenced in the text. For example, How to B provides detailed information on using streams and formatting output. By including the material in the How to appendix, it can be found quickly and it doesn't clutter a more general discussion of computer science and programming design with C++ specifics.

Chapter Coverage and Dependencies

Chapter 1 is an overview of computer science and programming. None of the material is used in subsequent chapters, though covering Chapter 1 doesn't take much time and sets a tone for using the book.

Part 1: Foundations of C++ Programming

Chapters 2 through 5 cover material essential to what is covered in the rest of the text. However, certain sections in this part can be skipped or treated less thoroughly since the material is repeated in other contexts later. The Balloon class used in Section 3.4 introduces a simple and compelling class, but the section can be skipped since the material on classes is studied again in Section 5.4. It's also possible to cover all the control statements early, then use the examples and classes introduced in Chapters 2 through 5. Chapters 2 through 5 should take less time to cover than Chapters 6 through 8. In general, the chapters later in the book take more time to digest than the earlier chapters, but offer more material.

Part 2: Program and Class Construction: Extending the Foundation

The material in Chapters 6 through 8, combined with earlier material, will form the basis of many first courses. It's possible to use sections of chapters from Part 3 to augment the material in the first eight chapters as noted below.

For those who prefer to cover vectors early, it's possible to cover Sections 6.1, 6.2 and 7.4, then cover Chapter 8. The material in Section 8.4 on built-in arrays is completely optional. The class tvector is modeled after the STL class vector, but performs range-checking for the overloaded indexing operator. The discussion of tvector relies on the method push_back for adding elements to a vector so that the vector resizes itself as needed. The differences between size and capacity for vectors are emphasized in Chapter 8.

The class WordStreamIterator introduced in Section 6.3 can be omitted each time it's used, though it's much easier to use the class to read a file more than once within the same program than using the stream functions described in How to B to reset a stream. The material on sets of strings in Section 6.5 is used in later chapters, but it can be skipped each time it's covered. The random walk classes discussed in Section 7.3 can be skipped, though they're used later in discussing inheritance and pointers.

Part 3: Design, Use, and Analysis: Building on the Foundation

Chapters 9 through 13 provide a wealth of material. It's unlikely that all the chapters can be covered in a single semester.

In general, most of the chapters in this part are independent of each other, though not completely. The material in Chapter 13 can be covered early, though it uses pointers. A quick discussion of allocation using new can finesse the use of pointers since the pointers are used to store vectors of elements in an inheritance hierarchy, not for linked structures.

Chapter 9, which covers getline, string streams, and overloaded operators, and Chapter 10 on recursion, can be covered in any order. Most of the material is not used in subsequent chapters, though the getline function is used in several examples and recursion is used in quick sort. These chapters could be covered before Chapter 8 on vectors, except that the example of recursion in Section 10.3.3 permutes the elements in a vector. The material on immutable lists in Section 10.5 can be skipped, though it is used in a few examples in later chapters.

Most of material in Chapter 11 can be skipped entirely or covered immediately after covering vectors. Section 11.3 on function objects is optional, though it's the right way of sorting by several criteria, and function objects are important in the STL and the Java Collections classes.

Thanks

Many people have contributed to this book and the material in it, and I hope that many more will. I must single out two people who have offered criticisms and suggestions that have been extremely useful during the development of this project: Rich Pattis (Carnegie Mellon University) and Dave Reed (Dickinson College). At Duke, Susan Rodger taught using a draft of the first edition, waited patiently while chapters were revised, and offered a nearly uncountable number of exercises, improvements, and programs. Her efforts have been very important in the development of this material. Greg Badros (then at Duke) reviewed the entire manuscript of the first edition and offered absolutely wonderful suggestions; he astonished me with his perspicacity. In the fall of 1995, David Levine used the first edition at Gettysburg College and made many constructive suggestions based on this use. In the fall of 1996, Dee Ramm learned and taught using the final draft, and made many useful suggestions. Through the auspices of McGraw-Hill, Marjorie Anderson offered wonderful suggestions for improving the quality of the first edition. Although I haven't vanquished the passive voice, any progress is due to her diligence, and all stylistic blunders are my own. Among the users of the first edition, Beth Katz at Millersville University stands out for providing feedback that I've tried to incorporate into this second edition.

The folks from McGraw-Hill involved with the second edition have been absolutely wonderful. Betsy Jones, Emily Gray, and Amy Hill have helped with time, patience, and support throughout the development of the second edition. John Rogosich at Techsetters created LATEX macros and supplied support for those macros with great alacrity. Pat Anton was my contact about the artwork at Techsetters; if it looks good it's due to her, and if it doesn't it's because I originated it all.

In addition, the following people have reviewed the material and offered many useful suggestions both for the first edition and for this second edition (if I've left someone out, I apologize): Robert Anderson, Deganit Armon, John Barr, Gail Chapman, Mike Clancy, Robert Duvall, Arthur Farley, Sarah Fix, Donald Gotterbarn, Karen Hay, Andrew Holey, Judy Hromcik, Beth Katz, David Kay, Joe Kmoch, Sharon Lee, Henry Leitner, David Levine, Clayton Lewis, John McGrew, Jerry Mead, Judy Mullins, David Mutchler, Richard Nau, Jeff Naughton, Chris Nevison, Bob Noonan, Richard Pattis, Robert Plantz, Richard Prosl, Dave Reed, Margaret Reek, Stuart Reges, Stephen Schach, David Teague, Beth Weiss, and Lynn Zeigler.

Development

The ideas and exercises in this book have been tested in the first course for majors at Duke since 1993. Many people using the first edition contributed thoughts and ideas. I'm grateful to all of them, especially students at Duke who saw many versions of the material before it was a book.

Versions of all the programs used in the book are available for Windows, Unix, and Macintosh operating systems. The software is currently available via anonymous ftp from `ftp.cs.duke.edu` in `pub/ola/book/ed2/code`. It is also accessible via the web at:

```
http://www.cs.duke.edu/csed/tapestry.
```

Although the first edition of the book went through extensive classroom testing, there are undoubtedly errors that persist and new ones introduced with this edition. Nevertheless, all code has been compiled and executed and is reproduced directly from the sources; it is not retyped.

I will respond to all email regarding errors and will attempt to fix mistakes in subsequent printings. I would be ecstatic to hear about suggestions that might improve certain sections, or comments about sections that caused problems even without suggestions for improvement. Of course, I love to hear that something worked well.

Please send all comments by email to:

```
ola@cs.duke.edu
```

I will try to acknowledge all mail received. Materials for the book are also accessible via the World Wide Web from the URL:

```
http://www.cs.duke.edu/csed/tapestry/
```

A mailing list is available for discussing any aspects of the book or the course. To subscribe, send email with the message:

```
subscribe tapestry
```

as the message body to:

```
majordomo@acpub.duke.edu
```

To unsubscribe, send the message:

```
unsubscribe tapestry
```

to the same address. To send mail to the list, use the address:

```
tapestry@acpub.duke.edu
```

Details

The second edition of the book was prepared using the LATEX package from Y & Y, Inc. Macros and LATEX support were supplied by Techsetters, Inc. I used hardware donated by Intel to Duke University running Windows NT donated by Microsoft. I also used RedHat Linux 5.1 running on a (now old) Pentium 100. I tested all programs using Codewarrior donated by Metrowerks, Visual C++ donated by Microsoft, and egcs C++ under Linux which is free from Cygnus Software. I used Emacs running under Windows NT and the Unix-like shell for NT created by Cygnus; both were indispensable (I could not survive without grep, for example). Screen images were captured using Snagit/32 and processed using SmartDraw Professional running under Windows NT. I also used XV and Xfig running under Linux to create drawings that were ultimately massaged by Techsetters using Adobe Photoshop. I printed preliminary versions of the manuscript on a Tektronix Color Laser/Phaser 740 and used Adobe Distiller to create pdf files from postscript.

Acknowledgments

To paraphrase Newton, the work in this book is not mine alone; I have stood on the shoulders of giants. Of course, Newton paraphrased Robert Burton, who said, "A dwarf standing on the shoulders of a giant may see farther than a giant himself." The styles used in several books serve as models for different portions of this text. In particular, Eric Roberts' *The Art and Science of C* [Rob95] provided style guidelines for formatting; the book *A Logical Approach to Discrete Math* [GS93] by David Gries and Fred B. Schneider motivated the biographies; books by Bjarne Stroustrup [Str94, Str97] and Scott Meyers [Mey92, Mey96] were indispensable in delving into C++. The way I think about programming was changed by [GHJ95] and other work from the patterns community. I've borrowed ideas from almost all of the textbooks I've read in 21 years of teaching, so I acknowledge them en masse.

Thanks to Duke University and the computer science department for providing an atmosphere in which teaching is rewarded and this book is possible.

The research that led to the inclusion of patterns and the apprentice style of learning used in this book was supported by the National Science Foundation under grants CCR-9702550 and DUE-9554910. This second edition was written during a sabbatical year in Vancouver, Canada where the salmon is great, the city is wonderful, and the rain isn't nearly as bad as people lead you to believe.

Finally, thanks to Laura for always understanding.

Owen Astrachan
Vancouver, Canada 1999

A Computer Science Tapestry

Exploring Programming and Computer Science
with C++

Computer Science and Programming   1

The computer is no better than its program.
ELTING ELMORE MORRISON
Men, Machines and Modern Times

Science and technology, and the various forms of art, all unite humanity in a single and interconnected system.
ZHORES MEDVEDEV
The Medvedev Papers

I want to reach that state of condensation of sensations which constitutes a picture.
HENRI MATISSE
Notes d'un Peintre

In this chapter we introduce you to computer science. Ideally, we would begin with a simple definition that could be expanded and refined throughout the book. Unfortunately, computer science, like other disciplines, has no simple definition. For example, we might say that biology is the study of life. But that doesn't explain much about the content of such subdisciplines as animal behavior, immunology, or genetics—all of which are part of biology. Nor does it explain much about the contributions that these disciplines make to biology in general. Similarly, is English the study of grammar and spelling, the reading of Shakespeare's plays, or the writing of poems and stories? In many cases it is easier to consider the subfields within an area of study than it is to define the area of study. So it is with computer science.

1.1   What Is Computer Science?

In some respects, computer science is a new discipline; it has grown and evolved along with the growth of computing technology and the cheaper, faster, and more accessible processing power of modern-day computers. As recently as 1970, many colleges and universities did not even have departments of computer science. But computer science has benefited from work done in such older disciplines as mathematics, psychology, electrical engineering, physics, and linguistics. Computer science inherits characteristics from all these fields in ways that we'll touch on in this book, but the thread that links these and the many subdisciplines of computer science is computer programming.

Some people prefer the term used in many European languages, *informatics*, over what is called *computer science* in the United States. Computer science is more the study of managing and processing information than it is the study of computers. Computer science is more than programming, but programming is at the core of information processing and computer science.

3

This book will guide you through the study of the design, building, and analysis of computer programs. Although you won't become an expert by working through this book, you will lay a foundation on which expertise can be built. Wherever possible, the programming examples will solve problems that are difficult to solve without a computer: a program might find the smallest of 10,000 numbers, rather than the smallest of 2 numbers. Longer examples are taken from various core areas of computer science. As this is a book about the design and analysis of computer programs, it must be used in conjunction with a computer. Reading alone cannot convey the same understanding that using, reading, and writing programs can.

1.1.1   The Tapestry of Computer Science

This chapter introduces computer science using a tapestry metaphor. A tapestry has much in common with computer science. A tapestry has many intricate scenes that form a whole. Similarly, computer science is a broad discipline with many intricate subdisciplines. In studying a tapestry, we can step back and view the work as a whole, move closer to concentrate on some particularly alluring or colorful region, and even study the quality of the fabric itself. We'll similarly explore computer science—studying some things in detail, but stepping back to view the whole when appropriate. We'll view programs as tapestries too. You'll study programs written by others, add to these programs to make them more useful, and write your own programs. You'll see that creating and developing programs is not only useful but is immensely satisfying, and often entertaining as well.

Several unifying threads run through a tapestry, and the various scenes and sections originate from and build on these threads. Likewise in computer science, we find basic themes and concepts on which the field is built and that we use to write programs and solve problems. In this chapter we introduce the themes of computer science, which are like the scenes in a tapestry, and the concepts, which are like the unifying threads.

Contexture is a word meaning both "an arrangement of interconnected parts" and "the act of weaving (assembling) parts into a whole." It can apply to tapestries and to computer programming. This book uses a contextural approach in which programming is the vehicle for learning about computer science. Although it is possible to study computer science without programming, it would be like studying food and cooking without eating, which would be neither as enjoyable nor as satisfying.

Computer science is *not* just programming. Too often this is the impression left after an initial exposure to the field. I want you to learn something of what a well-read and well-rounded computer scientist knows. You should have an understanding of what has been done, what might be done, and what cannot be done by programming a computer. After a brief preview of what is ahead, we'll get to it.

Alan Turing *(1913–1954)*

Alan Turing was one of the founders of computer science, studying it before there were computers! To honor his work, the highest achievement in the field of computer science—and the equivalent in stature to a Nobel prize—is the Turing award,

given by the Association for Computing Machinery (the ACM).

In 1937, Turing published the paper *On Computable Numbers, with an Application to the Entscheidungsproblem.* In this paper he invented an abstract machine, now known as a *Turing Machine,* that is (theoretically) capable of doing any calculation that today's supercomputers can. He used this abstract machine to show that there are certain problems in mathematics whose proofs cannot be found. This also shows that there are certain problems that cannot be solved with any computer. In particular, a program cannot be written that will determine whether an arbitrary program will eventually stop. This is called the **halting problem**.

During World War II, Turing was instrumental in breaking a German coding machine called the *Enigma.* He was also very involved with the design of the first computers in England and the United States. During this time, Turing practiced one of his loves—long-distance running. A newspaper account said of his second-place finish (by 1 foot) in a 3-mile race in a time of 15:51: "Antithesis of the popular notion of a scientist is tall, modest, 34-year-old bachelor Alan M. Turing. . . . Turing is the club's star distance runner. . . [and] is also credited with the original idea for the Automatic Computing Engine, popularly known as the Electronic Brain."

Turing was also fond of playing "running-chess," in which each player alternated moves with a run around Turing's garden. Turing was gay and, unfortunately, the 1940s and 50s were not a welcome time for homosexuals. He was found guilty of committing "acts of gross indecency" in 1952 and sentenced to a regimen of hormones as a "cure." More than a year after finishing this "therapy," and with no notice, Turing committed suicide in 1954.

For a full account of Turing's life see [Hod83].

1.2 Algorithms

To develop an initial understanding of the themes and concepts that make up the computer science tapestry, we'll work through an example. Consider two similar tasks of arranging objects into some predetermined order:

Arranging Cards

■   Arrange cards into four groups by suit: spades, hearts, clubs, diamonds.

■   Sort each group. To sort a group:

> For each rank (2, 3, 4, …, 10, J, Q, K, A) put the 2 first, followed by the 3, the 4, …, followed by the 10, J, Q, K, A (if any rank is missing, skip it).

Figure 1.1 Arranging cards in order.

1.   A hand of cards (arrange by rank and suit)
2.   100,000 exams (arrange by six-digit student ID number)

Card players often do the first task because it makes playing much simpler than if the cards in their hands are arranged in a random order. The second task is part of the administration of the Advanced Placement exams given each year to high school students. Many people are hired to sort the exam booklets by student ID number before the scores are entered into a computer. In both cases people are doing the arranging. The differences in the scale of the tasks and the techniques used to solve them will illuminate the study of computer science and problem solving.

1.2.1   Arranging 13 Cards

A hand of cards might look like this:

| 10♥ | 5♣ | Q♦ | 7♥ | 9♠ | A♣ | 8♦ | J♦ | 3♣ | 7♠ | K♥ | Q♣ | 8♠ |
| ♥10 | ♣5 | ♦Q | ♥7 | ♠9 | ♣A | ♦8 | ♦J | ♣3 | ♠7 | ♥K | ♣Q | ♠8 |

Most people arrange cards in order by suits (spades, hearts, diamonds, and clubs), and within suit by rank (2, …, 10, J, Q, K, A) with little thought. In fact, many people perform a slightly different sequence of steps in arranging different hands of cards, modifying their basic technique depending on the order in which the cards are dealt. However, if you are asked to describe the process of arranging a hand of cards to someone who has never seen cards before, the task becomes difficult. The careful description of such processes is one of the fundamental parts of computer science. The descriptions are called **algorithms** and are the focus of much study in computer science and in this book.

The algorithm for sorting cards shown in Figure 1.1 is both correct and concise, two traits to strive for in writing algorithms. The instructions to sort a group are applicable to all groups, not just the spades or to the diamonds. Instructions that apply in more than one situation are much more versatile than instructions that apply in a single situation.

Algorithms are often compared to recipes used in cooking: they are step-by-step plans used in some process (arranging cards or baking bread) to arrive at some end (a sorted hand of cards or a loaf of bread). Although this analogy is apt, cooking often allows for a larger margin of error than do algorithms that are to be implemented on a computer. Phrases like "beat until smooth," "sauté until tender," and "season to taste" are interpreted differently by cooks. A more appropriate analogy may be seen with the instructions that are used to knit a sweater or make a shirt. In such tasks, precise instructions are given and patterns must be followed or else a sweater with a front larger than the back or a shirt with mismatched buttons and buttonholes may result.

You can easily determine that the hand below is sorted correctly, in part because there are so few cards in a hand and because grouping cards by suit makes it easier to see if the cards are sorted. Verifying that the algorithm is correct in general is much more difficult than verifying that one hand of cards is sorted.

| 7♠ | 8♠ | 9♠ | 7♥ | 10♥ | K♥ | 3♣ | 5♣ | Q♣ | A♣ | 8♦ | J♦ | Q♦ |
| ♠7 | ♠8 | ♠9 | ♥7 | ♥10 | ♥K | ♣3 | ♣5 | ♣Q | ♣A | ♦8 | ♦J | ♦Q |

For example, suppose that an algorithm correctly sorts 1,000 hands of cards. Does this guarantee that the algorithm will sort all hands? No, it's possible that the next hand might not be sorted even though the first 1,000 hands were. This points out an important difference between verifying an algorithm and testing an algorithm. A *verified* algorithm has been proved to work in all situations. A *tested* algorithm has been rigorously tried with many examples to establish confidence that it works in all situations.

1.2.2 Arranging 100,000 exams

Arranging 100,000 exams by ID number is a much more cumbersome task than arranging 13 cards. Imagine being confronted with 100,000 exams to sort. Where would you begin? This task is more time-consuming and more prone to error than arranging cards. Although you probably don't need a precise description of the card-arranging algorithm to sort cards correctly, you'll need to think carefully about developing an algorithm to sort 100,000 exams using 40 people as assistants. Utilizing these "computational assistants" requires communication and organization beyond what is needed to arrange 13 cards in one person's hand. A sample of 32 student ID numbers is shown here:

```
672029  662497  118183  452603  637238  249262  617834  396939
483595  613046  361999  231519  695368  689831  346006  539184
712077  816735  540778  975985  950610  846581  931662  625487
278827  821759  131232  952606  547825  385646  880295  816645
```

These represent a small fraction of the number of exam booklets that must be arranged. Consider the algorithmic description in Figure 1.2. If this algorithm is implemented correctly, it will result in 32 numbers arranged from smallest to largest. If we had a computer to assist with the task, this might be an acceptable algorithm. (We'll see later that there are more efficient methods for use on a computer but that this is a method that works and is simple to understand.) We might be tempted to use it with 32 exams, but with 100,000 exams it would be extremely time-consuming and would make inefficient use of the resources at our disposal since using 40 people to find the smallest exam number is a literal waste of time.

Sorting Exams

Repeat the following until all 32 numbers (exams) have been arranged

- Scan the list of numbers (exams) looking for the smallest exam.
- Move the smallest number (exam) to another pile of exams that is maintained and arranged from smallest to largest.

Figure 1.2 Arranging exams in order.

1.3   Computer Science Themes and Concepts

The previous sorting example provides a context for the broad set of themes and concepts that comprises computer science.

1.3.1   Theory, Language, and Architecture

Three areas mentioned in [Ble90] as forming the core of computer science serve nicely as the essential themes, linking the various scenes of the computer science tapestry together. These themes are shown in Figure 1.3. Although we can develop algorithms for both sorting tasks, it would be useful to know if there are better algorithms or if there is a "best" algorithm in the sense that it can be proven to be the most efficient. Determining whether an algorithm is "better" than another may not be relevant for arranging cards because a nonoptimal algorithm will probably still work quickly. However, a "good" algorithm is very relevant when arranging 100,000 exams. Developing algorithms and evaluating them is the part of computer science known as **theory**.

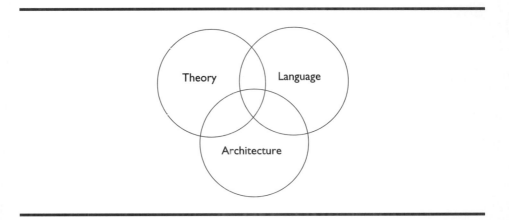

Figure 1.3 Essential computer science themes.

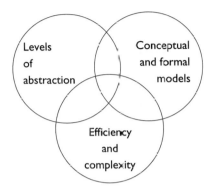

Figure 1.4 Recurring concepts.

If the algorithms are to be implemented on a computer or used by people (who are in some sense "computational engines"), there must be a **language** in which the algorithms are expressed. We have noted that cooking recipes, while similar to algorithms, often leave room for ambiguity. Although English (or other natural languages) may at some point become a viable language in which to "instruct" computers, specialized computer languages are needed now. Many programming languages exist, and often the choice of language has a large impact on how well a program is written and on how fast it is developed. Languages are necessary to implement algorithms on specific kinds of computers.

Although both these arranging tasks are similar, an algorithm for one may be inappropriate for the other. Viewing a person as a computational resource (or processor), we see that the card-arranging task is done using one processor while the exam-arranging task is done using several processors. Just as some people can sort cards more quickly than others, some computer processors are faster and work differently than other processors. The term **architecture** is used to describe how a computer is put together just as it is used to describe how a building is put together. One active research area in computer science involves developing algorithms and architectures for multiprocessor computing systems.

1.3.2 Abstractions, Models, and Complexity

In this section we continue our contextual approach, whereby we weave the essential themes into the fabric that is computer science and the scenes that make up its tapestry. In addition to the themes of theory, language, and architecture, we'll often refer to several of the recurring concepts presented in [ed91]. These form part of the foundation on which computer science is built; they are shown in Figure 1.4.

Both sorting tasks involve arranging things, yet the complexity of the second task makes it imperative that an efficient algorithm be used if the goal is to be achieved within a reasonable time frame. Both **efficiency** and **complexity** are parts of the computer science tapestry we are studying. In programming and computer science, these terms concern how difficult a problem is and the computational resources, such as time and memory, that a problem requires.

We have avoided many of the details inherent in these examples that might be of concern as rough ideas evolve into detailed algorithms. If 40 people are sorting exams we might be concerned, for example, with how many are left-handed. This might affect the arrangement of the exams as they are physically moved about during the sorting process. Some playing cards are embellished with beautiful designs; it might be necessary to explain to someone who has never played cards that these designs are irrelevant in the arrangement process. In general these levels of detail are examples of **levels of abstraction** (Figure 1.4). In one sense this entire chapter mirrors the fact that we are viewing the computer science tapestry at a very high level of abstraction, with few details. Each subsequent chapter of this book involves a study of some aspect of the tapestry at a level of greater detail.

Finally, both these tasks involve numbers. We all have an idea of what a number is, although the concept of number may be different to a mathematician and to an accountant. In computer science conceptual ideas must often be formalized to be well understood. For example, telling someone who is playing hide-and-go-seek to start counting from 1 and to stop when they reach the "last number" is an interesting way to teach the concept of infinity. The finite memory of computers, however, imposes a limit on the largest number that can be represented. This difference between **conceptual and formal models** is a concept that will recur and that completes the three concepts in Figure 1.4, forming common threads of the computer science tapestry.

Pause to Reflect

1.1 The *New Hacker's Dictionary* defines *bogo-sort* as described here.

> **Bogo-sort:** Repeatedly throw a hand of cards in the air, picking them up at random, and stopping the process when examining the hand reveals the cards are in order.

Using this "algorithm," what is the minimum number of "throws" that yields a sorted hand? What is the danger of using this algorithm?

1.2 In the algorithm for sorting cards, nothing is stated about forming a hand from each of the separate suits. Does something need to be stated? Is too much left as "understood by the player" so that someone unfamiliar with cards couldn't use the algorithm?

1.3 Write a concise description of the method or algorithm you use to sort a hand of cards.

1.4 Suppose that the 32 student ID numbers listed in the text are sorted. Is it a simple matter to verify that the numbers are in the correct order? Consider the same question for 100,000 numbers.

Charles Antony (Tony) Richard Hoare (b. 1934)

Perhaps best known for his invention of the sorting algorithm he modestly named Quicksort, Hoare has made profound contributions to many branches of computer

science, especially in programming and programming languages. Hoare received the ACM Turing award in 1980. In his award address he said this about learning from failure: "I have learned more from my failures than can ever be revealed in the cold print of a scientific article and now I would like you to learn from them, too.

Besides, failures are much more fun to hear about afterwards; they are not so funny at the time." In a collection of essays [Hoa89], Hoare describes the programmer of the current era as part apprentice and part wizard; he urges that computer science education should focus on both theoretical foundations and practical applications. In his last essay of that collection he states, "I salute the bravery of those who accept the challenge of

being the first to try out new ideas; and I also respect the caution of those who prefer to stick with ideas which they know and understand and trust."

I think Hoare may not like C++; it is too big, too full of features, and it doesn't have a formal foundation. However, according to his Web page, he set himself the following task for his 1993–1994 sabbatical year: to become acquainted with Visual Basic™. Of course as other goals for that year he listed:

To complete a work on unification of theories of programming and to start new work on a range of scientific theories of computational phenomena.

In describing computer science as, in part, an engineering discipline, Hoare states:

... the major factor in the wider propagation of professional methods is education, an education which conveys a broad and deep understanding of theoretical principles as well as their practical application, an education such as can be offered by our universities and polytechnics.

For more information, see [Hoa89].

1.4 Language, Architecture, and Programs

Language is necessary for expressing algorithms. For computers, a precise programming language is necessary. In this section we briefly touch on the process by which an algorithm is transformed from an idea into a working computer program. This process is the same regardless of the kind of computer being used.

The final computer program differs from machine to machine in the same manner that the same idea is expressed differently in German than it is in English. Consider the German word *Geländesprung* defined:

> **Geländesprung:** a jump made in skiing from a crouching position with the use of both poles.

An idea whose expression requires many English words can be expressed in a single German word. Different computers can offer the same economy of expression; what one computer might do in a single instruction can require several instructions (and a corresponding increase in time to execute the instructions) on another computer. For example, so-called **supercomputers** can add 100 numbers with a single instruction. On ordinary computers, one instruction can add only two numbers.

1.4.1 High- and Low-Level Languages

> High thoughts must have high language.
> ARISTOPHANES
> *Frogs*

How do computers work? We don't need to know this to use computers, just as we don't need to know how internal combustion engines work to drive a car. A little knowledge, however, can help to demystify what a computer is doing when it executes a program. A computer can be viewed from many levels, from the transistors that make up its circuits to the programs that are used to design the circuits.

At the lowest level, computers respond to electric signals at an extremely fast rate. Computers react to whether electricity is flowing or not; the computer merely responds to switches that are in one of two states: on or off. This method of using two states involves what is termed the **binary number system,** or the **base 2 system.** This system is based on counting using only the digits 0 and 1. The base 10 system, with which you are most familiar, uses the digits 0 through 9.

There are hundreds of different kinds of computers. You may have used Apple Macintosh computers, which are built using a computer chip called the *Power-PC*, or another kind of computer based on the Intel *Pentium* chip. (Pictures of these different chips are shown at the end of the chapter in Figures 1.9 and 1.11.) These chips are the foundation on which a computer is built. The chip determines how fast the computer runs and what kinds of software can be used with the computer. Since computers are constructed from different components and have different underlying architectures, they may respond differently to the same sequence of zeros and ones. Just as *chat* means "to converse informally" in English and means "a small domesticated feline (cat)" in

French, so might *00010100111010* instruct one computer to add two numbers and another computer to print the letter *q*.

Rather than instruct computers at this level of zeros and ones, languages have been developed that allow ideas to be expressed at a higher level—in a way more easily understood by people. In addition to being more easily understood, these high-level languages can be translated into particular sequences of zeros and ones for particular computers. Just as translators can translate English into both Japanese and Swahili, so can translating computer programs translate a high-level language into a low-level language for a particular computer. The concept of higher-level programming languages was a breakthrough. The first computers were "programmed" literally by flipping switches by hand or physically rewiring the computer to create different on/off states corresponding to a program. The use of higher-level languages made programming easier (although it is still an intellectually challenging task) and helped to make computer use more prevalent.

The computer language used in this book is called C++.[1] This language has its roots in the C programming language, which was developed in the 1970s. The language C is a high-level language[2] that allows low-level concepts to be expressed more readily than some other high-level languages. For example, in C it is easy to write a program to change a single bit (a 0 or a 1) in the computer's memory. This is hard, if not impossible, to do in other high-level languages, such as Pascal.

We're not studying C++ because it permits one bit to be changed. We're studying C++ because with it several programming styles are possible. In particular, it can be used with a style of programming called *object-oriented programming*, often abbreviated as OOP. We will use OOP throughout this book, but it will be an aid to our study of programming and computer science rather than the principal focus. We'll explore OOP briefly at the end of this chapter.

The intricacies of C++ are such that mastering the entire language, as well as the concepts of object-oriented programming, is a task too daunting and difficult for beginning programmers. In this book we present a significant subset of C++ and use it to write programs that permit the study of essential areas of computer science. At the same time the power of C++ is exploited where possible to allow you to create more complicated programs than would be feasible using other languages. Don't be disheartened that you won't learn absolutely all of C++ in this book—you'll be building a foundation on which subsequent study can add. The few parts of the language that aren't covered are mostly "shortcuts" that can be replaced using features of the language that are in the book.

A Concrete Example. To illustrate the difference between high- and low-level languages, we'll study how a C++ program is translated into a low-level language. The low-level language of 0's and 1's that a computer understands is called **machine language**. Because different computers have different machine languages, a program is needed to translate the high-level C++ language into machine language. A **compiler** is a program that does this translation. Often the compiling process involves an intermediate step wherein the code is translated into **assembly language**.

---

[1]This is pronounced as "see plus plus."

[2]Although some computer scientists might take exception to this statement, C is clearly a much higher-level language than machine or assembly language.

```
main:                                       main:
        save %sp,-128,%sp                           pushl %ebp
        mov 7,%o0                                   movl %esp,%ebp
        st %o0,[%fp-20]                             subl $12,%esp
        mov 12,%o0                                  movl $7,-4(%ebp)
        st %o0,[%fp-24]                             movl $12,-8(%ebp)
        ld [%fp-20],%o0                             movl -4(%ebp),%eax
        ld [%fp-24],%o1                             imull -8(%ebp),%eax
        call .umul,0                                movl %eax,-12(%ebp)
        nop                                         xorl %eax,%eax
        st %o0,[%fp-28]                             jmp .L1
        mov 0,%i0                                   .align 4
        b .LL1                                      xorl %eax,%eax
        nop                                         jmp .L1
        mov 0,%i0                                   .align 4
        b .LL1                              .L1:
        nop                                         leave
.LL1:                                               ret
        ret
        restore
```

Figure 1.5 Assembly code using g++ (Sparc on left, Pentium on right).

To keep the example simple, we'll use a program that stores two numbers in memory, then multiplies the numbers storing the product in a different memory location. The program follows:

```
int main()
{
    int x,y,z;
    x = 7; y = 12;
    z = x*y;
    return 0;
}
```

We will not discuss the C++ instructions here; we use the program only to illustrate the differences between high- and low-level languages.

The world is full of C++ compilers. Compilers exist for various kinds of computers, sizes of programs, and amounts of money. The code in this book has been tested using four different compilers. Some of these compilers cost hundreds of dollars, some are less expensive, and one is free.

The assembly code generated by the same compiler running on two different machines is shown in Figure 1.5. The compiler used is g++ running on two different machines: a Sun Sparcstation and a Pentium-based computer.[3] There is one column of assembly code for each machine. Note that although the programs are of roughly the same length, there are few similarities in the assembly instructions. Among the instruc-

---

[3]The characteristics of these machines are not important, but the same compiler runs on both machines, which facilitates a comparison.

tions are *ld*, *call*, and *nop* for the Sun assembly and *pushl*, *subl*, and *xorl* for the Pentium. The important point of Figure 1.5 is that you do *not* need to worry about assembly code to write programs in C++ or in any other high-level language. It is comforting to know that we can ignore most of the low-level details in writing programs and studying computer science and, perhaps, enticing to know that the details are there for those who are interested.

1.5 Creating and Developing Programs

How is a computer program created? Usually a problem arises whose solution requires computation. An algorithm for the solution is developed into a running program in several steps. The steps that lead to the program's execution on a computer are also important. We'll look at developing a program for the problem of multiplying two numbers as shown in Figure 1.6. The process of developing an idea into an algorithm that is eventually realized as a working computer program is illustrated in Figure 1.7.

From Problem to Algorithm. Consider the steps labeled 1 and 2 in Figure 1.7. The problem of multiplying two specific numbers (1,285 and 57) has been generalized to the problem of multiplying two arbitrary numbers (Y and Z). The two views of the problem, one concrete and one general, represent two levels of abstraction. A solution to the general problem will be useful for any two numbers, not just for 1,285 and 57. If you can develop a general solution that is useful in many situations, it is usually worth it. Sometimes, however, a solution to a specific problem is needed and solving a general version would take too long or be too difficult.

To write a program for solving this general problem, we must develop an algorithm for multiplication. Consider multiplying rational numbers (fractions), integers, real numbers, and complex numbers as illustrated in Figure 1.6.

You may not be familiar with each of these types of numbers, but each uses a different method for multiplication. If we're going to write a program to multiply, we'll need to determine what **type** of number is being used. The general form of $X \times Y$ can be used to express multiplication regardless of which type of number is multiplied. One of the advantages of C++ is that this conceptual similarity in notation is formalized in code: the same symbol, *, can be used to multiply many types of numbers.

In addition to the type of number, considerations in the development of the algorithm might include the size of the numbers being multiplied (an efficient algorithm would

Rational	Integer	Real	Complex
3/4 * 8/9	1,285 * 57	3.14 * 6.023	(3 + 5*i*) * (2 - 7*i*)
2/3	73,245	18.91222	41 - 11*i*

Figure 1.6 Multiplying different types of numbers.

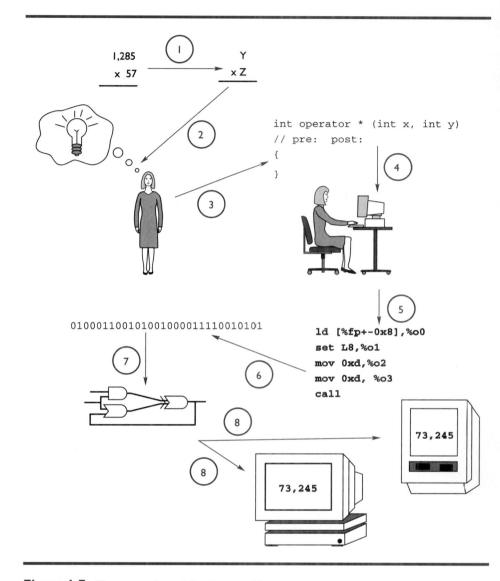

Figure 1.7 The steps of transition from problem to program.

be more important if the numbers were hundreds of digits long as opposed to three digits long), how many times numbers will be multiplied, and whether the result of multiplying the numbers can exceed the memory constraints of the computer. Although it's impossible for numbers to get "too big" conceptually, the inherent finiteness of a computer's memory requires that a formal model of computation take this into account.

From Algorithm to Program. In step 3 we translate the algorithm into the high-level language C++. The name *operator* * has been given to the C++ instructions that perform the multiplication. Translating the algorithm into code requires a knowledge of the programming language's syntax—the symbols and characters used in the language—as well as the meaning, or semantics, of these characters.

Once the algorithm is represented in a high-level language, a program must be entered into a computer. Step 4 consists of more than merely typing characters at a keyboard. Often the realization of the algorithm as a computer program has errors that become apparent as the program is tested. Testing can indicate that errors exist; removing the errors is another problem. Errors are often euphemistically called *bugs*.[4] This makes the process of removing errors **debugging**. Testing and debugging can uncover errors in the original algorithm in addition to errors in the C++ representation of the algorithm.

As you become more experienced at programming you can employ techniques called **defensive programming**: attempting to ensure that your programs are robust and error-free as part of the design process rather than relying on testing and debugging exclusively. Many computer scientists are currently developing methods that will permit programs to be proved correct in the same manner that mathematical theorems are proved. Although we will not use such formal methods in our study, we introduce some of the techniques.

From High-Level Program to Low-Level Program. In step 5, the high-level C++ program is translated into a lower-level language called **assembly language**. The name is derived from the notion of assembling the individual low-level instructions available on a particular computer into a form understandable by people. Although some programming is still done directly in assembly, the process of translation from high level to low level has been refined enough that programming at this level is often unnecessary.

Step 6 shows the translation of assembly language to **machine language**, the language of zeros and ones that a particular computer understands. Specific assembly language and machine language instructions differ according to the kind of computer being used (as shown in Figure 1.5), as opposed to high-level languages like C++, which are the same on various computers. The process of translation illustrated by steps 5 and 6 is accomplished by a computer program called a **compiler**, and the process is called **compiling**. A compiler translates code written in a high-level language into machine language. This translation process often includes an intermediate step in which the code is translated into assembly language.

Executing Machine Language. At the lowest level, the zeros and ones of machine language code cause switches to be turned on and off in the computer. These switches are extremely small and can be switched on and off quite rapidly. Technological advances have enabled transistors, which function as switches, to become increasingly smaller and faster. Switches are often represented by the diagrams in step 7.

The execution of a program is separate and different from the compilation of the program. Compiling a C++ program yields a low-level program, whereas executing a

---

[4]The derivation of the word *bug* is open to debate. Thomas Edison was reported to have discovered a "bug" in his phonograph in 1889. A literal example is the moth trapped in one of the first computers, the Harvard Mark II. The moth was placed into the system's logbook with the annotation "First actual case of bug being found" and is now on display in the Naval Museum in Dahlgren, Virginia.

machine language program results in the computer performing the tasks represented by the compiled machine code.

Coming Full Circle: Displaying the Results. Most current computers, and certainly the computers you will be using as you study computer science with this book, have a screen to display what happens when a program is run. Whether the program is a word processor or a C++ program for multiplying numbers, output is generally displayed on the screen. Note that the screens on the computers in Figure 1.7 display the answer to the original problem: $1,285 \times 57 = 73,245$.

1.6   Language and Program Design

One of the "eternal truths" of computer science and the computer industry is

Software is harder than hardware.

This statement means that new computers (hardware) are developed at a faster pace and more easily than new programs (software). There is certainly some truth to this, although new programming languages and new design methods have been developed in an attempt to alleviate this disparity. Many people believe that object-oriented programming, or OOP, will be of great assistance in making software easier to develop. OOP allows pieces of code to be reused in other contexts more easily.

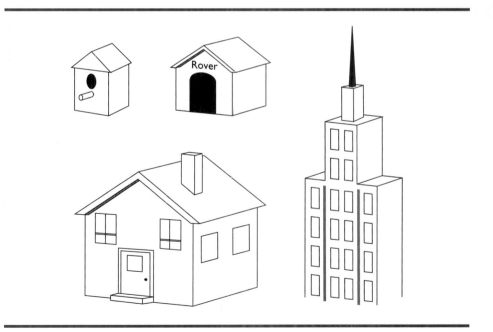

Figure 1.8 OOP: birdhouses and skyscrapers.

To try to understand what OOP is about, I use an analogy (suggested in [McC93]) that comes from construction (see Figure 1.8). Suppose you decide to build a birdhouse; you can probably nail some boards together in a couple of hours and provide a useful dwelling for your favorite flyers. You may not put much thought into the design of the house, although if you don't you may waste some wood. (A carpenter's adage is "measure twice, cut once.") Next suppose you're designing a doghouse for your favorite pet. You might take more care; you're probably more concerned with whether Rover gets wet than whether your neighborhood bluejay is inconvenienced by rain. You may buy a kit—a precut set of materials and plans for constructing the doghouse. Nevertheless, this is probably a day-long project, *if* you're used to using saws and hammers.

What about building a house? If you've been involved with house building, you know that it can take a long time, requiring contractors, plumbers, electricians, and usually a lot of headaches. However, it is certainly possible to build a house yourself. Most of the pieces of a house come prebuilt. For houses that don't use prebuilt pieces and instead require custom manufacturing, the price of construction can be very high. Finally, consider building a skyscraper such as the Empire State Building. Such a building requires careful planning and is much more complex than a typical family dwelling. Yet hundreds of such tall buildings are designed and built each year.

Computer scientists disagree about what OOP is and whether it is appropriate for use in an introductory course. By using a carefully chosen subset of C++, it is certainly possible to develop a mastery of basic programming concepts as well as an understanding and appreciation of OOP.

1.6.1 Off-the-Shelf Components

Using off-the-shelf components is one of the reasons that constructing large buildings is possible. The phrase *off-the-shelf* is used to mean a component that is manufactured in large quantity and that can be used in a variety of situations. Nails are no longer handcrafted by blacksmiths, and even houses can be purchased in a kit form. These components are often inexpensive but serve as well as (or better than) custom-built components. The same is true of building computers. One of the reasons that computers get less expensive every year is that the pieces that make up a computer get cheaper as more are produced—this is sometimes called *economy of scale*. Viewed differently, the key is *not* to do all the work yourself but to use what others provide.

Of course, off-the-shelf components don't always work. A roof of a birdhouse is different from the roof of the house you live in even though both share some common characteristics. It would be very useful to be able to order a standard roof, but then to be able to customize it easily to fulfill your specific needs.

In this book you will be using others' code in the writing of your own code, and you will be reusing the code you write for yet other programs. Code reuse is increasingly important, partly because of the graphical user interfaces (window systems) that are popular on computers. These interfaces are time-consuming to program but are very similar from program to program, so the potential for code reuse is great.

One of the goals of object-oriented programming is to provide **objects** to make code development easier. Objects are like off-the-shelf software components. You can imagine that using such objects might be much simpler than designing them yourself. Building a house from a kit is much simpler than designing the kit itself. The same is true of programming and program design—it's simpler to use software components supplied by others than to write everything yourself. In this book, however, OOP will be used in our study of programming and the examination of computer science rather than becoming the principal focus of study.

1.6.2 Using Components

As an example of how software components might be useful, consider digital clocks, the display on a CD player, a car's odometer, and a counter for Web-page hits. All of these devices require the display of numerals that are manipulated in some fashion. The numerals displayed are different according to how the device is used:

■   Clocks display time; the numerals represent hours, minutes, seconds.

■   CD players display information on how many tracks are available on a CD (some also display time).

■   Web-page counters display information about how many times the page has been accessed.

■   Odometers display mileage as recorded by a car's wheels.

It should be possible for the computer programs controlling these displays to share (reuse) the code that displays numerals, differing only in how it is determined which numerals should be displayed and, perhaps, where the numerals are displayed.

Object-oriented programming involves reusable components. In C++ the word **class** refers to a family of components sharing common characteristics. A class allows **operations** that are used to manipulate the **objects** that are components of the class. For example, the class *four-door sedan* describes many makes and models of car. A specific four-door sedan, the one in my driveway, is an object of the generalized "four-door sedan class." All objects in this class share the common characteristic of having four doors and being sedans. They share other characteristics too, such as having a steering wheel, an engine, and four wheels. These characteristics are shared by all cars, not just four-door sedans. Operations allowed by the class *four-door sedan* include being driven, storing luggage, and consuming fuel.

As another example, the display of a numeral might be a different class than the value being displayed. A numeral display class might support operations such as assigning a value to be displayed and actually "drawing" the numeral. Other classes, such as a clock class or a timer class, could supply the values to be displayed.

1.7 Chapter Review

This chapter provides an introduction to the field of computer science and places programming properly within the field. In subsequent chapters you'll begin the process of augmenting and constructing programs. The important concepts introduced in this chapter are outlined here.

- Computer science—is more than the study of computers. It includes many subfields that are linked by the study of programming. Key parts of computer science include theory, language, and architecture.

- Algorithm—is a plan for solving a problem. It's related to a set of instructions to accomplish a task, such as knitting a sweater, but we'll use it to refer to a plan for accomplishing a task, such as sorting a hand of cards (and often a computer will be involved).

- Theory—refers to underlying mathematical principles on which computer science is built. For example, being able to compare different algorithms to determine which is most efficient relies on theoretical tools.

- Architecture—refers to how a computer is designed and put together. Computers have different architectures: some computers rely on using several processors at one time rather than just one.

- Language—refers to computer programming languages, which come in many forms and flavors. Both high- and low-level languages are used in writing programs, but we'll concentrate on the high-level language C++.

- Efficiency and complexity—refer to how difficult a problem is to solve using a computer and how various algorithms compare in solving problems (e.g., in how fast they run).

- Conceptual and formal models—refer to different ways of thinking. Programs can be thought of as instructions for a computer, but a mathematical notion of programming is possible too.

- Levels of abstraction—refer to different ways of observing. An idea can be turned into an algorithm, which is implemented as a C++ program, which is executed as a machine-language program. The same idea is viewed at many different levels and has particular characteristics depending on the level.

- Compiler—is a computer program that translates a high-level language such as C++ into a low-level language that can be executed on a computer.

- Bug—is a mistake in a program. Finding such mistakes is called debugging.

- Object-oriented programming—is a method of programming that, in a nutshell, relies on the use of off-the-shelf software components.

- Class—is a family of objects sharing common characteristics. The integers are a class of numbers; four-door sedans are a class of cars.

1.8 Exercises

1.1 The process of looking up a word in a dictionary is difficult to describe in a precise manner. Write an algorithm that can be used to find the *page* in a dictionary on which a given word occurs (if the word is in the dictionary). You may assume that each page of the dictionary has guide words indicating the first and last words on the page, but you should assume that there are no thumb indexes on the pages (so you cannot turn immediately to a specific letter section).

1.2   Suppose that you have 10 loads of laundry, one washer, and one dryer. Washing a load takes 25 minutes, drying a load takes 25 minutes, and folding the clothes in a load takes 10 minutes, for a total of 1 hour per load (assuming that the time to transfer a load is built into the timings given). All the laundry can be done in 10 hours using the method of completing one load before starting the next one. Devise a method for doing all 10 loads in less than 10 hours by making better use of the resources. Carefully describe the method and how long it takes to do the laundry using the method.

1.3   Suppose that student ID numbers consist of two digits. The exams are sorted in a large room. Consider the following description of a sorting algorithm:

- Make 100 "in-boxes" labeled 00 to 99.
- Divide the exams among the people participating in the sort.
- Have each person put an exam in the correct box according to ID number.
- Collect the exams from the boxes in order (00–99).

This method will work correctly. Try to modify the method to work with four-digit ID numbers and six-digit ID numbers. In making the modification, assume you have only 100 boxes. (Hint: Consider examining only two digits at a time.)

1.4   The steps labeled 1–7 in Figure 1.7 illustrate the design, development, realization, and implementation of a computer program to multiply two numbers. Consider the following problem:

> **Develop a recipe for a chocolate cake with chocolate icing that tastes delicious and makes you swoon.**

Develop analogs or parallels to the steps 1–7 for developing such a recipe. Write a detailed description of the process you might go through to develop a recipe—*not* what the recipe is.

1.5   Assume that a young friend of yours knows how to multiply any two one-digit numbers (i.e., knows the times tables). Write an explanation (algorithm) of how to multiply an n-digit number by a one-digit number. Can you extend this algorithm into one that can be used to multiply two many-digit numbers (such as 1,285 and 57, as shown in Figure 1.7)?

1.6   There are many different high-level programming languages. Common languages include Pascal, FORTRAN, Scheme, BASIC, and COBOL. Can you think of a reason for why there are many languages as opposed to a single language? Why is more than one language in use today?

1.7   (Suggested by a description in *Computer Architecture,* by Blaauw and Brooks.) Consider clocks and watches as examples of different "architectures" used for telling time. For clocks and watches that have hands and dials, write an outline of an algorithm that can be used to tell time. How is the architecture of a wristwatch (with hands) similar to that of a grandfather clock? How is it different? What features of the face of a watch are essential for telling time? In particular, are numbers needed on the face of a watch to tell time? Make a list of different watch faces and try to distill the essential features of a watch face into a few descriptive sentences.

Consider the inner workings of watches: list at least three different methods used to "run" a watch. How are different levels of abstraction illustrated by the concept of a watch?

How is a digital watch different from a watch with hands? How is it similar?

1.8 C++ (and other high-level language) programs are written in a language that is a compromise between natural languages such as English and the language of zeros and ones, which is "spoken" by computers. Consider musical compositions written for different instruments or groups of musicians. Is music written in a high-level language or a low-level language? Are there different languages for expressing musical compositions as there are different natural languages and different computer languages? Why?

1.9 Suppose that you are playing in a large field with several friends and one of you discovers that a house key has been lost. Write an algorithm for finding the key that is designed to find it as quickly as possible. Write another algorithm designed to take a long time to find the key. Can you reason about whether your algorithms are the best possible or worst possible algorithms for this particular task?

How is this task related to how you look for a key when you have misplaced it inside your house?

Figure 1.9 A Pentium chip.

1.10 The program used to generate the assembler output in Figure 1.5 is used in Figure 1.10 on two different computers; the assembler code below on the right is generated on a Macintosh G3 computer, the code on the left on a Pentium computer running Windows NT. Both machines use the same compiler: Metrowerks Codewarrior. A Pentium chip is shown in Figure 1.9 (see p. 23) and a G3 chip is shown in Figure 1.11.

What is similar in these two versions of assembly language and what is different? Can you find instructions that would be common to all the different assembly codes? Why do you think different compilers generate different code for the same program?

```
_main                                    ".main"(1)
  push      ebp
  mov       ebp,esp                        stw      r31,-4(SP)
  sub       esp,16                         stw      r30,-8(SP)
  mov       dword ptr [ebp-12],7           li       r31,7
  mov       dword ptr [ebp-8],12           li       r30,12
  mov       edx,dword ptr [ebp-12]         mullw    r0,r31,r30
  imul      edx,dword ptr [ebp-8]          stw      r0,-16(SP)
  mov       dword ptr [ebp-4],edx          li       r3,0
  mov       eax,0                          lwz      r31,-4(SP)
  leave                                    lwz      r30,-8(SP)
  ret       near                           blr
```

Figure 1.10 Windows NT code on the left, Macintosh G3 code on the right.

Figure 1.11 A PowerPC chip.

1.11 The cards that were used in the context of sorting in this chapter (ace, king, queen, etc.) provide a good example of an object. If a card is one object, and a hand and deck are other objects composed of card objects, list a few operations that might be useful in manipulating cards, hands, and decks.

1.12 Vending machines are objects composed of several different objects. Pick a specific kind of vending machine and list several objects that are used to "make up" the vending machine (e.g., buttons used to specify items to be bought). For each object, and for the vending machine as a whole, list several operations that might be useful in reasoning about or manipulating the objects.

Are there some characteristics that all vending machines have in common? Are there classes of vending machines, each of which differs fundamentally from other kinds of vending machines?

1

Foundations of C++ Programming

C++ Programs: Form and Function   2

Scientists build to learn; engineers learn to build.
FRED BROOKS

tem·plate (têm´plît) *n.* A pattern, . . . used as a guide in making something accurately …
The American Heritage Dictionary

Art is the imposing of a pattern on experience, and our aesthetic
enjoyment in recognition of the pattern.
Dialogues of Alfred North Whitehead (June 10, 1943)

It is a bad plan that admits of no modification.
Publius Syrus, Maxim 469

To learn to write programs, you must write programs and you must read programs. Although this statement may not seem profound, it is a lesson that is often left unpracticed and, subsequently, unmastered. In thinking about the concepts presented in this chapter, and in practicing them in the context of writing C++ programs, you should keep the following three things in mind.

1. Programming has elements of both art and science. Just as designing a building requires both a sense of aesthetics and a knowledge of structural engineering, designing a program requires an understanding of programming aesthetics, knowledge of computer science, and practice in software engineering.

2. Use the programs provided as templates when designing and constructing programs of your own—use what's provided along with your own ingenuity. When some concept is unclear, stop to work on it and think about it before continuing. This work will involve experimenting with the programs provided. Experimenting with a program means reading, executing, testing, and modifying the program. When you experiment with a program, you can try to find its weak points and its strengths.

3. Practice.

This book is predicated on the belief that you learn best by doing new things and by studying things similar to the new things. This technique applies to learning carpentry, learning to play a musical instrument, or learning to program a computer. Not everyone can win a Grammy award and not everyone can win the Turing award,[1] but becoming adept programmers and practitioners of computer science is well within your grasp.

---

[1]The former is awarded for musical excellence, the latter for excellence in computer science.

Ultimately programs are a means of expressing algorithms in a form that computers execute. Before studying complicated and large programs, it's necessary to begin with the basics of what a program is, how programs are executed, and what C++ programs can do. However, understanding a program *completely* requires a great deal of experience and knowledge about C++. We'll use some simple programs to illustrate basic concepts. Try to focus on the big picture of programming; don't get bogged down by every detail. The details will eventually become clearer, and you'll master them by studying many programming examples.

2.1   Simple C++ Programs

In this section we introduce simple C++ programs to demonstrate how to use the C++ language. These programs produce **output**; they cause characters to be displayed on a computer screen. The first C++ program is *hello.cpp*, Program 2.1. This program is based on the first program in the book [KR78], written by the inventors of C; and it is the first program in [Str97], written by the inventor of C++. It doesn't convey the power of C++, but it's a tradition for C and C++ programmers to begin with this program.

All programs have names, in this case *hello*, and suffixes, in this case *.cpp*. In this book all programs have the suffix *.cpp*, which is one convention (other suffixes used include *.cc* and *.cxx*). If this program is compiled and executed, it generates the material shown in the box labeled "output."

Program 2.1   hello.cpp

```
#include <iostream>
using namespace std;

//traditional first program
// author: Owen Astrachan, 2/27/99

int main()
{
    cout << "Hello world" << endl;
    return 0;
}
```

hello.cpp

```
prompt> hello
Hello world
```

Program 2.2, *hello2.cpp,* produces output identical to that of Program 2.1. We'll look at why one of these versions might be preferable as we examine the structure of C++ programs. In general, given a specific programming task there are many, many different programs that will perform the task.

Program 2.2   hello2.cpp

```
#include <iostream>
using namespace std;

// traditional first program with user defined function
// author: Owen Astrachan, 02/27/99

void Hello()
{
    cout << "Hello world" << endl;
}

int main()
{
    Hello();
    return 0;
}
```
hello2.cpp

2.1.1   Syntax and Semantics

Programs are run by computers, not by humans. There is often much less room for error when writing programs than when writing English In particular, you'll need to be aware of certain rules that govern the use of C++. These rules fall into two broad categories: rules of syntax and rules of semantics.

What are syntax and semantics? In English and other natural languages, syntax is the manner in which words are used to construct sentences, and semantics is the meaning of the sentences. We'll see that similar definitions apply to syntax and semantics in C++ programs. Before reviewing rules for C++ programs, we'll look at some rules that govern the use and construction of English words and sentences:

- Rules of spelling:
  i before *e* except after *c* or when sounding like $\bar{a}$ as in ... *neighbor* and *weigh.*
- Rules of grammar:
  "with *none* use the singular verb when the word means 'no one' ... a plural verb is commonly used when *none* suggests more than one thing or person—'None are so fallible as those who are sure they're right' " [JW89].
- Rules of style:
  "Avoid the use of qualifiers. *Rather, very, little, pretty*—these are the leeches that infest the pond of prose, sucking the blood of words" [JW89].

Similar rules exist in C++. One difference between English and C++ is that the meaning, or **semantics,** of a poorly constructed English sentence can be understood although the syntax is incorrect:

> Its inconceivable that someone can study a language and not know whether or not a kind of sentence—the ungainly ones, the misspelled ones, those that are unclear—are capable of understanding.

This sentence has at least four errors in spelling, grammar, and style; its meaning, however, is still discernible.

In general, programming languages demand more precision than do natural languages such as English. A missing semicolon might make an English sentence fall into the run-on category. A missing semicolon in a C++ program can stop the program from working at all.

Dennis Ritchie (b. 1941)

Dennis Ritchie developed the C programming language and codeveloped the UNIX operating system. For his work with UNIX, he shared the 1983 Turing award with the codeveloper, Ken Thompson. In his Turing address, Ritchie writes of what computer science is.

> *Computer science research is different from these [physics, chemistry, mathematics] more traditional disciplines. Philosophically it differs from the physical sciences because it seeks not to discover, explain, or exploit the natural world, but instead to study the properties of machines of human creation. In this it is analogous to mathematics, and indeed the "science" part of computer science is, for the most part, mathematical in spirit. But an inevitable aspect of computer science is the creation of computer programs: objects that, though intangible, are subject to commercial exchange.*

Ritchie completed his doctoral dissertation in applied mathematics but didn't earn his doctorate because "I was so bored, I never turned it in." In citing the work that led to the Turing award, the selection committee mentions this:

> *The success of the UNIX system stems from its tasteful selection of a few key ideas and their elegant implementation. The model of the UNIX system has led a generation of software designers to new ways of thinking about programming.*

For more information see [Sla87, ACM87].

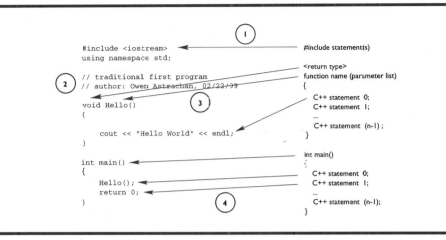

Figure 2.1 Format of a C++ program.

We'll illustrate the important syntactic details of a C++ program by studying *hello.cpp* and *hello2.cpp*, Programs 2.1 and 2.2. We'll then extend these into a typical and general program framework. Four rules for C++ program syntax and style will also be listed. A useful tool for checking the syntax of programs is the C++ compiler, which indicates whether a program has the correct form—that is, whether the program statements are "worded correctly." You should *not* worry about memorizing the syntactic details of C++ (e.g., where semicolons go). The details of the small subset of C++ covered in this chapter will become second nature as you read and write programs.

All the C++ programs we'll study in this book have the format shown in Figure 2.1 and explained below. Although this format will be used, the spacing of each line in a program does not affect whether a program works. The amount of **white space** and the blank lines between functions help make programs easier for humans to read but do not affect how a program works. *White space* refers to the space, tab, and return keys.

1. Programs begin with the appropriate #include statements.[2] Each include statement provides access, via a **header** file, to a **library** of useful functions. We normally think of a library as a place from which we can borrow books. A programming library consists of off-the-shelf programming tools that programmers can borrow. These tools are used by programmers to make the task of writing programs easier.

    In most C++ programs it is necessary to import information from such libraries into the program. In particular, information for output (and input) is stored in the iostream library, accessible by including the header file <iostream>, as shown in Figure 2.1. If a program has no output (or input), it isn't necessary to include <iostream>.

---

[2]The # sign is read as either "sharp" or "pound"; I usually say "pound-include" when reading to myself or talking with others.

All programs using standard C++ libraries should have `using namespace std;` after the `#include` statements. Namespaces[3] are explained in Section A.2.3 of How to A.

2. All programs should include comments describing the purpose of the program. As programs get more complex, the comments become more intricate. For the simple programs studied in this chapter, the comments are brief. The compiler ignores comments; programmers put comments in programs for human readers. C++ comments extend from a double slash, `//`, to the end of the line. Another style of commenting permits multiline comments—any text between `/*` and `*/` is treated as a comment. It's important to remember that people read programs, so writing comments should be considered mandatory although programs will work without them.

3. Zero, one, or more **programmer-defined** functions follow the `#include` statements and comments. Program 2.2, *hello2.cpp,* has two programmer-defined functions, named `Hello` and `main`. Program 2.1, *hello.cpp,* has one programmer-defined function, named `main`. In general, a function is a way of grouping C++ statements together so that they can be referred to by a single name. The function is an abstraction used in place of the statements. As shown in Figure 2.1, each programmer-defined function consists of the function's **return type,** the function's **name,** the function's **parameter list,** and the statements that make up the function's **body.** For the function `Hello` the return type is `void`, the name of the function is `Hello`, and there is an empty parameter list. There is only one C++ statement in `Hello`.

    The return type of the function `main` is `int`. In C++, an `int` represents an integer; we'll discuss this in detail later. The name of the function is `main`, and it too has an empty parameter list. There are two statements in the function body; the second statement is `return 0`. We'll also discuss the return statement in some detail later. The last statement in the function `main` of each program you write should be `return 0`.

4. Every C++ program must have exactly one function named **main.** The statements in `main` are executed first when a program is run. Some C++ compilers will generate a warning if the statement `return 0` is not included as the last statement in `main` (such statements are explained in the next chapter). It's important to spell `main` with lowercase letters. A function named `Main` is different from `main` because names are case-sensitive in C++. Finally, the return type of `main` should be specified as `int` for reasons we'll explore in Chapter 4.[4]

Since program execution begins with `main`, it is a good idea to start reading a program beginning with `main` when you are trying to understand what the program does and how it works.

---

[3]Compilers that support the C++ standard require `using namespace std;` but older compilers don't support namespaces. How to A explains this in more detail.

[4]Some books use a return type of `void` for `main`. According to the C++ standard, this is not legal; the return type *must* be `int`.

2.1 Find four errors in the ungainly sentence given above (and reproduced below) whose semantics (meaning) is understandable despite the errors.

> Its inconceivable that someone can study a language and not know whether or not a kind of sentence—the ungainly ones, the misspelled ones, those that are unclear—are capable of understanding.

Are humans better "processors" than computers because of the ability to compre-hend "faulty" phrases? Explain your answer.

2.2 Find two syntax errors and one semantic error in the sentence "There is three things wrong with this sentence."

2.3 Given the four rules for C++ programs, what is the smallest legal C++ program? (Hint: it doesn't produce any output, so it doesn't need a #include statement.)

2.4 No rules are given about using separate lines for C++ functions and statements. If main from Program 2.2 is changed as follows, is the program legal C++?

```
int main () { Hello(); return 0;}
```

2.2 How a Program Works

Computer programs execute sequences of statements, often producing some form of output. Statements are executed whether the program is written in a high- or low-level language. Determining what statements to include in a program is part of the art and science of programming. Developing algorithms and classes, and the relationship between classes, is also part of this art and science.

When you execute a program, either by typing the name of the program at a prompt or by using a mouse to click on "run" in a menu, the execution starts in the function main. When the program is running it uses the processor of the computer; when the program is finished it returns control of the processor to the operating system. The explicit return 0 statement in main makes it clear that control is returning to the operating system.

The output of Program 2.1, *hello.cpp,* results from the execution of the statement beginning cout << followed by other characters, followed by other symbols. This statement is in the body of the function main. The characters between the double quotation marks appear on the screen exactly as they appear between the quotes in the statement. (Notice that the quotes do not appear on the screen.) If the statement

```
cout << "Hello world" << endl;
```

is changed to

```
cout << "Goodbye cruel planet" << endl;
```

then execution of the program *hello.cpp* results in the output that follows:

Goodbye cruel planet

2.2.1   Flow of Control

In every C++ program, execution begins with the first statement in the function `main`. After this statement is executed, each statement in `main` is executed in turn. When the last statement has been executed, the program is done. Several uses of << can be combined into a single statement as shown in *hello.cpp,* Program 2.1. Note that `endl` indicates that an end-of-line is to be output (hence "end ell"). For example, if the statement

```
cout << "Hello world" << endl;
```

is changed to

```
cout << "Goodbye" << endl << "cruel planet" << endl;
```

then execution of the program *hello.cpp* results in the output shown below, where the first `endl` forces a new line of output.

Goodbye
cruel planet

This modified output could be generated by using two separate output statements:

```
cout << "Goodbye" << endl;
cout << "cruel planet" << endl;
```

Since each statement is executed one after the other, the output generated will be the same as that shown above.

In C++, statements are terminated by a semicolon. This means that a single statement can extend over several lines since the semicolon is used to determine when the statement ends.

```
cout << "Goodbye"       << endl
     << "cruel planet" << endl;
```

Just as run-on sentences in English can obscure the meaning, long statements in C++ can be hard to read. However, the output statement above that uses two lines isn't really too long; some programmers prefer it to the two-statement version since it is easy to read.

Function Calls. If a statement invokes, or **calls**, a function—such as when the statement `Hello();` in main invokes the function `Hello` in Program 2.2—then each of the statements in the called function is executed. For example, while the statements in the function `Hello` are executing, the statements in `main` are suspended, waiting for the statements in `Hello` to finish. When all the statements in a function have executed, **control** returns to the statement after the call to the function. In Program 2.2 this is the statement `return 0` after the function call `Hello()`. When the last statement in a program has executed, control returns from `main` to the computer just as control returns from `Hello` to `main` when the last statement in `Hello` is executed. If the `return 0` statement in `main` is missing, control will still return to the computer.

In the case of Program 2.2, three statements are executed:

1. The call `Hello();` in the function `main`.
2. The statement `cout << "Hello world" << endl;` in `Hello`.
3. The statement `return 0;` in `main`.

The execution of the second statement above results in the appearance of 11 "visible" characters on the computer's screen (note that a space is a character just as the letter *H* is a character).

Output Streams. To display output, the **standard output stream** `cout` is used. This stream is accessible in a program via the included library `<iostream>`. If this header file is not included, a program cannot make reference to the stream `cout`. You can think of an output stream as a stream of objects in the same way that a brook or a river is a stream of water. Placing objects on the output stream causes them to appear on the screen eventually just as placing a toy boat on a stream of water causes it to flow downstream. Objects are placed on the output stream using `<<`, the **insertion operator,** so named since it is used to insert values onto an output stream. Sometimes this operator is read as "put-to." The word `cout` is pronounced "see-out."

2.3   What Can Be Output?

Computers were originally developed to be number crunchers, machines used for solving large systems of equations. Not surprisingly, numbers still play a large part in programming and computer science. The output stream `cout` can be used for the output of numbers and words. In Program 2.1 characters appeared on the screen as a result of executing a statement that uses the standard output stream `cout`. Sequences of characters appearing between quotes are called **string literals.** Characters include letters a–z (and uppercase versions), numbers, symbols such as !+S%&*, and many other non-visible "characters," such as the backspace key, the return key, and in general any key that can be typed from a computer keyboard. String literals cannot change during a program's execution. The number 3.14159 is a **numeric literal** (it approximates the number π). In addition to string literals, it is possible to output numeric literals and arithmetic expressions.

For example, if the statement

```
cout << "Hello world" << endl;
```

is changed to

```
cout << "Goodbye" << endl << "cruel planet #" << 1 + 2
    << endl;
```

then execution of the program *hello.cpp* results in the output shown below.

```
Goodbye
cruel planet #3
```

The arithmetic expression $1 + 2$ is evaluated and 3, the result of the evaluation, is placed on the output stream. To be more precise, each of the chunks that follow a << is evaluated and causes the output stream to be modified in some way. The string literal `"Goodbye"` evaluates to itself and is placed on the output stream as seven characters. The arithmetic expression $1 + 2$ evaluates to 3, and the character 3 is placed on the output stream. Each `endl` begins a new line on the output stream.[5]

The C++ compiler ensures that arithmetic expressions are evaluated correctly and, with the help of the stream library, ensures that the appropriate characters are placed on the output stream.

Changing the output statement in *hello.cpp* to the statement here:

```
cout << "The radius of planet #" << 1+2
    << " is " << 6378.38 << " km," << endl
    << "which is " << 6378.38 * 0.62137 << " miles" << endl;
```

results in the output shown below. The symbol * is used to multiply two values, and the number 0.62137 is the number of miles in 1 kilometer.

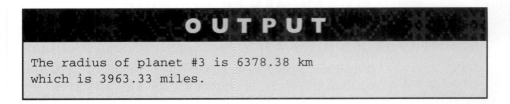

```
The radius of planet #3 is 6378.38 km
which is 3963.33 miles.
```

The ability of the output stream to handle strings, numbers, and other objects we will encounter later makes it very versatile.

---

[5]An `endl` also flushes the output buffer. Some programmers think it is bad programming to flush the output buffer just to begin a new line of output. The escape sequence \n can be used to start a new line.

2.5 Suppose that the body of the function `Hello` is as shown here:

```
cout << "PI = " << 3.14159 << endl;
```

What appears on the screen? Would the output of

```
cout << "PI = 3.14159" << endl;
```

be the same or different?

2.6 We've noted that more than one statement may appear in a function body:

```
void Hello()
{
  cout << "PI = " << 3.14159 << endl;
  cout << "e  = " << 2.71828 << endl;
  cout << "PI*e = " << 3.14159 * 2.71828 << endl;
}
```

What appears on the screen if the function `Hello` above is executed?

2.7 If the third `cout <<` statement in the previous problem is changed to

```
cout << "PI*e = 3.14159 * 2.71828" << endl;
```

what appears on the screen? Note that this statement puts a single string literal onto the output stream (followed by an `endl`). Why is this output different from the output in the previous question?

2.8 What does the computer display when the statement

```
cout << "1 + 2 = 5" << endl;
```

is executed? Can a computer generate output that is incorrect?

2.9 What modifications need to be made to the output statement in Program 2.1 (the *hello.cpp* program) to generate the following output?

```
I think I think, therefore I think I am
```

2.10 All statements in C++ are terminated by a semicolon. Is the programmer-defined function

```
void Hello()
{
    cout << "Hello World" << endl;
}
```

a statement? Why? Is the function call Hello() in main a statement?

2.11 If the body of the function main of Program 2.2 is changed as shown in the following, what appears on the screen?

```
cout << "I rode the scrambler at the amusement park"
     << endl; Hello();
```

2.4   Using Functions

The flow of control in *hello.cpp*, Program 2.1, is different from *hello2.cpp*, Program 2.2. The use of the function Hello in *hello2.cpp* doesn't make the program better or more powerful; it just increases the number of statements that are executed: a function call as well as an output statement. In this section we'll explore programs that use functions in more powerful ways. I say *powerful* in that the resulting programs are easier to modify and are useful in more applications than when functions are not used. Using functions can make programs longer and appear to be more complicated, but sometimes more complicated programs are preferred because they are more general and are easier to modify and maintain. Using functions to group statements together is part of managing the complex task of programming.

We'll now investigate Program 2.3 (*drawhead.cpp*) in which several cout << statements are used in the programmer-defined function Head. In *drawhead.cpp* the body of the main function consists of a call of the programmer-defined function Head and the statement return 0.

For the moment we will assume that all programmer-defined functions are constructed similarly to the manner in which the function main is constructed except that the word void is used before each function. This is precisely how the syntactic properties of functions were given in Section 2.1.1. The word void will be replaced with other words in later examples of programmer-defined functions; for example, we've seen that int is used with the function main.

Program 2.3   drawhead.cpp

```
#include <iostream>
using namespace std;

// print a head, use of functions
```

```
void Head()
{
    cout << "  ||||||||||||||||  " << endl;
    cout << "  |              |  " << endl;
    cout << "  |    o    o    |  " << endl;
    cout << " _|            |_ " << endl;
    cout << "|_            _|" << endl;
    cout << "  |    |_____|    |  " << endl;
    cout << "  |            |  " << endl;

}

int main()
{
    Head();
    return 0;
}
```

drawhead.cpp

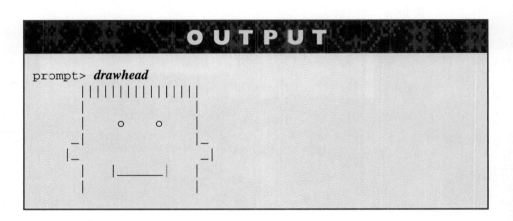

At this point the usefulness of functions may not be apparent in the programs we've presented. In the program *parts.cpp* that appears as Program 2.4, many functions are used. If this program is run, the output is the same as the output generated when *drawhead.cpp*, Program 2.3, is run.

Program 2.4 parts.cpp

```
#include <iostream>
using namespace std;

// procedures used to print different heads

void PartedHair()
// prints a "parted hair" scalp
{
    cout << "  ||||||||//////// " << endl;
```

```
    }

    void Hair()
    // prints a "straight-up" or "frightened" scalp
    {
        cout << "  |||||||||||||||  " << endl;
    }

    void Sides()
    // prints sides of a head -- other functions should use distance
    // between sides of head here as guide in creating head parts
       (e.g., eyes)
    {
        cout << "  |                |  " << endl;
    }

    void Eyes()
    // prints eyes of a head (corresponding to distance in Sides)
    {
        cout << "  |    o   o    |  " << endl;
    }

    void Ears()
    // prints ears (corresponding to distance in Sides)
    {
        cout << "  _|            |_ " << endl;
        cout << " |_            _|" << endl;
    }

    void Smile()
    // prints smile (corresponding to distance in Sides)
    {
        cout << "  |    |_____|    |  " << endl;
    }

    int main()
    {
        Hair();
        Sides();
        Eyes();
        Ears();
        Smile();
        Sides();
        return 0;
    }
```

parts.cpp

The usefulness of functions should become more apparent when the body of main is modified to generate new "heads." This program is longer than the previous programs and may be harder for you to understand. You should begin reading the program starting with the function main. Starting with main you can then move to reading the functions called from main, and the functions that these functions call, and so on. If each call of the function Sides in the body of main is replaced with two calls to Sides, then the new body of main and the output generated by the body are as shown here (as shown, Sides is called to add space between the eyes and the ears.)

```cpp
int main()
{
    Hair();
    Sides(); Sides();
    Eyes();
    Sides();
    Ears();
    Smile();
    Sides(); Sides();
    return 0;
}
```

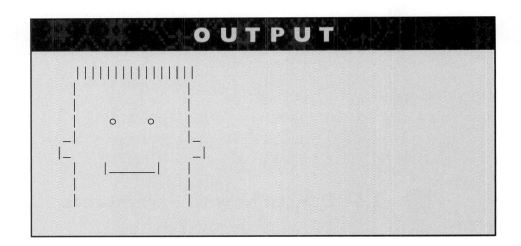

Although *parts.cpp,* Program 2.4, is more complicated than *drawhead.cpp*, Program 2.3, it is easier to modify. Creating heads with different hairstyles or adding a nose is easier when *parts.cpp* is used, because it is clear where the changes should be made because of the names of the functions. It's also possible not only to have more than one hairstyle appear in the same program, but to change what is displayed. For example, adding a nose can be done using a function Nose:

```cpp
void Nose()
// draw a mustached nose
{
    cout << " |        O        | " << endl;
    cout << " |       |||||     | " << endl;
}
```

On the other hand, the original program clearly showed what the printed head looks like; it's not necessary to run the program to see this. As you gain experience as a programmer, your judgment as to when to use functions will get better.

2.12 If you replace the call to the function `Hair` by a call to the function `PartedHair`, what kind of picture is output? How can one of the hair functions be modified to generate a flat head with no hair on it? What picture results if the call `Hair()` is replaced by `Smile()`?

2.13 Design a new function named `Bald` that gives the drawn head the appearance of baldness (perhaps a few tufts of hair on the side are appropriate).

2.14 Modify the function `Smile` so that the face either frowns or shows no emotion. Change the name of the function appropriately.

2.15 What functions should be changed to produce the head shown below? Modify the program to draw such a head.

```
| | | | | | |/ / / / / / / /
|                          |
|      ___     ___         |
|---|o|--|o|---|
|      ---     ---         |
 _|                      |_
|  _                    _|
|      |_____|        |
|                          |
```

2.5 Functions with Parameters

Program 2.4, *parts.cpp,* showed that the use of programmer-defined functions enabled the program to be more versatile than the program *drawhead.cpp.* Nevertheless, the program had to be re-edited and recompiled to produce new "heads." In this section and the next chapter, you will learn design methods that allow programs to be useful in more contexts.

2.5.1 What Is a Parameter?

In all the programs studied so far, the insertion operator << has been more useful than any programmer-defined function. The insertion operator is versatile because it can be used to write *any message* to the screen. Any sequence of characters between quotes (recall that such a sequence is termed a string literal) and any arithmetic expression can be inserted onto an output stream using the << operator.

■   `cout << "Hello world" << endl;`

■   `cout << "Goodbye cruel planet" << endl;`

■   `cout << "  ||||||||/////i////  " << endl;`

■   `cout << "The square of 10 is " << 10*10 << endl;`

The << operator can be used to output various things just as the addition operator + can be used to add them. It's possible to write programmer-defined functions that have this same kind of versatility. You've probably used a calculator with a square root button: $\sqrt{}$. When you find the square root of a number using this button, you're invoking the square root function with an **argument**. In the mathematical expression $\sqrt{101}$, the 101 is the argument of the square root function. Functions that take arguments are called **parameterized functions.** The parameters serve as a means of controlling what the functions do—setting a different parameter results in a different outcome just as $\sqrt{101}$ has a different value than $\sqrt{157}$. The words *parameter* and *argument* are synonyms in this context.

To see how parameters are useful in making functions more general, consider an (admittedly somewhat loose) analogy to a CD player. It is conceivable that one might put a CD of Gershwin's *Rhapsody in Blue* in such a machine and then glue the machine shut. From that point on, the machine becomes a "Gershwin player" rather than a CD player. One can also purchase a "weather box," which is a radio permanently tuned to a weather information service. Although interesting for determining whether to carry an umbrella, the weather box is less general-purpose than a normal (tunable) radio in the same way that the Gershwin player is less versatile than a normal CD player. In the same sense, the << operator is more versatile than the Head function in Program 2.3, which always draws the same head.

Functions with parameters are more versatile than functions without parameters although there are times when both kinds of function are useful. Functions that receive parameters must receive the correct kind of parameter or they will not execute properly (often such functions will not compile). Continuing with the CD analogy, suppose that you turn on a CD player with no CD in it. Obviously nothing will be played. Similarly, if it were possible to put a cassette tape into a CD player without damaging the player, the CD player would not be able to play the cassette. Finally, if a 2.5-inch mini-CD is forced into a normal CD player, still nothing is played. The point of this example is that the "parameterized" CD player must be used properly—the appropriate "parameter" (a CD, not a cassette or mini-CD) must be used if the player is to function as intended.

2.5.2 An Example of Parameterization: Happy Birthday

Suppose you are faced with the unenviable task of writing a program that displays the song "Happy Birthday" to a set of quintuplets named Grace, Alan, John, Ada, and Blaise.[6] In designing the program, we employ a concept called **iterative enhancement**, whereby a rough draft of the program is repeatedly refined until the desired program is finished.

A naive, first attempt with this problem might consist of 24 cout << statements; that is, 5 "verses" × 4 lines per verse + 4 blank lines (note that there is one blank line between each verse so that there is one less blank line than there are verses). Such a program would yield the desired output—but even without much programming experience this solution should be unappealing to you. Indeed, the effort required to generate a new

---

[6]Coincidentally, these are the first names of five pioneers in computer science: Grace Hopper, Alan Turing, John von Neumann, Ada Lovelace, and Blaise Pascal.

verse in such a program is the same as the effort required to generate a verse in the original program. Nevertheless, such a program has at least one important merit: it is easy to make work. Even though "cut-and-paste" techniques are available in most text editors, it is very likely that you will introduce typos using this approach.

We want to develop a program that mirrors the way people sing "Happy Birthday." You don't think of a special song *BirthdayLaura* to sing to a friend Laura and *Birthday-Dave* for a friend Dave. You use one song and fill in (with a parameter!) the name of the person who has the birthday.

OUTPUT

```
Happy birthday to you
Happy birthday to you
Happy birthday dear
Happy birthday to you

Happy birthday to you
Happy birthday to you
Happy birthday dear
Happy birthday to you

Happy birthday to you
Happy birthday to you
Happy birthday dear
Happy birthday to you

Happy birthday to you
Happy birthday to you
Happy birthday dear
Happy birthday to you

Happy birthday to you
Happy birthday to you
Happy birthday dear
Happy birthday to you
```

Program 2.5 bday.cpp

```cpp
#include <iostream>
using namespace std;

// first attempt at birthday singing
```

```
void Sing()
{
    cout << "Happy birthday to you" << endl;
    cout << "Happy birthday to you" << endl;
    cout << "Happy birthday dear  " << endl;
    cout << "Happy birthday to you" << endl;
    cout << endl;
}

int main()
{
    Sing(); Sing(); Sing(); Sing(); Sing();
    return 0;
}
```

bday.cpp

We need to print five copies of the song. We will design a function named Sing whose purpose is to generate the birthday song for each of the quintuplets. Initially we will leave the name of the quintuplet out of the function so that five songs are printed, but no names appear in the songs. Once this program works, we'll use parameters to add a name to each song. This technique of writing a preliminary version, then modifying it to lead to a better version, is one that is employed throughout the book. It is the heart of the concept of iterative enhancement.

The first pass at a solution is *bday.cpp*, Program 2.5. Execution of this program yields a sequence of printed verses close to the desired output, but the name of each person whose birthday is being celebrated is missing. One possibility is to use five different functions (SingGrace, SingAlan, etc.), one function for each verse, but this isn't really any better than just using 24 cout statements. We need to parameterize the function Sing so that it is versatile enough to provide a song for each quintuplet. This is done in Program 2.6, which generates exactly the output required. Note that the statement

```
cout << "Happy birthday dear " << endl;
```

from Program 2.5 has been replaced with

```
cout << "Happy birthday dear " << person << endl;
```

Program 2.6 bday2.cpp

```
#include <iostream>
using namespace std;

#include <string>

// working birthday program

void Sing(string person)
{
    cout << "Happy birthday to you" << endl;
    cout << "Happy birthday to you" << endl;
```

```
        cout << "Happy birthday dear " << person << endl;
        cout << "Happy birthday to you" << endl;
        cout << endl;
    }

    int main()
    {
        Sing("Grace");
        Sing("Alan");
        Sing("John");
        Sing("Ada");
        Sing("Blaise");
        return 0;
    }                                                                    bday2.cpp
```

This statement can be spread over several lines without affecting its behavior.

```
cout << "Happy birthday dear "
    << person
    << endl;
```

Because only one endl is used in the output statement, only one line of output is written.

2.5.3 Passing Parameters

When the function call Sing("Grace") in main is executed, the string literal "Grace" is the argument **passed** to the string parameter person. This is diagrammed by the solid arrow in Figure 2.2. When the statement

```
 cout << "Happy birthday dear " << person << endl"
```

in Sing is executed, the parameter person is replaced by its value, as indicated by the dashed arrow in Figure 2.2. In this case the value is the string literal "Grace". Since person is not between quotes, it is not a string literal. As shown in Figure 2.2, the parameter person is represented by a box. When the function Sing is called, the value that is passed to the parameter is stored in this box. Then each statement in the function is executed sequentially. After the last statement, cout << endl, executes, control returns from the function Sing to the statement that follows the function call Sing("Grace"). This means that the statement Sing("Alan") is executed next. This call passes the argument "Alan", which is stored in the box associated with the parameter person.

If you review the format of a C++ function given in Figure 2.1, you'll see that each function has a parameter list. In a parameter list, each parameter must include the name of the parameter and the **type** of the parameter. In the definition of Sing the parameter is given the name person. The parameter has the type string. Recall that a string is any sequence of characters and that string literals occur between double quotes. All parameters must have an indication as to their structure—that is, what type of thing the parameter is. A parameter's type determines what kinds of things can be done with the parameter in a C++ program.

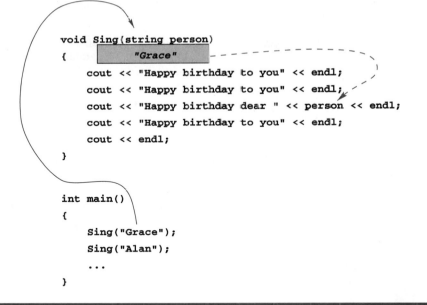

```
void Sing(string person)
{            "Grace"

    cout << "Happy birthday to you" << endl;
    cout << "Happy birthday to you" << endl;
    cout << "Happy birthday dear " << person << endl;
    cout << "Happy birthday to you" << endl;
    cout << endl;
}


int main()
{
    Sing("Grace");
    Sing("Alan");
    ...
}
```

Figure 2.2 Parameter passing.

The type `string` is not a built-in type in standard C++ but is made accessible by using the appropriate `#include` directive:

```
#include<string>
```

at the top of the program. Some older compilers do not support the standard string type. Information is given in How to C about `tstring`, an implementation of strings that can be used with older compilers. Include directives are necessary to provide information to the compiler about different types, objects, and classes used in a program, such as output streams and strings. Standard include files found in all C++ programming environments are indicated using angle brackets, as in `#include <iostream>`. Include files that are supplied by the user rather than by the system are indicated using double quotes, as in `#include "tstring.h"`.[7]

There is a vocabulary associated with all programming languages. Mastering this vocabulary is part of mastering programming and computer science. To be precise about explanations involving parameterized functions, I will use the word **parameter** to refer to usage within a function and in the function header (e.g., *person*). I will use the word **argument** to refer to what is passed to the function (e.g., *"Grace"* in the call `Sing("Grace")`.) Another method for differentiating between these two is to call the argument an **actual parameter** and to use the term **formal parameter** to refer to the

---

[7]The C++ standard uses header files that do not have a .h suffix, such as iostream rather than iostream.h. We use the .h suffix for header files associated with code supplied with this book.

parameter in the function header. Here we use the adjective *formal* because the form (or type — as in `string`) of the parameter is given in the function header.

We must distinguish between the occurrence of *person* in the statement `cout << ...` and the occurrence of the string literal `"Happy birthday dear "`. Since *person* does not appear in quotes, the value of the parameter *person* is printed. If the statement `cout << "person"` was used rather than `cout << person`, the use of quotes would cause the string literal *person* to appear on the screen.

```
Happy birthday to you
Happy birthday to you
Happy birthday dear person
Happy birthday to you
```

The use of the parameter's name causes the value of the parameter to appear on the screen. The value of the parameter is different for each call of the function *Sing*. The parameter is a **variable** capable of representing values in different contexts just as the variable x can represent different values in the equation $y = 5 \cdot x + 3$.

Pause to Reflect

2.16 In the following sequence of program statements, is the string literal `"Me"` an argument or a parameter? Is it an actual parameter?

```
cout << "  A Verse for My Ego" << endl;
Sing("Me");
```

2.17 What happens with your compiler if the statement `Sing("Grace")` is changed to `Sing(Grace)`? Why?

2.18 What modifications should be made to Program 2.6 to generate a song for a person named *Bjarne*?

2.19 What modifications should be made to Program 2.6 so that each song emphasizes the personalized line by ending it with three exclamation points?

```
Happy birthday dear Bjarne !!!
```

2.20 What happens if the name of the formal parameter *person* is changed to *celebrant* in the function `Sing`? Does it need to be changed everywhere it appears?

2.21 What call of function `Sing` would generate a verse with the line shown here?

```
Happy birthday dear Mr. President
```

2.22 What is the purpose of the final statement `cout << endl;` in function `Sing` in the birthday programs?

2.23 What is a minimal change to the Happy Birthday program that will cause each verse (about one person) to be printed three times before the next verse is printed three times (rather than once each) for a total of 15 verses? What is a minimal change that will cause all five verses (for all five people) to be printed, then all five printed again, and then all five printed again for a different ordering of 15 verses?

2.24 It is possible to write the Happy Birthday program so that the body of the function `Sing` consists of a single statement. What is that statement? Can you make one statement as readable as several?

Ada Lovelace *(1816–1853)*

Ada Lovelace, daughter of the poet Lord Byron, had a significant impact in publicizing the work of Charles Babbage. Babbage's designs for two computers, the

Difference Engine and the Analytical Engine, came more than a century before the first electronic computers were built but anticipated many of the features of modern computers.

Lovelace was tutored by the British mathematician Augustus De Morgan. She is characterized as *"an attractive and charming flirt, an accomplished musician, and a passionate believer in physical exercise. She combined these last two interests by practicing her violin as she marched around the family billiard table for exercise."* [McC79] Lovelace translated an account of Babbage's work into English. Her translation, and the accompanying notes, are credited with making Babbage's work accessible. Of Babbage's computer she wrote, "It would weave algebraic patterns the way the Jacquard loom weaved patterns in textiles."

Lovelace was instrumental in popularizing Babbage's work, but she was not one of the first programmers as is sometimes said. The programming language Ada is named for Ada Lovelace. For more information see [McC79, Gol93, Asp90].

2.6 Functions with Several Parameters

In this section we will investigate functions with more than one parameter. As a simple example, we'll use the children's song *Old MacDonald,* partially reproduced below. We would like to write a C++ program to generate this output.

OUTPUT

```
Old MacDonald had a farm, Ee-igh, Ee-igh, oh!
And on his farm he had a cow, Ee-igh, Ee-igh, oh!
With a moo moo here
And a moo moo there
Here a moo, there a moo, everywhere a moo moo
Old MacDonald had a farm, Ee-igh, Ee-igh, oh!

Old MacDonald had a farm, Ee-igh, Ee-igh, oh!
And on his farm he had a pig, Ee-igh, Ee-igh, oh!
With a oink oink here
And a oink oink there
Here a oink, there a oink, everywhere a oink oink
Old MacDonald had a farm, Ee-igh, Ee-igh, oh!
```

As always, we will strive to design a general program, useful in writing about, for example, ducks quacking, hens clucking, or horses neighing. In designing the program we first look for similarities and differences in the verses to determine what parts of the verses should be parameterized. We'll ignore for now the ungrammatical construct of *a oink*. The only differences in the two verses are the name of the animal, cow and pig, and the noise the animal makes, moo and oink, respectively. Accordingly, we design two functions: one to "sing" about an animal and another to "sing" about the animal's sounds, in Program 2.7, *oldmac1.cpp.*

This program produces the desired output but is cumbersome in many respects. To generate a new verse (e.g., about a quacking duck) we must write a new function and call it. In contrast, in the happy-birthday-generating program (Program 2.6), a new verse could be constructed by a new call rather than by writing a new function and calling it. Also notice that the flow of control in Program 2.7 is more complex than in Program 2.6. We'll look carefully at what happens when the function call Pig() in main is executed.

Program 2.7   oldmac1.cpp

```cpp
#include <iostream>
#include <string>
using namespace std;

// working version of old macdonald, single parameter procedures

void EiEio()
{
    cout << "Ee-igh, Ee-igh, oh!" << endl;
```

```
}

vcid Refrain()
{
    cout << "Old MacDonald had a farm, ";
    EiEio();
}

vcid HadA(string animal)
{
    cout << "And on his farm he had a " << animal << ", ";
    EiEio();
}

void WithA(string noise)
// the principal part of a verse
{
    cout << "With a ' << noise << " " << noise << " here" << endl;
    cout << "And a " << noise << " " << ncise << " there" << endl;

    cout << "Here a " << noise << ", "
        << "there a ' << noise << ", "
        << " everywhere a " << noise << " " << noise << endl;
}

void Pig()
{
    Refrain();
    HadA("pig");
    WithA("oink");
    Refrain();
}

void Cow()
{
    Refrain();
    HadA("cow");
    WithA("moo");
    Refrain();
}

irt main()
{
    Cow();
    cout << endl;
    Pig();
    return 0;
}
```

oldmacl.cpp

There are four statements in the body of the function Pig. The first statement, the function call Refrain(), results in two lines being printed (note that Refrain calls the function EiEiO). When Refrain finishes executing, control returns to the statement following the function call Refrain(); this is the second statement in Pig, the function call HadA("pig"). The argument "pig" is passed to the (formal)

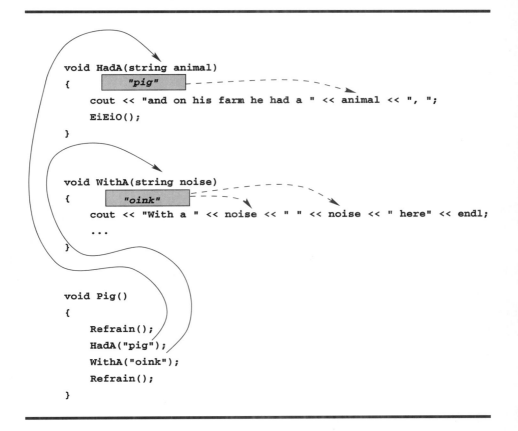

Figure 2.3 Passing arguments in Old MacDonald.

parameter `animal` and then statements in the function `HadA` are executed. When
the function `HadA` finishes, control returns to the third statement in `Pig`, the function
call `WithA("oink")`. As shown in Figure 2.3, this results in passing the argument
`"oink"`, which is stored as the value of the parameter `noise`. After all statements in
the body of `WithA` have executed, the flow of control continues with the final statement
in the body of the function `Pig`, another function call `Refrain()`. After this call
finishes executing, `Pig` has finished and the flow of control continues with the statement
following the call of `Pig()` in the main function. This is the statement `return 0` and
the program finishes execution.

   This program works, but it needs to be redesigned to be used more easily. This redesign process is another stage in program development. Often a programmer redesigns
a working program to make it "better" in some way. In extreme cases a program that
works is thrown out because it can be easier to redesign the program from scratch (using
ideas learned during the original design) rather than trying to modify a program. Often
writing the first program is necessary to get the good ideas used in subsequent programs.

   In this case we want to dispense with the need to construct a new function rather
than just a function call. To do this we will combine the functionality of the functions

HadA and WithA into a new function Verse. When writing a program, you should look for similarities in code segments. The bodies of the functions in Pig and Cow have the same pattern:

```
Refrain()
call to HadA(...)
call to WithA(...)
Refrain()
```

Incorporating this pattern into the function Verse, rather than repeating the pattern elsewhere in the program, yields a more versatile program.

In general, a programmer-defined function can have any number of parameters, but once written this number is fixed. The final version of this program, Program 2.8, is shorter and more versatile than the first version, Program 2.7. By looking for a way to combine the functionality of functions HadA and WithA, we modified a program and generated a better one. Often as versatility goes up so does length. When the length of a program decreases as its versatility increases, we're on the right track.

Program 2.8 oldmac2.cpp

```cpp
#include <iostream>
#include <string>
using namespace std;

// working version of old macdonald, functions with more than one
   parameter

void EiEio()
{
    cout << "Ee-igh, Ee-igh, oh!" << endl;
}

void Refrain()
{
    cout << "Old MacDonald had a farm, ".
    EiEio();
}

void HadA(string animal)
{
    cout << "And on his farm he had a " << animal << ", ";
    EiEio();
}

void WithA(string noise)
// the principal part of a verse
{
    cout << "With a " << noise << " " << noise << " here" << endl;
    cout << "And a " << noise << " " << noise << " there" << endl;
```

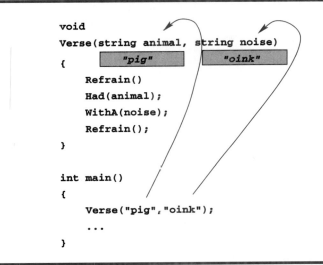

```
void
Verse(string animal, string noise)
{        "pig"           "oink"

    Refrain()
    Had(animal);
    WithA(noise);
    Refrain();

}


int main()
{

    Verse("pig","oink");
    ...

}
```

Figure 2.4   Passing multiple arguments.

```
    cout << "Here a " << noise << ", "
         << "there a " << noise << ", "
         << " everywhere a " << noise << " " << noise << endl;
}

void Verse(string animal, string noise)
{
    Refrain();
    HadA(animal);
    WithA(noise);
    Refrain();
}

int main()
{
    Verse("pig","oink");
    cout << endl;
    Verse("cow","moo");
    return 0;
}
```
oldmac2.cpp

I will sometimes use the word *elegant* as a desirable program trait. Program 2.8 is elegant compared to Program 2.7 because it is easily modified to generate new verses.

Note that the order in which arguments are passed to a function determines their use, not the actual values of the arguments or the names of the parameters. This is diagrammed in Figure 2.4.

In particular, the names of the parameters have nothing to do with their purpose. If *animal* is replaced everywhere it occurs in Program 2.8 with *vegetable,* the program will produce exactly the same output. Furthermore, it is the order of the parameters in the function header and the corresponding order of the arguments in the function call that determine what the output is. In particular, the function call

```
Verse("cluck","hen");
```

would generate a verse with the lines shown below since the value of the parameter *animal* will be the string literal `"cluck"`.

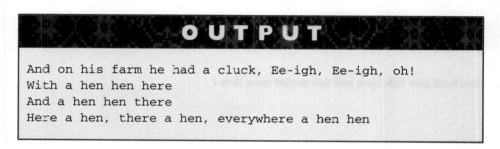

```
OUTPUT

And on his farm he had a cluck, Ee-igh, Ee-igh, oh!
With a hen hen here
And a hen hen there
Here a hen, there a hen, everywhere a hen hen
```

The importance of the *order of the arguments and parameters* and the lack of importance of the names of parameters often leads to confusion. Although the use of such parameter names as *param1* and *param2* (or, even worse, *x* and *y*) might at first glance seem to be a method of avoiding such confusion, parameter names that correspond roughly to their purpose are far more useful as the programs and functions we study get more complex. In general, parameters should be named according to the purpose just as functions are named. Guidelines for using lowercase and uppercase characters are provided at the end of this chapter.

Pause to Reflect

2.25 Write a function for use in Program 2.7 that produces output for a gobbling turkey. The function should be invoked by the call `Turkey`, which appears in the body of the function `main`.

2.26 Is it useful to have a separate function `EiEiO`?

2.27 How would the same effect of the function `Turkey` be achieved in Program 2.8?

2.28 If the order of the parameters of the function `Verse` is reversed so that the header is

```
void Verse(string noise, string animal)
```

but no changes are made in the body of `Verse`, then what changes (if any) must be made in the calls to `Verse` so that the output does not change?

2.29 What happens if the statement `Verse("pig",'cluck");` is included in the function `main`?

2.30 The statement `Verse("lamb");` will not compile. Why?

2.31 What happens if you include the statement Verse("owl",2) in the function main? What happens if you include the statement Verse("owl",2+2)?

Stumbling Block

You must be careful organizing programs that use functions. Although we have not discussed the order in which functions appear in a program, the order is important to a degree. Program 2.9 is designed to print a two-line message. As written, it will not compile.

Program 2.9   order.cpp

```cpp
#include <iostream>
#include <string>
using namespace std;

// order of procedures is important

void Hi (string name)
{
    cout << "Hi " << name << endl;
    Greetings();
}

void Greetings()
{
    cout << "Things are happening inside this computer" << endl;
}

int main()
{
    Hi("Fred");
    return 0;
}
```
order.cpp

When this program is compiled using the g++ compiler, the compilation fails with the following error messages.

```
order.cpp: In function 'void  Hi (class string)':
order.cpp:10: warning: implicit declaration of function
              'Greetings'
undefined reference to 'Greetings'
collect2: ld returned 1 exit status
```

With the Turbo C++ compiler the compilation fails, with the following error message.

```
Error order.cpp 8:
Function 'Greetings' should have a prototype
```

These messages are generated because the function `Greetings` is called from the function `Hi` but occurs physically after `Hi` in Program 2.9. In general, functions must appear (be defined) in a program before they are called.

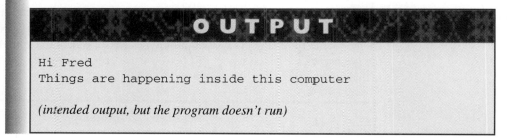

```
Hi Fred
Things are happening inside this computer
```

(intended output, but the program doesn't run)

This requirement that functions appear before they're called is too restrictive. Fortunately, there is an alternative to placing an entire function before it's called. It's possible to put information about the function before it's called rather than the function itself. This information is called the **signature** of a function, often referred to as the function's **prototype.** Rather than requiring that an entire function appear before it is called, only the prototype need appear. The prototype indicates the order and type of the function's parameters as well as the function's return type. All the functions we have studied so far have a `void` return type, but we'll see in the next chapter that functions (such as square root) can return `double` values, `int` values, `string` values, and so on. The return type, the function name, and the type and order of each parameter together constitute the prototype. The names of the parameters are not part of the prototype, but I always include the parameter names because names are useful in thinking and talking about functions.

> **Syntax: function prototype**
>
> *return type*
> *function name (type param-name, type param-name, ...) ;*

For example, the prototype for the function `Hi` is

```
void Hi (string name);
```

The prototype of the `Verse` function in Program 2.8 is different:

```
void Verse (string animal, string noise);
```

Just as arguments and parameters must match, so must a function call match the function's prototype. In the call to `Greetings` made from `Hi`, the compiler doesn't know the prototype for `Greetings`. If a function header appears physically before any call of the function, then a prototype is not needed. However, in larger programs it can be necessary to include prototypes for functions at the beginning of a program. In either case the compiler sees a function header or prototype before a function call so that the matching of arguments to parameters can be checked by the compiler.

The function `main` has a return type of `int`, and the default return type in C++ is `int`. Thus the error messages generated by the g++ compiler warn of an "implicit declaration" of the function Greetings, meaning that the default return of an integer is assumed. Since there is no function Greetings with such a return type, the "undefined reference" message is generated.

The error message generated by the Turbo C++ compiler is more informative and indicates that a prototype is missing. Program 2.10 has function prototypes. Note that the prototype for function Hi is not necessary since the function appears before it is called. Some programmers include prototypes for all functions, regardless of whether the prototypes are necessary. In this book we use prototypes when necessary but won't include them otherwise.

Program 2.10   order2.cpp

```cpp
#include <iostream>
#include <string>
using namespace std;

// illustrates function prototypes

void Hi(string);
void Greetings();

void Hi (string name)
{
    cout << "Hi " << name << endl;
    Greetings();
}

void Greetings()
{
    cout << "Things are happening inside this computer" << endl;
}

int main()
{
    Hi("Fred");
    return 0;
}
```

order2.cpp

2.7   Program Style

The style of indentation used in the programs in this chapter is used in all programs in the book. In particular, each statement within a function or program body is indented four spaces. As programs get more complex in subsequent chapters, the use of a consistent indentation scheme will become more important in ensuring ease of understanding. I recommend that you use the indentation scheme displayed in the programs here. If you adopt a different scheme you must use it consistently.

Indentation is necessary for human readers of the programs you write. The C++ compiler is quite capable of compiling programs that have no indentation, have multiple statements per line (instead of one statement per line as we have seen so far), and that have function names like `He553323xlo3`.

2.7.1 Identifiers

The names of functions, parameters, and variables are **identifiers**—a means of referral both for program designers and for the compiler. Examples of identifiers include *Hello, person,* and *Sing.* Just as good indentation can make a program easier to read, I recommend the use of identifiers that indicate to some degree the purpose of the item being labeled by the identifier. As noted above, the use of *animal* is much more informative than *param1* in conveying the purpose of the parameter to which the label applies. In C++ an identifier consists of any sequence of letters, numbers, and the underscore character (_). Identifiers may not begin with a number. And identifiers are *case-sensitive* (lower- and uppercase letters): the identifier *verse* is different from the identifier *Verse.* Although some compilers limit the number of characters in an identifier, the C++ standard specifies that identifiers can be arbitrarily long.

Traditionally, C programmers use the underscore character as a way of making identifiers easier to read. Rather than the identifier `partedhair`, one would use `parted_hair`. Some recent studies indicate that using upper- and lowercase letters to differentiate the parts of an identifier can make them easier to read. In this book I adopt the convention that all programmer-defined functions and types[8] begin with an uppercase letter. Uppercase letters are also used to separate subwords in an identifier, such as `PartedHair` rather than `parted_hair`. Parameters (and later variables) begin with lowercase letters although uppercase letters may be used to delimit subwords in identifiers. For example, a parameter for a large power of 10 might be `largeTenPower`. Note that the identifier begins with a lowercase letter, which signifies that it is a parameter or a variable. You may decide that `large_ten_power` is more readable. As long as you adopt a consistent naming convention, you shouldn't feel bound by conventions I employ in the code here.

In many C++ implementations identifiers containing a double underscore (__) are used in the libraries that supply code (such as `<iostream>`), and therefore identifiers in your programs must avoid double underscores. In addition, differentiating between single and double underscores (_ and __) is difficult.

Finally, some words have special meanings in C++ and cannot be used as identifiers. We will encounter most of these **keywords,** or **reserved** words, as we study C++. A list of keywords is provided in Table 2.1.

2.8 Chapter Review

In this chapter we studied the form of C++ programs, how a program executes, and how functions can make programs easier to modify and use. We studied programs that displayed songs having repetitive verses so that an efficient use of functions would reduce

---

[8]The type `string` used in this chapter is not built into C++ but is supplied as a standard type. In C++, however, it's possible to use programmer-defined types just like built-in types.

Table 2.1   C++ keywords.

asm	default	for	private	struct	unsigned
auto	delete	friend	protected	switch	using
bool	do	goto	public	template	virtual
break	double	if	register	this	void
case	dynamic_cast	inline	reinterpret_cast	throw	volatile
catch	else	int	return	true	wchar_t
char	enum	long	short	try	while
class	explicit	mutable	signed	typedef	
const	extern	namespace	sizeof	typeid	
const_cast	false	new	static	typename	
continue	float	operator	static_cast	union	

our programming efforts. At the same time, the verses had sufficient variation to make the use of parameters necessary in order to develop clean and elegant programs—programs that appeal to your emerging sense of programming style.

- C++ programs have a specific form:
  - #include statements to access libraries
  - comments about the program
  - programmer-defined functions
  - one function named main

- Libraries make "off-the-shelf" programming components accessible to programmers. System library names are enclosed between < and >, as in <iostream>. Libraries that are part of this book and nonsystem libraries are enclosed in double quotation marks, as in "tstring.h".

- Output is generated using the insertion operator, <<, and the standard output stream, cout. These are accessible by including the proper header file <iostream>.

- Strings are sequences of characters. The type string is not a built-in type but is accessible via the header file <string>.

- Functions group related statements together so that the statements can be executed together when the function is called.

- Parameters facilitate passing information between functions. The value passed is an *argument*. The "box" that stores the value in the function is a *parameter*.

- Iterative enhancement is a design process by which a program is developed in stages. Each stage is both an enhancement and a refinement of a working program.

- In designing programs, look for patterns of repeated code that can be combined into a parameterized function to avoid code duplication, as we did in Verse of Program 2.8.

- Prototypes are function signatures that convey to the compiler information that is used to determine if a function call is correctly formed.

■ Identifiers are names of functions, variables, and parameters. Identifiers should indicate the purpose of what they name. Your programs will be more readable if you are consistent in capitalization and underscores in identifiers.

2.9 Exercises

2.1 Add a function Neck to *parts.cpp*, Program 2.4, to generate output similar to that shown below.

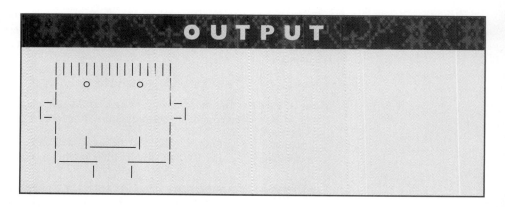

2.2 Modify the appropriate functions in Program 2.4 to display the head shown below.

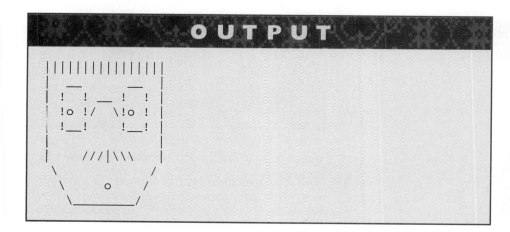

2.3 Write a program whose output is the text of *hello.cpp*, Program 2.1. Note that the output is a program!

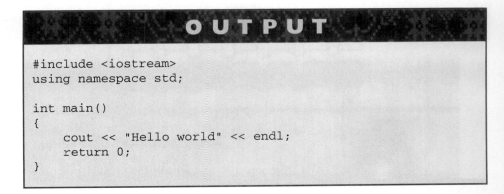

```
#include <iostream>
using namespace std;

int main()
{
    cout << "Hello world" << endl;
    return 0;
}
```

To display the character " you'll need to use an **escape sequence.** An escape sequence is a backslash \ followed by one character. The two-character escape sequence represents a single character; the escape sequence \" is used to print one quotation mark. The statement

```
cout << "\"Hello\" " << endl;
```

can be used to print the characters "Hello" on the screen, including the quotation marks! Be sure to comment your program-writing program appropriately.

2.4   A popular song performed by KC and the Sunshine Band repeats many verses using the words "That's the way Uh-huh Uh-huh I like it Uh-huh Uh-huh," as shown below.

O U T P U T

```
That's the way
Uh-huh Uh-huh
I like it
Uh-huh Uh-huh

That's the way
Uh-huh Uh-huh
I like it
Uh-huh Uh-huh
```

Write a program that generates four choruses of the song.

2.5   Write a program that generates the verses of a children's song shown below. Don't worry about the ungrammatical qualities inherent in the use of "goes" and "go" in your first attempt at writing the program. You should include a function with two parameters capable of generating any of the verses when the appropriate arguments are passed. Strive to make your program "elegant."

```
O U T P U T

The wheel on the bus goes round round round
round round round
round round round
The wheel on the bus goes round round round
All through the town

The wipers on the bus goes swish swish swish
swish swish swish
swish swish swish
The wipers on the bus goes swish swish swish
All through the town

The horn on the bus goes beep beep beep
beep beep beep
beep beep beep
The horn on the bus goes beep beep beep
All through the town

The money on the bus goes clink clink clink
clink clink clink
clink clink clink
The money on the bus goes clink clink clink
All through the town
```

Is it possible to generate a verse of the song based on the lines

```
The driver on the bus goes move on back
move on back
move on back
```

with small modifications? How many parameters would the `Verse` function of such a song have?

2.6 Consider the song about an old woman with an insatiable appetite, one version of which is partially reproduced in the following.

```
O U T P U T

There was an old lady who swallowed a fly
I don't know why she swallowed a fly
Perhaps she'll die.

There was an old lady who swallowed a spider
That wiggled and jiggled and tiggled inside her
She swallowed the spider to catch the fly
I don't know why she swallowed a fly
Perhaps she'll die.

There was an old lady who swallowed a bird
How absurd to swallow a bird
She swallowed the bird to catch the spider
That wiggled and jiggled and tiggled inside her
She swallowed the spider to catch the fly
I don't know why she swallowed a fly
Perhaps she'll die.
```

This song may be difficult to generate via a program using just the predefined output stream cout, the operator <<, and programmer-defined parameterized functions. Write such a program or sketch its solution, and indicate why it might be difficult to write a program for which it is easy to add new animals while maintaining program elegance. You might think about adding a verse about a cat (imagine that!) that swallows the bird.

2.7 In a song made famous by Bill Haley and the Comets, the chorus is

```
One, two, three o'clock, four o'clock rock
Five, six, seven o'clock, eight o'clock rock
Nine, ten, eleven o'clock, twelve o'clock rock
We're going to rock around the clock tonight
```

Rather than using words to represent time, you are to use numbers and write a program that will print the chorus above but with the line

```
1, 2, 3  o'clock, 4  o'clock rock
```

as the first line of the chorus. Your program should be useful in creating a chorus that could be used with military time; i.e., another chorus might end thus:

```
21, 22, 23 o'clock, 24 o'clock rock
We're going to rock around the clock tonight
```

You should use the arithmetic operator + where appropriate and strive to make your program as succinct as possible, calling functions with different parameters rather than writing similar statements.

Program Design and Implementation   3

GIGO—Garbage In, Garbage Out
Common computer aphorism

GIGO—Garbage In, Gospel Out
New Hacker's Dictionary

Civilization advances by extending the number of important operations which we can perform without thinking about them.
ALFRED NORTH WHITEHEAD
An Introduction to Mathematics

The memory of all that—No, no! They can't take that away from me.
IRA GERSHWIN
They Can't Take That Away from Me

The song-writing and head-drawing programs in Chapter 2 generated the same output for all executions unless the programs were modified and recompiled. These programs do not respond to a user of the program at **run time,** meaning while the programs are running or executing. The solutions to many programming problems require input from program users during execution. Therefore, we must be able to write programs that process input during execution. A typical framework for many computer programs is one that divides a program's execution into three stages.

1.   Input—information is provided to the program.
2.   Process—the information is processed.
3.   Output—the program displays the results of processing the input.

This **input/process/output (IPO)** model of programming is used in the simple programs we'll study in this chapter as well as in million-line programs that forecast the weather and predict stock market fluctuations. Breaking a program into parts, implementing the parts separately, and then combining the parts into a working program is a good method for developing programs. This is often called **divide and conquer;** the program is divided into pieces; each piece is implemented, or "conquered"; and the final program results from combining the conquered pieces. We'll employ divide and conquer together with iterative enhancement when designing classes and programs.

3.1 The Input Phase of Computation

In this chapter we'll discuss how the user can input values that are used in a program. These input values can be strings like the name of an animal or the noise the animal makes, as we'll see in Program 3.1, *macinput.cpp*. The input values can also be numbers like the price and diameter of a pizza, as we'll see in Program 3.5, *pizza.cpp*.

Two runs of a modified version of Program 2.8, *oldmac2.cpp*, are in the following output box. Input entered by the user (you) is shown in a bold-italic font. The computing environment displays `prompt>` as a cue to the user to enter a command—in this case, the name of a program. Prompts may be different in other computing environments. In your programming environment the program may be run using a menu-driven system rather than a command-line prompt, but we'll use the prompt to show the name of the program generating the output.

```
OUTPUT

prompt> macinput

Enter the name of an animal: cow
Enter noise that a cow makes: moo

Old MacDonald had a farm, Ee-igh, ee-igh, oh!
And on his farm he had a cow, Ee-igh, ee-igh, oh!
With a moo moo here
And a moo moo there
Here a moo, there a moo, everywhere a moo moo
Old MacDonald had a farm, Ee-igh, ee-igh, oh!

prompt> macinput

Enter the name of an animal: hen
Enter noise that a cow makes: cluck

Old MacDonald had a farm, Ee-igh, ee-igh, oh!
And on his farm he had a hen, Ee-igh, ee-igh, oh!
With a cluck cluck here
And a cluck cluck there
Here a cluck, there a cluck, everywhere a cluck cluck
Old MacDonald had a farm, Ee-igh, ee-igh, oh!
```

Each run of the program produces different output according to the words you enter. If the function `main` in Program 2.8 is modified as shown in the code segment in Program 3.1, the modified program generates the runs shown above.

Program 3.1   macinput.cpp

```
//  see program oldmac2.cpp for function Verse and #includes


int main()
{
    string animal;
    string noise;

    cout << "Enter the name of an animal: ";
    cin >> animal;

    cout << "Enter noise that a " << animal << " makes: ";
    cin >> noise;

    cout << endl;
    Verse(animal,noise);
    return 0;
}
```

macinput.cpp

3.1.1   The Input Stream, `cin`

We'll investigate each statement in `main` of Program 3.1. When you run the program, you enter information and the program reacts to that information by printing a verse of Old MacDonald's Farm that corresponds to what you enter. In C++, information you enter comes from the input stream `cin` (pronounced "cee-in"). Just as the output stream, `cout`, generates output, the input stream accepts input values used in a program. In the run of Program 3.1, the output statement

```
cout << "Enter the name of an animal: "
```

is *not* followed by an `endl`. As a result, your input appears on the same line as the words that prompt you to enter an animal's name.

When you enter input, it is taken from the input stream using the **extraction** operator, `>>` (sometimes read as "takes-from"). When the input is taken, it must be stored someplace. Program **variables,** in this case `animal` and `noise`, are used as a place for storing values.

3.1.2   Variables

The following statements from Program 3.1 **define** two `string` variables, named *animal* and *noise*.

```
string animal;
string noise;
```

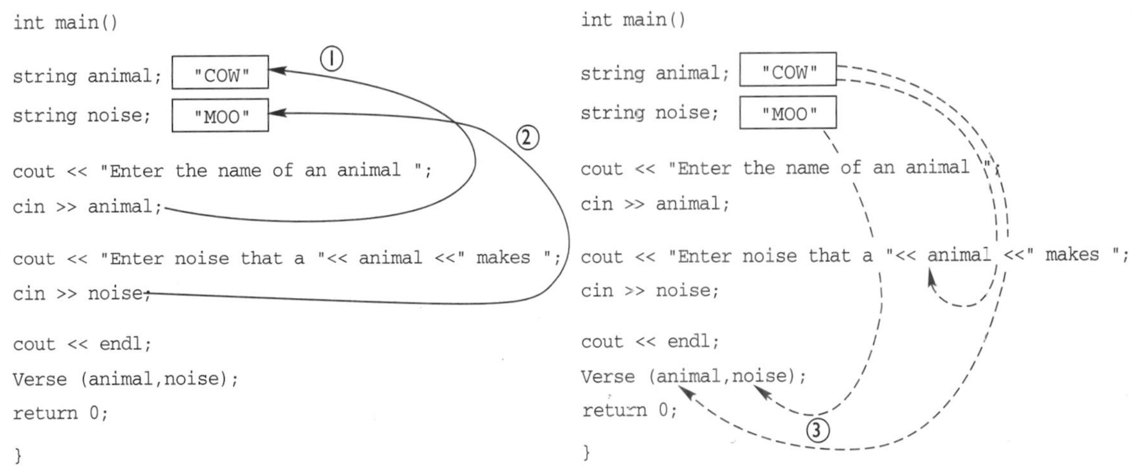

Figure 3.1 Using variables and streams for input.

These variables are represented in Figure 3.1 as boxes that store the variable values in computer memory. The value stored in a variable can be used just as the values stored in a function's formal parameters can be used within the function (see Figure 2.3). Parameters and variables are similar; each has a name such as `animal` or `noise` and an associated storage location. Parameters are given initial values, or **initialized,** by calling a function and passing an argument. Variables are often initialized by accepting input from the user.

Variables in a C++ program must be **defined** before they can be used. Sometimes the terms *allocate* and *create* are used instead of *define*. Sometimes the word **object** is used instead of *variable*. You should think of *variable* and *object* as synonyms. Just

> **Syntax: variable definition**
>
> *type name;*   **OR**
> *type name₁, name₂,..., nameₖ;*

as all formal parameters have a type or class, all variables in C++ have a type or class that determines what kinds of operations can be performed with the variable. The variable `animal` has the type or class `string`. In this book we'll define each variable in a separate statement as was done in Program 3.1. It's possible to define more than one variable in a single statement. For example, the following statement defines two `string` variables:

```
string animal,noise;
```

In the run of Program 3.1 diagrammed in Figure 3.1, values taken from the input stream are stored in a variable's memory location. The variable `animal` gets a value in the statement labeled 1; the variable `noise` gets a value in the statement labeled 2. The value of `animal` is used to prompt the user; this is shown by the dashed arrow. The

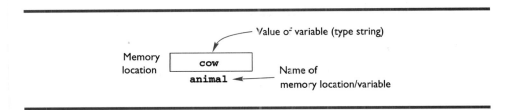

Figure 3.2 Variables as named memory locations.

arrow labeled 3 shows the values of both variables used as arguments to the function Verse. In the interactive C++ environments used in the study of this book, the user must almost always press the return (enter) key before an input statement completes execution and stores the entered value in animal. This allows the user to make corrections (using arrow keys or a mouse, for example) before the final value is stored in memory.

An often-used metaphor associates a variable with a mailbox. Mailboxes usually have names associated with them (either 206 Main Street, or the Smith residence) and offer a place in which things can be stored. Perhaps a more appropriate metaphor associates variables with dorm rooms.[1] For example, a room in a fraternity or sorority house (say, $\Psi\Upsilon$ or $\Delta\Delta\Delta$) can be occupied by any member of the fraternity or sorority but *not* by members of other residential groups.[2] The occupant of the room may change just as the value of a variable may change, but the type of the occupant remains the same, just as a variable's type remains fixed once it is defined. Thus we think of variables as named memory storage locations capable of storing a specific type of object. In the foregoing example the name of one storage location is animal and the type of object that can be stored in it is a string; for example, the value cow can be stored as shown in Figure 3.2.

In C++, variables can be defined anywhere, but they must be defined before they're used. Some programmers prefer to define all variables immediately after a left brace, {. Others define variables just before they're first used. (We'll have occasion to use both styles of definition.) When all variables are defined at the beginning of a function, it is easy to find a variable when reading code. Thus when one variable is used in many places, this style makes it easier to find the definition than searching for the variable's first use. Another version of the code in Program 3.1 is shown in the following block of code with an alternate style of variable definition:

```
int main()
{
    cout << "Enter the name of an animal ";
    string animal;
    cin >> animal;

    cout << "Enter noise that a " << animal << " makes ";
```

---

[1]This was suggested by Deganit Armon.

[2]The room could certainly not be occupied by independents or members of the opposite sex except in the case of co-ed living groups.

```
        string noise;
        cin >> noise;

        cout << endl;
        Verse(animal,noise);
        return 0;
}
```

Before the statement `cin >> animal` in Program 3.1 is executed, the contents of the memory location associated with the variable `animal` are undefined. You can think of an undefined value as garbage. Displaying an undefined value probably won't cause any trouble, but it might not make any sense. In more complex programs, accessing an undefined value can cause a program to crash.

Program Tip 3.1:   When a variable is defined give it a value. Every variable must be given a value before being used for the first time in an expression or an output statement, or as an argument in a function call.

One way of doing this is to define variables just before they're used for the first time; that way you won't define lots of variables at the beginning of a function and then use one before it has been given a value. Alternatively, you can define all variables at the beginning of a function and program carefully.

Pause to Reflect

3.1 If you run Program 3.1, *macinput.cpp*, and enter *baah* for the name of the animal and *sheep* for the noise, what is the output? What happens if you enter *dog* for the name of the animal and *bow wow* for the noise? (You probably need to run the program to find the answer.) What if *bow-wow* is entered for the noise?

3.2 Why is there no `endl` in the following statement prompting for the name of an animal, and why is there a space after the ell in `animal`?

```
    cout << "Enter the name of an animal ";
```

3.3 Write a function *main* for Program 2.5 (the Happy Birthday program) that prompts the user for the name of a person for whom the song will be "sung."

3.4 Add statements to the birthday program as modified in the previous exercise to prompt the user for his or her age and print a message about the age after the song is printed.

3.5 What happens if the statement `cin >> noise;` is removed from Program 3.1 and the program is run?

John Kemeny *(1926–1992)*

John Kemeny, with Thomas Kurtz, invented the programming language BASIC (Beginner's All-purpose Symbolic Instruction Code). The language was designed to be simple to use but as powerful as FORTRAN, one of the languages with which it competed when first developed in 1964. BASIC went on to become the world's most popular programming language.

Kemeny was a research assistant to Albert Einstein before taking a job at Dartmouth College. At Dartmouth he was an early visionary in bringing computers to everyone. Kemeny and Kurtz developed the Dartmouth Time Sharing System, which allowed hundreds of users to use the same computer "simultaneously." Kemeny was an inspiring teacher. While serving as president of Dartmouth College he still taught at least one math course each year. With a cigarette in a holder and a distinct, but very understandable, Hungarian accent, Kemeny was a model of clarity and organization in the classroom.

In a book published in 1959, Kemeny wrote the following, comparing computer calculations with the human brain. It's interesting that his words are still relevant more than 35 years later.

> *When we inspect one of the present mechanical brains we are overwhelmed by its size and its apparent complexity. But this is a somewhat misleading first impression. None of these machines compare with the human brain in complexity or in efficiency. It is true that we cannot match the speed or reliability of the computer in multiplying two ten-digit numbers, but, after all, that is its primary purpose, not ours. There are many tasks that we carry out as a matter of course that we would have no idea how to mechanize.*

For more information see [Sla87, AA85].

3.2 Processing Numbers

All the examples we've studied so far have used strings. Although many programs manipulate strings and text, numbers are used extensively in computing and programming. In this section we'll discuss how to use numbers for input, processing, and output. As we'll see, the syntax for the input and output of numbers is the same as for strings, but processing numbers requires a new set of symbols based on those you learned for ordinary math.

We'll start with a simple example, but we'll build toward the programming knowledge we need to write a program that will help us determine what size pizza is the best bargain. Just as printing "Hello World" is often used as a first program, programs that convert temperature from Fahrenheit to Celsius are commonly used to illustrate the use of numeric literals and variables in C++ programs.[3] Program 3.2 shows how this is done. The program shows two different types of numeric values and how these values are used in doing arithmetic in C++ programs.

Program 3.2 fahrcels.cpp

```cpp
#include <iostream>
using namespace std;

// illustrates i/o of ints and doubles
// illustrates arithmetic operations

int main()
{
    int ifahr;
    double dfahr;

    cout << "enter a Fahrenheit temperature ";
    cin >> ifahr;
    cout << ifahr << " = "
         << (ifahr - 32) * 5/9
         << " Celsius" << endl;

    cout << "enter another temperature ";
    cin >> dfahr;
    cout << dfahr << " = "
         << (dfahr - 32.0) * 5/9
         << " Celsius" << endl;

    return 0;
}
```

fahrcels.cpp

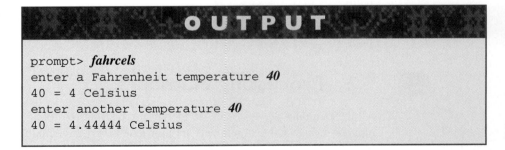

```
prompt> fahrcels
enter a Fahrenheit temperature 40
40 = 4 Celsius
enter another temperature 40
40 = 4.44444 Celsius
```

---

[3]Note, however, that using a computer program to convert a single temperature is probably overkill. This program is used to study the types int and double rather than for its intrinsic worth.

Two variables are defined in Program 3.2, ifahr and dfahr. The type of ifahr is int, which represents an integer in C++: what we think of mathematically as a value from the set of numbers $\{\ldots -3, -2, -1, 0, 1, 2, 3 \ldots\}$. The type of dfahr is double, which represents in C++ what is called a **floating-point number** in computer science and a *real number* in mathematics. Floating-point numbers have a decimal point; examples include $\sqrt{17}$, 3.14159, and 2.0. In Program 3.2 the input stream cin extracts an integer value entered by the user with the statement cin >> ifahr and stores the entered value in the variable ifahr. A floating-point number entered by the user is extracted and stored in the variable dfahr by the statement cin >> dfahr. Except for the name of the variable, both these statements are identical in form to the statements in Program 3.1 that accepted strings entered by the user. When writing programs using numbers, the type double should be used for all variables and calculations that might have decimal points.[4] The type int should be used whenever integers, or numbers without decimal points, are appropriate.

3.2.1 Numeric Data

Although there is no largest integer in mathematics, the finite memory of a computer limits the largest and smallest int values in C++. On computers using 16-bit compilers, the values of an int can range from $-32,768$ to $32,767$. When more modern 32-bit compilers are used, the typical range of int values is $-2,147,483,648$ to $2,147,483,647$. You shouldn't try to remember these numbers; you should remember that there are limits. The smaller range of int values is really too small to do many calculations. For example, the number of seconds in a day is 86,400, far exceeding the value that can be stored in an int using C++ on most 16-bit compilers. To alleviate this problem the type **long int** should be used instead of int. The variable ifahr could be defined to use this modified long int type as long int ifahr. The type long int is usually abbreviated simply as long. This makes long secs; a definition for a variable secs.

Program 3.3 shows the limitations of the type int. The first run after the program listing is generated using a 32-bit compiler. The same run on a computer using a 16-bit compiler generates a much different set of results, as shown.

Program 3.3   daysecs.cpp

```
#include <iostream>
using namespace std;

// converts days to seconds
// illustrates integer overflow

int main()
{
    int days;
```

---

[4]The type float can also be used for floating-point numbers. We will not use this type, since most standard mathematical functions use double values. Using the type float will almost certainly lead to errors in any serious mathematical calculations.

```
cout << "how many days: ";
cin >> days;
cout << days << " days = "
     << days*24*60*60
     << " seconds" << endl;

return 0;
}
```
daysecs.cpp

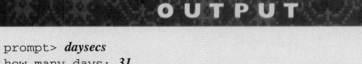

```
prompt> daysecs
how many days: 31
31 days = 2678400 seconds
prompt> daysecs
how many days: 365
365 days = 31536000 seconds
prompt> daysecs
how many days: 13870
13870 days = 1198368000 seconds
```

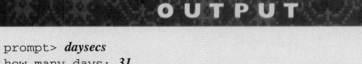

```
run using a 16-bit compiler
prompt> daysecs
how many days: 31
31 days = -8576 seconds
prompt> daysecs
how many days: 365
365 days = 13184 seconds
prompt> daysecs
how many days: 13870
13870 days = -23296 seconds
```

If the definition int days is changed to long days, then the runs will be the same on both kinds of computers.

> **Program Tip 3.2:**   Use `long` (`long int`) rather than `int` if you are using a 16-bit compiler. This will help ensure that the output of any program you write using integer arithmetic is correct.

It's also possible to use the type `double` instead of either `int` or `long int`. In mathematics, real numbers can have an infinite number of digits after a decimal point. For example, $1/3 = 0.333333\ldots$ and $\sqrt{2} = 1.41421356237\ldots$, where there is no pattern to the digits in the square root of two. Data represented using `double` values are approximations since it's not possible to have an infinite number of digits. When the definition of `days` is changed to `double days` the program generates the same results with 16- or 32-bit compilers.

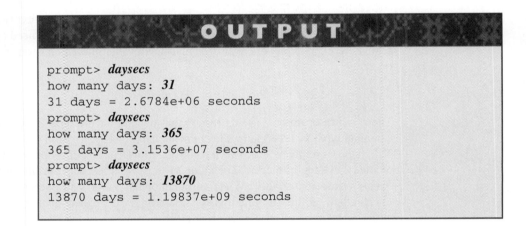

```
prompt> daysecs
how many days: 31
31 days = 2.6784e+06 seconds
prompt> daysecs
how many days: 365
365 days = 3.1536e+07 seconds
prompt> daysecs
how many days: 13870
13870 days = 1.19837e+09 seconds
```

The output in this run is shown using **exponent,** or **scientific,** notation. The expression `2.6784e+06` is equivalent to 2,678,400. The `e+06` means "multiply by 10^6." The same run results if the definition `int days` is used, but the output statement is changed as shown below.

```
cout << days*24.0*60*60 << " seconds" << endl;
```

We'll explore why this is the case in the next section. In How to B you can see examples that show how to format numeric output so that, for example, the number of digits after the decimal place can be specified in your programs.

3.2.2   Arithmetic Operators

Although the output statements in *fahrcels.cpp*, Program 3.2, are the same except for the name of the variable storing the Fahrenheit temperature, the actual values output by the statements are different. This is because arithmetic performed using `int` values behaves differently than arithmetic performed using `double` values. An **operator,** such as $+$, is used to perform some kind of computation. Operators combine **operands** as in $15 + 3$; the operands are 15 and 3. An **expression** is a sentence composed of operands

Table 3.1   The arithmetic operators.

Symbol	Meaning	Example
*	multiplication	`3*5*x`
/	division	`5.2/1.5`
%	mod/remainder	`7 % 2`
+	addition	`12 + x`
–	subtraction	`35 - y`

and operators, as in $(X - 32) * 5/9$. In this expression, X, 32, 5, and 9 are operands. The symbols –, *, and / are operators.

To understand why different output is generated by the following two expressions when the same value is entered for both `ifahr` and `dfahr`, we'll need to explore how arithmetic expressions are evaluated and how evaluation depends on the types of the operands.

```
(ifahr - 32) * 5/9          (dfahr - 32.0) * 5/9
```

The division operator / yields results that depend on the types of its operands. For example, what is $7/2$? In mathematics the answer is 3.5, but in C++ the answer is 3. This is because division of two integer quantities (in this case, the literals 7 and 2) is defined to yield an integer. The value of $7.0/2$ is 3.5 because division of `double` values yields a `double`. When an operator has more than one use, the operator is **overloaded.** In this case the division operator is overloaded since it works differently with `double` values than with `int` values.

The arithmetic operators available in C++ are shown in Table 3.1. Most should be familiar to you from your study of mathematics except, perhaps, for the modulus operator, %. The modulus operator % yields the remainder when one integer is divided by another. For example, executing the statement

```
cout << "47 divides 1347 " << 1347/47 << " times, "
     << "with remainder " << 1347 % 47 << endl;
```

would generate the following output because $1347 = 28 * 47 + 31$.

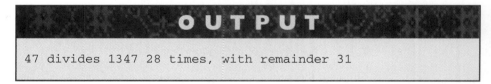

```
47 divides 1347 28 times, with remainder 31
```

In general the result of `p % q` (read this as "p mod q") for two integers should be a value `r` with the property that `p = x*q + r` where $x = p/q$. The % operator is often used to determine if one integer divides another—that is, divides with no remainder, as in 4/2 or 27/9. If `x % y = 0`, there is a remainder of zero when `x` is divided by `y`,

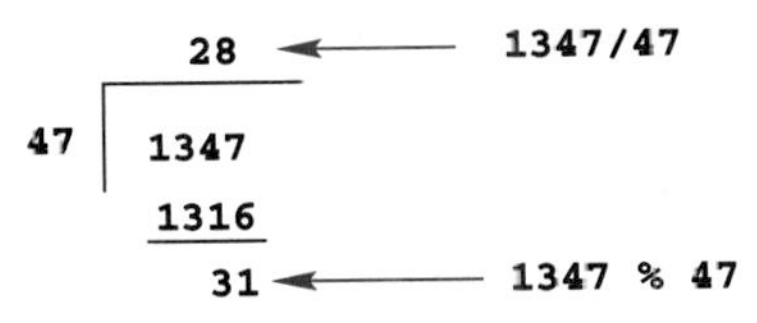

```
        28  ←————— 1347/47

   47 | 1347
        1316
        31  ←————— 1347 % 47
```

Figure 3.3 Using the modulus operator.

indicating that y evenly divides x. A calculation showing the modulus operator and how it relates to remainders is diagrammed in Figure 3.3. The following examples illustrate several uses of the modulus operator.

```
25 % 5 = 0        13 % 2 = 1        4 % 3 = 1
25 % 6 = 1        13 % 3 = 1        4 % 4 = 0
48 % 8 = 0        13 % 4 = 1        4 % 5 = 4
48 % 9 = 3        13 % 5 = 3        5 % 4 = 1
```

If either p or q is negative, however, the value calculated may be different on different systems.

> **Program Tip 3.3: Avoid negative values when using the % operator, or check the documentation of the programming environment you use.** In theory, the result of a modulus operator should be positive since it is a remainder. In practice the result is usually negative and not the result you expect when writing code. The C++ standard requires that a = ((a/b) * b) + (a % b).

3.2.3 Evaluating Expressions

The following rules are used for evaluating arithmetic expressions in C++ (these are standard rules of arithmetic as well):

1. Evaluate all parenthesized expressions first, with nested expressions evaluated "inside-out."
2. Evaluate expressions according to **operator precedence:** evaluate *, /, and % before + and -.
3. Evaluate operators with the same precedence left to right—this is called left-to-right **associativity.**

We'll use these rules to evaluate the expression (ifahr - 32) * 5/9 when ifahr has the value 40 (as in the output of Program 3.2). Tables showing precedence rules and associativity of all C++ operators are given in How to A: see Table A.4.

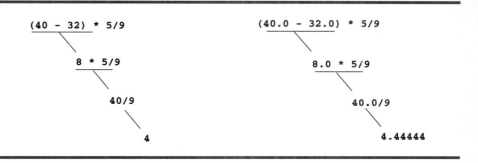

Figure 3.4 Evaluating arithmetic expressions.

■   Evaluate (ifahr - 32) first; this is 40 − 32, which is 8. (This is rule 1 above: evaluate parenthesized expressions first.)

■   The expression is now 8 * 5/9; because * and / have equal precedence, they are evaluated left to right (rule 3 above). This yields 40/9, which is 4.

In the last step above 40/9 evaluates to 4. This is because in integer division any fractional part is truncated, or removed. Thus although 40/9 = 4.444 . . . mathematically, the fractional part .444 . . . is truncated, leaving 4.

At this point it may be slightly mysterious why Program 3.2 prints 4.44444 when the expression (dfahr - 32.0) * 5/9 is evaluated. The subexpression (dfahr - 32.0) evaluates to the real number 8.0 rather than the integer 8. The expression (dfahr - 32) would evaluate to 8.0 as well because subtracting an int from a double results in a double value. Similarly, the expression 8.0 * 5/9 evaluates to 40.0/9, which is 4.44444, because when / is used with double values or a mixed combination of double and int values, the result is a double. The evaluation of both expressions from Program 3.2 is diagrammed in Figure 3.4.

This means that if the first cout << statement in Program 3.2 is modified so that the 5 is replaced by 5.0, as in (ifahr - 32) * 5.0/9, then the expression will evaluate to 4.44444 when 40 is entered as the value of ifahr because 5.0 is a double whereas 5 is an int.

Program 3.4 express.cpp

```
#include <iostream>
using namespace std;

// illustrates problems with evaluating
// arithmetic expressions

int main()
{
    double dfahr;
```

```
cout << "enter a Fahrenheit temperature ";
cin >> dfahr;
cout << dfahr << " = "
    << 5/9 * (dfahr - 32.0)
    << " Celsius' << endl;

return 0;
}
```

express cpp

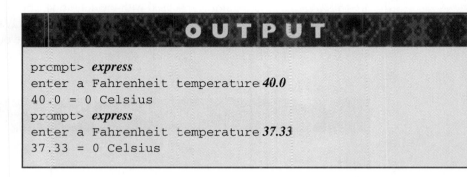

```
prompt> express
enter a Fahrenheit temperature 40.0
40.0 = 0 Celsius
prompt> express
enter a Fahrenheit temperature 37.33
37.33 = 0 Celsius
```

Often arithmetic is done by specialized circuitry built to add, multiply, and do other arithmetic operations. The circuitry for int operations is different from the circuitry for double operations, reflecting the different methods used for multiplying integers and real numbers. When numbers of different types are combined in an arithmetic operation, one circuit must be used. Thus when 8.0 * 5 is evaluated, the 5 is **converted** to a double (and the double circuitry would be used). Sometimes the word **promoted** is used instead of *converted*.

Stumbling Block

Pitfalls with Evaluating Expressions. Because arithmetic operators are overloaded and because we're not used to thinking of arithmetic as performed by computers, some expressions yield results that don't meet our expectations. Referring to Program 3.4, we see that in the run of *express.cpp* the answer is 0, because the value of the expression 5/9 is 0 since integer division is used. It might be a better idea to use 5.0 and 9.0 since the resulting expression should use double operators. If an arithmetic expression looks correct to you but it yields results that are not correct, be sure that you've used parentheses properly, that you've taken double and int operators into account, and that you have accounted for operator precedence.

Pause to Reflect

3.6 If the output expressions in Program 3.2 are changed so that subexpressions are enclosed in parentheses as shown, why do both statements print zero?

```
(ifahr - 32) * (5/9)
```

3.7 What is printed if parentheses are not used in either of the expressions in Program 3.2?

```
ifahr - 32 * 5/9
```

3.8 If the expression using `ifahr` is changed as shown, what will the output be if the user enters 40? Why?

```
(ifahr - 32.0) * 5/9
```

3.9 What modifications are needed to change Program 3.2 so that it converts degrees Celsius to Fahrenheit rather than vice versa?

3.10 If *daysecs.cpp*, Program 3.3, is used with the definition `long  day`, but the output is changed to `cout << 24*60*60*days << endl`, then the program behavior with a 16-bit compiler changes as shown here. The output is incorrect. Explain why the change in the output statement makes a difference.

```
                       O U T P U T

prompt> daysecs
how many days: 31
31 days = 646784 seconds
prompt> daysecs
how many days: 365
365 days = 7615360 seconds
```

3.11 The quadratic formula, which gives the roots of a quadratic equation, is

$$\frac{-b \pm \sqrt{b^2 - 4ac}}{2a}$$

The roots of $2x^2 - 8x + 6$ should be 3 and 1, where $a = 2$, $b = -8$, $c = 6$, and $\sqrt{b^2 - 4ac} = 4$. Explain why the statements below print 12 and 4 instead of 3 and 1.

```
cout << (8 + 4)/2*2 << endl;
cout << (8 - 4)/2*2 << endl;
```

3.2.4 The Type `char`

The individual letters used to construct C++ `string` values are called *characters*; the type `char` is used to represent characters. The type `char` is actually an integral type; in many ways `char` values act like `int` values. This means it's possible to add `char` values; however, we'll avoid using characters as though they were integers. We'll use chars almost exclusively as a way to build `string` values, and we'll study how to do this in later chapters.

A `char` prints differently than an integer; otherwise, it can be used like an integer. Single quotes (apostrophes) are used to indicate `char` values; for example, `'a'`, `' '`, and `'Z'` are all valid C++ characters.

3.3 Case Study: Pizza Slices

In this section we'll look at one program in some detail. The program uses the types `int` and `double` in calculating several statistics about different sizes of pizza. The program might be used, for example, to determine whether a 10-inch pizza selling for $10.95 is a better buy than a 14-inch pizza selling for $14.95.

3.3.1 Pizza Statistics

Pizzas can be ordered in several sizes. Some pizza parlors cut all pizzas into eight slices, whereas others get more slices out of larger pizza pies. In many situations it would be useful to know what size pie offers the best deal in terms of cost per slice or cost per square inch of pizza. Program 3.5, *pizza.cpp*, provides a first attempt at a program for determining information about pizza prices.

Program 3.5 pizza.cpp

```
#include <iostream>
using namespace std;

// find the price of one slice of pizza
// and the price per square inch

void SlicePrice(int radius, double price)
// compute pizza statistics
{
    // assume all pizzas have 8 slices

    cout << "sq in/slice = ";
    cout << 3.14159*radius*radius/8 << endl;

    cout << "one slice: $" << price/8 << endl;
    cout << "$" << price/(3.14159*radius*radius);
    cout << " per sq. inch" << endl;
}

int main()
{
    int radius;
    double price;
    cout << "enter radius of pizza ";
    cin >> radius;
```

```
        cout << "enter price of pizza ";
        cin >> price;

        SlicePrice(radius,price);

        return 0;
    }
```

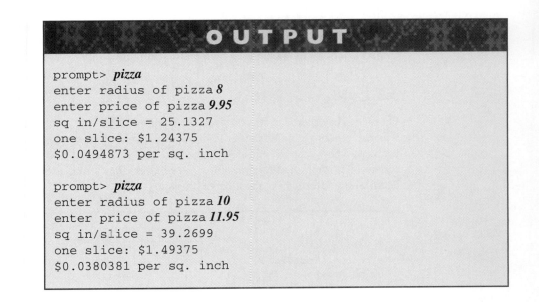

```
prompt> pizza
enter radius of pizza 8
enter price of pizza 9.95
sq in/slice = 25.1327
one slice: $1.24375
$0.0494873 per sq. inch

prompt> pizza
enter radius of pizza 10
enter price of pizza 11.95
sq in/slice = 39.2699
one slice: $1.49375
$0.0380381 per sq. inch
```

The function `SlicePrice` is used for both the processing and the output steps of computation in *pizza.cpp*. The input steps take place in `main`. Numbers entered by the user are stored in the variables `radius` and `price` defined in `main`. The values of these variables are sent as **arguments** to `SlicePrice` for processing. This is diagrammed in Figure 3.5.

If the order of the arguments in the call `SlicePrice(radius,price)` is changed to `SlicePrice(price,radius)`, the compiler issues a warning:

```
pizza.cpp: In function 'int main()':
pizza.cpp:30: warning: 'double' used for argument 1 of
              'SlicePrice(int, double)'
```

It's not generally possible to pass a `double` value to an `int` parameter without losing part of the value, so the compiler issues a warning. For example, passing an argument of 11.95 to the parameter `radius` results in a value of 11 for the parameter because `double` values are truncated when stored as integers. This is called **narrowing**. Until we discuss how to convert values of one type to another type, you should be sure that the type of an argument matches the type of the corresponding formal parameter. Since

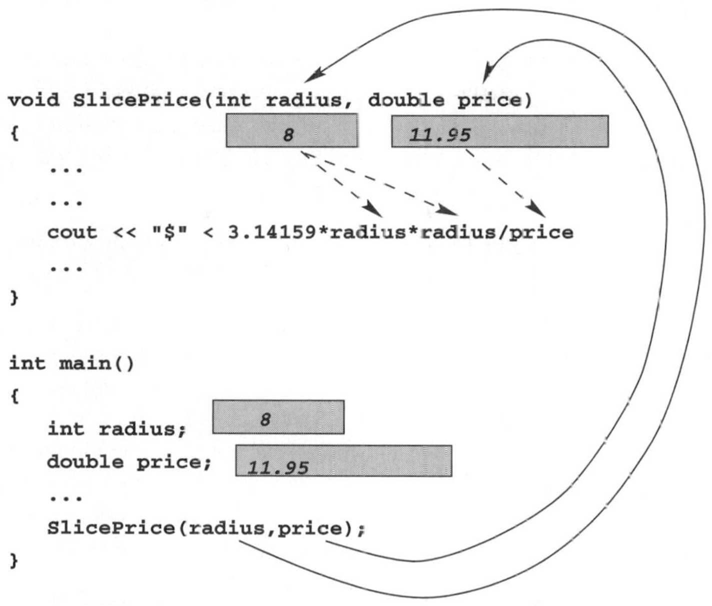

```
    void SlicePrice(int radius, double price)
    {                        8            11.95
        ...
        ...
        cout << "$" < 3.14159*radius*radius/price
        ...
    }

    int main()
    {
        int radius;        8
        double price;    11.95
        ...
        SlicePrice(radius,price);
    }
```

Figure 3.5 Passing arguments.

different types may use different amounts of storage and may have different internal representations in the computer, it is a good idea to ensure that types match properly.

> **Program Tip 3.4: Pay attention to compiler warnings.** When the compiler issues a warning, interpret the warning as an indication that your program is not correct. Although the program may still compile and execute, the warning indicates that something isn't proper with your program.

The area of a circle is given by the formula $\pi \times r^2$, where r is the radius of the circle. In `SlicePrice` the formula determines the number of square inches in a slice and the price per square inch; the parentheses used to compute the price per square inch are necessary.

```
cout << "$" << price/(3.14159*radius*radius)
```

If parentheses are not used, the rules for evaluating expressions lead to a value of $380.331 per square inch for a 10-inch pizza costing $11.95. The value of `price/3.14159` is multiplied by 10 twice—the operators / and * have equal precedence and are evaluated from left to right. In the exercises you'll modify this program so that a user can enter the number of slices as well as other information. Such changes make the program useful in more settings.

3.4 Classes and Types: An Introduction

The types int and double are built-in types in C++, whereas string is a class. In object-oriented programming terminology, programmer-defined types are often called **classes.** Although some people make a distinction between the terms *type* and *class,* we'll treat them as synonyms. The term *class* is apt as indicated by the definition below from the *American Heritage Dictionary:*

> **class** 1. A set, collection, group, or configuration containing members having or thought to have at least one attribute in common.

All variables of type, or class, string share certain attributes that determine how they can be used in C++ programs. As we've seen in several examples, the types int and double represent numbers with different attributes. In the discussion that follows, I'll sometimes use the word **object** instead of the word *variable.* You should think of these as synonyms. The use of classes in object-oriented programming gives programmers the ability to write programs using off-the-shelf components. In this section we'll examine a programmer-defined class that simulates a computer-guided hot-air balloon as shown in Program 3.6; the graphical output is shown as Figure 3.6.

Program 3.6   *gfly.cpp*
<hr style="width:30%">

```cpp
#include <iostream>
using namespace std;
#include "gballoon.h"

// auto-pilot guided balloon ascends, cruises, descends

int main()
{
    Balloon b(MAROON);
    int rise;                   // how high to fly      (meters)
    int duration;               // how long to cruise  (seconds)

    cout << "Welcome to the windbag emporium." << endl;
    cout << "You'll rise up, cruise a while, then descend." << endl;
    cout << "How high (in meters) do you want to rise: ";
    cin >> rise;
    cout << "How long (in seconds) do you want to cruise: ";
    cin >> duration;

    b.Ascend(rise);             // ascend to specified height
    b.Cruise(duration);         // cruise for specified time-steps
    b.Descend(0);               // come to earth
    WaitForReturn();            // pause to see graphics window
    return 0;
}
```

gfly.cpp

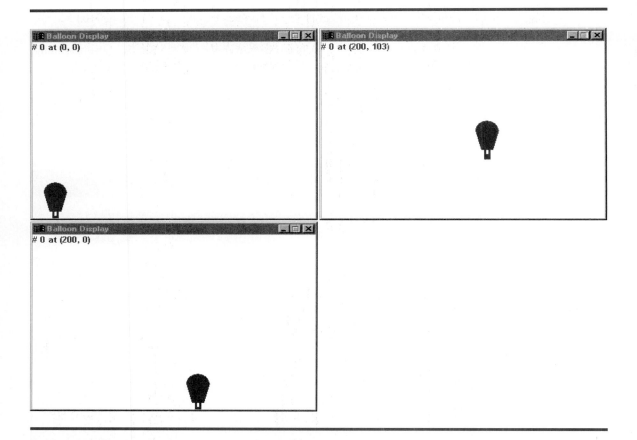

Figure 3.6 Screendumps from a run of *gfly.cpp*; rise to 100 m., cruise for 200 secs.

You won't know all the details of how the simulated balloon works, but you'll still be able to write a program that guides the balloon. This is also part of object-oriented programming: using classes without knowing exactly how the classes are implemented, that is, without knowing about the code used "behind the scenes." Just as many people drive cars without understanding exactly what a spark plug does or what a carburetor is, programmers can use classes without knowing the details of how the classes are written.

A fundamental property of a class is that its behavior is defined by the functions by which objects of the class are manipulated. Knowing about these functions should be enough to write programs using the objects; intimate knowledge of how the class is implemented is not necessary. This should make sense since you've worked with `double` variables without knowledge of how `double` numbers are stored in a computer.

In *gfly.cpp*, an object (variable) b of type, or class, `Balloon` is defined and used to simulate a hot-air balloon rising, cruising for a specified duration, and then descending to earth. Running this program causes both a **graphics window** and a **console window** to appear on your screen. The console window is the window we've been using in all our programs so far. It is the window in which output is displayed and in which you enter input when running a program. The graphics window shows the balloon actually moving across part of the computer screen. The run below shows part of the text output that appears in the console window. Snapshots of the graphics window at the beginning, middle (before the balloon descends), and end of the run are shown in Figure 3.6.

Clearly there is something going on behind the scenes since the statements in Program 3.6 do not appear to be able to generate the output shown. In subsequent chapters we'll study how the Balloon class works; at this point we'll concentrate on understanding the three function calls in Program 3.6.

OUTPUT

Part of a run, the balloon rises and travels for seven seconds
```
prompt> gfly
Welcome to the windbag emporium.
You'll rise up, cruise a while, then descend.
How high (in meters) do you want to rise: 100
How long (in seconds) do you want to cruise: 200

balloon #0 at (0, 0)    **** rising to 50 meters
balloon #0 at (0, 0)    burn
balloon #0 at (0, 10)   burn
balloon #0 at (0, 20)   burn
balloon #0 at (0, 30)   burn
balloon #0 at (0, 40)   burn

balloon #0 at (0, 50)   ***** Cruise at 50 m. for 100 secs.
balloon #0 at (0, 50)   wind-shear -1
balloon #0 at (1, 49)
balloon #0 at (2, 49)
balloon #0 at (3, 49)   wind-shear -4
balloon #0 at (4, 45)   wind-shear -1   too low!   burn
balloon #0 at (5, 54)   wind-shear -3
balloon #0 at (6, 51)
balloon #0 at (7, 51)
```

3.4.1   Member Functions

We have studied several programs with user-defined functions. In *macinput.cpp*, Program 3.1, the function Verse has two string parameters. In *pizza.cpp*, Program 3.5, the function SlicePrice has one int parameter and one double parameter. In Program 3.6, *gfly.cpp*, three function calls are made: *Ascend, Cruise,* and *Descend.* Together, these functions define the behavior of a Balloon object. You can't affect a balloon or change how it behaves except by using these three functions to access the balloon. These functions are applied to the object b as indicated by the "dot" syntax as in

```
b.Ascend(rise);
```

which is read as "*b dot ascend rise*." These functions are referred to as **member functions** in C++. In other object-oriented languages, functions that are used to manipulate objects of a given class are often called **methods.** In this example, the object b invokes its member function Ascend with rise as the argument.

Note that definitions of these functions do *not* appear in the text of Program 3.6 before they are called. The prototypes for these functions are made accessible by the statement

```
#include "gballoon.h"
```

which causes the information in the **header file** *gballoon.h* to be included in Program 3.6. The header file is an interface to the class Balloon. Sometimes an **interface diagram** is used to summarize how a class is accessed. The diagram shown in Figure 3.7 is modeled after diagrams used by Grady Booch [Boo91]. Each member function[5] is shown in an oval, and the name of the class is shown in a rectangle. Details about the member function prototypes as well as partial specifications for what the functions do are found in the header file. The interface diagram serves as a reminder of what the names of the member functions are.

Detailed information on the Balloon class and all other classes that are provided for use with this book is found in How to G.

3.4.2 Reading Programs

One skill you should begin to learn is how to read a program and the supporting documentation for the program. Rich Pattis, the author of *Karel the Robot*, argues that you should read a program carefully, not like a book but like a contract you desperately want to break. The idea is that you must pay close attention to the "fine print" and not just read for plot or characterization. Sometimes such minute perusal is essential, but it is often possible to gain a general understanding without such scrutiny.

The header file *gballoon.h* is partially shown in Program 3.7. The private section of the code is not shown here but is available if you look at the header file with the code that comes with this book.

Program 3.7 gballoonx.h

```
#ifndef _GBALLOON_H
#define _GBALLOON_H
```

---

[5]We will not use the functions GetAltitude and GetLocation now but will return to them in a later chapter.

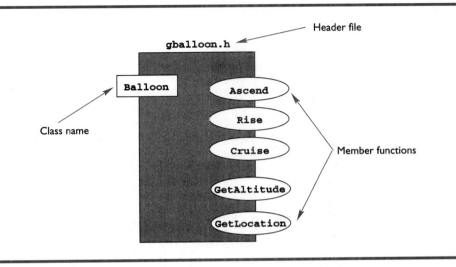

Figure 3.7 Interface diagram for Balloon class.

```
// class for balloon manipulation using simulated auto pilot
// (based on an idea of Dave Reed) graphics version 3/22/99
//
// Ascend: rise to specified height in a sequence of burns
//         Each burn raises the altitude by 10 meters
//
// Cruise: cruise for specified time-steps/seconds
//         Random wind-shear can cause balloon to rise and fall,
//         but vents and burns keep balloon within 5 m. of start
//         altitude
//
// Descend:  descend to specified height in sequence of vents
//           Each vent drops the balloon 10 m. or to ground if < 10 m.
//
// int GetAltitude: returns altitude (in meters)  (y-coord)
// int GetLocation: returns how many time-steps/secs elapsed (x-coord)

#include "canvas.h"
#include "utils.h"

class Balloon
{
  public:
    Balloon();                   // use default color (gold)
    Balloon(color c);            // balloon of specified color

    void Ascend  (int height);   // ascend so altitude >= parameter
    void Descend (int height);   // descend so altitude <= parameter
    void Cruise  (int steps);    // cruise for parameter time-steps
    int GetAltitude() const;     // returns height above ground
                                 //   (y-coord)

    int GetLocation() const;     // returns # time-steps (x-coord)
  private:
```

```
        void Burn();
        void Vent();
        int myAltitude;
        int mySteps;          // ... see gballcon.h for details
    };
    #endif                                                        gballoonx.h
```

There are three important details of this header file.

1. Comments provide users and readers of the header file with an explanation of what the member functions do.

2. Member functions are declared in the **public** section of a class definition and may be called by a user of the class as is shown in Program 3.6. We'll discuss the special member function `Balloon` later. The other functions, also shown in the interface diagram in Figure 3.7, each have prototypes showing they take one `int` parameter except for `GetAltitude` and `GetLocation`.

3. Functions and data in the **private** section are *not* accessible to a user of the class. As a programmer using the class, you may glance at the private section, but the compiler will prevent your program from accessing what's in the private section. Definitions in the private section are part of the class's implementation, *not* part of the class's interface. As a user, or **client,** of the class, your only concern should be with the interface, or public section.

3.4.3 Private and Public

The declaration of the class `Balloon` in Program 3.7 shows that the parts of the class are divided into two sections: the private and the public sections. The public section is how an object of a class appears to the world, how the object behaves. Objects are manipulated in programs like Program 3.6, *gfly.cpp,* by calling the object's public member functions. Private member functions[6] exist only to help implement the public functions. Imagine a company that publishes a list of its company phone numbers. For security reasons, some numbers are accessible only by those calling from within the company building. An outsider can get a copy of the company phonebook and see the inaccessible phone numbers, but the company switchboard will allow only calls from within the building to go through to the inaccessible numbers.

In general, the designation of what should be private and what should be public is a difficult task. At this point, the key concept is that you access a class via its public functions. Some consider it a drawback of C++ that information in the private section can be seen and read, but many languages suffer from the same problem. To make things simple, you should think of the private section as invisible until you begin to design your own classes.

There are often variables in the private section. These variables, such as `myAltitude`, define an object's **state**—the information that determines the object's characteristics. In the case of a `Balloon` object, the altitude of the balloon, represented

---

[6]Prototypes for private member functions like `Burn` and `AdjustAltitude` are visible in the full listing of *gballoon.h,* but are not shown in the partial listing of *gballoonx.h* in Program 3.7.

by the `int` variable `myAltitude`, is part of this state. Knowledge of the private section isn't necessary to understand how to use `Balloon` objects.

Donald Knuth (b. 1938)

Donald Knuth is perhaps the best-known computer scientist and is certainly the foremost scholar of the field. His interests are wide-ranging, from organ play-

ing to word games to typography. His first publication was for *MAD* magazine, and his most famous is the three-volume set *The Art of Computer Programming*.

In 1974 Knuth won the Turing award for "major contributions to the analysis of algorithms and the design of programming languages." In his Turing award address he says:

The chief goal of my work as educator and author is to help people learn how to write beautiful programs. My feeling is that when we prepare a program, it can be like composing poetry or music; as Andrei Ershov has said, programming can give us both intellectual and emotional satisfaction, because it is a real achievement to master complexity and to establish a system of consistent rules.

In discussing what makes a program "good," Knuth says:

In the first place, it's especially good to have a program that works correctly. Secondly it is often good to have a program that won't be hard to change, when the time for adaptation arises. Both of these goals are achieved when the program is easily readable and understandable to a person who knows the appropriate language.

Of computer programming Knuth says:

We have seen that computer programming is an art, because it applies accumulated knowledge to the world, because it requires skill and ingenuity, and especially because it produces objects of beauty.

For more information see [Sla87, AA85, ACM87].

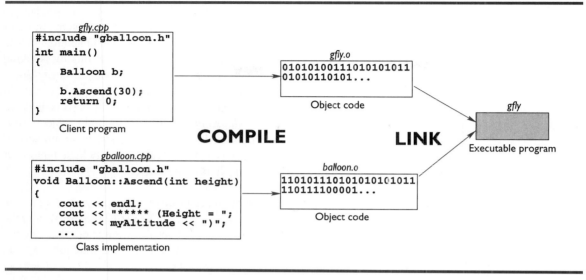

Figure 3.8 Compiling and linking.

The public section describes the interface to an object, that is, what a client or user needs to know to manipulate the object. In a car, the brake pedal is the interface to the braking system. Pressing the pedal causes the car to stop, regardless of whether antilock brakes, disc brakes, or drum brakes are used. In general, the public interface provides "buttons" and "levers" that a user can push and pull to manipulate the object as well as dials that can be used to read information about the object state.

All header files we'll use in this book will have statements similar to the #ifndef _BALLOON_H statement and others that begin with the # sign, as shown in *balloon.h*. For the moment we'll ignore the purpose of these statements; they're necessary but are not important to the discussion at this point. The ifndef statement makes it impossible to include the same header file more than once in the same program. We'll see why this is important when programs get more complex.

3.5   Compiling and Linking

In Chapter 1 we discussed the differences between **source code,** written in a high-level language like C++, and machine code, written in a low-level language specific to one kind of computer. The compiler translates the source code into machine code. Another step is almost always necessary in making an executable program. Code from libraries needs to be **linked** together with the machine code to form an executable program. For example, when the header file <iostream> is used, the code that implements input and output streams must be linked. When the header file "balloon.h" is used, the code that implements the balloon class must be linked. This process of compiling and linking is illustrated in Figure 3.8.

The compiler translates source code into machine, or **object,** code. The word *object* here has nothing to do with object-oriented programming; think of it as a synonym for *machine code*. In some environments object code has a `.o` extension; in other environments it has a `.obj` extension. The different object files are linked together to form an executable program. Sometimes you may not be aware that linking is taking place. But when you develop more complex programs, you'll encounter errors in the linking stage. For example, if you try to compile *gfly.cpp*, Program 3.6, you *must* link-in the code that implements the balloon class. The implementation of the class is declared in *gballoon.h* and is found in the file *balloon.cpp*. The corresponding object code, as translated by the compiler, is in *balloon.o*. It's often convenient to group several object files together in a code **library.** The library can be automatically linked into your programs so that you don't need to take steps to do this yourself.

Pause to Reflect

3.12 Some pizza parlors cut larger pies into more pieces than small pies: a small pie might have 8 pieces, a medium pie 10 pieces, and a large pie 12 pieces. Modify the function `SlicePrice` so that the number of slices is a parameter. The function should have three parameters instead of two. How would the function `main` in Program 3.5 change to accommodate the new `SlicePrice`?

3.13 In *pizza.cpp*, what changes are necessary to allow the user to enter the diameter of a pizza instead of the radius?

3.14 Based on the descriptions of the member functions given in the header file `balloonx.h` (Program 3.7), why is different output generated when Program 3.6 is run with the same input values? (Run the program and see if the results are similar to those shown above.)

3.15 What would the function `main` look like of a program that defines a `Balloon` object, causes the balloon to ascend to 40 meters, cruises for 10 time-steps, ascends to 80 meters, cruises for 20 time-steps, then descends to earth?

3.16 What do you think happens if the following two statements are the only statements in a modified version of Program 3.6?

```
b.Ascend(50);
b.Ascend(30);
```

What would happen if these statements are reversed (first ascend to 30 meters, then to 50)?

3.6 Chapter Review

In this chapter we studied the input/process/output model of computation and how input is performed in C++ programs. We also studied numeric types and operations and a user-defined class, `Balloon`. The importance of reading programs and documentation in order to be able to modify and write programs was stressed.

- Input is accomplished in C++ using the extraction operator, >>, and the standard input stream, cin. These are accessible by including <iostream>.

- Variables are memory locations with a name, a value, and a type. Variables must be defined before being used in C++. Variables can be defined anywhere in a program in C++, but we'll define most variables at the beginning of the function in which they're used.

- Numeric data represent different kinds of numbers in C++. We'll use two types for numeric data: int for integers and double for floating-point numbers (real numbers, in mathematics). If you're using a microcomputer, you should use the type long (long int) instead of int for quantities over 5,000.

- Operators are used to form arithmetic expressions. The standard math operators in C++ are + - * / %. In order to write correct arithmetic expressions you must understand operator precedence rules and the rules of expression evaluation.

- Conversion takes place when an int value is converted to a corresponding double value when arithmetic is done using both types together.

- The type char represents characters, which are used to construct strings. In C++ characters are indicated by single quotes: 'y' and 'Y'.

- Classes are types, but are defined by a programmer rather than being built into the language like int and double. The interface to a class is accessible by including the right header file.

- Member functions manipulate or operate on objects. Only member functions defined in the public section of a class definition can be used in a client program.

- A class is divided into two sections, the private section and the public section. Programs that use the class access the class by the public member functions.

- Executable programs are created by compiling source code into object code and linking different object files together. Sometimes object files are stored together in a code library.

3.7 Exercises

3.1 Write a program that prompts the user for a first name and a last name and that prints a greeting for that person. For example:

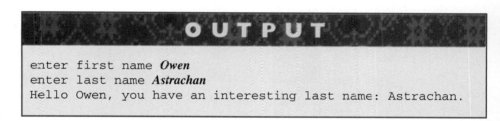

```
OUTPUT

enter first name Owen
enter last name Astrachan
Hello Owen, you have an interesting last name: Astrachan.
```

3.2 Write a program that prompts the user for a quantity expressed in British thermal units (BTU) and that converts it to Joules. The relationship between these two units of measure is given as 1 BTU = 1054.8 Joules.

3.3   Write a program that prompts the user for a quantity expressed in knots and that converts it to miles per hour. The relationship needed is that 1 knot = 101.269 ft/min (and that 5,280 ft = 1 mile).

3.4   Write a program using the operators / and % that prompts the user for a number of seconds and then determines how many hours, minutes, and seconds this represents. For example, 20,000 seconds represents 5 hours, 33 minutes, and 20 seconds.

3.5   Write a program that prints three verses of the classic song "One hundred bottles of _____ on the wall" as shown here.

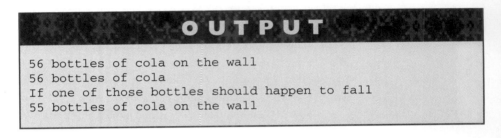

```
56 bottles of cola on the wall
56 bottles of cola
If one of those bottles should happen to fall
55 bottles of cola on the wall
```

The function's **prototype** is

```
void BottleVerse(string beverage, int howMany)
```

The first parameter, beverage, is a string representing the kind of beverage for which a song will be printed. The second parameter, howMany, is not a string but is a C++ integer. The advantage of using an int rather than a string is that arithmetic operations can be performed on ints. For example, given the function BottleVerse shown below, the function call BottleVerse("cola",56) would generate the abbreviated verse shown here.

```
void BottleVerse(string beverage, int howMany)
{
  cout << howMany << " bottles of "
      << beverage << ", ";
  cout << "one fell, " << howMany - 1
      << " exist" << endl;
}
```

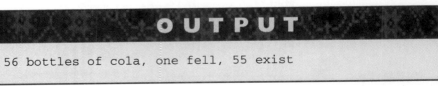

```
56 bottles of cola, one fell, 55 exist
```

Note how the string parameter is used to indicate the specific kind of beverage for which a verse is to be printed. The int parameter is used to specify how many bottles

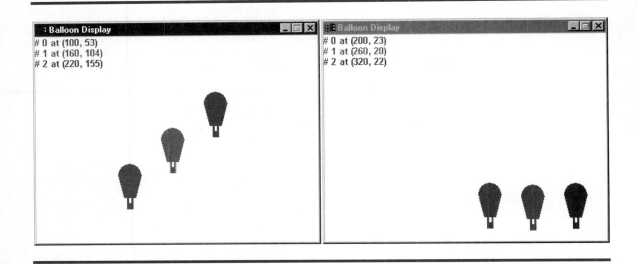

Figure 3.9 Screendumps from a run of *gfly2.cpp*.

are "in use." Note that because int parameters support arithmetic operations, the expression howMany - 1 is always 1 less than the just-printed number of bottles. In the program you write, three verses should be printed. The number of bottles in the first verse can be any integer. Each subsequent verse should use 1 bottle less than the previous verse. The user should be prompted for the kind of beverage used in the song.

3.6 Write a program that calculates pizza statistics but takes into account both the number of slices and the thickness of the pizza. The user should be prompted for both quantities.

3.7 Write a program that can be used as a simplistic trip planner. Prompt the user for the number of car passengers, the length of the trip in miles, the capacity of the fuel tank in gallons, the price of gas, and the miles per gallon that the car gets. The program should calculate the number of tanks of gas needed, the total price of the gas needed, and the price per passenger if the cost is split evenly.

3.8 Write a program that uses a variable of type Balloon that performs the following sequence of actions:

1. Prompt the user for an initial altitude and a number of time steps.
2. Cause the balloon to ascend to the specified altitude, then cruise for the specified time steps.
3. Cause the balloon to descend to half the altitude it initially ascended to, then cruise again for the specified time steps.
4. Cause the balloon to descend to earth (height = 0).

3.9 The program *gfly2.cpp* is shown on the next page as Program 3.8. Several different balloons are used in the same program. A screendump is shown in Figure 3.9. Modify the program so the user is prompted for how high the first balloon should rise. The other two balloons should rise to heights two and three times as high, respectively. The user should be prompted for how far the balloons cruise. The balloons should cruise for one-third this distance, then the function WaitForReturn should be called so that the user can see the balloons paused in flight. Repeat this last step twice so that the balloons all fly for the specified time, but in three stages.

Program 3.8   gfly2.cpp
————————————

```cpp
#include <iostream>
using namespace std;
#include "gballoon.h"

// illustrates graphical balloon class
// auto-pilot guided balloon ascends, cruises, descends

int main()
{

    Balloon b1(MAROON);
    Balloon b2(RED);
    Balloon b3(BLUE);

    WaitForReturn();

    b1.Ascend(50);   b1.Cruise(100);
    b2.Ascend(100);  b2.Cruise(160);
    b3.Ascend(150);  b3.Cruise(220);

    WaitForReturn();

    b1.Descend(20);  b1.Cruise(100);
    b2.Descend(20);  b2.Cruise(100);
    b3.Descend(20);  b3.Cruise(100);

    WaitForReturn();
    return 0;
}
```

gfly2.cpp

Control, Functions, and Classes

4

> If *A* equals success, then the formula is $A = X + Y + Z$.
> *X* is work. *Y* is play. *Z* is keep your mouth shut.
> ALBERT EINSTEIN
> *quoted in SIGACT News, Vol. 25, No. 1, March 1994*

> Your "if" is the only peacemaker; much virtue in "if."
> WILLIAM SHAKESPEARE
> *As You Like It, V, iv*

> Leave all else to the gods.
> HORACE
> *Odes, Book I, Ode ix*

In the programs studied in Chapter 3, statements executed one after the other to produce output. This was true both when all statements were in main and when control was transferred from main to another function, as it was in SlicePrice in *pizza.cpp*, Program 3.5. However, code behind the scenes in *gfly.cpp*, Program 3.6, executed differently in response to the user's input and to a simulated wind-shear effect. Many programs require nonsequential control. For example, transactions made at automatic teller machines (ATMs) process an identification number and present you with a screen of choices. The program controlling the ATM executes different code depending on your choice—for example, either to deposit money or to get cash. This type of control is called **selection:** a different code segment is selected and executed based on interaction with the user or on the value of a program variable.

Another type of program control is **repetition:** the same sequence of C++ statements is repeated, usually with different values for some of the variables in the statements. For example, to print a yearly calendar your program could call a PrintMonth function 12 times:

```
PrintMonth("January", 31);
//...
PrintMonth("November",30);
PrintMonth("December",31);
```

Here the name of the month and the number of days in the month are arguments passed to PrintMonth. Alternatively, you could construct the PrintMonth function to determine the name of the month as well as the number of days in the month given the year and the number of the month. This could be done for the year 2000 by repeatedly executing the following statement and assigning values of 1, 2, ..., 12 to month:

```
PrintMonth(month, 2000);
```

In this chapter we'll study methods for controlling how the statements in a program are executed and how this control is used in constructing functions and classes. To do this we'll expand our study of arithmetic operators, introduced in the last chapter, to include operators for other kinds of data. We'll also study C++ statements that alter the flow of control within a program. Finally, we'll see how functions and classes can be used as a foundation on which we'll continue to build as we study how programs are used to solve problems. At the end of the chapter you'll be able to write the function PrintMonth, but you'll also see a class that encapsulates the function so you don't have to write it.

4.1   The Assignment Operator

In the next three sections we'll use a program that makes change using U.S. coins to study relational and assignment statements and conditional execution. We'll use the same program as the basis for what could be a talking cash register.

A run of *change.cpp,* Program 4.1, shows how change is made using quarters, dimes, nickels, and pennies. The program shows how values can be stored in variables using the **assignment operator,** =. In previous programs the user entered values for variables, but values can also be stored using the assignment operator. The code below assigns values for the circumference and area of a circle according to the radius value, then prints the values.[1]

```
double radius, area, circumference;
cout << "enter radius: ";
cin >> radius;
area = 3.14159*radius*radius;
circumference = 3.14159*2*radius;
cout << "area = " << area
     << " circumference = " << circumference << endl;
```

The assignment operator in Program 4.1 has two purposes. It assigns the number of each type of coin needed to the appropriate variable (e.g., quarters and dimes) and it resets the value of the variable amount so that change will be correctly calculated.

Syntax: assignment operator =

variable = expression

The assignment operator = stores values in variables. The expression on the right-hand side of the = is evaluated, and this value is stored in the memory location associated with the variable named on the left-hand side of the =. The use of the equal sign to assign values to variables can cause confusion, especially if you say "equals" when you read an expression like quarters = amount/25. Operationally, the value on the right is stored in quarters, and it would be better to write quarters ← amount / 25. The assignment statement can be read as *"The memory location of the variable quarters is assigned the value of amount/25,"* but that is cumbersome (at best). If you can bring

---

[1]The formula for the area of a circle is πr^2; the formula for circumference is $2\pi r$ where r is the radius.

yourself to say "gets" for =, you'll find it easier to distinguish between = and == (the Boolean equality operator). Verbalizing the process by saying "*Quarters gets amount divided by twenty-five*" will help you understand what's happening when assignment statements are executed.

Program 4.1   change.cpp

```cpp
#include <iostream>
using namespace std;

// make change in U.S. coins
// Owen Astrachan, 03/17/99

int main()
{
    int amount;
    int quarters, dimes, nickels, pennies;

    // input phase of program

    cout << "make change in coins for what amount: ";
    cin >> amount;

    // calculate number of quarters, dimes, nickels, pennies

    quarters = amount/25;
    amount = amount - quarters*25;

    dimes = amount/10;
    amount = amount - dimes*10;

    nickels = amount/5;
    amount = amount - nickels*5;

    pennies = amount;

    // output phase of program

    cout << "# quarters =\t" << quarters << endl;
    cout << "# dimes =\t"    << dimes    << endl;
    cout << "# nickels =\t"  << nickels  << endl;
    cout << "# pennies =\t"  << pennies  << endl;

    return 0;
}
```

change.cpp

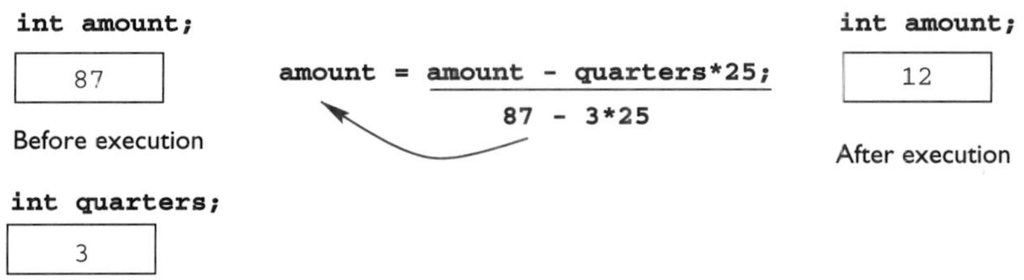

```
int amount;                                                      int amount;

┌──────────┐      amount  =  amount  -  quarters*25;            ┌──────────┐
│    87    │                 87  -  3*25                        │    12    │
└──────────┘                                                     └──────────┘
Before execution                                                 After execution

int quarters;
┌──────────┐
│    3     │
└──────────┘
```

Figure 4.1   Updating a variable via assignment.

O U T P U T

```
prompt> change
make change in coins for what amount: 87
# quarters =      3
# dimes =         1
# nickels =       0
# pennies =       2
prompt> change
make change in coins for what amount: 42
# quarters =      1
# dimes =         1
# nickels =       1
# pennies =       2
```

The statement amount = amount - quarters*25 updates the value of the variable amount. The right-hand side of the statement is evaluated first. The value of this expression, amount - quarters*25, is stored in the variable on the left-hand side of the assignment statement—that is, the variable amount. This process is diagrammed in Figure 4.1 when amount is 87.

A sequence of assignments can be chained together in one statement:

$$x = y = z = 13;$$

This statement assigns the value 13 to the variables x, y, and z. The statement is interpreted as x = (y = (z = 13)). The value of the expression (z = 13) is 13, the value assigned to z. This value is assigned to y, and the result of the assignment to y is 13. This result of the expression (y = 13) is then assigned to x. Parentheses aren't needed in the statement x = y = z = 13 because the assignment operator = is **right-associative:** in the absence of parentheses the rightmost = is evaluated first.

Table 4.1 Escape sequences in C++.

Escape sequence	Name	ASCII
\n	newline	NL (LF)
\t	horizontal tab	HT
\v	vertical tab	VT
\b	backspace	BS
\r	carriage return	CR
\f	form feed	FF
\a	alert (bell)	BEL
\\	backslash	\
\?	question mark	?
\'	single quote (apostrophe)	'
\"	double quote	"

In contrast, the subtraction operator is **left-associative.** The expression 8 – 3 – 2 is equal to 3 because it is evaluated as (8 – 3) – 2 rather than 8 – (3 – 2): here the leftmost subtraction is evaluated first. Most operators are left-associative; the associativity of all C++ operators is shown in Table A.4 in How to A.

Escape Sequences. The output of *change.cpp* is aligned using a tab character '\t'. The tab character prints one tab position, ensuring that the amounts of each kind of coin line up. The backslash and t to print the tab character are an example of an **escape sequence.** Common escape sequences are given in Table 4.1. The table is repeated as Table A.5 in How to A. Each escape sequence prints a single character. For example, the following statement prints the four-character string "\'":

```
cout << "\"\\\'\"" << endl;
```

4.2 Choices and Conditional Execution

> I shall set forth from somewhere, I shall make the reckless choice
> ROBERT FROST
> *The Sound of the Trees*

In this section we'll alter Program 4.1 so that it prints only the coins used in giving change. We'll also move the output part of the program to a separate function. By parameterizing the output and using a function, we make it simpler to incorporate modifications to the original program.

> **Program Tip 4.1:   Avoid duplicating the same code in several places in the same program.** Programs will be modified. If you need to make the same change in more than one place in your code it is very likely that you will leave some changes out, or make the changes inconsistently. In many programs more time is spent in **program maintenance** than in **program development**. Often, moving duplicated code to a function and calling the function several times helps avoid code duplication.

Program 4.2   change2.cpp

```cpp
#include <iostream>
#include <string>
using namespace std;

// make change in U.S. coins
// Owen Astrachan, 03/17/99

void Output(string coin, int amount)
{
    if (amount > 0)
    {   cout << "# " << coin << " =\t" << amount << endl;
    }
}

int main()
{
    int amount;
    int quarters, dimes, nickels, pennies;

    // input phase of program

    cout << "make change in coins for what amount: ";
    cin >> amount;

    // calculate number of quarters, dimes, nickels, pennies

    quarters = amount/25;
    amount = amount - quarters*25;

    dimes = amount/10;
    amount = amount - dimes*10;

    nickels = amount/5;
    amount = amount - nickels*5;

    pennies = amount;

    // output phase of program

    Output("quarters",quarters);
    Output("dimes",dimes);
```

```
Output("nickels",nickels);
Output("pennies",pennies);

return 0;
}
```

change2.cpp

OUTPUT

```
prompt> change2
make change in coins for what amount: 87
# quarters =    3
# dimes =       1
# pennies =     2
```

In the function Output an if statement is used for **conditional execution**—that is, if makes the execution depend on the value of amount. In the C++ statement

```
if (amount > 0)
{    cout << "# " << coin << " =\t" << amount << endl;
}
```

the **test expression** (amount > 0) controls the cout << statement so that output appears only if the value of the int variable amount is greater than zero.

4.2.1 The if/else Statement

An if statement contains a test expression and a **body:** a group of statements within curly braces { and }. These statements are executed *only* when the test expression, also called a **condition** or a **guard,** is true. The test *must* be enclosed by parentheses. In the

Syntax: if statement
if (*test expression*)
{
statement list;
}

next section we'll explore operators that can be used in tests, including <, <=, >, and >=. The body of the if statement can contain any number of statements. The curly braces that are used to delimit the body of the if statement aren't needed when there's only one statement in the body, but we'll always use them as part of a **defensive programming** strategy designed to ward off bugs before they appear.

Program 4.3 shows that an `if` statement can have an `else` part, which also controls, or guards, a body of statements within curly braces { and } that is executed when the test expression is false. Any kind of statement can appear in the body of an `if/else` state-

> **Syntax: if/else statement**
>
> ```
> if  (test expression)
> {
>     statement list;
> }
> else
> {
>     statement list;
> }
> ```

ment, including other `if/else` statements. We'll discuss formatting conventions for writing such code after we explore the other kinds of operators that can be used in the test expressions that are part of `if` statements. You may find yourself writing code with an **empty** `if` or `else` body: one with no statements. This can always be avoided by changing the test used with the `if` using rules of logic we'll discuss in Section 4.7.

In Program 4.3, if the value of `response` is something other than `"yes"`, then the `cout <<` statements associated with the `if` section are not executed, and the statements in the `else` section of the program are executed instead. In particular, if the user enters `"yeah"` or `"yup"`, then the program takes the same action as when the user enters `"no"`. Furthermore, the answer `"Yes"` is also treated like the answer `"no"` rather than `"yes"` because a capital letter is different from the equivalent lowercase letter. As we saw in Program 4.1, *change.cpp,* the rules of C++ do *not* require an `else` section for every `if`.

Program 4.3   broccoli.cpp

```cpp
#include <iostream>
#include <string>
using namespace std;

// illustrates use of if-else statement

int main()
{
    string response;
    cout << "Do you like broccoli [yes/no]> ";
    cin >> response;
    if ("yes" == response)
    {   cout << "Green vegetables are good for you" << endl;
        cout << "Broccoli is good in stir-fry as well" << endl;
    }
    else
    {   cout << "De gustibus non disputandum" << endl;
        cout << "(There is no accounting for taste)" << endl;
    }
    return 0;
}
```

broccoli.cpp

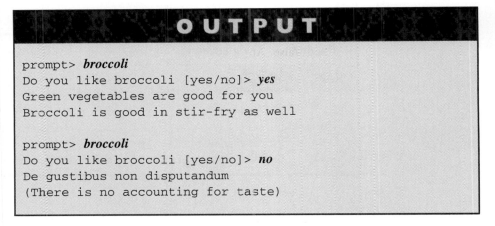

```
prompt> broccoli
Do you like broccoli [yes/no]> yes
Green vegetables are good for you
Broccoli is good in stir-fry as well

prompt> broccoli
Do you like broccoli [yes/no]> no
De gustibus non disputandum
(There is no accounting for taste)
```

The else section in Program 4.3 could be removed, leaving the following:

```
int main()
{
  string response;
  cout << "Do you like broccoli [yes/no]> ";
  cin >> response;
  if ("yes" == response)
  { cout << "Green vegetables are good for you" << endl;
    cout << "Broccoli is good in stir-fry as well" << endl;
  }
  return 0;
}
```

In this modified program, if the user enters any string other than "yes", nothing is printed.

> **Program Tip 4.2: Use an if statement to guard a sequence of statements and an if/else statement to choose between two sequences.** The if statement solves the problem of guarding the sequence of statements in the body of the if so that these statements are executed only when a certain condition holds. The if/else statement solves the problem of choosing between two different sequences. Later in the chapter we'll see how to choose between more than two sequences using cascaded if/else statements.

4.3 Operators

We've seen arithmetic operators such as +, *, %, the assignment operator =, and the < operator used in if/else statements. In this section we'll study the other operators available in C++. You'll use all these operators in constructing C++ programs.

Table 4.2 The relational operators.

Symbol	Meaning	Example
==	equal to	`if ("yes" == response)`
>	greater than	`if (salary > 30000)`
<	less than	`if (0 < salary)`
!=	not equal to	`if ("yes" != response)`
>=	greater than or equal to ($\geq$)	`if (salary >= 10000)`
<=	less than or equal to ($\leq$)	`if (20000 <= salary)`

4.3.1 Relational Operators

> Comparisons are odious.
> JOHN FORTESCUE
> *De Laudibus Legum Angliae, 1471*

The expressions that form the test of an `if` statement are built from different operators. In this section we'll study the **relational operators,** which are used to determine the relationships between different values. Relational operators are listed in Table 4.2.

The parenthesized expression that serves as the test of an `if` statement can use any of the relational operators shown in Table 4.2. The parenthesized expressions evaluate to true or false and are called **Boolean** expressions, after the mathematician George Boole. Boolean expressions have one of two values: **true** or **false.** In C++ programs, any nonzero value is considered "true," and zero-valued expressions are considered "false." The C++ type **bool** is used for variables and expressions with one of two values: *true* and *false*. Although `bool` was first approved as part of C++ in 1994, some older compilers do not support it.[2] We'll use `true` and `false` as values rather than zero and one, but remember that zero is the value used for false in C++ .

The relational operators < and > behave as you might expect when used with `int` and `double` values. In the following statement the variable `salary` can be an `int` or a `double`. In either case the phrase about minimum wage is printed if the value of `salary` is less than 10.0.

---

[2]If you're using a compiler that doesn't support `bool` as a built-in type, you can use the header file `bool.h` supplied with the code from this book via `#include"bool.h"` to get access to a programmer-defined version of type `bool`.

```
if (salary < 10.0)
{   cout << "you make below minimum wage" << endl;
}
```

When `string` values are compared, the behavior of the inequality operators < and > is based on a dictionary order, sometimes called **lexicographical** order:

```
string word;
cout << "enter a word: ";
cin >> word;
if (word < "middle")
{   cout << word << " comes before middle" << endl;
}
```

In the foregoing code fragment, entering the word `"apple"` generates the following output.

```
apple comes before middle
```

Entering the word `"zebra"` would cause the test (`word < "middle"`) to evaluate to false, so nothing is printed. The comparison of strings is based on the order in which the strings would appear in a dictionary, so that `'A"` comes before `"Z"`. Sometimes the behavior of string comparisons is unexpected. Entering `"Zebra"`, for example, generates this output:

```
Zebra comes before middle
```

This happens because capital letters come before lowercase letters in the ordering of characters used on most computers.[3]
To see how relational operators are evaluated, consider the output of these statements:

```
cout << (13 < 5) << endl;
cout << (5 + 1 < 6 * 2) << endl;
```

---

[3]We'll explore the ASCII character set, which is used to determine this ordering, in Chapter 9.

```
0
1
```

The value of $13 < 5$ is false, which is zero; and the value of $6 < 12$ is true, which is one. (In How to B, a standard method for printing `bool` values as `true` and `false`, rather than 1 and 0, is shown.) In the last output statement, the arithmetic operations are executed first because they have higher precedence than relational operators. You've seen precedence used with arithmetic operators; for example, multiplication has higher precedence than addition, so that $3 + 4 \times 2 = 11$. You can use parentheses to bypass the normal precedence rules. The expression $(3 + 4) \times 2$ evaluates to 14 rather than 11. A table showing the relative precedence of all C++ operators can be found in Table A.4 in How to A.

> **Program Tip 4.3: When you write expressions in C++ programs, use parentheses liberally.** Trying to uncover precedence errors in a complex expression can be very frustrating. Looking for precedence errors is often the last place you'll look when trying to debug a program. As part of defensive programming, use parentheses rather than relying exclusively on operator precedence.

Because execution of an `if` statement depends only on whether the test is true or false (nonzero or zero), the following code is legal in C++ :

```cpp
if (6 + 3 - 9)
{   cout << "great minds think alike" << endl;
}
else
{   cout << "fools seldom differ" << endl;
}
```

These statements cause the string "fools seldom differ" to be output, because the expression $(6 + 3 - 9)$ evaluates to 0, which is false in C++ . Although this code is legal, it is not necessarily good code. It is often better to make the comparison explicit, as in

```cpp
if (x != 0)
{   DoSomething();
}
```

rather than relying on the equivalence of "true" and any nonzero value:

```cpp
if (x)
{   DoSomething();
}
```

which is equivalent in effect, but not in clarity. There are situations, however, in which the second style of programming is clearer. When such a situation arises, I'll point it out.

4.3.2 Logical Operators

As we will see (for example, in *usemath.cpp*, Program 4.6), it can be necessary to check that a value you enter is in a certain range (e.g., not negative). In *change.cpp*, Program 4.1, the program should check to ensure that the user's input is valid (e.g., between 0 and 99). The following code implements this kind of check:

```
if (choice < 0)
{    cout << "illegal choice" << endl;
}
else if (choice > 99)
{    cout << "illegal choice" << endl;
}
else
{    // choice ok, continue
}
```

This code has the drawback of duplicating the code that's executed when the user enters an illegal choice. Suppose a future version of the program will require the user to reenter the choice. Modifying this code fragment would require adding new code in two places, making the likelihood of introducing an error larger. In addition, when code is duplicated, it is often difficult to make the same modifications everywhere the code appears. Logical operators allow Boolean expressions to be combined, as follows:

```
if (choice < 0 || choice > 99)
{    cout << "illegal choice" << endl;
}
else
{    // choice ok, continue
}
```

The test now reads, "If choice is less than 0 or choice is greater than 99." The test is true (nonzero) when either `choice < 0` or `choice > 99`. The operator `||` is the **logical or** operator. It evaluates to true when either or both of its Boolean arguments are true. The **logical and** operator `&&` operates on two Boolean expressions and returns true only when both are true.

The preceding test for valid input can be rewritten using logical and as follows:

```
if (0 <= choice && choice <= 99)
{    // choice ok, continue
}
else
{    cout << "illegal choice" << endl;
}
```

Be careful when translating English or mathematics into C++ code. The phrase "choice is between 0 and 99" is often written in mathematics as $0 \leq choice \leq 99$. In C++ relational operators are left-associative, so the following `if` test, coded as it would be in mathematics, will evaluate to true for *every* value of `choice`.

Table 4.3 Truth table for logical operators.

A	B	A || B	A && B	!A
false	false	false	false	true
false	true	true	false	true
true	false	true	false	false
true	true	true	true	false

```
if (0 <= choice <= 99)
{   // choice ok, continue
}
```

Since the leftmost <= is evaluated first (the relational operators, like all binary operators, are left-associative), the test is equivalent to ((0 <= choice) <= 99). The value of the expression (0 <= choice) is either false (0) or true (1), both of which are less than or equal to 99, thus satisfying the second test.

There is also a unary operator ! that works with Boolean expressions. This is the **logical not operator.** The value of !expression is false if the value of expression is true, and true when the value of expression is false. The two expressions below are equivalent.

$$x \; != \; y \qquad !(x \; == \; y)$$

Logical operators are given in Table 4.3. Because ! has a very high precedence, the parentheses in the expression on the right are necessary (see Table A.4).

4.3.3 Short-Circuit Evaluation

The following statement is designed to print a message when a grade-point average is higher than 90%:

```
if (scoreTotal/numScores > 0.90)
{   cout << "excellent!  very good work" << endl;
}
```

This code segment might cause a program to exit abnormally[4] if the value of numScores is zero because the result of division by zero is not defined. The abnormal exit can be avoided by using another **nested** if statement (the approach required in languages such as Pascal):

```
if (numScores != 0)
{
   if (scoreTotal/numScores > 0.90)
   {   cout << "excellent!  very good work" << endl;
   }
}
```

---

[4]The common phrase for such an occurrence is **bomb,** as in "The program bombed." If you follow good defensive programming practices, your programs should not bomb.

However, in languages like C, C++, and Java another approach is possible:

```
if (numScores != 0 && scoreTotal/numScores > 0.90)
{    cout << "excellent!  very good work" << endl;
}
```

The subexpressions in an expression formed by the logical operators && and || are evaluated from left to right. Furthermore, the evaluation automatically stops as soon as the value of the entire test expression can be determined. In the present example, if the expression numScores != 0 is false (so that numScores is equal to 0), the entire expression must be false, because when && is used to combine two Boolean subexpressions, both subexpressions must be true (nonzero) for the entire expression to be true (see Table 4.3). When numScores == 0, the expression scoreTotal/numScores > 0.90 will *not* be evaluated, avoiding the potential division by zero.

Similarly, when || is used, the second subexpression will not be evaluated if the first is true, because in this case the entire expression must be true—only one subexpression needs to be true for an entire expression to be true with ||. For example, in the code

```
if (choice < 1 || choice > 3)
{    cout << "illegal choice" << endl;
}
```

the expression choice > 3 is not evaluated when choice is 0. In this case, choice < 1 is true, so the entire expression must be true.

The term **short-circuit evaluation** describes this method of evaluating Boolean expressions. The short circuit occurs when some subexpression is not evaluated because the value of the entire expression is already determined. We'll make extensive use of short-circuit evaluation (also called "lazy evaluation") in writing C++ programs.

4.3.4 Arithmetic Assignment Operators

C++ has several operators that serve as "contractions," in the grammatical sense that "I've" is a contraction of "I have." These operators aren't necessary, but they can simplify and shorten code that changes the value of a variable. For example, several statements in *change.cpp,* Program 4.1, alter the value of amount; these statements are similar to the following:

```
amount = amount - quarters*25;
```

This statement can be rewritten using the operator -=:

```
amount -= quarters*25;
```

Similarly, the statement number = number + 1, which increments the value of number by one, can be abbreviated using the += operator: number += 1;. In general, the statement *variable = variable + expression;* has exactly the same effect as the statement *variable += expression;*

Using such assignment operators can make programs easier to read. Often a long variable name appearing on both sides of an assignment operator = will cause a lengthy

Table 4.4   Arithmetic assignment operators.

Symbol	Example	Equivalent
+=	x += 1;	x = x + 1;
*=	doub *= 2;	doub = doub * 2;
-=	n -= 5;	n = n - 5;
/=	third /= 3;	third = third / 3;
%=	odd %= 2;	odd = odd % 2;

expression to wrap to the next line and be difficult to read. The arithmetic assignment operators summarized in Table 4.4 can alleviate this problem.

It's not always possible to use an arithmetic assignment operator as a contraction when a variable appears on both the left and right sides of an assignment statement. The variable must occur as the *first* subexpression on the right side. For example, if x has the value zero or one, the statement x = 1 - x changes the value from one to zero and vice versa. This statement cannot be abbreviated using the arithmetic assignment operators.

4.4   Block Statements and Defensive Programming

Following certain programming conventions can lead to programs that are more understandable (for you and other people reading your code) and more easily developed.

In this book we follow the convention of using **block delimiters,** { and }, for each part of an if/else statement. This is shown in *change2.cpp,* Program 4.2. It is possible to write the if statement in Program 4.2 without block delimiters:

```
if (amount > 0)
    cout << "# " << coin << " =\t" << amount << endl;
```

The test of the if statement controls the output statement so that it is executed only when amount is greater than zero.

As we've seen, it is useful to group several statements together so that all are executed precisely when the test of an if/else statement is true. To do this, a **block** (or **compound**) **statement** is used. A block statement is a sequence of one or more statements enclosed by curly braces, as shown in Program 4.2. If no braces are used, a program may compile and run, but its behavior might be other than expected. Consider the following program fragment:

```
int salary;
cout << "enter salary ";
cin >> salary;
if (salary > 30000)
    cout << salary << " is a lot to earn " << endl;
    cout << salary*0.55 << " is a lot of taxes << endl;
```

```
cout << "enter \# of hours worked ";
. . .
```

Two sample runs of this fragment follow:

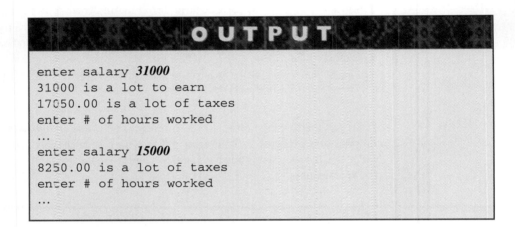

```
enter salary 31000
31000 is a lot to earn
17050.00 is a lot of taxes
enter # of hours worked
...
enter salary 15000
8250.00 is a lot of taxes
enter # of hours worked
...
```

Stumbling Block

Note that the indentation of the program fragment might suggest to someone reading the program (but not to the compiler!) that the "lot of taxes" message should be printed only when the salary is greater than 30,000. However, the taxation message is *always* printed. The compiler interprets the code fragment as though it were written this way:

```
int salary;
cout << "enter salary ";
cin >> salary;
if (salary > 30000)
{    cout << salary << " is a lot to earn " << endl;
}
cout << salary*0.55 << " is a lot of taxes " << endl;
cout << "enter # of hours worked ";
```

When 15000 is entered, the test `salary > 30000` evaluates to false, and the statement about "a lot to earn" is not printed. The statement about a "lot of taxes," however, is printed because it is not controlled by the test.

Indentation and spacing are ignored by the compiler, but they are important for people reading and developing programs. For this reason, we will always employ braces {} and a block statement when using `if/else` statements, even if the block statement consists of only a single statement.

4.4.1 Defensive Programming Conventions

This convention of always using braces is an example of a **defensive programming** strategy: writing code to minimize the potential for causing errors. Suppose you decide to add another statement to be controlled by the test of an `if` statement that is initially written without curly braces. When the new statement is added, it will be necessary to include the curly braces that delimit a block statement, but that is easy to forget to do. Since the missing braces can cause a hard-to-detect error, we adopt the policy of including them even when there is only a single statement controlled by the test.

> **Program Tip 4.4: Adopt coding conventions that make it easier to modify programs.** You'll rarely get a program right the first time. Once a program works correctly, it's very likely that you'll need to make modifications so that the program works in contexts unanticipated when first designed and written. More time is spent modifying programs than writing them, so strive to make modification as simple as possible.

To see that indentation makes a difference, note that *noindent.cpp,* Program 4.4, compiles and executes without error but that no consistent indentation style is used. Notice that the program is much harder for people to read, although the computer "reads" it with no trouble.

Program 4.4 noindent.cpp

```
#include <iostream>
#include <string>
using namespace std;
int main() { string response; cout
<< "Do you like C++ programming [yes/no]> "; cin >> response;
        if ("yes" == response) { cout <<
"It's more than an adventure, it can be a job"
                    << endl; } else {  cout
<< "Perhaps in time you will" << endl; } return    0;}
```

noindent.cpp

In this book the left curly brace { always follows an `if/else` on the next line after the line on which the `if` or `else` occurs. The right curly brace } is indented the same level as the `if/else` to which it corresponds. Other indentation schemes are possible; one common convention follows. This is called *K&R* style after the originators of C, Kernighan and Ritchie.

```
if ("yes" == response) {
    cout << "Green vegetables are good for you" << endl;
    cout << "Broccoli is good in stir-fry as well" << endl;
}
```

You can adopt either convention, but your boss (professor, instructor, etc.) may require a certain style. If you're consistent, the particular style isn't that important, although it's often the cause of many arguments between supporters of different indenting styles.

In this book we usually include the first statement between curly braces on the same line as the first (left) brace. If you use this style of indenting, you will not press return after you type the left curly brace {. However, we sometimes do press return, which usually makes programs easier to read because of the extra white space.[5]

Stumbling Block

Problems with = and ==. Typing = when you mean to type == can lead to hard-to-locate bugs in a program. A coding convention outlined here can help to alleviate these bugs, but you must keep the distinction between = and == in mind when writing code. Some compilers are helpful in this regard and issue warnings about "potentially unintended assignments."

The following program fragment is intended to print a message depending on a person's age:

```
string age;
cout << "are you young or old [young/old]: ";
cin >> age;
if (age = "young")
{ cout << "not for long, time flies when you're having fun";
}
else
{ cout << "hopefully you're young at heart";
}
```

If the user enters old, the message beginning "not for long..." is printed. Can you see why this is the case? The test of the if/else statement should be read as "if age gets young." The string literal "young" is assigned to age, and the result of the assignment is nonzero (it is "young", the value assigned to age). Because anything nonzero is regarded as true, the statement within the scope of the if test is executed.

You can often prevent such errors by putting constants on the left of comparisons as follows:

```
if ("young" == age)
  // do something
```

If the assignment operator is used by mistake, as in if ("young" = age), the compiler will generate an error.[6] It is much better to have the compiler generate an error message than to have a program with a bug in it.

Putting constants on the left in tests is a good defensive programming style that can help to trap potential bugs and eliminate them before they creep into your programs.

---

[5]In a book, space is more of a premium than it is on disk—hence the style of indenting that does not use the return. You should make sure you follow the indenting style used by your boss or programming role model.

[6]On one compiler the error message "error assignment to constant" is generated. On another, the less clear message "sorry, not implemented: initialization of array from dissimilar array type" is generated.

4.4.2 Cascaded `if/else` Statements

Sometimes a sequence of `if/else` statements is used to differentiate among several possible values of a single expression. Such a sequence is called **cascaded.** An example is shown in *monthdays.cpp,* Program 4.5.

Program 4.5 monthdays.cpp

```cpp
#include <iostream>
#include <string>
using namespace std;

// illustrates cascaded if/else statements

int main()
{
    string month;
    int days = 31;               // default value of 31 days/month

    cout << "enter a month (lowercase letters): ";
    cin >> month;

    // 30 days hath september, april, june, and november

    if ("september" == month)
    {   days = 30;
    }
    else if ("april" == month)
    {   days = 30;
    }
    else if ("june" == month)
    {   days = 30;
    }
    else if ("november" == month)
    {   days = 30;
    }
    else if ("february" == month)
    {   days = 28;
    }
    cout << month << " has " << days << " days" << endl;

    return 0;
}
```

monthdays.cpp

It's possible to write the code in *monthdays.cpp* using **nested** `if/else` statements as follows. This results in code that is much more difficult to read than code using cascaded `if/else` statements. Whenever a sequence of `if/else` statements like this is used to test the value of one variable repeatedly, we'll use cascaded `if/else` statements. The rule of using a block statement after an `else` is not (strictly speaking) followed, but the code is much easier to read. Because a block statement follows the `if`, we're not violating the spirit of our coding convention.

```
if ("april" == month)
{    days = 30;
}
else
{
    if ("june" == month)
    {    days = 30;
    }
    else
    {
        if ("november" == month)
        {    days = 30;
        }
        else
        {
            if ("february" == month)
            {    days = 28;
            }
        }
    }
}
```

OUTPUT

```
prompt> days4
enter a month (lowercase letters): january
january has 31 days
prompt> days4
enter a month (lowercase letters): april
april has 30 days
prompt> days4
enter a month (lowercase letters): April
April has 31 days
```

Pause to Reflect

4.1 The statements altering amount in *change.cpp,* Program 4.1, can be written using the mod operator %. If amount = 38, then amount/25 == 1, and amount % 25 == 13, which is the same value as 38 - 25*1. Rewrite the program using the mod operator. Try to use an arithmetic assignment operator.

4.2 Describe the output of Program 4.3 if the user enters the string "Yes", the string "yup", or the string "none of your business".

4.3 Why is days given a "default" value of 31 in *monthdays.cpp,* Program 4.5?

4.4 How can *monthdays.cpp,* Program 4.5, be modified to take leap years into account?

4.5 Modify *broccoli.cpp,* Program 4.3, to include an `if` statement in the `else` clause so that the "taste" lines are printed only if the user enters the string `"no"`. Thus you might have lines such as

```
if ("yes" == response)
{
}
else if ("no" == response)
{
}
```

4.6 Using the previous modification, add a final `else` clause (with no `if` statement) so that the output might be as follows:

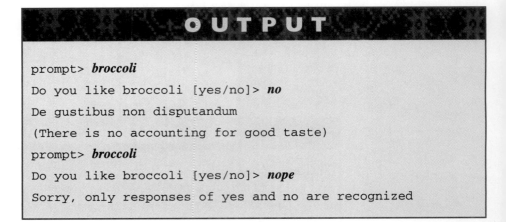

```
O U T P U T

prompt> broccoli
Do you like broccoli [yes/no]> no
De gustibus non disputandum
(There is no accounting for good taste)
prompt> broccoli
Do you like broccoli [yes/no]> nope
Sorry, only responses of yes and no are recognized
```

4.7 Write a sequence of `if/else` statements using `>` and, perhaps, `<` that prints a message according to a grade between 0 and 100, entered by the user. For example, high grades might get one message and low grades might get another message.

4.8 Explain why the output of the first statement below is 0, but the output of the second is 45:

```
cout << (9 * 3 < 4 * 5) << endl;
cout << (9 * (3 < 4) * 5) << endl;
```

Why are the parentheses needed?

4.9 What is output by each of the following statements? Why?

```
cout << (9 * 5 < 45)    << endl;
cout << (9*5 < 45 < 30) << endl;
```

4.10 Write a code fragment in which a `string` variable `grade` is assigned one of three states (`"High Pass"`, `"Pass"`, and `"Fail"`) according to whether an input integer grade is between 80 and 100, between 60 and 80, or below 60, respectively. It may be useful to write the fragment so that a message is printed and then modify it so that a `string` variable is assigned a value.

Stumbling Block

The Dangling Else Problem. Using the block delimiters { and } in all cases when writing `if/else` statements can prevent errors that are very difficult to find because the indentation, which conveys meaning to a reader of the program, is ignored by the compiler when code is generated. Using block delimiters also helps in avoiding a problem that results from a potential ambiguity in computer languages such as C++ that use `if/else` statements (C and Pascal have the same ambiguity, for example).

The following code fragment attempts to differentiate odd numbers less than zero from other numbers. The indentation of the code conveys this meaning, but the code doesn't execute as intended:

```
if (x % 2 == 1)
    if (x < 0)
        cout << " number is odd and less than zero" << endl;
else
    cout << " number is even " << endl;
```

What happens if the `int` object x has the value 13? The indentation seems to hint that nothing will be printed. In fact, the string literal `"number is even"` will be printed if this code segment is executed when x is 13. The segment is read by the compiler as though it is indented as follows:

```
if (x % 2 == 1)
    if (x < 0)
        cout << " number is odd and less than zero" << endl;
    else
        cout << " number is even " << endl;
```

The use of braces makes the intended use correspond to what happens. Nothing is printed when x has the value 13 in

```
if (x % 2 == 1)
{   if (x < 0)
        cout << " number is odd and less than zero" << endl;
}
else
{   cout << " number is even " << endl;
}
```

As we have noted before, the indentation used in a program is to assist the human reader. The computer doesn't require a consistent or meaningful indentation scheme. Misleading indentation can lead to hard-to-find bugs where the human sees what is intended rather than what exists.

One rule to remember from this example is that an `else` always corresponds to the most recent `if`. Without this rule there is ambiguity as to which `if` the `else` belongs; this is known as the **dangling-else** problem. Always employ curly braces { and } when using block statements with `if/else` statements (and later with looping constructs). If braces are always used, there is no ambiguity because the braces serve to delimit the scope of an `if` test.

Claude Shannon *(b. 1916)*

Claude Shannon founded **information theory**—a subfield of computer science that is used today in developing methods for encrypting information. Encryption is used to store data in a secure manner so that the information can be read only by designated people.

In his 1937 master's thesis, Shannon laid the foundation on which modern computers are built by equating Boolean logic with electronic switches. This work enabled hardware designers to design, build, and test circuits that could perform logical as well as arithmetic operations. In an interview in [Hor92], Shannon responds to the comment that his thesis is "possibly the most important master's thesis in the century" with "It just happened that no one else was familiar with both those fields at the same time." He then adds a wonderful non sequitur: "I've always loved that word 'Boolean.'"

Shannon is fond of juggling and riding unicycles. Among his inventions are a juggling "dummy" that looks like W. C. Fields and a computer THROBAC: Thrifty Roman Numeral Backward Computer.

Although much of Shannon's work has led to significant advances in the theory of communication, he says:

I've always pursued my interests without much regard for financial value or the value to the world; I've spent lots of time on totally useless things.

Shannon's favorite food is vanilla ice cream with chocolate sauce.

Shannon received the National Medal of Science in 1966. For more information see [Sla87, Hor92].

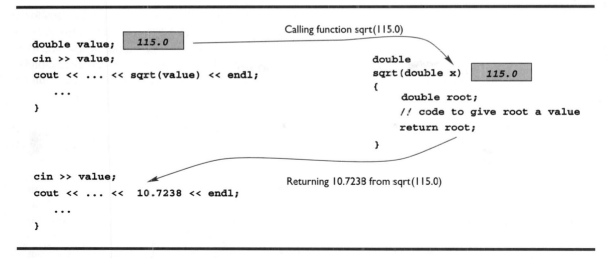

Figure 4.2 Evaluating the function call `sqrt115.0`.

4.5 Functions That Return Values

> Civilization advances by extending the number
> of important operations which we can perform without thinking about them.
> ALFRED NORTH WHITEHEAD
> *An Introduction to Mathematics*

In Chapter 3 we studied programmer-defined functions, such as `SlicePrice` in *pizza.cpp*, Program 3.5, whose prototype is

```
void SlicePrice(int radius, double price)
```

The return type of `SlicePrice` is `void`. Many programs require functions that have other return types. You've probably seen mathematical functions on hand-held calculators such as $\sin(x)$ or $\sqrt{x}$. These functions are different from the function `SlicePrice` in that they return a value. For example, when you use a calculator, you might enter the number 115, then press the square-root key. This displays the value of $\sqrt{115}$ or 10.7238. The number 115 is an **argument** to the square root function. The value returned by the function is the number 10.7238. Program 4.6 is a C++ program that processes information in the same way: users enter a number, and the square root of the number is displayed.

Control flow from *usemath.cpp* is shown in Figure 4.2. The value 115, entered by the user and stored in the variable `value`, is copied into a memory location associated with the parameter `x` in the function `sqrt`. The square root of 115 is calculated, and a **return** statement in the function `sqrt` returns this square root, which is used in place of the expression `sqrt(value)` in the `cout` statement. As shown in Figure 4.2, the value 10.7238 is displayed as a result.

The function `sqrt` is accessible by including the header file `<cmath>`. Table 4.5 lists some of the functions accessible from this header file. A more complete table of functions is given as Table F.1 in How to F. In the sample output of *usemath.cpp*, Program 4.6, the square roots of floating-point numbers aren't always exact. For example, $\sqrt{100.001} = 10.0000499998$, but the value displayed is 10. Floating-point values cannot always be exactly determined. Because of inherent limits in the way these values are stored in the computer, the values are rounded off to the most precise values that can be represented in the computer. The resulting **roundoff error** illustrates the theme of *conceptual* and *formal* models introduced in Chapter 1. Conceptually, the square root of 100.001 can be calculated with as many decimal digits as we have time or inclination to write down. In the formal model of floating-point numbers implemented on computers, the precision of the calculation is limited.

Program 4.6   usemath.cpp

```
#include <iostream>
#include <cmath>
using namespace std;

// illustrates use of math function returning a value

int main()
{
    double value;
    cout << "enter a positive number ";
    cin >> value;
    cout << "square root of " << value << " = " << sqrt(value) << endl;

    return 0;
}
```

usemath.cpp

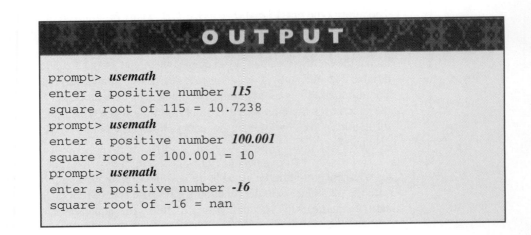

```
OUTPUT

prompt> usemath
enter a positive number 115
square root of 115 = 10.7238
prompt> usemath
enter a positive number 100.001
square root of 100.001 = 10
prompt> usemath
enter a positive number -16
square root of -16 = nan
```

Table 4.5 Some functions in `<cmath>`.

Function Name	Prototype	Returns
double fabs	(double x)	absolute value of x
double log	(double x)	natural log of x
double log10	(double x)	base-ten log of x
double sin	(double x)	sine of x (x in radians)
double cos	(double x)	cosine of x (x in radians)
double tan	(double x)	tangent of x (x in radians)
double asin	(double x)	arc sine of x $[-\pi/2, \pi/2]$
double acos	(double x)	arc cosine of x $[0, \pi]$
double atan	(double x)	arc tangent of x $[-\pi/2, \pi/2]$
double pow	(double x, double y)	x^y
double sqrt	(double x)	$\sqrt{x}$, square root of x
double floor	(double x)	largest integer value $\leq$ x
double ceil	(double x)	smallest integer value $\geq$ x

Finally, although the program prompts for positive numbers, there is no check to ensure that the user has entered a positive number. In the output shown, the symbol nan stands for "not a number."[7] Not all compilers will display this value. In particular, on some computers, trying to take the square root of a negative number may cause the machine to lock up. It would be best to guard the call `sqrt(value)` using an `if` statement such as the following one:

```
if (0 <= value)
{   cout << "square root of " << value << " = "
        << sqrt(value) << endl;
}
else
{   cout << "nonpositive number " << value
        << " entered" << endl;
}
```

Alternatively, we could **compose** the function `sqrt` with the function `fabs`, which computes absolute values.

```
cout << "square root of " << value << " = "
     << sqrt(fabs(value)) << endl;
```

The result returned by the function `fabs` is used as an argument to `sqrt`. Since the return type of `fabs` is `double` (see Table 4.5), the argument of `sqrt` has the right type.

---

[7]Some compilers print NaN; others crash rather than printing an error value.

4.5.1 The Math Library `<cmath>`

In C and C++ several mathematical functions are available by accessing a math library using #include `<cmath>`.[8] Prototypes for some of these functions are listed in Table 4.5, and a complete list is given as Table F.1 in How to F.

All of these functions return `double` values and have `double` parameters. Integer values can be converted to `double`s, so the expression `sqrt(125)` is legal (and evaluates to 11.18033). The function `pow` is particularly useful because there is no built-in exponentiation operator in C++. For example, the statement

```
cout << pow(3,13) << endl}
```

outputs the value of 3^{13}: three to the thirteenth.

The functions declared in `<cmath>` are tools that can be used in any program. As programmers, we'll want to develop functions that can be used in the same way. On occasion, we'll develop functions that aren't useful as general-purpose tools but make the development of one program simpler. For example, in *pizza.cpp,* Program 3.5, the price per square inch of pizza is calculated and printed by the function `SlicePrice`. If the value were returned by the function rather than printed, it could be used to determine which of several pizzas was the best buy. This is shown in *pizza2.cpp,* Program 4.7. Encapsulating the calculation of the price per square inch in a function, as opposed to using the expression `smallPrice/(3.14159 * smallRadius * smallRadius)`, avoids errors that might occur in copying or retyping the expression for a large pizza. Using a function also makes it easier to include other sizes of pizza in the same program. If it develops that we've made a mistake in calculating the price per square inch, isolating the mistake in one function makes it easier to change than finding all occurrences of the calculation and changing each one.

Program 4.7 pizza2.cpp

```
#include <iostream>
using namespace std;

// find the price per square inch of pizza
// to compare large and small sizes for the best value
//
// Owen Astrachan
// March 29, 1999
//

double Cost(double radius, double price)
// postcondition: returns the price per sq. inch
{
    return price/(3.14159*radius*radius);
}

int main()
{
```

---

[8]The name `cmath` is the C++ math library, but with many older compilers you will need to use `math.h` rather than `cmath`.

```
    double smallRadius, largeRadius;
    double smallPrice, largePrice;
    double smallCost,largeCost;

    // input phase of computation

    cout << "enter radius and price of small pizza ';
    cin >> smallRadius >> smallPrice;

    cout << "enter radius and price of large pizza ";
    cin >> largeRadius >> largePrice;


    // process phase of computation

    smallCost = Cost(smallRadius,smallPrice);
    largeCost = Cost(largeRadius,largePrice);

    // output phase of computation

    cout << "cost of small pizza = " << smallCost << " per sq.inch" << endl;
    cout << "cost of large pizza = " << largeCost << " per sq.inch" << endl;

    if (smallCost < largeCost)
    {   cout << "SMALL is the best value " << endl;
    }
    else
    {   cout << "LARGE is the best value " << endl;
    }

    return 0;
}
```

pizza2.cpp

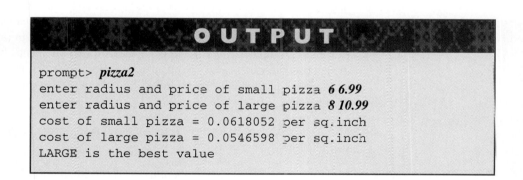

```
prompt> pizza2
enter radius and price of small pizza 6 6.99
enter radius and price of large pizza 8 10.99
cost of small pizza = 0.0618052 per sq.inch
cost of large pizza = 0.0546598 per sq.inch
LARGE is the best value
```

From the user's point of view, Program 3.5 and Program 4.7 exhibit similar, though not identical, behavior. When two programs exhibit identical behavior, we describe this sameness by saying that the programs are identical as **black boxes.** We cannot see the inside of a black box; the behavior of the box is discernible only by putting values into the box (running the program) and noting what values come out (are printed by the program). A black box specifies input and output, but not how the processing step takes place. The balloon class and the math function sqrt are black boxes; we don't know how they are implemented, but we can use them in programs by understanding their input and output behavior.

4.5.2 Pre- and Postconditions

In the function SlicePrice of *pizza2.cpp,* Program 4.7, a comment is given in the form of a **postcondition.** A postcondition of a function is a statement that is true when the function finishes executing. Each function in this book will include a postcondition that describes what the function does. Some functions have **preconditions**. A precondition states what parameter values can be passed to the function. Together a function's pre-condition and postcondition provide a contract for programmers who call the function: if the precondition is true the postcondition will be true. For example, a precondition of the function sqrt might be that the function's parameter is nonnegative.

> **Program Tip 4.5: When calling functions, read postconditions carefully. When writing functions, provide postconditions.** When possible, provide a precondition as well as a postcondition since preconditions provide programmers with information about what range of values can be passed to each parameter of a function.

In the main function of *pizza2.cpp,* the extraction operator >> extracts two values in a single statement. Just as the insertion operator << can be used to put several items on the output stream cout, the input stream cin continues to flow so that more than one item can be extracted.

Pause to Reflect

4.11 Write program fragments or complete programs that convert degrees Celsius to degrees Fahrenheit, British thermal units (Btu) to joules (J), and knots to miles per hour. Note that x degrees Celsius equals $(9/5)x + 32$ degrees Fahrenheit; that x J equals $9.48 \times 10^{-4}(x)$Btu; and that 1 knot = 101.269 ft/min (and that 5,280 ft = 1 mile). At first do this *without* using assignment statements, by incorporating the appropriate expressions in output statements. Then define variables and use assignment statements as appropriate. Finally, write functions for each of the conversions.

4.12 Modify *pizza2.cpp,* Program 4.7, to use the function pow to square radius in the function Cost.

4.13 If a negative argument to the function sqrt causes an error, for what values of x does the following code fragment generate an error?

```
if (x >= 0 && sqrt(x) > 100)
    cout << "big number" << endl;
```

4.14 Heron's formula gives the area of a triangle in terms of the lengths of the sides of the triangle: a, b, and c.

$$\text{area} = \sqrt{s \cdot (s - a) \cdot (s - b) \cdot (s - c)} \qquad (4.1)$$

where s is the semiperimeter, or half the perimeter $a + b + c$ of the triangle. Write a function `TriangleArea` that returns the area of a triangle. The sides of the triangle should be parameters to `TriangleArea`.

4.15 The law of cosines gives the length of one side of a triangle, c, in terms of the other sides a and b and the angle C formed by the sides a and b:

$$c^2 = a^2 + b^2 - 2 \cdot a \cdot b \cos(C)$$

Write a function `SideLength` that computes the length of one side of a triangle, given the other two sides and the angle (in radians) between the sides as parameters to `SideLength`.

4.16 The following code fragment allows a user to enter three integers:

```
int a,b,c;
cout << "enter three integers ";
cin >> a >> b >> c;
```

Add code that prints the average of the three values read. Does it make a difference if the type is changed from `int` to `double`? Do you think that `>>` has the same kind of associativity as `=`, the assignment operator?

4.5.3 Function Return Types

The functions `sqrt` and `SlicePrice` used in previous examples both returned `double` values. In this section we'll see that other types can be returned.

Determining Leap Years. Leap years have an extra day (February 29) not present in nonleap years. We use arithmetic and logical operators to determine whether a year is a leap year. Although it's common to think that leap years occur every four years, the rules for determining leap years are somewhat more complicated, because the period of the Earth's rotation around the Sun is not exactly 365.25 days but approximately 365.2422 days.

- If a year is evenly divisible by 400, then it is a leap year.
- Otherwise, if a year is divisible by 100, then it is *not* a leap year.
- The only other leap years are evenly divisible by 4.[9]

---

[9]These rules correspond to a year length of 365.2425 days. In the *New York Times* of January 2, 1996 (page B7, out-of-town edition), a correction to the rules used here is given. The year 4000 is *not* a leap year, nor will any year that's a multiple of 4000 be a leap year. Apparently this rule, corresponding to a year length of 365.24225 days, will have to be modified too, but we probably don't need to worry that our program will be used beyond the year 4000.

For example, 1992 is a leap year (it is divisible by 4), but 1900 is not a leap year (it is divisible by 100), yet 2000 is a leap year, because, although it is divisible by 100, it is also divisible by 400.

The Boolean-valued function `IsLeapYear` in Program 4.8 uses multiple `return` statements to implement this logic.

Recall that in the expression `(a % b)` the modulus operator `%` evaluates to the remainder when `a` is divided by `b`. Thus, `2000 % 400 == 0`, since there is no remainder when 2000 is divided by 400.

The sequence of cascaded `if` statements in `IsLeapYear` tests the value of the parameter `year` to determine whether it is a leap year. Consider the first run shown, when `year` has the value 1996. The first test, `year % 400 == 0`, evaluates to false, because 1996 is not divisible by 400. The second test evaluates to false, because 1996 is not divisible by 100. Since $1996 = 4 \times 499$, the third test, `(year % 4 == 0)`, is true, so the value `true` is returned from the function `IsLeapYear`. This makes the expression `IsLeapYear(1996)` in `main` true, so the message is printed indicating that 1996 is a leap year. You may be tempted to write

```
if (IsLeapYear(year) == true)
```

rather than using the form shown in *isleap.cpp*. This works, but the `true` is redundant, because the function `IsLeapYear` is Boolean-valued: it is either true or false.

The comments for the function `IsLeapYear` are given in the form of a **precondition** and a **postcondition**. For our purposes, a precondition is what must be satisfied for the function to work as intended. The "as intended" part is what is specified in the postcondition. These conditions are a *contract* for the caller of the function to read: if the precondition is satisfied, the postcondition will be satisfied. In the case of `IsLeapYear` the precondition states that the function works for any year greater than 0. The function is *not* guaranteed to work for the year 0 or if a negative year such as −10 is used to indicate the year 10 B.C.

It is often possible to implement a function in many ways so that its postcondition is satisfied. Program 4.9 shows an alternative method for writing `IsLeapYear`. Using a black-box test, this version is indistinguishable from the `IsLeapYear` used in Program 4.8.

Program 4.8   isleap.cpp

```
#include <iostream>
using namespace std;

// illustrates user-defined function for determining leap years

bool IsLeapYear(int year)
// precondition: year > 0
// postcondition: returns true if year is a leap year, else returns false
{
    if (year % 400 == 0)         // divisible by 400
    {   return true;
    }
```

```
        else if (year % 100 == 0)      // divisible by 100
        {   return false;
        }
        else if (year % 4 == 0)        // divisible by 4
        {   return true;
        }
        return false;
    }

    int main()
    {
        int year;
        cout << "enter a year ";
        cin >> year;
        if (IsLeapYear(year))
        {   cout << year << " has 366 days, it is a leap year" << endl;
        }
        else
        {   cout << year << " has 365 days, it is NOT a leap year" << endl;
        }
        return 0;
    }
```

isleap.cpp

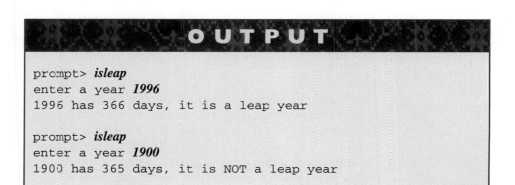

```
prompt> isleap
enter a year 1996
1996 has 366 days, it is a leap year

prompt> isleap
enter a year 1900
1900 has 365 days, it is NOT a leap year
```

Program 4.9 isleap2.cpp

```
bool IsLeapYear(int year)
// precondition: year > 0
// postcondition: returns true  if year is a leap year, else false
{
    return (year % 400 == 0) || ( year % 4 == 0 && year % 100 != 0 );
}
```

isleap2.cpp

A Boolean value is returned from IsLeapYear because the logical operators &&
and || return Boolean values. For example, the expression IsLeapYear(1974)
causes the following expression to be evaluated by substituting 1974 for year:

```
(1974 % 400 == 0) || ( 1974 % 4 == 0 && 1974 % 100 != 0 );
```

Since the logical operators are evaluated left to right to support short-circuit evaluation, the subexpression 1974 % 400 == 0 is evaluated first. This subexpression is false because 1974 % 400 is 374. The rightmost parenthesized expression is then evaluated, and its subexpression 1974 % 4 == 0 is evaluated first. Since this subexpression is false, the entire && expression must be false (why?), and the expression 1974 % 100 != 0 is not evaluated. Since both subexpressions of || are false, the entire expression is false, and false is returned.

Boolean-valued functions such as IsLeapYear are often called **predicates.** Predicate functions often begin with the prefix Is. For example, the function IsEven might be used to determine whether a number is even; the function IsPrime might be used to determine whether a number is prime (divisible by only 1 and itself, e.g., 3, 17); and the function IsPalindrome might be used to determine whether a word is a palindrome (reads the same backward as forward, e.g., mom, racecar).

Program Tip 4.6: Follow conventions when writing programs. Conventions make it easier for other people to read and use your programs and for you to read them long after you write them. One common convention is using the prefix Is for predicate/Boolean-valued functions.

Converting Numbers to English. We'll explore a program that converts some integers to their English equivalents. For example, 57 is "fifty-seven" and 14 is "fourteen." Such a program might be the basis for a program that works as a talking cash register, speaking the proper coins to give as change. With speech synthesis becoming cheaper on computers, it's fairly common to encounter a computer that "speaks." The number you hear after dialing directory assistance is often spoken by a computer. There are many home finance programs that print checks; these programs employ a method of converting numbers to English to print the checks. In addition to using arithmetic operators, the program shows that functions can return strings as well as numeric and Boolean types, and it emphasizes the importance of pre- and postconditions.

Program 4.10   numtoeng.cpp

```
#include <iostream>
#include <string>
using namespace std;

// converts two-digit numbers to English equivalents
// Owen Astrachan, 3/30/99

string DigitToString(int num)
// precondition: 0 <= num < 10
// postcondition: returns English equivalent, e.g., 1->one,...9->nine
```

```
{
    if (0 == num)         return "zero";
    else if (1 == num)    return "one";
    else if (2 == num)    return "two";
    else if (3 == num)    return "three";
    else if (4 == num)    return "four";
    else if (5 == num)    return "five";
    else if (6 == num)    return "six";
    else if (7 == num)    return "seven";
    else if (8 == num)    return "eight";
    else if (9 == num)    return "nine";
    else return "?';
}

string TensPrefix(int num)
// precondition: 10 <= num <= 99 and num % 10 == 0
// postcondition: returns ten, twenty, thirty, forty, etc.
//                corresponding to num, e.g., 50->fifty
{
    if (10 == num) return "ten";
    else if (20 == num) return "twenty';
    else if (30 == num) return "thirty";
    else if (40 == num) return "forty";
    else if (50 == num) return "fifty";
    else if (60 == num) return "sixty";
    else if (70 == num) return "seventy";
    else if (80 == num) return "eighty";
    else if (90 == num) return "ninety";
    else return "?";
}

string TeensToString(int num)
// precondition: 11 <= num <= 19
// postcondition: returns eleven, twelve, thirteen, fourteen, etc.
//                corresponding to num, e.g., 15 -> fifteen
{
    if (11 == num) return "eleven";
    else if (12 == num) return "twelve";
    else if (13 == num) return "thirteen';
    else if (14 == num) return "fourteen";
    else if (15 == num) return "fifteen";
    else if (16 == num) return "sixteen";
    else if (17 == num) return "seventeen";
    else if (18 == num) return "eighteen";
    else if (19 == num) return "nineteen";
    else return "?";
}

string NumToString(int num)
// precondition: 0 <= num <= 99
// postcondition: returns English equivalent, e.g., 1->one, 13->thirteen
{
    if (0 <= num && num < 10)
    {   return DigitToString(num);
    }
```

```
        else if (10 < num && num < 20)
        {    return TeensToString(num);
        }
        else if (num % 10 == 0)
        {    return TensPrefix(num);
        }
        else
        {    // concatenate ten's digit with one's digit
             return TensPrefix(10 * (num/10)) + "-" + DigitToString(num % 10);
        }
}

int main()
{
        int number;
        cout << "enter number between 0 and 99: ";
        cin >> number;
        cout << number  << " = " << NumToString(number) << endl;
        return 0;
}
```

numtoeng.cpp

```
                            O U T P U T

prompt> numtoeng
enter number between 0 and 99: 22
22 = twenty-two

prompt> numtoeng
enter number between 0 and 99: 17
17 = seventeen

prompt> numtoeng
enter number between 0 and 99: 103
103 = ?-three
```

The code in the DigitToString function does not adhere to the rule of using block statements in every if/else statement. In this case, using { } delimiters would make the program unnecessarily long. It is unlikely that statements will be added (necessitating the use of a block statement), and the form used here is clear.

Program Tip 4.7:   White space usually makes a program easier to read and clearer.   Block statements used with if/else statements usually make a program more robust and easier to change. However, there are occasions when these rules are not followed. As you become a more practiced programmer, you'll develop your own aesthetic sense of how to make programs more readable.

A new use of the operator + is shown in function NumToString. In the final else statement, three strings are joined together using the + operator:

```
return TensPrefix(10*(num/10))+ "-" + DigitToString(num%10);
```

When used with string values, the + operator joins or **concatenates** (sometimes "catenates") the string subexpressions into a new string. For example, the value of "apple" + "sauce" is a new string, "applesauce". This is another example of operator overloading; the + operator has different behavior for string, double, and int values.

Robust Programs. In the sample runs shown, the final input of 103 does not result in the display of one hundred three. The value of 103 violates the precondition of NumToString, so there is no guarantee that the postcondition will be satisfied. **Robust** programs and functions do not bomb in this case, but either return some value that indicates an error or print some kind of message telling the user that input values aren't valid. The problem occurs in this program because "?" is returned by the function call TensPrefix(10 * (num/10)). The value of the argument to TensPrefix is $10 \times (103/10) == 10 \times 10 == 100$. This value violates the precondition of TensPrefix. If no final else were included to return a question mark, then nothing would be returned from the function TensPrefix when it was called with 103 as an argument. This situation makes the concatenation of "nothing" with the hyphen and the value returned by DigitToString(num % 10) problematic, and the program would terminate because there is no string to join with the hyphen.

Many programs like *numtoeng.cpp* prompt for an input value within a range. A function that ensures that input is in a specific range by reprompting would be very useful. A library of three related functions is specified in *prompt.h*. We'll study these functions in the next chapter, and you can find information about them in How to G. Here is a modified version of main that uses PromptRange:

```
int main()
{
    int number = PromptRange("enter a number",0,99);
    cout << number << " = " << NumToString(number) << endl;

    return 0;
}
```

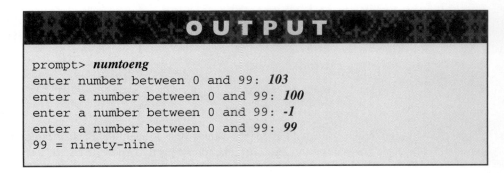

```
prompt> numtoeng
enter number between 0 and 99: 103
enter a number between 0 and 99: 100
enter a number between 0 and 99: -1
enter a number between 0 and 99: 99
99 = ninety-nine
```

You don't have enough programming tools to know how to write `PromptRange` (you need loops, studied in the next chapter), but the specifications of each function make it clear how the functions are called. You can treat the functions as black boxes, just as you treat the square-root function *sqrt* in `<cmath>` as a black box.

Pause to Reflect

4.17 Write a function `DaysInMonth` that returns the number of days in a month encoded as an integer with 1 = January, 2 = February,..., 12 = December. The year is needed because the number of days in February depends on whether the year is a leap year. In writing the function, you can call `IsLeapYear`. The specification for the function is

```
int DaysInMonth(int month,int year)
// pre: month coded as: 1 = january, ..., 12 = december
// post: returns # of days in month in year
```

4.18 Why are parentheses needed in the expression `TensPrefix(10*(num/10))`? For example, if `TensPrefix(10*num/10)` is used, the program generates a nonnumber when the user enters 22.

4.19 Write a predicate function `IsEven` that evaluates to true if its `int` parameter is an even number. The function should work for positive and negative integers. Try to write the function using only one statement: `return` *expression.*

4.20 Write a function `DayName` whose header is

```
string DayName(int day)
// pre: 0 <= day <= 6
// post: returns string representing day, with
//       0 = "Sunday", 1 = "Monday", ..., 6 = "Saturday"
```

so that the statement `cout << DayName(3) << endl;` prints `Wednesday`.

4.21 Describe how to modify the function `NumToString` in *numtoeng.cpp*, Program 4.10, so that it works with three-digit numbers.

4.22 An Islamic year y is a leap year if the remainder, when $11y + 14$ is divided by 30, is less than 11. In particular, the 2nd, 5th, 7th, 10th, 13th, 16th, 18th, 21st, 24th, 26th, and 29th years of a 30-year cycle are leap years. Write a function `IsIslamicLeapYear` that works with this definition of leap year.

4.23 In the Islamic calendar [DR90] there are also 12 months, which strictly alternate between 30 days (odd-numbered months) and 29 days (even-numbered months), except for the twelfth month, *Dhu al-Hijjah,* which in leap years has 30 days. Write a function `DaysInIslamicMonth` for the Islamic calendar that uses only three `if` statements.

4.6 Class Member Functions

Section 3.4 discusses a class named `Balloon` for simulating hot-air balloons. We've used the class `string` extensively in our examples, but we haven't used all of the functionality provided by strings themselves. Recall from Section 3.4 that functions provided by a class are called **member functions**. In this section we'll study three `string` member functions, and many more are explained in How to C. We'll also have a sneak preview at the class `Date`, which is covered more extensively in the next chapter. We'll show just one example program using the class, but the program provides a glimpse of the power that classes bring to programming.

4.6.1 `string` Member Functions

The functions we've studied so far, like those in `<cmath>`, are called **free functions** because they do not belong to a class. Member functions are part of a class and are invoked by applying a function to an object with the dot operator. Program 4.11 shows the `string` member functions `length` and `substr`. The function `length` returns the number of characters in a string; the function `substr` returns a *substring* of a string given a starting position and a number of characters.

Program 4.11 strdemo.cpp

```
#include <iostream>
#include <string>
using namespace std;

// illustrates string member functions length() and substr()

int main()
{
    string s;
    cout << "enter string: ";
    cin >> s;
    int len = s.length();
    cout << s << " has " << len << " characters" << endl;
    cout << "first char is " << s.substr(0, 1)   << endl;
```

```
cout << "last char is  " << s.substr(s.length()-1, 1) << endl;
cout << endl << "all but first is " << s.substr(1,s.length()) << endl;
return 0;
}
```

strdemo.cpp

```
prompt> strdemo
enter string: theater
theater has 7 characters
first char is t
last char is r
all but first is heater
prompt> strdemo
enter string: slaughter
theater has 9 characters
first char is s
last char is r
all but first is laughter
```

The first position or **index** of a character in a string is zero, so the last index in a string of 11 characters is 10. The prototypes for these functions are given in Table 4.6.

Each `string` member function used in Program 4.11 is invoked using an object and the dot operator. For example, `s.length()` returns the length of s. When I read code, I read this as "s dot length" and think of the length function as applied to the object s, returning the number of characters in s.

Table 4.6 Three `string` member functions.

Function Prototype and Description

`int length()`
postcondition: returns the number of characters in the string

`string substr(int pos, int len)`
precondition: 0 <= pos < length()
postcondition: returns substring of `len` characters beginning at position `pos`
(as many characters as possible if `len` too large, but error if `pos` is out of range)

`int find(string s)`
postcondition: returns first position/index at which string s begins
(returns `string::npos` if `s` does not occur)

> **Program Tip 4.8: Ask not what you can do to an object; ask what an object can do to itself.** When you think about objects, you'll begin to think about what an object can tell you about itself rather than what you can tell an object to do.

In the last use of substr in Program 4.11 more characters are requested than can be supplied by the arguments in the call s.substr(1, s.length()). Starting at index 1, there are only s.length()-1 characters in s. However, the function substr "does the right thing" when asked for more characters than there are, and gives as many as it can without generating an error. (For a full description of this and other string functions see How to C.) Although the string returned by substr is printed in *strdemo.cpp*, the returned value could be stored in a string variable as follows:

```
string allbutfirst = s.substr(1,s.length());
```

The string *Member Function* find. The member function find returns the index in a string at which another string occurs. For example, "plant" occurs at index three in the string "supplant", occurs at index five in "transplant", and does not occur in "vegetable". Program 4.12, *strfind.cpp*, shows how find works. The return value string::npos indicates that a substring does not occur. Your code should not depend on string::npos having any particular value.[10]

Program 4.12 strfind.cpp

```cpp
#include <iostream>
#include <string>
using namespace std;

int main()
{
    string target = "programming is a creative process";
    string s;
    cout << "target string: " << target << endl;
    cout << "search for what substring: ";
    cin >> s;
    int index = target.find(s);
    if (index != string::npos)
    {   cout << "found at " << index << endl;
    }
    else
    {   cout << "not found" << endl;
    }
    return 0;
}
```

strfind.cpp

---

[10] Actually, the value of string::npos is the largest positive index; see How to C.

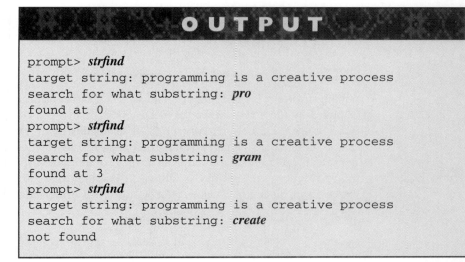

```
prompt> strfind
target string: programming is a creative process
search for what substring: pro
found at 0
prompt> strfind
target string: programming is a creative process
search for what substring: gram
found at 3
prompt> strfind
target string: programming is a creative process
search for what substring: create
not found
```

The double colon `::` used in `string::npos` separates the value, in this case npos, from the class in which the value occurs, in this case `string`. The `::` is called the **scope resolution operator**; we'll study it in more detail in the next chapter.

4.6.2   Calling and Writing Functions

When you first begin to use functions that return values, you may forget to process the return value. All nonvoid functions return a value that should be used in a C++ expression (e.g., printed, stored in a variable, used in an arithmetic expression). The following C++ statements show how three of the functions studied in this chapter (`sqrt`, `NumToString`, and `IsLeap`) are used in expressions so that the values returned by the functions aren't ignored:

```
double hypotenuse = sqrt{side1*side1 + side2*side2);
cout << NumToString(47) << endl;
bool millenniumLeaps = IsLeap(2000) || IsLeap(3000);
```

It doesn't make sense, for example, to write the following statements in which the value returned by sqrt is ignored:

```
double s1, s2;
cout << "enter sides: ";
cin >> s1 >> s2;
double root;
sqrt(s1*s1 + s2*s2);
```

The programmer may have meant to store the value returned by the function call to sqrt in the variable `root`, but the return value from the function call in the last statement is ignored.

Whenever you call a function, think carefully about the function's prototype and its postcondition. Be sure that if the function returns a value you use the value.[11]

Program Tip 4.9: Do not ignore the value returned by nonvoid functions. Think carefully about each function call you make when writing programs, and do something with the return value that makes sense in the context of your program and that is consistent with the type and value returned.

Write Lots of Functions. When do you write a function? You may be writing a program like *pizza2.cpp*, Program 4.7, where the function Cost is used to calculate how much a square inch of pizza costs. The function is reproduced here.

```
double Cost(double radius, double price)
// postcondition: returns the price per sq. inch
{
    return price/(3.14159*radius*radius);
}
```

Is it worth writing another function called CircleArea like this?

```
double CircleArea(double radius)
// postcondition: return area of circle with given radius
{
    return radius*radius*3.14159;
}
```

In general, when should you write a function to encapsulate a calculation or sequence of statements? There is no simple answer to this question, but there are a few guidelines.

Program Tip 4.10: Functions encapsulate abstractions and lead to code that's often easier to read and modify. Do not worry about so-called execution time "overhead" in the time it takes a program to execute a function call. Make your programs correct and modifiable before worrying about making them fast.

As an example, it's often easier to write a complex Boolean expression as a function that might include if/else statements, and then call the function, than to determine what the correct Boolean expression is. In the next section we'll study a tool from logic that helps in writing correct Boolean expressions, but writing functions is useful when you're trying to develop appropriate loop tests. For example, if you need to determine

---

[11]Some functions return a value but are called because they cause some change in program state separate from the value returned. Such functions are said to have **side effects** since they cause an effect "on the side," or in addition to the value returned by the function. In some cases the returned value of a function with side effects is ignored.

if a one-character string represents a consonant, it's probably easier to write a function
`IsVowel` and use that function to write `IsConsonant`, or to use `!IsVowel()` when
you need to determine if a string is a consonant.

```
bool IsVowel(string s)
// pre: s is a one-character string
// post: returns true if s is a vowel, return false
{
    if (s.length() != 1)
    {   return false;
    }
    return s == "a" || s == "e" || s == "i" ||
           s == "o" || s == "u";
}
```

The `return` *Statement.* In the function `IsVowel()` there are two `return` statements and an `if` without an `else`. When a `return` statement executes, the function
being returned from immediately exits. In `IsVowel()`, if the string parameter s has
more than one character, the function immediately returns `false`. Since the function
exits, there is no need for an `else` body, though some programmers prefer to use an
`else`. Some programmers prefer to have a single `return` statement in every function.
To do this requires introducing a local variable and using an `else` body as follows:

```
bool IsVowel(string s)
// pre: s is a one-character string
// post: returns true if s is a vowel, else return false
{
    bool retval = false;    // assume false
    if (s.length() == 1)
    {   retval = (s == "a" || s == "e" || s == "i" ||
                  s == "o" || s == "u");
    }
    return retval;
}
```

You should try to get comfortable with the assignment to `retval` inside the `if` statement. It's often easier to think of the assignment using this code.

```
if (s == "a"|| s == "e"|| s == "i"|| s == "o"|| s == "u")
{   retval = true;
}
else
{   retval = false;
}
```

This style of programming uses more code. It's just as efficient, however, and it's ok to
use it though the single assignment to `retval` is more terse and, to many, more elegant.

4.6.3 The Date Class

At the beginning of this chapter we discussed writing a function PrintMonth that prints a calendar for a month specified by a number and a year. As described, printing a calendar for January of the year 2001 could be done with the call PrintMonth(1,2001). You could write this function with the tools we've studied in this chapter though it would be cumbersome to make a complete calendar. However, using the class Date makes it much simpler to write programs that involve dates and calendars than writing your own functions like IsLeap. In general, it's easier to use classes that have been developed and debugged than to develop your own code to do the same thing, though it's not always possible to find classes that serve your purposes.

We won't discuss this class in detail until the next chapter, but you can see how variables of type Date are defined, and two of the Date member functions are used in Program 4.13. More information about the class is accessible in How to G. To use Date objects you'll need to add #include"date.h" to your programs.

Program 4.13 datedemo.cpp

```
#include <iostream>
using namespace std;
#include "date.h"

// simple preview of using the class Date

int main()
{
    int month, year;
    cout << "enter month (1-12) and year ";
    cin >> month >> year;

    Date d(month, 1, year);
    cout << "that day is " << d << ", it is a " << d.DayName() << endl;
    cout << "the month has " << d.DaysIn() << " days in it " << endl;

    return 0;
}
```

datedemo.cpp

After examining the program and the output on the next page, you should think about how you would use the class Date to solve the following problems; each can be solved with just a few lines of code.

Pause to Reflect

4.24 Determine if a year the user enters is a leap year.

4.25 Determine the day of the week of any date (month, day, year) the user enters.

4.26 Determine the day of the week your birthday falls on in the year 2002.

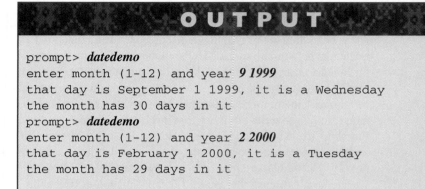

```
prompt> datedemo
enter month (1-12) and year 9 1999
that day is September 1 1999, it is a Wednesday
the month has 30 days in it
prompt> datedemo
enter month (1-12) and year 2 2000
that day is February 1 2000, it is a Tuesday
the month has 29 days in it
```

4.7   Using Boolean Operators: De Morgan's Law

Many people new to the study of programming have trouble developing correct expressions used for the guard of an *if* statement. For example, suppose you need to print an error message if the value of an int variable is either 7 or 11.

```
if (value == 7 || value == 11)
{   cout << "**error** illegal value: " << value << endl;
}
```

The statement above prints an error message for the illegal values of 7 and 11 only and not for other, presumably legal, values. On the other hand, suppose you need to print an error message if the value is anything other than 7 or 11 (i.e., 7 and 11 are the only legal values). What do you do then? Some beginning programmers recognize the similarity between this and the previous problem and write code like the following:

```
if (value == 7 || value == 11)
{   // do nothing, value ok
}
else
{   cout << "**error** illegal value: " << value << endl;
}
```

This code works correctly, but the empty block guarded by the if statement is not the best programming style. One simple way to avoid the empty block is to use the logical negation operator. In the code below the operator ! negates the expression that follows so that an error message is printed when the value is anything other than 7 or 11.

```
if ( ! (value == 7 || value == 11) )
{   cout << "**error** illegal value: " << value << endl;
}
```

Table 4.7 De Morgan's Laws for logical operators.

Expression	Logical Equivalent by De Morgan's Law
! (a && b)	(!a) || (!b)
! (a || b)	(!a) && (!b)

Alternatively, we can use De Morgan's law[12] to find the logical negation, or opposite, of an expression formed with the logical operators && and ||. De Morgan's laws are summarized in Table 4.7.

The negation of an && expression is an || expression, and vice versa. We can use De Morgan's law to develop an expression for printing an error message for any value other than 7 or 11 by using the logical equivalent of the guard in the if statement above.

```
if ( (value != 7 && (value != 11) )
{   cout << "**error** illegal value: " << value << endl;
}
```

De Morgan's law can be used to reason effectively about guards when you read code. For example, if the code below prints an error message for illegal values, what are the legal values?

```
if (s != "rock" && s != "paper" && s != "scissors")
{    cout << "** error** illegal value: " << s << endl;
}
```

By applying De Morgan's law twice, we find the logical negation of the guard that tells us the legal values. (What would be an else block in the statement above?)

```
if (s == "rock" || s == "paper" || s == "scissors") //legal
```

This shows the legal values are "rock" or "paper" or "scissors," and all other strings represent illegal values.

---

[12]Augustus De Morgan (1806–1871), first professor of mathematics at University College, London, as well as teacher to Ada Lovelace (see Section 2.5.3).

Richard Stallman (b. 1953)

Richard Stallman is hailed by many as "the world's best programmer." Before the term *hacker* became a pejorative, he used it to describe himself as "someone

fascinated with how things work, [who would see a broken machine and try to fix it]."

Stallman believes that software should be free, that money should be made by adapting software and explaining it, but not by writing it. Of software he says, "I'm going to make it free even if I have to write it all myself." Stallman uses the analogy that for software he means "free as in free speech, not as in free beer." He is the founder of the GNU software project, which creates and distributes free software tools. The GNU g++ compiler, used to develop the code in this book, is widely regarded as one of the best compilers in the world. The free operating system Gnu/Linux has become one of the most widely used operating systems in the world. In 1990 Stallman received a MacArthur "genius" award of $240,000 for his dedication and work. He continues this work today as part of the League for Programming Freedom, an organization that fights against software patents (among other things). In an interview after receiving the MacArthur award, Stallman had a few things to say about programming freedom:

> *I disapprove of the obsession with profit that tempts people to throw away their ideas of good citizenship.... businesspeople design software and make their profit by obstructing others' understanding. I made a decision not to do that. Everything I do, people are free to share. The only thing that makes developing a program worthwhile is the good it does.*

4.8   Chapter Review

In this chapter we discussed using and building functions. Changing the flow of control within functions is important in constructing programs. Encapsulating information in functions that return values is an important abstraction technique and a key concept in building large programs.

The `if/else` statement can be used to alter the flow of control in a program. You can write programs that respond differently to different inputs by using `if/else` statements. The test in an `if` statement uses relational operators to yield a Boolean value whose truth determines what statements are executed. In addition to relational operators, logical (Boolean), arithmetic, and assignment operators were discussed and used in several different ways.

The following C++ and general programming features were covered in this chapter:

■ The `if/else` statement is used for conditional execution of code. Cascaded `if` statements are formatted according to a convention that makes them more readable.

■ A function's return type is the type of value returned by the function. For example, the function `sqrt` returns a `double`. Functions can return values of any type.

■ The library whose interface is specified in `<cmath>` supplies many useful mathematical functions.

■ Boolean expressions and tests have values of true or false and are used as the tests that guard the body of code in `if/else` statements. The type `bool` is a built-in type in C++ with values of `true` and `false`.

■ A block (compound) statement is surrounded by { and } delimiters and is used to group several statements together.

■ Relational operators are used to compare values. For example, 3 < 4 is a relational expression using the < operator. Relational operators include ==, !=, <, >, <=, >=. Relational expressions have Boolean values.

■ Logical operators are used to combine Boolean expressions. The logical operators are | |, &&, !. Both | | and && (logical or and logical and, respectively) are evaluated using **short-circuit** evaluation.

■ Boolean operators in C++ use short-circuit evaluation so that only as much of an expression is evaluated from left-to-right as needed to determine whether the expression is true (or false).

■ Defensive programming is a style of programming in which care is taken to prevent errors from occurring rather than trying to clean up when they do occur.

■ Pre- and postconditions are a method of commenting functions; if the preconditions are true when a function is called, the postconditions will be true when the function has finished executing. These provide a kind of contractual arrangement between a function and the caller of a function.

■ Several **member functions** of the `string` class can be used to determine the length of a string and to find substrings of a given string. Nonmember functions are called **free functions**.

■ Functions encapsulate abstractions, such as when a leap year occurs and in calculating a square root. Functions should be used with regularity in programs.

■ Classes encapsulate related functions together. The class `string` encapsulates functions related to manipulating strings, and the class `Date` encapsulates functions related to calendar dates.

■ De Morgan's laws are useful in developing Boolean expressions for use in `if` statements and in reasoning about complex Boolean expressions.

4.9   Exercises

4.1   Write a program that prompts the user for a person's first and last names (be careful; more than one `cin >>` statement may be necessary). The program should print a message that corresponds to the user's names. The program should recognize at least four different names. For example:

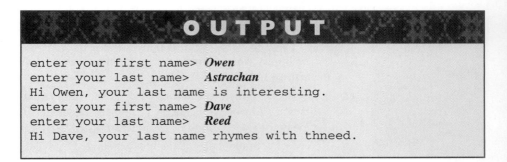

```
enter your first name> Owen
enter your last name> Astrachan
Hi Owen, your last name is interesting.
enter your first name> Dave
enter your last name> Reed
Hi Dave, your last name rhymes with thneed.
```

4.2   Write a function whose specification is

```
string IntToRoman(int num)
// precondition: 0 <= num <= 10
// postcondition: returns Roman equivalent of num
```

so that `cout << IntToRoman(7) << endl;` would cause `"VII"` to be printed. Note the precondition. Write a program to test that the function works.

4.3   Write a function with prototype `int Min2(int,int)` that returns the minimum value of its parameters. Then use this function to write another function with prototype `int Min3(int,int,int)` that returns the minimum of its three parameters. `Min3` can be written with a single line:

```
int Min3(int x, int y, int z)
// post: returns minimum of x, y, and z
{
    return Min2(                      );
}
```

where the two-parameter function is called with appropriate actual parameters. Write a test program to test both functions.

  You can then rewrite the minimum functions, naming them both `Min`. In C++, functions can have the same name if their parameters differ (this is another example of overloading).

4.4   Write a program in which the user is prompted for a real number (of type `double`) and a positive integer and that prints the `double` raised to the integer power. Use the function pow from `<cmath>`. For example:

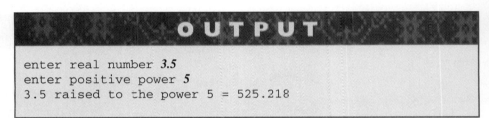

```
enter real number 3.5
enter positive power 5
3.5 raised to the power 5 = 525.218
```

4.5 Write a program that is similar to *numtoeng.cpp,* Program 4.10, but that prints an English equivalent for any number less than one million. If you know a language other than English (e.g., French, Spanish, Arabic), use that language instead of English.

4.6 Use the function sqrt from the math library[13] to write a function PrintRoots that prints the roots of a quadratic equation whose coefficients are passed as parameters.

```
PrintRoots(1,-5,6);
```

might cause the following to be printed, but your output doesn't have to look exactly like this:

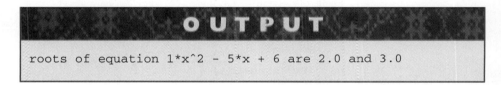

```
roots of equation 1*x^2 - 5*x + 6 are 2.0 and 3.0
```

4.7 (from [Coo87]) The surface area of a person is given by the formula

$$7.184^{-3} \times \text{weight}^{0.452} \times \text{height}^{0.725} \tag{4.2}$$

where weight is in kilograms and height is in centimeters. Write a program that prompts for height and weight and then prints the surface area of a person. Use the function pow from <cmath> to raise a number to a power.

4.8 Write a program using the class Date that prints the day of the week on which your birthday occurs for the next seven years.

4.9 Write a program using ideas from the head-drawing program *parts.cpp,* Program 2.4, that could be used as a kind of police sketch program. A sample run could look like the following:

---

[13]On some systems you may need to link the math library to get access to the square root function.

```
                         O U T P U T

prompt> sketch
Choices of hair style fcllow

(1)   parted
(2)   brush cut
(3)   balding

enter choice: 1
Choices of eye style follow

(1)   beady-eyed
(2)   wide-eyed
(3)   wears glasses

enter choice: 3
Choices of mouth style follow

(1)   smiling
(2)   straightfaced
(3)   surprised

enter choice: 3

        | | | | | | | / / / / / / / /
        |                         |
        |     ---     ---         |
        |---|o|--|o|---|
        |     ---     ---         |
       _|                       |_
      |_                         _|
        |           o           |
        |                       |
```

4.10 Write a function that allows the user to design different styles of T-shirts. You should allow choices for the neck style, the sleeve style, and the phrase or logo printed on the T-shirt. For example:

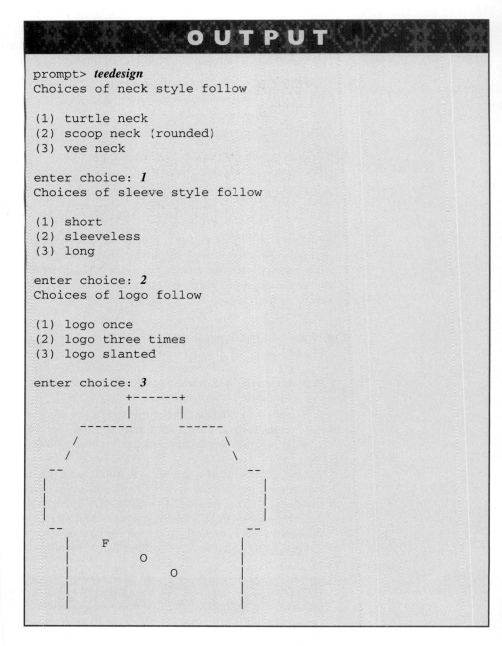

```
                        O U T P U T

prompt> teedesign
Choices of neck style follow

(1) turtle neck
(2) scoop neck (rounded)
(3) vee neck

enter choice: 1
Choices of sleeve style follow

(1) short
(2) sleeveless
(3) long

enter choice: 2
Choices of logo follow

(1) logo once
(2) logo three times
(3) logo slanted

enter choice: 3
                    +------+
                    |      |
            -------        ------
           /                     \
          /                       \
        --                         --
        |                           |
        |                           |
        --                         --
          |        F              |
          |            O          |
          |                O      |
          |                       |
          |                       |
```

4.11 (from [KR96]) The wind chill temperature is given according to a somewhat complex formula derived empirically. The formula converts a temperature (in degrees Fahrenheit) and a wind speed to an equivalent temperature (eqt) as follows:

$$\text{eqt} = \begin{cases} \text{temp} & \text{if wind} \leq 4 \\ a - (b + c \times \sqrt{\text{wind}} - d \times \text{wind}) \times (a - \text{temp})/e & \text{if temp} \leq 45 \\ 1.6 * \text{temp} - 55.0 & \text{otherwise} \end{cases} \quad (4.3)$$

where $a = 91.4, b = 10.45, c = 6.69, d = 0.447, e = 22.0$. Write a program that prompts for a wind speed and a temperature and prints the corresponding wind chill temperature. Use a function `WindChill` with the following prototype:

```
double WindChill(double temperature, double windSpeed)
// pre: temperature in degrees Fahrenheit
// post: returns wind-chill index/
//       comparable temperature
```

4.12 (also from [KR96]) The U.S. CDC (Centers for Disease Control—this time, not Control Data Corporation) determine obesity according to a "body mass index," computed by

$$\text{index} = \frac{\text{weight in kilograms}}{(\text{height in meters})^2} \quad (4.4)$$

An index of 27.8 or greater for men or 27.3 or greater for nonpregnant women is considered obese. Write a program that prompts for height, weight, and sex and that determines whether the user is obese. Write a function that returns the body mass index given the height and weight in inches and pounds, respectively. Note that one meter is 39.37 inches, one inch is 2.54 centimeters, one kilogram is 2.2 pounds, and one pound is 454 grams.

4.13 Write a program that converts a string to its Pig-Latin equivalent. To convert a string to Pig-Latin use the following algorithm:

1. If the string begins with a vowel, add `"way"` to the string. For example, Pig-Latin for "apple" is "appleway."

2. Otherwise, find the first occurrence of a vowel, move all the characters before the vowel to the end of the word, and add `"ay"`. For example, Pig-Latin for "strong" is "ongstray" since the characters "str" occur before the first vowel.

Assume that vowels are a, e, i, o, and u. You'll find it useful to write several functions to help in converting a string to its Pig-Latin equivalent. You'll need to use string member functions `substr`, `find`, and `length`. You'll also need to concatenate strings using +. Finally, to find the first vowel, you may find it useful to write a function that returns the minimum of two values. You'll need to be careful with the value `string::npos` returned by the string member function `find`. Sample output for the program follows.

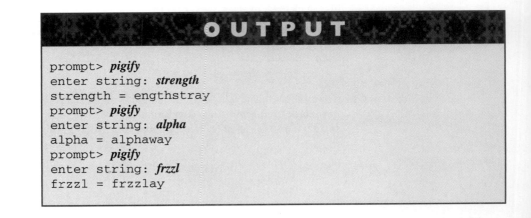

```
prompt> pigify
enter string: strength
strength = engthstray
prompt> pigify
enter string: alpha
alpha = alphaway
prompt> pigify
enter string: frzzl
frzzl = frzzlay
```

Iteration with Programs and Classes

5

> "What IS the use of repeating all that stuff,"
> the Mock Turtle interrupted, "if you don't explain it as you go on?
> It's by far the most confusing thing I ever heard!"
> LEWIS CARROLL
> *Alice's Adventures in Wonderland*

> I shall never believe that God plays dice with the world.
> ALBERT EINSTEIN
> *Einstein, His Life and Times,* by Philipp Frank

The if/else statement selects different code fragments depending on values calculated at run time by the program. In this chapter we will study control statements called **loops,** which are used to execute code segments repeatedly. Repetition significantly extends the kinds of programs we can write. We will also study several classes that extend the domain of problems we can solve by writing programs.

To extend the range of problems and programs, we will use some basic design guidelines that help in writing code, functions, and programs. As programs get larger and more complicated, these design guidelines will help in managing the complexity that comes with harder and larger problems.

In the first part of the chapter we'll introduce a basic loop statement. We'll use loops to study applications in different areas of computer science. We'll end the chapter with a study of two classes used in this book that extend the kind of programs you can write. Using loops and these classes will make it possible to write programs to print calendars for any year, to simulate gambling games, and to solve complex mathematical equations.

5.1 The while Loop

> **banana problem**: Not knowing where or when to bring a
> production to a close. "I know how to spell 'banana,'
> but I don't know when to stop."
> *The New Hacker's Dictionary*

In the last chapter Program 4.10, *numtoeng.cpp*, printed English text for integers in the range of 1–99. Converting this program to handle all C++ integer values would be difficult without using loops. Loops are used to execute a group of statements repeatedly. Repeated execution is often called **iteration**. The most basic statement in C++ for looping is the **while** statement. It is similar syntactically to the if statement, but very different semantically. Both statements have tests whose truth determines whether a block of

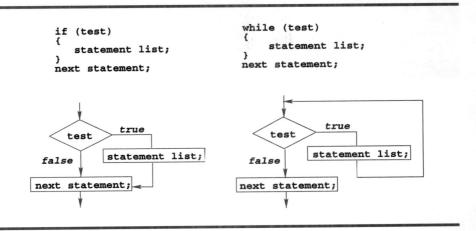

Figure 5.1   Flow control for `if` and `while` statements.

statements is executed. When the test of an `if` statement is true, the block of statements that the test controls is executed once. In contrast, the block of statements controlled by the test of a `while` loop is executed repeatedly, as long as the test is true.

The control flow for `if` statements and `while` statements is shown in Figure 5.1. In a `while` loop, after execution of the last statement in the **loop body** (the block of statements guarded by the test), the test expression is evaluated again. If it is true, the statements in the loop body are executed again, and the process is repeated until the test becomes false. The test of a loop must be false when the loop exits. The body of a

---

Syntax: while statement

```
while (test expression)
{
    statement list;
}
```

---

while loop is the group of statements in the curly braces guarded by the parenthesized test. The test is evaluated once before all the statements in the loop body are executed, *not* once after each statement. If the test is true, *all*

the statements in the body are executed. After the last statement in the body is executed, the test is evaluated again. If the test evaluates to true, the statements in the loop body are executed again, and this process of test/execute repeats until the test is false. (We will learn methods for "breaking" out of loops later that invalidate this rule, but it is a good rule to keep in mind when designing loops.)

When writing loops, remember that the loop test is *not* reevaluated after each statement in the loop body, only after the last statement. To ensure that loops do not execute forever, it's important that at least one statement in the loop changes the values that are part of the test expression. As a simple example, Program 5.1 prints a string backward.

Program 5.1 revstring.cpp

```cpp
#include <iostream>
#include <string>
using namespace std;

int main()
{
    int k;
    string s;
    cout << "enter string: ";
    cin >> s;
    cout << s << " reversed is ";

    k = s.length() - 1;    // index of last character in s
    while (k >= 0)
    {   cout << s.substr(k,1);
        k -= 1;
    }
    return 0;
}
```

revstring.cpp

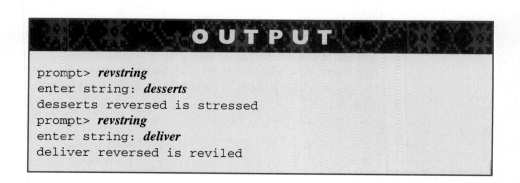

```
prompt> revstring
enter string: desserts
desserts reversed is stressed
prompt> revstring
enter string: deliver
deliver reversed is reviled
```

In Program 5.1 the value of the indexing variable k changes each time the loop executes. Since k is used in the loop guard, and k decreases each time the loop executes, you can reason informally that the loop will terminate: the loop executes exactly as many times as there are characters in the string s. Developing loop tests/guards can be difficult, and we'll study techniques that will help you develop loops that execute correctly. In general there are three conceptual parts in developing a loop test.

1. The **initialization** of variables/expressions that are part of the loop, in particular of the loop guard. In *revstring.cpp* the initialization is the following statement:

```
k = s.length() - 1;    // index of last character in s
```

2.   The loop guard or test, which is a Boolean expression whose truth determines if the loop body executes. This is k >= 0 in *revstring.cpp*.

3.   The **update** of variables/expressions. The update must have the potential to make the loop test false. Usually this means changing the value of a variable used in the test. In *revstring.cpp* the following statement is the update:

```
k -= 1;
```

For the string "flow", the initial value of k is 3. The loop body executes for k having the values 3, 2, 1, and 0. When k is zero, the letter 'f' is printed, and k is decremented to have the value −1. The loop guard is tested and is false, so the loop exits when k has the value −1.

5.1.1   Infinite Loops

You must be careful when writing loops because it is possible for a loop to execute forever—a so-called **infinite loop.** As a simple example, consider the loop

```
while (6 != 4)
{   cout << "this will be printed many times" << endl;
}
```

which will execute forever (or until the user stops the program) because 6 is not equal to 4, and the truth of the loop test is unchanged by any of the statements in the loop body. On many systems, typing Ctrl-C will stop an infinite loop.

Usually infinite loops aren't as easy to spot as the loop above. You may, for example, forget to update a variable and thus create an infinite loop. For example, leaving out the statement k -= 1 in *revstring.cpp*, Program 5.1, creates an infinite loop that prints the last character of the string "forever." The following loop is infinite for some values of num.

```
int num;
cin >> num;
int start = 0;
while (start != num)
{   start += 2;
}
```

The values for start are {0, 2, 4, . . .}. If num is an odd number, the loop is infinite. If the purpose of the loop is to increment start until it "passes" num, then it would be better to use the following loop test.

```
int num;
cin >> num;
int start = 0;
while (start <= num)
{   start += 2;
}
```

Pause to Reflect

5.1 Write a loop to print the numbers from 1 up to a value entered by the user, one number per line. Modify the loop to print the numbers from the user-entered value down to 1.

5.2 Complete the following loop so that it prints all powers of two less than 30,000, starting with 1 2 4 8 16. You can do this by adding a single *= statement to the loop.

```
num = 1;
while (num < 30000)
{   cout << num << endl;


}
```

5.3 How can you determine quickly that the following loop is an infinite loop (and will execute "forever") whenever num is less than 100?

```
cout << "enter number ";
cin >> num;
while (num < 100)
{   product = product * num;
    answer = answer + 1;
}
```

5.4 Write a loop that allows the user to enter a string and that prints the first vowel that occurs in the string. Assume a Boolean-valued function IsVowel exists that takes a string as a parameter and returns true if the string is a vowel; otherwise the function returns false.

5.5 Write the function with the following specification:

```
string revstring(string s)
// pre: returns reverse of s, that is, "stab" for "bats"
```

Assuming revstring works, write a Boolean-valued function IsPalindrome that returns true if a string is a **palindrome** (i.e , is the same forward as backward like "mom" and "racecar").

5.1.2 Loops and Mathematical Functions

The first computers were used almost exclusively as "number crunchers"—machines that solved numerical problems and equations. The very word "computer" formerly meant a person employed to perform such extensive calculations. For that reason, one of the first machines to do the job had the name ENIAC, for *E*lectronic *N*umerical *I*ntegrator *And* *C*omputer. This special-purpose computer eventually evolved into a more general machine called UNIVAC, for *Uni*versal *A*utomatic *C*omputer.

Today the machines we call "computers" are much more general-purpose, and many people find it difficult to imagine writing without using a word processor, movies without digital special effects, and banking without automatic tellers. All these applications require computers used in ways that at least on the surface don't involve numerical computations. Nevertheless, all information stored in today's computers is represented at some level by a number (even words are "converted" to 0's and 1's when stored in a computer's memory). **Numerical analysis** is a branch of computer science in which mathematical methods for solving many kinds of equations using computers are designed and developed. Although we won't delve deeply into this branch of computer science, we'll use some simple mathematical examples to study some broader concepts.

We'll investigate three mathematical functions: one to calculate the **factorial** of an integer, one to determine whether an integer is **prime,** and one to do **exponentiation** or raising a number to a power. These functions provide simple examples of loops and loop development, reinforce the concept of programmer-defined functions, and introduce functions to which we will return later.

5.1.3 Computing Factorials

The factorial function, usually denoted mathematically as $f(x) = x!$, is used in statistics, probability, and an area of computer science and mathematics called *combinatorics*. One definition of the function is

$$n! = 1 \times 2 \times \cdots \times (n - 1) \times n \tag{5.1}$$

so that $6! = 1 \times 2 \times 3 \times 4 \times 5 \times 6 = 720$. As a special case, by definition $0! = 1$. Program 5.2 implements and tests a function for computing factorials.

Program 5.2 fact.cpp

```cpp
#include <iostream>
#include "prompt.h"
using namespace std;

// illustrates loop and integer overflow

long Factorial(int num);

int main()
{
    int highValue = PromptRange("enter max value for factorial",1,30);
    int current = 0;   // compute factorial of this value

    while (current <= highValue)
    {   cout << current << "! = " << Factorial(current) << endl;
        current += 1;
    }
    return 0;
}
```

```
long Factorial(int num)
// precondition: num >= 0
// postcondition returns num!
{
    long product = 1;
    int count = 0;

    while (count < num)           // invariant: product == count!
    {   count += 1;
        product *= count;
    }
    return product;
}
```

fact.cpp

In the function Factorial the variable product accumulates the result with the statement product *= count; this result is returned when the loop finishes executing. The values of the variables product and count change each time that the loop test is evaluated in computing 6!, as shown in Figure 5.2.

OUTPUT

```
prompt> fact
enter max value for factorial between 1 and 30: 17
 0! = 1
 1! = 1
 2! = 2
 3! = 6
 4! = 24
 5! = 120
 6! = 720
 7! = 5040
 8! = 40320
 9! = 362880
10! = 3628800
11! = 39916800
12! = 479001600
13! = 1932053504
14! = 1278945280
15! = 2004310016
16! = 2004189184
17! = -288522240
```

Each time that the loop test is evaluated, the value of the variable product is always equal to (count)! (that's count factorial), as shown. Since 0! = 1 (by definition), this is true the first time the loop test is evaluated as well as after each iteration of the

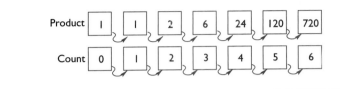

Figure 5.2 Relationship between variables `product` and `count` in *fact.cpp*.

loop body. A statement that is true each time a loop test is evaluated is called a **loop invariant**—the truth of the statement does not vary or change. Loop invariants can help us reason about the correctness of programs that use loops. Since `product == count!` is an invariant, and `product` is returned, we can reason that the `Factorial` function calculates the correct value if `count == num`. Since the loop test is false when the loop exits, and the logical negation of `count < num` is `count >= num`, we're almost there. Since `count` is incremented by one, it cannot go past `num` without being equal to `num` first. Thus the loop test's negation, in conjunction with the invariant, help us reason about the correctness of the loop.

Conceptually, the function `Factorial` in Program 5.2 will always return the correct value. However, in practice the correct value may not be returned, as is evident from the foregoing run of the program. Note that 16! < 15!; that 17! is a negative number; and that although 13! = 13 × 12!, the value for 13! ends in a four while 12! ends in a zero. None of these results represents mathematical truth. Because integers stored in a computer have a largest value, it is possible for seemingly bizarre results to occur when this largest value is exceeded. Keep in mind that the limitation on integer values is one of many ways that a computer program can function exactly as it should (although not, perhaps, as intended) but produce unanticipated and often inexplicable results. I used `long` as the return type of `Factorial` and as the type of `product` to ensure that the function returns "correct" results through 12 factorial even on 16-bit machines.

Using the class `BigInt` instead of `int` or `long` allows calculations with arbitrarily large integers.[1] Details of the class `BigInt` can be found in How to G; but you can program with them as though they were integers—that is, use arithmetic operators, print them, and read them. Program 5.3, *bigfact.cpp*, shows how simple it is to use `BigInt`. (You must use `#include "bigint.h"` when programming with `BigInt` values.)

Program 5.3   bigfact.cpp

```
#include <iostream>
#include "prompt.h"
#include "bigint.h"
using namespace std;
```

[1]The integers aren't really arbitrarily large; they're limited by the memory in the computer. In practice `BigInt` values are as big as you want; your programs will most likely run out of time in making calculations with them before running out of memory.

```cpp
// illustrates loop and integer overflow

BigInt Factorial(int num);

int main()
{
    int highValue = PromptRange("enter max value for factorial",1,50);
    int current = 0;   // compute factorial of this value

    while (current <= highValue)
    {   cout << current << "! = " << Factorial(current) << endl;
        current += 1;
    }
    return 0;
}

BigInt Factorial(int num)
// precondition: num >= 0
// postcondition returns num!
{
    BigInt product = 1;
    int count = 0;

    while (count < num)             // invariant: product == count!
    {   count += 1;
        product *= count;
    }
    return product;
}
```

bigfact.cpp

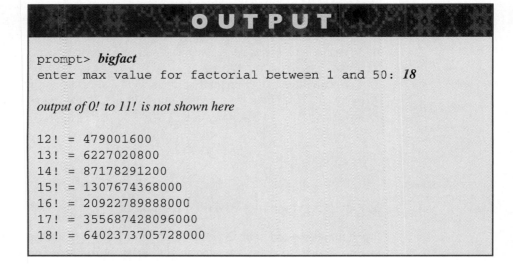

```
prompt> bigfact
enter max value for factorial between 1 and 50: 18

output of 0! to 11! is not shown here

12! = 479001600
13! = 6227020800
14! = 87178291200
15! = 1307674368000
16! = 20922789888000
17! = 355687428096000
18! = 6402373705728000
```

Unlike the results generated by Program 5.2, *fact.cpp*, the factorial calculations from *bigfact.cpp* are correct.

Cryptography and Computer Science

Before the 1970s, encryption techniques were largely based on sharing a private key that was used to encrypt messages. Both the sender and the receiver needed to have the private key. This was a potential security leak: how is the key transmitted from one person to another? In old movies couriers transported keys in briefcases strapped to their wrists. Apparently this method was used in real life as well.

In the mid-1970s several people developed **public-key** cryptography. The essence of these methods is that there are two keys: one private and one public. Everyone in the world has access to the public key and can use it to encrypt messages. Only the receiver of the message has the private key, and this key is required to decrypt the message. The keys are numbers and are calculated by choosing two large prime numbers, multiplying them together, and then doing a few other mathematical operations. The August 1977 "Mathematical Games" section of the magazine *Scientific American* explained this method of cryptography and had a challenge from the inventors of the method: Decrypt a message based on factoring the number called RSA-129 (it has 129 digits and is named for the inventors of the encryption method: Rivest, Shamir, and Adleman):

```
114,381,625,757,888,867,669,235,779,976,146,
612,010,218,296,721,242,352,562,561,842,935,
706,935,245,733,897,830,597,123,563,958,705,
058,989,075,147,599,290,026,879,543,541
```

The column claimed that it would take 40 quadrillion years to decrypt the message and offered $100.00 to the first person to do it. In 1994, more than 1600 computers around the world were put to work for eight months using new factoring methods to factor RSA-129. Coordinated by Arjen Lenstra, the computers used "wasted cycles"—time that the computers would have been otherwise idle—to factor RSA-129. The number was successfully factored, and the message from the *Scientific American* article was decrypted. The message was THE MAGIC WORDS ARE SQUEAMISH OSSIFRAGE.

For an illuminating account of the method and history of public-key cryptography, and of a public-domain program called PGP that can be used for encrypting/decrypting, see [Gar95].

5.1.4 Computing Prime Numbers

Prime numbers used to be the domain of pure mathematicians specializing in number theory. Today they play an increasingly important role in computer science applications. Current **encryption** techniques, used to encode data so that information cannot be read (electronically or visually), are largely based on efficient methods for determining whether a number is prime. Data encryption is a big business with many ethical and privacy considerations. In addition, writing programs to determine whether numbers are prime is part of the rites of passage one traditionally undergoes in studying programming.

By definition, a number is prime if its only divisors are 1 and the number itself. For example, 5, 7, 53, and 97 are prime, but 91 is not prime because it is divisible by 7 (and 13). The only even prime number is 2. By convention, 1 is not considered prime.

It seems that we'll need to check divisors of a number N to see whether the number is prime. We could naïvely check all numbers from 1 to N as potential divisors, checking the remainder each time. This method can be improved by checking only potential divisors less than the square root of a number. For example, to determine whether 119 is prime, we check divisors up to 11 (because $11^2 = 121 > 119$). Any number greater than 11 that divides 119 must have a corresponding factor less than 11 because factors come in pairs. Thus 7 and 17 are both factors of 119, but only one factor is needed to show that 119 is not prime (and the second factor is easily obtained by dividing by the first).

We need to be careful. We don't want to check that 1 is a divisor because it divides every number evenly. We can also avoid testing even numbers as potential divisors because 2 is the only even number that's prime. The approach used in the Boolean-valued function `IsPrime` shown in Program 5.4 tests numbers less than or equal to 2 explicitly, avoids testing even numbers other than 2, then uses a loop to check all potential divisors less than the square root of n, the parameter of `IsPrime`.

Program 5.4 primes.cpp

```cpp
#include <iostream>
#include <cmath>              // for sqrt
using namespace std;

// program to check for primeness
// Owen Astrachan, 4/1/99

bool IsPrime(int n);         // determines if n is prime

int main()
{
    int k,low,high;
    int numPrimes = 0;
    cout << "low number> ";
    cin >> low;

    cout << "high number> ";
    cin >> high;

    cout << "primes between " << low << " and " << high <<  endl;
    cout << "----------------------------------" << endl;

    k = low;
    while (k <= high)
    {   if (IsPrime(k))
        {   cout << k << endl;
            numPrimes += 1;
```

```cpp
        }
        k += 1;
    }
    cout << "-----------------" << endl;
    cout << numPrimes << " primes found between " << low
        << " and " << high << endl;

    return 0;
}


bool IsPrime(int n)
// precondition: n >= 0
// postcondition: returns true if n is prime, else returns false
//                returns false if precondition is violated
{
    if (n < 2)                          // 1 and 0 aren't prime
    {   return false;                   // treat negative #'s as not prime
    }
    else if (2 == n)                    // 2 is only even prime number
    {   return true;
    }
    else if (n % 2 == 0)                // even, can't be prime
    {   return false;
    }
    else                                // number is odd
    {   int limit = int(sqrt(n) + 1);   // largest divisor to check
        int divisor = 3;                // initialize to smallest divisor

        // invariant: n has no divisors in range [2..divisor)

        while (divisor <= limit)
        {   if (n % divisor == 0)       // n is divisible, not prime
            {   return false;
            }
            divisor += 2;               // check next odd number
        }
        return true;                    // number must be prime
    }
}
```

primes.cpp

Each `return` statement in `IsPrime` exits the function. Flow of control continues with the statement that follows the call of `IsPrime`. In particular, the `return` statement in the `while` loop permits a kind of premature loop exit. As soon as a divisor is found, the function exits and returns `false`. If control reaches the `return` statement after the `while` loop, the loop test must be false; that is, `divisor > limit`. In this case n is prime.

OUTPUT

```
prompt> primes
low number> 100000
high number> 100100
primes between 100000 and 100100
----------------------------------
100003
100019
100043
100049
100057
100069
------------------
6 primes found between 100000 and 100100
```

Program Tip 5.1: When a `return` statement is executed, flow of control immediately leaves the function in which the `return` is located and continues with the statement that follows the function call. No other statements within the function are executed. One school of thought says that each function should have exactly one `return` statement. This is always possible, but it often requires the introduction of extra variables or more complicated code. You will find that judicious use of multiple `return`s within one function can make the function simpler to write and easier to reason about.

On some computers the assignment `int limit = sqrt(n) + 1` may cause a warning:

```
primes.cpp: In function 'bool IsPrime(int)':
primes.cpp:53: warning: initialization to 'int' from 'double'
```

The value returned by `sqrt` is a `double`. Assigning a `double` to an `int` is not always possible because the largest `double` value may be greater than the largest `int` value. Even though a program compiles, compiler warnings should not be ignored; they are often an indication that you have misused the language. In this case, you can avert the warning by explicitly converting the `double` value to an `int`. This is shown in *primes.cpp* in the statement assigning a value to `limit`:

```
int limit = int(sqrt(n) + 1);     // largest divisor to check
```

Using the type `int` like a function call explicitly converts the value `sqrt(n) + 1` into an integer. This is called a **type cast.** The cast prevents the warning because you, the programmer, explicitly converted one type to another. We'll study casts in more detail in Section 6.3.6.[2]

The value sqrt(n) + 1 is used instead of sqrt(n) because of the limited precision of floating-point numbers. For example, the square root of 49 might be calculated as 6.9999 rather than 7.0. In this case, the assignment int limit = sqrt(49) stores the value 6 in limit because the double is truncated when it's assigned to an int. Adding 1 avoids this kind of problem.

5.1.5 Kinds of Loops

The loop in main of *primes.cpp* iterates exactly high-low+1 times, so if low is 10 and high is 20, the loop executes 11 times for k having values 10, 11, ..., 19, 20. When the value of a simple arithmetic expression like high-low+1 gives the number of loop iterations (and the value can be calculated before the loop executes the first time), the loop is called a **definite loop**. When the update of the expression used in the loop test is an increment by one, such as k += 1, or a decrement by one, such as k -= 1 in Program 5.1, *revstring.cpp*, the definite loop is often called a **counting loop**.

In contrast, the loop in the function IsPrime of *primes.cpp* is not a definite loop. Although the maximum number of iterations can be calculated in advance,[3] the loop exits as soon as a divisor is found. The early exit means that no simple expression determines the number of loop iterations. However, in some sense the loop is a kind of counting loop because the value of divisor is incremented by two for each iteration.

5.1.6 Efficiency Considerations

How important is it to check divisors up to $\sqrt{n}$ rather than n in determining whether a number is prime? People often suggest using $n/2$ rather than n. Is this better than $\sqrt{n}$? These questions are important in determining the efficiency or **complexity** of the algorithm used in IsPrime, but they don't affect the correctness of the algorithm. Consider that $\sqrt{50,000} = 223.6$ but that $50,000/2 = 25,000$. This difference means that using $n/2$ as the limit in IsPrime could result in approximately 12,388 more numbers being checked as potential divisors in determining that 49,999 is prime (it is). The extra number of divisors is 12,388 rather than 24,776 because only odd numbers are checked as potential divisors in the loop. I timed two versions of Program 5.4: one that used limit = sqrt(n) + 1 and one that used limit = n/2 + 1. It took 1.44 seconds to determine that there are 5,133 primes between 1 and 50,000 when the square root limit was used, but 45.78 seconds when the limit based on half of n was used. Interestingly, even checking only divisors less than the square root of a number is much too slow for the encryption algorithms that are based on using large prime numbers. These encryption algorithms use pairs of large prime numbers, so they need to determine whether 200-digit numbers are prime. The square root of such a number has 100 digits. Testing 10^{100} numbers as potential divisors would require more time

---

[2]As we'll see in Section 6.3.6, the latest C++ standard has a casting operator static_cast, whose use is preferred to the style of cast we've shown here. Not all compilers support static_cast.

[3]The maximum number of iterations is roughly $\sqrt{n}/2$.

than the universe has been in existence. What makes the encryption algorithms feasible? Computer scientists and mathematicians developed efficient methods for determining whether a number is prime. These methods don't actually factor a number; they just yield a yes or no answer to the question "Is this number prime?" However, no one has developed an efficient algorithm for factoring numbers. The keys to the encryption methods used are (1) efficiently determining that a number is prime and (2) difficulty in factoring the product of the two primes.

5.1.7 Exponentiation: A Case Study in Loop Development

We'll use the mathematical operation of raising a number to a power, called **exponentiation**, as an illustration of algorithm efficiency and of using invariants to develop a loop.

Today's businesses and governments rely increasingly on electronic messages and transactions. With powerful computers to assist in electronic spying, many worry that no message is safe from being stolen and deciphered. However, computer scientists have developed methods of data encryption that result in messages that are provably difficult to decrypt or decode.

These techniques of data encryption require that large prime numbers (approximately 150 digits) be manipulated by raising these numbers to large powers.[4] Data encryption is used to prevent people from "spying" on electronic information. For example, someone sending an electronic message from an office in Europe to an office in Canada might be worried that the message will be intercepted by electronic eavesdroppers. Instead of being sent as **plain text** (i.e., understandable by anyone), the message might be **encrypted** so that it cannot be intercepted and understood.

Efficient methods for computing x^n, the operation of exponentiation, are essential when both x and n are large. In C++, the exponentiation operation is not a built-in operator, as addition, subtraction, multiplication, division, and some others are (e.g., the % operator for remainder). The library of routines specified in the header file <cmath> does include an exponentiation routine called pow (see Table F.1), but it is useful for us to examine ways of implementing a function to perform exponentiation. Not only will doing so illuminate concepts of programming and C++; it is sometimes necessary to implement such a function when the one provided in the math library won't work, such as in raising a BigInt value to a power.

Exponentiation can be defined in at least three ways. The first method is the one you may be accustomed to:

$$a^n = \underbrace{a \times a \times \cdots \times a}_{n \text{ times}} \tag{5.2}$$

An equivalent **inductive** or **recursive** definition follows:

$$a^n = \begin{cases} 1 & \text{if } n = 0 \\ a \times a^{(n-1)} & \text{otherwise} \end{cases} \tag{5.3}$$

---

[4]This is part of how *RSA* encryption works; the powers are computed modulo another number m so that the result is constrained to be between 0 and $m - 1$.

Table 5.1   Calculating 3^{16} efficiently. The **Answer** column cannot be filled in until the **Depends on** column is filled in from the bottom to the top. x_i indicates a value to fill in.

Power	Depends on	Answer
$3^{16} = (3^8)^2$	$(x_4)^2$	43,046,721
$x_4 = 3^8 = (3^4)^2$	$(x_3)^2$	6,561
$x_3 = 3^4 = (3^2)^2$	$(x_2)^2$	81
$x_2 = 3^2 = (3^1)^2$	$(x_1)^2$	9
$x_1 = 3^1$	none	3

Finally, it's possible to take advantage of properties of exponents such as $3^8 = 3^4 \times 3^4$ to define exponentiation:

$$a^n = \begin{cases} 1 & \text{if } n = 0 \\ a^{n/2} \times a^{n/2} & \text{if } n \text{ is even} \\ a \times a^{n/2} \times a^{n/2} & \text{if } n \text{ is odd (note that } n/2 \text{ truncates to an integer)} \end{cases} \tag{5.4}$$

This last definition has the advantage that it may lead to fewer multiplications than the first two definitions when we develop a program to translate the definitions into code. For example, given the task of computing 3^{16}, you might break the problem down as shown in Table 5.1, where 3^{16} is calculated by computing 3^8 and squaring the result. In turn, 3^8 is calculated by computing 3^4 and squaring it. This process of breaking down a number continues until the simple case of $3^1 = 3$ is reached. Note that only four multiplications are required—one for squaring each of the numbers $3, 9, 81, 6,561$. This is many fewer multiplications than the 16 required by the naïve method used in the first definition of exponentiation above.

Definition 5.2 leads to the following relatively simple counting loop in the function Power for raising a number to an integer power:

```
double Power(double base,int expo)
// precondition:  expo >= 0
// postcondition: returns base^expo (base to the power expo)
{
    double result = 1.0;
    while (expo > 0)
    {   result *= base;
        expo -= 1;
    }
    return result;
}
```

The loop iterates exactly expo times so that calculating x^n requires n multiplications and n subtractions. We want to develop a similar function, one that is black-box equivalent to Power but that uses fewer multiplications as with definition 5.4. We'll use a loop guard similar to the one above, but we'll use a loop invariant to help explain the loop and reason about its correctness. The invariant will also help you remember how to develop the code on your own. We'll start with the following code that accumulates the final answer in the variable result:

```
double Power(double base, int expc)
// precondition: expc >= 0
// postcondition: returns base^expo (base to the power expo)
{
    double result = 1.0;
    // invariant:  result * (base^expo) == answer
    while (expo > 0)
    {
    }
    return result;
}
```

Recall that a loop invariant is true each time the loop test is evaluated. In particular, it is true the first time the test is evaluated. The invariant is expressed as a comment:

$$\text{result} \times \text{base}^{\text{expo}} = \text{answer} \tag{5.5}$$

Since the initial value of result is 1.0, the invariant is true the first time the loop test is evaluated. Since expo is used in the loop test, the value of expo must change as the loop iterates. For the invariant to remain true, the value of either result or base must change as well. When the loop terminates, we'll want the value of expo to be zero. Since the invariant is true, this will guarantee that the correct answer is returned since $x^0 = 1$ for all x.

When the exponent is even, definition 5.4 dictates dividing the exponent by 2, that is, taking advantage of the property that $3^{20} = 3^{10} \times 3^{10}$. If the exponent is divided in half then either result or base (or both) must change to establish the truth of the invariant. We'll use the following properties of even exponents:

$$a^b = a^{b/2} \times a^{b/2} = (a \times a)^{b/2} \tag{5.6}$$

Using this property, when we divide expo by 2 we'll square base so that the value of the expression in the invariant shown in Equation 5.5 remains the same.

$$\text{result} \times \text{base}^{\text{expo}} = \text{result} \times (\text{base} \times \text{base})^{\text{expo}/2} \tag{5.7}$$

This relationship leads to the following loop (the function header isn't duplicated):

```
double result = 1.0;
// invariant:  result * (base^expo) == answer
while (expo > 0)
{   if (expo % 2 == 0)              // exponent is even
    {   expo /= 2;
        base *= base;              // (a*a)^(b/2) == a^b
    }
    else  // must handle this case
}
return result;
```

The loop is almost done, but we must still deal with odd exponents. Definition 5.4 for odd exponents is similar to the case for even exponents, but an additional factor of base is involved:

$$\text{result} \times \text{base}^{\text{expo}} = (\text{result} \times \text{base}) \times \text{base}^{\text{expo}/2} \times \text{base}^{\text{expo}/2} \qquad (5.8)$$

The part of this expression involving expo/2 is identical to the expression used for even exponents. To incorporate the additional factor of base we'll multiply result by base. This reestablishes the invariant.

```
double result = 1.0;
// invariant:  result * (base^expo) == answer
while (expo > 0)
{   if (expo % 2 == 0)              // exponent is even
    {   expo /= 2;
        base *= base;              // (a*a)^(b/2) == a^b
    }
    else
    {   expo /= 2;
        result *= base;
        base *= base;
    }
}
return result;
```

Before we look at the code one final time, we'll review how the invariant helps reason about the correctness of the program.

1. The invariant is true each time the loop test is evaluated. In particular, it must be true the first and last times the test is evaluated.

2. When the loop finishes, the loop test must be false. We can use this, in conjunction with the truth of the invariant, to reason about a loop's correctness.

In the loop from Power, the value of expo will be zero when the loop exits. We can infer this because the loop test is false, so we know that expo <= 0. But expo can never be negative since it is only changed when it is divided by two. Since the invariant is true, and the value of expo is zero, we have the following:

$$\text{result} \times \text{base}^{\text{expo}} = \text{result} \times \text{base}^{0} = \text{result} = \text{final answer} \qquad (5.9)$$

Since result is returned, we have "proved" that the function correctly satisfies its postcondition. Of course this is an informal proof, but I hope it is effective in convincing you about the loop and the function.

Before you decide you're "done" in writing a function, class, or program, you should review the code. In the function Power the same statements appear in both the if and the else block. You should always **factor out** duplicated code by moving it before or after the if/else statement as appropriate. Here we can factor out two statements and leave an if without an else. To do this, we negated the original test used in the if so that now the code tests for odd exponents.

```
double Power(double base, int expc)
// precondition: expo >= 0
// postcondition: returns base^expo (base to the power expo)
{
    double result = 1.0;
    // invariant:  result * (base^expo) = answer
    while (expo > 0)
    {   if (expo % 2 != 0)        // exponent is odd
        {   result *= base;
        }
        expo /= 2;               // 4/2 == 2, 5/2 == 2
        base *= base;            // (a*a)^(b/2) == a^b
    }
    return result;
}
```

Program Tip 5.2: Invariants are useful in developing and documenting loops. You should try to include an invariant in every loop you write. At first this will seem difficult or useless. But what's obvious to you today won't be obvious to someone else, or to you, tomorrow, so document your code.

Program Tip 5.3: Factor out common code. Don't be satisfied when your function or program works. Be sure that your code is easy to understand and is not uselessly redundant, and that code duplication is minimized.

Pause to Reflect

5.6 Assume that the factorial of a negative number is defined to be the factorial of the corresponding absolute value so that, for example, $(-5)! = 5! = 120$. Modify the function Factorial in Program 5.2 so that the correct value is returned for any value of num. Be sure to change the comments.

5.7 What value is returned by the call Factorial(-7) in the program *fact.cpp*, Program 5.2?

5.8 Write a function to calculate $x!!$ where $x!! = (x!)!$. For example, $3!! = 6! = 720$.

5.9 Generalizing the previous exercise, write a function with two parameters to calculate $x(!)^n$, where $x(!)^n = x \underbrace{!!...!}_{n \text{ times}}$. Use BigInts for the calculations.

5.10 Here is another version of `Factorial`; this version is changed only slightly from that given in Program 5.2. Does this version pass a black-box test comparing it with the original? What is a good invariant for the loop?

```
int Factorial(int num)
{
    int product = 1;
    int count = 1;

    while (count <= num)
    {   product *= count;
        count += 1;
    }
    return product;
}
```

5.11 If the statement `divisor += 2` is changed to `divisor += 1`, does the function `IsPrime` still work as intended?

5.12 What value is returned by the call `IsPrime(1)`? Is this what should be returned?

5.13 It is possible to write a loop without a return from the middle of the loop in the function `IsPrime`. The `while` loop can be replaced by the following:

```
while (divisor <= limit && n % divisor != 0)
{   divisor += 2;
}
```

What statement is needed after the loop to ensure that the correct value is returned?

5.14 What values does `expo` have each time the loop test is evaluated in the final version of the function `Power` if the original value is 1,024? If the original value is 1,000? (The last value is 0 in all cases.)

5.15 Why is the invariant for the loop of `IsPrime` in *primes.cpp*, Program 5.4, true the first time the loop test is evaluated? Write an informal argument about the correctness of `IsPrime` using the invariant and the loop test together.

5.16 Before common code was factored out in the loop for calculating powers, the two statements below were part of the `else` clause.

```
result *= base;
base *= base;
```

Can the order of these statements be changed? Why?

5.17 Modify the function `Power` to work with negative exponents, where $a^{-n} = 1/a^n$.

5.1.8   **Numbers Written in English**

As another example of a loop we'll use DigitToString from *numtoeng.cpp*, Program 4.10, to convert a number to an English equivalent string formed from the digits. For example, 123 is represented by "one two three", and 4017 is represented by "four zero one seven".

We'll need a loop to do two things:

- Extract one digit at a time from the number.
- Build up the string one word at a time.

The modulus operator % makes it easy to determine the rightmost digit of any number. It's difficult to get the leftmost digit because we don't know how many digits are in the number. To build the English equivalent, we'll have to build a string by concatenating each digit-string in the proper order. Each time a digit is peeled off the number, its corresponding string is concatenated to the front of the string being built.

Program 5.5   digits.cpp
_____

```
#include <iostream>
#include <string>
using namespace std;

// illustrates loops, convert a number to a string of English digits
// i.e., 1346 -> one three four six
// Owen Astrachan, 6/8/95

string DigitToString(int num);
string StringOut(long int number);

int main()
{
    long number;

    cout << "enter an integer: ";
    cin >> number;
    cout << StringOut(number) << endl;

    return 0;
}

string DigitToString(int num)
// precondition: 0 <= num < 10
// postcondition: returns English equivalent, e.g., 1->one,...9->nine
{
    if (0 == num)       return "zero";
    else if (1 == num)  return "one";
    else if (2 == num)  return "two";
    else if (3 == num)  return "three";
    else if (4 == num)  return "four";
    else if (5 == num)  return "five";
```

```
        else if (6 == num)   return "six";
        else if (7 == num)   return "seven";
        else if (8 == num)   return "eight";
        else if (9 == num)   return "nine";
        else return "?";
}


string StringOut(long number)
// precondition: 0 < number
// postcondition: returns string formed from digits written in English
//                e.g., 123 -> "one two three"
{
    string s = "";
    int digit;
    while (number != 0)
    {   digit = number % 10;
        s = DigitToString(digit) + " " + s;
        number /= 10;
    }
    return s;
}
```

digits.cpp

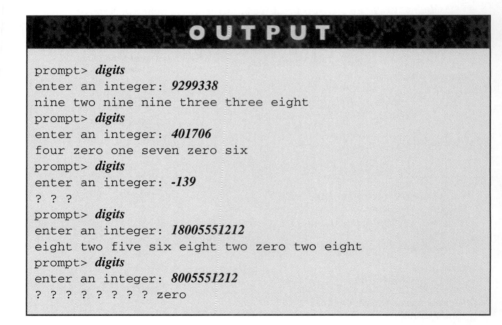

```
prompt> digits
enter an integer: 9299338
nine two nine nine three three eight
prompt> digits
enter an integer: 401706
four zero one seven zero six
prompt> digits
enter an integer: -139
? ? ?
prompt> digits
enter an integer: 18005551212
eight two five six eight two zero two eight
prompt> digits
enter an integer: 8005551212
? ? ? ? ? ? ? ? zero
```

The first time the loop test is evaluated, s represents the empty string " ": a string with no characters. The value of digit is undefined because no value has been assigned to digit. Since a space is always added after the digit string added to the front of string s, there is a space at the end of s. This space won't be "visible" if s is printed, unless another string is printed immediately after s. The space will be included in calculating the length of s, so StringOut(111).length() == 12 because the string is "one one one ".

5.1.9 Fence Post Problems

The extra space after the last English digit of the string made by StringOut in Program 5.5, *digits.cpp*, is undesirable. Spaces should occur between each two digits rather than after each digit. A similar problem occurs with the following loop, intended to print the numbers 1 through 10 separated by commas: 1,2,3,4,5,6,7,8,9,10. The loop doesn't work properly:

```
int num = 1;
while (num <= 10)
{    cout << num << ",";
     num += 1;
}
cout << endl;
```

The loop prints 1,2,3,4,5,6,7,8,9,10, instead (note the trailing comma). The problem here is that the number of numbers is one more than the number of commas, just as the number of digits is one more than the number of spaces in the function *StringOut*.

This kind of problem is often called a **fence post** problem because a fence (see picture below) has one more fence post than fence crosspieces. In our example, the numbers are the posts and the commas are the crosspieces.

The correct number of posts and crosspieces cannot be printed in a loop that outputs both fences and crosspieces because the loop generates the same number of each. There are three alternatives: print the first fence post (number) before the loop; print the last post (number) after the loop; or guard the printing of the crosspiece inside the loop. The three approaches are coded as follows:

Program 5.6 threeloops.cpp

```
int n = 1;                int n = 1;                  int n = 1;
cout << n;                while (n < 10)              while (n <= 10)
n += 1;                   {    cout << n << ",";       {    cout << n;
while (n <= 10)               n += 1;                      if (n < 10)
{    cout << "," << n;    }                                    ccut << ",";
     n += 1;              cout << n << endl;                n += 1;
}                                                      }
cout << endl;                                          cout << erdl;
```

threeloops.cpp

In the solution on the left, the comma is printed before each number is printed in the loop. This requires an increment before the loop or a different initialization of n.

Printing the comma after each number requires printing the final number after the loop. This is shown in the code in the middle, where the loop test is modified to use < instead of <=.

Both solutions share the problem of code duplication. In the code segment at the top left, n is incremented by one in two places. In the segment at the top right, there are two cout << n statements. Code duplication often causes maintenance problems because changes must be made identically in more than one place. The solution on the right avoids the code duplication but mimics the loop test inside the loop, which is a slightly different kind of code duplication. Each of these solutions is an acceptable way to solve fence post problems.

Pause to Reflect

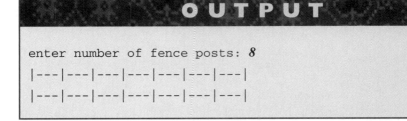

5.18 Write code that permits the user to enter the number of fence posts in a fence and then "draws" a fence as shown in the following sample output:

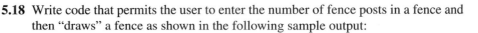

```
enter number of fence posts: 8
|---|---|---|---|---|---|---|
|---|---|---|---|---|---|---|
```

5.19 Alter the code in the function *StringOut* in Program 5.5, *digits.cpp,* so that spaces occur between each digit as opposed to after each digit.

5.20 Modify *StringOut* to generate a string that's backward—for example, "three two one" for the number 123.

5.21 Write a function that returns the number of characters in an int, accounting for a minus sign for negative numbers. For example, NumDigits(1234) returns 4, and NumDigits(-1234) returns 5.

5.22 Write a loop that prints the numbers 1 through 100 with each group of 10 numbers starting on a new line. There should be a space between each of the numbers on a line:

```
1 2 3 4 5 6 7 8 9 10
11 12 13 14 15 16 17 18 19 20
. . .
91 92 93 94 95 96 97 98 99 100
```

You may find it useful to use the statement

```
if (num % 10 == 0)
{    cout << endl;
}
```

in the loop body.

5.23 Write a loop using the operator `/=` that calculates how many times a number can be divided in half before 0 is reached. For example, 2 can be divided twice (attaining 1 then 0), 3 can be divided twice, 511 can be divided 9 times, and 512 can be divided 10 times. Use this loop to write a function `IntegerLog` that has two parameters, `number` and `n`, and returns how many times `number` can be divided by `n`.

5.2 Alternative Looping Statements

Writing loops can be difficult. It's not always easy to determine what the loop test should be, what statements belong in the loop body, and how variables should be initialized and updated before, in, and after a loop. Loops tend to have four sections:

- **Initialization:** This step occurs prior to the loop. Variables that need to be initialized are given values prior to the first time the loop test is evaluated.
- **Loop test:** The test determines whether the loop body will be executed. When the loop test is false, the loop body is not executed. If the loop test is always true, an infinite loop results, unless the loop is exited with a `return` statement, as used in `IsPrime` in *primes.cpp*, Program 5.4.
- **Loop body:** The statements that are executed each time the loop test evaluates to true.
- **Update:** The statements that affect values in the loop test. These statements ensure that the loop will eventually terminate. Values of variables in the loop test will be changed by the update statements.

These sections are diagrammed in Figure 5.3 for the two loops in *primes.cpp*, Program 5.4.

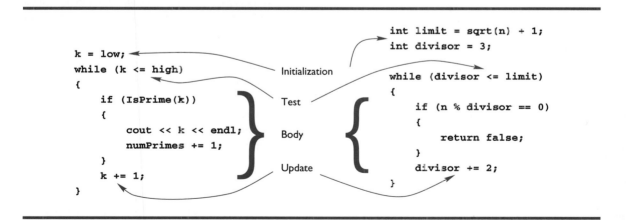

Figure 5.3 The four sections of a loop.

5.2.1 The `for` Loop

These loops are often written using an alternative looping construct to the `while` loop. The **for loop** is just a kind of shorthand, or **syntactic sugar,**[5] that can be used instead of a `while` loop. Anything written with one loop can be written with the other and vice versa.

The `for` loop offers some economy in terms of lines of code when compared with its `while` loop equivalent. The **initialization** statement is executed only once, before the evaluation of the test for the first time. The **test expression** is evaluated; if it is true, the loop body executes. After the last statement in the loop body is executed, the **update** statement executes. The test is then evaluated again, and the process continues (without initialization) until the test is false. Since all the information in a `for` loop appears at the beginning of the loop, it is often easier to understand than the corresponding `while` loop. The update statement should change values used in the test expression so that the loop makes progress toward termination.

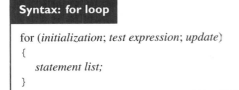

Syntax: for loop

```
for (initialization; test expression; update)
{
    statement list;
}
```

Here is the `while` loop from `main` in *primes.cpp*, Program 5.4, with the corresponding `for` loop:

```
k = low;                          for(k=low; k <= high; k += 1)
while (k <= high)                 {   if (IsPrime(k))
{   if (IsPrime(k))                   {   cout << k << endl;
    {   cout << k << endl;                numPrimes += 1;
        numPrimes += 1;               }
    }                             }
    k += 1;
}
```

The parentheses following the `for` loop enclose three separate parts of a loop: initialization, test, and update. These parts are separated by semicolons as shown. Block statement delimiters enclose the body of the `for` loop just as they enclose the body of the `while` loop.

I adhere to a style of programming in which `for` loops are used only when a bound on the number of iterations can be simply calculated. Such loops are sometimes called **definite** loops. Typically, these loops are counting loops—loops that execute a sequence of statements a fixed number of times, as shown in the example above from *primes.cpp*. Many C++ programmers use `for` loops exclusively; the economy of code makes programs *appear* shorter. Choosing the style of loop to use should not be a major decision point in developing a program. Sticking with the style adopted in this book is one way of ensuring that little time is spent on deciding what kind of loop to use. As an example of when I choose *not* to use a `for` loop, a `while` loop from *digits.cpp*, Program 5.5, is shown in Program 5.7 on the left with the corresponding `for` loop on the right:

---

[5] The term **syntactic sugar** is used for constructs that don't have a new meaning but are more aesthetically pleasing in some way. Often this means "easier for a human reader to understand."

Program 5.7 digitloops.cpp

```
while (number != 0)                    for(; number != 0; number /= 10)
{   digit = number % 10;               {   s = DigitToString (digit) + " " + s;
    s = DigitToString(digit) + " " + s;    }
    number /= 10;
}
```

digitloops.cpp

This is *not* a counting loop. The number of times the loop body is executed depends on how many times number can be divided by 10.[6] This example shows that the initialization part of a for loop can be omitted. The other parts of a for loop can be omitted too, but omitting the test part results in an infinite loop.

5.2.2   The Operators ++ and −−

Counting loops often require statements such as k += 1. Because incrementing by one is such a common operation, C++ includes an operator that can be used to increment by one in place of += 1. The statement

```
k++;
```

can be used in place of k += 1. Similarly, the statement k-- can be used in place of k -= 1 to decrement a value by one. The operator ++ is the **postincrement** operator, and the operator -- is the **postdecrement** operator. In all the code in this book, the expression x++ is used only as shorthand for x += 1. Similarly, x-- is used only as shorthand for x -= 1. If you read other books on C++, you may find these operators used as parts of other expressions. For example, the statement x = z + y++ is legal in C++. This statement stores z + y in x, and then increments the value of y by one. Don't try to use the operator this way—it will invariably get you into trouble. Instead, use ++ and -- only as abbreviations as already described. When used in this way, the statements below on the left affect x the same way: its value is incremented by one Similarly, the statements on the right decrement x by one.

```
x += 1;            x -= 1;
x++;               x--;
++x;               --x;
```

I don't use the **preincrement operator** ++x or the **predecrement operator** --x in this book. When used in expressions like x = z + ++y, the value of y is incremented first, then the value of z + y is stored in x. Since I don't use ++ and -- except as abbreviations for += 1 and -= 1, I use only the postincrement and postdecrement operators.

An example of a counting for loop using the postincrement operator follows; this is the while loop from main of *primes.cpp,* Program 5.4:

---

[6]Although this number of iterations can be calculated using logarithms, this isn't done in this loop.

```
for(k = low;  k <= high;  k++)
{    if (IsPrime(k))
     {    cout << k << endl;
          numPrimes++;
     }
}
```

5.24 The function `Factorial` in *fact.cpp*, Program 5.2, uses a `while` loop to calculate the factorial of a number. Rewrite the function so that a `for` loop is used instead.

5.25 Write a `while` loop equivalent to the following `for` loop:

```
double total = 0.0;
double val;
for(val = 1.0; val < 10000; val *= 1.5)
{    total += val;
}
```

5.26 Write a `for` loop equivalent to the following `while` loop:

```
int k = 1;
int sum = 0;
while (k <= num)
{    sum += k;
     k += 2;
}
```

5.27 What is printed by the following `for` loop?

```
int k;
for(k=1024;  k >= 0  ;k/=2)
{    cout << k << endl;
}
```

5.2.3 The do-while Loop

Many programs prompt for an input value within a range. For example, Program 4.10, *numtoeng.cpp*, prompts for an `int` between 0 and 100. The `PromptRange` functions declared in `"prompt.h"` ensure that input is within a range specified by the programmer. Think for a moment about how to write a loop that continually reprompts if input is not within a specific range. Since you must enter a value before any test can determine whether the value is valid, using a `while` loop leads to a fence post problem. Instead, a **do-while** loop can be used. The `do-while` loop works similarly to a `while` loop, but the loop test occurs at the end of the loop rather than at the beginning. This means that the body of a `do-while` loop is executed at least once. In contrast, a `while` loop does not iterate at all if the loop test is false the first time it is evaluated. Here is the body of one of the `PromptRange` functions:

```
int PromptRange(string prompt, int low, int high)
// pre: low <= high
// post: returns a value between low and high (inclusive)
{
    int value;
    do
    {   cout << prompt << " between ";
        cout << low << " and " << high << ": ";
        cin >> value;
    } while (value < low || high < value);

    return value;
}
```

Note that the output statements for the prompt are executed prior to the input statement. If the value entered is not valid, the loop continues to execute until a valid value is entered.

5.2.4 Pseudo-Infinite Loops

Because of errors in design, loops sometimes execute forever. It's fairly common to forget to increment a counter when writing a while loop. This is a good reason to use a for loop—it's harder to forget the update statement in a for loop.

Sometimes, however, it's useful to write seemingly infinite loops with an exit condition from within the loop body. We'll use this style of loop with an exit only in situations that would cause code to be duplicated otherwise. Consider the following loop, which sums user-entered values until the user enters zero:

```
int sum = 0;
int number;
cin >> number;
while (number != 0)
{   sum += number;
    cin >> number;
}
cout << "total = " << sum << endl;
```

To evaluate the test while (number != 0), the variable number is given a value before the test is evaluated for the first time as well as each time the loop body is executed. Reading an initial value so that the loop test can be evaluated the first time is called **priming** the loop. A word is read again within the loop body before the next evaluation. Eric Roberts, author of *The Art and Science of C*, calls these "loop-and-a-half" loops [Rob95]. Studies show that loop-and-a-half[7] loops are easier for students to write as infinite loops with an exit.

---

[7]It would be nice to say that four out of five programmers surveyed prefer while (true) with break loops. Studies do indicate that students find it easier to write code using this kind of loop than using a primed while loop.

The following loop avoids duplicating the code that extracts a value for `number` from `cin`:

```
while (true)              // until break from within loop
{   cin >> number;
    if (number == 0)
    {   break;            // OUT OF LOOP
    }
    sum += number;
}
cout << "total = " << sum << endl;
```

Since the loop test is always true, the loop appears to be an infinite loop. There is no way for the test to become false. The **break** statement in the loop causes an abrupt change in the flow of control. When executed, a `break` causes execution to break out of the innermost loop in which the `break` occurs. In the example here, execution continues with the output statement `cout << "total = ..."` when the `break` is executed. As an alternative to `while(true)`, the loop test `for(;;)` is a special C++ idiom that also means "execute forever." I don't use this style of infinite loop since its purpose doesn't seem as clear as the `while(true)` loop.

It is easy to carry this style of writing loops to extremes and write only infinite loops with break statements. You should try to write loops with explicit loop tests and use `while(true)` loops only for loop-and-a-half problems.

> **Program Tip 5.4:** **The `break` statement causes termination of the innermost loop in which it occurs. Control passes to the next statement after the innermost loop. Use the `break` statement judiciously in situations where code would be duplicated otherwise.** As we'll see in later chapters, loop tests often provide meaningful clues when it becomes necessary to reason about how a loop works and whether or when the loop terminates. A test of `true` doesn't provide many clues. However, used properly, infinite loops avoid code duplication and thus lead to programs that are easier to maintain.

Some programmers find it easier to understand the logic of the following loop than that of the loop used in `PromptRange` shown previously:

```
while (true)
{   cout << prompt << " between ";
    cout << low << " and " << high << ": ";
    cin >> value;
    if (low <= value && value <= high) return value;
}
```

The `return` statement exits the function (and the loop) when the user-entered value is within the specified range. Sometimes it's easier to develop the logic for loop termination, as shown above, than for loop continuation, as shown in the function `PromptRange`. De Morgan's law from Section 4.7 can help in converting logical expressions for continuation into expressions for termination because one is typically the logical negation of the other.

5.2.5 Choosing a Looping Statement

The `while` loop is the kind of loop to use in most situations. For writing definite loops, a `for` loop may be appropriate. For writing loops that must iterate once, a do-while loop may be appropriate. Given that there are three different kinds of loops, it's natural to wonder whether there are rules that can make the "correct" choice of what kind of loop to apply easier to determine. Since any loop can be made to do the work of any other with appropriate statements, we won't worry too much about this kind of decision. In summary, however, the following guidelines may prove helpful:

- The `while` loop is a general-purpose loop. The test is evaluated before the loop body, so the loop body may never execute.
- The `for` loop is best for definite loops—loops in which the number of iterations is known before loop entry.
- The do-while loop is appropriate for loops that must execute at least once because the test is evaluated after the loop body.
- Infinite loops, with a `break` (or `return` from function) statement, are often useful alternatives, especially when loop priming is necessary or when it's difficult to develop the logic used in the loop test.

In all three types of loop the braces { } that surround the loop body are not required by the compiler if the loop body is a single statement. However, the style guidelines for code in this book require the bodies of loops and `if`/`else` statements to be enclosed in braces, even if they consist of single comments.

5.2.6 Nested Loops

When one loop occurs in the body of another loop, the loops together are called **nested loops**. In *primes.cpp*, Program 5.4, there is a "virtual nested loop" because the loop in the function `IsPrime` is executed repeatedly by the call from the loop in `main`.

An example adapted from [KR96] shows how nested loops can be used to print a table of wind chill values. The effective temperature is significantly decreased when the wind speed is high. For example, a 20-mile-per-hour wind on a 50-degree day reduces the temperature to an equivalent wind chill index of 32 degrees. The desired output is a table of wind speed and temperature, with the wind chill index temperature given as follows:

```
  O U T P U T

prompt> windchill
deg. F:    50   40   30   20   10    0  -10  -20  -30  -40

 0 mph:    50   40   30   20   10    0  -10  -20  -30  -40
 5 mph:    47   37   26   16    5   -4  -15  -25  -36  -47
10 mph:    40   28   15    3   -9  -21  -33  -46  -58  -70
15 mph:    35   22    8   -4  -18  -31  -45  -58  -72  -85
20 mph:    32   17    3  -10  -24  -39  -53  -67  -82  -96
25 mph:    29   14    0  -14  -29  -44  -59  -74  -89 -104
30 mph:    28   12   -2  -17  -33  -48  -63  -79  -94 -109
35 mph:    26   11   -4  -20  -35  -51  -67  -82  -98 -113
40 mph:    25    9   -5  -21  -37  -53  -69  -85 -101 -116
45 mph:    25    9   -6  -22  -38  -54  -70  -86 -102 -118
50 mph:    25    9   -7  -23  -39  -55  -71  -87 -103 -119
```

Because the table must be printed one row at a time, a first cut at the code is row-oriented, with one row for each wind speed between 0 and 50 miles per hour:

```
for(windspeed=0; windspeed <= 50; windspeed += 5)
    print a row of temperatures;
```

Printing a row also requires a loop, and this leads to the nested loops shown in *windchill.cpp*, Program 5.8. Each wind chill temperature is printed by the **inner loop,** in which temperature varies from 50 down to −40 degrees; the inner loop prints a complete row of the table. The inner loop executes completely before one iteration of the **outer loop** has finished.

Program 5.8   windchill.cpp

```cpp
#include <iostream>
#include <iomanip>        // for setw
#include <cmath>          // for sqrt
using namespace std;

// Owen Astrachan
// nested loops to print wind-chill chart
//
// idea: Programming with Class by Kamin and Reingold, McGraw-Hill
// formula for wind-chill from
// UMAP Module 658, COMAP, Inc., Lexington, MA 1984, Bosch and Cobb

double WindChill(double temperature, double windSpeed);

int main()
```

```
{
    const int WIDTH = 5;
    const int MIN_TEMP = -40;
    const int MAX_TEMP = 50;
    const string LABEL = "deg. F: ";
    int temp,wind;

    // print column headings

    cout << LABEL;
    for(temp = MAX_TEMP; temp >= MIN_TEMP; temp -=10)
    {   cout << setw(WIDTH) << temp;
    }
    cout << endl << endl;

    // print table of wind chill temperatures

    for(wind = 0; wind <= MAX_TEMP; wind += 5) // row heading
    {   cout   << wind << " mph:\t";

        for (temp = MAX_TEMP; temp >= MIN_TEMP; temp -= 10)  // print the row
        {   cout << setw(WIDTH) << int(WindChill(temp,wind));
        }
        cout << endl;
    }
    return 0;
}

double WindChill(double temperature, double windSpeed)
// precondition: temperature in degrees Fahrenheit
// postcondition: returns wind-chill index/comparable temperature
{
    if (windSpeed <= 4)             // low wind, temperature unaltered
    {   return temperature;
    }
    else if (windSpeed <= 45)    // high wind
    {   return
            91.4 - (10.45 + 6.69*sqrt(windSpeed) - 0.447 * windSpeed) *
            (91.4 - temperature)/22.0;
    }
    else
    {   return (1.6 * temperature - 55.0);
    }
}
```

windchill.cpp

Because the function WindChill returns a double value and there is no reason to print several numbers after a decimal point in the table, the value returned by the WindChill function is stored in an int variable. The value is converted to an int using the expression int(WindChill(temp,wind)) just as the value returned by the function sqrt was converted to an int in *primes.cpp*, Program 5.4. To make each column of the table line up properly, a stream manipulator setw for the input stream cout is used. The argument to setw specifies a **field width** used to print the next value. Printing a number like 27 in a field width of five requires three extra spaces in addition to the two characters of 27 to pad the output to five characters. If the output occupies three spaces (e.g., the number 123 or the string `"cat"`), then two literal blanks '   ' will pad the output to five spaces. If the value being printed requires more than five spaces (e.g., for the number 123456), the entire value is still printed. You don't need `setw`; it's possible to print the right number of spaces by testing the value being printed as follows and padding with spaces as shown below, but using `setw` is much simpler.

```
if (num < 10)
{    cout << "   ";     // twc spaces
}
else if (num < 100)
{    cout << " ";       // one space
}
cout << num;
```

Program output should be easy to read, but you should not concentrate on well-formatted output when first implementing a program. Information on `setw` and other functions that help in formatting output is in How to B.

Sometimes it is useful to use the value of the outer loop to control how many times the inner loop iterates. This is shown in *multiply.cpp*, Program 5.9, which prints the lower half of a multiplication table (the upper half is the same because multiplication is commutative: $2 \times 5 = 5 \times 2$). Both loops are counting loops. The outer loop, whose loop control variable is `j`, determines how many rows appear in the output. The statement `cout << endl` is executed once each time the body of the outer loop is executed. The number of iterations of the inner loop is determined by the value of `j`. As can be seen in the output, the number of entries in each row increases by 1 in each successive row. When `j` is one, there is one number, 1, in the first row. When `j` is three, there are three numbers, 3 6 9, in the third row. The `width` member function ensures that three-digit numbers and two-digit numbers line up properly in columns.

Program 5.9 multiply.cpp

```
#include <iostream>
#include <iomanip>    // for setw
#include "prompt.h"
using namespace std;

// simple illustration of nested loops

int main()
{
    int j,k;
    int limit = PromptRange("number for multiply table",2,15);

    for(j=1; j <= limit; j++)
    {   for(k=1; k <= j; k++)
        {   cout << setw(3) << k*j << " ";
        }
```

```
        cout << endl;
    }
    return 0;
}
```

```
O U T P U T

prompt> multiply
number for multiply table between 2 and 15: 5
   1
   2    4
   3    6    9
   4    8   12   16
   5   10   15   20   25

prompt> multiply
number for multiply table between 2 and 15: 10
   1
   2    4
   3    6    9
   4    8   12   16
   5   10   15   20   25
   6   12   18   24   30   36
   7   14   21   28   35   42   49
   8   16   24   32   40   48   56   64
   9   18   27   36   45   54   63   72   81
  10   20   30   40   50   60   70   80   90  100
```

If a break statement is inserted as the last statement of the inner loop, immediately
following cout << setw(3) << k*j << " ", the output changes:

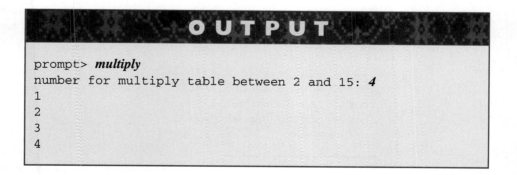

```
O U T P U T

prompt> multiply
number for multiply table between 2 and 15: 4
1
2
3
4
```

Note that the outer loop is *not* exited early. The `break` statement causes the inner loop (in which the loop control variable is k) to exit before the loop test k <= j becomes false. This means that the inner loop executes exactly once.

You should think very carefully when you decide that nested loops are necessary, especially if you're using `while` loops. Nested loops are often necessary when data are printed or processed in a tabular format; but it is often possible to use a single loop with an `if` statement in the loop body, and one loop is usually easier to code properly than two nested loops are.

> **Program Tip 5.5:   Coding is often easier if you move the inner loop of a nested loop into a separate function, and then call the function.** It's often easier to test a function than to test a loop, and keeping the inner loop in a separate function helps in developing correct programs.

5.2.7   Defining Constants

In *windchill.cpp*, Program 5.8, several **constant** identifiers are defined.

```
const int WIDTH = 5;
const int MIN_TEMP = -40;
const int MAX_TEMP = 50;
```

The type modifier **const** means that `MIN_TEMP` is a constant. Because it is constant, `MIN_TEMP` cannot be assigned a new value or changed in any way. For example, if the line

```
MIN_TEMP = -80;
```

is added immediately after the definition of `MIN_TEMP`, one compiler generates the error message below.[8]

```
Error : not an lvalue
windchill.cpp line 19    MIN_TEMP = -80;
```

In general, it is good programming practice to use constants to represent values that do not change during the execution of a program. Some examples of constant definitions are the following:

```
const double PI = 3.14159265;
const double INCHES_PER_CM = 0.39370;
const int January = 1;
const string cpp = "C++";
```

---

[8] An *lvalue* is an object to which a value can be assigned; the "l" is for left, since assignment changes the variable on the left.

Using named constants not only improves the readability of a program; it permits edit changes in a program to be localized in one place. For example, if you need a more precise value of π of 3.1415926535897, only one constant is changed (and the program recompiled). Mnemonic names, or names that indicate the purpose they serve, also pro-

Syntax: const value
const *type identifier = value*;

vide meaning and make it easier to read and understand code. Using the constant January instead of 1 in a calendar-making program can make the code much easier to follow. It is a common convention for constant identifiers to consist of all capital letters and to use underscores to separate different words.

Using constants also protects against inadvertent modification of a variable. The compiler can be an important tool in developing code if you use language features like const appropriately.

Pause to Reflect

5.28 Write a loop that accepts input from the user until the number zero is entered. The output should be the number of positive numbers entered and the number of negative numbers entered.

5.29 There is a fence post problem in *multiply.cpp*: a space is printed after every number rather than between numbers. Modify the loop so that no space is printed after the last number in a row. (*Hint:* It's possible to do this by modifying how setw is used.)

5.30 Write nested loops to print (a) the pattern of stars on the left and (b) the pattern of stars on the right. The number of rows should be entered by the user; there are k stars in row k.

5.31 Write appropriate constant definitions to represent the number of feet in a mile (5,280); the number of ounces in a pound (16); the mathematical constant e (2.71828); the number of grams in a pound (453.59); and the number foot-pounds in an erg (1.356 × 10^7).

5.3 Variable Scope

In Section 3.1.2 we discussed where variables are defined, and we showed that it is possible to define variables anywhere, not just immediately following a curly brace {. You need to be aware of how the location of a variable's definition affects the use of the variable. For example, the variable numPrimes, defined in main of *primes.cpp*, Program 5.4, is not accessible from the function IsPrime. A variable defined within a function is **local** to the function and cannot be accessed from another function. Parameters provide a mechanism for passing values from one function to another.

Similarly, a variable defined between two curly braces { } is accessible only within the curly braces. To be more precise, a variable name can be used only from the point at which it is defined to the first right curly brace }. For example, consider the following fragment from the function IsPrime. The variables limit and divisor are accessible only within the else block in which they are defined. The added comment after the else block indicates that these variables cannot be accessed at that point.

```
else                               // number is odd
{
    int limit = int(sqrt(n) + 1);
    int divisor = 3;   // smallest divisor

    while (divisor <= limit)
    {   if (n % divisor == 0)  // n is divisible, not prime
        {   return false;
        }
        divisor += 2;            // check next odd number
    }
    return true;                 // number must be prime
}

// comment added: limit and divisor NOT defined here
```

The following code fragment shows a variable count that can be accessed only in the bottom "half" of a loop:

```
while(total <= limit)
{   // count NOT accessible here

    int count = 0;

    // count IS accessible here
}
// count NOT accessible here
```

The variable count is accessible only from within the loop, and only from its definition to the bottom of the loop. The part of a program in which a variable name is accessible is called the variable name's **scope**.

You should be careful when defining variables in loop bodies (or if/else blocks) because these variables will not be accessible outside the loop body. In particular, be careful of for loops written as follows:

```
for(int k=0; k < 10; k++)
{   // loop body
}
```

The variable k is not, strictly speaking, defined within the curly braces that delimit the body of the loop. Nevertheless, the scope of k is local to the loop; k cannot be accessed after the loop. Not all compilers support this kind of scoping with for loops, but according to the C++ standard the scoping should be supported. It is common to need to access the value of a loop index variable (k in the example above) after the loop has finished. In such a case, the loop index cannot be local to the loop.

5.4 Using Classes

In addition to built-in C++ types like int and double, we've made extensive use of the class string in the programs we've studied so far. In Section 5.1.3 we showed how the BigInt class was useful for representing integers without the limits on values inherent in using the int type. In this section we extend our programming toolkit by looking briefly at two classes: the Date for representing calendar dates and the class Dice for simulating the kind of dice used in board games. We'll look at these classes as **client** programmers or users of the classes rather than implementers. In the next chapter we'll look more closely at how classes are implemented, but here we're more interested in extending the kinds of programs we can write by using classes, rather than studying the classes themselves.

5.4.1 The Date Class

In general, manipulating and understanding dates and calendars is an integral part of many software products. The so-called *year 2000 problem* has cost companies billions of dollars as they try to cope with software written when memory and disk space were expensive. Such software typically uses two digits to represent a year; that is, 99 represents 1999. The year 2000 causes problems with much of this software because, for example, a credit card issued in 1998 that expires in two years might be stored in software as expiring in the year 100 (two years after the year 98). Careless programming and design can lead to serious problems with such products. In [Neu95] several potential problems with software that manipulates dates and times are illustrated:

- With COBOL (COmmon Business-Oriented Language), a programming language used extensively in business and finance, most software allocates only two digits for the year part of a date. This causes problems in switching from December 31, 1999, to January 1, 2000.
- Early releases of the spreadsheet program Lotus 1-2-3 treated 2000 as a nonleap year and 1900 as a leap year when, in fact, the opposite is the case. Later versions of the software corrected the problem for the year 2000, but not for 1900, which remains a leap year according to the software.
- A Washington, D.C., hospital computer crashed on September 19, 1989, precisely 32,768 days after January 1, 1900. Note that 32,767 is the largest integer representable by an int on typical microcomputers.

We'll examine a class that represents calendar dates for any month in any year after October 1752.[9] Some of the tools for implementing a calendar date class have been developed already in previous programs: determining the number of days in a month and determining when a year is a leap year.

Rather than use these tools to develop code that calculates the day of the week, we'll use a class `Date`, accessible using the include file `"date.h"`. In making a calendar, not all of the member functions of the `Date` class will be used. (Full details of the class can be found in How to G.) Instead, we'll rely on a simple example program to understand how to use some of the member functions of the class `Date`.

Program 5.10   usedate.cpp

```cpp
#include <iostream>
#include "date.h"
using namespace std;

// show Date member functions

int main()
{
    Date today;
    Date birthDay(7,4,1776);
    Date million(1000000L);
    Date badDate(3,38,1999);
    Date y2k(1,1,2000);

    cout << "today    \t: "  << today    << endl;
    cout << "US bday \t: "   << birthDay << endl;
    cout << "million \t: "   << million  << endl;
    cout << "bad date \t: " << badDate   << endl << endl;

    cout << y2k << " is a " << y2k.DayName() << endl << endl;

    Date one = million - 999999L;
    Date birthDay2000(birthDay.Month(), birthDay.Day(), 2000);
    today++;

    cout << "day one \t: "   << one << " on a " << one.DayName() << endl;
    cout << "bday2K  \t: "   << birthDay2000 << endl;
    cout << "tomorrow \t: "  << today << endl;

    return 0;
}
```

usedate.cpp

---

[9] The calendar used in the United States is the *Gregorian* calendar, which went into effect in 1582, but not in the English-speaking world until 1752. Several countries did not adopt this calendar until the 1900s, but it is adopted almost universally today. In-depth and interesting information about calendars can be found in [DR90, RDC93].

In reading the output below it might help to know that I ran the program on March 15, 1999. Think about what appears on each line of the output and how the Date class works.

```
                         O U T P U T

prompt> usedate
today              : March 15 1999
US bday            : July 4 1776
million            : November 28 2738
bad date           : March 1 1999


January 1 2000 is a Saturday


day one            : January 1 1 on a Monday
bday2K             : July 4 2000
tomorrow           : March 16 1999
```

Constructors and Initialization. The technical word that describes object initialization and definition is **construction.** Construction initializes the state of an object. For programmer-defined classes like Date, a special member function, called a **constructor,** performs this initialization. The first line of output from *usedate.cpp* will differ depending on the day the program is run. This is because the variable today, defined using the parameterless or **default** constructor, constructs a variable with "today's date" according to the documentation in *date.h,* Program G.2. The variable birthDay is constructed using the three-parameter constructor. According to the documentation in *date.h* the parameters specify the month, day, and year of a Date object. The variable million is constructed using the single-parameter constructor. The documentation in *date.h* indicates that the value of the parameter specifies the absolute number of days from January 1, A.D. 1; one million days from this date is November 28, 2738.[10] Finally, the variable badDate is constructed with an invalid date in March; the invalid date is converted to March 1 (as described in the beginning of the header file). Invalid months (i.e., outside the range 1–12) are converted to January.

Classes often have more than one constructor, especially when there is more than one way to specify the value of an object. The compiler can determine which constructor to use since the parameter lists are different.

---

[10]In the constant value 1000000L, the L is used to indicate that this is a long int value. On 32-bit machines the L isn't necessary, but it is needed on 16-bit machines where the largest int value is 32,767.

Other `Date` *Member Functions.* Based on the output of *usedate.cpp* you may be able to determine that the `Date` member function `DayName()` returns the day of the week on which a date occurs. You can check a calendar to see that New Year's day in 2000 is a Saturday (which makes it convenient to celebrate on Friday night!). The functions `Month()` and `Day()` return the number of the month (1 . . . 12) and day, respectively, for a given date. These return `int` values, as you might have determined by the similarity of the construction of `birthDay2000` to `birthDay`.

It's also possible to perform arithmetic with `Date` objects. The variable `one` is constructed by subtracting a (long) integer value from the `Date` object `million`. This yields another date, in the same way that the value of `today - 1` is a `Date` representing yesterday. The statement `today++` changes `today` to represent the next day, or tomorrow. Of course it's confusing that the value of `today` becomes tomorrow after the statement executes.

You can compare dates using the relational operators, such as `<`, `<=`, and others. For complete information, see the header file `"date.h"` and the exercises at the end of this chapter.

Pause to Reflect

5.32 How would you use a `Date` variable to determine on what day of the week you were born?

5.33 How would you use the `Date` class to determine how many days you've been alive? (Hint: Subtract two `Date` objects.)

5.34 Using one `Date` variable and the member function `DaysIn()` (which returns the number of days in the month—see `date.h`), write the Boolean-valued function `IsLeapYear` as specified in *isleap.cpp,* Program 4.8.

5.35 If the one-millionth day is November 28, 2738 (see Program 5.10, *usedate.cpp*), do we need to worry that the `Date` class is not robust and might cause problems when the absolute number of days since 1 A.D. exceeds the largest value of a `long`?

5.36 In Canada and Europe dates are usually specified by giving the day first rather than the month. In the United States, 4/8/2000 means April 8, 2000. The same date means August 4, 2000, in Canada. Is it possible to write a program using the `Date` class for dates in Canada? How?

5.37 Write a function that determines and returns the date on which Thanksgiving (a U.S. holiday) occurs in any year. Thanksgiving is the fourth Thursday in November. Use the following header:

```
Date Thanksgiving(int year)
// post: returns the Date for Thanksgiving in year
```

5.38 Many people prefer Fridays to Mondays. Write a function that prints all the months in a given year that have more Fridays than Mondays.

5.4.2 The Dice Class

In this section you'll learn about a programmer-defined class, named Dice, that permits the computer to simulate the kind of dice used in board games. The class simulates dice with any number of sides, not just common six-sided dice. It's even possible to have one-sided dice and million-sided dice, both of which are easy to simulate but hard to carve. Six- and twelve-sided dice are shown in the following figure:

The class Dice is very general and permits simulation of an N-sided die for any N.

These simulated dice, and the computer-generated random numbers on which they are based, are part of an application area of computer science called **simulation.** Simulations model real-world phenomena using a computer, which becomes a virtual laboratory for experimenting with models of physical systems without the expense of building the systems. Computer-based simulations are used to design planes, trains, and automobiles; to predict the weather; and to build and design computers and programs. We'll study simulation in more detail in the later chapters, but we'll use the Dice[11] class to study program and class construction.

To use the Dice class in a program you must include "dice.h" just as you must include "date.h" to use the Date class and <string> to use the string class. (The header file for the Dice class is in How to G.) Program 5.11 is a simple program showing all the Dice member functions.

Program 5.11 roll.cpp

```
#include <iostream>
using namespace std;
#include "dice.h"

// simple program illustrating use of Dice class
// roll two dice, print results, Owen Astrachan, 3/31/99

int main()
{
    Dice cube(6);              // six-sided die
    Dice dodeca(12);           // twelve-sided die

    cout << "rolling " << cube.NumSides() << " sided die" << endl;
    cout << cube.Roll() << endl;
    cout << cube.Roll() << endl;
    cout << "rolled " << cube.NumRolls() << " times" << endl;
```

---

[11]The word *dice* is the plural form of the word *die*, but a class named Die seems somewhat macabre. Also, using Dice prevents professors from jokingly saying "Die Class" to their students.

```
cout << "rolling " << dodeca.NumSides() << " sided die" << endl;
cout << dodeca.Roll() << endl;
cout << dodeca.Roll() << endl;
cout << dodeca.Roll() << endl;
cout << "rolled " << dodeca.NumRolls() << " times" << endl;
return 0;
}
```
roll.cpp

OUTPUT

```
prompt> roll
rolling 6 sided die
5
3
rolled 2 times
rolling 12 sided die
8
1
12
rolled 3 times

prompt> roll
rolling 6 sided die
1
6
rolled 2 times
rolling 12 sided die
8
9
2
rolled 3 times
```

Dice Construction. When you define a Dice object like cube or dodeca you must specify the number of sides for the simulated Dice object. Unlike the class Date, which has a default (parameterless) constructor, the Dice class does not; you must supply the number of sides. Many people think it makes sense to have a default constructor yield a six-sided Dice object, so that Dice x1,x2,x3; defines three six-sided dice. However, when I designed the Dice class I decided to require a parameter. You can, of course, change the implementation of the class to permit a default constructor. We'll study how classes are implemented in the next chapter.

In C++ a constructor is a member function with the same name as the class. Constructors are functions with no return type. Neither void, int, double, nor any other type can be specified as the return type of a constructor. If a Dice variable is defined without providing arguments to the constructor, as shown in *tryroll.cpp*, Program 5.12, an error message will be generated. Different compilers issue different error messages, and the messages are not always intuitive for beginning programmers. However, the compilers always identify the line on which an error occurs.

Program 5.12 tryroll.cpp

```
#include <iostream>
using namespace std;
#include "dice.h"

int main()
{
    Dice spinner;

    cout << "# of sides = " << spinner.NumSides() << endl;
    return 0;
}
```

tryroll.cpp

The error message generated by the g++ compiler follows:

```
tryroll: In function 'int main()':
tryroll:7: no matching function for call to 'Dice::Dice ()'
tryroll:7: in base initialization for class 'Dice'
```

Note that the error messages indicate that the compiler tries to find a constructor with no parameters, Dice::Dice(), but cannot find one. We'll discuss the :: operator later. Using Metrowerks Codewarrior the error is less helpful:

```
Error    : function call '?0()' does not match
'Dice::Dice(int)'
'Dice::Dice(const Dice &)'
tryroll.cpp line 7    Dice spinner;
```

Using Visual C++ the error indicates that no **default constructor** can be found:

```
Compiling...
tryroll.cpp
C:\tryroll.cpp(7) : error C2512: 'Dice' : no appropriate
                   default constructor available
Error executing cl.exe.
```

A default constructor is one with no parameters; see the error message from the g–+ compiler.

> **Program Tip 5.6:** **When compilation errors occur at the point where an object is constructed in a program, look carefully at the constructors in the corresponding header file to see why the error occurs.** You must try to find a constructor whose parameters correspond to the the arguments passed when the object is defined.

5.4.3 Testing the Dice Class

When a new class is designed and implemented, it must be tested. Testing usually requires programs specifically designed for testing rather than for general use or for a specific application. For the Dice class we'd like to know whether the simulated dice behave as we'd expect real dice to behave. Are the simulated dice truly random? Do the simulated dice conform to the mathematical models that exist for random events such as dice rolls? To test the Dice class, we'll use a program to see whether the theoretical outcomes of rolling dice are matched by the empirical results of the test program.

We'll use a program *dicetest.cpp,* designed to toss two six-sided dice and to determine how many rolls are needed to obtain a specific sum. For example, we should expect that fewer rolls of a pair of dice are required to obtain a sum of 7 than to obtain a sum of 2. Furthermore, given that there is exactly one way to obtain a sum of 2 and one way to obtain a sum of 12 (rolling two ones and two sixes, respectively), we should expect the same number of simulated rolls to obtain either the sum of 2 or 12. The program will simulate tossing two dice and record the number of rolls needed to obtain some target between 2 and 12. We'll repeat this experiment several times and output the average number of rolls needed to obtain each sum. We wouldn't be surprised, for example, if a program needed only one roll to obtain a sum of 12—tossing double sixes does happen. We should be surprised, however, if the experiment of trying for a 12 was repeated 1,000 times and the average number of rolls before rolling a 12 was reported to be 1—this doesn't match either our intuitive expectation or the mathematical expectation of how many rolls it takes to obtain a 12 with two six-sided dice.

Program 5.13 testdice.cpp

```
#include <iostream>
using namespace std;
#include "prompt.h"
#include "dice.h"

// simulate rolling two dice to obtain all possible sums
// repeat the "experiment" specified number of times
// Owen Astrachan, 8/9/94, modified 6/9/95, 4/20/99

double RollTest(int target,int experiments);

int main()
{
    int numTimes;                       // for one trial
```

```
      long totalRolls;                         // accumulate for all trials
      int k;

      numTimes = PromptRange("number of 'trials' ",100,20000);

      totalRolls = 0;
      for(k=2; k <= 12; k++)
      {   cout << k << "\t" << RollTest(k,numTimes) << endl;
      }

      return 0;
}

double RollTest(int target, int trials)
// precondition: 2 <= target <= 12, 0 < trials
// postcondition: returns average # of rolls needed to obtain target
//                  trying 'trials' times
{
      Dice d1(6);
      Dice d2(6);

      int total = 0;
      int k;
      for(k=0; k < trials; k++)
      {   int numRolls = 1;                      //first time through loop is 1 roll
          while (d1.Roll() + d2.Roll() != target)
          {   numRolls += 1;
          }
          total += numRolls;
      }
      return double(total)/trials;
}
```

testdice.cpp

OUTPUT

```
number of 'trials'  between 100 and 20000: 10000
2        35.9015
3        18.0322
4        11.9391
5        9.0508
6        7.1973
7        5.9474
8        7.2554
9        8.9598
10       12.0036
11       17.9579
12       36.9615
```

The results obtained for trying to roll a 2 and a 12 are very close. Consulting a book on discrete mathematics provides an answer that is correct theoretically[12] and might further validate these empirical results. The average returned by the function `RollTest()` in Program 5.13 is converted to a `double` value by casting:

```
return double(total)/trials;
```

Casting is needed because both `total` and `trials` are int values, and the result of dividing an `int` by an `int` value is an `int`. A `long` is used for `totalRolls` in `main` instead of an `int` because the total number of rolls over many trials will exceed the largest `int` value on 16-bit computers.

Pause to Reflect

5.39 Modify the loop in *testdice.cpp*, Program 5.13, so that the values of the dice rolls are printed for each simulated roll (run the program for only one trial). You'll need to define two integer variables to store the values of the dice rolls to print them (this can be tricky).

5.40 Write a function that rolls two n-sided dice and returns how many rolls are needed before the dice show the same number—that is, until doubles are rolled. The function should have one parameter: the number of sides on the dice.

5.41 Write a function that "flips a coin" (a two-sided `Dice` object) n times, where n is a parameter, and returns the number of times "heads" is flipped.

5.42 Write a function that rolls three six-sided dice and returns the number of rolls needed before all three dice show the same number. De Morgan's law may be useful in developing a loop test.

5.43 Write code that picks a random month of the year and a random day in that month, then prints the date. The `Dice` objects you use should never cause an error. This means that for February you'll need either a 28-sided die or a 29-sided die depending on whether it's a leap year.

5.44 Write a loop to count how many times three six-sided dice must be rolled until the values showing are all different. De Morgan's law may be useful in developing a loop test.

---

[12]Mathematically, the expected number of rolls to obtain either a 2 or a 12 is 36. This is a property of independent, discrete random variables. The expected number of rolls to obtain a 7 is 6.

Grace Murray Hopper (1906–1992)

Grace Hopper was one of the first programmers of the Harvard Mark I, the first programmable computer built in the United States. In her words she was "the third programmer on the world's first large-scale digital computer" [Gü95].

This work was done while she was in the Navy in the last years of World War II. It was while working on the Mark II that Hopper was involved with the first documented "bug": the famous moth inside one of the computer's relays that led to the use of the term *debugging*.

She developed the first compiler, called A-0, while working for Remington Rand in 1952. Until that time, many people believed that computers were good only for "number crunching," that computers were not capable of programming—which is what a compiler does (it produces a working program from a higher-level language). After a period of retirement, Hopper returned to naval duty in 1967 at the age of 60. She remained on active duty for 19 more years and was promoted to commodore in 1983 and to admiral in 1985. She was a proponent of innovative thinking and kept a clock on her desk that ran counterclockwise to show that things could be done differently. Although very proud of her career in the Navy, Hopper had little tolerance for bureaucracies, saying:

> *"It's better to show that something can be done and apologize for not asking permission, than to try to persuade the powers that be at the beginning."*

The Grace M. Hopper award for contributions to the field of computer science is given each year by the ACM (Association for Computing Machinery) for work done before the age of 30. In 1994 this award was given to Bjarne Stroustrup for his work in inventing and developing the language C++.

For more information see [Sla87], from which some of this biography is taken.

5.5 Chapter Review

In this chapter we discussed how classes are implemented. We also covered different looping and selection statements. Guidelines were given to assist in determining what kind of loop statement should be used and how loops are developed. The important topics covered in this chapter are summarized here.

- Interface (`.h` file) and implementation (`.cpp` files) provide an abstraction mechanism for writing and using C++ classes.

- Constructors are member functions that are automatically called to construct and initialize an object.

- Member functions are used to access an object's behavior or to get information about the object's state.

- The `for` loop is an alternative looping construct used for definite loops (where the number of iterations is known before the loop executes for the first time).

- The `do-while` loop body is always executed once, in contrast to a `while` loop body, which may never be executed.

- Infinite loops formed using `while(true)` or `for(;;)` are often used with `break` statements to avoid duplicated code and complex loop tests. However, you should be judicious in using `break` statements because overreliance on them can lead to code that is hard to understand logically.

- A loop invariant is a statement that helps reason about and develop loops. A loop invariant is true each time the loop test is evaluated, although its truth must often be reestablished during the loop's execution.

- The built-in types `int` and `double` represent a limited range of values in computing, compared to the infinite range of values of integers and real numbers in mathematics. You must be careful to take this limited range of values into account when interpreting data and developing programs.

- Often small differences in a program can have a drastic effect on program efficiency. Determining whether a number is prime illustrates some considerations in making a program efficient.

- A `return` statement causes a function to stop, and control is returned to the calling statement. It is possible and often convenient to use `return` to exit a function early, much as a `break` statement is used to exit infinite loops.

- Fence post problems are typical in code that loops. A fence post problem is often solved using a special case before the loop or after the loop.

- The postincrement and postdecrement operators `++` and `--` are convenient shortcuts for adding and subtracting one, respectively.

- Variables modified with `const` have values that do not change. Using such constants can make programs more readable; for example, the constant AVOGADRO or MOLE carries more meaning than `6.023e23`.

- A variable is accessible only within its scope, usually delimited by curly braces: `{` and `}`. Private data variables in a class are global to all member functions of the class.

- Constructors are special member functions used to initialize an object. A default constructor is one with no parameters. A class can have more than one constructor, like the `Date` class, or only one constructor, like the `Dice` class.
- Develop test programs when you design and implement classes. Testing should be an integral part of the process of program and class design.

5.6 Exercises

5.1 Write a program modeled after the *100 bottles of X on the wall* song (see the exercises in Chapter 3) that will print as many verses of the song as the user specifies (both the kind of beverage and the number of bottles should be specified by the user). Try to make the program grammatical so that it doesn't print

```
one bottles of sarsaparilla on the wall
```

(note the incorrect plural of bottle).

5.2 Write a program that prints a totem pole of random heads. Prompt the user for the number of heads; each head of the totem pole should be randomly drawn by using a `Dice` variable to choose among different choices for hair, eyes, mouth, and so on.

```
                         O U T P U T

prompt> totem
how many head: 2
        ||||||///////////
        |                   |
        |                   |
        |    O    O         |
        |                   |
       _|                  _|
      |_                    _|
        |    --------        |
        |                   |
        ||||||||||||||||||
        |                   |
        |                   |
        |    .    .         |
        |                   |
       _|                  _|
      |_                    _|
        |    |_____|     |
        |                   |
```

5.3 Modify *testdice.cpp,* Program 5.13, so that it calculates the average number of rolls to obtain all possible sums for two *n*-sided dice, where *n* is a value entered by the user. The number of trials should also be entered by the user. Write functions that can be used to minimize the amount of code that appears in `main`. As an example, you might consider a function with the following prototype:

```
double AverageRolls(int target, int trials, int numSides)
// pre:   2 <= target <= 2*numSides
// post: returns average # of rolls needed to obtain
//        sum 'target' rolling two dice with 'numSides'
//        sides, repeating the experiment 'trials' times
```

Can you modify this program easily to work for three *n*-sided dice rather than two?

5.4 Write a program that finds the greatest common divisor, or gcd, of two numbers. The gcd of two numbers *x* and *y* is the largest number that evenly divides both *x* and *y*. For example, the gcd of 12 and 42 is 6, and the gcd of 14 and 74 is 2. Euclid developed an algorithm for determining the gcd more than 2,000 years ago. You should use this algorithm in calculating the greatest common divisor of *x* and *y*:

```
assign r the value x % y
if r equals 0
then
    STOP, gcd is y
else
    assign x the value y
    assign y the value r
    repeat (back to top)
```

Write a function that returns the gcd of two numbers, and use the function to create a table of gcds similar to the following table, where the ranges of *x* and *y* are entered by the user:

```
      y
  x | 1  2  3  4  5  6  7
 ---+----------------------
 11 | 1  1  1  1  1  1  1
 12 | 1  2  3  4  1  6  1
 13 | 1  1  1  1  1  1  1
 14 | 1  2  1  2  1  2  7
 15 | 1  1  3  1  5  3  1
```

5.5 Write a program to simulate tossing a coin (use a two-sided die). The program should toss a coin 10,000 times (or some number of times specified by the user) and keep track of the longest run of heads or tails that occurs in a sequence of simulated coin flips. Thus, in the sequence HTHTTTHHHHT there is a sequence of three tails and a sequence of four heads.

To keep track of the runs, four variables—headRun, tailRun, maxHeads, and maxTails—are defined and initialized to zero. These variables keep track of the length of the current head run, the length of the current tail run, and the maximum runs of heads and of tails, respectively. After the statement heads++ the value of headRun is incremented. After the statement tails++ the value of tailRun is incremented.

In addition, these variables must be reset to zero at the appropriate time, and the values of the max head run and max tail run variables must be set appropriately.

5.6 Write a program that computes all **twin primes** between two values entered by the user. Twin primes are numbers that differ by two and are both primes, such as 1019 and 1021.

5.7 Write a function with prototype `int NumDigits(num)` that determines the number of digits in its parameter. Use the ideas of the previous exercise, but be sure that the function works for *all* integer values (including zero, which has one digit, and negative numbers—don't forget about the function `fabs`).

5.8 Write a Boolean-valued predicate function similar to `IsPrime` that returns true if its parameter is a **perfect number** and false otherwise. A number is perfect if it is equal to the sum of its proper divisors (i.e., not including itself). For example, $6 = 1+2+3$ and $28 = 1+2+4+7+14$ are the first two perfect numbers. Recall that the expression `num % divisor` has value zero exactly when `divisor` divides num exactly; for example, `30 % 6 == 0` but `30 % 7 = 2`. The function should be named `IsPerfect`.

5.9 Write a function `SumOfNums` that calculates and returns the sum of the numbers from 1 to *n* (where *n* is a parameter). The statement

```
cout << SumOfNums(100) << endl;
```

should cause 5050 to be printed since $1+2+\cdots+100 = 5050$. It's possible to write this program without using a loop (such a solution is often attributed to the mathematician C. F. Gauss, who supposedly discovered it when he was a boy).

5.10 The following loop sums all numbers entered by the user (and stops when the user enters a nonpositive number):

```
int num;
cin >> num;
int sum = 0;
while (num >= 0)
{    sum += num;
     cin >> num;
}
```

Explain how the two uses of `cin >>` correspond to a kind of fence post problem. Then write a program based on the foregoing loop to calculate the average of a sequence of nonnegative numbers entered by the user.

5.11 Write a function that simulates a slot machine by printing three randomly chosen strings as the values displayed by the slot machine. Each string should be chosen randomly from among four different choices, such as `"orange"`, `"lemon"`, `"lime"`, `"cherry"` (but any words will do). Choose the random values eight times and display each choice of three as shown in the following sample run. If the strings are all the same or are all different when the final sequence of these strings appears, then print a message that the user wins; otherwise the user loses.

```
                        O U T P U T

prompt> slots
Welcome to the slot machine simulation
Here's a spin....
cherry orange cherry
lime    lemon  cherry
lime    lemon  lemon
lime    cherry cherry
lemon  lime    cherry
lemon  lemon  lime
orange lime    lime
you lose!!

prompt> slots
Welcome to the slot machine simulation
Here's a spin....
lime    lime    orange
orange cherry orange
orange cherry lime
cherry orange lime
lime    orange orange
cherry orange lemon
lemon  lemon  lemon
all values equal, you win!!

prompt> slots
Welcome to the slot machine simulation
Here's a spin....
lemon   cherry orange
lemon   orange lemon
cherry orange lime
lime    cherry lime
cherry cherry cherry
orange cherry cherry
orange lime    cherry
all values different, you win!!
```

5.12 Using the class `BigInt`, make a table of how many times each of the digits $0\ldots 9$ occurs in huge numbers like 200! or 2^{5000}. You can determine digits by peeling off digits one at a time, as in *digits.cpp*, Program 5.5, or you can use the `BigInt` member function `ToString()`, which returns a string of digits, such as `"1234567"` for the value 1,234,567; then look at each character of the string.

5.13 Write a program that displays the prime factors of a number. The prime factors of 60 are $2 \times 2 \times 3 \times 5$. Use the program to display the prime factors of all numbers between two user-entered numbers.

5.14 Consider the following U.S. holidays:

- Mother's Day, the second Sunday in May
- Labor Day, the first Monday in September
- Thanksgiving, the fourth Thursday in November

Write one function that determines the date on which these holidays fall in any year. The same function should be called with different parameters for the different holidays. For example, for Labor Day you would pass parameters "Monday", 1, and 9 for the first Monday in September (the ninth month); for Mother's Day you would pass "Sunday", 2, and 5 (for May). Use this function and write code to determine how many school days (Mon–Fri) there are between Labor Day and Thanksgiving in any year.

5.15 Daylight-saving time causes clocks to be reset in the spring and fall in many (but not all) parts of the United States. Daylight saving begins on the first Sunday of April (set clocks ahead one hour, "spring ahead") and ends on the last Sunday of October (set clocks back one hour, "fall back"). Write a program that shows the number of days in which daylight-saving time is in effect for all years from 1990 to 2010. You may find it useful to write a function that returns the number of daylight-saving days given the year (as a parameter).

5.16 Some people believe that our physical, emotional, and intellectual habits are governed by *biorhythms*. A biorhythm cycle exists for each of these three traits; the length of the cycle differs, but all cycles start when we are born. The physical cycle is 23 days long, the intellectual cycle is 33 days long, and the emotional cycle is 28 days long. The cycles repeat as sine waves, with the period of each wave given by the cycle length. A critical day occurs when all three cycles cross at the equivalent of $y = 0$ if the cycles are plotted on x and y axes. When a cycle is at its peak (e.g., as $\sin(\pi/2)$ is the peak of a sine wave), we are favored for that cycle, so that a peak on the intellectual cycle is a good day to take an exam.

Use the Date class to determine when your next critical day is and when your next peak and low days are for each of the three cycles.

5.17 Here are rules for one version of the game of craps, played with six-sided dice.

A player rolls two dice. If the sum of the two is 7 or 11, the roller wins immediately; if the sum is a 2, 3, or 12, the roller loses at once. If the sum is 4, 5, 6, 8, 9, or 10, the roller rolls again. By repeating the initial number, the roller "makes his or her point" and wins. By rolling a 7 the roller "craps out" and loses. Otherwise, the roller keeps on rolling again until he or she wins or loses.

Write a program that simulates a game of craps, then modify the program to simulate 10,000 games, reporting how many simulated games are "won."

5.18 Write a program that prints a calendar for any month in any year as shown here:

```
 O U T P U T

prompt> calendar
enter month between 1 and 12: 6
enter year between 1752 and 2500: 1999

    June 1999
 Su Mo Tu We Th Fr Sa
           1  2  3  4  5
  6  7  8  9 10 11 12
 13 14 15 16 17 18 19
 20 21 22 23 24 25 26
 27 28 29 30
```

For a real challenge, make it possible for the user to specify how large the calendar should be, something like this:

```
 Su    Mo    Tu    We    Th    Fr    Sa
+---+---+---+---+---+---+---+
|    |  1 |  2 |  3 |  4 |  5 |  6 |
+---+---+---+---+---+---+---+
|  7 |  8 |  9 | 10 | 11 | 12 | 13 |
+---+---+---+---+---+---+---+
| 14 | 15 | 16 | 17 | 18 | 19 | 20 |
+---+---+---+---+---+---+---+
| 21 | 22 | 23 | 24 | 25 | 26 | 27 |
+---+---+---+---+---+---+---+
| 28 | 29 | 30 |    |    |    |    |
+---+---+---+---+---+---+---+
```

or like this

```
  Sunday     Monday     Tuesday
+---------+---------+---------+
|       1 |       2 |       3 |
|         |         |         |   . . .
|         |         |         |
|         |         |         |
|         |         |         |
+---------+---------+---------+
```

5.19 Write a program to track the number of times each sum for two 12-sided dice occurs over 10,000 rolls, or more generally, the number of times each sum for two n-sided dice occurs. We'll learn how to do this simply in Chapter 8, but with the programming tools you have, you'll need to write a program to write the program for you! Write a program, named *metadice.cpp*, that reads the number of sides of the dice and outputs *a program* that can be compiled and executed. For example, the following function might be part of the program; it defines and initializes variables to track each dice sum:

```
void Definitions(int sides)
// post: variable definitions for c2, c3, ...
//          are output int cX = 0;   2 <= x <= 2*sides
{
    int k;
    for(k=2; k <= 2*sides; k++)
    {   cout << "\t" << "int c" << k << " = 0;" << endl;
    }
    cout << endl << endl;
}
```

The function Definitions creates the variable definitions shown below; these are part of the program *that is output* by the program *metadice.cpp* that you write (and of which the function Definitions is a part).

```
                            O U T P U T

prompt> metadice
enter # sides: 5
#include <iostream>
using namespace std;
#include "dice.h"

int main()
{
        int c2 = 0;
        int c3 = 0;
        int c4 = 0;
        int c5 = 0;
        int c6 = 0;
        int c7 = 0;
        int c8 = 0;
        int c9 = 0;
        int c10 = 0;

        program continues here

        return 0;
}
```

2

Program and Class Construction: Extending the Foundation

Classes, Iterators, and Patterns

6

Nature uses only the longest threads to weave her pattern, so each small piece of the fabric
reveals the organization of the entire tapestry.
RICHARD FEYNMAN
in Grady Booch, *Object Solutions*

The control structures we studied in Chapters 4 and 5 permit program statements to be executed selectively or repeatedly according to values entered by the user or calculated by the program. In Section 5.4 we saw how using classes like Dice and Date extends the domain of problems we can solve by programming. In this chapter we'll extend the idea of repetition by processing various data in several applications. A common pattern emerges from all these applications: the pattern of iterating over a sequence of data. Examples of such iteration include processing each word in one of Shakespeare's plays, processing the elements of a set, and processing movement of a simulated molecule. We'll also explore classes in more depth, studying class implementation as well as class use. We'll explore design guidelines for constructing classes and programs.

In particular, we'll cover classes used to read information from files stored on a disk rather than entered from the keyboard. We'll use a standard stream class that behaves in the same way cin behaves but that allows data to flow from text files. We'll develop a new class for reading words from files and build on the pattern of iteration developed for the class to develop new classes. Writing programs and functions that use these classes requires a new kind of parameter, called a *reference parameter,* which we'll discuss in some detail.

6.1 Classes: From Use to Implementation

In Section 5.4 we studied code examples using classes Dice and Date. These classes complement the standard C++ class string and will be part of the toolkit of classes we'll extend and use throughout the book. In this section we'll examine classes more closely. This will help you get comfortable with the syntax of **class implementation** in addition to the syntax of using classes that you've already seen. You'll learn how to modify classes and how to implement your own.

6.1.1 Class Documentation: The Interface (.h File)

C++ classes encapsulate **state** and **behavior.** The behavior of a class is what the class does. Behavior is often described with verbs: cats eat, sleep, and play; dice are rolled. The state of a class depends on physical properties. For example, dice have a fixed number of sides.

Class behavior is defined by **public member functions**; these are the class functions that client programs can call. Public member functions of the class Dice are the Dice constructor and the functions NumRolls(), NumSides(), and Roll(). The **class declaration** for Dice is shown below; the entire header file *dice.h* is found in How to G as Program G.3. (The header file includes many comments that aren't shown below.)

```
class Dice
{
  public:
    Dice(int sides);        // constructor
    int Roll();             // return the random roll
    int NumSides() const;   // how many sides this die has
    int NumRolls() const;   // # times this die rolled

  private:
    int myRollCount;        // # times die rolled
    int mySides;            // # sides on die
};
```

The state of an object is usually specified by class **private data** like myRollCount and mySides for a Dice object. Private state data are often called **member data**, **data members**, **instance variables**, or **data fields**. As we'll see, the term *instance variable* is used because each Dice instance (or object) has its own data members.

When an object is **defined,** by a call to a constructor, memory is allocated for the object, and the object's state is initialized. When a built-in variable is defined, the variable's state may be uninitialized. For programmer-defined types such as Dice, initialization takes place when the Dice variable is defined. As a programmer using the Dice class, you do not need to be aware of how a Dice object is initialized and constructed or what is in the private section of the Dice class. You do need to know some properties, such as when a Dice object is constructed it has been rolled zero times. As you begin to design your own classes, you'll need to develop an understanding of how the state of an object is reflected by its private data and how member functions use private data. Class state as defined by private data is not directly accessible by client programs. A **client program** is a program like *roll.cpp*, Program 5.11, that uses a class. We'll soon see how a class like Dice is implemented so that client programs that use Dice objects will work.

6.1.2 Comments in *.h* Files

The documentation for a class, in the form of comments in the **header file** in which the class is declared, furnishes information about the constructor's parameters and about all public member functions.

The names of header files traditionally end with a *.h* suffix. When the C++ standard was finalized, the *.h* suffix was no longer used so that what used to be called <iostream.h> became <iostream>. I continue to use the *.h* suffix for classes supplied with this book, but I use the standard C++ header file names.

In this book the name of a header file almost always begins with the name of the class that is declared in the header file. The header file provides the compiler with the information it needs about the form of class objects. For programmers using the header file, the header file may serve as a manual on how to use a class or some other set of routines (as <cmath> or <math.h> describes math functions such as sqrt). Not all header files are useful as programmer documentation, but the compiler uses the header files to determine if functions and classes are used correctly in client programs. The compiler *must* know, for example, that the member functions NumSides and Roll are legal Dice member functions and that each returns an int value. By reading the header file you can see that two **private data variables**, myRollCount and mySides, define the state of a Dice object. As the designer and writer of client programs, you do *not* need to look at the private section of a class declaration. Since client programs can access a class only by calling public member functions, you should take the view that class behavior is described only by public member functions and not by private state.

A header file is an **interface** to a class or to a group of functions. The interface is a description of what the behavior of a class is, but not of how the behavior is implemented. You probably know how to use a stereo—at least how to turn one on and adjust the volume. From a user's point of view, the stereo's interface consists of the knobs, displays, and buttons on the front of the receiver, CD player, tuner, and so on. Users don't need to know how many watts per channel an amplifier delivers or whether the tuner uses phase-lock looping. You may know how to drive a car. From a driver's point of view, a car's interface is made up of the gas and brake pedals, the steering wheel, and the dashboard dials and gauges. To drive a car you don't need to know whether a car engine is fuel-injected or whether it has four or six cylinders.

The *dice.h* header file is an interface to client programs that use Dice objects. Just as you use a stereo without (necessarily) understanding fully how it works, and just as you use a calculator by pressing the $\sqrt{}$ button without understanding what algorithm is used to find a square root, a Dice object can be used in a client program without knowledge of its private state. As the buttons and displays provide a means of accessing a stereo's features, the public member functions of a class provide a means of accessing (and sometimes modifying) the private fields in the class. The displays on an amp, tuner, or receiver are like functions that show values; the buttons that change a radio station actually change the state of a tuner, just as some member functions can change the state of a class object.

When a stereo is well-designed, one component can be replaced without replacing all components. Similarly, several models of personal computer offer the user the ability to upgrade the main chip in the computer (the central processing unit, or CPU) without buying a completely new computer. In these cases the implementation can be replaced, provided that the interface stays the same. The user won't notice any difference in how the buttons and dials on the box are arranged or in how they are perceived to work. Replacing the implementation of a class may make a user's program execute more quickly, or use less space, or execute more carefully (by checking for precondition violations) but should not affect whether the program works as intended. Since client programs depend only on the interface of a class and not on the implementation, we say that classes provide a method of **information hiding**—the state of a class is hidden from client programs.

William H. (Bill) Gates *(b. 1955)*

Bill Gates is the richest person in the United States and CEO of Microsoft. He began his career as a programmer writing the first BASIC compiler for early microcomputers while a student at Harvard.

When asked whether studying computer science is the best way to prepare to be a programmer, Gates responded:

No, the best way to prepare is to write programs, and to study great programs that other people have written. In my case, I went to the garbage cans at the Computer Science Center and I fished out listings of their operating system. You've got to be willing to read other people's code, then write your own, then have other people review your code.

Gates is a visionary in seeing how computers will be used both in business and in the home. Microsoft publishes best-selling word processors, programming languages, and operating systems as well as interactive encyclopedias for children. Some people question Microsoft's business tactics, but in late 1994 and again in 1999 antitrust proceedings did little to deter Microsoft's progress. There is no questioning Gates's and Microsoft's influence on how computers are used.

Although Gates doesn't program anymore, he remembers the satisfaction that comes from programming.

When I compile something and it starts computing the right results, I really feel great. I'm not kidding, there is some emotion in all great things, and this is no exception.

For more information see [Sla87].

6.1.3   Class Documentation: The Implementation or *.cpp* File

The header file `<cmath>` (or `<math.h>`) contains function prototypes, or headers, for functions like `sqrt` and `sin`. The bodies of the functions are not part of the header file. A function prototype provides information that programmers need to know to call the function. A prototype also provides information that enables the compiler to determine if a function is called correctly. The prototype is an interface, just as the class declaration in *dice.h* is an interface for users of the Dice class.

The bodies of the Dice member functions are not part of the header file *dice.h*, Program G.3. These function bodies provide an implementation for each member function and are put in a separate file. As a general rule (certainly one we will follow in this book), the name of the **implementation file** will begin with the same prefix as the header file but will end with a .cpp suffix, indicating that it consists of C++ code.[1]

Like all functions we've studied, a member function has a return type, a name, and a parameter list. However, there must be some way to distinguish member functions from nonmember functions when the function is defined. The double colon :: **scope resolution operator** specifies that a member function is part of a given class. The prototype int Dice::NumSides() indicates that NumSides() is a member function of the Dice class. Constructors have no return type. The prototype Dice::Dice(int sides) is the Dice class constructor. The prototype for the constructor of the Balloon class described in *gballoon.h,* Program 3.7, is Balloon::Balloon() because no parameters are required. As an analogy, when I'm with my family, I'm known simply as Owen, but to the world at large I'm Astrachan::Owen. This helps identify which of many possible Owens I am; I belong to the Astrachan "class." The implementation of each Dice member function

> **Syntax: member function prototype**
>
> ClassName::ClassName (parameters)
> //constructor (cannot have return type)
>
> *type* ClassName::FunctionName (parameters)
> //nonconstructor member function

is in *dice.cpp*, Program 6.1. Each Dice member function is implemented with only a few lines of code. The variable mySides, whose value is returned by Dice::NumSides, is not a parameter and is not defined within the function. Similarly, the variable myRollCount, incremented within the function Dice::Roll, is neither a parameter nor a variable locally defined in Dice::Roll.

Program 6.1 dice.cpp

```
#include "dice.h"
#include "randgen.h"

// implementation of dice class
// written Jan 31, 1994, modified 5/10/94 to use RandGen class
// modified 3/31/99 to move RandGen class here from .h file

Dice::Dice(int sides)
// postcondition: all private fields initialized
{
    myRollCount = 0;
    mySides = sides;
}

int Dice::Roll()
```

---

[1]A suffix of .cc is used in the code provided for use in Unix/Linux environments.

```
// postcondition: number of rolls updated
//                 random 'die' roll returned
{
    RandGen gen;      // random number generator

    myRollCount= myRollCount + 1;          // update # of times die rolled
    return gen.RandInt(1,mySides);         // in range [1..mySides]
}

int Dice::NumSides() const
// postcondition: return # of sides of die
{
    return mySides;
}

int Dice::NumRolls() const
// postcondition: return # of times die has been rolled
{
    return myRollCount;
}
```

dice.cpp

The variables myRollCount and mySides are private variables that make up the state of a Dice object. As shown in Figure 6.1, each object or **instance** of the Dice class has its own state variables. Each object may have a different number of sides or be rolled a different number of times, so different variables are needed for each object's state. The convention of using the prefix my with each private data field emphasizes that the data belongs to a particular object. The variable cube in *roll.cpp,* Program 5.11, has a mySides field with value 6, whereas the mySides that is part of the dodeca variable has value 12. This is why dodeca.NumSides() returns 12 but cube.NumSides() returns 6; the member function NumSides returns the value of mySides associated with the object to which it is applied with ., the dot operator.

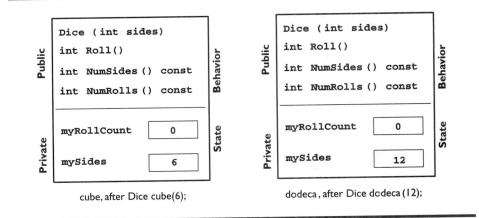

Figure 6.1 After Dice constructors have executed.

If the interface (header file) is well designed, you can change the implementation without changing or recompiling the client program.[2] Similarly, once the implementation is written and compiled, it does not need to be recompiled each time the client program changes. For large programs this can result in a significant savings in the overhead of designing and testing a program. With the advent of well-constructed class **libraries** that are available for a fee or for free, users can write programs much more easily and without the need for extensive changes when a new implementation is provided. This process of compiling different parts of a program separately is described in Section 3.5.

6.1.4 Member Function Implementation

We'll look briefly at the implementation of each member function of the `Dice` class as given in *dice.cpp*, Program 6.1.

The `Dice` Constructor. A class's constructor must initialize all private data (instance variables), so each data member should be given a value explicitly by the constructor. In the body of the constructor `Dice::Dice()` both instance variables `mySides` and `myRollCount` are initialized.

> **Program Tip 6.1:** **Assign a value to all instance variables in every class constructor.** It's possible that you won't know what value to assign when an object is constructed because the actual value will be determined by another member function. In this case, provide some known value, such as zero for an `int` instance variable. Known values will help as you debug your code.

The Member Functions `Dice::NumRolls` and `Dice::NumSides`. Class member functions are often divided into two categories:

- **Accessor functions** that access state but do not alter the state.
- **Mutator functions** that alter the state.

The functions `Dice::NumRolls()` and `Dice::NumSides()` are **accessor functions** since they return information about a `Dice` object, but they do not change the object's state. Note that the implementation of these functions is a single line that returns the value of the appropriate instance variable. Accessor functions often have simple implementations like this. Nearly every programmer that designs classes adheres to the **design heuristic** of making all state data private. A heuristic is a rule of thumb or guideline. As a guideline, there may be exceptional situations in which the guideline is not followed, but in this book all class states will be private.

---

[2] You *will* need to relink the client program with the new implementation.

> **Program Tip 6.2:   All state or instance variables in a class should be private.** You can provide accessor functions for clients to get information about an object's state, but all access should be through public member functions; no instance variables should be public.

Accessor functions in C++ almost always have the keyword **const** following the parameter lists, both in the *.h* file and in the *.cpp* file. We discuss this use of const in detail in How to D. Since accessor functions like Dice::NumSides do not change an object's state, the word const is used by the compiler to actually prohibit changes to state.

> **Program Tip 6.3:   Make accessor functions const.** You make a member function a const function by putting the keyword const after the parameter list.

The Member Function Dice::Roll. The function Dice::Roll() is a **mutator function** because it alters the state of a Dice object. State is altered because a Dice object keeps track of how many times it has been rolled. The private instance variable myRollCount is modified as follows:

```
myRollCount = myRollCount + 1;
```

Because the state changes, the function Dice::Roll() cannot be a const function.

The other lines in Dice::Roll() actually generate the random roll using another class RandGen that generates pseudo-random numbers.

6.1.5   Scope of Private Variables

The instance variables defined in the private section of a class declaration are accessible in all member functions of the class. Private variable names are **global** to all member functions because they can be accessed in each member function. In the Dice class the instance variable mySides is initialized in the constructor and used in Dice::Roll() to generate a random roll. The instance variable myRollCount is initialized in the constructor, incremented in Dice::Roll(), and used to return a value in Dice::NumRolls().

> **Program Tip 6.4:   If a variable is used in only one member function, it's possible that the variable should be defined locally within the function, and not as a private instance variable.** There are occasions when this heuristic doesn't hold (e.g., when a variable must maintain its value over multiple calls of the same member function), but it's a good, general class design heuristic.

By defining a variable at the beginning of a program and outside of any function, you can make it global to all the functions in a program. A **global variable** is accessible everywhere in a program without being passed as a parameter. This is considered poor programming style because the proliferation of global variables in large programs makes it difficult to modify one part of the program without affecting another part. Because global variables cannot be used in large programs without great care (and even then global variables can cause problems), we will not use any global variables even in small programs.

> **Program Tip 6.5: Avoid using global program variables.** Global variables don't work in large programs, so practice good coding style by avoiding their use in small programs.

Pause to Reflect

6.1 How do the displays and buttons on a stereo receiver provide an interface to the receiver? If you purchase a component stereo system (e.g., a CD player, a tuner, a receiver, and a cassette deck), do you need to buy a new receiver if you upgrade the CD player? How is this similar to or different from a header file and its corresponding implementation?

6.2 Do you know how a soda-vending machine works (on the inside)? Can you "invent" a description of how one works that is consistent with your knowledge based on using such machines?

6.3 Why are there so many comments in the header file *dice.h*?

6.4 What is the purpose of the member functions NumSides and NumRolls? For example, why won't the lines

```
Dice tetra(4);
cout << "# of sides = " << tetra.mySides << endl;
```

compile, and what is an alternative that will compile?

6.5 In the member function Dice::Roll() the value returned is specified by the following:

```
gen.RandInt(1,mySides)
```

What type/class of variable is gen and where is the class declared?

6.6 What changes to *roll.cpp*, Program 5.11, permit the user to enter the number of sides in the simulated die?

6.7 Can the statement myRollCount++ be used in place of myRollCount = myRollCount + 1 in Dice::Roll()?

6.8 Suppose a member function `Dice::LastRoll()` is added to the class `Dice`. The function returns the value of the most recent roll. Should function `Dice::LastRoll()` be `const`? What changes to private data and to other member functions are needed to implement the new member function?

```
int Dice::LastRoll()   // is const needed here?
// post: returns value of last time Roll() was called
```

6.2   Program Design with Functions

To see how useful classes are in comparison to using only free functions[3] in the design and implementation of programs, we'll study a program that gives a simple quiz on arithmetic using addition. For example, you might be asked to write a program like this to help your younger sibling practice with math problems or to help an elementary school teacher with a drill-and-practice program for the computer. We'll begin with a program that uses free functions to implement the quiz. In the next chapter we'll modify the quiz programs from this chapter so that several collaborating classes are used instead of free functions. The version developed in this chapter serves as a prototype of the final version. A **prototype** is not a finished product but is useful in understanding design issues and in getting feedback from users.

> **Program Tip 6.6:   A prototype is a good way to start the implementation phase of program development and to help in the design process.** A prototype is a "realistic model of a system's key functions" [McC93]. Booch says that "prototypes are by their very nature incomplete and only marginally engineered." [Boo94] A prototype is an aid to help find some of the important issues before design and implementation are viewed as frozen, or unchanging. For those developing commercial software, prototypes can help clients articulate their needs better than a description in English.

Program 6.2 uses classes and functions we've used in programs before. The header file *randgen.h* for class RandGen is in How to G, but we'll need only the function `RandGen::RandInt` that returns a random integer between (and including) the values of the two parameters as illustrated in Program 6.2.

Program 6.2   simpquiz.cpp

```
#include <iostream>
#include <iomanip>        // for setw
#include <string>
using namespace std;
#include "randgen.h"      // for RandInt
#include "prompt.h"
```

---

[3]Recall that a free function is any function defined outside of a class.

```cpp
// simple quiz program

int MakeQuestion()
// postcondition: creates a random question, returns the answer
{
    const WIDTH = 7;
    RandGen gen;
    int num1 = gen.RandInt(10,20);
    int num2 = gen.RandInt(10,20);

    cout << setw(WIDTH) << num1 << endl;
    cout << "+" << setw(WIDTH-1) << num2 << endl;
    cout << "-------" << endl;

    return num1 + num2;
}


int main()
{
    string name = PromptString("what is your name? ");
    int     correctCount = 0;
    int     total = PromptRange(name + ", how many questions, ",1,10);
    int     answer,response, k;

    for(k=0; k < total; k++)
    {   answer = MakeQuestion();
        cout << "answer here: ";
        cin >> response;
        if (response == answer)
        {   cout << "correct! " << endl;
            correctCount++;
        }
        else
        {   cout << "incorrect, answer = " << answer << endl;
        }
    }
    int percent = double(correctCount)/total * 100;
    cout << name << ", your score is " << percent << "%" << endl;

    return 0;
}
```

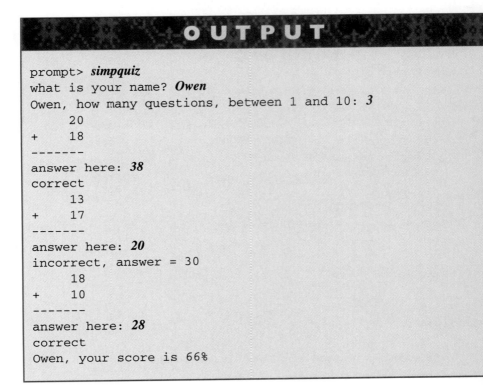

```
prompt> simpquiz
what is your name? Owen
Owen, how many questions, between 1 and 10: 3
        20
+       18
-------
answer here: 38
correct
        13
+       17
-------
answer here: 20
incorrect, answer = 30
        18
+       10
-------
answer here: 28
correct
Owen, your score is 66%
```

6.2.1   Evaluating Classes and Code: Coupling and Cohesion

This program works well for making simple quizzes about arithmetic, but it's hard to modify the program to make changes such as these:

1. Allow the student (taking the quiz) more than one chance to answer the question. A student might be allowed several chances depending on the difficulty of the question asked.
2. Allow more than one student to take a quiz at the same time, say two students sharing the same keyboard.
3. Record a student's results so that progress can be monitored over several quizzes.

As we noted in Program Tips 4.4 and 4.10, writing code that's simple to modify is an important goal in programming. You can't always anticipate what changes will be needed, and code that's easy to modify will save lots of time in the long run.

The modifications above are complicated for a few reasons.

1. There's no way to repeat the same question. If the student is prompted for an answer several times, the original question may scroll off the screen.
2. The body of the `for` loop could be moved into another function parameterized by

name. This might be the first step in permitting a quiz to be given to more than one student at the same time, but in the current program it's difficult to do this.

3. Once we learn about reading and writing information from and to files we'll be able to tackle this problem more easily, but it will still be difficult using the current program. It's difficult in part because the code for giving the quiz and the code for recording quiz scores will be mixed together, making it hard to keep the code dealing with each part separate. Keeping the code separate is a good idea because it will be easier to modify each part if it is independent of the other parts.

The last item is very important. It is echoed by two program and class design heuristics.

> **Program Tip 6.7:   Code, classes, and functions should be as cohesive as possible.** A **cohesive function** does one thing rather than several things. A **cohesive class** captures one idea or set of related behaviors rather than many more unrelated ideas and behaviors. When designing and implementing functions and classes you should make them highly cohesive.

The function MakeQuestion from Program 6.2 does two things: it makes a question and it returns the answer to the question. Doing two things at the same time makes it difficult to do just one of the two things (e.g., ask the same question again). Functions that do one thing are more cohesive than functions that do two things.

> **Program Tip 6.8:   Code, classes, and functions should not be coupled with each other.** Each function and class should be as independent from others as possible, or **loosely coupled**. It's impossible to have no coupling—functions and classes wouldn't be able to call or use each other. But loose coupling is a goal in function and class design.

A function is tightly coupled with another function if the functions can't exist independently or if a change in one causes a change in the other. Ideally, changing a function's implementation without changing the interface or prototype should cause few changes in other functions. In Program 6.2, *simpquiz.cpp*, the function MakeQuestion, which makes questions, and main, which gives a quiz, are tightly coupled with each other and with the student taking the quiz. These three parts of the program should be less coupled than they are.

6.2.2   Toward a Class-Based Quiz Program

We want to develop a quiz program that will permit different kinds of questions—that is, not just different kinds of arithmetic problems, but questions about state capitals, English literature, rock and roll songs, or whatever you think would be fun or instructive. We'd like the program to be able to give a quiz to more than one student at the same time, so that two people sharing a keyboard at one computer could both participate. If possible, we'd like to allow a student to have more than one chance at a question.

In the next chapter we'll study one design of a program that will permit different kinds of quizzes for more than one student. That program will use three collaborating classes. However, we need to study a few more C++ language features and some new classes before we tackle the quiz program.

Before we develop the class design we must study another mode of parameter passing that we'll need in developing more complex classes, functions, and programs. We'll use a modified version of *simpquiz.cpp*, Program 6.2.

As we move toward a new quiz program, think about how the program changes. You'll find that there is no "best design" or "correct design" when it comes to writing programs. However, there are criteria by which classes and programs can be evaluated, such as **coupling** and **cohesion** as outlined in Program Tips 6.8 and 6.7.

6.2.3 Reference Parameters

Program 6.3, *simpquiz2.cpp,* is a modified version of Program 6.2 that uses a function `GiveQuiz` as an encapsulation of the code in `main` of Program 6.2. This encapsulation makes it easier to give a quiz to more than one person in the same program and is a step toward developing a class-based program. The output of Program 6.2 and Program 6.3 are exactly the same (given that the random questions may be different). The function `GiveQuiz` passes two values back to `main` when `GiveQuiz` is called: the number of questions answered correctly and the total number of questions. Since two values are passed back, it's not possible to use a return type that passes only one value back.

In the header of `GiveQuiz` in Program 6.3, *simpquiz2.cpp,* note that the last two parameters are preceded by an ampersand, `&`. Using an ampersand permits values to be passed back from the function to the calling statement.

Program 6.3 simpquiz2.cpp

```cpp
#include <iostream>
#include <iomanip>         // for setw
#include <string>
using namespace std;
#include "randgen.h"       // for RandInt
#include "prompt.h"

// simple quiz program

int MakeQuestion()
// postcondition: creates a random question, returns the answer
{
    const WIDTH = 7;
    RandGen gen;
    int num1 = gen.RandInt(10,20);
    int num2 = gen.RandInt(10,20);

    cout << setw(WIDTH) << num1 << endl;
```

```
    cout << "+" << setw(WIDTH-1) << num2 << endl;
    cout << "-------" << endl;

    return num1 - num2;
}

void GiveQuiz(string name, int & correct, int & total)
// precondition:  name = person taking the quiz
// postcondition: correct = # correct answers, total = # questions
{
    correct = 0;
    total = PromptRange(name + ", how many questions, ',1,10);
    int   answer,response, k;

    for(k=0; k < total; k++)
    {   answer = MakeQuestion();
        cout << 'answer here: ";
        cin >> response;
        if (response == answer)
        {   cout << "correct! " << endl;
            correct++;
        }
        else
        {   cout << "incorrect, answer = " << answer << endl;
        }
    }
}

int main()
{
    int correctCount, total;
    string student = PromptString("what is your name? ");
    GiveQuiz(student, correctCount, total);
    int percent = double(correctCount)/total * 100;
    cout << student << ", your score is " << percent << "%" << endl;

    return 0;
}
```

simpquiz2.cpp

The first parameter of the function GiveQuiz represents the name of the student taking the quiz. This value is passed into the function. The other parameters are used to pass values back from the function GiveQuiz to the statement calling the function. These last three parameters are **reference** parameters; the ampersand appearing between the type and name of the parameter indicates a reference parameter. The diagram in Figure 6.2 shows how information flows between GiveQuiz and the statement that calls GiveQuiz from main. The ampersand modifier used for the last three parameters in the prototype of GiveQuiz makes these references to integers rather than integers. We'll elaborate on this distinction, but a reference is used as an alias to refer to a variable that has already been defined. The memory for a reference parameter is defined somewhere else, whereas the memory for a nonreference parameter, also called a **value** parameter, is allocated in the function.

The value of student (*Owen,* in the figure) is copied from main into the memory location associated with the parameter name in GiveQuiz. Once the value is copied,

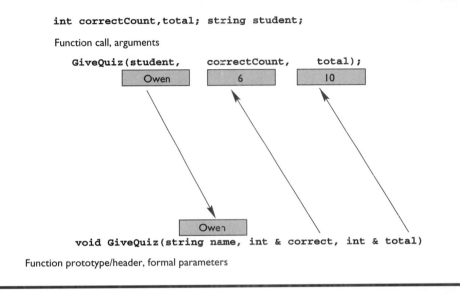

Figure 6.2 Passing parameters by value and by reference in `simpquiz2.cpp`.

the variable `student` defined in `main` and the parameter `name` in `GiveQuiz` are not connected or related in any way. For example, if the value of `name` in `GiveQuiz` is changed, the value of `name` in `main` is *not* affected. This is very different from how reference parameters work. As indicated in Figure 6.2, the storage for the last two arguments in the function call is referenced, or referred to, by the corresponding parameters in `GiveQuiz`. For example, the variable `correctCount` defined in `main` is referred to by the name `correct` within the function `GiveQuiz`. When one storage location (in this case, defined in `main`) has two different names, the term **aliasing** is sometimes used. Whatever happens to `correct` in `GiveQuiz` is really happening to the variable `correctCount` defined in `main` because `correct` refers to `correctCount`. This means that if the statement `correct++;` assigns 3 to `correct` in `GiveQuiz`, the value is actually stored in the memory location allocated in `main` and referred to by the name `correctCount` in `main`. Rich Pattis, author of *Get A-Life: Advice for the Beginning C++ Object-Oriented Programmer* [Pat96], calls reference parameters "voodoo doll" parameters: if you "stick" `correct` in `GiveQuiz`, the object `correctCount` in `main` yells "ouch."

One key to understanding the difference between the two kinds of parameters is to remember where the storage is allocated. For reference parameters, the storage is allocated somewhere else, and the name of the parameter refers back to this storage. For value parameters, the storage is allocated in the function, and a value is copied into this storage location. This is diagrammed by the leftmost arrow in Figure 6.2. When reference parameters are used, memory is allocated for the arguments, and the formal parameters are merely new names (used within the called function) for the memory locations associated with the arguments. This is shown in Figure 6.2 by the arrows that point "up" from the identifiers `correct` and `total`, which serve as aliases for the memory locations allocated for the variables `correctCount` and `total` in `main`.

6.2.4 Pass by Value and Pass by Reference

Program 6.4, *pbyvalue.cpp*, shows a contrived (but I hope illustrative) example of parameter passing.

Program 6.4 pbyvalue.cpp
_____

```cpp
#include <iostream>
#include <string>
using namespace std;

// illustrates pass-by-value/pass-by-reference semantics

void DoStuff(int number, string & word)
{
    cout << "DoStuff in:\t" << number << " " << word << endl;
    number *= 2;
    word = "What's up Doc?";
    cout << "DoStuff out:\t" << number << " " << word << endl;
}

void DoStuff2(int & one, int & two, string & word)
{
    cout << "DoStuff2 in:\t" << one << " " << two << " " << word << endl;
    one *= 2;
    cout << "DoStuff2 mid:\t" << one << " " << two << " " << word << endl;
    two += 1;
    word = "What's up Doc?";
    cout << "DoStuff2 out:\t" << one << " " << two << " " << word << endl;
}

int main()
{
    int num = 30;
    string name = "Bugs Bunny";

    DoStuff(num,name);
    cout << endl << "DoStuff main:\t" << num << " " << name << endl << endl;

    DoStuff2(num,num,name);
    cout << endl << "DoStuff2 main:\t" << num << " " << name << endl;
    return 0;
}
```

pbyvalue.cpp

The parameter `number` in the function `DoStuff` is passed by value, not by reference, so assignment to `number` does *not* affect the value of the argument `num`. The same does not hold for the reference parameter `word`; the changed value does change the value of the argument `name` in `main`.

In contrast, all parameters are reference parameters in `DoStuff2`. What's very tricky[4] about `DoStuff2` is that the reference parameters `one` and `two` both alias the same memory location `num` in `main`. Assignment to `one` is really assignment to `num` and thus also assignment to `two` since both `one` and `two` reference the same memory. It helps to draw a diagram like the one in Figure 6.2, but with arrows from `one` and `two` both pointing to the same memory location associated with `num` in `main`.

```
                        O U T P U T

prompt> pbyvalue
DoStuff in:        30  Bugs Bunny
DoStuff out:       60  What's up Doc?


DoStuff main:      30  What's up Doc?


DoStuff2 in:       30 30 What's up Doc?
DoStuff2 mid:      60 60 What's up Doc?
DoStuff2 out:      61 61 What's up Doc?


DoStuff2 main:     61 What's up Doc?
```

The first line of output prints the values that are passed to `DoStuff`. The value of the parameter `number` in `DoStuff` is the same as the value of `num` in `main` because this value is copied when the argument is passed to `DoStuff`. After the value is copied, there is no relationship between `number` and `num`. This can be seen in the first line of output generated in `main`: `num` is still 30. However, the change to parameter `word` does change `name` in `main`. Values are *not* copied when passed by reference. The identifiers `word` and `name` are aliases for the same memory location.

When a function is called and an argument passed to a reference parameter, we use the term **call by reference**. When an argument is copied into a function's parameter, we use the term **call by value**. Value parameters require time to copy the value and require memory to store the copied value; it's possible for this time and space to have an impact on a program's performance. Sometimes reference parameters are used to save time and space. Unfortunately, this permits the called function to change the value of the argument—the very reason we used reference parameters in Program 6.3. You can, however, protect against unwanted change and still have the efficiency of reference parameters when needed.

---

[4]I could have written "what's verwy twicky," but I didn't.

6.2.5 `const` Reference Parameters

Value parameters are copied from the corresponding argument, as shown in *pbyvalue.cpp,* Program 6.4. For parameters that require a large amount of memory, making the copy takes time in addition to the memory used for the copy. In contrast, reference parameters are not copied, and thus no extra memory is required and less time is used.

Some programs must make efficient use of time and memory space. Value parameters for large objects are problematic in such programs. Using **const reference** or **constant reference** parameters yields the efficiency of reference parameters and the safety of value parameters. "Safety" means that it's not possible to change a value parameter so that the argument is also changed. The argument is protected from accidental or malicious change. Like value parameters, `const` reference parameters cannot be changed by a function so that the argument changes (as we'll see, assignments to `const` reference parameters are prohibited by the compiler). A `const` reference parameter is defined using the `const` modifier in conjunction with an ampersand as shown in *constref.cpp,* Program 6.5. `Const` reference parameters are also called **read-only** parameters.

Program 6.5 constref.cpp

```
#include <iostream>
#include <string>
using namespace std;
#include "prompt.h"

// illustrates const reference parameters
// Owen Astrachan, 7/11/96, 4/19/99

void Print(const string & word);

int main()
{
    string word = PromptString("enter a word: ");

    Print("hello world");
    Print(word);
    Print(word + " " + word);

    return 0;
}

void Print(const string & word)
{
    cout << "printing: " << word << endl;
}
```

constref.cpp

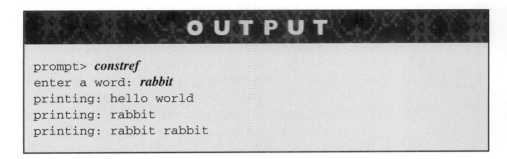

```
prompt> constref
enter a word: rabbit
printing: hello world
printing: rabbit
printing: rabbit rabbit
```

The parameter word in Print is a const reference parameter. The use of const prevents the code in Print from "accidentally" modifying the value of the argument corresponding to word. For example, adding the statement word = "hello" just before the output statement generates the following error message with one compiler:

```
Error   : cannot pass const/volatile data object to
           non-const/volatile member function
constref.cpp line 23  {word = "hello";
```

In addition, const reference parameters allow literals and expressions to be passed as arguments. In *constref.cpp,* the first call of Print passes the literal "hello world", and the third call passes the expression word + " " + word. Literals and expressions can be arguments passed to value parameters since the value parameter provides the memory. However, literals and expressions cannot be passed to reference parameters since there is no memory associated with either a literal or an expression. Fortunately, the C++ compiler will generate a temporary variable for literals and expressions when a const reference parameter is used. If the const modifier is removed from Print in *constref.cpp,* the program will fail to compile with most compilers.

> **Program Tip 6.9:   Parameters of programmer-defined classes like string should be const reference parameters rather than value parameters.** (Occasionally a copy is needed rather than a const reference parameter, but such situations are rare.) There is no reason to worry about this kind of efficiency for built-in types like int and double; these use relatively little memory, so that a copy takes no more time to create than a reference does, and no temporary variables are needed when literals and expressions are passed as arguments.

For some classes a specific function is needed to create a copy. If a class does not supply such a "copy-making" function—actually a special kind of constructor called a **copy constructor**—one will be generated by the compiler. This default copy constructor may not behave properly in certain situations that we'll discuss at length later. A brief discussion of copy constructors can be found in Chapter 12.

The compiler will allow only accessor functions (see Section 6.1) labeled as const member functions to be applied to a const reference parameter. If you try to invoke a mutator (non-const) member function on a const reference parameter, the compilation will catch this error and fail to compile the program.[5]

We want to develop question classes for different kinds of quizzes, but we need some more programming tools. In the next sections we'll see how to read from files instead of just from the keyboard. We'll also see how to write to files.

Pause to Reflect

6.9 What is the function header and body of a function GetName that prompts for a first and last name and returns two strings, one representing each name?

6.10 Write a function Roots having the following function header:

```
void Roots(double a, double b, double c,
           double & root1, double & root2)
// precondition:    a,b,c coefficients of
//                  ax^2 + bx + c
// postcondition:   sets root1 and root2 to roots
//                  of quadratic
```

that uses the quadratic formula

$$\frac{-b \pm \sqrt{b^2 - 4ac}}{2a}$$

to find the roots of a quadratic. The call Roots(1,5,6,r1,r2) would result in r1 and r2 being set to −2 and −3. You'll have to decide what to do if there are no real roots.

6.11 Suppose that a function Mystery has only value parameters. What is printed by the following statements? Why?

```
int num = 3;
double top = 4.5;
Mystery(num,top);
cout << num << " " << top << endl;
```

6.12 Write the header for a function that returns the number of weekdays (Monday through Friday) and weekend days (Saturday and Sunday) in a month and year that are input to the function as integer values using 1 for January and 12 for December. Don't write the function, just a header with pre- and postconditions.

6.13 Two formal parameters can alias the same argument as shown in Change:

---

[5]Some older compilers may issue a warning rather than an error, but 32-bit compilers will catch const errors and fail.

```
void Change(int & first, int & second)
{
    first += 2;
    second *= 2;
}
```

Using the function `Change` above, explain why 20 is printed by the code fragment below and determine what is printed if `num` is initialized to 3 rather than 8.

```
int main()
{
    int num = 8;
    Change(num,num);
    cout << num << endl;
    return 0;
}
```

6.14 It is often necessary to interchange, or swap, the values of two variables. For example, if $a = 5$ and $b = 7$, then swapping values would result in $a = 7$ and $b = 5$. Write the body of the function `Swap`. (*Hint:* You'll need to define a variable of type `int`.)

```
void Swap(int & a, int & b)
// postcondition: interchanges values of a and b
```

6.3   Reading Words: Stream Iteration

> If you steal from one author, it's plagiarism;
> if you steal from many, it's research.
> WILSON MIZNER

Word-processing programs merely manipulate words and characters, but scholars sometimes use programs that process character data to determine authorship. For example, literary investigators have sought to determine the authorship of Shakespeare's plays and sonnets. Some have argued that they were written by philosopher Francis Bacon or dramatist Christopher Marlowe, but most Shakespearean authorities doubt these claims. To amass evidence regarding the authorship of a literary work, it is possible to gather statistics to create a "literary fingerprint." Such a fingerprint can be based on frequently used words, phrases, or allusions. It can also include a count of uncommon words. Computer programs facilitate the gathering of these data.

In this section, we demonstrate the pattern of iterating over words and characters by simpler, but similar, kinds of programs. These programs will count words and letters—the kind of task that is built into many word-processing programs and used when a limit on the number of words in an essay is set (e.g., by newspaper columnists and students writing English papers). We'll first write a program that counts words entered by the user or stored in a text file. A text file is the kind of file in which C++ programs are stored or word-processing documents are saved when the latter are saved as plain text.[6]

I'll adopt a four-step process in explaining how to develop the program. As you write and develop programs, you should think about these steps and use them if they make sense. These steps are meant as hints or guidelines, not rules that should be slavishly followed.

6.3.1 Recommended Problem-Solving and Programming Steps

1. Think about how to solve the problem with paper, pencil, and brain (but no computer). Consider how to extend the human solution to a computer-based solution. You may find it useful to sketch a solution using **pseudocode,** a mixture of English and C++.

2. If, after thinking about how to solve the problem with a computer (and perhaps writing out a solution), you are not sure how to proceed, pause. Try thinking about solving a related problem whose solution is similar to a program previously studied.

3. Develop a working program or class in an iterative manner, implementing one part at a time before implementing the entire program. This can help localize problems and errors because you'll be able to focus on small pieces of the program rather than the entirety.

4. When you've finished, pause to reflect on what you've learned about C++, programming, and program design and implementation. You may be able to develop guidelines useful in your own programming, and perhaps useful to others as well.

We will use these steps to solve the word count problem. First we'll specify the problem in more detail and develop a pseudocode solution. This step will show that we're missing some knowledge of how to read from files, so we'll solve a related problem on the way to counting the words in a text file. After writing a complete program we'll develop a class-based alternative that will provide code that's easier to reuse in other contexts.

6.3.2 A Pseudocode Solution

Counting the words in this chapter or in Shakespeare's play *Hamlet* by hand would be a boring and arduous task. However, it's an easy task for a computer program—simply scan the text and count each word. It would be a good idea to specify more precisely what a "word" is. The first part of any programming task is often a careful **specification** of exactly what the program should do. This may require defining terms such as *word*. In this case, we'll assume that a word is a sequence of characters separated from other words by white space. White space characters are included in the escape characters in Table A.5 in How to A; for our purposes, white space is ' ', '\t', and '\n': the space, tab, and newline characters.[7] Escape sequences represent certain characters such

---

[6]The adjective *plain* is used to differentiate text files from files in word processors that show font, page layout, and formatting commands. Most word processors have an option to save files as plain text.

[7]Other white space characters are formfeed, return, and vertical tab.

as the tab and newline in C++. To print a backslash requires an escape sequence; \\ prints as a single backslash.[8]

For this problem, we'll write a pseudocode description of a loop to count words. Pseudocode is a language that has characteristics of C++ (or Java, or some other language), but liberties are taken with syntax. Sketching such a description can help focus your attention on the important parts of a program.

```
numWords = 0;
while (words left to read)
{    read a word;
     numWords++;
}
print number of words read
```

White Space–Delimited Input for Strings. These pseudocode instructions are very close to C++, except for the test of the while loop and the statement read a word. In fact, we've seen code that reads a word using the extraction operator >> (e.g., Program 3.1, *macinput.cpp*). White space separates one string from another when the extraction operator >> is used to process input. This is just what we want to read words. As an example, what happens if you type steel-gray tool-box when the code below is executed?

```
string first, second;
cout << "enter two words:";
cin >> first >> second;
cout << first << " : " << second << endl;
```

Since the space between the *y* of *steel-gray* and the *t* of *tool-box* is used to delimit the words, the output is the following:

```
steel-gray : tool-box
```

As another example, consider this loop, which will let you enter six words:

```
string word;
int numWords;
for(numWords=0; numWords < 6; numWords++)
{    cin >> word;
     cout << numWords << " " << word << endl;
}
```

---

[8]Consider buying groceries. Often a plastic bar is used to separate your groceries from the next person's. What happens if you go to a store to buy one of the plastic bars? If the person behind you is buying one too, what can you use to separate your purchases?

Suppose you type the words below with a tab character between `it` and `ain't`, the return key pressed after `broke`, and two spaces between `don't` and `fix`.

```
If it        ain't broke,
don't    fix it.
```

OUTPUT

```
0   If
1   it
2   ain't
3   broke,
4   don't
5   fix
```

Although the input typed by the user appears as two lines, the input stream `cin` processes a sequence of characters, not a sequence of words or lines. The characters on the input stream appear as literally a stream of characters (the symbol ⊔ is used to represent a space).

```
If⊔it\tain\'t⊔broke,\ndon\'t⊔⊔fix it.
```

There are three different escape characters in this stream: the tab character, `\t`, the newline character, `\n`, and the apostrophe character, `\'`. We don't need to be aware of these escape characters, or any other individual character, to read a sequence of words using the loop shown above. At a low level a stream is a sequence of characters, but at a higher level we can use the extraction operator, `>>`, to view a stream as a sequence of words.

The extraction operator, `>>`—when used with `string` variables—groups adjacent, non-white space characters on the stream to form words as shown by the output of the `while` loop above. Note that punctuation is included as part of the word `broke,` because all non-white space characters, including punctuation, are the same from the point of view of the input stream `cin`. Since the operator `>>` treats all white space the same, the newline is treated the same as the spaces or tabs between adjacent words. Any sequence of white space characters is treated as white space, as can be seen in the example above, where a tab character space separates `it` from `ain't` and two spaces separate `don't` from `fix`.

Now that we have a better understanding of how the extraction operator works with input streams, characters, and words, we need to return to the original problem of counting words in a text file. We address two problems: reading an arbitrary number of words and reading from a file. We cannot use a definite loop because we don't know in advance how many words are in a file—that's what we're trying to determine.

6.3.3   Solving a Related Problem

How can a loop be programmed to stop when there are no more words in the input? Step two of our method requires solving a familiar but related problem when confronted with a task whose solution isn't immediately apparent. In this case, suppose that words are to be entered and counted until you enter some specific word signaling that no more words will be entered. The test of a `while` loop used to solve this task can consist of `while (word != LAST_WORD)`, where `LAST_WORD` is the special word indicating the end of the input and `word` holds the value of the string that you enter.

This is an example of a **sentinel** loop—the sentinel is the special value that indicates the end of input. Such loops are classic fence post problems: you must enter a word before the test is made and, if the test indicates there are more words, you must enter another word. Program 6.6 shows such a sentinel loop accepting entries until the user enters the word *end*. The special sentinel value is *not* considered part of the data being processed. Sometimes it's difficult to designate a sentinel value because no value can be singled out as invalid data. In the second run the number of words does not appear immediately after the word *end* is entered because more typing takes place afterward. The number of words is not output until after the return key is pressed, and this occurs several words after the word *end* is entered.

Program 6.6   sentinel.cpp

```cpp
#include <iostream>
#include <string>
using namespace std;

    // count words in the standard input stream, cin

int main()
{
    const string LAST_WORD = "end";

    string word;
    int numWords = 0;                    // initially, no words

    cout << "type '" << LAST_WORD << "' to terminate input" << endl;

    cin >> word;
    while (word != LAST_WORD)            // read succeeded
    {   numWords++;
        cin >> word;
    }
    cout << "number of words read = " << numWords << endl;

    return 0;
}
```

sentinel.cpp

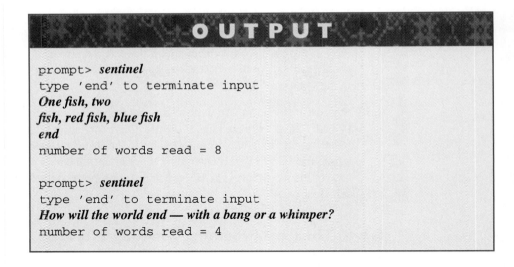

```
prompt> sentinel
type 'end' to terminate input
One fish, two
fish, red fish, blue fish
end
number of words read = 8

prompt> sentinel
type 'end' to terminate input
How will the world end — with a bang or a whimper?
number of words read = 4
```

This apparent delay is a side effect of **buffered input,** which allows the user to make corrections as input is entered. When input is buffered, the program doesn't actually receive the input and doesn't do any processing until the return key is pressed. The input is stored in a memory area called a *buffer* and then passed to the program when the line is finished and the return key pressed. Most systems use buffered input, although sometimes it is possible to turn this buffering off.

Although we still haven't solved the problem of developing a loop that reads all words (until none are left), the sentinel loop is a start in the right direction and will lead to a solution in the next section.

Pause to Reflect

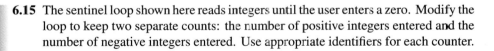

6.15 The sentinel loop shown here reads integers until the user enters a zero. Modify the loop to keep two separate counts: the number of positive integers entered and the number of negative integers entered. Use appropriate identifiers for each counter.

```
const int SENTINEL = 0;
int count = 0;

int num;
cin >> num;
while (num != SENTINEL)
{   count++;
    cin >> num;
}
```

6.16 Does your system buffer input in the manner described in this section? What happens if Program 6.6 is run and the user enters the text below? Why?

```
This is the start, this is the end --- nothing
is in between.
```

6.17 Another technique used with sentinel loops is to force the loop to iterate once. This is called **priming** the loop.[9] If the statement cin >> word before the while loop in Program 6.6 is replaced with the statement word = "dummy";, how should the body of the while loop be modified so that the program counts words in the same way?

6.18 Suppose that you want to write a loop that stops after either of two sentinel values is read. Using the technique of the previous problem in which the loop is forced to iterate once by giving a dummy value to the string variable used for input, write a loop that counts words entered by the user until the user enters either the word end or the word finish. Be sure to use appropriate const definitions for both sentinels.

6.3.4   The Final Program: Counting Words

We are finally ready to finish a program that counts all the words in a text file or all the words a user enters. We would like to refine the loop in Program 6.6, *sentinel.cpp,* so that it reads all input but does not require a sentinel value to identify the last word in the input stream. This will let us calculate the number of words (or characters, or occurrences of the word *the*) in any text file since we won't need to rely on a specific word to be the sentinel last word. This is possible in C++ because the extraction operator not only extracts strings (or numbers) from an input stream, but returns a result indicating whether the extraction succeeds. For example, a code fragment used earlier read the words steel-gray and tool-box using the statement

```
cin >> first >> second;
```

This statement is read, or parsed, by the C++ compiler as though it were written as

```
(cin >> first) >> second;
```

because >> is left-associative (see Table A.4 in How to A). Think of the input stream, cin, as flowing through the extraction operators, >>. The first word on the stream is extracted and stored in first, and the stream continues to flow so that the second word on the stream can be extracted and stored in second. The result of the first extraction, the value of the expression (cin >> first), is the input stream, cin, without the word that has been stored in the variable first.

The Return Value of operator >>. The most important point of this explanation is that the expression (cin >> first) not only reads a string from cin but returns the stream so that it can be used again, (e.g., for another extraction operation). Although it may seem strange at first, the stream itself can be tested to see if the extraction succeeded. The following code fragment shows how this is done.

---

[9]The derivation of priming probably comes from old water pumps that had to be *primed* or filled with water before they started.

```
int num;
cout << "enter a number: ";
if (cin >> num)
{   cout << "valid integer: "   << num << endl;
}
else
{   cout << "invalid integer: " << num << endl;
}
```

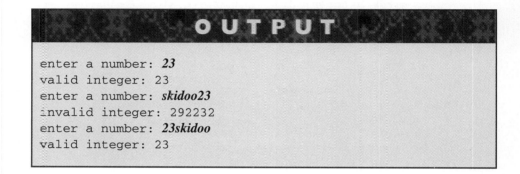

```
enter a number: 23
valid integer: 23
enter a number: skidoo23
invalid integer: 292232
enter a number: 23skidoo
valid integer: 23
```

The expression (cin >> num) evaluates to true when the extraction of an integer from cin has succeeded. The characters skidoo23 do not represent a valid integer, so the message invalid integer is printed. The integer printed here is a garbage value. Since no value is stored in the variable num when num is first defined, whatever value is in the memory associated with num is printed. Other runs of the program may print different values. Note that when 23skidoo is entered, the extraction succeeds and 23 is stored in the variable num. In this case, the characters skidoo remain on the input stream and can be extracted by a statement such as cin >> word, where word is a string variable. The use of the extraction operator to both extract input and return a value used in a Boolean test can be confusing because the extraction operation does two things.

Some people prefer to write the if statement using the fail member function of the stream cin:

```
cin >> num;
if (! cin.fail())
{   cout << "valid integer: "   << num << endl;
}
```

The member function fail returns true when an extraction operation has failed and returns false otherwise. You do not need to use fail explicitly because the extraction operator returns the same value as fail; but some programmers find it clearer to use fail. The stream member function fail returns true whenever a stream operation has failed, but the only operations we've seen so far are I/O operations. Details of all the stream member functions can be found in How to B.

Program 6.7 correctly counts the number of words in the input stream `cin` by testing the value returned by the extraction operator in a `while` loop.

Program 6.7 countw.cpp

```cpp
#include <iostream>
#include <string>
using namespace std;

    // count words in the standard input stream, cin

int main()
{
    string word;
    int numWords = 0;                      // initially, no words

    while (cin >> word)                    // read succeeded
    {   numWords++;
    }
    cout << "number of words read = " << numWords << endl;
    return 0;
}
```

countw.cpp

The test of the `while` loop is false when the extraction operation fails. When reading strings, extraction fails only when there is no more input. As shown above, input with integers (and `doubles`) can fail if a noninteger value is entered. Since any sequence of characters is a string, extraction fails for strings only when there is no more input. If you're using the program interactively, you indicate no more input by typing a special character called the **end-of-file** character. This character should be typed as the first and only character on a line, followed by pressing the return key. When UNIX or Macintosh computers are used, this character is Ctrl-D, and on MS-DOS/Windows machines this character is Ctrl-Z. To type this character the control key must be held down at the same time as the D (or Z) key is pressed. Such control characters are sometimes not shown on the screen but are used to indicate to the system running the program that input is finished (end of file is reached).

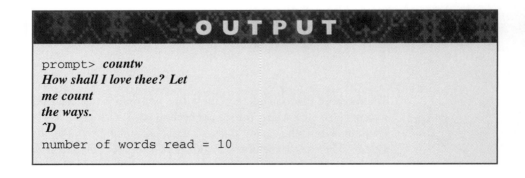

```
prompt> countw
How shall I love thee? Let
me count
the ways.
^D
number of words read = 10
```

The end-of-file character was typed *not* as the string ^D but by holding down the control key and pressing the D key simultaneously.

We'll modify *countw.cpp* so that it will count words stored in a text file; then we'll see how to turn this program into a class that makes it a general-purpose programming tool.

6.3.5 Streams Associated with Files

In Program 6.6, *sentinel.cpp,* and Program 6.7, *countw.cpp,* the standard input stream, cin, was used as the source of words. Clearly you can't be expected to type in all of *Hamlet* to count the words in that play. Instead, you need some way to create a stream associated with a text file (rather than with the keyboard and the standard input stream, cin). A class ifstream, accessible by including the file <fstream> (or <fstream.h> on some systems), is used for streams that are associated with text files. Program 6.8, *countw2.cpp,* is a modification of Program 6.7 but uses an ifstream variable.

Program 6.8   countw2.cpp

```
#include <iostream>
#include <fstream>                 // for ifstream
#include <string>
#include "prompt.h"

   // count words in a file specified by the user

int main()
{
    string word;
    int numWords = 0;                        // initially no words
    int sum = 0;                             // sum of all word lengths
    ifstream input;

    string filename = PromptString("enter name of file: ");

    input.open(filename.c_str());            // bind input to named file

    while (input >> word)                    // read succeeded
    {   numWords++;
        sum += word.length();
    }
    cout << "number of words read = " << numWords << endl;
    cout << "average word length = " << sum/numWords << endl;

    return 0;
}
```

countw2.cpp

In the following runs, the file melville.txt is the text of Herman Melville's *Bartleby, The Scrivener: A Story of Wall-Street.* The file hamlet.txt is the complete text of William Shakespeare's *Hamlet.* These, as well as other works by Shakespeare, Edgar Allen Poe, Mark Twain, and others, are accessible as text files.[10]

```
OUTPUT

prompt> countw2
enter name of file: melville.txt
number of words read = 14353
average word length = 4
prompt> countw2
enter name of file: hamlet.txt
number of words read = 31956
average word length = 4


prompt> countw2
enter name of file: macbet.txt
number of words read = 0
Floating exception
```

The variable `input` is an instance of the class `ifstream`—an **input file stream**— and supports extraction using `>>` just as `cin` does. The variable `input` is associated, or **bound,** to a particular user-specified text file with the member function `ifstream::open()`.

```
input.open(filename.c_str());    // bind input to named file
```

The string `filename` that holds the name of the user-specified file is an argument to the member function `ifstream::open()`. The standard string member function `c_str()` returns a C-style string required by the prototype for the function `open()`. The `open()` function may be modified to accept standard strings, but the conversion function `c_str()` will always work. Once `input` is bound to a text file, the extraction operator `>>` can be used to extract items from the file (instead of from the user typing at the keyboard as is the case with `cin`).

There is a similar class **ofstream** (for *output file stream*) also accessible by including the header file `<fstream>`. This class supports the use of the insertion operator, `<<`, just as `ifstream` supports extraction, using the `>>` operator. The code fragment below writes the numbers 1 to 1,024 to a file named `"nums.dat"`, one number per line.

```
ofstream output;
output.open("nums.dat");
int k;
for(k=0; k < 1024; k++)
```

---

[10]The files containing these literary works are available with the material that supports this book. These texts are in the public domain, which makes on-line versions of them free.

```
{   output << k << endl;
}
```

In the example of using Program 6.8, file `macbet.txt` has no words. I made a mistake when entering the name of the file to read (I meant to type `macbeth.txt`), which caused the extraction operation to fail because the file does not exist. Because no words were read, the average calculation resulted in a division-by-zero error. On some systems, division by zero can cause the machine to crash. A **robust** program protects against errors. Program 6.8 could be made robust by guarding the average calculation with an `if` statement to check whether `numWords == 0`. It's also possible to check the result of the function `ifstream::open` as shown:

```
input.open(filename.c_str());
if (input.fail())
{   cout << "open for " << filename << " failed " << endl;
}
```

You should always look carefully at program output to determine if it meets your expectations. The average printed for both *Hamlet* and *Melville* is four. This is surprising; you probably do not expect the averages to be exactly the same. To fix this problem we'll need to change how the average is calculated; we need to use `double` values.

6.3.6 Type Casting

Since both `numWords` and `sum` are `int` variables, the result of the division operator, `/`, is an `int`. How can the correct average be calculated? One method is to define `sum` to be a `double` variable. Since the statement

```
sum += word.length();
```

will correctly accumulate a sum of integers even when `sum` is a `double` variable, this method will work reasonably well. However, it may not be the best method because the wrong type (`double`) is being used to accumulate the sum of integers. Instead we can use a **type cast.** This is a method that allows one type to be converted (sometimes called **coerced**) into another type. For example, the statement

```
cout << "average length = " << double(sum)/numWords << endl;
```

yields the correct average of 4.705 for *Melville* and 4.362 for *Hamlet*. The expression `double(sum)` shows that the type `double` is used like a function name with an argument `sum`. The result is a `double` that is as close to the integer value of `sum` as possible. Since the result of a mixed-type arithmetic expression is of the highest type (in this case, `double`), 3.5 will be printed. You can also write a cast as `((double) sum)/numWords`.[11] A cast has higher precedence than arithmetic operators (see Table A.4 in How to A), so `(double) sum/numWords` will also work because `sum` is cast to a `double` value before the division occurs.

---

[11]This is the C-style of casting but can be used in C++ and is useful if the cast is to a type whose name is more than one word, such as `long int`.

Alternatively, the statement

```
cout << "average length = " << sum/double(numWords) << endl;
```

also gives a correct result since the mixed-type expression yields a `double` result.

> **Program Tip 6.10: Be careful when casting a value of one type to another.**
> It is possible that a type cast will result in a value changing. Casting is sometimes necessary, but you should be cautious in converting values of one type to another type.

For example, using Turbo C++, the output of the three statements

```
cout << int(32800.2) << endl;
cout << double(333333333333333) << endl;
cout << int(3.6) << endl;
```

follows:

```
-32736
9.214908e+08
3
```

The third number printed is easy to explain—casting a double to an `int` **truncates,** or chops off, the decimal places. The first two numbers exceed the range of valid values for `int` and `double`, respectively, using Turbo C++.

In general, casting is sometimes necessary, but you must be careful that the values being cast are valid values in the type being cast to.

Casting with `static_cast`. Four cast operators are part of standard C++. In this book the operator `static_cast` will be used.[12] As an example, the statement

```
cout << double(sum)/numWords << endl;
```

is written as shown in the following to use the `static_cast` operator:

```
cout << static_cast<double>(sum)/numWords << endl;
```

Your C++ compiler may not support `static_cast`, but this will change soon as the C++ standard is adopted. Using `static_cast` makes casts easier to spot in code. Also, since casting a value of one type to another is prone to error, some people prefer to use `static_cast` because it leads to ugly code and will be less tempting to use.

---

[12]The other cast operators are `const_cast`, `dynamic_cast`, and `reinterpret_cast`; we'll have occasion to use these operators, but rarely.

6.3.7 A Word-Reading Class Using `ifstream`

The third of the program development guidelines given in Section 6.3.1 calls for programs to be developed using an iterative process. Sometimes this means redesigning an already working program so that it will be useful in different settings. In the case of Program 6.7, *countw.cpp,* we want to reimplement the program in a new way to study a programming pattern that we will see on many occasions throughout this book. The resulting program will be longer, but it will yield a C++ class that is easier to modify for new situations than the original program. It will also help us focus on a pattern you can use in other classes and programs: the idea of processing "entries." In this case we'll process all the words in a text file. The same design pattern can be used to process all the prime numbers between 1000 and 9999, all the files in a computer disk directory, and all the tracks on a compact disk.

The pattern of iteration over entries is expressed in pseudocode as

```
find the first entry;
while (the current entry is valid)
{
   process the current entry;
   advance to the next entry;
}
```

We'll use a `WordStreamIterator` class to get words one at a time from the text file.

As an example of how to use the class, the function `main` below is black-box equivalent to Program 6.7, *countw.cpp.* For any input, the output of these two programs is the same.

```
int main()
{
    string word;
    int numWords = 0;            // initially, no words
    WordStreamIterator iter;

    iter.Open(PromptString("enter name of file: "));

    for(iter.Init(); iter.HasMore(); iter.Next())
    {   numWords++;
    }
    cout << "number of words read = " << numWords << endl;

    return 0;
}
```

This program fragment may seem more complex than the code in *countw2.cpp,* Program 6.8. This is often the case; using a class can yield code that is lengthier and more verbose than non–class-based code. However, class-based code is often easier to adapt to different situations. Using classes also makes programs easier to develop on more than one computing platform. For example, if there are differences in how text files are read using C++ on different computers, these differences can be encapsulated in classes and made invisible to programmers who can use the classes without knowing the implementation details. This makes the code more portable. The process of developing code in one computing environment and moving it to another is called **porting** the code. The member functions `Init`, `HasMore`, `Next`, and `Current` together form a programming pattern called an **iterator**. This iterator pattern is used to loop over values stored somewhere, such as in an `ifstream` variable. By using the same names in other iterating contexts we may be able to develop correct code more quickly. Using the same names also lets us use programming tools developed for iterators.

We have focused on how to use classes rather than on how to design classes. In general, designing classes and programs is a difficult task. One design rule that helps is building new designs based on proven designs. This is especially true when a design pattern can be reused.

> **Program Tip 6.11:** **A pattern is a solution to a problem in a context.** In the case of the `WordStreamIterator` class, the problem is accessing the strings in a stream many times within the same program. The class hides the details of the stream functions and lets us concentrate on accessing a sequence of strings rather than on details of how to reread a stream.

The class declaration for `WordStreamIterator` is found in *worditer.h*, Program G.6 in How to G. We won't look at the implementation in *worditer.cpp*, but the code is provided for use with this book. You need to understand how to use the class, but to use the class you don't need to understand the implementation.

In the case of a `WordStreamIterator` object, you should know that the member function `WordStreamIterator::HasMore` will return true if there is more input to be read. When `HasMore` returns false, accessing the current word using the `Current` member function is not a valid operation.

The constructor `WordStreamIterator::WordStreamIterator` leaves the object `iter` in a state where accessing the current word is *not* valid. In this state the function `HasMore` will return false. You must call the function `Init` to access words. The call `iter.Init` reads the first word from the input stream and updates the internal state accordingly.

Pause to Reflect

6.19 What statements can be added to *countw2.cpp*, Program 6.8, so that three values are tracked: the number of small (one- to three-letter) words, the number of medium (four- to seven-letter) words, and the number of large (eight-letter or longer) words?

6.20 What is the function header for a function that accepts a file name and returns the number of small, medium, and large words as defined in the previous exercise? (The function has four parameters, the file name is passed into the function, and the other values are returned from the function via parameters.)

6.21 What is the value of $1/2$ and why is it different from $1/2.0$? What is the value of `20/static_cast<double>(6)`?

6.22 Write code that prompts for two file names, one for input and one for output. Every word in the input file should be written to the output file, one word per line.

6.23 The statement below reads one string and two `ints`:

```
string s; int m,n;
cin >> s >> m >>n;
```

The statement succeeds in reading three values if the user types `"hello 12 3 "` (without the quotes). What is the value of n in this case? If the user types `"hello 1 2 3 4 5"` the statement succeeds (what is the value of n?), but if it is executed immediately again, the value of n will be 5. Why, and what is the value of s after the statement executes again?

6.24 Suppose a text file named `"quiz.dat"` stores student information, one student per line. Each student's first name, last name, and five test scores are on one line (there are no spaces other than between names and scores).

```
owen astrachan 70 85 80 70 60
josh astrachan 100 100 95 97 93
gail chapman 88 90 92 94 96
susan rodger 91 91 91 55 91
```

Write a loop to read information for all students and to print the average for each student.

6.25 Why can't the `WordStreamIterator` class be used to solve the problem in the previous exercise? (Knowing what you've learned so far, there is a way to solve the problem using the function `atoi` from *strutils.h*; see How to G.)

6.4 Finding Extreme Values

> We ascribe beauty to that which is simple,
> which has no superfluous parts;
> which exactly answers its end,
> which stands related to all things,
> which is the mean of many extremes.
> RALPH WALDO EMERSON
> *The Conduct of Life*

The maximum and minimum values in a set of data are sometimes called **extreme** values. In this section we'll examine code to find the maximum (or minimum) values in a set of data. For example, instead of just counting the number of words in Shakespeare's *Hamlet*, we might like to know what word occurs most often. Using the `WordStreamIterator` class we can do so, although the program is very slow.

Later in the chapter I will introduce a mechanism for speeding up the program. As a preliminary step, we'll look at *mindata.cpp,* Program 6.9, designed to find the minimum of all numbers in the standard input stream.

The `if` statement compares the value of the number just read with the current minimum value. A new value is assigned to `minimum` only when the newly read number is smaller. However, Program 6.9 does not always work as intended, as you may be able to see from the second run of the program. Using the second run, you may reason about a mistake in the program: the variable `minimum` is initialized incorrectly. You may wonder about what happens when the string `"apple"` is entered when a number is expected. As you can see from the output, the program counts only four numbers as read in the second run.

The operator `>>` fails when you attempt to extract an integer but enter a noninteger value such as `"apple"`. The operator `>>` fails in the following situations:

1. There are no more data to be read (extracted) from the input stream (i.e., all input has been processed).

2. There was never any data because the input stream was not bound to any file. This can happen when an `ifstream` object is constructed and initialized with the name of a file that doesn't exist or isn't accessible.

3. The data to be read are not of the correct type (e.g., attempting to read the string `"apple"` into an integer variable).

Program 6.9 mindata.cpp
_____

```cpp
#include <iostream>
using namespace std;

    // determine minimum of all numbers in input stream

int main()
{
    int numNums = 0;                    // initially, no numbers
    int minimum = 0;                    // tentative minimal value is 0

    int number;
    while (cin >> number)
    {   numNums++;
        if (number < minimum)
        {   minimum = number;
        }
    }
    cout << "number of numbers = " << numNums << endl;
    cout << "minimal number is " << minimum << endl;

    return 0;
}
```

mindata.cpp

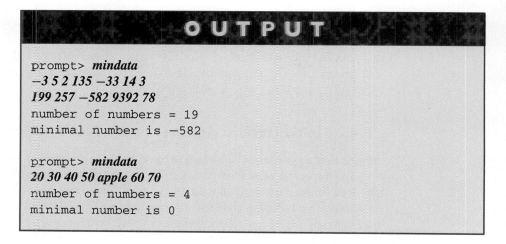

```
prompt> mindata
−3 5 2 135 −33 14 3
199 257 −582 9392 78
number of numbers = 19
minimal number is −582

prompt> mindata
20 30 40 50 apple 60 70
number of numbers = 4
minimal number is 0
```

There are two methods for fixing the program so that it will work regardless of what integer values are entered; currently the test in the `if` statement of *mindata.cpp* will never be true if the user enters only positive numbers.

■ Initialize `minimum` to "infinity" so the first time the `if` statement is executed the entered value will be less than `minimum`.

■ Initialize `minimum` to the first value entered on the input stream.

We'll elaborate on each of these approaches in turn.

6.4.1 Largest/Smallest Values

To implement the first approach we'll take advantage of the existence of a largest integer in C++. Since integers (and other types such as `double`) are stored in a computer using a fixed amount of memory, there cannot be arbitrarily large or small values. In the standard system file `<climits>` (or `limits.h`), several useful constants are defined:

```
INT_MAX    INT_MIN    LONG_MAX    LONG_MIN
```

These constants represent, respectively, the largest and smallest `int` values and the largest and smallest `long` values. We can now initialize `minimum` from Program 6.9 as follows (assuming `<climits>` is included):

```
int main()
{
    int numNums = 0;         // initially, no numbers
    int minimum = INT_MAX;   // all values less than this
}
```

The program finds the correct minimum because the `if` test evaluates to true the first time, since any integer value is less than or equal to `INT_MAX`. However, if only values of INT_MAX are encountered, the test of the if statement will never be true. In this case the program still finds the correct minimum of INT_MAX.

Similar constants exist for double values; these are accessed in <cfloat> (or <float.h>). The largest and smallest double values are represented by the constants DBL_MIN and DBL_MAX, respectively.

6.4.2   Initialization: Another Fence Post Problem

Implementing the second approach to the extreme value problem—using the first item read as the initial value for minimum—is a typical fence post problem. An item must be read before the loop to initialize minimum. Items must continue to be read within the loop. In developing code for this approach, we must decide what to do if no items are entered. What is the minimum of no values? Perhaps the safest approach is to print an error message as shown in Program 6.10.

Program 6.10 mindata2.cpp

```cpp
#include <iostream>
using namespace std;

    // determine minimum of all numbers in input stream
    // illustrates fencepost problem: first item is minimum initialization

int main()
{
    int numNums = 0;                // initially, no numbers
    int minimum;                    // smallest number entered
    int number;                     // user entered number

    if (cin >> number)              // read in first value
    {   minimum = number;           // to initialize minimum
        numNums++;
    }
    while (cin >> number)           // read in any remaining values
    {   numNums++;
        if (number < minimum)
        {   minimum = number;
        }
    }
    if (numNums > 0)
    {   cout << "number of numbers = " << numNums << endl;
        cout << "minimal number is " << minimum << endl;
    }
    else
    {   cout << "no numbers entered, no minimum found" << endl;
    }
    return 0;
}
```

mindata2.cpp

The input statement `cin >> number` is the test of the `if` statement. It ensures that a number was read. Another approach to using the first number read as the initial value of `minimum` uses an `if` statement in the body of the `while` loop to differentiate between the first number and all other numbers. The value of `numNums` can be used for this purpose.

```
while (cin >> number)
{   numNums++;
    if (numNums == 1 || number < minimum)
    {   minimum = number;
    }
}
```

Many people prefer the first approach because it avoids an extra check in the body of the `while` loop. The check `numNums == 1` is true only once, but it is checked every time through the loop. In general, you should prefer an approach that does not check a special case over and over when the special case can occur only once. On the other hand, the check in the loop body results in shorter code because there is no need to read an initial value for `minimum`. Since code isn't duplicated (before the loop and in the loop), there is less of a maintenance problem because code won't have to be changed in two places. The extra check in the loop body may result in slightly slower code, but unless you have determined that this is a time-critical part of a program, ease of code maintenance should probably be of greater concern than a very small gain in efficiency. There is no single rule you can use to determine which is the best method. As with many problems, the best method depends on the exact nature of the problem.

Program Tip 6.12: The safest approach to solving extreme problems is to use the first value for initialization of all variables that track the extreme (minimum or maximum). If you're finding the minimum or maximum of numeric values represented by `int` or `double`, then constants like `INT_MIN` can be used, but using the first value is always safe.

Pause to Reflect

6.26 If *mindata.cpp,* Program 6.9, is modified so that it reads floating-point numbers (of type `double`) instead of integers, which variables' types change? What other changes are necessary?

6.27 If the largest and smallest in a sequence of `BigInt` values are being determined, what is the appropriate method for initializing the variables tracking the extreme values? (The type `BigInt` was introduced in Section 5.1.3.)

6.28 What happens if each of the following statements is used to calculate the average of the values entered in Program 6.8? Why?

```
cout << "average word length = "
     << (double) sum/numWords << endl;
```

Does the statement below produce different output?

```
cout << "average word length = "
     << (double sum/numWords) << endl;
```

6.29 Write and run a small program to output the largest and smallest integer values on your system.

6.30 Modify *mindata.cpp*, Program 6.9, and *mindata2.cpp*, Program 6.10, to calculate the maximum of all values read.

6.31 Strings can be compared alphabetically (also called *lexicographically*) using the operators < and > so that "apple" < "bat" and "cabin" > "cabana". What is the function header and body of a function that exhaustively reads input and returns the alphabetically first and last word read?

6.4.3 Word Frequencies

We can use the method of finding extreme values from *mindata.cpp*, Program 6.9, and the WordStreamIterator class to find the word that occurs most often in a text file. The idea is to read one word at a time using a WordStreamIterator object and to use another iterator to read the entire text file from beginning to end counting how many times the given word occurs. This is shown in Program 6.11. Using nested iterators in this way results in a very slow program because if there are 2000 words in a file, the file will be read 2000 times. Redundancy occurs because we don't have the programming tools to track whether a word is already counted; thus we may count the number of times *the* occurs more than 100 times.

Program 6.11   maxword.cpp

```
#include <iostream>
#include <string>
using namespace std;
#include "worditer.h"

#include "prompt.h"

// illustrates nested loops using WordStreamIterator class
// to find the word that occurs most often in a file
// Owen Astrachan, 2/13/96, 4/10/99

int main()
{
    int maxOccurs = 0;
    int wordCount = 0;
    string word,maxWord;
    string filename = PromptString("enter file name: ");
    WordStreamIterator outer,inner;
```

```
    outer.Open(filename);          // open two iterators
    inner.Open(filename);

    for(outer.Init(); outer.HasMore(); outer.Next())
    {   wordCount++;
        word = outer.Current();    // current word for comparison
        int count = 0;             // count # occurrences

        for(inner.Init(); inner.HasMore(); inner.Next())
        {   if (inner.Current() == word)   // found another occurrence
            {   count++;
            }
        }
        if (count > maxOccurs)             // maximal so far
        {   maxOccurs = count;
            maxWord = word;
        }
        if (wordCount % 100 == 0)          // update "progress bar"
        {   cout << "..";
            if (wordCount % 1000 == 0) cout << endl;
        }
    }
    cout << endl << "word \"" << maxWord << "\" occurs "
        << maxOccurs << " times" << endl;
    return 0;
}
```
maxword.cpp

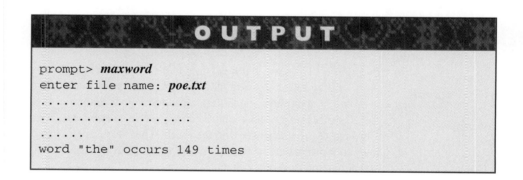

```
prompt> maxword
enter file name: poe.txt
. . . . . . . . . . . . . . . . . . .
. . . . . . . . . . . . . . . . . . .
. . . . . .
word "the" occurs 149 times
```

The outer loop, using the iterator `outer`, processes each word from a text file one at a time. The inner loop reads the entire file, counting how many times `word` occurs in the file. Since each `WordStreamIterator` object has its own state, the iterator `outer` keeps track of where it is in the input stream, even as the iterator `inner` reads the entire stream from beginning to end.

Pause to Reflect

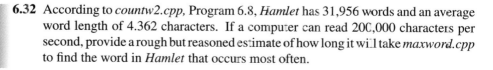

6.32 According to *countw2.cpp,* Program 6.8, *Hamlet* has 31,956 words and an average word length of 4.362 characters. If a computer can read 200,000 characters per second, provide a rough but reasoned estimate of how long it will take *maxword.cpp* to find the word in *Hamlet* that occurs most often.

6.33 Suppose that the code in `main` from *mindata.cpp*, Program 6.9, is moved to a function named `ReadNums` so that the new body of `main` is

```
{
    ....
    ReadNums(numNums,minimum);
    cout << "number of numbers = " << numNums << endl;
    cout << "minimal number is " << minimum << endl;
}
```

What is the function header and body of `ReadNums`? How would the function header and body change if only the average of the numbers read is to be returned?

6.34 How can you modify *maxword.cpp* so that instead of printing two dots every 100 words as it does currently, it prints a percentage of how much it has processed, like this:

```
10%...20%...30%...40%...50%...60%...70%...80%...90%...
 word "the" occurs 149 times
```

(Hint: Count the total words first.)

6.4.4   Using the `CTimer` class

Program 6.11 is slow, but how slow is it? User-interface studies show that people are more willing to put up with slow programs, or slow Internet connections, if feedback is provided about how much time a program or download is expected to take.[13] Using the class `CTimer`, whose interface is given in *ctimer.h* as Program G.5 in How to G, allows us to provide a user with feedback. The `CTimer` class also allows us to time how long code fragments or functions take to execute, which, in turn, allows us to evaluate algorithm and program efficiency.

Program 6.12 shows how `CTimer` can be used to time loop execution. The program shows all but one of the `CTimer` member functions. The `CTimer::Reset` function resets a `CTimer`'s internal stopwatch to zero. The precision or **granularity** of the timing done by `CTimer` may depend on the machine on which it's run. On many machines, the class "ticks" in increments of one-sixtieth of a second.[14]

---

[13]Have you ever watched the progress bar in an Internet browser as it updates the time to complete a download?

[14]The tick value is found as the constant `CLOCKS_PER_SEC` in the header file `<ctime>` or `time.h`.

Program 6.12   usetimer.cpp

```cpp
#include <iostream>
using namespace std;

#include "ctimer.h"
#include "prompt.h"

// illustrate CTimer class and loop timings

int main()
{
    int inner = PromptRange("# inner iterations x 10,000 ",1,10000);
    int outer = PromptRange("# outer iterations",1,20);

    long j,k;
    CTimer timer;

    for(j=0; j < outer; j++)
    {   timer.Start();
        for(k=0; k < inner*10000L; k++)
        {
            // nothing done here
        }
        timer.Stop();
        cout << j << "\t" << timer.ElapsedTime() << endl;
    }
    cout << "-------" << endl;
    cout << "total = " << timer.CumulativeTime() << "\t"
         << inner*outer*10000L << " iterations "<< endl;

    return 0;
}
```

```
                          O U T P U T

run on a PII, 300 Mhz machine running Windows NT
prompt> usetimer
#inner iterations x 10,000  between 1 and 10000: 10000
# outer iterations between 1 and 20: 3
0       2.364
1       2.353
2       2.373
-------
total = 7.090   300000000 iterations

run on a P100 machine running Linux
prompt> usetimer
#inner iterations x 10,000  between 1 and 10000: 10000
# outer iterations between 1 and 20: 3
0       17.11
1       17.11
2       17.12
-------
total = 51.34   300000000 iterations
```

Using the `CTimer` class we can add code to Program 6.11 to give the user an estimate of how long the program will take to run. The modified program is `maxword2.cpp`. The entire program is accessible online, or with the code that comes with this book. The timing portions of the code are shown as Program 6.13 after the output.

```
                          O U T P U T

prompt> maxword2
enter file name: poe.txt
2.314   of 46.5

timing data removed

46.197  of 46.5
48.5    of 46.5
50.804  of 46.5
53.107  of 46.5
word "the" occurs 149 times
```

Program 6.13 maxword2time.cpp

```
CTimer timer;
timer.Start();
for(outer.Init(); outer.HasMore(); outer.Next())
{   wordCount++;
}
timer.Stop();
double totalTime = timer.ElapsedTime()*wordCount;
wordCount = 0;
timer.Reset();

for(outer.Init(); outer.HasMore(); outer.Next())
{    word = outer.Current();        // current word for comparison
     wordCount++;

     int count = 0;                  // count # occurrences
     timer.Start();
     for(inner.Init(); inner.HasMore(); inner.Next())
     {   if (inner.Current() == word)   // found another occurrence
         {   count++;
         }
     }
     if (count > maxOccurs)            // maximal so far
     {   maxOccurs = count;
         maxWord = word;
     }
     if (count > maxOccurs)            // maximal so far
     {   maxOccurs = count;
         maxWord = word;
     }
     timer.Stop();
     if (wordCount % 100 == 0)
     {   cout  << timer.CumulativeTime() << "\tof " << totalTime << endl;
     }
}
```

maxword2time.cpp

As you can see in the output, the time-to-completion is underestimated by the program. The loop that calibrates the time-to-completion reads all the words but does not compare words. The string comparisons in the inner nested loop take time that's not accounted for in the time-to-completion calibrating loop.

6.5 Case Study: Iteration and String Sets

We'll take one step toward speeding up *maxword.cpp*, Program 6.11, by studying the class StringSet and its associated iterator class StringSetIterator.

Sets used in programming are based on the mathematical notion of set: a collection of elements with no duplicates. Examples include sets of integers: $\{1, 3, 2, 4\}$; sets of shapes: $\{\triangle, \triangledown, \bowtie, \bigcirc\}$; and sets of spices: {"paprika", "cayenne", "chili"}. The collection {1, 3, 2, 3, 4, 3, 1} is not a set because it contains duplicate elements.

Program 6.14 illustrates how to program using the class StringSet and the associated class StringSetIterator. The member functions of StringSetIterator have the same names as those of the class WordStreamIterator.

Program 6.14 setdemo.cpp

```cpp
#include <iostream>
using namespace std;
#include "stringset.h"

// demonstrate string set use

int main()
{
    StringSet sset;
    sset.insert("watermelon");
    sset.insert("apple");
    sset.insert("banana");
    sset.insert("orange");
    sset.insert("banana");
    sset.insert("cherry");
    sset.insert("guava");
    sset.insert("banana");
    sset.insert("cherry");

    cout << "set size = " << sset.size() << endl;

    StringSetIterator it(sset);
    for(it.Init(); it.HasMore(); it.Next())
    {   cout << it.Current() << endl;
    }
    return 0;
}
```

setdemo.cpp

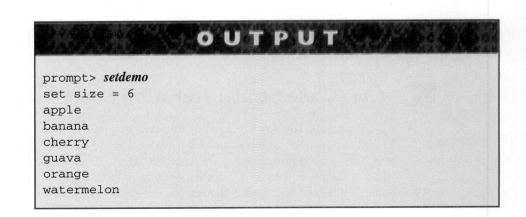

```
prompt> setdemo
set size = 6
apple
banana
cherry
guava
orange
watermelon
```

Client programs can call `StringSet::insert` hundreds of times with the same argument, but only the first call succeeds in inserting a new element into the set. Other `StringSet` member functions include `StringSet::clear`, which removes all elements from a set, and `StringSet::erase`, which removes one element, if it is present; that is, `sset.erase("apple")` decreases the size of the set used in *setdemo.cpp*, Program 6.14, by removing `"apple"`. The header file *stringset.h* is Program G.7 in How to G.

6.5.1 Iterators and the *strutils.h* Library

Program 6.15, *setdemo2.cpp*, shows two different kinds of iterators used in the same program. The program reads a file and stores all the words in a `StringSet` object. The words are first converted to lowercase, and all leading and trailing punctuation is removed using functions `ToLower` and `StripPunc` from *strutils.h* (for details see Program G.8 in How to G). This reduces the number of different words in many of the English text files used in this book. For example, the line below occurs in *The Cask of Amontillado*, used in this book as the file *poe.txt*.

```
``Yes, yes,'' I said; ``yes, yes.''
```

If we don't strip punctuation and convert to lowercase, this line contains four occurrences of the word "yes" (each word is shown surrounded by double quotes that aren't part of the word as read by the program): "``Yes,", "yes,''", "``yes,", and "yes.''".

6.5.2 The Type `ofstream`

Program 6.15, *setdemo2.cpp*, shows how to print to a text file of type `ofstream`. Opening an `ofstream` variable uses the same syntax as opening an `ifstream` variable. Writing to an `ifstream` uses the same syntax as writing to `cout` as shown by the function `Print`, which accepts either `cout` or the `ifstream` variable output as arguments. The reason that both streams can be arguments is that the parameter has type **ostream**. We'll explore why both `cout` and an `ifstream` object have the type `ostream` in a later chapter.[15]

> **Program Tip 6.13: When passing streams as parameters, use `ostream` for output streams and `istream` for input streams.** Using the most general kind of stream as a parameter ensures that you'll be able to pass many different kinds of streams as arguments.

Although we've only studied `cin` and `ifstream` for input, and `cout` and `ofstream` for output, you'll encounter other kinds of streams later in this book and your study of C++.

---

[15]This works because of inheritance, but you do not need to understand inheritance conceptually, or how it is implemented in C++, to use streams.

Program Tip 6.14:   Streams must be passed by reference. The compiler may not complain if you pass a stream by value, but your program will not work properly. Streams are almost never `const` reference parameters because stream functions invariably change the state of the stream.

Program 6.15   setdemo2.cpp

```cpp
#include <iostream>
#include <fstream>    // for ifstream and ofstream
#include <string>
using namespace std;

#include "worditer.h"
#include "stringset.h"
#include "strutils.h"
#include "prompt.h"

Print(StringSetIterator& ssi, ostream& output)
{
    for(ssi.Init(); ssi.HasMore(); ssi.Next())
    {   output << ssi.Current() << endl;
    }
}

int main()
{
    string filename = PromptString("enter file name: ");
    WordStreamIterator wstream;
    wstream.Open(filename);
    string word;

    StringSet wordset;
    for(wstream.Init(); wstream.HasMore(); wstream.Next())
    {   word = wstream.Current();
        ToLower(word);
        StripPunc(word);
        wordset.insert(word);
    }
    StringSetIterator ssi(wordset);
    Print(ssi,cout);
    cout << "# different words = " << wordset.size() <<  endl;

    filename = PromptString("file for output: ");
    ofstream output(filename.c_str());
    Print(ssi,output);

    return 0;
}
```

setdemo2.cpp

```
OUTPUT

prompt> hamlet.txt
1
1604
a
a'mercy

output words removed

yourself
yourselves
youth
zone
# different words = 4832
file for output: hamwords.dat
```

When the program is run on Shakespeare's *Hamlet* as shown, a file hamwords.dat is created and contains the 4,832 different words occurring in *Hamlet*. The words are printed in alphabetical order because of how the StringSet class is implemented. Note that words include "1" and "1604" and that these appear before words beginning with "a" because of the character system used in computers, in which digits come before letters.

6.5.3 Sets and Word Counting

Using a StringSet object greatly speeds up the execution time for *maxword.cpp*, Program 6.11. The original program used nested iterators to find the most frequently occurring word in a file. The modified version below, *maxword3.cpp*, Program 6.16, puts the words in a set, then the outer iterator goes over the set while the inner iterator reads the file each time. The program uses an object of type CircleStatusBar to monitor how much time remains as it's reading a file and finding the most frequently occurring word.[16] Three snapshots of the CircleStatusBar timing a run using Poe's *The Cask of Amontillado* are shown in Figure 6.3. The program does not use the *strutils.h* functions StripPunc and ToLower that were used in *setdemo2.cpp*, Program 6.15. This is why the number of different words is shown as 1,040 for *maxword3.cpp* but as 810 for *setdemo2.cpp*.

---

[16]The CircleStatusBar class in *tstatusbar.h* requires the use of the graphics library discussed in How to H.

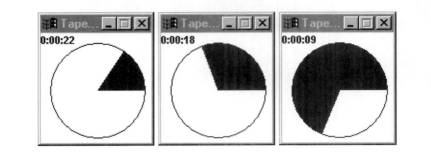

Figure 6.3   Timed output from *maxword3.cpp* using `StatusCircle`, `WordIter`, and `StringSet` classes.

Program 6.16   maxword3.cpp

```cpp
#include <iostream>
#include <string>
using namespace std;
#include "worditer.h"
#include "stringset.h"
#include "prompt.h"
#include "statusbar.h"

// 4/23/99, find most frequently occurring word using stringsets/iterators

int main()
{
    int maxOccurs = 0;
    int wordsRead = 0;
    string word,maxWord;
    StringSet wordSet;
    StatusCircle circle(50);

    string filename = PromptString("enter file name: ");
    WordStreamIterator ws;
    ws.Open(filename);

    for(ws.Init(); ws.HasMore(); ws.Next())
    {    wordSet.insert(ws.Current());
    }
    cout << "read " << wordSet.size() << " different words" << endl;

    StringSetIterator ssi(wordSet);
    for(ssi.Init(); ssi.HasMore(); ssi.Next())
    {    circle.update(wordsRead/double(wordSet.size())*100);
        int count = 0;
        wordsRead++;
```

```
        word = ssi.Current();
        for(ws.Init(); ws.HasMore(); ws.Next())
        {   if (ws.Current() == word)
            {   count++;
            }
        }
        if (count > maxOccurs)
        {   maxOccurs = count;
            maxWord = word;
        }
    }
    cout << endl << "word \"" << maxWord << "\" occurs "
         << maxOccurs << " times" << endl;

    return 0;
}
```

maxword3.cpp

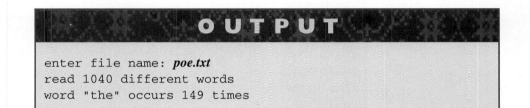

```
enter file name: poe.txt
read 1040 different words
word "the" occurs 149 times
```

If the functions `StripPunc` and `ToLower` are used, the word "the" will occur more than 149 times.

Pause to Reflect

6.35 Write the body of the function below that creates the union of two string sets.

```
void union(const StringSet& lhs, const StringSet& rhs,
           StringSet& result)
// post: result contains elements in either lhs or rhs
```

6.36 Write the body of the function below that creates the intersection of two string sets.

```
void intersect(const StringSet& lhs, const StringSet& rhs,
               StringSet& result)
// post: result contains elements in both lhs and rhs
```

(If you compare the sizes of `lhs` and `rhs` you can make the function more efficient by looping over the smallest set.)

6.37 Write a loop that prints all the strings in a set that are still elements of the set if the first character is removed (e.g., like `"eat"` and `"at"` if both were in the set).

6.38 Write a loop to print all the strings in a set that are "pseudo-palindromes" — different words when written backward, such as `"stressed"` and `"desserts"` (if both are in the set).

6.6   Chapter Review

In this chapter we studied how classes were implemented, with an in-depth look at the class `Dice`. Member functions of classes are categorized as constructors and accessor and mutator functions; private data make up the state of a class. We studied different modes of parameter/argument passing. We saw how (relatively) simple it is to read and write text files in C++ because of the similarity of file streams to `cin` and `cout`. We saw a pattern of iteration using functions `Init`, `HasMore`, and `Next` used with both streams and with sets of strings. The pattern was used to permit programs to access the elements of a collection without real knowledge of how the collection is implemented. By using the same names for iterator functions, we'll make it easier to understand new iterators when we encounter them. We also studied how to solve extreme problems, such as finding the maximum and minimum in a collection.

Important topics covered include the following:

- Accessor and mutator functions allow a class's state to be examined and changed, respectively.

- Private instance variables are accessible only in member functions, not in client programs.

- Coupling and cohesion are important criteria for evaluating functions, classes, and programs.

- Reference parameters permit values to be returned from functions via parameters. This allows more than one value to be returned. `Const` reference parameters are used for efficiency and safety.

- Parameters are passed by value (a copy is made) unless an ampersand, &, is used for passing by reference. In this case the formal parameter identifier is an alias for the memory associated with the associated function argument.

- A variable is **defined** when storage is allocated. A variable is **declared** if no storage is allocated, but the variable's type is associated with the variable's identifier.

- Parameters for programmer-defined classes are often declared as `const` reference parameters to save time and space while ensuring safety.

- Programs are best designed in an iterative manner, ideally by developing a working program and adding pieces to it so that the program is always functional to some degree. Writing pseudocode first is often a good way of starting the process of program development.

- The extraction operator, >>, uses white space to delimit, or separate, one string from another.

- In sentinel loops, the sentinel value is *not* considered part of the data.

- The extraction operator returns a value that can be tested in a loop to see whether the extraction succeeds, so `while (cin >> word)` is a standard idiom for reading streams until there are no more data (or until the extraction fails). The stream member function `fail` can be used too.

- Files can be associated with streams using `ifstream` variables. The extraction operator works with these streams. The `ifstream` member function `open` is used to bind a named disk file to a file stream. An `ofstream` variable is used to associate an output file stream with a named disk file.

- If you enter a nonnumeric value when a numeric value (e.g., an `int` or a `double`) is expected, the extraction will fail, and the nonnumeric character remains unprocessed on the input stream.

- Types sometimes need to be cast, or changed, to another type. Casting often causes values to change; that is, when casting from a `double` to an `int`, truncation occurs. A new cast operator, `static_cast`, should be used if your compiler supports it.

- Constants for the largest `int` and `double` values are accessible and can be found in the header files `<limits.h>` and `<float.h>`, respectively. The constants defining system extreme values are `INT_MAX`, `INT_MIN`, `LONG_MAX`, `LONG_MIN`, `DBL_MAX`, and `DBL_MIN`.

- Finding extreme (highest and lowest) values is a typical fence post problem. Initializing with the first value is usually a good approach, but sometimes a value of "infinity" is available for initialization (e.g., `INT_MAX`).

- The class `CTimer` can be used to time program segments. The granularity of its underlying clock may differ among different computers.

- The `WordStreamIterator` class encapsulates file reading so that the same file can be easily read many times within the same program.

- The `StringSet` class is used to represent sets of strings (no duplicates). An associated class `StringSetIterator` allows access to each value in a set.

6.7 Exercises

6.1 Create a data file in the format

```
firstname lastname testscore
firstname lastname testscore
```

where the first two entries on a line are `string` values and the last entry is an `int` test score in the range 0–100. For example:

```
Owen Astrachan 95
Dave Reed 56
Steve Tate 99
Dave Reed 77
Steve Tate 92
Owen Astrachan 88
Mike Clancy 100
Mike Clancy 95
Dave Reed 47
```

Write a program that prompts for a name and then reads the text file and computes and outputs the average test score for the person whose name is entered. Use the following `while` statement to read entries from an `ifstream` variable `input`:

```
string first, last;
int score;
while (input >> first >> last >> score)
{
    // read one line, process it
}
```

6.2 Implement a class similar to the class `Dice` but like the child's game *Magic 8-Ball*. Call the class `Fortune`. A `Fortune` object should represent a many-sided fortune-teller. You can choose 6 sides, or 8 sides, or even 20 sides like the "real" Magic 8-Ball, but the number of sides is fixed. It is not specified at construction as it is for the class `Dice`. Each time the object is "rolled" (or shaken, or asked to tell the future), a different fortune is returned. For example, consider the code below and the sample output:

```
#include "fortune.h"

int main()
{
    int rolls = PromptRange("# of fortunes ", 1, 10);
    Fortune f;
    int k;
    for(k=0; k < rolls; k++)
    {   cout << f.Shake() << endl;
    }
    return 0;
}
```

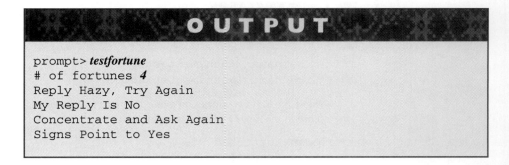

```
prompt> testfortune
# of fortunes 4
Reply Hazy, Try Again
My Reply Is No
Concentrate and Ask Again
Signs Point to Yes
```

Be creative with your fortunes, and develop a program that illustrates all the member functions of your class. For an added challenge, make the class behave so that after it has told more than 100 fortunes it breaks and tells the same one every time.

6.3 Create a class `WordDice` similar to the class from the previous exercise, but with a constructor that takes a file name and reads strings from the specified file. The strings can be stored in a `StringSet` instance variable. One of the strings is returned at random each time the function `WordDice::Roll` is called. For example, the code segment below might print any one of seven different colors if the data file `"spectrum.dat"` contains the lines

```
red orange yellow
green blue indigo violet
```

The code fragment using this file follows:

```
WordDice wd("spectrum.dat");
cout << wd.Roll() << endl;
cout << wd.Roll() << endl;
cout << wd.Roll() << endl;
```

```
prompt> testwordie
red
green
yellow
```

You should test the program with different data files. For an added challenge, test the program by rolling a WordDice object as many times as needed until all the different words are "rolled." Print the number of rolls needed to generate all the possible words.

6.4 Create a data file where each line has the format

```
item size retail-price-sold-for
```

For example, a file might contain information from a clothing store (prices aren't meant to be realistic):

```
coat small 110.00
coat large 130.00
shirt medium 22.00
dress tiny 49.00
pants large 78.50
coat large 140.00
```

Write a program that prompts the user for the name of a data file and then prompts for the name of an item, the size of the item, and the wholesale price paid for the item. The program should generate several statistics as output:

- Average retail price paid for the item.
- Total profit made by selling the item.
- Percentage of all sales accounted for by the specified item and size, both by price and by units sold.
- Percentage of all item sales, where the item is the same as specified, both by price and by units sold.

For example, in the data file above, if the wholesale price of a large coat is $100.00, then the output should include

- Average retail price for large coats is $135.00.
- Total profit is $70.00.
- Percentage of all sales is one-third (2 out of 6).
- Percentage of all coat sales is two-thirds (2 out of 3).

6.5 Write a program based on the word game *Madlibs*. The input to *Madlibs* is a vignette or brief story, with words left out. Players are asked to fill in missing words by prompting for adjectives, nouns, verbs, and so on. When these words are used to replace the missing words, the resulting story is often funny when read aloud.

In the computerized version of the game, the input will be a text file with certain words annotated by enclosing the words in brackets. These enclosed words will be replaced after prompting the user for a replacement. All words are written to another text file (use an `ofstream` variable).[17] Since words will be read and written one at a time, you'll need to keep track of the number of characters written to the output file so that you can use an `endl` to finish off, or flush, lines in the output file. For example, in the sample run below, output lines are flushed using `endl` after writing 50 characters (the number of characters can be accumulated using the `string` member function `length`).

The output below is based on an excerpt from *Romeo and Juliet* annotated for the game. Punctuation must be separated from words that are annotated so that the brackets can be recognized (using `substr`). Alternatively, you could search for brackets using `find` and maintain the punctuation.

The text file `mad.in` is

```
But soft! What [noun] through yonder window [verb] ?
It is the [noun] , and [name] is the [noun] !
Arise, [adjective] [noun] , and [verb] the [adjective]
[noun] , Who is already [adjective] and
[another_adjective] with [emotion]
```

The output is shown on the next page. Because we don't have the programming tools to read lines from files, the lines in the output aren't the same as the lines in the input. In the following run, the output file created is reread to show the user the results.

---

[17]You may need to call the member function `close` on the `ofstream` object. If the output file is truncated so that not all data is written, call `close` when the program has finished writing to the stream.

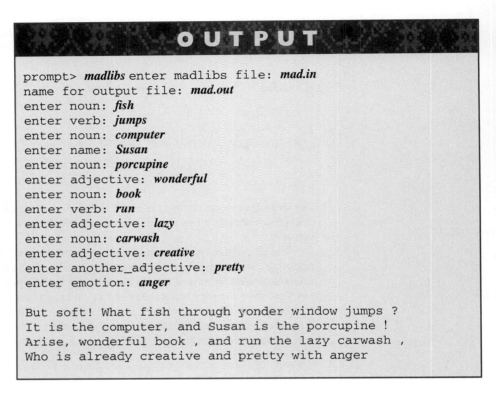

```
OUTPUT

prompt> madlibs enter madlibs file: mad.in
name for output file: mad.out
enter noun: fish
enter verb: jumps
enter noun: computer
enter name: Susan
enter noun: porcupine
enter adjective: wonderful
enter noun: book
enter verb: run
enter adjective: lazy
enter noun: carwash
enter adjective: creative
enter another_adjective: pretty
enter emotion: anger

But soft! What fish through yonder window jumps ?
It is the computer, and Susan is the porcupine !
Arise, wonderful book , and run the lazy carwash ,
Who is already creative and pretty with anger
```

6.6 Write a program to compute the average of all the numbers stored in a text file. Assume the numbers are integers representing test scores; for example,

```
70 85 90
92 57 100 88
87 98
```

First use the extraction operator, >>. Then use a WordStreamIterator object. Since WordStreamIterator::Current returns a string, you'll need to convert the string to the corresponding integer; that is, the string "123" should be converted to the int 123. The function atoi in *strutils.h* in How to G will convert the string.

```
int atoi(string s)
// pre: s represents an int, that is "123", "-457", etc.
// post: returns int equivalent of s
//       if s isn't properly formatted (that is "12a3")
//       then 0 (zero) is returned
```

6.7 The **standard deviation** of a group of numbers is a statistical measure of how much the numbers spread out from the average (the average is also called the *mean*). A low standard deviation shows that most of the numbers are near the mean. If numbers are denoted as $(x_1, x_2, x_3, \ldots, x_n)$, then the mean is denoted as $\bar{x}$. The standard deviation is the square root of the **variance**. (The standard deviation is usually denoted by the Greek letter sigma, σ, and the variance is denoted by σ^2.)

The mathematical formula for calculating the variance is

$$\sigma^2 \;=\; \frac{1}{n-1}[(x_1 - \bar{x})^2 + (x_2 - \bar{x})^2 + \cdots (x_n - \bar{x})^2]$$

$$=\; \frac{1}{n-1}[\sum_{i=1}^{n}(x_i - \bar{x})^2]$$

Using algebra this formula can be rearranged to yield the formula

$$\sigma^2 = \frac{1}{n-1}[\sum_{i=1}^{n} x_i^2 - \frac{1}{n}(\sum_{i=1}^{n} x_i)^2] \qquad (6.1)$$

This formula does not involve the mean, so it can be computed with a single pass over all the data rather than two passes (one to calculate the mean, the other to calculate the variance).

Write a program to compute the variance and standard deviation using both formulae. Although these formulae are mathematically equivalent, they often yield very different answers because of errors introduced by floating-point computations. Use the technique from the previous exercise so that you can read a file of data twice using a `WordStreamIterator` object. If the data consist of floating-point values instead of integers, you can use the function `atof` to convert a string to the `double` value it represents, such as `atof("123.075") == 123.075`.

6.8 The **hailstone** sequence, sometimes called the $3n + 1$ sequence, is defined by a function $f(n)$:

$$f(n) = \begin{cases} n/2 & \text{if } n \text{ is even} \\ 3 \times n + 1 & \text{otherwise, if } n \text{ is odd} \end{cases} \qquad (6.2)$$

We can use the value computed by f as the argument of f as shown below; the successive values of n form the hailstone sequence.[18]

```
while (n != 1)
{   n = f(n);
}
```

Although it is conjectured that this loop always terminates, no one has been able to prove it. However, it has been verified by computer for an enormous range of numbers. Several sequences are shown below with the initial value of n on the left.

```
7 22 11 34 17 52 26 13 40 20 10 5 16 8 4 2 1

11 34 17 52 26 13 40 20 10 5 16 8 4 2 1

22 11 34 17 52 26 13 40 20 10 5 16 8 4 2 1

14 7 22 11 34 17 52 26 13 40 20 10 5 16 8 4 2 1

8 4 2 1
```

---

[18]It's called a *hailstone sequence* because the numbers go up and down, mimicking the process that forms hail.

9 28 14 7 22 11 34 17 52 26 13 40 20 10 5 16 8 4 2 1

Write a program to find the value of n that yields the longest sequence. Prompt the user for two numbers, and limit the search for n to all values between the two numbers.

6.9 Use the CTimer class to test two methods for computing powers outlined in Section 5.1.7. The first method outlined there makes n multiplications to compute x^n; the second method makes roughly $\log_2(n)$ multiplications, that is, 10 multiplications to compute x^{1024} (here x is a double value but n is an int).

Write two functions, with different names but the same parameter lists, for computing x^n based on the two methods. Call these functions thousands of times each with different values of n. For example, you might calculate 3.0^{50}, 3.0^{100}, 3.0^{150}, and so on. You'll need to do several calculations for a fixed n to make a CTimer object register. Plot the values with values of n on the x-axis and time (in seconds) on the y-axis. If you have access to a spreadsheet program you can make the plots automatically by writing the data to an output file.

You should also compare the time required by these two methods using the function pow from <cmath>. Finally, you should test both methods of exponentiation using BigInt values rather than double values for the base (the exponent can still be an integer). You should try to explain the timings you observe with BigInt values, which should be different from the timings observed for double values.

6.10 Data files for several of Shakespeare's plays are available on the Web pages associated with this book. Write a program that reads the words from at least five different plays, putting the words from each play in a StringSet object. You should find the words that are in the intersection of all the plays. Finding the intersection may take a while, so test the program with small data files before trying Shakespeare's plays.

After you've found the words in common to all five plays (or more plays), find the top 10 most frequently occurring of these words. There are many ways to do this. One method is to find the most frequently occurring word using code from Program 6.16, *maxword3.cpp*. After this word is found, remove it from the set of common words and repeat the process. You can use this method to rank order (most frequent to least frequent) all the words in common to the plays, but this will take a long time using the WordStreamIterator class.

6.11 Do the last exercise, but rather than reading a file of words many times (e.g., once for each word in the list of common words), adopt a different approach. First read all the words from a file into a list, using the class StringList from *clist.h*. Program 6.17, *listcount.cpp*, shows how StringList is used. The only function that's needed other than iterating functions is the function cons, which attaches an element to the front of a list and returns the new list (the old list is not changed).

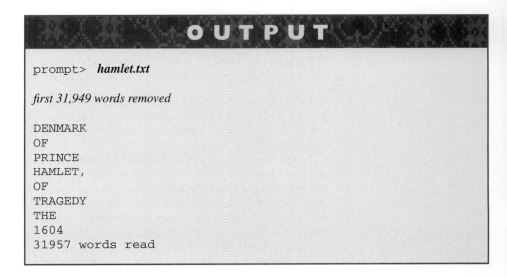

O U T P U T

prompt> *hamlet.txt*

first 31,949 words removed

DENMARK
OF
PRINCE
HAMLET,
OF
TRAGEDY
THE
1604
31957 words read

Program 6.17 listcount.cpp

```cpp
#include <iostream>
#include <fstream>
#include <string>
using namespace std;

#include "clist.h"
#include "prompt.h"

int main()
{
    string filename = PromptString("enter filename ");
    ifstream input(filename.c_str());
    string word;

    StringList slist;
    while (input >> word)
    {   slist = cons(word,slist);
    }

    StringListIterator it(slist);
    for(it.Init(); it.HasMore(); it.Next())
    {   cout << it.Current() << endl;
    }
    cout << slist.Size() << " words read " << endl;

    return 0;
}
```

listcount.cpp

Since new words are added to the front using cons, the words are stored in the list so that the first word read is the last word in the list. Using the class StringList can make string-processing programs faster than using the class WordStreamIterator because strings are read from memory rather than from disk. For example, on my 300 MHz Pentium, using *maxword.cpp*, Program 6.11, takes approximately 53 seconds to process `poe.txt`. Using *maxword3.cpp*, Program 6.16, takes approximately 28 seconds. Replacing the inner `WordStreamIterator` by a `StringListIterator` reduces the time to 3.4 seconds because memory is so much faster than disk.

Class Interfaces, Design, and Implementation 7

> There is no single development, in either technology or management technique, which by itself
> promises even one order-of-magnitude improvement within a decade in productivity, in
> reliability, in simplicity.
>
> FRED P. BROOKS
> *No Silver Bullet — Essence and Accident in Software Engineering*

One tenet of object-oriented programming is that a library of well-designed classes makes it easier to design and write programs. The acronym *COTS*, for *commercial, off-the-shelf* software, is often used to identify the process of reusing (commercial) libraries of classes and code. Classes are often easier to reuse in programs than nonclass code. For example, we've used the `Dice` and `RandGen` classes and the functions from `"prompt.h"` in many programs. In almost every program we've used `cout` and `cin`, objects that are part of the hierarchy of stream classes. As programmers and designers, we need to be familiar with what classes are available and with patterns of design that we can use. Reusing concepts is often as important as reusing code.

In this chapter we'll discuss the design and implementation of a class-based program for administering on-line quizzes. We'll see that careful planning makes it possible to reuse the same class interface so that different kinds of quizzes can be given. We'll study another example of class interface reuse in a program that simulates random walks in one and two dimensions.

7.1 Designing Classes: From Requirements to Implementation

Choosing classes and member functions is a difficult design process. It's very hard to choose the right number of classes with the right member functions so that the classes are cohesive, loosely coupled, and easy to modify and yield an elegant, correctly working program. Many programmers and computer scientists are good algorithmic thinkers but bad class designers, and vice versa. You shouldn't expect to become an accomplished designer early in your studies, but you can build expertise by studying other designs and by modifying existing designs before creating your own. In this way you'll learn as an apprentice learns any craft.[1]

---

[1] Programming is both an art and a science. To some, it's only a science or only an art/craft. In my view there are elements of both in becoming an accomplished programmer. You must understand science and mathematics, but good design is not solely a scientific enterprise.

7.1.1   Requirements

The **requirements** of a problem or programming task are the constraints and demands asked by the person or group requesting a programming solution to a problem. As a designer/programmer your task in determining requirements is to interact with the users (here *users* means both the person using the program and the person hiring you) to solicit information and feedback about how the program will be used, what it must accomplish, and how it interacts with other programs and users. In this book and in most early courses, the requirements of a problem are often spelled out explicitly and in detail. However, sometimes you must infer requirements or make a best guess (since you don't have a real user/software client with whom to interact).

The **specification** of the quiz problem from Section 6.2.2 is reproduced below. From the specification you may be able to infer the requirements. We'll use the specification as a list of requirements and move toward designing classes.

> We want to develop a quiz program that will permit different kinds of questions—that is, not just different kinds of arithmetic problems, but questions about state capitals, English literature, rock and roll songs, or whatever you think would be fun or instructive. We'd like the program to be able to give a quiz to more than one student at the same time, so that two people sharing a keyboard at one computer could both participate. If possible, we'd like to allow a student to have more than one chance at a question.

Thinking about this specification leads to the following requirements (in no particular order):

1. More than one kind of question can be used in a quiz.
2. Several students can take a quiz sharing a keyboard.
3. Students may be allowed more than one chance to answer a question.

With a real client you would probably get the chance to ask questions about the requirements. Should a score be reported as in Programs 6.2 and 6.3? Should the scores be automatically recorded in a file? Should the user have the choice of what kind of quiz to take? We'll go forward with the requirements we've extracted from the problem specification. We'll try to design a program that permits unanticipated demands (features?) to be incorporated.

As we develop classes we'll keep the examples simple and won't go deeply into all the issues that arise during design. Our goal here is to see the process simply, glossing over many details but giving a real picture of the design process. In later chapters and future courses you'll delve more deeply into problems and issues of designing classes.

7.1.2   Nouns as Classes

The nouns in a specification are usually good candidates for classes. In the specification above the nouns that seem important include

quiz, question, problem, student, computer, keyboard, chance

Our program doesn't need to deal with the nouns computer and keyboard, so we'll use the other nouns as candidates for classes. As you become more experienced, you'll develop a feel for separating important nouns/classes from less important ones. You'll learn to identify some candidate class nouns as synonyms for others. For this quiz program we'll develop three classes: quiz, question, and student. A question object will represent a kind of question factory that can generate new problems. For example, an arithmetic question class might generate problems like "what is $2 + 2$?" or "what is 3×7?" On the other hand, an English literature question class might generate problems like "Who wrote *Charlotte's Web*?" or "In what work does the character Holden Caulfield appear?" As you'll see, a problem will be a part of the question class rather than a separate class.

7.1.3 Verbs as Member Functions (Methods)

The first step in designing identified classes is determining class behavior and responsibility. A class's public member functions determine its **behavior**. In some object-oriented languages member functions are called **methods**; I'll often use the terms member function and method interchangeably. Sometimes you may think at first that a method belongs to one class, but during the design process it will seem better to place it in another class. There isn't usually one right way to design classes or a program. The **responsibilities** of a class are the methods associated with the class and the interactions between classes. Sometimes candidate class methods can be found as verbs in a specification. Often, however, you'll need to anticipate how a program and classes are used to find methods.

7.1.4 Finding Verbs Using Scenarios

It's not always clear what member functions are needed. Sometimes creating **scenarios** of how a program works helps determine class behavior and responsibility. A scenario is a description, almost like a dialog, between the user and the program or between classes in a program.

In the quiz example scenarios could include the following:

- Two students sit at a keyboard, each is asked to enter her name, then a quiz is given and students alternate providing answers to questions.

- When a quiz is given, the student determines the number of questions that will be asked before the quiz starts. If two people are taking a quiz together, both are asked the same number of questions.

- Students have two chances to respond to a question. A simple "correct" or "incorrect" is given as feedback to each student response. If a student doesn't type a correct response, the correct answer is given.

- At the end of a quiz, each student taking the quiz is given a score.

Some verbs from these scenarios follow (long, descriptive names are chosen to make the verbs more clear):

EnterName, ChooseNumberOfQuestions, ChooseKindOfQuestion, RespondTo-Question, GetCorrectAnswer, GetScore, AskQuestion, ProvideFeedback

Which of these verbs goes with which class? In assigning responsibilities we'll need to return to the scenarios to see how the classes interact in a program. At this point we're concentrating only on public behavior of the classes, not on private state or implementation of the classes.

> **Program Tip 7.1:   Concentrate on behavior rather than on state in initial class design.** You can change how a class is implemented without affecting client programs that use the class, but you cannot change the member functions (e.g., the parameters used) without affecting client programs.

Client programs depend on the **interface** provided in a header file. If the interface changes, client programs must change too. Client programs should not rely on how a class is implemented. If code is written to conform to an interface, rather than to an implementation, changes in client code will be minimized when the implementation changes.[2]

Pause to Reflect

7.1 The method `Dice::Roll` in *dice.cpp*, Program 6.1, uses a local `RandGen` variable to generate simulated random dice rolls. If the `RandGen` class is changed, does a client program like *roll.cpp*, Program 5.11, change? Why?

7.2 What are the behaviors of the class `CTimer` declared in the header file *ctimer.h*, Program G.5, and used in the client code *usetimer.cpp*, Program 6.12?

7.3 Write a specification for a class that simulates a coin. "Tossing" the coin results in either heads or tails.

7.4 Write a specification and requirements for a program to help a library with overdue items (libraries typically loan more than books). Make up whatever you don't know about libraries, but try to keep things realistic. Develop some scenarios for the program.

7.5 Suppose you're given an assignment to write a program to simulate the gambling game roulette using a computer (see Exercise 7.9 at the end of this chapter for an explanation of the game). Write a list of requirements for the game; candidate classes drawn from nouns used in your description; potential methods; and scenarios for playing the game.

---

[2]Client programs may depend indirectly on an implementation, that is, on how fast a class executes a certain method. Changes in class performance may not affect the correctness of a client program, but the client program will be affected.

Mary Shaw

Mary Shaw is Professor of Computer Science at Carnegie Mellon University. Her research interests are in the area of software engineering, a subfield of computer science concerned with developing software using well-defined tools and techniques. In [EL94] Shaw says this about software engineering:

Science often grows hand-in-hand with related engineering. Initially, we solve problems any way we can. Gradually a small set of effective techniques enters the folklore and passes from one person to another. Eventually the best are recognized, codified, taught, perhaps named. Better understanding yields theories to explain the techniques, to predict or analyze results, and to provide a base for systematic extension. This improves practice through better operational guidance and tools that automate details. The software developer, thus freed from certain kinds of detail, can tackle bigger, more complex problems.

In discussing her current research interests, Shaw combines the themes of both language and architecture. She describes her research in the following:

Software now accounts for the lion's share of the cost of developing and using computer systems. My research is directed at establishing a genuine engineering discipline to support the design and development of software systems and reduce the costs and uncertainties of software production. My current focus is on design methods, analytic techniques, and tools used to construct complete software systems from subsystems and their constituent modules. This is the software architecture level of design, which makes me a software architect. (This is from her World Wide Web home page at Carnegie Mellon.)

In 1993 Shaw received the Warnier prize for contributions to software engineering. Among her publications are guides to bicycling and canoeing in western Pennsylvania.

7.1.5 Assigning Responsibilities

Not all responsibilities will be assigned to a class. Some will be free functions or code that appears in main, for example. In my design, I decided on the following assignments of responsibilities to classes.

- **Student**
  - Construct using name (ask for name in `main`)
  - RespondTo a question
  - GetScore
  - GetName (not in scenario, but useful accessor)
- **Quiz**
  - ChooseKindOfQuestion
  - AskQuestion of/GiveQuestion to a student
- **Question**
  - Create/Construct question type
  - AskQuestion
  - GetCorrectAnswer

These assignments are not the only way to assign responsibilities for the quiz program. In particular, it's not clear that a `Student` object should be responsible for determining its own score. It might be better to have the `Quiz` track the score for each student taking the quiz. However, we'll think about how scores are kept (this is state, and we shouldn't think about state at this stage; but we can think of which class is responsible for keeping the state). If `Quiz` keeps score, then it may be harder to keep score for three, four, or more students. If each `Student` keeps score, we may be able to add students more easily.

We haven't assigned to any class the responsibilities of determining the number of questions and of providing feedback. We'll prompt the student for the number of questions in `main`, and feedback will be part of either `Quiz::GiveQuestionTo` or `Student::RespondTo`. We're using the **scope resolution operator** :: to associate a method with a class because this makes it clear how responsibilities are assigned.

7.1.6 Implementing and Testing Classes

At this point you could write a header (.h) file for each class. This helps solidify our decisions, and writing code usually helps in finding flaws in the initial design. Design is not a sequential process but is a process of **iterative enhancement**. At each step, you may need to revisit previous steps and rethink decisions that you thought were obviously correct. As you begin to implement the classes, you may develop scenarios unanticipated in the first steps of designing classes.

> **Program Tip 7.2:   One cornerstone of iterative enhancement is adding code to a working program.** This means that the software program grows; it doesn't spring forth fully functional. The idea is that it's easier to test small pieces and add functionality to an already tested program than it is to test many methods or a large program at once.

Ideally we'll test each class separately from the other classes; but some classes are strongly coupled, and it will be difficult to test one such class without having the other class already implemented and tested. For example, testing the `Student::RespondTo` method probably requires passing a question to this method that the student can respond to. If we don't have a question, what can we do? We can use **stub functions** that are not fully functional (e.g., the function might be missing parameters) but that generate output we'll use to test our scenarios. We might use the stub shown as Program 7.1.

Program 7.1 studentstub.cpp

```cpp
void Student::RespondTo( missing Question parameter )
{
    string answer;
    cout << endl << "type answer after question " << endl;
    cout << "what is your favorite color? ";
    cin >> answer;
    if (answer == "blue")
    {   cout << "that is correct" << endl;
    myCorrect++;
    }
    else
    {   cout << "No! your favorite color is blue" << endl;
    }
}
```

studentstub.cpp

We could use this stub function to test the other member functions `Student::Name()` and `Student::Score()`. Program 7.2 shows a test program for the class `Student`.

Program 7.2 mainstub.cpp

```cpp
#include <iostream>
#include <string>
using namespace std;
#include "student.h"
#include "prompt.h"

int main()
{
    string name = PromptString("enter name: ");
    int numQuest = PromptRange("number of questions: ",1,10);
    Student st(name);
    int k;
    for(k=0; k < numQuest; k++)
    {   st.RespondTo();    // question parameter missing
    }
    cout << st.Name() << ", your score is "
         << st.Score() << " out of " << numQuest << endl;
    return 0;
}
```

mainstub.cpp

In testing the class `Student` I created a program *teststudent.cpp* like *mainstub.cpp* above. I put the class interface/declaration (.h file) and implementation/definition (.cpp file) in *teststudent.cpp* rather than in separate files (although the program above shows a

#include"student.h", that's not how I originally wrote the test program). After the class was tested, I cut-and-pasted the code segments into the appropriate student.h and student.cpp files. Although not shown here, a test program similar to the one above is available as *teststudent.cpp* in the on-line programs available for this book (but see *quiz.cpp*, Program 7.8, for a complete program with classes Student and Quiz). A run of *teststudent.cpp* (or *mainstub.cpp*, Program 7.2) follows.

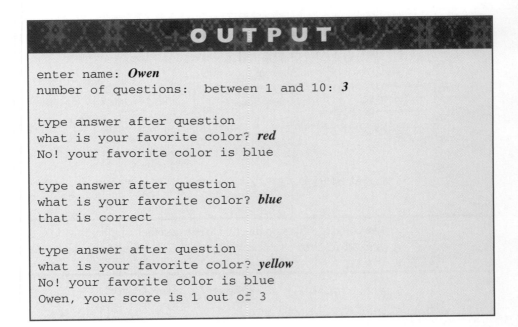

```
enter name: Owen
number of questions:   between 1 and 10: 3

type answer after question
what is your favorite color? red
No! your favorite color is blue

type answer after question
what is your favorite color? blue
that is correct

type answer after question
what is your favorite color? yellow
No! your favorite color is blue
Owen, your score is 1 out of 3
```

After testing the Student class we can turn to the Quiz class. In general the order in which classes should be implemented and tested is not always straightforward. In [Ben88] John Bentley offers the following "tips" from Al Schapira:

Program Tip 7.3:   Always do the hard part first. If the hard part is impossible, why waste time on the easy part? Once the hard part is done, you're home free.

Program Tip 7.4:   Always do the easy part first. What you think at first is the easy part often turns out to be the hard part. Once the easy part is done, you can concentrate all your efforts on the hard part.

7.1.7 Implementing the Class `Quiz`

There are two behaviors in the list of responsibilities for the class `Quiz`: choosing the kind of question and giving the question to a student. The kind of question will be an integral part of the class `Question`. It's not clear what the class `Quiz` can do in picking a type of question, but if there were different kinds of questions perhaps the `Quiz` class could choose one. Since we currently have only one type of question we'll concentrate on the second responsibility: giving a question to a student.

In designing and implementing the function `Quiz::GiveQuestionTo` we must decide how the `Quiz` knows which student to ask. There are three possibilities. The important difference between these possibilities is the responsibility of creating `Student` objects.

1. A `Quiz` object knows about all the students and asks the appropriate student. In this case all `Student` objects would be private data in the `Quiz` class, created by the `Quiz`.

2. The student of whom a question will be asked is passed as an argument to the `Quiz::GiveQuestionTo` member function. In this case the `Student` object is created somewhere like `main` and passed to a `Quiz`.

3. The student is created in the function `Quiz::GiveQuestionTo` and then asked a question.

These are the three ways in which a `Quiz` member function can access any kind of data, and in particular a `Student` object. The three ways correspond to how `Student` objects are defined and used:

1. As instance variables of the class `Quiz` because private data is global to all `Quiz` methods and so is accessible in `Quiz::GiveQuestionTo`.

2. As parameter(s) to `Quiz::GiveQuestionTo`. Parameters are accessible in the function to which they're passed.

3. As local variables in `Quiz::GiveQuestionTo` because local variables defined in a function are accessible in the function.

In our quiz program, the third option is not a possibility. Variables defined within a function are not accessible outside the function, so `Student` objects defined within the function `Quiz::GiveQuestionTo` are not accessible outside the function. This means no scores could be reported, for example. If we choose the first option, the `Quiz` class must provide some mechanism for getting student information because the students will be private in the `Quiz` class and not accessible, for example, in `main` to print scores unless the `Quiz` class provides accessor functions for students.

The second option makes the most sense. `Student` objects can be defined in `main`, as can a `Quiz` object. We can use code like the following to give a quiz to two students:

```
int main()
{
    Student owen("Owen");
    Student susan("Susan");
    Quiz q;
    q.GiveQuestionTo(owen);
    q.GiveQuestionTo(susan);

    cout << owen.Name()  << " score = "
         << owen.Score() << endl;
    cout << susan.Name() << " score = "
         << susan.Score() << endl;
    return 0;
}
```

This code scenario corresponds to one of the original requirements: allow two students to take a quiz at the same time using the same program. The code should also provide a clue as to how the Student parameter is passed to Quiz::GiveQuestionTo—by value, by reference, or by const reference.

If you think carefully about the code, you'll see that the score reported for each student must be calculated or modified as part of having a question asked. This means the score of a student changes (potentially) when a question is asked. For changes to be communicated, the Student parameter must be a reference parameter. A value parameter is a copy, so any changes will not be communicated. A const reference parameter cannot be changed, so the number of correct responses cannot be updated. Reference parameters are used to pass values back from functions (and sometimes to pass values in as well), so the Student parameter must be passed by reference.

We'll design the function Quiz::GiveQuestionTo() to permit more than one attempt, one of the original program requirements. The code is shown in Program 7.3.

Program 7.3 quizstub.cpp

```
void Quiz::GiveQuestionTo(Student & s)
// postcondition: student s asked a question
{
  cout << endl << "Ok, " << s.Name() << " it's your turn" << endl;
  cout << "type answer after question " << endl;

  myQuestion.Create();
  if (! s.RespondTo(myQuestion))
  { cout << "try one more time" << endl;
    if (! s.RespondTo(myQuestion))
    {  cout << "correct answer is " << myQuestion.Answer() << endl;
    }
  }
}
```

quizstub.cpp

This code shows some of the methods of the class `Question`. From the code, and the convention of using the prefix `my` for private data, you should be able to reason that the object `myQuestion` is private data in `Quiz` and that methods for the `Question` class include `Question::Create()` and `Question::Answer()`. The other method listed in the original responsibilities for `Question`, which we'll call `Question::Ask()`, is responsible for asking the question. As we'll see, this method is called in `Student::RespondTo()`.

Pause to Reflect

7.6 If `myQuestion` is an instance variable of the class `Quiz`, where is `myQuestion` constructed?

7.7 Why is `s`, the parameter of `Quiz::GiveQuestionTo()`, a reference parameter? Why can't it be a `const` reference parameter? (Think about the scenarios and what happens to parameter `s` after a question is given.)

7.8 As shown in Program 7.3, the function `Student::RespondTo()` returns a `bool` value. Based on the value's use, what is an appropriate postcondition for the function?

7.9 How is the function `Student::RespondTo()` in Program 7.3 different from the version used in *mainstub.cpp*, Program 7.2? Is it appropriate that the function changed?

7.10 What is the prototype of the method `Student::RespondTo()` as it is used in Program 7.3? In particular, how is the parameter passed: by value, by reference, or by `const` reference (and why)?

7.11 `Question::Answer()` returns the correct answer in some printable form. When do you think the correct answer is determined?

7.1.8 Implementing the Class `Question`

In testing the function `Quiz::GiveQuestionTo` above, I didn't have the class `Question` implemented. I could have implemented a simple version of the class, a version good enough for testing other classes. Alternatively I could use output statements in place of calling the `Question` methods, much as the quiz about favorite colors was used in testing the class `Student`. Since a simple version of the class is useful in testing other classes, I implemented the version shown in *question.h*, Program 7.4. Note that each member function is implemented in the class rather than as a separate function outside the class. In general, the class declaration (interface) should be kept separate from the definition (implementation). For a test implementation like this one, which will eventually be replaced by separate .h and .cpp files, making all the code part of the class declaration is acceptable practice. When function definitions are included in a class declaration, the functions are called **in-line** functions. In general you should not use in-line member functions but should define them in a separate .cpp file.

> **Program Tip 7.5:   Some programmers use in-line member functions for "small" classes — those classes that have few member functions and few instance variables.** However, as you're learning to design and implement classes it's a good idea to use the generally accepted practice of separating a class's interface from its implementation by using separate .h and .cpp files.

Program 7.4   question.h

```cpp
#include <iostream>
#include <string>
using namespace std;

// simple Question class for testing other classes

class Question
{
  public:
    Question()
    {   // nothing to initialize
    }
    void Create()
    {   // the same question is used every time
    }
    void Ask()
    {   cout << "what is your favorite color? ";
    }
    string Answer() const
    {   return "blue";
    }
};
```

question.h

Our test version of `Student::RespondTo` can be modified to use the simple `Question` class as shown. The output of the program will not change from the original version in *teststudent.cpp*.

```cpp
void Student::RespondTo(Question & q)
{
    string answer;
    cout << endl << "type answer after question " << endl;
    q.Ask();
    cin >> answer;

    if (answer == q.Answer())
    {   cout << "that is correct" << endl;
        myCorrect++;
    }
    else
```

```
{   cout << "No! your favorite color is "
        << q.Answer() << endl;
}
}
```

With this simple version of Question done, we can test the implementations of Student and Quiz completely. Then we can turn to a complete implementation of a Question class for implementing quizzes in arithmetic as called for in the requirements for this problem.

7.1.9   Sidebar: Converting int and double Values to strings

In our test version of the Question class the function Question::Answer() returns a string. As we turn to the final implementation it seems that we'll need to change this return type to be an int since the answer to a question about an arithmetic operation like addition is almost certainly an integer, not a string. There's a compelling reason to leave the return type as string, however. One of the original requirements was to design and implement a program that allows quizzes about a wide variety of topics, such as English literature and rock and roll songs in the original list of topics. The answers to these questions will almost certainly be strings rather than numbers. How can we accommodate all possible quiz answers?

If we could convert int values to strings, such as the number 123 to the string "123", we could continue to use strings to represent answers. Since almost any kind of answer can be represented as a string, we'd like to use strings. For example, the string "3.14159" prints just like the double value 3.14159. We built functions for converting integers to an English representation in *numtoeng.cpp*, Program 4.10, and in *digits.cpp*, Program 5.5. These programs converted an int value like 123 to "one hundred twenty three" and "one two three", respectively. We could use these as a basis for writing our own conversion functions. Fortunately, there are functions already written that convert numeric values to equivalent strings and vice versa. These functions are demonstrated in *numtostring.cpp*, Program 7.5.

As shown in the output, the functions tostring, atoi, and atof do no error checking (nonnumeric strings are converted to zero by both atoi and atof). These conversion functions are part of the string-processing functions accessible using *strutils.h* given in How to G as Program G.8.[3]

With the conversion functions from *strutils.h* now in our programming tool kit, we can tackle the problem of implementing the Question class for questions about arithmetic problems.

---

[3]The functions atoi and atof are **adapter functions** for standard conversion functions with the same names in <cstdlib> (or <stdlib.h>). The functions atoi and atof in <cstdlib> take C-style, char * strings as parameters, so functions accepting string parameters are provided in *strutils.h* as adapters for the standard functions.

Program 7.5   numtostring.cpp

```cpp
#include <iostream>
#include <string>
using namespace std;

#include "strutils.h"   // for tostring, atoi

// illustrate string to int/double conversion and vice versa

int main()
{
    int    ival;
    double dval;
    string s;

    cout << "enter an int ";
    cin >> ival;

    s = tostring(ival);
    cout << ival << " as a string is " << s << endl;

    cout << "enter a double ";
    cin >> dval;
    cout << dval << " as a string is " << tostring(dval) << endl;

    cout << "enter an int (to store in a string) ";
    cin >> s;
    ival = atoi(s);
    cout << s << " as an int is " << ival << endl;

    cout << "enter a double (to store in a string) ";
    cin >> s;
    cout << s << " as a double is " << atof(s) << endl;

    return 0;
}
```

```
                           O U T P U T

prompt> numtostring
enter an int 1789
1789 as a string is 1789
enter a double 2.7182
2.7182 as a string is 2.7182
enter an int (to store in a string) -639
-639 as an int is -639
enter a double (to store in a string) 17e2
17e2 as a double is 1700
prompt> numtostring
enter an int -123
-123 as a string is -123
enter a double 17e2
1700 as a string is 1700
enter an int (to store in a string) 23skidoo
23skidoo as an int is 23
enter a double (to store in a string) pi
pi as a double is 0
```

The member function `Question::Ask()` must ask the question last created by the function `Question::Create()`. Since these functions are called independently by client programs, the `Create` function must store information in private, state variables of the `Question` class. These state variables are then used by `Question::Ask()` to print the question. We'll use simple addition problems like "what is 20 + 13?" We'll store the two numbers that are part of a question in instance variables myNum1 and myNum2. Values will be stored in these variables by `Question::Create()`, and the values will be accessed in `Question::Ask()`. We'll also store the answer in the instance variable myAnswer so that it can be accessed in the accessor function `Question::Answer()`.

> **Program Tip 7.6: Instance variables are useful for communicating values between calls of different member functions.** The values might be set in one function and accessed in a different function. Sometimes instance variables are used to maintain values between calls of the same function.

As the last step in our design we'll think about frequent uses of the class that we can make easier (or at least simpler). Client code will often check if a student response is correct, using code like this:

```
if (response == q.Answer()) // correct
```

We'll make this easier by using a `bool`-valued function `Question::IsCorrect` so that checking code will change to this:

```
if (q.IsCorrect(response)) // correct
```

This opens the possibility of changing how the function `Question::Answer` works. For example, we could allow `albany` to be a match for `Albany` by making `IsCorrect` ignore the case of the answers. We could even try to allow for misspellings. We might also try to prevent clients from calling `Answer`, but allow them to check if an answer is correct. We'll leave the `Answer` function in place for now, but in designing classes the goal of hiding information and minimizing access to private state should be emphasized. Consider the unnecessary information revealed in some campus debit-card systems. If a student buys some food, and the register shows a balance of $1,024.32 to everyone in the checkout line, too much information has been revealed. The only information that's needed to complete the purchase is whether the student has enough money in her account to cover the purchase. It's fine for everyone to see "Purchase OK," but it's not acceptable for everyone to see all balances. A student balance, for example, could be protected by using a password to access this sensitive information.

Finally, we decide which functions are accessors and which are mutators. Accessor functions don't change state, so they should be created as `const` functions. The final class declaration is shown as *mathquest.h*, Program 7.6.

Program 7.6 mathquest.h

```
#ifndef _MATHQUEST_H
#define _MATHQUEST_H

// ask a question involving arithmetic
//
// This class conforms to the naming conventions
// of quiz questions in "A Computer Science Tapestry" 2e,
// this convention requires the following functions:
//
// void Create()      -- ask a new question
// void Ask() const   -- ask the last question Create()'d
//
// bool IsCorrect(const string& answer) const
//      -- return true iff answer is correct to last (Create()) question
// string Answer() const
//      -- return the answer to the last (Create()) question
//
#include <string>
using namespace std;

class Question
{
  public:
    Question();

    bool IsCorrect(const string& answer) const;
    string Answer()                       const;
```

```
    void Ask()                                const;


    void Create();   // create a new question

  private:


    string myAnswer;   // store the answer as a string here
    int myNum1;         // numbers used in question
    int myNum2;
};
```

The final class definition/implementation is shown as *mathquest.cpp*, Program 7.7. Some new syntax is shown in Program 7.7 for initializing instance variables in a constructor. In previous constructors like the Dice constructor in *dice.cpp*, Prog 6.1, instance variables were assigned values in the body of the constructor using syntax identical to variable assignment in other contexts.

The code in the *Question::Question* constructor uses an **initializer list** to give initial values to all instance variables. Each instance variable must be constructed. Construction of instance variables takes place before the body of the constructor executes. When parameters must be supplied to a variable at construction time, the values are supplied in an initializer list that appears between the constructor header and the body of the constructor. A single colon ' : ' is used to begin the initializer list, and each item in the list is separated from other items by a comma ' , ' — but note that the last item is not followed by a comma because commas separate items (this is a fence post problem). Because some instance variables require parameters at construction time, such as a Dice variable requiring a parameter, I'll use initializer lists for constructors in code shown from now on. When an instance variable doesn't need a constructor, you can show it with a parameterless constructor as shown for myVar3 in the syntax diagram. Alternatively, you can omit this constructor call, but then one of the instance variables won't appear in the list. I'll try to be consistent in initializing all instance variables. Instance variables are initialized in the order in which they appear in a class declaration, and *not* in the order in which they appear in the initializer list. To avoid problems, make the order of construction in the initializer list the same as the order in which instance variables appear in the private section of a class declaration. Some compilers will catch inconsistent orderings and issue a warning.

Syntax: initializer list

```
ClassName::ClassName  (parameters)
     :   myVar1(parameters),
         myVar2(parameters),
         myVar3( ),
         myVarN(parameters)
  {
      code as needed for further initialization
  }
```

Program 7.7   mathquest.cpp

```cpp
#include <iostream>
#include <iomanip>
using namespace std;

#include "mathquest.h"
#include "randgen.h"
#include "strutils.h"


Question::Question()
    : myAnswer("*** error ***"),
      myNum1(0),
      myNum2(0)
{
    // nothing to initialize
}

void Question::Create()
{
    RandGen gen;

    myNum1 = gen.RandInt(10,20);
    myNum2 = gen.RandInt(10,20);
    myAnswer = tostring(myNum1 + myNum2);
}

void Question::Ask() const
{
    const int WIDTH = 7;
    cout << setw(WIDTH) << myNum1 << endl;
    cout << "+" << setw(WIDTH-1) << myNum2 << endl;
    cout << "-------" << endl;
    cout << setw(WIDTH-myAnswer.length()) << " ";
}

bool Question::IsCorrect(const string& answer) const
{
    return myAnswer == answer;
}

string Question::Answer() const
{
    return myAnswer;
}
```

mathquest.cpp

Program 7.8, *quiz.cpp*, uses all the classes in a complete quiz program. The class declarations and definitions for Student and Quiz are included in *quiz.cpp* rather than in separate .h and .cpp files. The Question class is placed into separate files to make it easier to incorporate new kinds of questions.

Program 7.8   quiz.cpp

```cpp
#include <iostream>
#include <string>
using namespace std;
#include "mathquest.h"
#include "prompt.h"

// quiz program for illustrating class design and implementation

class Student
{
  public:
    Student(const string& name);    // student has a name

    int    Score() const;           // # correct
    string Name()  const;           // name of student

    bool RespondTo(Question & q);   // answer a question, update stats

  private:

    string myName;          // my name
    int    myCorrect;       // my # correct responses
};

Student::Student(const string& name)
  : myName(name),
    myCorrect(0)
{
    // initializer list does the work
}

bool Student::RespondTo(Question & q)
// postcondition: q is asked, state updated to reflect responses
//                return true iff question answered correctly
{
    string answer;
    q.Ask();
    cin >> answer;

    if (q.IsCorrect(answer))
    {   myCorrect++;
        cout << "yes, that's correct" << endl;
        return true;
    }
    else
    {   cout << "no, that's not correct" << endl;
        return false;
    }
}

int Student::Score() const
```

```cpp
// postcondition: returns # correct
{
    return myCorrect;
}

string Student::Name() const
// postcondition: returns name of student
{
    return myName;
}

class Quiz
{
  public:
    Quiz();
    void GiveQuestionTo(Student & s); // ask student a question

  private:

    Question myQuestion; // question generator
};

Quiz::Quiz()
  : myQuestion()
{
  // nothing to do here
}

void Quiz::GiveQuestionTo(Student & s)
// postcondition: student s asked a question
{
    cout << endl << "Ok, " << s.Name() << " it's your turn" << endl;
    cout << "type answer after question " << endl;

    myQuestion.Create();
    if (! s.RespondTo(myQuestion))
    {   cout << "try one more time" << endl;
        if (! s.RespondTo(myQuestion))
        {   cout << "correct answer is " << myQuestion.Answer() << endl;
        }
    }
}

int main()
{
    Student owen("Owen");
    Student susan("Susan");
    Quiz q;
    int qNum = PromptRange("how many questions: ",1,5);
    int k;
    for(k=0; k < qNum; k++)
    {   q.GiveQuestionTo(owen);
        q.GiveQuestionTo(susan);
    }
    cout << owen.Name()  << " score:\t" << owen.Score()
```

```
        << " out of " << qNum
        << " = " << double(owen.Score())/qNum * 100 << "%" << endl;
cout << susan.Name() << " score:\t" << susan.Score()
        << " out of " << qNum
        << " = " << double(susan.Score())/qNum * 100 << "%" << endl;

    return 0;
}
```

cuiz.cpp

```
================ O U T P U T ================

prompt> quiz
how many questions:   between 1 and 5: 3

Ok, Owen it's your turn
type answer after question
        19
+       17
-------
        36
yes, that's correct

Ok, Susan it's your turn
type answer after question

        11
+       16
-------
        27
yes, that's correct

Ok, Owen it's your turn
type answer after question

        17
+       15
-------
        34
no, that's not correct
try one more time

output continued
```

OUTPUT

```
       17
+      15
-------
       32
yes, that's correct

Ok, Susan it's your turn
type answer after question
       20
+      17
-------
       37
yes, that's correct

Ok, Owen it's your turn
type answer after question
       16
+      17
-------
       23
no, that's not correct
try one more time
       16
+      17
-------
       27
no, that's not correct
correct answer is 33

Ok, Susan it's your turn
type answer after question
       15
+      17
-------
       32
yes, that's correct
Owen score:    2 out of 3 = 66.6667%
Susan score:   3 out of 3 = 100%
```

7.12 What (simple) modifications can you make to the sample `Question` class in *question.h*, Program 7.4, so that one of two colors is chosen randomly as the favorite color? The color should be chosen in `Question::Create()` and used in the other methods, `Ask()` and `Answer()`.

7.13 Why is the string `"pi"` converted to the `double` value zero by `atof` in the sample run of Program 7.5, *numtostring.cpp*?

7.14 Does conversion of `"23skidoo"` to the `int` value 23 mirror how the string would be read if the user typed `"23skidoo"` if prompted by the following?

```
int num;
cout << "enter value ";
cin >> num;
```

7.15 Why is the function `Question::Ask()` declared as `const` in *mathquest.h*, Program 7.6?

7.16 The declaration for a class `Game` is partially shown below:

```
class Game
{
  public:
    Game();
    ...
  private:
    Dice myCube;
    int  myBankRoll;
};
```

The constructor should make `myCube` represent a six-sided `Dice` and should initialize `myBankRoll` to 5000. Explain why an initializer list is required because of `myCube` and show the syntax for the constructor `Game::Game()` (assuming there are only the two instance variables shown in the class).

7.17 The statements for reporting quiz scores for two students in `quiz.cpp`, Program 7.8, duplicate the code used for the output. Write a function that can be called to generate the output for either student, so that the statements below replace the score-producing output statements in `quiz.cpp`:

```
reportScores(owen, qNum);
reportScores(susan, qNum);
```

7.18 What question is asked if a client program calls `Question::Ask()` without ever calling `Question::Create()`?

7.2 A Conforming Interface: A New Question Class

We want to develop a new `Question` class for a different kind of quiz. As an illustration, we'll develop a class for asking questions about U.S. state capitals. We don't have the programming tools needed to easily store the state/capital pairs within the new `Question` class.[4] Instead, we'll put the state/capital pairs in a text file and read the text file repeatedly using a `WordStreamIterator` object. To generate a random state/capital question we'll skip a random number of lines of the file when reading it. Suppose the first five lines of the text file are as follows.

```
Alabama     Montgomery
Alaska    Juneau
Arizona    Phoenix
Arkansas    Little_Rock
California    Sacramento
```

If we skip two lines of the file we'll ask what the capital of Arizona is; if we skip four lines we'll ask about the capital of California; and if we don't skip any lines we'll ask about Alabama.

7.2.1 Using the New Question Class

We'll call the new class `Question`. This will allow us to use the class without changing the program *quiz.cpp*, Program 7.8, except to replace the `#include "mathquest.h"` line by `#include "capquest.h"`. The class about capitals declared in *capquest.h* has the same interface (i.e., the same class name and the same public member functions) as the class declared in *mathquest.h*, so the client program in *quiz.cpp* doesn't change at all. A run of the program *quiz.cpp*, Program 7.8, modified to include `"capquest.h"`, is shown below.

The downside of this approach is that we can't let the user choose between math questions and capital questions while the program is running; the choice must be made before the program is compiled. This is far from ideal: we wouldn't expect a real student-user to compile a program to take a quiz using a computer. However, until we study inheritance in Chapter 13, we don't really have any other options.

---

[4]Perhaps the simplest way to do this is to use a vector or array, but the method used in the `Question` class developed in this chapter is fairly versatile without using a programming construct we haven't yet studied.

```
O U T P U T
```

```
prompt> quiz
how many questions:  between 1 and 5: 2

it's your turn Owen
type answer after question
the capital of Wisconsin is Madison
yes, that's correct

it's your turn Susan
type answer after question
the capital of Washington is Seattle
no, try one more time
the capital of Washington is Tacoma
no, correct answer is Olympia

it's your turn Owen
type answer after question
the capital of Utah is Salt_Lake_City
yes, that's correct

it's your turn Susan
type answer after question

the capital of New_Mexico is Albuquerque
no, try one more time
the capital of New_Mexico is Santa_Fe
yes, that's correct
Owen score:      2 out of 2 = 100%
Susan score:     1 out of 2 = 50%
```

7.2.2 Creating a Program

Before looking briefly at the new implementation of Question, we'll review the process of creating a working C++ program. This will help you understand how the different Question classes work with the quiz program.

Three steps are needed to generate an executable program from source files:

1. The **preprocessing** step handles all #include directives and some others we haven't studied. A **preprocessor** is used for this step.

2. The **compilation** step takes input from the preprocessor and creates an **object file** (see Section 3.5) for each .cpp file. A **compiler** is used for this step.

3. One or more object files are combined with libraries of compiled code in the **linking** step. The step creates an executable program by linking together system-dependent libraries as well as client code that has been compiled. A **linker** is used for this step.

7.2.3 The Preprocessor

The preprocessor is a program run on each source file before the source file is compiled. A source file like *hello.cpp*, Program 2.1, is translated into something called a **translation unit**, which is then passed to the compiler. The source file isn't physically changed by the preprocessor, but the preprocessor does use **directives** like #include in creating the translation unit that the compiler sees. Each preprocessor directive begins with a sharp (or number) sign # that must be the first character on the line.

Processing #include Statements. A #include statement literally cuts and pastes the code in the file specified into the translation unit that is passed to the compiler. For example, the preprocessor directive #include<iostream> causes the preprocessor to find the file named iostream and insert it into the translation unit. This means that what appears to be a seven-line program like the following might actually generate a translation unit that causes the compiler to compile 10,000 lines of code.

```
#include<iostream>
using namespace std;
int main()
{
    cout << "hello world" << endl;
    return 0;
}
```

I tried the program above with three different C++ environments. The size of the translation unit ranged from 2,986 lines using g++ with Linux, to 16,075 using Borland CBuilder, to 17,261 using Metrowerks Codewarrior.

Compilers are fast. At this stage of your programming journey you don't need to worry about minimizing the use of the #include directive, but in more advanced courses you'll learn techniques that help keep compilation times fast and translation units small.

Where Are include Files Located? The preprocessor looks in a specific list of directories to find include files. This list is typically called the **include path**. In most environments you can alter the include path so that the preprocessor looks in different directories. In many environments you can specify the order of the directories that are searched by the preprocessor.

> **Program Tip 7.7:** **If the preprocessor cannot find a file specified, you'll probably get a warning. In some cases the preprocessor will find a different file than the one you intend—one that has the same name as the file you want to include.** This can lead to compilation errors that are hard to fix. If your system lets you examine the translation unit produced by the preprocessor, you may be able to tell what files were included. You should do this only when you've got real evidence that the wrong header file is being included.

Most systems look in the directory in which the .cpp file that's being preprocessed is located. More information about setting options in your programming environment can be found in How to I.

Other Preprocessor Directives. The only other preprocessor directive we use in this book is the **conditional compilation** directive. Each header file begins and ends with preprocessor directives as follows (see also *dice.h*, Program G.3). Suppose the file below is called *foo.h*.

```
#ifndef _FOO_H
#define _FOO_H


header file for Foo goes here


#endif
```

The first line tells the preprocessor to include the file *foo.h* in the current translation unit only if the symbol _FOO_H is *not* defined. The *n* in ifndef means "if NOT defined," then proceed. The first thing that happens if the symbol _FOO_H is not defined is that it becomes defined using the directive #define. The final directive #endif helps limit the extent of the first #ifndef. Every #ifndef has a matching #endif. The reason for bracketing each header file with these directives is to prevent the same file from being included twice in the same translation unit. This could easily happen, for example, if you write a program in which you include both <iostream> and "date.h". The header file "date.h" also includes <iostream>. When you include one file, you also include all the files that it includes (and all the files that they include, and all the files that they include). Using the #ifndef directive prevents an infinite chain of inclusions and prevents the same file from being included more than once.

Occasionally it's useful to be able to prevent a block of code from being compiled. You might do this, for example, during debugging or development to test different versions of a function. The directive #ifdef causes the preprocessor to include a section of a file only if a specific symbol is defined.

```
#ifdef FOO
void TryMe(const string& s)
{   cout << s << " is buggy" << endl;
}
#endif
```

```
void TryMe(const string& s)
{   cout << s << "is correct' << endl;
}
```

In the code segment above, the call `TryMe("rose")` generates `rose is correct` as output. The first version (on top) of `TryMe` isn't compiled because the preprocessor doesn't include it in the translation unit passed to the compiler unless the symbol `FOO` is defined. You can, of course, define the symbol `FOO` if you want to. Some programmers use `#ifdef 0` to block out chunks of code because zero is never defined.

7.2.4 The Compiler

The input to the compiler is the translation unit generated by the preprocessor from a source file. The compiler generates an **object file** for each compiled source file. Usually the object file has the same prefix as the source file but ends in .o or .obj. For example, the source file *hello.cpp* might generate *hello.obj* on some systems. In some programming environments the object files aren't stored on disk but remain in memory. In other environments the object files are stored on disk. It's also possible for the object files to exist on disk for a short time so that the linker can use them. After the linking step the object files might be automatically erased by the programming environment.

Object files are typically larger than the corresponding source file, but may be smaller than the translation unit corresponding to the source file. Many compilers have options that generate **optimized code**. This code will run faster, but the compiler will take longer to generate the optimized code. On some systems you won't be able to use a debugger with optimized code.

> **Program Tip 7.8:   Turn code optimization off.** Unless you are writing an application that must execute very quickly, and you've used profiling and performance tools that help pinpoint execution bottlenecks, it's probably not worth optimizing your programs. In some systems, debuggers may get confused when using optimized code, and it's more important for a program to be correct than for it to be fast.

Since the compiler uses the translation unit provided by the preprocessor to create an object file, any changes in the translation unit from a .cpp source file will force the .cpp file to be recompiled. For example, if the header file *question.h* is changed, then the source program *quiz.cpp*, Program 7.8, will need to be recompiled. Since the file *question.h* is part of the translation unit generated from *quiz.cpp*, the recompilation is necessary because the translation unit changed. In general, a source file has several **compilation dependencies**. Any header file included by the source file generates a dependency. For example, Program 7.8, *quiz.cpp*, has four direct dependencies:

- ■   `<iostream>` and `string`, two system dependencies.
- ■   `"prompt.h"` and `"mathquest.h"`, two nonsystem dependencies.

There may be other indirect dependencies introduced by these. Since both `"prompt.h"` and `"mathquest.h"` include `<string>`, another dependency would be introduced, but `<string>` is already a dependency.

> **Program Tip 7.9:   You should try to minimize the number of dependencies for each source file.** Since a change in a dependency will force the source file to be recompiled, keeping the number of dependencies small means you'll need to recompile less often during program development.

Notice that *mathquest.cpp*, Program 7.7, depends directly on the files *randgen.h* and *strutils.h*. These two files are *not* dependencies for *quiz.cpp* because they're not part of the translation unit for *quiz.cpp*.

Libraries.   Often you'll have several object files that you use in all your programs. For example, the implementations of `iostream` and `string` functions are used in nearly all the programs we've studied. Many programs use the classes declared in *prompt.h*, *dice.h*, *date.h*, and so on. Each of these classes has a corresponding object file generated by compiling the .cpp file. To run a program using all these classes, you need to combine the object files in the linking phase. However, nearly all programming environments make it possible to combine object files into a library that can then be linked with your own programs. Using a library is a good idea because you need to link with fewer files, and it's usually simple to get an updated library when one becomes available.

7.2.5   The Linker

The linker combines all the necessary object files and libraries together to create an executable program. Libraries are always needed, even if you are not aware of them. Standard libraries are part of every C++ environment and include classes and functions for streams, math, and so on. Often you'll need to use more than one library. For example, I use a library called *tapestry.lib* for all the programs in this book. This library contains the object files for classes `Dice`, `Date`, `RandGen` and functions from `strutils`, among many others. The suffix `.lib` is typically used for libraries.

You aren't usually aware of the linker as you begin to program because the libraries are linked in automatically. However, as soon as you begin to write programs that use several .cpp files, you'll probably encounter linker errors.

For example, if I try to create an executable program from *quiz.cpp*, Program 7.8, but I forget to link in the code from the class `Question` in *mathquest.cpp*, Program 7.7, the following errors are generated. The first two errors using Metrowerks Codewarrior follow:

```
Link Error : Undefined symbol: ?Ask@Question@@QBEXXZ
(Question::Ask) in file: quiz.cpp

Link Error : Undefined symbol:?IsCorrect@Question@@QBE_NABV?
$basic_string@DU?$char_traits@D@std@@V?$
```

```
                                          allocator@D@2@@std@@@Z
(Question::IsCorrect) in file:quiz.cpp
```

Using Microsoft Visual C++ the first two errors follow:

```
quiz.obj : error LNK2001: unresolved external symbol
 "public: void__thiscall Question::Ask(void)const "
          (?Ask@Question@@QBEXXZ)
quiz.obj : error LNK2001: unresolved external symbol
 "public: bool__thiscall Question::IsCorrect
(class std::basic_string<char,struct std::char_traits<char>,
class std::allocator<char> > const &)const "
(?IsCorrect@Question@@QBE_NABV?$basic_string@DU
```

These errors may be hard to understand. The key thing to note is that they are **linker errors**. Codewarrior specifically identifies the errors as linker errors. If you look at the Visual C++ output you'll see a clue that the linker is involved: the errors are identified as error LNK2001.

Program Tip 7.10: **If you get errors about unresolved references, or undefined/unresolved external symbols, then you've got a linker error.** This means that you need to combine the object files from different .cpp files together. In most C++ environments this is done by adding the .cpp file to a project, or by changing a Makefile to know about all the .cpp files that must be linked together.

String Compilation and Linker Errors. The other reason the errors are hard to read is because of the standard class string. The string class is complicated because it is intended to be an industrial-strength class used with several character sets (e.g., ASCII and UNICODE) at some point. The string class is actually built on top of a class named basic_string, which you may be able to identify in some of the linker errors above.

7.2.6 A New Question Class

The new question class in *capquest.h* has the same public member functions as, but a different private section from, the class in *mathquest.h*. Part of *capquest.h* follows:

```
class Question
{
  public:
    Question(const string& filename);

    bool IsCorrect(const string& answer) const;
    string Answer()                      const;
    void Ask()                           const;
```

```
        void Create();  // create a new question

    private:

        string myAnswer;            // answer (state capital)
        string myQuestion;          // the state
        WordStreamIterator myIter;  // iterates over file
    };
```

The instance variable myIter processes the file of states and capitals, choosing one line at random as the basis for a question each time Question::Create() is called (see Program 7.9, *capquest.cpp*). The instance variable myQuestion replaces the two instance variables myNum1 and myNum2 from *mathquest.h*, Program 7.6. The method Question::Create() in *capquest.cpp* does most of the work. In creating the new Question class three goals were met:

■ Using the same interface (public methods) as the class in *mathquest.h* helped in writing the new class. When I wrote the new class I concentrated only on the implementation since the interface was already done.

■ The client program *quiz.cpp* did not need to be rewritten. It did need to be recompiled after changing #include"mathquest.h" to use "capquest.h".

■ The new class Question can be used for questions other than states and capitals. The modifications are straightforward and discussed in the following Pause to Reflect exercises.

Program 7.9 capquest.cpp

```cpp
#include <iostream>
#include <iomanip>
using namespace std;

#include "randgen.h"
#include "strutils.h"

Question::Question(const string& filename)
    : myAnswer("*** error ***"),
      myQuestion("*** error ***")
{
    myIter.Open(filename.c_str());
}

void Question::Create()
{
    RandGen gen;

    int toSkip = gen.RandInt(0,49);   // skip this many lines
    int k;
```

```
    myIter.Init();
    for(k=0; k < toSkip; k++)
    {   myIter.Next();    // skip the state
        myIter.Next();    // and the capital
    }
    myQuestion = myIter.Current();
    myIter.Next();
    myAnswer = myIter.Current();
}


void Question::Ask() const
{
    cout << "the capital of " << myQuestion << " is ";
}


bool Question::IsCorrect(const string& answer) const
{
    return myAnswer == answer;
}


string Question::Answer() const
{
    return myAnswer;
}
```

capquest.cpp

Pause to Reflect

7.19 Why are the state New York and the capital Little Rock stored in the data file as New_York and Little_Rock, respectively? (Why aren't spaces used?)

7.20 The class Question declared in *capquest.h* uses a WordStreamIterator instance variable, so it has #include"worditer.h" at the top of the file. This means that *quiz.cpp*, Program 7.8, depends directly on "worditer.h" and indirectly on <string> since <string> is included in *worditer.h*. What prevents the file <string> from being included multiple times when the preprocessor creates a translation unit for *quiz.cpp*?

7.21 The file *capquest.cpp*, Program 7.9, includes "randgen.h". Does *quiz.cpp* depend on "randgen.h"? Why?

7.22 If the class RandGen declared in "randgen.h" is rewritten so that the header file changes, does *quiz.cpp* need to be recompiled? Relinked (to create an executable program about state capitals)? Why?

7.23 The constant 49 is **hardwired** into the definition of Question::Create() for skipping lines in the file of states and capitals. Explain how myIter could be used in the constructor of the class to count the lines in the file so that the number 49 would be computed by the class itself at run time.

7.24 Suppose you want to create a quiz based on artists/groups and their recordings. Data are stored in a text file as follows:

```
Lawn_Boy Phish
A_Live_One Phish
Automatic_for_the_People R.E.M.
Broken Nine_Inch_Nails
The_Joshua_Tree U2
Nick_of_Time Bonnie_Raitt
```

The idea is to ask the user to identify the group that made a recording. How can you change the class `Question` in *capquest.h* and *capquest.cpp* so that it can be used to give both state/capital and group/recording quizzes? With the right modifications you should be able to use questions of either type in the same quiz program. (Hint: The new `Question` class constructor could have two parameters, one for the file of data and one for the prompt for someone taking the quiz.)

7.3 Random Walks

> When you can measure what you are speaking about,
> and express it in numbers, you know something about it…
> LORD KELVIN
> *Popular Lectures and Addresses*

> We must never make experiments to confirm our ideas, but simply to control them.
> CLAUDE BERNARD
> *Bulletin of New York Academy of Medicine, vol. IV, p. 997*

In this section we'll explore some programs and classes that are simulations of natural and mathematical events. We'll also use the pattern of iteration introduced with the `WordStreamIterator` class in *worditer.h*, Program G.6 (see How to G), and used in *maxword.cpp*, Program 6.11. We'll design and implement several classes. Classes for one- and two-dimensional random walks will share a common interface, just as the class `Question` declared in both *mathquest.h* and *capquest.h* did. Because of this common interface, a class for observing random walks (graphically or by printing the data in the walk to a file) will be able to observe both walks. First we'll write a simple program to simulate random walks, then we'll design and implement a class based on this program. Comparing the features of both programs will add to your understanding of object-oriented programming. We'll also study `structs`, a C++ feature for storing data that can be used instead of a class.

A random walk is a model built on mathematical and physical concepts that is used to explain how molecules move in an enclosed space. It's also used as the basis for several mathematical models that predict stock market prices. First we'll investigate a random walk in one dimension and then move to higher dimensions.

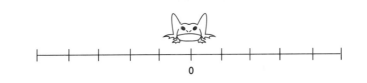

Figure 7.1   Initial position of a frog in a one-dimensional random walk.

7.3.1   One-Dimensional Random Walks

Suppose a frog lives on a lily pad and there are lily pads stretching in a straight line in two directions. The frog "walks" by flipping a coin. If the coin comes up heads, the frog jumps to the right; otherwise the frog jumps to the left. Each time the frog jumps, it jumps one unit, but the length of the jump might change. This jumping process is repeated for a specific number of steps and then the walk stops. The initial configuration for such a random walk is shown in Figure 7.1. We can gather several interesting statistics from a random walk when it is complete (and sometimes during the walk). In a walk of n steps we might be interested in how far from the start the frog is at the end of the walk. Also of interest are the furthest points from the start reached by the frog (both east and west or positive and negative if the walk takes place on the x-axis) and how often the frog revisits the "home" lily pad.

We'll look at a simple program for simulating random walks, then think about designing a class that encapsulates a walk but is more general than the walk we've described. The size of a frog's world might be limited, for example, if the frog lives in a drain pipe.

We'll use a two-sided `Dice` object to represent the coin that determines what direction the frog jumps. Program 7.10, *frogwalk.cpp,* simulates a one-dimensional random walk. The program uses the C++ **switch** instead of an `if`/`else` statement. The `switch` statement is the final control statement we'll use in our programs. A switch statement is often shorter than the corresponding sequence of cascaded `if`/`else` statements, but it's also easier to make programming errors when writing code using `switch` statements. We'll discuss the statement after the program listing.

With a graphical display, the frog could be shown moving to the left and right. Alternatively, a statement that prints the position of the frog could be included within the `for` loop. This would provide clues as to whether the program is working correctly. In the current program, the only output is the final position of the frog. Without knowing what this position should be in terms of a mathematical model, it's hard to determine if the program accurately models a one-dimensional random walk.

Program 7.10 frogwalk.cpp

```cpp
#include <iostream>
using namespace std;
#include "dice.h'
#include "prompt.h"

// simulate one-dimensional random walk
// Owen Astrachan, 8/13/94, modified 5/1/99

int main()
{
    int numSteps = PromptRange("enter # of steps",0,20000);
    int position = 0;            // "frog" starts at position 0
    Dice die(2);                 // used for "coin flipping"
    int k;
    for(k=0; k < numSteps; k++)
    {    switch (die.Roll())
        {
          case 1:
            position++;    // step to the right
            break;
          case 2:
            position--;    // step to the left
            break;
        }
    }
    cout << "final position = " << position << endl;
    return 0;
}
```

frogwalk.cpp

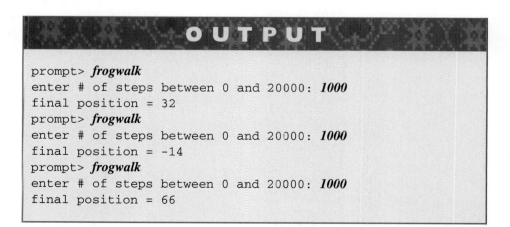

```
O U T P U T

prompt> frogwalk
enter # of steps between 0 and 20000: 1000
final position = 32
prompt> frogwalk
enter # of steps between 0 and 20000: 1000
final position = -14
prompt> frogwalk
enter # of steps between 0 and 20000: 1000
final position = 66
```

7.3.2   Selection with the `switch` Statement

In Exercise 4.9 of Chapter 4 a program was specified for drawing different heads as part of a simulated police sketch program. The following function `Hair` comes from one version of this program:

```
void Hair(int choice)
// precondition: 1 <= choice <= 3
// postcondition: prints hair in style specified by choice
{
    if (1 == choice)
    {   cout << "  ||||||//////// " << endl;
    }
    else if (2 == choice)
    {   cout << "  ||||||||||||||| " << endl;
    }
    else if (3 == choice)
    {   cout << "  |_____|  " << endl;
    }
}
```

The cascaded `if`/`else` statements work well. In some situations, however, an alternative conditional statement can lead to code that is shorter and sometimes more efficient. You shouldn't be overly concerned about this kind of efficiency, but in a program differentiating among 100 choices instead of 3 the efficiency might be a factor. The **switch** statement provides an alternative method for writing the code in `Hair`.

```
void Hair(int choice)
// precondition: 1 <= choice <= 3
// postcondition: prints hair in style specified by choice
{
    switch(choice)
    {
        case 1:
            cout << "  ||||||//////// " << endl;
            break;
        case 2:
            cout << "  ||||||||||||||| " << endl;
            break;
        case 3:
            cout << "  |_____|  " << endl;
            break;
    }
}
```

Each **case** label, such as `case 1`, determines what statements are executed based on the value of the expression used in the `switch` test (in this example, the value of the variable `choice`). There should be one `case` label for each possible value of the `switch` test expression.

All of the labels are *constants* that represent *integer* values known at compile time. Examples include `13,53 - 7,true,and 'a'`. It's not legal to use `double` values like 2.718, `string` values like `"spam"`, or expressions that use variables like `2*choice`

Syntax: switch statement

```
switch (expression)
{
    case constant₁:
        statement list;
        break;
    case constant₂:
        statement list;
        break;
    ...
    default :
        statement list;
}
```

---

for `case` labels in a `switch` statement. If the value of *expression* in the `switch` test matches a `case` label, then the corresponding statements are executed. The `break` causes flow of control to continue with the statement following the `switch`. If no matching `case` label is found, the `default` statements, if present, are executed. Most programmers put the `default` statement last inside a `switch`, but a few argue that it should be the first label. There are no "shortcuts" in forming cases. You cannot write `case 1,2,3:`, for example, to match either one, two, or three. For multiple matches, each case is listed separately as follows:

```
case 1 :
case 2 :
case 3 :
    statement list
    break;
```

In the `switch` statement shown in `Hair`, exactly one `case` statement is executed; the `break` causes control to continue with the statement following the `switch`. (Since there is no following statement in `Hair`, the function exits and the statement after the call of `Hair` is executed next.) In general, a `break` statement is required, or control will **fall through** from one case to the next.

Program Tip 7.11: **It's very easy to forget the break needed for each case statement, so when you write switch statements, be very careful.**

Program Tip 7.12: **As a general design rule, don't include more than two or three statements with each case label.** If more statements are needed, put them in a function and call the function. This will make the `switch` statement easier to read.

A missing `break` statement often causes hard-to-find errors. If the `break` corresponding to `case 2` in the function `Hair` is removed, and the value of `choice` is 2, two lines of output will be printed.

(*Warning! Incorrect code follows!*)

```cpp
void Hair(int choice)
// precondition: 1 <= choice <= 3
// postcondition: prints hair in style specified by choice
{
    switch(choice)
    {
        case 1:
            cout << "   |||||||//////// " << endl;
            break;
        case 2:
            cout << "   ||||||||||||||||   " << endl;
        case 3:
            cout << "   |_____|   " << endl;
            break;
    }
}
```

OUTPUT

```
||||||||||||||||
|_____|
```

Because there is no `break` following the hair corresponding to `case 2`, execution falls through to the next statement, and the output statement corresponding to `case 3` is executed.

The efficiency gained from a `switch` statement occurs because only one expression is evaluated and the corresponding `case` statements are immediately executed. In a sequence of `if/else` statements it is possible for all the `if` tests to be evaluated. As mentioned earlier, it's not worth worrying about this level of efficiency until you've timed a program and know what statements are executed most often. The `switch` statement does make some code easier to read, and the efficiency gains can't hurt.

7.3.3   A RandomWalk Class

Program 7.10, *frogwalk.cpp*, is short. It's not hard to reason that it correctly simulates a one-dimensional random walk. However, modifying the program to have more than one frog hopping on the lily pads is cumbersome because the program is not designed to be extended in this way. If we encapsulate the state and behavior of a random-walking frog in a class, it will be easier to have more than one frog in the same program. With a class we may be able to have different random-walkers jump with different probabilities, that is, one walker might jump left 50% of the time, another 75% of the time. Using a class will also make it easier to extend the program to simulate a two-dimensional walk.

We'll use a class RandomWalk whose interface is shown in *walk.h*, Program 7.11. Member functions Init, HasMore, and Next behave similarly to their counterparts in the WordStreamIterator class (see Program 6.11, *maxword.cpp*) and the *StringSetIterator* class (see *maxword2.cpp*). This usage of the **iterator** pattern is somewhat different from what we've used in previous classes and programs, but we use the same names since the random walk is an iterative process. There are two differences in the use of an iterator here:

- The iterator functions are part of the class RandomWalk rather than belonging to a separate class. In the other uses the iterator class was separate from the class being iterated over.

- In the StringSetIterator and WordStreamIterator classes the collection being iterated over was complete when the iterators executed. For the RandomWalk class the iterating functions create the random walk — using the functions again results in a different random walk rather than reiterating over the same walk.

Program 7.11   walk.h

```
#ifndef _RANDOMWALK_H
#define _RANDOMWALK_H


// Owen Astrachan, 6/20/96, modified 5/1/99
// class for implementing a one dimensional random walk
//
// constructor specifies number of steps to take, random walk
// goes left or right with equal probability
//
// two methods for running simulation:
//
// void Simulate()  -- run a complete simulation
//
// Init(); HasMore(); Next() -- idiom for starting and iterating
//                              one step at a time
// accessor functions:
//
// int Position()     -- returns x coordinate
//                       (# steps left/right from origin)
// int Current()      -- alias for GetPosition()
//
// int TotalSteps()  -- returns total # steps taken

class RandomWalk
```

```
{
  public:
    RandomWalk(int maxSteps);    // constructor, parameter = max # steps
    void Init();                 // take first step of walk
    bool HasMore();              // returns false if walk finished, else true
    void Next();                 // take next step of random walk

    void Simulate();             // take all steps in simulation

    int Position()    const;     // returns position (x coord) of walker
    int Current()     const;     // same as position
    int TotalSteps()  const;     // returns total # of steps taken

  private:

    void TakeStep();             // simulate one step of walk
    int myPosition;              // current x coordinate
    int mySteps;                 // # of steps taken
    int myMaxSteps;              // maximum # of steps allowed
};
```
                                                                          walk.h
```
#endif
```

A parameter to the RandomWalk constructor specifies the number of steps in the walk. A main function that uses the class follows:

```
int main()
{
    int numSteps = PromptRange("enter # steps",0,1000000);

    RandomWalk frog(numSteps);
    frog.Simulate();
    cout << "final position = " << frog.GetPosition() << endl;
}
```

In this program an entire simulation takes place immediately using the member function Simulate. The output from this program is the same as the output from *frogwalk.cpp*. Using the RandomWalk class makes it easier to simulate more than one random walk at the same time. In *frogwalk2.cpp,* Program 7.12, two random walkers are defined. The program keeps track of how many times the walkers are located at the same position during the walk. It would be very difficult to write this program based on *frogwalk.cpp*, Program 7.10. Since the number of steps in the simulation is a parameter to the RandomWalk constructor, variables frog and toad must be defined *after* you enter the number of steps. One alternative would be to have a member function SetSteps used to set the number of steps in the simulation.

Program 7.12 frogwalk2.cpp

```
#include <iostream>
using namespace std;
#include "prompt.h"
```

```
#include "walk.h"

// simulate two random walkers at once
// Owen Astrachan, 6/29/96, modified 5/1/99

int main()
{
    int numSteps = PromptRange("enter # steps",0,30000);

    RandomWalk frog(numSteps);          // define two random walkers
    RandomWalk toad(numSteps);
    int samePadCount = 0;               // # times at same location

    frog.Init();                        // initialize both walks
    toad.Init();

    while (frog.HasMore() && toad.HasMore())
    {   if (frog.Current() == toad.Current())
        {   samePadCount++;
        }
        frog.Next();
        toad.Next();
    }
    cout << "frog position = " << frog.Position() << endl;
    cout << "toad position = " << toad.Position() << endl;
    cout << "# times at same location = " << samePadCount << endl;
    return 0;
}
```

frogwalk2.cpp

Because both random walkers take the same number of steps, it isn't necessary to have checks using both frog.HasMore() and toad.HasMore(); but since both walkers must be initialized using Init and updated using Next, we use HasMore for both to maintain symmetry in the code.[5]

Reviewing Program Tip 7.1 we find that it's good advice to concentrate first on class methods and behavior, then move to instance variables and state.

---

[5]Checking both HasMore functions will be important if we modify the classes to behave differently. Write programs anticipating that they'll change.

```
                        O U T P U T

prompt> frogwalk2
enter # steps between 0 and 30000: 10000
frog position = -6
toad position = -26
# times at same location = 87
prompt> frogwalk2
enter # steps between 0 and 30000: 10000
frog position = 16
toad position = 40
# times at same location = 392
```

For `RandomWalk` I first decided to use the iteration pattern of `Init`, `HasMore`, and `Next`. Since it may be useful to execute an entire simulation at once I decided to implement a `Simulate` function to do this. As we'll see, it will be easy to implement this function using the iterating member functions. Finally, the class must provide some accessor functions. In this case we need functions to determine the current location of a `RandomWalk` object and to determine the total number of steps taken.

Determining what data should be private is not always a simple task (see Program Tip 7.6 for some guidance). You'll often need to revise initial decisions and add or delete data members as the design of the class evolves. As a general guideline, private data should be an intrinsic part of what is modeled by the class. For example, the current position of a `RandomWalk` object is certainly an intrinsic part of a random walk. The `Dice` object used to determine the direction to take at each step is not intrinsic. The state of one `Dice` object does not need to be accessed by different member functions, nor does the state need to be maintained over several invocations of the same function. Even if a `Dice` object is used in several member functions, there is no compelling reason for the same `Dice` object to be used across more than one function.

When you implement a class you should use the same process of iterative enhancement we used in previous programs. For classes this means you might not implement all member functions at once. For example, you could leave a member function out of the public section at first and add it later when the class is partially complete. Alternatively, you could include a declaration of the function, but implement it as an empty **stub function** with no statements.

When I implemented `RandomWalk` I realized that there would be code duplicated in `Init` and `Next` since both functions simulate one random step. Since it's a good idea to avoid code duplication whenever possible, I decided to factor the duplicate code out into another function called `TakeStep` called from both `Init` and `Next`.[6] This kind of **helper function** should be declared in the private section so that it is not accessible to client programs. Member functions, however, can call private helper functions.

---

[6]Actually, I wrote the code for `Init` and `Next` and then realized it was duplicated after the fact, so I added the helper function.

It's not unreasonable to make TakeStep public so that client programs could use either the iteration member functions or the TakeStep function. Similarly, you may decide that the function Simulate is superfluous since client programs can implement it by using Init, HasMore, and Next (see Program 7.13, *walk.cpp*). There is often a tension between including too many member functions in an effort to provide as much functionality as possible and too few member functions in an effort to keep the public interface simple and easy to use. There are usually many ways of writing a program, implementing a class, skinning a cat, and walking a frog.

In [Rie96] Arthur Riel offers two design heuristics we'll capture as one programming tip.

Program Tip 7.13: Minimize the number of methods in the interface (protocol) of a class. You should also implement a minimal public interface that all classes understand.

The RandomWalk member functions are fairly straightforward. All private data are initialized in the constructor; the function RandomWalk::TakeStep() simulates a random step and updates private data accordingly, and the other member functions are used to simulate a random walk or to access information about a walk, such as the current location of the simulated walker. The implementation is shown in Program 7.13.

Program 7.13 walk.cpp

```cpp
#include "walk.h"
#include "dice.h"

RandomWalk::RandomWalk(int maxSteps)
   : myPosition(0),
     mySteps(0),
     myMaxSteps(maxSteps)
// postcondition: no walk has been taken, but walk is ready to go
{
    // work done in initializer list
}

void RandomWalk::TakeStep()
// postcondition: one step of random walk taken
{
    Dice coin(2);
    switch (coin.Roll())
    {
      case 1:
        myPosition--;
        break;
      case 2:
        myPosition++;
        break;
    }
```

```
        mySteps++;
}

void RandomWalk::Init()
// postcondition: first step of random walk taken
{
    myPosition = 0;
    mySteps = 0;
    TakeStep();
}

bool RandomWalk::HasMore()
// postcondition: returns true when random walk still going
//                i.e., when # of steps taken < max. # of steps
{
    return mySteps < myMaxSteps;
}

void RandomWalk::Next()
// postcondition: next step in random walk simulated
{
    TakeStep();
}

void RandomWalk::Simulate()
// postcondition: one simulation completed
{
    for(Init(); HasMore(); Next())
    {
    // simulation complete using iterator methods
    }
}

int RandomWalk::Position() const
// postcondition: returns position of walker (x coordinate)
{
    return myPosition;
}

int RandomWalk::Current() const
// postcondition: retrns position of walker (x coordinate)
{
    return Position();
}

int RandomWalk::TotalSteps() const
// postcondition: returns number of steps taken by walker
{
    return mySteps;
}
```

walk.cpp

Each member function requires only a few lines of code. The brevity of the functions makes it easier to verify that they are correct. As you design your own classes, try to keep the implementations of each member function short. Using private helper functions can help both in keeping code short and in factoring out common code.

Program Tip 7.14: Use private helper functions to avoid code duplication in public methods. The helper functions should be private because client programs don't need to know how a class is implemented, and helper functions are an implementation technique.

7.3.4 A Two-Dimensional Walk Class

In this section we'll extend the one-dimensional random walk to two dimensions. A two-dimensional random walk is a more realistic model of a large molecule moving in a gas or liquid, although it is still much simpler than the physical forces that govern molecular motion. Nevertheless, the two-dimensional walk provides insight into the phenomenon known as *Brownian motion*, named after the botanist Robert Brown who, in the early 1800s, investigated pollen grains moving in water. His observations were modeled physically by Albert Einstein, whose hypotheses were confirmed by Jean-Baptiste Perrin, who won a Nobel prize for his work.

The class `RandomWalk2D` models a two-dimensional random walk, the implementation and use of which are shown in *brownian.cpp,* Program 7.14. In two dimensions, a molecule can move in any direction. This direction can be specified by a random number of degrees from the horizontal. A random number between 1 and 360 can be generated by a 360-sided die. However, using a `Dice` object would constrain the molecule to use a direction that is an integer. We'd like molecules to be able to go in any direction, including angles such as 1.235157 and 102.3392. Instead of using a `Dice` object, we'll use an object from the class `RandGen`, specified in *randgen.h,* Program G.4. Since the sine and cosine functions `sin` and `cos` from `<cmath>` are needed for this simulation, and since these functions require an angle specified in radians[7] rather than degrees, we need to use random `double` values.

The geometry to translate a random direction into *x* and *y* distances follows:

$$\cos(a) = X / \text{step size}$$
$$\sin(a) = Y / \text{step size}$$

If a random angle *a* is chosen, the distance moved in the *X*-direction is $\cos(a) \times$ step size as shown in the diagram. The distance in the *Y*-direction is a similar function

---

[7]There are 360 degrees in a circle and 2π radians in a circle. It's not necessary to understand radian measure, but $180° = \pi$ radians. This means that $a° = d(3.14159/180)$ radians. You can also use conversion functions `deg2rad` and `rad2deg` in *mathutils.h,* Program G.9 in How to G.

of the sine of the angle *a*. In the member function RandomWalk2D::TakeStep()
these properties are used to update the coordinates of a molecule in simulating a two-
dimensional random walk. The manner in which a direction is calculated changes in
moving from one to two dimensions. We also need to change how a position is stored so
that we can track both an *x* and a *y* coordinate. We could use two instance variables, such
as myXcoord and myYcoord. Instead, we'll use the Point class for representing
points in two dimensions (the header file *point.h* is Program G.10 in How to G). As
we'll see in Section 7.4, Point acts like a class but is in some ways different because
it has public data. These are the principal differences between the class RandomWalk
and RandomWalk2D:

▪ The implementation of the member function TakeStep to cope with a two-
   dimensional random direction.

▪ The change of type for instance variable myPosition from int to Point to
   cope with two dimensions.

▪ The change in return type for methods Position and Current from int to
   Point.

Program 7.14 browrian.cpp
_____

```
#include <iostream>
#include <cmath>              // for sin, cos, sqrt
#include "randgen.h"
#include "prompt.h"
#include "mathutils.h"        // for PI
#include "point.h"
using namespace std;

// simluate two-dimensional random walk
// Owen Astrachan, 6/20/95, modified 6/29/96, modified 5/1/99

class RandomWalk2D
{
  public:
     RandomWalk2D(long maxSteps,
                  int size);     // # of steps, size of one step
     void Init();               // take first step of walk
     bool HasMore();            // returns false if walk finished, else true
     void Next();               // take next step of random walk
     void Simulate();           // complete an entire random walk

     long  TotalSteps() const;   // total # of steps taken by molecule
     Point Position()    const;  // current position
     Point Current()     const;  // alias for Position

  private:
     void TakeStep();           // simulate one step of walk
     Point myPosition;          // coordinate of current position
     long  mySteps;             // # of steps taken
```

```
    int   myStepSize;       // size cf step
    long  myMaxSteps;       // maximum # of steps allowed
};

RandomWalk2D::RandomWalk2D(long maxSteps,int size)
  : myPosition(),
    mySteps(0),
    myStepSize(size),
    myMaxSteps(maxSteps)
// postcondition: walker initialized
{

}

void RandomWalk2D::TakeStep()
// postcondition: one step of random walk taken
{
    RandGen gen;                     // random number generator
    double randDirection = gen.RandReal(0,2*PI);

    myPosition.x += myStepSize * cos(randDirection);
    myPosition.y += myStepSize * sin(randDirection);
    mySteps++;
}

void RandomWalk2D::Init()
// postcondition: Init step of random walk taken
{
    mySteps = 0;
    myPosition = Point(0,0);
    TakeStep();
}

bool RandomWalk2D::HasMore()
// postcondition: returns false when random walk is finished
//                i.e., when # of steps taken >= max. # of steps
//                return true if walk still in progress
{
    return mySteps < myMaxSteps;
}

void RandomWalk2D::Next()
// postcondition: next step in random walk simulated
{
    TakeStep();
}

void RandomWalk2D::Simulate()
{
    for(Init(); HasMore(); Next())
    {
        // simulation complete using iterator methods
    }
}
```

```cpp
long RandomWalk2D::TotalSteps() const
// postcondition: returns number of steps taken by molecule
{
    return mySteps;
}


Point RandomWalk2D::Position() const
// postcondition: return molecule's position
{
    return myPosition;
}


Point RandomWalk2D::Current() const
// postcondition: return molecule's position
{
    return myPosition;
}


int main()
{
    long numSteps= PromptRange("enter # of random steps",1L,1000000L);
    int stepSize=  PromptRange("size of one step",1,20);
    int trials=    PromptRange("number of simulated walks",1,1000);
    RandomWalk2D molecule(numSteps,stepSize);

    int k;
    double total = 0.0;
    Point p;
    for(k=0; k < trials; k++)
    {
        molecule.Simulate();
        p = molecule.Position();
        total += p.distanceFrom(Point(0,0));   // total final distance from origin
    }
    cout << "average distance from origin = " << total/trials << endl;
    return 0;
}
```

brownian.cpp

OUTPUT

```
prompt> brownian
enter # of random steps between 1 and 1000000: 1024
size of one step between 1 and 20: 1
number of simulated walks between 1 and 1000: 100
average distance from origin = 26.8131
prompt> brownian
enter # of random steps between 1 and 1000000: 1024
size of one step between 1 and 20: 4
number of simulated walks between 1 and 1000: 100
average distance from origin = 108.861
```

If the output of one simulation is printed and used in a plotting program, a graph of the random walk can be made. Two such graphs are shown in Figures 7.2 and 7.3. Note that the molecule travels in completely different areas of the plane. However, the molecule's final distance from the origin doesn't differ drastically between the two runs. The distance from the origin of a point (x, y) is calculated by the formula $\sqrt{x^2 + y^2}$. The distances are accumulated in Program 7.14 using the method `Point::distanceFrom()` so that the average distance can be output.

The paths of the walk shown in the plots are interesting because they are **self-similar.** If a magnifying glass is used for a close-up view of a particular part of the walk, the picture will be similar to the overall view of the walk. Using a more powerful magnifying glass doesn't make a difference; the similarity still exists. This is a fundamental property of **fractals,** a mathematical concept that is used to explain how seemingly random phenomena aren't as random as they initially seem.

The results of both random walks illustrate one of the most important relationships of statistical physics. In a random walk, the average (expected) distance D from the start of a walk of N steps, where each step is of length L, is given by the following equation:

$$D = \sqrt{N} \times L \tag{7.1}$$

The results of the simulated walks above don't supply enough data to validate this relationship, but the data are supportive. In the exercises you'll be asked to explore this further.

Pause to Reflect

7.25 Modify *frogwalk.cpp*, Program 7.10, so the user enters a distance from the origin— say, 142—and the program simulates a walk until this distance is reached (in either the positive or negative direction). The program should output the number of steps needed to reach the distance.

7.26 Only one simulation is performed in Program 7.10. The code for that one simulation could be moved to a function. Write a prototype for such a function that returns both the final distance from the start as well as the maximum distance from the start reached during the walk.

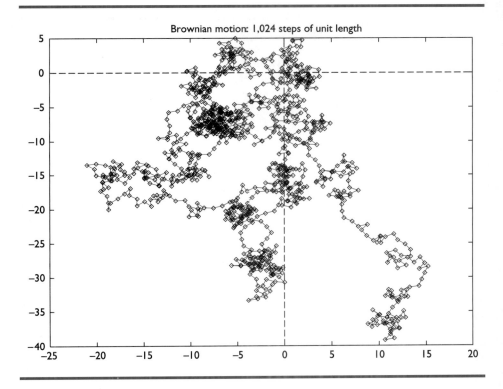

Brownian motion: 1,024 steps of unit length

Figure 7.2 Fractal characteristics of two-dimensional random walks.

7.27 Can you find an expression for use in *frogwalk.cpp,* Program 7.10, so that no switch or if/else statement is needed when the position is updated? For example: position += die.Roll() would add either 1 or 2 to the value of position. What's needed is an expression that will add either −1 or 1 with equal probability.

7.28 A two-dimensional walk on a lattice constrains the random walker to take steps in the compass point directions: north, east, south, west. How can the class RandomWalk be modified to support a frog that travels on lattice points? How can the class RandomWalk2D be modified?

7.29 If you modified the random walking classes RandomWalk2D and RandomWalk with code to track the number of times the walker returned to the starting position, either (0,0) or 0 respectively, would you expect the results to be similar?

7.30 Suppose the one-dimensional walker is restricted to walking in a circle instead of on an infinite line. Outline a modification to the class RandomWalk so that the number of "lily pads" on a circle is specified as well as the number of steps in a walk. Strive for a modification that entails minimal change to the class.

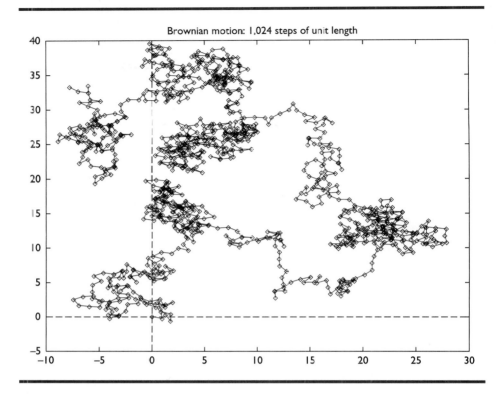

Figure 7.3 Fractal characteristics of two-dimensional random walks (*continued*).

7.3.5 The Common Interface in `RandomWalk` and `RandomWalk2D`

Because the methods of `RandomWalk` and `RandomWalk2D` have the same names, we can modify Program 7.12, *frogwalk2.cpp*, very easily. That program keeps track of how many times two walkers have the same position (we used the metaphor of two frogs sharing the same lily pad). The only difference between the one-dimensional walk class declared in *walk.h* and the two-dimensional class whose declaration and definition are both given in *brownian.cpp*, Program 7.14, is that the functions `Current()` and `Position()` return an `int` in the one-dimensional case and a `Point` in the two-dimensional case. As we'll see in Section 7.4, `Point` objects can be compared for equality and printed, so the only change needed to the code in *frogwalk2.cpp* to accommodate two-dimensional walkers is a change in the `#include` from `"walk.h"` to `"walk2d.h"`. Here I'm assuming that the class `RandomWalk2D` has been defined and implemented in .h and .cpp files rather than in *brownian.cpp*. Actually a small change must be made in the constructor calls of `frog` and `toad` since the size of the step is specified for the two-dimensional walkers.

Program 7.15   twodwalk.cpp

```cpp
#include <iostream>
using namespace std;
#include "prompt.h"
#include "walk2d.h"

// simulate two random walkers at once
// Owen Astrachan, 6/29/96, modified 5/1/99

int main()
{
    int numSteps = PromptRange("enter # steps",0,30000);

    RandomWalk2D frog(numSteps,1);   // define two random walkers
    RandomWalk2D toad(numSteps,1);
    int samePadCount = 0;                 // # times at same location

    frog.Init();                          // initialize both walks
    toad.Init();

    while (frog.HasMore() && toad.HasMore())
    {   // if (frog.Current() == toad.Current())
        if (frog.Current().distanceFrom(toad.Current()) < 1.0)
        {   samePadCount++;
    }
        frog.Next();
    toad.Next();
    }
    cout << "frog position = " << frog.Position() << endl;
    cout << "toad position = " << toad.Position() << endl;
    cout << "# times at same location = " << samePadCount << endl;
    return 0;
}
```

twodwalk.cpp

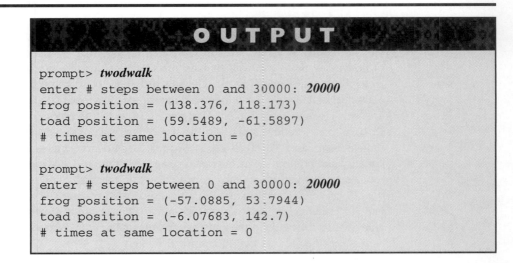

```
prompt> twodwalk
enter # steps between 0 and 30000: 20000
frog position = (138.376, 118.173)
toad position = (59.5489, -61.5897)
# times at same location = 0

prompt> twodwalk
enter # steps between 0 and 30000: 20000
frog position = (-57.0885, 53.7944)
toad position = (-6.07683, 142.7)
# times at same location = 0
```

It's probably not surprising that the two-dimensional walkers never occupy the same position. Even if the walkers are very close to each other it's extraordinarily unlikely that the double values representing both *x* and *y* coordinates will be exactly the same. This is due in part to accumulated round-off errors introduced when small double values are added together. In general you should avoid comparing double values for exact equality, but use a function like FloatEqual in *mathutils.h* (Program G.9 and discussed in How to G).

A simple change in Program 7.15, *twodwalk.cpp*, can track if two walkers are very close rather than having exactly the same position. Using Point::distanceFrom() (see Program 7.14, *brownian.cpp*) lets us do this if we change the if test as follows:

```
if (frog.Current().distanceFrom(toad.Current()) < 1.0)
```

Two runs with this test show a change in behavior.

OUTPUT

```
prompt> twodwalk
enter # steps between 0 and 30000: 20000
frog position = (-37.9018, 63.9209)
toad position = (-4.6354, 18.2154)
# times at same location = 6

prompt> twodwalk
enter # steps between 0 and 30000: 20000
frog position = (-125.509, 98.8204)
toad position = (82.7206, -24.1438)
# times at same location = 11
```

7.4   structs as Data Aggregates

Suppose you're writing a function to find the number of words in a text file that have fewer than four letters, between four and seven letters, and more than seven letters. The prototype for such a function might look like this:

```
void fileStats(const string& filename, int& smallCount,
               int& medCount, int& largeCount)
// postcondition: return word counts for text-file filename
//          smallCount  = # words with length() < 4
//          medCount    = # words with 4 <= length() <= 7
//          largeCount  = # words with 7 < length()
```

It's easy to imagine a more lengthy and elaborate set of statistics for a text file; the parameter list for a modified fileStats function would quickly become cumbersome.

We could write a class instead, with instance variables recording each count or other statistic. However, if we write a single member function to get all the statistics, we have the same prototype as the function fileStats shown above. If we use one member function for each statistic, that quickly gets cumbersome in a different way.

Instead of using several related parameters, we can group the related parameters together so that they can be treated as a single structure. A class works well as a way to group related data together, but if we adhere to the guideline in Program Tip 6.2, all data should be private with public accessor functions when clients need access to some representation of a class's state. Object-oriented programmers generally accept this design guideline and implement accessor and mutator methods for retrieving and updating state data.

Sometimes, rather than using a class to encapsulate both data (state) and behavior, a **struct** is used. In C++ a struct is similar to a class but is used for storing related data together. Structs are implemented almost exactly like classes, but the word struct replaces the word class. The only difference between a struct and a class in C++ is that by default all data and functions in a struct are public, whereas the default in a class is that everything is private. We'll use structs to combine related data together so that the data can be treated as a single unit. A struct used for this purpose is described in the C++ standard as *plain old data,* or *pod.*

In the file statistics example we could use this declaration:

```
struct FileStats
{
    string fileName;    // name of text file
    int     smallCount; // # words with length() < 4
    int     medCount;   // # words with 4 <= length() <= 7
    int     largeCount; // # words with 7 < length()
};
```

Since the combined data have different types, that is, string and int, a struct is often called a **heterogeneous aggregate,** a means of encapsulating data of potentially different types into one new type. As a general design rule we won't require any member functions in a struct and will rely on all data fields being public by default. As we'll see, it may be useful to implement some member functions, including constructors, but we won't insist on these as we do for the design and implementation of a new class. In general, we'll use structs when we want to group data (state) and perhaps some behavior (functions) together, but we won't feel obligated to use the same kinds of design rules that we use when we design classes (e.g., all data are private). You should know that other programmers use structs in a different way and do not include constructors or other functions in structs. Since constructors often make programs shorter and easier to develop without mistakes, we'll use them when appropriate.

Using the struct FileStats we might have the following code:

```
void computeStats(FileStats& fs)
// precondition:  fs.fileName is name of a text file
// postcondition: data fields of fs represent statistics
{  // code here
```

```
    }
int main()
{
    FileStats fs;
    fs.fileName = "poe.txt";
    computeStats(fs);
    cout << "# large words in " << fs.fileName
        << " = " << fs.largeCount << endl;
    return 0;
}
```

> **Program Tip 7.15:** **If you're designing a class with little or no behavior, but just data that are accessed and modified, consider implementing the class as a struct.** A class should have behavior beyond setting and retrieving the value of each instance variable. Using structs for encapsulating data (with helper functions when necessary, such as for construction and printing) is a good compromise when development of a complete class seems like overkill.

7.4.1   structs for Storing Points

We've used objects of type Point in programs for simulating two-dimensional random walks (see Program 7.14, *brownian.cpp*, for an example). The type Point declared in *point.h*, Program G.10 in How to G, is implemented as struct rather than a class. With our design guidelines, a struct allows us to make the data public. For Point the data are *x* and *y* coordinates. Using a struct means we don't need to provide methods for getting and setting the coordinates, but can access them directly as shown in Program 7.16, *usepoint.cpp*.

Program 7.16   usepoint.cpp

```
#include <iostream>
using namespace std;

#include "point.h"

int main()
{
    Point p;
    Point q(3.0, 4.0);

    // print the points
    cout << "p = " << p << " q = " << q << endl;

    q.x *= 2;
    q.y *= 2;
```

```
cout << "q doubled = " << q << endl;

p = q;
if (p == q)
{   cout << "points are now equal" << endl;
}
else
{   cout << "points are NOT equal" << endl;
}

p = Point(0,0);
cout << q.distanceFrom(p) << " = distance of q from " << p << endl;

return 0;
}
```

usepoint.cpp

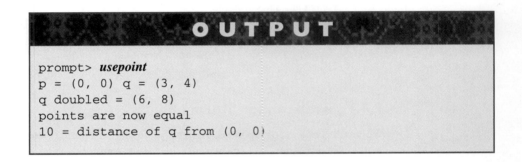

```
prompt> usepoint
p = (0, 0)  q = (3, 4)
q doubled = (6, 8)
points are now equal
10 = distance of q from (0, 0)
```

The data members of the `structs` p and q are accessed with a dot notation just as member functions of a class are accessed. However, because the data fields are public, they can be updated and accessed without using member functions. Sometimes the decision to use a `struct`, or several variables, or a class will not be simple. Using a `struct` instead of several variables makes it easy to add more data at a later time.

> **Program Tip 7.16: Be wary when you decide to use a `struct` rather than a class.** When you use a `struct`, client programs will most likely depend directly on the implementation of the `struct` rather than only on the interface. If the implementation changes, all client programs may need to be rewritten rather than just recompiled or relinked, as when client programs use only an interface rather than direct knowledge of an implementation.

If you reason carefully about the output from *usepoint.cpp* you'll notice several properties of `Point`. You can verify some of these by examining the header file *point.h* in How to G.

■   The default (parameterless) `Point` constructor initializes to the origin: (0,0).

■ Point objects can be assigned to each other, as in p = q, and compared for equality, as in if (p == q).

■ A **temporary** (or **anonymous**) Point object can be created by calling a constructor and using the constructed Point in a statement. The following statement from *usepoint.cpp* creates a temporary Point representing the origin (0,0) and assigns it to p:

```
p = Point(0,0);
```

A temporary is also used in *brownian.cpp*, Program 7.14, to compute a walker's final distance from the origin.

■ The method Point::distanceFrom() computes the distance of one point from another.

7.4.2 Operators for structs

In the programs using Point objects we printed points and compared them for equality. These operations are possible on Point objects because the relational operators and the output insertion operator << are **overloaded** for the class Point. The definition of the overloaded stream insertion operator is shown below (see also *point.cpp* with the files provided for use with this book):

```
ostream& operator << (ostream& os, const Point& p)
// postcondition: p inserted on output as (p.x,p.y)
{
    os << p.tostring();
    return os;
}
```

The parameter output can be any output stream, that is, either cout or an ofstream object. After the point p is inserted onto stream output, the stream is returned so that a chain of insertions can be made in one statement as shown in *usepoint.cpp*. A full description of how to overload the insertion operator and all other operators is found in How to E.

> **Program Tip 7.17: Many classes should have a member function named tostring that produces a representation of the class as a string.** Using the tostring method makes it very simple to overload the stream insertion operator, but is also useful in other contexts.

If you use the graphics package associated with this book you'll probably use the tostring method to "print" on the graphics screen since the screen displays strings but not streams.

As another example, here is the relational operator == for Point objects:

```
bool operator == (const Point& lhs, const Point& rhs)
```

```
{
    return lhs.x == rhs.x && lhs.y == rhs.y;
}
```

Note that the prototype for this function is declared in *point.h*, but the definition above is found in *point.cpp* (just as methods are declared in a header file and implemented in the corresponding .cpp file).

> **Program Tip 7.18:** **When possible, design a class to behave as users will expect from the behavior of built-in types like int and double.** This often means overloading relational operators and the stream insertion operator and ensuring that objects can be assigned to each other.

As we'll see in How to E and study in later chapters, overloaded operators can make the syntax of developing programs with new classes much simpler than if no overloaded operators were implemented.

7.5   Chapter Review

- The first step in developing programs and classes is to develop a specification and a list of requirements.

- Nouns in a problem statement or specification help identify potential classes; verbs help identify potential methods.

- When designing and implementing classes, first concentrate on behavior (methods), then concentrate on state (private data).

- Use scenarios to help develop classes and programs.

- Use stub functions when you want to test a class (or program) without implementing all the functions at once. Test classes in isolation from each other whenever possible.

- Factor out common code accessed by more than one function into another function that is called multiple times. For member functions, make these helping functions private so that they can be called from other member functions but not from client programs.

- Try to keep the bodies of each member function short so that the functions are easy to verify and modify.

- Functions atoi and atof allow conversion from strings to ints and doubles, respectively. These and the overloaded function tostring to convert from ints and doubles to strings are found in strutils.h.

- Keep classes to a single purpose. Use more than one class rather than combining different or unrelated behaviors in the same class.

- Program by conforming to known interfaces whenever possible. This reduces both conceptual hurdles and potential recompilation and relinking.

- Creating a program from source files in C++ consists of preprocessing, compiling, and linking. Libraries are often accessed in the linking phase.

- Compilation errors and linking errors have different causes.

- Initializer lists are used to construct private data in a class. You should use initializer lists rather than assigning values in the body of a constructor.

- Random walks are useful models of many natural phenomenon with a basis in mathematics and statistical physics.

- The `switch` statement is an alternative to cascaded `if`/`else` statements.

- `Structs` are used as heterogeneous aggregates. When related data should be stored together without the programming and design overhead of implementing a class, `structs` are a useful alternative. `Structs` are classes in which the data are public by default. `Structs` can also have constructors and helper functions to make them easier to use.

- The insertion operator can be overloaded for programmer-defined types, as can relational operators.

7.6 Exercises

7.1 Write a quiz program similar to *quiz.cpp* Program 7.8, but using different levels of mathematical drill questions. Give the user a choice of easy, medium, or hard questions. An easy question involves addition of two-digit numbers, but no carry is required, so that 23 + 45 is ok, but 27 + 45 is not. A medium question uses addition, but a carry is always required. A hard question involves multiplication of a two-digit number by a one-digit number, but the answer must be less than 100.

7.2 Modify Program 7.10, *frogwalk.cpp*, to keep track of all the locations that are visited more than once, not just the number of times the walkers are at the same location. To do this, use a `StringSet` object (see Programs 6.14 and 6.15 in Section 6.5). Use the functions `tostring` from *strutils.h* to convert walker positions to strings so that they can be stored in a `StringSet`. Then change the program so that two two-dimensional walkers are used as in *twodwalk.cpp*. You'll need to use `Point::tostring()` to store two-dimensional locations in a `StringSet`.

7.3 A result of Dirichlet (see [Knu98a], Section 4.5) says that if two numbers are chosen at random, the probability that their greatest common divisor equals 1 is $6/\pi^2$. Write a program that repeatedly chooses two integers at random and calculates the approximation to π. For best results use a `RandGen` variable `gen` (from *randgen.h*) and generate a random integer using `gen.RandInt(1, RAND_MAX)`.

7.4 A reasonable but rough approximation of the mathematical constant π can be obtained by simulating throwing darts. The simulated darts are thrown at a dartboard in the shape of a square with a quarter-circle in it.

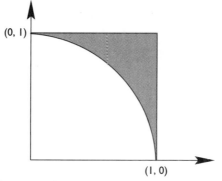

If 1000 darts are thrown at the square, and 785 land in the circle, then 785/1000 is an approximation for $\pi/4$ since the area of the circle (with radius 1) is $\pi/4$. The approximation for π is $4 \times 0.785 = 3.140$. Write a program to approximate π using this method. Use a unit square as shown in the figure, with corners at (0,0), (1,0), (1,1), and (0,1). Use the RandGen class specified in *randgen.h* and the member function RandReal, which returns a random double value in the range $(0 . . 1)$. For example, the following code segment generates random x and y values inside the square and increments a counter hits if the point (x, y) lies within the circle:

```
x = gen.RandReal();
y = gen.RandReal();

if (x*x + y*y <= 1.0)
{   hits++;
}
```

This works because the equation of the unit circle is $x^2 + y^2 = 1$. Allow the user to specify the number of darts (random numbers) thrown or use a varying number of darts to experiment with different approximations. This kind of approximation is called a **Monte Carlo** approximation.

7.5 This problem (adapted from [BRE71]) is a simplistic simulation of neutrons in a nuclear reactor. Neutrons enter the lead wall of a nuclear reactor and collide with the lead atoms in the wall. Each time a neutron collides with a lead atom it rebounds in a random direction (between 0 and 2π radians) before colliding with another lead atom, reentering the reactor, or leaving the wall. To simplify the simulation we'll assume that all neutrons enter the wall at a right angle; each neutron travels a distance d before either colliding, reentering the reactor, or leaving the wall; and the wall is $3d$ units thick. Figure 7.4 diagrams a wall; the reactor is at the bottom. The neutron at the left reenters the reactor, the neutron in the middle leaves the wall outside the reactor, and the neutron on the right is absorbed in the wall (assume that after 10 collisions within the wall a neutron is absorbed).

If p is the depth of penetration inside the wall, then p is changed after each collision by p += d * cos(angle), where angle is a random angle (see *brownian.cpp,* Program 7.14). If $p < 0$, then the neutron reenters the reactor, and if $3d < p$, then the neutron leaves the wall; otherwise it collides with another lead atom or is absorbed.

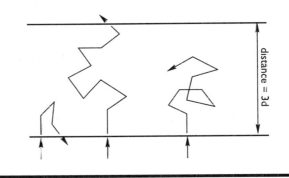

Figure 7.4 Collisions in a nuclear reactor.

Write a program to simulate this reactor. Use 10,000 neutrons in the simulation and determine the percentages of neutrons that return to the reactor, are absorbed in the wall, and penetrate the wall to leave the reactor. Use the simulation to determine the minimal wall thickness (as a multiple of d) required so that no more than 5% of the neutrons escape the reactor. To help test your simulation, roughly 26% of the neutrons should leave a $3d$-thick wall and roughly 22% should be absorbed.

7.6 Repeat the simulation from the previous exercise but assume the neutrons enter the wall at a random angle rather than at a right angle. Then implement a neutron observer class that records the movements of a neutron. Record the motion of 10 neutrons and graph the output if you have access to a plotting program.

7.7 Write a program to test the relationship $D = \sqrt{N} \times L$ from statistical physics, described in Equation 7.1. Use a one-dimensional random walk and vary both the length of each step L and the number of steps N. You'll need to run several hundred experiments for each value; try to automate the process.

If you have access to a graphing program, graph the results. If you know about curve fitting, try to fit a curve to the results and see if the empirical observations match the theoretical equation. You can repeat this experiment for the two-dimensional random walk.

7.8 Write a program for two-dimensional random walks in which two frogs participate at the same time. Keep track of the closest and furthest distances the frogs are away from each other during the simulation. Can you easily extend this to three frogs or four frogs?

7.9 Write a program to simulate a roulette game. In roulette you can place bets on which of 38 numbers is chosen when a ball falls into a numbered slot. The numbers range from 1 to 36, with special 0 and 00 slots. The 0 and 00 slots are colored green; each of the numbers 1 through 36 is red or black. The red numbers are 1, 3, 5, 7, 9, 12, 14, 16, 18, 19, 21, 23, 25, 27, 30, 32, 34, and 36. Gamblers can make several different kinds of bet, each of which pays off at different odds as listed in Table 7.1. A payoff of 1 to 1 means that a \$10.00 bet earns \$10.00 (plus the bet \$10.00 back); 17 to 1 means that a \$10.00 bet earns \$170.00 (plus the \$10.00 back). If the wheel spins 0 or 00, then all bets lose except for a bet on the single number 0/00 or on the two consecutive numbers 0 and 00. You may find it useful to implement a separate Bet class to keep track of the different kinds of bets and odds. For example, when betting on a number, you'll need to keep

Table 7.1　Roulette bets and payoff odds.

Bet	Payoff Odds
Red/black	1 to 1
Odd/even	1 to 1
Single number	35 to 1
Two consecutive numbers	17 to 1
Three consecutive numbers	11 to 1

track of the number, but betting on red/black requires only that you remember the color chosen.

7.10 Design and implement a struct for representing points in three dimensions. Then program a random walk in three dimensions and determine how often two walkers are within 10 units of each other. Use a class `RandomWalk3D` patterned after the class `RandomWalk2D` in *brownian.cpp*, Program 7.14.

Arrays, Data, and Random Access

8

A teacher who can arouse a feeling for one single good action . . . accomplishes more than he who fills our memory with rows on rows of natural objects, classified with name and form.

GOETHE
Elective Affinities, Book II, Ch. 7

Computers are useless; they can only give you answers.

PABLO PICASSO
21st Century Dictionary of Quotations

A compact disc (CD), a computer graphics monitor, and a group of campus mailboxes share a common characteristic, as shown in Figure 8.1: Each consists of a sequence of items, and each item is accessible independently of the other items. In the case of a CD, any track can be played without regard to whether the other tracks are played. This arrangement is different from the way songs are recorded on a cassette tape, where, for example, the fifth song is accessible only after playing or fast-forwarding past the first four. In the case of a graphics monitor, any individual picture element, or **pixel**, can be turned on or off, or changed to a different color, without concern as to what the values of the other pixels are. The independence of each pixel to display different colors permits images to be displayed very rapidly. The address of a student on many campuses, or a person living in an apartment building, is typically specified by a box number.

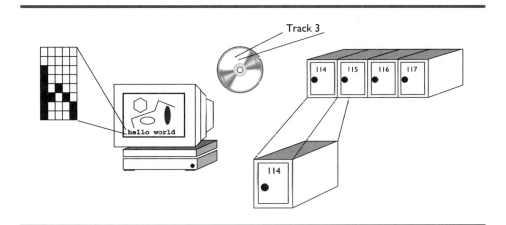

Figure 8.1 Random or constant-time access.

Postal workers can deliver letters to box 117 without worrying about the location of the first 100 boxes, the last 100 boxes, or any boxes other than 117.

This characteristic of instant access is useful in programming applications. The terminology used is **random access,** as opposed to the **sequential access** to a cassette tape. Most programming languages include a construct that allows data to be grouped together so that each data item is accessible independently of the other items. For example, a collection of numbers might represent test scores; a collection of strings could represent the different words in *Hamlet;* and a collection of strings and numbers combined in a `struct` might represent the words in *Hamlet* and how many times each word occurs.

We've studied three ways of structuring data in C++ programs: classes, `structs`, and files accessible using streams. In this chapter you will learn about a data structure called an **array**—one of the most useful data structures in programming. Examples of array use in this chapter include

- Using an array as many counters—for example, to keep track of how many times all sums of rolling *n*-sided dice occur or to keep track of how many times each letter of the alphabet occurs in *Hamlet*.
- Using an array to store a list of words in a file, keeping track of each different word and then extending this array to track how many times each different word occurs.
- Using an array to maintain a database of on-line information for over 3,000 different CD titles, or alternatively, an on-line address book.

8.1   Arrays and Vectors as Counters

Consider Program 8.1, *dieroll.cpp*, which tracks the number of times each sum between 2 and 8 occurs when two four-sided dice are rolled. Modifying this program to track the number of times each possible dice roll occurs for six-sided dice would be very ugly.

Program 8.1   dieroll.cpp

```
#include <iostream>
using namespace std;
#include "dice.h"
#include "prompt.h"

// illustrates cumbersome programming
// roll two dice and track occurrences of all possible rolls

const int DICE_SIDES = 4;

int main()
{
    int twos=    0;                      // counters for each possible roll
    int threes=  0;
    int fours=   0;
    int fives=   0;
```

```
    int sixes=   0;
    int sevens=  0;
    int eights=  0;

    int rollCount = PromptRange("how many rolls",1,20000);
    Dice d(DICE_SIDES);

    int k;
    for(k=0; k < rollCount; k++)          // simulate all the rolls
    {   int sum = d.Roll() + d.Roll();
        switch (sum)
        {
          case 2:
            twos++;
            break;
          case 3:
            threes++ ;
            break;
          case 4:
            fours++;
            break;
          case 5:
            fives++;
            break;
          case 6:
            sixes++;
            break;
          case 7:
            sevens++;
            break;
          case 8:
            eights++;
            break;
        }
    }
    // output for each possible roll # of times it occurred

    cout << "roll\t# of occurrences" << endl;
    cout << "2\t" << twos   << endl;
    cout << "3\t" << threes << endl;
    cout << "4\t" << fours  << endl;
    cout << "5\t" << fives  << endl;
    cout << "6\t" << sixes  << endl;
    cout << "7\t" << sevens << endl;
    cout << "8\t" << eights << endl;

    return 0;
}
```

dieroll.cpp

```
                            O U T P U T

prompt> dieroll
how many rolls between 1 and 20000    10000
roll             # of occurrences
2                623
3                1204
4                1935
5                2474
6                1894
7                1246
8                624
```

The code in *dieroll.cpp* would be much more compact if loops could be used to initialize the variables and generate the output. To do this we need a new kind of variable that maintains several different values at the same time; such a variable could be used in place of twos, threes, fours, and so on. Most programming languages support such variables; they are called **arrays.** An array structures data together and has three important properties:

1.   An array is a *homogeneous* collection. Each item stored in an array is the same type; for example, all integers, all doubles, or all strings. It is not possible to store both integers and strings in the same array.

2.   Items in an array are numbered, or ordered; that is, there is a first item, a fifteenth item, and so on. The number that refers to an item is the item's **index,** sometimes called the **subscript.**

3.   An array supports **random access.** The time to access the first item is the same as the time to access the fifteenth item or the hundredth item.

In C++ the built-in array type has many problems; it is difficult for beginning programmers to use, and its use is too closely coupled with its low-level implementation.[1] We'll study built-in arrays, but we want to study the concept of homogeneous collections and random access without the hardships associated with using the built-in array type. Instead, we'll use a class that behaves like an array from a programming perspective but insulates us from the kind of programming problems that are common with built-in arrays. We'll use a class tvector, defined in the header file *tvector.h.*[2] The "t" in tvector stands for "Tapestry." You can use the standard vector class in any of

---

[1] The built-in array type in C++ is the same as its C-based counterpart. It is based on pointers, designed to be very efficient, and prone to hard-to-find errors, especially for beginning programmers.

[2] The class vector is defined as part of the STL library in standard C++. The class tvector declared in *tvector.h* is consistent with this standard class. The class apvector, defined for use in the Advanced Placement computer science course, is based on the class tvector. All member functions of the apvector class are also member functions of the tvector class. However, the tvector class supports push_back and pop_back functions not supported by apvector.

the programs in this book, but you'll find the `tvector` class is much more forgiving of the kinds of mistakes that beginning and experienced programmers make. Because `tvector` catches some errors that `vector` doesn't catch, `tvector` is slightly less efficient. If you really need the efficiency, develop using `tvector` and then switch to `vector` when you know your program works correctly.

Before studying Program 8.2, a program that is similar to *dieroll.cpp* but uses a `tvector` to track dice rolls, we'll discuss important properties of the `tvector` class and how to define `tvector` variables.

8.1.1 An Introduction to the Class `tvector`

The simplest definition of a `tvector` variable includes the variable's name, the type of item being stored, and an integer value passed to the constructor that indicates how many items the vector can store. The definitions below define a variable `numbers` that can store seven integer values and a variable `words` that can store five string values.

```
tvector<int>     numbers(7);
tvector<string>  words(5);
```

Because a `tvector` is a homogeneous collection, you can think of a `tvector` variable as a collection of boxes:

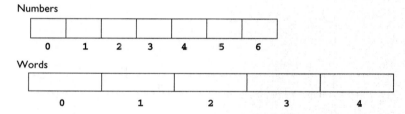

Each box or item in the `tvector` is referenced using a numerical index. In C++ the first item stored in a `tvector` has index zero. Thus, in the diagram here, the five items in `words` are indexed from zero to four. In general, the valid indexes in a `tvector` with n elements are $0, 1, \ldots, n - 1$.

An element of a `tvector` is selected, or referenced, using a numerical index and brackets: [ ]. The following statements store the number 13 as the first element of *numbers* and the string `"fruitcake"` as the first element of *words* (remember that the first element has index zero):

```
numbers[0]  = 13;
words[0]    = "fruitcake";
```

`tvector` variables can be indexed using a loop as follows, where all the elements of `numbers` are assigned the value zero:

```
int k;
for(k=0; k < 5; k++)
{   numbers[k] = 0;
}
```

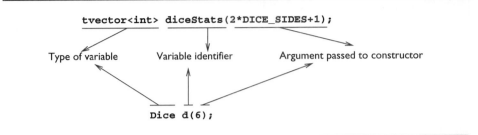

Figure 8.2 Comparing a `tvector` variable definition to a `Dice` variable definition. Both variables have names and a constructor parameter.

The number of elements in a vector variable is specified by a parameter to the `tvector` constructor, just as the number of sides of a `Dice` variable is specified when the `Dice` variable is constructed, as shown in Figure 8.2. This value can be a variable whose value is entered by the user; an expression; or, in general, any integer value. More details on defining `tvector` variables are given in Section 8.2.1.

8.1.2 Counting with `tvectors`

Program 8.2, *dieroll2.cpp*, uses a `tvector` to keep track of different dice rolls but otherwise performs the same tasks as Program 8.1, *dieroll.cpp*.

From a black-box viewpoint there is no difference between the programs *dieroll.cpp* and *dieroll2.cpp*. The `tvector` variable `diceStats` can store nine different integer values. The capacity of `diceStats` is determined when the variable is defined by the statement `tvector<int> diceStats(2*DICE_SIDES+1)`.

Program 8.2 dieroll2.cpp

```cpp
#include <iostream>
using namespace std;
#include "dice.h"
#include "prompt.h"
#include "tvector.h"

// use vector to simulate rolling of two dice
// Owen Astrachan, March 9, 1994, modified 5/2/99

const int DICE_SIDES = 4;

int main()
{
    int sum;
    int k;
    Dice d(DICE_SIDES);
    tvector<int> diceStats(2*DICE_SIDES+1);  // room for largest dice sum
    int rollCount = PromptRange("how many rolls",1,20000);
```

```
for(k=2; k <= 2*DICE_SIDES; k++)        // initialize counters to zero
{   diceStats[k] = 0;
}

for(k=0; k < rollCount; k++)            // simulate all the rolls
{   sum = d.Roll() + d.Roll();
    diceStats[sum]++;
}

cout << "roll\t\t# of occurrences" << endl;
for(k=2; k <= 2*DICE_SIDES; k++)
{   cout << k << "\t\t" << diceStats[k] << endl;
}
return 0;
}
```

dieroll2.cpp

```
                        O U T P U T

prompt> dieroll2
how many rolls between 1 and 2000010000
roll            # of occurrences
2               523
3               1204
4               1935
5               2474
6               1894
7               1246
8               624
```

There is one major difference between the definition of diceStats as a tvector variable and that of d as a Dice variable: the tvector definition indicates that the tvector contains integers. We'll discuss this in depth after examining other parts of the program.

Because the indexing begins with 0, the last location in a nine-element array has index 8. This is why space for nine integer values is allocated in Program 8.2 even though only seven of the locations are accessed in the program—diceStats[2] through diceStats[8]—as shown in Figure 8.3. The conceptual simplicity of using diceStats[sum] to represent the number of times two dice are rolled more than compensates for the two memory locations that could be saved by defining an array of seven values and using diceStats[sum-2] to store the number of times sum is obtained.

In Figure 8.3 the switch statement used to increment the appropriate counter in Program 8.1 is contrasted with the single statement diceStats[sum]++, which increments the corresponding vector location serving as a counter in Program 8.2.

When a vector is defined, the values in each vector location, or **cell,** are initially undefined. The vector cells can be used as variables, but they must be indexed, as shown here for a vector named `diceStats` containing nine cells:

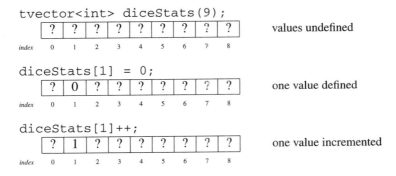

The indexing expression determines which of the many array locations is accessed. Indexing makes arrays extraordinarily useful. One array variable represents potentially thousands of different values, each value specified by the array variable name and the indexing value. The expression `diceStats[1]` is read as "diceStats sub one," where the word "sub" comes from the mathematical concept of a *subscripted* variable such as n_1.

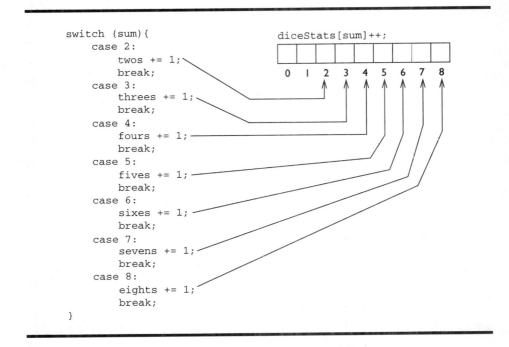

Figure 8.3 Using a `tvector` to store counts for tracking dice rolls.

8.2 Defining and Using tvectors

8.2.1 tvector Definition

When you define a tvector variable you'll normally specify the number of entries, or cells, in the tvector. As we'll see later in this chapter, when you use a vector so that it grows to accommodate more cells, it's possible that you won't specify the number of cells when the vector is first constructed.

Since vectors are homogeneous collections, you must also specify the type stored in each entry, such as int, string, or double. The following statements define three tvector variables: values stores 200 doubles, names stores 50 strings, and scores stores some number between 1 and 1000 of int values.

```
tvector<double> values(200);
tvector<string> names(50);
tvector<int>     scores(PromptRange("# of scores",1,1000));
```

The type of value stored in each cell of a tvector variable is specified between angle brackets (the less-than and greater-than symbols) before the name of the variable is given. The size of the tvector is an argument to the constructor, as illustrated in Figure 8.2.

Syntax: tvector definition

tvector<*type*> varname;
tvector<*type*> varname (*size expression*);
tvector<*type*> varname (*size expression*,
              value);

The type that defines what *kind* of element is stored in each array cell can be any built-in type (e.g., int, double, bool). It can also be a programmer-defined type such as string. The only qualification on programmer-defined types is that the type must have a default (or parame-terless) constructor. For example, it is *not* possible to have a definition tvector<Dice> dielist(10) for an array of 10 dice elements because a Dice object requires a parameter indicating the number of sides that the Dice object has. It is possible to define a vector of Date elements (see *date.h* in How to G or Program 5.10, *usedate.cpp*) because there is a default constructor for the Date class.

The *expression* in the tvector constructor determines the number of cells of the tvector variable. This integer expression can use variables, arithmetic operators, and function calls. For example, it is possible to use

```
tvector<int> primes(int(sqrt(X)));
```

to allocate a variable named primes whose number of cells is given by the (integer) truncated value of the square root of a variable X. If no integer expression is used, as in tvector<int> list, a vector with zero cells is created. We'll see later that sometimes this is necessary and that the number of cells in a vector can grow or shrink. The third form of constructor initializes all the cells to the value passed as the second argument to the constructor.

8.2.2 `tvector` Initialization

For vectors of user-defined types like `string`, all vector elements are initialized using the default constructor unless an argument is supplied the `tvector` constructor for initalization as shown below. For built-in types the `tvector` class does not initialize each vector cell, so the values will most likely be undefined.[3] For example, when a variable is used to represent several counters, as it is in Program 8.2, *dieroll2.cpp*, each element of the vector must be initialized to zero. As shown in the syntax diagram for `tvector` construction, it's possible to initialize all elements of a vector when the vector is constructed. For example, the statements below create a vector of 20 strings in which each string has the value `"Fred Brooks "` and a vector of 100 ints in which each `int` has the value 25.

```
tvector<string> names(20,"Fred Brooks");
tvector<int>    nums(100,25);
```

8.2.3 `tvector` Parameters

`tvector` variables can be passed as parameters just like any other variable in C++.[4] To illustrate how vectors are used and passed as parameters, we'll study another example in which a vector is used to count several quantities. First we'll count how many times each different character occurs in an input file. For example, we can count the number of occurrences of the letter *e* in *Hamlet* using Program 8.3, *letters.cpp*. Just as a vector of counters was used to count dice rolls in *dieroll2.cpp,* Program 8.2, a `tvector` of counters is used to track how many times each character occurs in the file.

Counting characters is similar to counting dice rolls: each `tvector` element records the number of occurrences of one character. We mentioned the type `char` briefly in Section 3.2.4. You can find more information on the type `char` in How to A and in Chapter 9. Two character-processing functions are used in *letters.cpp* that we haven't seen before, but I hope you'll understand their use from the context and the comments. The function `isalpha` from <cctype> (or <ctype.h>) returns `true` if its `char` parameter is a letter, either 'a'–'z' or 'A'–'Z' (see Table F.2 in How to F for more information). The stream function `get()` reads one character at a time from a stream; white space is not skipped. More information on `get` is found in How to B and in Chapter 9.

Program 8.3 letters.cpp

```
#include <iostream>
#include <fstream>        // for ifstream
#include <cstdlib>        // for exit()
```

---

[3]The standard `vector` class initializes all vector elements, including built-in types. Built-in types are initialized to 0, where 0 means `false` for `bool` values and 0.0 for `double` values, for example. The `tvector` class uses a different method to allocate memory than the standard vector class, so cells will not necessarily have a defined value unless one is supplied when the `tvector` is constructed.

[4]This is not quite true of arrays, as we'll see later in this chapter. This is another reason to prefer using the `tvector` class to using built-in arrays.

```
#include <cctype>            // for tolower()
#include <climits>           // for CHAR_MAX
#include <string>
#include <iomanip>
using namespace std;

#include "prompt.h"
#include "tvector.h"

// count # occurrences of all characters in a file
// written: 8/5/94, Owen Astrachan, modified 5/1/99

void Print(const tvector<int> & counts, int total);
void Count(istream & input, tvector<int> & counts, int & total);

int main()
{
    int totalAlph = 0;
    string filename = PromptString("enter name of input file: ");
    ifstream input(filename.c_str());

    if (input.fail() )
    {   cout << "could not open file " << filename << endl;
        exit(1);
    }
    tvector<int> charCounts(CHAR_MAX+1,0);    // all initialized to 0

    Count(input,charCounts,totalAlph);
    Print(charCounts,totalAlph);

    return 0;
}

void Count(istream & input, tvector<int> & counts, int & total)
// precondition: input open for reading
//               counts[k] == 0, 0 <= k < CHAR_MAX
// postcondition: counts[k] = # occurrences of character k
//                total = # alphabetic characters
{
    char ch;
    while (input.get(ch))            // read a character
    {   if (isalpha(ch))             // is alphabetic (a-z)?
        {   total++;
        }
        ch = tolower(ch);            // convert to lower case
        counts[ch]++;                // count all characters
    }
}

void Print(const tvector<int> & counts, int total)
// precondition: total = total of all entries in counts['a']..counts['z']
// postcondition: all values of counts from 'a' to 'z' printed
{
    const int MIDALPH = 13;
    cout.setf(ios::fixed);     // print 1 decimal place
```

```
cout.precision(1);
char k;
for(k = 'a'; k <= 'm'; k++)
{   cout << k << setw(7) << counts[k] << " ";
    cout << setw(4) << 100 * double(counts[k])/total << "% \t\t";
    cout << char(k+MIDALPH) << setw(7) << counts[k+MIDALPH] << " ";
    cout << setw(4) << 100 * double(counts[k+MIDALPH])/total << "%" << endl;
}
```
```
}
```

letters.cpp

For all practical purposes, a `char` variable is an integer constrained to have a value between zero and CHAR_MAX. Since `char` variables can be used as integers, we can use a `char` variable to index an array. We'll use the vector element with index `'a'` to count the occurrences of `'a'`, the element with index `'b'` to count the b's, and so on. The constant CHAR_MAX is defined in `<climits>` (or `<limits.h>`). We use it to initialize `charCounts`, a `tvector` of counters, so that all counters are initially zero.

```
tvector<int> charCounts(CHAR_MAX+1,0);
```

Only the 26 vector elements corresponding to the alphabetic characters `'a'` through `'z'` are printed, but every character is counted.[5] An alternative method of indexing `charCounts` that uses only 26 array elements rather than CHAR_MAX elements is explored in the Pause to Reflect exercises. To make the output look nice, we use stream member functions to limit the number of places after a decimal point when a `double` value is printed. These member functions are discussed in How to B.

`tvector` parameters should always be passed by reference, unless you need to pass a copy of the `tvector` rather than the `tvector` itself, but it's very rare to need a copy. Avoid copying because it takes time and uses memory. Some functions require value parameters, but these are rare when `tvector` parameters are used, so you should use reference or `const` reference parameters all the time. Use a `const` reference parameter, as shown in `Print` in Program 8.3, when a `tvector` parameter isn't changed. A `const` reference parameter is efficient and also allows the compiler to catch inadvertent attempts to change the value of the parameter. The parameter `counts` in the function `Print` is *not* changed; its contents are used to print the values of how many times each letter occurs.

> **Program Tip 8.1: `tvector` parameters should be passed by reference (using &) or by `const` reference.** Use a `const` reference parameter as part of a defensive programming strategy when a parameter is not changed but is passed by reference because of efficiency considerations.

---

[5] I had a bug in the version of this program that appeared in the first edition: I used CHAR_MAX instead of CHAR_MAX+1 as the size of the vector. If CHAR_MAX has the value 255, then the array will have 255 elements, but the largest index will be 254, and a character with value 255 will cause an illegal-index error. I never encountered this error in practice because I use *letters.cpp* to read text files, and the characters in text files typically don't have values of CHAR_MAX. This kind of off-by-one indexing error is common when using vectors. Some people call this an OBOB error (off-by-one bug).

Notice that the `for` loop in the function `Print` uses a `char` variable to index the values between `'a'` and `'z'`. The loop runs only from `'a'` to `'m'` because each line of output holds data for two letters, such as `'a'` and `'n'` or `'b'` and `'o'`. The result of adding 13 to `'a'` is `'n'`, but the explicit cast to `char` in `Print()` of Program 8.3 ensures that a character is printed. When ASCII values are used, these characters 'a' to 'z' correspond to array cells 97 to 122 (see Table F.3 in How to F).

O U T P U T

prompt> *letters*
enter name of input file: *hamlet.txt*

a	9950	7.6%		n	8297	6.4%
b	1830	1.4%		o	11218	8.6%
c	2606	2.0%		p	2016	1.5%
d	5025	3.9%		q	220	0.2%
e	14960	11.5%		r	7777	6.0%
f	2698	2.1%		s	8379	6.4%
g	2420	1.9%		t	11863	9.1%
h	8731	6.7%		u	4343	3.3%
i	8511	6.5%		v	1222	0.9%
j	110	0.1%		w	3132	2.4%
k	1272	1.0%		x	179	0.1%
l	5847	4.5%		y	3204	2.5%
m	4253	3.3%		z	72	0.1%

Pause to Reflect

8.1 In Program 8.1, how many lines must be changed or added to simulate two 12-sided dice? How many lines must be changed or added in Program 8.2 to simulate two 12-sided dice?

8.2 What changes must be made to Program 8.2 to simulate the rolling of three 6-sided dice?

8.3 Write definitions for a `tvector doubVec` of 512 `doubles` and `intVec` of 256 `ints`. Write code to initialize each vector location to twice its index so that `doubVec[13] = 26.0` and `intVec[200] = 400`.

8.4 Is it possible to create a vector of `Balloons` as declared in Program 3 7, *gballoon.h*? Why?

8.5 Write a definition for a `tvector` of strings that stores the names of the computer scientists for whom "Happy Birthday" was printed in Program 2.6, *bday2.cpp*. Write a loop that would print the song for all the names stored in the vector.

8.6 Suppose *letters.cpp* is modified so that the count of how many times `'a'` occurs is kept in the vector element with index zero (and the count of `'z'` occurrences is in the vector element with index 25). What changes are needed to do this? (Hint: If `'a' + 13 == 'n'` as shown in `Print`, the value of `'b' - 'a'` is 1 and the value of `'z' - 'a'` is 25.)

8.7 Write a short program, with all code in `main`, that determines how many 2-letter, 3-letter, ..., up to 15-letter words there are in a text file.

8.2.4 A `tvector` Case Study: Shuffling CD Tracks

Many CD players have an option for "random play." Pressing the random-play or shuffle button causes the tracks on the CD to be "shuffled" and played in some arbitrary order, which may be different each time the CD is played. CD jukeboxes shuffle collections of CDs rather than just the collection of tracks on a single CD. In this section we'll develop the program *shuffle.cpp,* Program 8.4, to simulate this random-play feature for a single CD.

We'll need to store the tracks in a `tvector` and rearrange the elements in the `tvector` to simulate the shuffling. We'll want to identify the original track number as well as the title of the track, so we'll use a `struct` to encapsulate this information.

Developing the Program. We'll start with the declaration below for a `struct Track` to store information about each track on a CD. All the tracks on a CD are stored in a `tvector<Track>` object.

```
struct Track
{
    string title;   // title of song/track
    int     number;   // the original track number
};
```

Rather than designing, coding, and testing the entire program at once, we'll concentrate first on the two main features of the program: printing and shuffling CD track information. Before shuffling, we'll need to print, so we'll implement `Print` first. Programming Tip 7.2 reminds us to grow a program — develop a program by adding to a working program rather than implementing the entire program at once.

A function to print the contents of a vector will need the vector and the number of elements in the vector. We'll write a function to encapsulate the loop below that prints the first `count` elements of a vector `tracks`.

```
int k;
for(k=0; k < count; k++)
{   cout << tracks[k].number << "\t"
         << tracks[k].title << endl;
}
```

Sometimes it is hard to interpret (and even read) the expressions from the loop above that follow:

```
tracks[k].title;
tracks[k].number;
```

To decipher such expressions, you can read them inside out, one piece at a time.[6] The [ ] are used to indicate an entry in a vector. The identifier to the left of them indicates that the name of the tvector is tracks. The identifier k is used to select a particular cell—note that the initial value of k is 0, indicating the first cell. I read the first expression as "tracks sub k dot title."

Now you should think about what kind of element is represented by tracks[k]: what is stored in tracks? We're dealing with a vector of Track structs. Now you should think about what Track is. It's a struct, so, as with a class, a period or dot . is needed to access one of its fields. The struct Track has two fields: title and number. Examining the struct declaration may remind you what type each field is. In particular, title is a string.

Initializing a tvector. To test a print function we'll need to store track information in a vector. Instead of reading track names from a file, we'll test by hard-wiring several tracks in main, then pass the vector to the print function. Given the declaration for the struct Track above, we're stuck writing code like the following:

```
tvector<Track> tracks(9);

tracks[0].title=  "The Squirming Coil";
tracks[0].number= 1;
tracks[1].title=  "Reba";
tracks[1].number= 2;
...
```

When you find yourself writing ugly code like this you should say to yourself, "There must be a better way."

Program Tip 8.2:   If you find yourself writing code that seems unnecessarily redundant, tedious, or that just offends your sense of aesthetics (it's ugly), step back and think if there might be a way to improve the code. Sometimes you'll just have to write code you don't consider ideal because you don't know enough about the language, because you can't think of the right approach, or because there just isn't any way to improve the code. Ugly code is often a maintenance headache, and some time invested early in program development can reap benefits during the lifetime of developing and maintaining a program.

In this case, adding a constructor to the struct Track makes initialization simpler. We want to write code like the following:

```
tvector<Track> tracks(10);
```

---

[6]Sometimes the most inside piece isn't obvious, but there are often several places to start.

```
tracks[0] = Track("The Squirming Coil",1);
tracks[1] = Track("Reba",2);
tracks[2] = Track("My Sweet One",3);
...
```

Adding a two-parameter constructor to the `struct` lets us write this code; see the new declaration for `Track` in *shuffle.cpp*, Program 8.4. Since we want to make a vector of `Track` `struct`s we must supply a default/parameterless constructor as well (see the syntax diagram for `tvector` construction). With initialization in `main` and the implementation of `Print`, we're ready to remove compilation errors, test the program, and then add the shuffling function. When we write `Print` we'll need to pass the number of elements in the vector. As we'll see in the next section, we can avoid using two parameters by having the vector keep track of how many elements it has, but for now we'll pass two parameters to `Print`: a vector and a count of how many elements are in the vector.

> **Program Tip 8.3:   Functions that have `tvector` parameters sometimes require an `int` parameter that specifies the number of values actually stored in the `tvector`.** The number of values stored is often different from the capacity of the `tvector`. We'll see that it's easy to avoid this second size parameter if the vector itself keeps track of the number of values it stores as well as its capacity.

We'll discuss the shuffling algorithm and code after the program listing.

Program 8.4   shuffle.cpp

```cpp
#include <iostream>
#include <string>
using namespace std;

#include "tvector.h"
#include "randgen.h"

struct Track
{
    string title;    // title of song/track
    int    number;   // the original track number

    Track::Track()
      : title("no title"),
        number(0)
    { }

    Track::Track(const string& t, int n)
      : title(t),
        number(n)
    { }
```

```cpp
};

void Print(const tvector<Track>& tracks, int count)
// precondition: there are count locations in tracks
// postcondition: contents of tracks printed
{
    int k;
    for(k=0; k < count; k++)
    {   cout << tracks[k].number << "\t" << tracks[k].title << endl;
    }
}

void Shuffle(tvector<Track> & tracks,int count)
// precondition: count = # of entries in tracks
// postcondition: entries in tracks have been randomly shuffled
{
    RandGen gen;      // for random # generator
    int randTrack;
    Track temp;
    int k;
    // choose a random song from [k..count-1] for song # k

    for(k=0; k < count - 1; k++)
    {   randTrack = gen.RandInt(k,count-1);    // random track
        temp = tracks[randTrack];              // swap entries
        tracks[randTrack] = tracks[k];
        tracks[k] = temp;
    }
}

int main()
{
    tvector<Track> tracks(10);

    tracks[0] = Track("Box of Rain",1);
    tracks[1] = Track("Friend of the Devil",2);
    tracks[2] = Track("Sugar Magnolia",3);
    tracks[3] = Track("Operator",4);
    tracks[4] = Track("Candyman",5);
    tracks[5] = Track("Ripple",6);
    tracks[6] = Track("Brokedown Palace",7);
    tracks[7] = Track("Till the Morning Comes",8);
    tracks[8] = Track("Attics of my Life",9);
    tracks[9] = Track("Truckin",10);

    Print(tracks,10);
    Shuffle(tracks,10);
    cout << endl << "---- after shuffling ----" << endl << endl;
    Print(tracks,10);
}
```

shuffle.cpp

Each time the program is run a different order of tracks is generated.

```
                          O U T P U T

prompt> shuffle
1         Box of Rain
2         Friend of the Devil
3         Sugar Magnolia
4         Operator
5         Candyman
6         Ripple
7         Brokedown Palace
8         Till the Morning Comes
9         Attics of my Life
10        Truckin

---- after shuffling ----

5         Candyman
2         Friend of the Devil
8         Till the Morning Comes
4         Operator
10        Truckin
7         Brokedown Palace
6         Ripple
3         Sugar Magnolia
9         Attics of my Life
1         Box of Rain
```

Shuffling Tracks. The shuffling algorithm we'll employ is simple and is good theoretically—that is, it really does shuffle things in a random way. In this case each of the possible arrangements, or **permutations,** of the tracks is equally likely to occur.

The basic algorithm consists of picking a track at random to play first. This can be done by rolling an N-sided die, where there are N tracks on the CD, or by using the RandGen class used in Program 7.14, *brownian.cpp*. Once the first random track is picked, one of the remaining tracks is picked at random to play second. This process is continued until a song is picked for the first track, second track, and so on through the Nth track. Without a tvector this would be difficult (though not impossible) to do. Program 8.4, *shuffle.cpp*, performs this task.

The expression randTrack = gen.RandInt(k,count-1) is used in the function Shuffle to choose a random track from those remaining. The first time the for loop is executed, the value of k is 0, all the tracks are eligible for selection, and the random number is a valid index between 0 and count-1 (which is a number from 0 to 9 in *shuffle.cpp*). The contents of the tvector cell at the randomly generated index are swapped with the contents of the cell with index 0 so that the random-index track is now the first track. The next time through the loop, the random number chosen is between 1 and `count-1` so that the first track (at index 0) cannot be chosen as the random track.

Pause to Reflect

8.8 Suppose a new function `Initialize` is added to *shuffle.cpp* to initialize the elements of a vector of `Track structs`. Write the header/prototype, pre-, and postconditions for the function. You'll need two parameters, just as the two functions `Print` and `Shuffle` have.

8.9 In `Print`, why can't the output be generated by this statement?

```
cout << tracks[k] << endl;
```

8.10 In `Shuffle`, is it important that the test of the `for` loop be `k < count - 1` instead of `k < count`? What would happen if the test were changed?

8.11 The statement below from `Shuffle` assigns the contents of one vector element to another.

```
tracks[randTrack] = tracks[k];
```

What kind of object is assigned in this statement? How many assignments do you think are part of this assignment?

8.12 Suppose no items are specifically assigned in `main`, but instead this code is used:

```
tvector<Track> tracks(10);
Print(tracks,10);
Shuffle(tracks,10);
Print(tracks,10);
return 0;
```

Would you be able to tell if the shuffle function works? Why? (What's printed?)

8.13 A different method of shuffling is suggested by the following idea. Pick two random track numbers and swap the corresponding vector entries. Repeat this process 1,000 times (or some other time as specified by a constant). Write code that uses this method for shuffling tracks. Do you have any intuition as to why this method is "worse" than the method used in *shuffle.cpp*?

8.3 Collections and Lists Using `tvectors`

Our first example programs used vectors as counters to determine how many times each of several possible simulated dice rolls occurs and how many times each character in an input file occurs. As we saw with the CD track-shuffling program, it's possible to use vectors to store objects other than counters. For example, we could store all the words from a text file in a vector and write a program like Program 6.16, *maxword3.cpp*, to find the most frequently occurring word. Using a vector will make the program execute quickly since words will be in memory (in a vector) rather than on disk as they're scanned repeatedly to find the word that occurs most often.

In many programs, the number of items stored in a vector will not be known when the program is compiled but will be determined at runtime. This would be the case, for example, if we store all the words in a text file in a vector. How big should we define vectors to be in order to accommodate the many situations that may arise? If we make a vector that can hold lots of data, to accommodate large text files, then we'll be wasting memory when the program is run on small text files. Conversely, if the vector is too small we won't be able to process large files. Fortunately, vectors can grow during a program's execution so that vector usage can be somewhat efficient. There will be some inefficiency because to grow a vector we'll actually have to make a new one and throw out the old one. As a metaphor, suppose you keep addresses and phone numbers of friends in an electronic personal organizer. You may become so popular, with so many friends, that you run out of memory for all the addresses you store. You may be able to buy more memory, but with most organizers you'll need to replace the old memory chip with a larger chip. This means you'll need to copy the addresses you've saved (to a computer, for example, but onto paper if you're really unlucky), install the new memory, then copy the addresses into the new memory.

8.3.1   Size and Capacity

In general, the number of elements stored in a vector will not be the same as the capacity of the vector. The capacity is how many elements could be stored, or how many cells the vector has. The size is the number of elements that are actually stored in the vector. These are different ideas conceptually, and programs will usually need to track both quantities separately. Using the electronic organizer as an example again, the capacity is how many names and addresses the organizer is capable of storing (how much memory it has) whereas the size is how many names are currently stored in it. Although client code can grow a vector explicitly, it's usually simpler and more efficient to have the vector grow itself.

8.3.2   Using `push_back`, `resize`, and `reserve`

When a vector is defined with an explicit size as an argument to the constructor, this argument determines both the capacity and the size of the vector. The size is determined since default objects will be constructed in each vector cell. Member function `tvector::size()` returns the size.

```
tvector<Date>   holidays(17);      // holidays.size() == 17
tvector<double> values(1000);      // values.size() == 1000
tvector<int>    scores;            // scores.size() == 0
tvector<string> names(10,"Joe');   // names.size() == 10
```

The member function `tvector::push_back` is used to add elements to the end of a vector; the vector resizes itself as needed by doubling its capacity. The lines below illustrate push_back and how size and capacity change each time an element is added.

```
tvector<string> names;        // size() == 0, capacity() == 0
names.push_back("Fred");       // size() == 1, capacity() == 2
names.push_back("Wilma");      // size() == 2, capacity() == 2
names.push_back("Barney");     // size() == 3, capacity() == 4
names.push_back("Betty");      // size() == 4, capacity() == 4
names.push_back("Pebbles");    // size() == 5, capacity() == 8
```

The size of a vector is determined by three thirgs:

- The number of times push_back is called; each call increases the size by one.
- The initial size of a vector when an argument is supplied at construction; this initial value is the size and the capacity.
- The argument in a call to tvector::resize(), which changes the size and can change the capacity when the vector grows (resizing cannot shrink the capacity).

The code below prints the values stored in names in the example above:

```
int k;
for(k=0; k < names.size(); k++)
{   cout << names[k] << endl;
}
```

O U T P U T

```
Fred
Wilma
Barney
Betty
Pebbles
```

If a vector is given a size at construction, with subsequent elements added using push_back, the method tvector::size will not return the number of elements added by calling push_back.

```
tvector<string> names(7); // size() == capacity() == 7
names.push_back("Grace");  // size() == 8, capacity() == 14
names.push_back("Alan");   // size() == 9, capacity() == 14
```

The value of names[0] is " " because this value is constructed by the default string constructor. The value of names[7] is "Grace" since the initial size puts default string values in array elements 0–6.

A vector grows when its size and capacity are equal and push_back adds a new element to the vector. When a vector grows itself by client programs calling push_back, the capacity doubles.[7]

Since the capacity doubles, it might go from 8 to 16 to 32 and so on. If you're writing a program and you know you'll need to store at least 5,000 elements, this growing process can be inefficient.[8] The member function tvector::reserve() is used to create an initial capacity, but the size remains at zero.

```
tvector<string> names;     // size() == 0, capacity() == 0
names.reserve(2048);       // size() == 0, capacity() = 2048
```

> **Program Tip 8.4:** If you're going to use push_back do not define a vector by giving a size when the vector is constructed. If you construct with a size, the method tvector::size won't return the number of elements added by push_back; it will return that number plus the initial size. If you want to allocate space for efficiency reasons use tvector::reserve.

We'll use two functions in Program 8.5 that read words from a file and store them in a vector to illustrate the differences between using push_back and calling resize explicitly. The runs also show that using tvector::reserve can lead to increased efficiency when a vector would double frequently otherwise.

Program 8.5 growdemo.cpp

```
#include <iostream>
#include <string>
using namespace std;

#include "prompt.h"
#include "tvector.h"
#include "worditer.h"
#include "ctimer.h"

// show differences between push_back and calling resize explicity

void ReadAll(WordStreamIterator& iter, tvector<string>& list)
// postcondition: all words from iter stored in list
{
    for(iter.Init(); iter.HasMore(); iter.Next())
    {    list.push_back(iter.Current());
    }
}
```

---

[7]The class tvector doubles its capacity each time except when the capacity is initially zero, that is, when the vector is first constructed. The capacity goes from 0 to 2, and then doubles each time. The standard vector class should double in capacity too, but implementations are not required to double the capacity. Most implementations use doubling, but there may be some that don't.

[8]Recall that doubling requires copying the elements into a new vector that's twice as large.

```cpp
void ReadAll2(WordStreamIterator& iter,
              tvector<string>& list, int& count)
// postcondition: all words from iter stored in list,
//                count = number of words read
{
    count = 0;
    for(iter.Init(); iter.HasMore(); iter.Next())
    {   if (count >= list.capacity())
        {   list.resize(list.capacity()*2 + 1);  // grow by doubling
        }
        list[count] = iter.Current();
        count++;
    }
}


int main()
{
    CTimer timer;
    string filename = PromptString("enter filename ");
    WordStreamIterator iter;
    iter.Open(filename);

    tvector<string> listA;  // listA.reserve(100000);
    tvector<string> listB;  // listB.reserve(100000);

    timer.Start();
    ReadAll(iter,listA);
    timer.Stop();
    cout << "# words: " << listA.size()
         << " capacity: " << listA.capacity()
         << " time: " << timer.ElapsedTime() << endl;

    int count;              // # elements stored in listB
    timer.Start();
    ReadAll2(iter,listB,count);
    timer.Stop();
    cout << "# words: " << count
         << " capacity: " << listB.capacity()
         << " time: " << timer.ElapsedTime() << endl;
    return 0;
}
```

growdemo.cpp

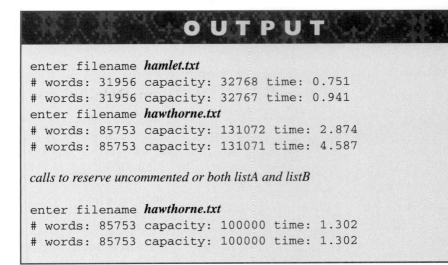

```
OUTPUT

enter filename hamlet.txt
# words: 31956 capacity: 32768 time: 0.751
# words: 31956 capacity: 32767 time: 0.941
enter filename hawthorne.txt
# words: 85753 capacity: 131072 time: 2.874
# words: 85753 capacity: 131071 time: 4.587

calls to reserve uncommented or both listA and listB

enter filename hawthorne.txt
# words: 85753 capacity: 100000 time: 1.302
# words: 85753 capacity: 100000 time: 1.302
```

The code in `ReadAll` is considerably simpler than the code in `ReadAll2`. As the runs show, `ReadAll` is also more efficient when there is considerable doubling.[9]

Pause to Reflect

8.14 If the `WordStreamIterator` is replaced by an `ifstream` variable in Program 8.5, the call to `ReadAll` returns the same values, but the call to `ReadAll2` returns a value of zero in reference parameter `count`, with nothing stored in the vector. Why?

8.15 Why is the expression `list.capacity()*2 + 1` used in `ReadAll2` of *growdemo.cpp* rather than `list.capacity()*2`?

8.16 What value would be returned by `listB.size()` during the middle run shown in the output box (when `listB.capacity()` returns 131071)?

8.17 What changes are needed in `main` of Program 8.4, *shuffle.cpp*, to use `push_back`? How could the functions `Print` and `Shuffle` change to take advantage of using `push_back` in `main`?

8.18 A `tvector` is constructed with size zero, then grows itself to a size of 2, 4, 8, 16, …vector elements (assuming `reserve` is not used). Each time the vector grows, new memory is allocated and old memory de-allocated. When the capacity of the vector is 512, how many vector elements have been allocated (including the final 512)? If the capacity is 16,384, how many vector elements have been allocated?

8.19 If a `tvector` grows by one vector element instead of doubling (e.g., grows to 1, 2, 3, 4, …elements), then how many elements have been allocated when the capacity is 32 (including the final 32)? When the capacity is 128? When the capacity is 16,384? (Hint: $1 + 2 + \cdots + n = n(n + 1)/2$.)

---

[9]The efficiency improvements are a property of the `tvector` implementation. When the standard class `vector` is used instead of `tvector` in `growdemo.cpp` the efficiency gains are not nearly as pronounced.

8.20 Why do you think the time used in *growdemo.cpp*, Program 8.5, by the `push_back` function ReadAll is less than the time used by the function ReadAll2 (when `reserve` isn't used)?

8.3.3   Vector Idioms: Insertion, Deletion, and Searching

To illustrate common vector operations, we'll use a small program that reads information representing a portfolio of stocks. We'll show examples of adding a new stock, deleting a stock, and finding stocks that match certain criteria—that is, stocks trading below $50.00, stocks above $100.00, stocks on the NASDAQ exchange,[10] or stocks whose symbols begin with the letter "Q."

We'll read a file of information similar to what's shown below, but without the company name on the end of each line.[11] The information below is out of date; it is from 1996 and not meant to reflect current stock prices. The data for each stock include its symbol, such as *KO*, the exchange (N = New York, T = NASDAQ), the price, the number of shares traded, and the name of the company. which doesn't appear in the data file we'll use.

```
KO       N       50.5     735000     COCA COLA CO
DIS      N       64.125   282200     DISNEY CO WALT HLDG CO
ABPCA    T       5.688    49700      AU BON PAIN CO INC CL A
NSCP     T       42.813   385900     NETSCAPE COMM CORP
F        N       32.125   798900     FORD MOTOR CO
```

Program 8.6 uses a class `Portfolio` to read and print a collection of stocks.

Program 8.6   stocks.cpp

```cpp
#include <iostream>
#include <fstream>
#include <string>
#include <iomanip>
using namespace std;

#include "tvector.h"
#include "strutils.h"   // for atoi and atof
#include "prompt.h"

struct Stock
{
    string name;
    string exchange;
    double price;
```

---

[10]There are several stock exchanges in the world. Examples include the New York Exchange, the NASDAQ exchange, the Toronto Exchange, and others.

[11]The other information on a line can be read using >>, but the company name requires the use of the function getline because the name consists of more than one word. We'll study getline in Chapter 9.

```
    int     shares;

    Stock()
      : name("dummy"),
        exchange("none"),
        price(0.0),
        shares(0)
      { }

    Stock(const string& n, const string& xc,
          double p, int ns)
      : name(n),
        exchange(xc),
        price(p),
        shares(ns)
      { }
};

class Portfolio
{
  public:
    Portfolio();
    void Read(const string& filename);

    void Print(ostream& out)    const;

  private:
    tvector<Stock> myStocks;
};

Portfolio::Portfolio()
  : myStocks(0)
{
    myStocks.reserve(20);    // start with room for 20 stocks
}

void Portfolio::Read(const string& filename)
{
    ifstream input(filename.c_str());
    string symbol, exchange, price, shares;

    while (input >> symbol >> exchange >> price >> shares)
    {    myStocks.push_back(Stock(symbol,exchange,atof(price),atoi(shares)));
    }
}

void Portfolio::Print(ostream& out) const
{
    int k;
    int len = myStocks.size();

    out.precision(3);        // show 3 decimal places
    out.setf(ios::fixed);    // for every stock price

    for(k=0; k < len; k++)
```

```
    {   out  << myStocks[k].name << "\t"
            << myStocks[k].exchange << "\t"
            << setw(8) << myStocks[k].price << "\t"
            << setw(12) << myStocks[k].shares << endl;
    }
    cout << endl << "----" << endl << '# stocks: " << len << endl;
}

int main()
{
    string filename = PromptString("stock file ");
    Portfolio pcrt;

    port.Read(filename);
    port.Print(cout);

    return 0;
}
```

stocks.cpp

The conversion functions `atoi` and `atof` from *strutils.h* are discussed in How to G. The formatting functions `precision` and `setf` for displaying a fixed number of decimal places are discussed in How to B.

```
O U T P U T

prompt> stocks
stock file stocksmall.dat
KO       N        50.500           735000
DIS      N        64.125           282200
ABPCA    T         5.688            49700
NSCP     T        42.813           385900
F        N        32.125           798900
----
# stocks: 5
```

The `Portfolio` constructor initializes the instance variable `myStocks` to have zero elements in the initializer list, then reserves space for 20 stocks in the body of the constructor. `tvector` instance variables *must be* constructed in an initializer list. It's not possible to include the size of a vector in the class declaration. For example, the following code does not work:

```
class Thing
{   ...
    private:
        tvector<int> myData(30);  // ***illegal***
};
```

A class declaration does not allocate memory; memory is allocated in the class definition, specifically in a constructor. This means you must construct each private `tvector` data field in the initializer list of each constructor.[12]

> **Program Tip 8.5: When a `tvector` instance variable is used in a class, each constructor for the class should explicitly construct the `tvector` in the constructor's initializer list.** A vector can be given a size, or sized to zero with space reserved by a call to `tvector::reserve` in the constructor body.

8.3.4 Insertion into a Sorted Vector

As shown in *stocks.cpp*, the function `push_back` is simple to use and effectively adds a new element to the end of a vector. What can you do if you want to add a new element to the middle of a vector or to some other location? If the list of stocks is kept in alphabetical order by symbol, for example, new stocks should be added in the correct location to keep the list in sorted order. The only way to do this with a vector is to shift elements to create an empty vector cell for the new element.

Suppose, for example, that you keep books arranged alphabetically by author, or a collection of compact discs (CDs) arranged alphabetically by artist. When you get a new book (or a new CD), you'll probably have to move or shift several books to make a spot for the new one. If you're facing a bookshelf, you might start at the rightmost end and slide the books to the right until you find where the new book belongs. This mimics exactly how new elements are inserted into a vector when the vector is maintained in sorted order.

We'll write code to shift vector elements to the right. The key statement follows:

```
myStocks[loc] = myStocks[loc-1];
```

When `loc` has the value 8, for example, this copies the element with index 7 into the vector cell with index 8, effectively shifting an element to the right. After this statement executes, the element in the vector cell with index 7 is still there, but has been copied into the cell with index 8 as well. We'll stop shifting when we've looked at every vector element or when we find where the new stock belongs in the sorted order. The code below inserts a stock `s` in sorted order by symbol.[13]

```
void Portfolio::Add(const Stock& s)
// postcondition: s added to porfolio in sorted order
{
    int count = myStocks.size(); // size before adding
    myStocks.push_back(s);       // vector size is updated
    int loc = count;
```

---

[12]If you don't include an explicit `tvector` constructor in a class's initializer list, the vector will have zero elements, which is actually the right thing to do if you're using `push_back`.

[13]This code is from *stocks2.cpp*, not shown in the book, but available with the programs that come with the book or from the book's Web site.

```
    while (0 < loc && s.symbol <= myStocks[loc-1].symbol)
    {   myStocks[loc] = myStocks[loc-1];
        loc--;
    }
    myStocks[loc] = s;
}
```

The new stock is first inserted at the end of the vector using `push_back` simply to allow the vector to update its count of how many elements are in the vector. Elements are then shifted, and the stock `s` is stored in the proper location when the loop finishes.

To understand and reason about the loop that shifts elements to the right, we'll concentrate on three properties of the variable `loc`. These properties are true each time the loop test is evaluated, so they constitute a **loop invariant** and should help us reason about the correctness of the loop.

- ▌ `loc-1` is the index of the item that will be shifted right if necessary; this is the rightmost element not yet processed.
- ▌ `loc` is the index of the cell in which the new stock will be inserted in sorted order.
- ▌ All items with index `loc + 1` through index `count` are greater than the new stock being inserted.

Figure 8.4 illustrates the process of inserting a stock with symbol "D" into a sorted vector (for the purposes of illustration, all symbols are single characters). Initially the vector has eight elements, so the value of `loc` is 8. The three properties that make up the loop invariant hold the first time the loop test is evaluated.

- ■ `loc-1`, or 7, is the index of *V*, the rightmost unprocessed element. It will be shifted as necessary.
- ■ `loc`, or 8, is the cell in which the new stock will be stored (if the new stock has symbol "Z," it is stored in location 8).
- ■ All items with indexes 9 through 8 are greater than the stock being inserted. In this case the range 9 ... 8 represents an **empty range** because 9 > 8. There are no elements in this empty range, so it's true that all the elements in the range are greater than the element being inserted.[14]

When `loc` is 4, as shown in Figure 8.4, the three properties still hold. At this point the letters *Q, S, T,* and *V* have been shifted to the right because the loop body has been executed for values of `loc` of 7, 6, 5, 4.

Since the loop test is true, the body is executed, and *M* is shifted to the right. Finally, when `loc == 2`, the three properties still hold:

---

[14]Don't worry too much about this. The key here is that it's impossible to find a word in the range 9 ... 8 that's smaller than the word being inserted. It's impossible because there are no words in the empty range.

- `loc-1`, or 1, is the rightmost unprocessed element.
- `loc`, or 2, is the index where the new stock will be inserted.
- All items with indexes between 3 and 8 have values greater than "D."

However, the loop test is false because `s.symbol > myStocks[loc].symbol` (because `D > C`). The loop exits, and the new stock is inserted in the cell with index `loc`, as described by the invariant.

8.3.5 Deleting an Element Using `pop_back`

Deleting the last element of a vector is very simple; the method `tvector::pop_back` reduces a vector's size by one, effectively deleting the last element. The capacity of the vector is unchanged, but since client programs use `tvector::size()` to determine the number of elements stored in a vector, calling `pop_back` removes the element.

The following code shows a simple method for removing an element from the middle of a vector when the vector is *not* maintained in sorted order. The last element is copied into the vector cell that will be "deleted." Calling `pop_back` ensures that the vector updates its internal state properly.

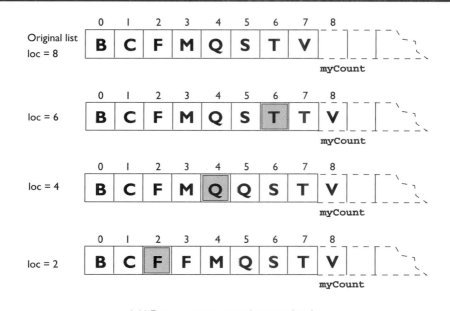

Add **D** to vector maintained in sorted order

Figure 8.4 Maintaining a vector in sorted order. The new element will go in the vector cell with index `loc` when shifting is finished. The shaded location is being considered as the location of the new element.

```
// remove element with index loc from vector v
int lastIndex = v.size() - 1;
v[loc] = v[lastIndex];
v.pop_back();
```

If the vector is maintained in sorted order, vector elements must be shifted to delete an element while maintaining the sorted order. In contrast to the code that shifted elements to the right to make space for a new element, deletion requires shifts to the left.

```
// delete element with index loc
int k;
for(k=loc; k < myStocks.size()-1; k++)
{  myStocks[k] = myStocks[k+1];
}
myStocks.pop_back();
```

8.3.6 Searching a Vector

Searching and sorting are common applications in programming. In the stock portfolio example from *stocks.cpp*, Program 8.6, the program was modified to keep stocks in sorted order. In this section we'll see how to search for stocks that match some criterion. Sometimes searching will yield an exact, or single, match. If we search for the stock with symbol *HRL* we expect only one match. In general, searching for a stock by symbol should yield zero or one matches since stock symbols are unique. On the other hand, if we search for all stocks below $10.00, or that traded more than 500,000 shares, there may be many matches.

Searching for a Unique Match. In a **sequential search** (sometimes called a **linear** search), elements in a vector are scanned in sequence, one after the other. Sequential search is necessary, for example, if you want to find the person whose phone number is 555-2622 in your local phone book. Phone books are arranged alphabetically by name rather than numerically by phone number, so you must scan all numbers, one after the other, hoping to find 555-2622.

A search function must return something. Typically the returned value is an index into the vector, or the matching element found during the search. Using an index as a return value makes it possible to encode a failed search by returning a bad index value like −1. If a vector element is returned, it's not possible, in general, to return a value indicating a failed search. Some people code search functions to return two values: a bool to indicate if the search is successful and the matching element. If the bool value is false, the matching element has no defined value. The code below shows a function that returns the index of a match in a vector of strings. This code can also be found in Program 8.7, *timesearch.cpp*.

```
int search(const tvector<string>& list, const string& key)
// pre:  list.size() == # elements in list
// post: returns index of key in list, -1 if key not found
{
```

```
    int k;
    for(k=0; k < list.size(); k++)
    {   if (list[k] == key)
        {   return k;
        }
    }
    return -1;    // reach here only when key not found
}
```

Counting Matches.   You may want to know how many stocks sell for more than $150.00 or traded more than 500,000 shares, but not care which stocks they are. This is an example of a **counting search** or **counting match**. Modifying the linear search code to count matches is straightforward. The sequential search code returned as soon as a match was found, but in counting all matches no early return is possible.

```
int countMatches(const tvector<Stock>& list, int minShares)
// pre:   list.size() == # stocks in list
// post:  returns # stocks trading more than minShares shares
{
    int k, count = 0;
    for(k=0; k < list.size(); k++)
    {   if (list[k].share > minShares)
        {   count++;
        }
    }
    return count;
}
```

Collecting Matches.   In the previous example, the function `countMatches` could determine the number of stocks that traded more than 500,000 shares but could not determine which stocks these are. It would be simple to add an output statement to the function so that the stocks that matched were printed, but you may want to know the average price of the matching stocks rather than just a printed list of the stocks. The easiest way to collect matches in a search is to store the matches in a vector. The function below is a modication of `countMatches` that returns the matching stocks as elements of the parameter `matches`.

```
void collectMatches(const tvector<Stock>& list,
                    int minShares,tvector<Stock>& matches)
// pre: list.size() == # elements in list
// post: matches contains just the elements of list
//       that traded > minShares shares
{
    int k;
    matches.resize(0);   // initially no matches
```

```
for(k=0; k < list.size(); k++)
{   if (list[k].share > minShares)
    {   matches.push_back(list[k]);
    }
}
}
```

The call to `matches.resize()` ensures that matches contains just the stocks that match the criterion of trading more than minShares shares. Recall that `resize` cannot reduce the capacity of a vector, but it does make the size zero.

Pause to Reflect

8.21 The loop below is designed to find the index at which a new item should be inserted in an array to keep the array in sorted order. The loop finds the index but doesn't insert. For example, if list is ("avocado", "banana", "lemon", "orange") and s is "cherry" the function should return 2; if s is "watermelon" the function should return 4.

```
int insertionIndex(const tvector<string>& list,
                   const string& s)
// pre: list is sorted, list[0] <= ... <= list[n]
//      where n = list.size()-1
// post: return index i of s in list, so that i
//       is largest value with list[0]..list[i-1] < s
{
    int len = list.size();
    int k=0;
    // invariant: list[0]..list[k-1] < s
    while (k < len && list[k] < s)
    {   k++;
    }
    return k;
}
```

1. Why is list a const reference parameter?
2. What value should be returned if s is "apple"? Is this value returned?
3. Is 4 returned when s is "watermelon"?
4. Why is the text k < len needed?

8.22 Assuming the function insertionIndex from the previous problem satisfies its postcondition, write the function below, which could be used as the basis for a new Portfolio::Add from Section 8.3.4.

```
void insertAt(tvector<string>& list,
              const string& s, int loc)
// post: s inserted into list at index loc
//       order of list elements unchanged
```

To insert a string into a sorted vector, leaving it sorted, the following call should work:

```
string s = "apple";
insertAt(list, s, insertionIndex(list,s));
```

8.23 In a vector of *n* elements, what is the fewest number of elements that are shifted to insert a new element in sorted order? What is the most number of elements that are shifted?

8.24 The method `tvector::clear` makes the size of a vector 0; the call `t.clear()` has the same effect as `t.resize(0)`. If there were no functions `clear` or `resize` you could write a function to remove all the elements of vector by calling `pop_back`. Write such a function.

8.25 Write a function `deleteAt` that works like `insertAt` from the second Pause to Reflect exercise in this section.

```
void deleteAt(tvector<string>& list, int loc)
// post: item at index loc removed,
//       order of other items unchanged
```

How could you call `deleteAt` to remove `"banana"` from the vector (`"avocado"`, `"banana"`, `"lemon"`, `"orange"`)?

8.26 Assume the function `isVowel` exists.

```
bool isVowel(const string& s)
// post: returns true if s is 'a', 'e', 'i', 'o', 'u'
//       (or uppercase equivalent)
```

Write the function below:

```
int vowelCount(const tvector<string>& list)
// post:return # strings in list beginning with a vowel
```

Assuming `vowelCount` works, what expression returns the number of strings in a vector `list` that do *not* begin with a vowel?

8.27 Modify the function in the previous exercise to return a vector containing all the strings that begin with a vowel, instead of just the count of the number of strings.

8.28 Write a function to return the sum of all the elements in a vector of `int`s.

```
int sum(const tvector<int>& list)
// post: returns list[0] + ... + list[list.size()-1]
```

8.29 Write a function that removes duplicate elements from a sorted vector of strings.

```
void removeDups(tvector<string>& list)
// pre: list[0] <= ... <= list[list.size()-1] (sorted)
// post: duplicates removed from still sorted list
```

For example, the vector

```
("avocado","avocado","lemon','"lemon","lemon","orange")
```

should be changed to

```
("avocado","lemon","orange")
```

David Gries

David Gries is a computer scientist and educator at Cornell University. He is well known for his advocation of the use of formal methods in designing and implementing software and in the training of undergraduates in computer science. He has done perhaps more than any one person in making the study of loop invariants and formal methods accessible to students in introductory courses.

In his World Wide Web biography he writes of encounters with recursion when earning his master's degree in 1963: "it was fun, figuring out how to implement recursion efficiently before there were many papers on the topic." In an essay [Gri74] written in 1974 he provides timeless advice:

It must be made clear that one technique will never suffice (for example, top-down programming). A programmer needs a bag of tricks, a collection of methods for attacking a problem. Secondly, if we are to raise the level of programming, each programmer (no matter how good he feels he is) must become more conscious of the tools and techniques he uses. It is not enough to just program; we must discover how and why we do it.

Gries has twins, and in a coincidence of the highest order, the twins were born on the birthday of Gries and his twin sibling. In noting that he is (perhaps) better known for his educational work than his research work, Gries writes, "Do what you are good at; bloom where you are planted." For his work in education Gries was awarded the 1994 IEEE Taylor L. Booth Award, the 1991 ACM SIGCSE award, and the 1995 Karl V. Karlstrom Outstanding Educator Award.

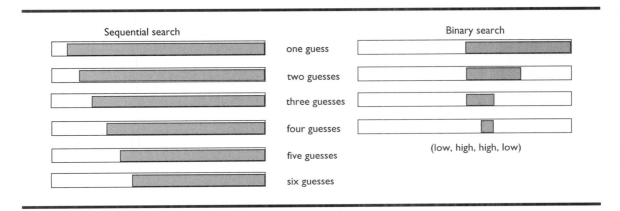

Figure 8.5   Comparing sequential/linear search, on the left, with binary search, on the right.

8.3.7   Binary Search

Phone books are arranged alphabetically by name rather than numerically by phone number, so you must scan all numbers, one after the other, if you hope to find 555-2622. Of course if you were doing this, you could easily miss the number; people aren't good at this kind of repetitive task, but computers are. On the other hand, you can look up John Armstrong's, Nancy Drew's, or Mr. Mxyzptlk's number without scanning every entry. Since name/number pairs are stored alphabetically by name, it's possible to search for a name efficiently. In this section we'll investigate **binary search:** a method of searching that takes advantage of sorted data to speed up search. As we'll see, binary search is not always better than sequential search. Choosing the right searching algorithm depends on the context in which the search will be used.

Binary search is based on the method you may have used in playing a guess-a-number game. Suppose someone thinks of a number between 1 and 100 and will tell you whether your guess is low, high, or correct. You'll probably use 50 as the first guess. This will eliminate half of the numbers from consideration and is considerably more fruitful than guessing 1 (which, invariably, is low). The strategy of guessing the middle number works regardless of the the range of numbers. For example, if someone initially thinks of a number between 1 and 1,024, you would guess 512. One guess shrinks the number of possibilities by half, from 1,024 to 512. The number of possibilities continues to shrink from 512 to 256, 128, 64, 32, 16, 8, 4, 2, and finally 1. This is a total of 10 guesses to find one of 1,024 possible different numbers. Consider what happens if you're told "yes" or "no" rather than high/low, and how this affects your guessing strategy. That example illustrates the difference between binary search and sequential search. Eliminating half of the numbers with one guess, rather than one number, is shown graphically in Figure 8.5. A `tvector` of 32 elements is shown; the shaded area represents the region of items still being considered after each guess is made. The size of the region being considered is reduced by half each time for binary search, but by only one for sequential search.

When binary search is used, each comparison cuts the range of potential matches in half. The total number of guesses will be how many times the initial number of items can be cut in half. As we've seen, 1,024 items require 10 guesses; it's not a coincidence that

$2^{10} = 1,024$. Doubling the number of items from 1,024 to 2,048 increases the number of guesses needed by only one because one guess cuts the list of 2,048 down to 1,024, and we know that 10 guesses are needed for 1,024 items. Again, it's not a coincidence that $2^{11} = 2,048$.

Looking up a name in a phone book of 1,024 names might require 11 guesses. When there is only one name left to check, it must be checked too because the name being sought might not be in the phone book (this doesn't happen with the guess-a-number game). How many guesses are needed using binary search to search a list of one million names? As we've seen, this depends on how many times one million can be cut in half. We want to find the smallest number n such that $2^n \geq 1,000,000$; this will tell us how many items must be checked (we might need to add 1 if there's a possibility that the item isn't in the list; this cuts the final list of one item down to a list of zero items). Since $2^{19} = 524,288$ and $2^{20} = 1,048,576$, we can see that 20 (or 21) guesses are enough to find an item using binary search in a list of one million items. If you're familiar with logarithms, you may recall that log functions are the inverse of exponential functions, and therefore that the number of times a number x can be cut in half is $\log_2(x)$, or log base 2 of x. Again, we may need to add 1 if we need to cut a number in half to get down to zero instead of 1. This is the analog of reducing the items down to a zero-element list or a one-element list.

8.3.8 Comparing Sequential and Binary Search

We're more concerned with comparing sequential search and binary search than with the exact number of items examined with binary search. The difference between 20 and 21 items examined is far less important than the difference between 21 items (binary search) and one million items (sequential search). Although it's possible that only one item is examined when a sequential search is used (consider looking up a word like "aardvark" in the dictionary), the worst case is that one million items might need to be examined (consider looking up "zzzz" in a million-word dictionary). Table 8.1 provides a comparison of the number of items that must be examined using sequential and binary search.

Examining 18 items will be much faster than examining 100,000 items, but how

Table 8.1 Comparing sequential/linear search with binary search.

	Number of Items Examined	
List Size	**Binary Search**	**Sequential Search**
1	1	1
10	4	10
1,000	11	1,000
5,000	14	5,000
100,000	18	100,000
1,000,000	21	1,000,000

much faster? If two strings can be compared in a microsecond (one millionth of a second)—which is very possible on moderately fast computers—both searches will take less than one second. Does it matter that binary search requires 0.000018 seconds and sequential search requires 0.1 seconds? The answer is "It depends." It probably won't matter to you if you're waiting for a response to appear on a computer monitor, but it may matter if the computer is "waiting" for the search and 100 million searches are necessary. On the computers I used to develop the code in this book, searching for one word in an on-line dictionary of 25,000 words appears to me to take no time using either sequential or binary search. To be precise, I can type a word to search for, press Enter, and see the word found in the dictionary on the screen instantaneously.

However, in Program 8.7, *timesearch.cpp*, a file of words is read, and then every different word in the file is searched for in a vector of all the words in the file. To be precise, the following sequence takes place in *timesearch.cpp*:

1. All the words in a file are read and stored in a vector. Words are converted to lowercase, and leading/trailing punctuation is removed.
2. A `StringSet` is created from the words in the vector. The set is effectively a list of the different words in the file (the vector contains duplicates).
3. A copy of the vector is made, and the copy is sorted. There are now two vectors: one sorted and one unsorted.[15]
4. Each word in the set is searched for in the vector. Sequential search is used with the unsorted vector; binary search is used with the sorted vector.

As you can see in the runs, the time to search using a sorted vector with binary search is very much faster than the time to search using sequential search. For Hawthorne's *The Scarlet Letter*, searching for 9,164 different strings in a vector of 85,754 strings took 267 seconds using sequential search and only 0.17 seconds using binary search in a sorted vector. Of course it took more than one minute to sort the vector in order to use binary search, but the total time is still much less than the time for sequential search. On the other hand, consider the times for Poe's *The Cask of Amontillado*. While still drastically different at 0.501 and 0.01 seconds, a user doesn't see much impact in a process that finishes in half a second. That's why the answer to whether binary search or sequential search is better is "It depends."

Program 8.7   timesearch.cpp

```
#include <iostream>
#include <fstream>
#include <string>
using namespace std;

#include "tvector.h"
#include "ctimer.h"
```

---

[15]The function `QuickSort` from *sortall.h* is used to sort. Sorting is discussed in Chapter 11, but you can call a sort function without knowing how it works.

```
#include "strutils.h"        // for StripPunc and ToLower
#include "stringset.h"
#include "prompt.h"
#include "sortall.h"

// demonstrate differences between sequential and binary search
// Owen Astrachan, 5/4/99

void Read(const string& filename, tvector<string>& list)
// post: list is unsorted collection of all the strings
//       in text file filename, each string is converted to
//       lowercase with leading/trailing punctuation removed
{
    ifstream input(filename.c_str());
    string word;
    while (input >> word)
    {   StripPunc(word);
        ToLower(word);
        list.push_back(word);
    }
}

void makeSet(const tvector<string>& list,StringSet& sset)
// post: sset is set of strings from list
{
    int k;
    int len = list.size();
    for(k=0; k < len; k++)
    {   sset.insert(list[k]);
    }
}

int search(const tvector<string>& list, const string& key)
// precondition: list.size() == # elements in list
// postcondition: returns index of key in list, -1 if key not found
{
    int k;
    for(k=0; k < list.size(); k++)
    {   if (list[k] == key)
        {   return k;
        }
    }
    return -1;    // reach here only when key not found
}

int bsearch(const tvector<string>& list, const string& key)
// precondition: list.size() == # elements in list
// postcondition: returns index of key in list, -1 if key not found
{
    int low = 0;              // leftmost possible entry
    int high = list.size()-1; // rightmost possible entry
    int mid;                  // middle of current range
    while (low <= high)
    {   mid = (low + high)/2;
        if (list[mid] == key)      // found key, exit search
```

```
        {    return mid;
        }
        else if (list[mid] < key)    // key in upper half
        {   low = mid + 1;
        }
        else                         // key in lower half
        {   high = mid - 1;
        }
    }
    return -1;                       // not in list
}

double timeLinear(const StringSet& sset, const tvector<string>& list)
{
    CTimer timer;
    StringSetIterator it(sset);

    timer.Start();
    for(it.Init(); it.HasMore(); it.Next())
    {   int index = search(list,it.Current());
        if (index == -1)
        {   cout << "missed a search for " << it.Current() << endl;
        }
    }
    timer.Stop();
    return timer.ElapsedTime();
}

double timeBinary(const StringSet& sset, const tvector<string>& list)
{
    CTimer timer;
    StringSetIterator it(sset);

    timer.Start();
    for(it.Init(); it.HasMore(); it.Next())
    {   int index = bsearch(list,it.Current());
        if (index == -1)
        {   cout << "missed a search for " << it.Current() << endl;
        }
    }
    timer.Stop();
    return timer.ElapsedTime();
}

int main()
{

    string filename = PromptString("enter file ");
    CTimer timer;
    tvector<string> list, sortedList;
    StringSet sset;

    timer.Start();
    Read(filename,list);
    timer.Stop();
```

```
    cout << timer.ElapsedTime() << " secs to read "
        << list.size() << " total words" << endl;

    timer.Start();
    makeSet(list,sset);
    timer.Stop();
    cout << "make set time:\t" << timer.ElapsedTime() << " set size: "
        << sset.size() << endl;

    timer.Start();
    sortedList = list;
    QuickSort(sortedList,sortedList.size());
    timer.Stop();
    cout << "make sorted time:\t" << timer.ElapsedTime() << endl;

    cout << "unsorted search time:\t" << timeLinear(sset,list) << endl;
    cout << "sorted search time:\t"   << timeBinary(sset,sortedList) << endl;
    return 0;
}
```

timesearch.cpp

O U T P U T

```
prompt> timesearch
enter file poe.txt
0.08 secs to read 2325 total words
make set time:  0.17 set size: 810
make sorted time:      0.09
unsorted search time:  0.501
sorted search time:    0.01

prompt> timesearch
enter file hamlet.txt
1.072 secs to read 31957 total words
make set time:  6.429 set size: 4832
make sorted time:      6.429
unsorted search time:  56.652
sorted search time:    0.08

prompt> timesearch
enter file hawthorne.txt
3.895 secs to read 85754 total words
make set time:  24.896 set size: 9164
make sorted time:      68.228
unsorted search time:  267.585
sorted search time:    0.17
```

The postconditions for functions `search` and `bsearch` in Program 8.7, *time-search.cpp*, are identical. You can use either function to search, but a vector must be sorted to use binary search.

8.4   Built-in Arrays

This section covers materials not used in this book other than in this section.

In this section we'll study the built-in C++ array type and compare it with the `tvector` class we've used to implement a homogeneous, random-access data structure. The `tvector` class is defined using the built-in C++ array type. Using built-in arrays results in code that will probably execute more quickly than when the `tvector` class is used because of overhead associated with checking `tvector` indexes.

However, it is much more difficult to develop correct programs with arrays than it is with vectors. Any integer value can be used to subscript an array, even if the value doesn't represent a valid array location. In some languages (e.g., Java), indexing values that do not represent valid array locations causes a program to generate an error message, which can be used to trace the program's behavior. In C and C++, on the other hand, an invalid subscript value can cause unexpected behavior that can lead to hard-to-find errors. Such invalid subscripts are not checked before being used to index a built-in array. Using the `tvector` class rather than the built-in array type provides some safety when using indexed variables because indexes are checked with the `tvector` class. Arrays in C++ have several properties that, at best, might be described as idiosyncratic and, at worst, are a programmer's nightmare.

There are three reasons to study arrays in addition to vectors:

- If you read programs written by other people you'll probably see lots of array code.
- Arrays are more low-level and so can offer some performance gains, though the built-in vector class (which has no range checking) should be just as fast with any reasonable implementation.
- It's easier to initialize an array than it is to initialize a vector.

8.4.1   Defining an Array

In C++ the size of an array must be specified by an expression whose value can be determined at compile time. The three statements below on the left define two arrays: one named `numList`, capable of storing 200 values of type `double`, and one named `names` that can store 50 `string` values. Corresponding `tvector` definitions are given on the right.

```
const int SIZE = 100;          const int SIZE = 100;
double numList[SIZE*2];        tvector<double> numList(SIZE*2);
string names[SIZE/2];          tvector<string> names(SIZE/2);
```

In contrast, the following definition of `numList` is illegal according to the C++ standard because the value of `size` must be determined at compile time but here is known only at run time. Nevertheless, some compilers may permit such definitions, and in Chapter 12 we will see how to define in a legal manner an array whose size is not known at compile time. There is no compile-time limit on the size of tvector variables—only on built-in array variables.

```
int size;
cout << "enter size ";
cin >> size;
double numList[size];          // not legal in standard C++
```

8.4.2 Initializing an Array

Arrays can be initialized by assigning values to the individual array locations, using a loop. It is also possible to assign values to individual array locations when an array is defined. For example, the following definitions assign values representing the number of days in each month to monthDays and the names of each month to monthNames:

```
int monthDays[13]  =  {0,31,28,31,30,31,30,
                       31,31,30,31,30,31};
string monthNames[13] = {"","January","February","March",
                         "April","May","June","July",
                         "August", "September","October",
                         "November","December"};
```

Given these definitions, it's possible to print the names of all the months, in order from January to December, and how many days are in each month, with the following loop:

```
for(k=1; k <= 12; k++)
{ cout << monthNames[k] << ", " << monthDays[k]
      << " days" << endl;
}
```

This kind of initialization is *not* possible with tvector variables—only with variables defined using built-in arrays. Note that the zeroth location of each array is unused, so that the *k*th location of each array stores information for the *k*th month rather than storing information for March in the location 2. Again, the conceptual simplicity of this scheme more than compensates for an extra array location.

Although the number of entries in each array (13) is specified in the definitions above, this is not necessary. It would be better stylistically to define a constant const int NUM_MONTHS = 12 and use the expression NUM_MONTHS + 1 in defining the arrays, but no number at all needs to be used, as follows:

```
int monthDays []   = {0,31,28,31,30,31,30,
                      31,31,30,31,30,31};
string dayNames [] = {"Sunday", "Monday", "Tuesday",
                      "Wednesday", "Thursday","Friday",
                      "Saturday"};
```

The definition for `dayNames` causes an array of seven strings to be allocated and initialized. The definition of `monthDays` allocates and initializes an array of 13 integers. Since the compiler can determine the necessary number of array locations (essentially by counting commas in the list of values between curly braces), including the number of cells is allowed but is redundant and not necessary.

It is useful in some situations to assign all array locations the value zero as is done in Program 8.2. This can be done when the array is defined, by using initialization values as in the preceding examples, but an alternative method for initializing all entries in an array to zero follows:

```
int diceStats[9] = {0};
```

The `int` array `diceStats` has nine locations, all equal to zero. When zero is used to initialize all array locations, the number of locations in the array is *not* redundant as it is in the earlier examples because there is no comma-separated list of values that the compiler can use to determine the number of array values. This method *cannot* be used to initialize arrays to values other than zero. The definition

```
int units[100] = {1};
```

results in an array with `units[0] == 1`, but all other locations in `units` are zero. When a list of values used for array initialization doesn't have enough values, zeros are used to fill in the missing values. This is essentially what is happening with the shortcut method for initializing an array of zeros. I don't recommend this method of initialization; it leads to confusion because zero is treated differently from other values.

In contrast, `tvector` variables can be initialized so that all entries contain any value, not just zero. This can be done using the two-parameter `tvector` constructor.

8.4.3 Arrays as Parameters

Arrays are fundamentally different from other types in C++ in two ways:

1. It is *not* possible to assign one array to another using an assignment operator =.
2. An array passed as a parameter is *not* copied; it is as though the array were passed by reference.

The reason for these exceptions to the normal rules of assignment and parameter passing in C++ (which permit assignment between variables of the same type and use call-by-value for passing parameters) is based on what an array variable name is: a *constant* whose value serves as a *reference* to the first (index 0) item in the array. Since constants cannot be changed, assignments to array variables are illegal:

```
int coins[] = {1,5,10,25};
int bills[] = {1,5,10,20};

coins = bills;        // illegal in C and C++
coins[3] = bills[3]; // legal, assigning to array location
```

Because the array name is a reference to the first array location, it can be used to access the entire contents of the array, with appropriate indexing. Only the array name is passed as the value of a parameter, but the name can be used to change the array's contents even though the array is not explicitly passed by reference. When an array is passed as a parameter, empty brackets [ ] are used to indicate that the parameter is an array. The number of elements allocated for the storage associated with the array parameter does not need to be part of the array parameter. This is illustrated in Program 8.8.

Program 8.8 fixlist.cpp

```cpp
#include <iostream>
using namespace std;

// illustrates passing arrays as parameters

void Change(int list[], int numElts);
void Print(const int list[], int numElts);

int main()
{
    const int SIZE = 10;

    int numbers[SIZE];
    int k;
    for(k=0; k < SIZE; k++){
        numbers[k] = k+1;
    }

    cout << "before" << endl << "---------" << endl;
    Print(numbers,SIZE);

    cout << endl << "after" << endl << "---------" << endl;
    Change(numbers,SIZE);
    Print(numbers,SIZE);
    return 0;
}

void Change(int list[], int numElts)
// precondition: list contains at least numElts cells
// postcondition: list[k] = list[0] + list[1] + ... + list[k]
//                for all 0 <= k < numElts
{
    int k;
    for(k=1; k < numElts; k++)
    {   list[k] += list[k-1];
    }
}

void Print(const int list[], int numElts)
// precondition: list contains at least numElts cells
// postcondition: all elements of list printed
{
```

```
    int k;
    for(k=0; k < numElts; k++)
    {   cout << list[k] << endl;
    }
}
```

fixlist.cpp

OUTPUT

```
before
---------
1
2
3
4
5
6
7
8
9
10

after
---------
1
3
6
10
15
21
28
36
45
55
```

The identifier numbers is used as the name of an array; its value is the location of the first array cell (which has index zero). In particular, numbers does *not* change as a result of being passed to Change(), but the *contents* of the array numbers do change. This is a subtle distinction, but the array name is passed by value, as are all parameters by default in C and C++. The name is used to access the memory associated with the array, and the values stored in this memory can change. Since it is not legal to assign a new value to an array variable (e.g., list = newlist), the parameter list cannot be changed in any case, although the values associated with the array cells can change.

> **Program Tip 8.6:** **An array name is like a handle that can be used to grab all the memory cells allocated when the array is defined.** The array name cannot be changed, but it can be used to access the memory cells so that they can be changed.

const Parameters. The parameter for the function `Print` in Program 8.8 is defined as `const` or a constant array. The values stored in the cells of a constant array *cannot* be changed; the compiler will prevent attempts to do so. The values stored in a `const` array can, however, be accessed, as is shown in `Print`. If the statement `list[k] = 0` is added in the `while` loop of `Print`, the g++ compiler generates the following error message:

```
fixlist.cpp: In function 'void Print(const int *, int)':
fixlist.cpp:46: assignment of read-only location

Compilation exited abnormally with code 1
at Sat Jun  4 14:02:18
```

> **Program Tip 8.7:** **Using a const modifier for parameters is good, defensive programming—it allows the compiler to catch inadvertent attempts to modify a parameter.** A `const` array parameter protects the values of the array cells from being modified.

Array Size as a Parameter. The number of elements in an array parameter is *not* included in the formal parameter. As a result, there must be some mechanism for determining the number of elements stored in an array parameter. This is commonly done by passing this value as another parameter, by using a global constant, by using the array in a class that contains the number of entries, or by using a sentinel value in the array to indicate the last entry. As an example, the following function `Average` returns the average of the first `numScores` test scores stored in the array `scores`:

```
double Average(const int scores, int numScores)
// precondition: numScores = # of entries in scores
// postcondition: returns average of
//                scores[0] ... scores[numScores-1]
{
    int total = 0;
    double average = 0.0;           // stores returned average
    int k;
    for(k=0; k < numScores; k += 1)
    {   total += scores[k];
```

```
    }

    if (numScores != 0)  // guard divide by zero
    {   average = double(total)/numScores;
    }
    return average;
}
```

Some other section of code might read numbers, store them in an array, and call the function `Average` to compute the average of the numbers read. Alternatively, the numbers stored in the formal parameter `scores` might be data generated from a simulation or some other computer program.

In the following program segment, numbers representing grades (for students in a hypothetical course) are read until the input is exhausted or until the number of grades would exceed the capacity of the array. The average of these grades is then calculated using the function `Average`.

```
const int MAX_GRADES = 100;   // maximum # of grades
int grades[MAX_GRADES];
int numGrades = 0;                    // # of grades entered

while (cin >> score && numGrades < MAX_GRADES)
{   grades[numGrades] = score;
    numGrades++;
}
cout << "average grade = " << Average(grades,numGrades)
     << endl;
```

This example is meant to illustrate how an array might be used. The approach of storing the grades in an array to calculate the average is not a good one. Because the size of an array is determined at compile time, the code in this example is limited to manipulating at most `MAX_GRADES` grades. Since it is possible to calculate the average of a set of numbers without storing all the numbers, the approach used above is unnecessarily limiting.

The value of `numScores` in `Average` is exactly the number of values stored in the array `scores` but is one more than the largest index of an array cell with a valid value. This off-by-one difference is potentially confusing, so be careful in writing loops that access all the elements in an array.

8.5   Chapter Review

We studied the vector class `tvector` used in place of built-in arrays to store collections of values accessible by random access. Vectors can store thousands of values, and the fifth, five-hundredth, and five-thousandth values can be accessed in the same amount of time. Vectors and their built-in counterparts, arrays, are very useful in writing programs that store and manipulate large quantities of data.

The important topics covered include the following:

- `tvectors` can be used as counters, for example to count the number of occurrences of each ASCII character in a text file or the number of times a die rolls each number over several trials.

- `tvectors` are constructed by providing the size of the vector (the number of elements that can be stored) as an argument to the constructor. Vectors are indexed beginning at zero, so a six-element vector has valid indexes 0, 1, 2, 3, 4, 5.

- `tvectors` can be grown by client programs using `resize` or can grow themselves when elements are added using `push_back`. Client programs should double the size when a vector is grown as opposed to growing the size by adding one element.

- When using `push_back`, vectors should be constructed without specifying a size, though space can be allocated using `tvector::reserve`.

- `tvectors` of all built-in types can be defined, and vectors of programmer-defined types (like `string`) can be defined if the type has a default constructor.

- `tvectors` can be initialized to hold the same value in every cell by providing a second argument to the constructor when the vector is defined.

- `tvectors` should always be passed by reference to save memory and the time that would be required to copy if pass by value were used. There are occasions when a copy is needed, but in general pass by reference is preferred. Use `const` reference parameters to protect the parameters from being altered even when passed by reference.

- Initializer lists should be used to construct vectors that are private data members of class objects.

- The function `pop_back` removes the last element of a vector and decreases by one the size of the vector.

- Sequential search is used to find a value in an unsorted vector. Binary search can be used to find values in sorted vectors. Binary search is much faster, needing roughly 20 comparisons to find an item in a list of one million different items. The drawback of binary search is that its use requires a sorted vector.

- Insertion and deletion in a sorted vector requires shifting elements to the right and left, respectively.

- Built-in arrays are cumbersome to use but may be more efficient than vectors. Nevertheless, you should use vectors and switch to arrays only when you've determined that speed is essential and that the use of vectors is making your program slow (which is probably not the case).

- Built-in arrays can be initialized with several values at once. Built-in arrays cannot be resized, cannot be assigned to each other, and do not support range-checked indexing. The size of a built-in array must be known at compile time (although we'll see in Chapter 12 that an alternative form of array definition does permit array size to be determined at run time).

8.6   Exercises

8.1 Modify Program 8.3, *letters.cpp,* so that a vector of 26 elements, indexed from 0 to 25, is used to track how many times each letter in the range $'a'-'z'$ occurs. To do this, map the character $'a'$ to 0, $'b'$ to 1,..., and $'z'$ to 25. Isolate this mapping in a function CharToIndex whose header is

```
int CharToIndex(char ch)
// pre: 'a' <= ch and ch <= 'z'
// post: returns 0 for 'a', 1 for 'b', ... 25 for 'z'
```

(Note that $'a' - 'a' == 0$, $'b' - 'a' == 1$, and $'z' - 'a' == 25$.)

8.2 Write a program that maintains an inventory of a CD collection, a book collection, or some other common collectible. Model the program on *stocks.cpp,* Program 8.6, but instead of implementing a class Portfolio, implement a class called CDCollection, for example. The user of the program should have the choice of printing all items, deleting items given an identification number or artist, searching for all work by a particular artist, reading data from a file, and saving data to a file. The data file *cd.dat* that comes with the on-line materials for this book contains thousands of CD entries. For example, the lines below show information for five CDs: an id, the price, the group, and the name of the CD.

```
100121 : 15.98 : R.E.M. : Automatic for the People
100122 : 14.98 : Happy Mondays : Yes, Please
100126 : 14.98 : 10,000 Maniacs : Our Time In Eden
100127 : 11.98 : Skid Row : B-Side Ourselves
```

You won't be able to read a file in this format using the extraction operator >> because the artist and title contain white space. To read these you'll need to use the function getline discussed in Chapter 9. The loop below shows how to read a file in the format above and store the information in a struct CD. The code is very similar to the function Portfolio::Read from *stocks.cpp.*

```
void CDCollection::Read(const string& filename)
{
    ifstream input(filename.c_str());
    string idnum, price, group, title;

    while (getline(input,idnum, ':') &&
           getline(input,price, ':') &&
           getline(input,grcup, ':') &&
           getline(input,title, '\n'))
    {   myCDs.push_back(CD(idnum, atof(price),
                            group, title));
    }
}
```

8.3 Modify the class RandomWalk found in *walk.h,* Program 7.11, so that the one-dimensional walker keeps track of how many times it visits every position in the range -100 to 100. You can use either one tvector with 201 elements or two tvector instance variables: one for nonnegative positions and one for negative positions. A RandomWalk object should also keep track of how many times it goes outside the -100–100 range. You'll need to add one or more member functions to get or print the data kept about how many times each position is visited. The simplest approach is to add a method `PrintStats` to print the data. Alternatively, you could return a vector of statistics to client programs. You'll need to think carefully about how to verify that the program is tracking visits properly.

For an extra challenge, keep track of every position visited, not just those in the range -100–100. You'll need to grow the vector(s) that keep track of visits to do this.

8.4 Write a program to implement the guess-a-number game described in Section 8.3.7 on binary search. The user should think of a number between 1 and 100 and respond to guesses made by the computer. Make the program robust so that it can tell whether the user cheats by providing inconsistent answers.

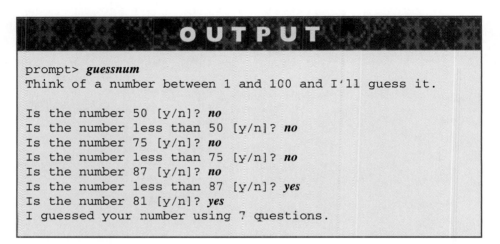

```
prompt> guessnum
Think of a number between 1 and 100 and I'll guess it.

Is the number 50 [y/n]? no
Is the number less than 50 [y/n]? no
Is the number 75 [y/n]? no
Is the number less than 75 [y/n]? no
Is the number 87 [y/n]? no
Is the number less than 87 [y/n]? yes
Is the number 81 [y/n]? yes
I guessed your number using 7 questions.
```

You'll find it useful to call the function `PromptYesNo` in *prompt.h* (see Program G.1 in How to G).

8.5 Write a program that reads a text file and keeps track of how many times each of the different words occurs. A `StringSet` object can keep track of the different words, but the program needs to keep track of how many times each word occurs. There are several ways you might solve this problem; one is outlined below:

> Create a `struct` containing a word and a count of how many times the word occurs. Each time a word is read from the file, it is looked up in a vector of these `struct`s. If the word has been seen before, the word's count is incremented; otherwise the word is added with one occurrence.

8.6 Design a `Histogram` class for displaying quantities stored in a `tvector`. A **histogram** is like a bar graph that displays a line relative to the size of the data being visualized. You can construct a `Histogram` object from a vector, and use the vector as a source of data that generates the histogram. For example, the results of using *letters.cpp*, Program 8.3, to find occurrences of each letter in *Hamlet* can be displayed as a histogram as follows:

```
                          O U T P U T

prompt> letters
enter name of input file: hamlet
   a (   9950 ) ***************************
   b (   1830 ) ****
   c (   2606 ) ******
   d (   5025 ) *************
   e ( 14960 ) ****************************************
   f (   2698 ) *******
   g (   2420 ) ******
   h (   8731 ) ***********************
   i (   8511 ) **********************
   j (    110 )
   k (   1272 ) ***
   l (   5847 ) ***************
   m (   4253 ) ***********
   n (   8297 ) **********************
   o ( 11218 ) ******************************
   p (   2016 ) *****
   q (    220 )
   r (   7777 ) ********************
   s (   8379 ) **********************
   t ( 11863 ) *******************************
   u (   4343 ) ***********
   v (   1222 ) ***
   w (   3132 ) ********
   x (    179 )
   y (   3204 ) ********
   z (     72 )
```

The absolute counts for each letter are shown in parentheses. The bars are scaled so that the longest bar (for the letter *e*) has 40 asterisks and the other bars are scaled relative to this. For example, the letter *h* has 23 asterisks and $8731/14960 \times 40 = 23.32$ (where we divide using `double` precision, but truncate the final result to an integer).

Member functions for the `Histogram` class might include setting the length of the longest bar, identifying labels for each bar drawn, plotting a range of values rather than all values, and grouping ranges; for example, for plotting data in the range 0–99, you might group by tens and plot 0–9, 10–19, 20–29, ..., 90–99.

It's difficult to write a completely general histogram class, so you'll need to decide how much functionality you will implement. The following histogram tracks 10,000 rolls of two six-sided dice and scales the longest bar to 40 characters:

```
                    O U T P U T

prompt> rollem
how many sides for dice: 6
how many rolls: 10000
    2 (    282 ) ******
    3 (    522 ) *************
    4 (    874 ) *********************
    5 (   1106 ) ***************************
    6 (   1376 ) **********************************
    7 (   1650 ) ******************************************
    8 (   1431 ) *************************************
    9 (   1131 ) ***************************
   10 (    815 ) ********************
   11 (    545 ) **************
   12 (    268 ) ******
```

8.7 Reimplement the histogram class from the previous exercise to draw a vertical histogram.
For example, a graph for rolling two six-sided dice (scaled to 10 asterisks in the longest
bar) is shown below, followed by the same graph drawn vertically.

```
    2 (    243 ) *
    3 (    594 ) ***
    4 (    827 ) ****
    5 (   1066 ) ******
    6 (   1327 ) *******
    7 (   1682 ) **********
    8 (   1465 ) ********
    9 (   1091 ) ******
   10 (    807 ) ****
   11 (    606 ) ***
   12 (    292 ) *
```

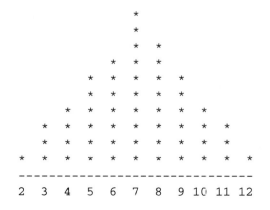

It's harder to get labels drawn well for the vertical histogram, so first try to determine how to draw the bars and don't worry initially about the labels.

8.8 Implement a *Sieve of Eratosthenes* to find prime numbers. A sieve is implemented using a tvector of bool values, initialized so that all elements are true. To find primes between 2 and N, use tvector indexes 2 through N, so you'll need an $(N+1)$-element tvector.

1. Find the first entry that is true (initially this entry has index 2 because 0 and 1 do not count in the search for primes). We'll call the index of the true entry p since this entry will be prime.
2. Set each entry whose index is a multiple of p to false.
3. Repeat until all tvector elements have been examined.

The process is illustrated in Figure 8.6 for the numbers 2 through 18. Circled numbers are true. In the topmost view of the array the first true cell has index 2, so all the even numbers (multiples of 2) are changed to false. These are shown as shaded entries in the diagram. The next true value is 3, so all multiples of 3 are changed to false (although 6, 12, and 18 have already been changed). In the third row no more new entries will be set to false that are not already false, and the primes have been determined (although the steps are repeated until all tvector elements have been examined).

8.9 Write a program that keeps track of important dates/events and reminds you of all the important dates that occur in the next two weeks each time you run the program. For example, you can store events in a data file as follows:

```
04 01   April Fools Day
02 08   Mom's birthday
01 01   New Year's Day
07 16   Laura's birthday
11 22   Margaret's birthday
```

To read data in this format you'll need to use the getline function from Chapter 9 to read all the words on a line after the month and day. The code below reads an ifstream named input in this format and prints all the events.

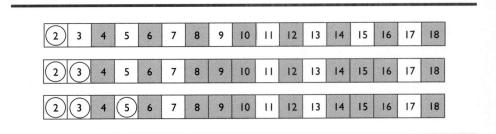

Figure 8.6 Using a Sieve of Eratosthenes to find primes.

```
int month, day;
string event;
while (input >> month >> day &&
       getline(input,event)
{
    Date dday(month,day,1999);
    cout << event << " occurs on " << dday << endl;
}
```

The program should prompt the user for a time frame, like one day, or one week, or 15 weeks, and print all the events that occur within that time frame of the current day (the day on which the program is run). See date.h, Program G.2 in How to G, for a review of the Date class.

You should allow the user the option of printing all the events in chronological order.

8.10 Write a program that determines the frequently used words in a text file. We'll define **frequently used** to mean that a word accounts for at least 1% of all the words in a file. For example, in the file *melville.txt* there are 14,353 total words, so any word that occurs more than 143 times is a frequently used word. For *melville.txt* the frequently used words are shown in Table 8.2 with their number of occurrences.

Table 8.2 Frequent words in *melville.txt*.

334	a	196	my
376	and	151	not
218	he	359	of
219	his	194	that
519	i	603	the
265	in	432	to
164	it	195	was

3

Design, Use, and Analysis: Extending the Foundation

Strings, Streams, and Operators $\quad$ 9

He was a poet and hated the approximate.
RAINER MARIA RILKE
The Journal of My Other Self

Computer programs require precision even when abstraction is required
to make them intelligible.
J.A. ZIMMER
Abstraction for Programmers

Abstraction . . . is seductive; forming generic abstract types can lead into confusing excess.
MARIAN PETRE
Psychology of Programming, 112

In 1936 Alan Turing, a British mathematician, published a famous paper titled "On Computable Numbers, with an Application to the Entscheidungsproblem." This paper helped lay the foundation for much of the work done in theoretical computer science, even though computers did not exist when the paper was written.[1] Turing invented a model of a computer, called a **Turing machine,** and he used this model to develop ideas and proofs about what kinds of numbers could be computed. His invention was an abstraction, not a real machine, but it provided a framework for reasoning about computers. The **Church–Turing thesis** says that, from a theoretical standpoint, all computers have the same power. This is commonly accepted; the most powerful computers in the world compute the same things that Turing's abstract machine could compute. Of course some computers are faster than others, and computers continue to get faster every year,[2] but the kinds of things that can be computed have not changed.

How can we define abstraction in programming? *The American Heritage Dictionary* defines it as "the act or process of separating the inherent qualities or properties of something from the actual physical object or concept to which they belong." The general user's view of a computer is an abstraction of what really goes on behind the scenes. You do not need to know how to program a pull-down menu or a tracking mouse to use these tools. You do not need to know how numbers are represented in computer memory to write programs that manipulate numeric expressions. In some cases such missing knowledge is useful because it can free you from worrying unnecessarily about issues that aren't relevant to programming at a high level.

Abstraction is a cornerstone of all computer science and certainly of our study of programming. The capability that modern programming languages and techniques

---

[1] At least, computers as we know them had not yet been invented. Several kinds of calculating machines had been proposed or manufactured, but no general-purpose computer had been built.

[2] No matter when you read this sentence, it is likely to be true.

provide us to avoid dealing with details permits more complex and larger programs to be written than could be written with assembly language, for example.

In this chapter we'll discuss characters, strings, files, and streams. These form an abstraction hierarchy with characters at the lowest level and streams at the highest level. A character is a symbol such as 'a'. Strings and files are both constructed from characters. We'll see that streams can be constructed from strings as well as from files. Although a character lies at the lowest level, we'll see that characters are also abstractions. We'll discuss programming tools that help in using and combining these abstractions.

9.1   Characters: Building Blocks for Strings

From the beginning of our study of C++ we have worked with the class string. Although we haven't worried about how the string class is implemented or about the individual characters from which strings are built, we have used the string class extensively in many programs. We have treated strings as abstractions—we understand strings by their use and behavior rather than by their construction or implementation. If we understand the string member functions (such as length, substr, operator ==, and operator <<), we do not need to understand the details and idiosyncrasies of the implementation. However, some programs manipulate the individual characters used to build strings, so we'll need to expand our understanding of characters.

9.1.1   The Type char as an Abstraction

We have discussed strings as sequences of characters but have not included detailed discussions of how a character is implemented in C++. The type char is used for characters in C++.[3]

A char variable stores legal character values. The range of legal values depends on the computer system being used and even the country in which the system is used. The range of legal characters that is supported in a computing system is called the **character set.** The most commonly used set is the ASCII set (pronounced "askee," an acronym for American Standard Code for Information Interchange); all programs in this book are run on a system with this character set. An emerging standard set is called Unicode, which supports international characters, such as ä, that are not part of the ASCII set. Chinese, Japanese, Arabic, and Cyrillic character sets may also be represented using Unicode. You must try to isolate your programs as much as possible from the particular character set being used in the program's development. This will help ensure that the program is **portable**—that is, useful in other computing environments than the one in which it was developed.

The type char is the smallest built-in type. A char variable uses less (actually, no more) memory than any other type of variable. A char literal is identified by single quotes, as shown in the first two of the following examples:

---

[3]Some people pronounce char as "care," short for "character." Others pronounce it "char" as in "charcoal." A third common pronunciation is "car" (rhymes with "star"). I don't like the "charcoal" pronunciation and use the pronunciation that has character.

```
char letter = 'a';
char digit = '9';
string word = "alphabetic";
```

Note that `string` literals use double quotes, which are different from two single quotes.

As an abstraction, a `char` is very different from an `int`. Unfortunately, in almost all cases a `char` can be treated as an `int` in C++ programs. This similarity has the potential to be confusing. From a programmer's view, a `char` is distinguished from an `int` by the way it is printed and, perhaps, by the amount of computer memory it uses. The relationship between `char` and `int` values is determined by the character set being used. For ASCII characters this relationship is given in Table F.3 in How to F.

Program 9.1 shows how the type `char` is very similar to the type `int` but prints differently. The `char` variable k is incremented just as an `int` is incremented, but, as the output shows, characters appear on the screen differently than integers.

The output of Program 9.1 shows that capital letters come before lowercase letters when the ASCII character set is used. Notice that the characters representing the digits '0' through '9' are contiguous and come before any alphabetic character.

Program 9.1 charlist.cpp

```cpp
#include <iostream>
using namespace std;

// illustrates use of char as an integral type

int main()
{
    char first,last;
    cout << "enter first and last characters" << endl;
    cout << "with NO SPACE separating them: ";
    cin >> first >> last;

    cout << first;          // print first char (fence post problem)
    char k;
    for(k=first+1; k <= last; k++)
    {   cout << " " << k;
    }
    cout << endl;
    return 0;
}
```

charlist.cpp

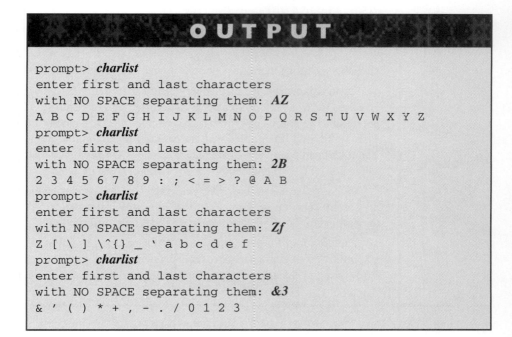

```
prompt> charlist
enter first and last characters
with NO SPACE separating them: AZ
A B C D E F G H I J K L M N O P Q R S T U V W X Y Z
prompt> charlist
enter first and last characters
with NO SPACE separating them: 2B
2 3 4 5 6 7 8 9 : ; < = > ? @ A B
prompt> charlist
enter first and last characters
with NO SPACE separating them: Zf
Z [ \ ] \^{} _ ` a b c d e f
prompt> charlist
enter first and last characters
with NO SPACE separating them: &3
& ' ( ) * + , - . / 0 1 2 3
```

If we change the output statement to cast the character to an `int`,

```
cout << " " << int(k);
```

the program will display the internal numeric representation of each `char` rather than its symbolic character representation.

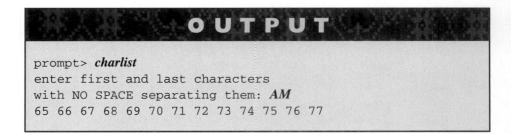

```
prompt> charlist
enter first and last characters
with NO SPACE separating them: AM
65 66 67 68 69 70 71 72 73 74 75 76 77
```

Using the cast makes it more difficult to verify that the output is correct because the symbolic form of each character isn't used. In general, there isn't any reason to be concerned with what the numerical representation of each character is because C++ provides many mechanisms that allow programs to use the type `char` abstractly without regard for the underlying character set. You can make the following assumptions about character codes on almost every system you'll use.

1. The digit characters `'0'` through `'9'` (ASCII values 48 through 57) are consecutive with no intervening characters.

Table 9.1 Some functions in <cctype>.

Function Prototype	Returns True When
int isalpha(int c)	c is alphabetic (upper- or lowercase)
int isalnum(int c)	c is alphabetic or a digit
int islower(int c)	c is a lowercase letter
int isdigit(int c)	c is a digit character '0'–'9'

2. The lowercase characters 'a' through 'z' (ASCII 97 through 122) are consecutive, and the uppercase characters 'A' through 'Z' (ASCII 65 through 90) are consecutive.

These assumptions are true for the ASCII character set and the Unicode character set, but not necessarily for all character sets.[4] In almost all programming environments you'll use either ASCII or Unicode. In the next section we'll study utility functions that help in writing portable programs.

9.1.2 The Library <cctype>

To be portable, your code must not rely on a specific character set. Just as the functions in the math library <cmath> make writing mathematical and scientific programs easier, a library of character functions helps in writing portable character-manipulating programs. This character library is accessible by using #include <cctype> or on some systems using <ctype.h>. The prototypes for some of the functions in <cctype> are given in Table 9.1; prototypes for all the functions are found in Table F.2 in How to F.

Although the formal parameter for each function is an int, these functions are intended to work with char arguments. Thus isalpha('9') evaluates to zero (false) because '9' is not an alphabetic character. In an ASCII environment isdigit(57) evaluates to nonzero (true) because 57 is the ASCII value for the character '9'. You should avoid using these functions in such a manner; treat characters as symbolic abstractions.

> **Program Tip 9.1: The functions in <cctype> return an int value rather than a bool value; but treat the value as a bool.** In particular, there is no guarantee that the return value will be 1 for true (although the return value will always be 0 for false). This means you should write if (isdigit(ch)) rather than if (isdigit(ch) == 1) in your code.

---

[4]The C++ standard requires that '0' through '9' be consecutive, but in the EBCDIC character set the letters 'a' through 'z' and 'A' through 'Z' are not consecutive.

To write portable programs, use the functions in <cctype> rather than writing equivalent functions. For example, if the ASCII character set is used, the following function could serve as an implementation of tolower:

```
int tolower(int c)
// postcondition: returns lowercase equivalent of c
//                if c isn't uppercase, returns c unchanged
{
    if ('A' <= c && c <= 'Z')        // c is uppercase
    {   return c + 32;
    }
    return c;
}
```

This function works only when the ASCII character set is used, and it relies on two properties of the character set:

- The uppercase letters occur in order with no intervening characters.
- The difference between a lowercase letter and its uppercase equivalent is always 32.

You can isolate some dependencies on ASCII by subtracting characters:

```
int tolower(int c)
// postcondition: returns lowercase equivalent of c
//                if c isn't uppercase, returns c unchanged
{
    if ('A' <= c && c <= 'Z')        // c is uppercase
    {   return c + ('a' - 'A');
    }
    return c;
}
```

The correctness of this code depends only on a character set in which 'a' through 'z' and 'A' through 'Z' are consecutive ranges. Since char values can be manipulated as int values, you can subtract one character from another, yielding an int value. However, although you can multiply 'a' * 'b', the result doesn't make sense; using ASCII, the result is 97*98 == 9506, which is not a legal character value. Although you can use char variables as integers, you should restrict arithmetic operations of characters to the following:

1. Adding an integer to a character—for example, '0' + 2 == '2'
2. Subtracting an integer from a character—for example, '9' - 3 == '6' and 'C' - 2 == 'A'
3. Subtracting two characters—for example, '8' - '0' == 8 and 'Z' - 'A' == 25

You can use a char value in a switch statement because char values can be used as integers. You can also compare two char values using the relational operators <, <=, >, and >=. Character comparisons are based on the value of the underlying character set, which will always reflect lexicographical (dictionary) order.

Now that we have covered the lowest level of the character–string–file–stream hierarchy, we'll see how characters are used to build strings and files. We'll investigate strings first.

9.1.3 Strings as char Sequences

The class string, accessible using the header file <string>,[5] is an abstraction that represents sequences of characters. However, we haven't yet studied any mechanism for extracting individual characters from a string. Although the substr member function extracts strings and operator + concatenates strings, until now we haven't been able to alter the individual characters of a string.

Basically, a string acts like a vector of characters. The characters are indexed from 0 to s.length()-1. For example, if str represents the string "computer", then 'c' has index 0 and 'r' has index 7. Individual characters in a string are accessed using the **indexing** operator [], shown in *spreader.cpp,* Program 9.2, which prints a string with spaces between each character.

Program 9.2 spreader.cpp

```cpp
#include <iostream>
#include <string>
using namespace std;
#include "prompt.h"

// spread a string by inserting spaces between characters

int main()
{
    string s = PromptString("enter a string: ");
    int k, limit = s.length();      // # of chars in s
    if (limit > 0)                  // at least one character
    {   cout << s[0];               // first character, fence post problem
        for(k=1; k < limit; k++)    // then loop over the rest
        {   cout << " " << s[k];
        }
        cout << endl;
    }
    return 0;
}
```

spreader.cpp

---

[5]The C++ standard string class is accessible using the header file <string>. You may be using "tstring.h" or "apstring.h" rather than the standard header file. Each of these implementations works with the programs in this book.

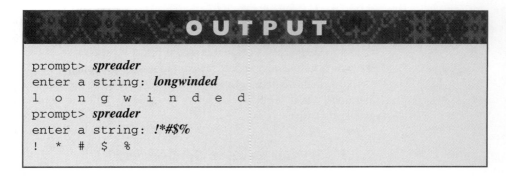

```
prompt> spreader
enter a string: longwinded
l    o    n    g    w    i    n    d    e    d
prompt> spreader
enter a string: !*#$%
!    *    #    $    %
```

Because the expression s[k] is used for output, and because the compiler can determine that the expression s[k] is a char, the symbolic form of each character is printed—that is, an 'o' instead of 111 (the ASCII value of 'o'). The indexing operator can also be used to change an individual character in a string. For example, the following sequence of statements would cause taste to be displayed:

```
string s = "paste";
s[0] = 't';
cout << s << endl;
```

A program that uses the [] operator with an index that is **out of range** (i.e., less than 0 or greater than or equal to the number of characters in a string) will cause undefined behavior if the standard string class is used because the standard class does not check for illegal indexes.[6]

Program Tip 9.2: Out-of-range string indexes can cause indeterminate and hard-to-find errors. The errors are indeterminate because the program may behave differently each time it is run, depending on what values are in memory. An out-of-range index will either read from or write to a memory location that is not part of the string. Such memory accesses invariably lead to errors.

---

[6]The implementations of string in "tstring.h" or "apstring.h" do check for illegal indexes. These implementations will generate an error message when a program indexes a string with an out-of-range value.

John von Neumann *(1903–1957)*

John von Neumann was a genius in many fields. He founded the field of game theory with his book *Theory of Games and Economic Behavior* (cowritten with Oskar Morgenstern). He helped develop the atomic bomb as part of the Manhattan Project. Almost all computers in use today are based on the von Neumann model of stored programs and use an architecture that he helped develop in the early years of computing

In 1944, von Neumann was working with the ENIAC (Electronic Numerical Integrator and Computer), a machine whose wires had to be physically rearranged to run a different program. The idea of storing a program in the computer, just as data are stored, is generally credited to von Neumann (although there has been a history of sometimes rancorous dispute; see [Gol93, Mac92]).

Hans Bethe, a Nobel Prize–winning physicist, graded academic seminars on a scale of 1 to 10:

Grade one was something my mother could understand. Grade two my wife could understand. Grade seven was something I could understand. Grade eight was something only the speaker and Johnny von Neumann could understand. Grade nine was something Johnny could understand, but the speaker didn't. Grade ten was something even Johnny could not yet understand, but there was little of that.

Von Neumann's powers of memory and calculation were prodigious, as were his contributions to so many fields. For a full account of von Neumann's life see [Mac92].

Pause to Reflect

9.1 The following function is intended to return the decimal equivalent of a digit character; for example, for ′0′ it should return 0, and for ′3′ it should return 3.

```
int todigit(int c)
// pre: c is a digit character: '0','1', ..., '9'
// post: returns digit equivalent,
//        e.g., 3 for '3'
{
    if (isdigit(c))
    {   return c - '0';
    }
}
```

This function does return the correct values for all digit characters. The function is not robust because it may cause programs to crash if the precondition isn't true. How would you make it more robust?

9.2 The underlying numeric value of a character (in ASCII and other character sets) reflects lexicographical order. For example, `'C'` < `'a'` because uppercase letters precede lowercase letters in the ASCII ordering. Why does this help to explain why `"Zebra"` < `"aardvark"` but `"aardvark"` < `"yak"`?

9.3 Explain why the statement `cout << 'a'+3 << endl` generates the integer 100 as output. Why does the statement `cout << char('a'+3) << endl` generate the character `'d'`?

9.4 If the ASCII set is used, what are the values of `iscntrl('\t')`, `isspace('\t')`, and `islower('\t')`?

9.5 Write a function `isvowel` that returns true when its parameter is a vowel: `'a'`, `'e'`, `'i'`, `'o'`, or `'u'` (or the uppercase equivalent). What is an easy way of writing `isconsonant` (assuming `isvowel` exists)?

9.6 Write a Boolean-valued function `IsPalindrome` that returns true when its string parameter is a palindrome and false otherwise. A **palindrome** is a word that reads the same backward as forward, such as "racecar," "mom," and "amanaplanacanalpanama" (which is "A man, a plan, a canal—Panama!" with no spaces, capitals, or punctuation).

For a challenge, make the function ignore spaces and punctuation so that "A man, a plan, a canal — Panama!" is recognized as a palindrome.

9.7 Write the body of the following function `MakeLower` so that all uppercase letters in s are converted to lowercase. Why is s a reference parameter?

```
void MakeLower(string & s)
// post: all letters in s are lower case
```

9.8 There are several functions in the library `"strutils.h"` (see *strutils.h*, Program G.8 in How to G) for converting strings to numbers: `atoi` converts a string to an `int` and `atof` converts a string to a `double`. (The "a" is for "alphabetic"; "atoi" is pronounced "a-to-i.")

Write a function with prototype `int atoi(string s)` that converts a string to its decimal equivalent; for example, `atoi("1234")` evaluates to 1234, and `atoi("-52")` evaluates to −52.

9.2 Streams and Files as Lines and Characters

A `string` variable is a sequence of characters, but we manipulate strings abstractly without knowing the details of how the characters are stored or represented. When information is hidden in this way, and a type is used independently of the underlying representation of the data, the type is sometimes called an **abstract data type,** or **ADT.** The data type is abstract because knowledge cf its underlying implementation is not necessary to use it. You probably don't know how individual 0s and 1s are stored to represent int and double values, but you can still write programs that use these numeric types.

In this section we'll see that a stream is also an abstract data type. Until now we have viewed a stream as a sequence of words or numbers. We extract words or numbers from a stream using >> and insert onto a stream using <<. We have developed programs using the standard streams cin and cout, as well as streams bound to files using the classes ifstream and ofstream. In this section we'll study functions that let us view streams as a sequence of lines rather than words and numbers. Other functions let us view streams as sequences of characters; different views are useful in different settings. We'll see some applications that are most easily implemented when streams are viewed as sequences of lines and others where a sequence of characters is a better choice.

9.2.1 Input Using getline()

Input operations on strings using >> result in word-at-a-time input, where words are treated as any sequence of non–white space characters. In some applications other methods of input are needed. In particular, an ifstream variable bound to a file may require line-oriented input. Consider, for example, processing a file in the following format, where an artist/group name is followed on the next line by the title of a compact disk (CD) by the artist:

```
Spin Doctors
Pocket Full of Kryptonite
The Beatles
Sergeant Pepper's Lonely Hearts Club Band
Strauss
Also Sprach Zarathustra
The Grateful Dead
American Beauty
```

There is no way to read all the words on one line of a file using the stream-processing tools currently at our disposal. Since many text files are arranged as a sequence of lines rather than white space–delimited words, we need a method for reading input other than the extraction operator >>. The function getline allows an entire line of input to be read at once. When we view a stream as line-oriented rather than word-oriented, we need to be able to include white space as part of the line read from a stream.

If the line cin >> s in Program 9.2 is replaced with getline(cin,s), the user can enter a string with spaces in it:

```
prompt> spreader
enter a string:   Green Eggs and Ham
G   r   e   e   n      E   g   g   s      a   n   d      H   a   m
```

In the original program the only word read by the program is `Green` because the space between "Green" and "Eggs" terminates the extraction operation when `>>` is used. The characters `"Eggs and Ham"` will not be processed but will remain on the input stream.

The function `getline` is used in Program 9.3 to count the total number of lines in a file. This gives a better count of the number of characters in a file too because a line can contain white space characters that would not be read if `>>` were used.

Program 9.3   filelines.cpp

```cpp
#include <iostream>
#include <fstream>
#include <cstdlib>
#include <string>
using namespace std;
#include "prompt.h"

// count # of lines in input file

int main()
{
    ifstream input;
    string s;                               // line entered by user
    long  numLines = 0;
    long  numChars = 0;
    string filename = PromptString("enter name of input file: ");
    input.open(filename.c_str());

    if (input.fail() )
    {   cout << "could not open file " << filename << endl;
        exit(1);
    }

    while (getline(input,s))
    {   numLines++;
        numChars += s.length();
    }
    cout << "number of lines = " << numLines
         << ", number of characters = " << numChars << endl;
    return 0;
}
```

filelines.cpp

The function `getline` extracts a line, stores the line in a `string` variable, and returns the state of the stream. Some programmers prefer to test the stream state explicitly:

```
while (getline(input,s) && ! input.fail())
```

However, it is fine to use `getline` in a loop test, both to extract a line and as a test to see whether the extraction succeeds, just as the expression `infile >> word` can be used as the test of a `while` loop to process all the white space–delimited words in a stream.

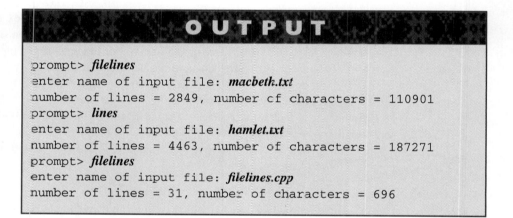

```
prompt> filelines
enter name of input file: macbeth.txt
number of lines = 2849, number of characters = 110901
prompt> lines
enter name of input file: hamlet.txt
number of lines = 4463, number of characters = 187271
prompt> filelines
enter name of input file: filelines.cpp
number of lines = 31, number of characters = 696
```

As used in Program 9.3, `getline` has two parameters: an input stream and a string for storing the line extracted from the stream. The stream can be a predefined stream such as `cin` or an `ifstream` variable such as `input`, as used in Program 9.3. An optional third parameter to `getline` indicates the **line delimiter** or sentinel character that identifies the "end of line." The `string` function `getline` extracts one line from the stream passed as the first parameter. The characters composing the line are stored in the `string` parameter `s`. The state of the stream after the extraction is returned as the value of the function. The return value is a reference to the stream because streams should not be passed or returned by value.

Syntax: getline

```
istream &
getline(istream & is,
        string & s,
        char sentinel = '\n');
```

Normally, the end of a line is marked by the newline character `'\n'`. However, it is possible to specify a different value that will serve as the end-of-line character. An optional third argument can be passed to `getline`. This `char` parameter (`sentinel` in the diagram) is used as the end-of-line character. The end-of-line character is extracted from the stream but is *not* stored in the string `s`.

For example, suppose a file is formatted with a CD artist and title on the same line, separated by a colon :, as follows:

```
Jimmy Buffet : Fruitcakes
Paul Simon : The Rhythm Of The Saints
Boyz II Men : Cooleyhighharmony
```

The following loop reads this file, storing the artist and title in two strings:

```
string artist,title;
while (getline(input,artist,':') && getline(input,title))
{   cout << artist << "\t" << title << endl;
}
```

> **Program Tip 9.3: Be very careful when using both get line and the extraction operator >> with the same stream.** Extraction skips white space but often leaves the white space on the stream. For example, if you type characters and press Enter when >> is used, the newline character that was input by pressing the Enter key is still on the cin stream. A subsequent getline operation reads all characters until the newline, effectively reading nothing. If your programs seem to be skipping input from the user, look for problems mixing these two input operations. It's better to use just getline to read strings, and the conversion operators atof and atoi (see *strutils.h* in How to G) to convert a string to an int or to a double, respectively, than to mix the two forms of stream input.

The value returned by getline is the same value that would be returned if the stream member function fail were called immediately after the call to getline. As we've seen, some programmers prefer to make the call to fail explicitly rather than to use the value returned by getline. A getline operation will fail if the stream cannot be read, either because it is bound to a nonexistent file or because no more lines are left on the stream.

A stream variable can be used by itself instead of the function fail. For example,

```
input.open(filename.c_str());
if (input.fail())
{   cout << "could not open file " << filename << endl;
    exit(1);
}
```

can be replaced by the statements

```
input.open(filename.c_str());
if (! input)
{   cout << "could not open file " << filename << endl;
    exit(1);
}
```

The use of !input in place of input.fail() is common in C++ programs. I'll use fail most of the time because it makes clear how the stream is being tested.

9.2.2 Parsing Line-Oriented Data Using `istringstream`

Data are often line-oriented because people find it easy to edit and read lines of words, numbers, and other data. Reading data is straightforward when the number of items per line is the same for an entire data set because a `for` loop can be used to iterate a set number of times for each input line. Another approach is needed when the number of items per line varies. For example, we might want to access the individual words in the titles of the CDs stored in a file:

```
The Beatles
Sergeant Pepper's Lonely Hearts Club Band
Strauss
Also Sprach Zarathustra
   . . .
```

We might need to write a program to average students' grades, where each student has a different number of grades stored in the following format (firstname lastname grades):

```
Dave Reed 55 60 75 67 72 59
Mike Clancy 88 92 91 97
Stuart Reges 99 94 98 91 95
```

In general, parsing input and reading data often make up the hardest part of developing a program. Reading data is not an algorithmically challenging problem, but dealing with badly formed data and different kinds of data can be an unpleasant part of programming.

We already know how to process stream input a word at a time using the extraction operator `>>`. We need a tool that lets us use `>>` on one line of a file. The class `istringstream` (for **input string stream**), accessible by including the file `<sstream>`[7], is just the tool we need. The `istringstream` class constructs a stream bound to a string as the source of the input, much as the `ifstream` class constructs a stream bound to a disk file as the source of input. Because an `istringstream` object is a stream, it supports the same functions and operators as `ifstream` objects and the standard input stream `cin`.

The code in *readnums.cpp,* Program 9.4, uses an `istringstream` variable to read line-oriented numerical data where the number of integers on each line varies. The average of the numbers on each line of input is calculated and printed.

Program 9.4 readnums.cpp

```cpp
#include <iostream>
#include <sstream>
#include <string>
using namespace std;

// illustrates use of input string streams
```

---

[7]The name `istringstream` is relatively new; older compilers that don't use this name will use `istrstream`. The header file for `istrstream` is `<strstream.h>`. On some systems this may be shortened to `<strstrea.h>`.

```cpp
int main()
{
    string s;
    cout << "program computes averages of lines of numbers."  << endl;
    cout << "to exit, use end-of-file" << endl << endl;

    while (getline(cin,s))
    {   int total = 0;
        int count = 0;
        int num;

        istringstream input(s);
        while (input >> num)
        {   count++;
            total += num;
        }
        if (count != 0)
        {   cout << "average of " << count << " numbers = "
                 << double(total)/count << endl;
        }
        else
        {   cout << "data not parsed as integers" << endl;
        }
    }
    return 0;
}
```

readnums.cpp

```
O U T P U T

prompt> readnums
program computes averages of lines of numbers.
to exit, use end-of-file

10 20 30
average of 3 numbers = 20
1 2 3 4 5 6 7 8
average of 9 numbers = 4.5
1 -1 2 -2 3 -3 4 -4 5 -5
average of 10 numbers = 0
apple orange guava
data not parsed as integers
2 4 apple 8 10
average of 2 numbers = 3
^Z
```

The `getline` function reads one line of input into the string s, and the `istringstream` variable `input` is constructed from s. Then `input` is used as a stream: integers are extracted using >> until the extraction fails. The variable `input` *must* be defined (and hence constructed) inside the `while (getline(cin,s))` loop of *readnums.cpp*. The source of data in an `istringstream` object is the `string` passed as an argument to the `istringstream` constructor. It is not possible to define `input` before the loop and then rebind `input` to a string entered by the user within the loop. The `istringstream` variable `input` is constructed anew at each iteration of the `while (getline(cin,s))` loop.

An `istringstream` is constructed from a standard string object, but it will work correctly when constructed from a C-style string.[8] Changing the value of the `string` used to construct an `istringstream` object while the stream is being used can lead to trouble.

9.2.3 Output Using `ostringstream`

It's relatively easy to learn to program with `istringstream` objects because they behave exactly like `cin` or an `ifstream` variable. Sometimes it's useful in programs to be able to form a string by joining different values, such as a string formed from the string `"the answer is "` and the int 257. The string formed by joining the different values can be passed as a parameter, printed, and in general be treated like any string object. You can use the conversion function `tostring` (from *strutils.h* in How to G) and string catenation for this:

```
string result = "the answer is " + tostring(257);
```

The value of `result` is the string `"the answer is 257"`. However, it's much easier to combine together different values using an `ostringstream` object (output string stream).

```
ostringstream output;
output << "the answer is " << 257;
string result = output.str();
```

An `ostringstream` (like `istringstream`, accessible from `<sstream>`) behaves like an output stream, that is, like `cout` or an `ofstream` variable. Values can be written to the output string stream using standard stream insertion, including formatting operators like `setw` (see How to B). The method `ostringstream::str()` returns a string that contains the characters written to the output string stream.

---

[8]If a nonstandard `string` class is used, (e.g., from `"apstring.h"` or `"tstring.h"`), you'll need to use the `c_str()` string member function when constructing an `istringstream` variable.

Niklaus Wirth (b. 1934)

Niklaus Wirth is perhaps best known as the inventor/developer of the programming language Pascal. He also was an early adherent of a methodology of programming he called "stepwise refinement," writing a paper in 1971 that called for developing programs in a style I've called *iterative enhancement* in this book. Pascal was developed in the early 1970s; it was not, as conventional wisdom would have it, developed solely as a language for educational use. In his 1984 Turing Award lecture Wirth says:

> *Occasionally, it has been claimed that Pascal was designed as a language for teaching. Although this is correct, its use in teaching was not the only goal. In fact, I do not believe in using tools and formalisms in teaching that are inadequate for any practical task. By today's standards, Pascal has obvious deficiencies for programming large systems, but 15 years ago it represented a sensible compromise between what was desirable and what was effective.*

Wirth continued to develop languages that were successors of Pascal, notably Modula-2 and Oberon. In discussing the difficulties of developing hardware and software, Wirth has this to say about the complexity of these tasks:

> *It is true that we live in a complex world and strive to solve inherently complex problems, which often do require complex mechanisms. However, this should not diminish our desire for elegant solutions, which convince by their clarity and effectiveness. Simple, elegant solutions are more effective, but they are harder to find than complex ones, and they require more time, which we too often believe to be unaffordable.*

When contacted about providing a picture for the second edition of this book, Wirth replied, "I must say that I have never been a friend of C++." Most of this material is taken from [Wir87].

9.2.4 Strings, Streams, and Characters

Sometimes it is useful to regard a file (and its associated stream) as a collection of characters rather than as a collection of lines. Of course, we could read a file a line at a time using `getline` and then access each character of the extracted string, but sometimes character-at-a-time input is more appropriate than line-at-a-time input. The stream member function `get` is used to read one character at a time. White space is *not* skipped when `get` is used. Program 9.5, *filelines2.cpp*, uses `get` to count the characters in a file one at a time. Note that `getline` is not a stream member function but that `get` is.

Program 9.5 filelines2.cpp

```cpp
#include <iostream>
#include <fstream>
#include <cstdlib>      // for exit
#include <string>
using namespace std;

#include "prompt.h"

// count # of lines and chars in input file

int main()
{
    long numChars = 0;
    long numLines = 0;
    char ch;
    string filename = PromptString("enter name of input file: ");
    ifstream input;
    input.open(filename.c_str());

    if (input.fail() )
    {   cout << "could not open file " << filename << endl;
        exit(1);
    }
    while (input.get(ch))           // reading char succeeds?
    {   if ('\n' == ch)             // read newline character
        {   numLines++;
        }
        numChars++;
    }

    cout << "number of lines = " << numLines
         << ", number of characters = " << numChars << endl;
    return 0;
}
```

filelines2.cpp

```
OUTPUT

prompt> filelines2
enter name of input file: macbeth.txt
number of lines = 2849, number of characters = 113750
prompt> filelines2
enter name of input file: hamlet.txt
number of lines = 4463, number of characters = 191734
```

The number of lines printed by *filelines2.cpp,* Program 9.5, is the same as the number of lines calculated by *filelines.cpp,* Program 9.3, but the number of characters printed is different. If you look carefully at all the numbers printed by both programs, you may be able to determine what the "missing" characters are. In the on-line version of *Hamlet,* both programs calculate the number of lines as 4,463, but Program 9.3 calculates 187,271 characters, compared to the 191,734 calculated by Program 9.5. Not coincidentally, $187{,}271 + 4{,}463 = 191{,}734$. The newline character '\n' is not part of the total number of characters calculated by Program 9.3. This points out some subtle behavior of the getline function. getline reads a line of text, terminated by the newline character '\n'. The newline character is read but is *not* stored in the string parameter to getline. You can change Program 9.3 to count newlines by changing the calculation of numChars as follows:

```
numChars += s.length() + 1; // +1 for newline
```

The comment is important here; the reason for the addition of + 1 may not be apparent without it.

Pause to Reflect

9.9 Write a small program that prompts for the name of an artist and prints all CDs by the artist. Assume input is in the following format:

```
The Black Crowes
The Southern Harmony and Musical Companion
10,000 Maniacs
Blind Man's Zoo
The Beatles
Rubber Soul
```

For example, if the user enters The Beatles, the output might be

```
Sergeant Pepper's Lonely Hearts Club Band
The White Album
Revolver
Rubber Soul
```

depending on what CD titles are stored in the file.

9.10 From its use in *filelines2.cpp,* Program 9.5, the char parameter to get must be a reference parameter. Why is this the case?

9.11 Program 9.5, *filelines2.cpp,* can be modified so that it copies a file by writing every character (using <<) that is read. What modifications are necessary so that the user is prompted for the name of a new file to be written that will be a copy of the file that is read?

9.12 How can the copy program from the previous exercise be modified so that all uppercase letters in the input file are converted to lowercase letters in the output file? (*Hint:* The change is very straightforward.)

9.3 Case Study: Removing Comments with State Machines

With the stream and string functions we have studied, we now have the choice of reading streams in several ways:

- A word at a time, using >> and `string` variables.
- A line at a time, using `getline` and `string` variables.
- A character at a time, using `get` and `char` variables.

In this section we'll develop a program to remove all comments from a file. We'll see that character-at-a-time input facilitates this task, and we'll study an approach that extends to other parsing-related problems.[9] We'll use a new syntactic feature of C++ called an **enum**.

9.3.1 Counting Words

To make the method used to remove comments more familiar, we'll modify *filelines2.cpp* to count words in addition to counting lines and characters. We'll use the same specification for words that the extraction operator >> uses: a white space–delimited sequence of characters.

Since we're reading one character at a time, we'll need a method to determine when a word starts and when it ends. We'll use the function `isspace` from <cctype> (see Table F.2 in How to F) to determine if a character is white space, but how can we keep track of word boundaries? The key is recognizing that the program is in one of two **states**. It is either reading a word, or not reading a word. When the program reads a space, it is not in a word. When it reads a nonspace character it is in a word. The transition from the in-a-word state to the not-in-a-word state marks a word, so whenever this transition occurs we'll update the word count. The transitions are diagrammed in Figure 9.1 and shown in code in Program 9.6, *wc.cpp*.[10]

Program 9.6 wc.cpp

```
#include <iostream>
#include <fstream>
#include <cstdlib>      // for exit
#include <cctype>       // for isspace
#include <string>
using namespace std;

#include "prompt.h"
```

---

[9] A program is **parsed** by the compiler in the process of converting it into assembly or machine language. "Parse" usually refers to the process of reading input in identifiable chunks such as C++ identifiers, reserved words, etc.

[10] The Unix program *wc* counts words, lines, and characters, hence the name.

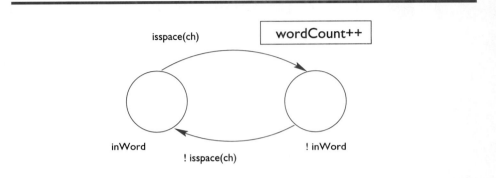

Figure 9.1 States for counting words.

```
// count # of lines and chars in input file

int main()
{
    long numChars = 0;
    long numLines = 0;
    long numWords = 0;
    char ch;
    bool inWord = false;   // initially not reading a word

    string filename = PromptString("enter name of input file: ");
    ifstream input;
    input.open(filename.c_str());

    if (input.fail() )
    {   cout << "could not open file " << filename << endl;
        exit(1);
    }
    while (input.get(ch))       // reading char succeeds?
    {   if ('\n' == ch)         // read newline character
        {   numLines++;
        }
        numChars++;
        if (isspace(ch))
        {   if (inWord)         // just finished a word
            {   inWord = false;
                numWords++;
            }
        }
        else                    // not a space
        {   if (! inWord)       // just started a word
            {   inWord = true;
            }
        }
    }
```

```
if (inWord) numWords++;    // ended in a word

cout << "lines = " << numLines
     << "\tchars = " << numChars
     << "\twords = " << numWords << endl;
return 0;
}
```

wc.cpp

```
prompt> wc
enter name of input file: melville.txt
lines = 1609     chars = 82140     words = 14353
prompt> wc
enter name of input file: bible10.txt
lines = 228760   chars = 4959549 words = 822899
```

9.3.2   Problem Specification: What Is a Comment?

The first step in writing almost any program is to specify the problem properly. We must decide what a comment is, and we should try to identify potential problems in our definition. We'll write a program that removes comments beginning with //. These comments extend to the end of a line and are simpler to remove than /* ...*/ comments, which can extend over several lines. We'll read and echo all characters except those that are part of a comment.

9.3.3   A State Machine Approach to I/O

Our comment-removing program will prompt for the name of a program (actually any text file) and print the program with all the comments removed. Our first program will output using cout, but we'll design the program so that output to an ofstream object will be a simple change. We must decide whether to read a program a line at a time or a character at a time. Since // comments are line-oriented, reading input a line at a time makes sense. We could use the string member function find to determine whether each line contains the string "//" and, if so, where the "//" begins. However, this approach cannot be extended to removing /* ...*/ comments, which can extend over several lines, so we'll use character-at-a-time input instead.

We'll use a state machine approach in reading and removing comments. In a **state machine** program, each input character causes the program to change its behavior depending on the program's state. We'll use a three-state function to remove comments. The function will be in one of three states as it reads each character:

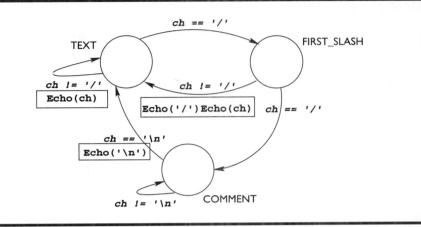

Figure 9.2 State machine diagram for removing // comments.

1.   Processing regular, uncommented text.
2.   A slash '//' has just been read.
3.   Processing commented text.

   In Figure 9.2, these states are labeled as *TEXT, FIRST_SLASH,* and *COMMENT.* Each state is shown as a circle, and state changes are shown with arrows. The program can change state each time a character is read, although it's possible to stay in the same state. Some state changes (or state transitions) are accompanied by an action, shown in a box. In the text-processing state *TEXT,* nonslash characters are echoed; a slash character is not echoed but causes a state transition to the state labeled *FIRST_SLASH.* In the state *FIRST_SLASH* we don't yet whether a comment follows or whether the division operator / was just read. The answer depends on the next character read. If a slash character is read, we know a comment follows, so we change state to *COMMENT;* otherwise there was only one slash, so we echo the slash and the character just read and return to *TEXT,* the state of parsing noncommented text. Finally, in the *COMMENT* state, we ignore all characters. However, when a newline character '\n' is read, we know the comment has ended, so the newline is echoed and the state changes back to *TEXT.*

   The advantage of the state approach is that we simply read one character at a time and take an action on the character depending on the current state of the program. In a way, the states serve as memory. For example, in the state *FIRST_SLASH* we know that one slash remains unprocessed. If the slash doesn't begin a comment, we'll echo the unprocessed slash and change to reading regular text.

   Program 9.7, *decomment.cpp,* implements this state machine approach. The method `Decomment::Transform` actually removes the comments. An enumerated type `Decomment::ReadState` is used so that symbolic values appear in code for each state. The symbolic label *FIRST_SLASH* is more informative than a number like 1 in reading code. We'll cover enumerated types after we discuss the program.

Program 9.7 decomment.cpp

```cpp
#include <iostream>
#include <fstream>
#include <cstdlib>      // for exit
using namespace std;
#include "prompt.h"

// Owen Astrachan 7/4/1996, revised 5/4/99
// state-machine approach for removing all // comments from a file
// (doesn't handle // in a string, e.g., " test // comment "

class Decomment
{
  public:
    Decomment();
    void Transform(istream& input, ostream& output);

  private:
    void Echo(char ch, ostream& output);

    const char SLASH;
    const char NEWLINE;

    enum ReadState{TEXT, FIRST_SLASH, COMMENT};
};

Decomment::Decomment()
 : SLASH('/'),
   NEWLINE('\n')
{
    // constants initialized
}

void Decomment::Echo(char ch, ostream& output)
{
    output << ch;
}

void Decomment::Transform(istream& input, ostream& output)
{
    char ch;
    ReadState currentState = TEXT;
    while (input.get(ch))                   // read one char at a time
    {   switch(currentState)
        {
          case TEXT:
            if (ch == SLASH)              // potential comment begins
            {   currentState = FIRST_SLASH;
            }
            else
            {   Echo(ch,output);
            }
```

```
                break;

            case FIRST_SLASH:
                if (ch == SLASH)
                {   currentState = COMMENT;
                }
                else                      // one slash not followed by another
                {   Echo(SLASH,output);   // print the slash from last time
                    Echo(ch,output);      // and the current character
                    currentState = TEXT;  // reading uncommented text
                }
                break;

            case COMMENT:
                if (ch == NEWLINE)        // end-of-line is end of comment
                {   Echo(NEWLINE,output); // be sure to echo end of line
                    currentState = TEXT;
                }
                break;
        }
    }
}


int main()
{
    string filename = PromptString("enter filename: ");
    ifstream input(filename.c_str());
    if (input.fail())
    {   cout << "could not open " << filename << " for reading" << endl;
        exit(1);
    }
    Decomment dc;
    dc.Transform(input,cout);

    return 0;
}
```

decomment.cpp

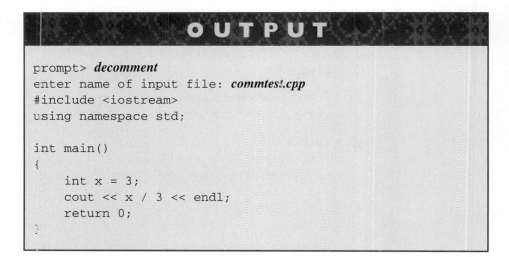

```
prompt> decomment
enter name of input file: commtest.cpp
#include <iostream>
using namespace std;

int main()
{
    int x = 3;
    cout << x / 3 << endl;
    return 0;
}
```

enum values are used as the values of the variable `currentState`. Otherwise the logic is precisely illustrated in Figure 9.2. The test input is the following file, named *commtest.cpp:*

```
#include <iostream>
using namespace std;
// this is a sample program for comment removal
int main()
{
    int x = 3;                      // meaningful identifier??
    cout << x / 3 << endl;    // complex math is fun
    return 0;                       // this is a useful comment
}
```

The program *decomment.cpp* does remove all comments properly, but there is a case that causes text to be removed when it shouldn't be. When the two-character sequence // is embedded in a string, it is not the beginning of a comment:

```
cout << "Two slashes // not a comment" << endl; // tricky?
```

This situation causes problems with the state machine used in *decomment.cpp*, but it's possible to add more states to fix the problem.

Pause to Reflect

9.13 Modify *decomment.cpp*, Program 9.7, so that the output goes to a file specified by the user.

9.14 Draw a state transition diagram similar to Figure 9.2 but for removing /* ...*/ comments. Don't worry about // comments; just remove the other kind of comment.

9.15 It's possible to use two states to remove // comments. Instead of using the state *COMMENT* in *decomment.cpp,* use getline to gobble up the characters on a line when a slash is read in the state *FIRST_SLASH*. Modify *decomment.cpp* to use this approach.

9.16 Add states to either the diagram or the program *decomment.cpp* to avoid removing the // sequence when it is embedded in a string.

9.17 Write a state transition diagram for word-at-a-time input that you could use to find all int variables. Solve a simple version of the problem, assuming that every variable is defined separately—that is, there are no definitions in the form

```
int x, y, z;
```

What other situations can cause problems for your approach?

9.3.4 Enumerated Types

An **enumerated type** allows you to create all the legal values for a new type. For example, a coin type might have the values *heads* and *tails,* and a color spectrum type might have the values *red, orange, yellow, green, blue, indigo,* and *violet.* Using enumerated types makes programs more readable. The type ReadState in the class Decomment from *decomment.cpp*, Program 9.7, has three values: TEXT, FIRST_SLASH, and COMMENT. A variable of type ReadState can have only these values.

An enum introduces a new type whose possible values are defined completely when the enum is declared. Each value of an enum type has an associated integer value; default values of 0, 1, ... are assigned to each enum value in succession. However, enums are most often used because they let values be represented symbolically rather than numerically. For example, the declaration

```
enum CardSuit{spade, heart, diamond, club};
```

creates a new type CardSuit. The variable definition CardSuit suit; creates a variable suit whose only possible values are spade, heart, diamond, and club. The assignment suit = spade is legal; the assignment suit = 1 is not legal. The integer values associated with CardSuit values make spade have the value 0 and club have the value 3. The statement cout << suit outputs an integer, either 0, 1, 2, or 3. enums are *not* printed symbolically except, perhaps, in a debugging environment. It's possible to assign explicit values using

```
enum CardSuit {spades=2, hearts=5, diamonds=7, clubs=9};
```

so that the value associated with diamonds is 7, for example, but there are very few good reasons to do this. enums let you use symbolic values in your code, and this can make code easier to read and maintain. Relying on a correspondence between the value 1 and a suit of hearts, which would be necessary if enums weren't used, can cause errors since it's easy to forget that 1 means hearts and 0 means spades.

Using enums: Conversion between enum and int. As noted earlier, an int value cannot be assigned to an enum variable. It is possible, however, to assign an enum to an int.

```
enum CardSuit{spades, hearts, diamonds, clubs};
int k = spades;                     // legal
CardSuit c = 3;                     // illegal
CardSuit s = CardSuit(3);          // legal
```

As this example shows, if an explicit cast is used, an int can be converted to an enum. Program 9.8 shows an enum used as an int as an argument to RandGen::RandInt and as the index of an array.

Program 9.8 enumdemo.cpp

```cpp
#include <iostream>
#include <string>
using namespace std;

#include "randgen.h"

int main()
{
    enum spectrum{red, orange, yellow, green, blue, indigo, violet};

    string specstrings[] = {"red", "orange", "yellow", "green",
                            "blue", "indigo", "violet"};
    RandGen gen;
    spectrum color = spectrum(gen.RandInt(red,violet));
    cout << specstrings[color] << endl;

    if (color == red)
    {   cout << "roses are red" << endl;
    }
    else
    {   cout << "that's a pretty color" << endl;
    }
    return 0;
}
```

enumdemo.cpp

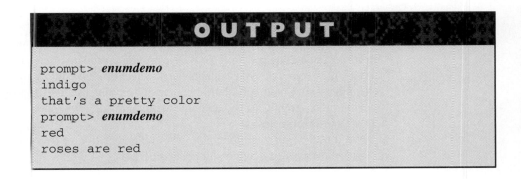

```
OUTPUT

prompt> enumdemo
indigo
that's a pretty color
prompt> enumdemo
red
roses are red
```

Class enums. By restricting an enum to be used as part of a class, several different classes can share the same enum symbolic names. For example, it is not legal to declare the following two enums in the same program unless they are declared inside separate classes because the value orange cannot be shared among different enumerated types.

```
enum spectrum {red, orange, yellow, green,
                blue, indigo, violet};
enum fruit {orange, apple, cherry, banana};
```

However, if the enumerated types are moved inside classes Spectrum and Fruit, respectively, then there is no conflict since the values are Spectrum::orange and Fruit::orange, which are different.

```
class Spectrum
{
  public:
    ...
    enum Color{red, orange, yellow, green,
              blue, indigo, violet};
};
class Fruit
{
  public:
    ...
    enum Kind{orange, apple, cherry, banana};
};
```

Here the new types introduced by the enum declaration are Spectrum::Color and Fruit::Kind; the scope-resolution operator :: is required as part of the enum type name except when the enum is used within a member function.

9.4 Case Study: Overloaded Operators and the ClockTime Class

Often the hardest part of writing a program is reading the data. This can be difficult because data are often stored in a form that is inconvenient from the point of view of the programmer. In general, this sentiment is aptly stated as

I/O is messy.

In this section we'll develop a program that calculates the total playing time for all the music stored on a compact disk (CD). The program could be extended with more options such as those found on typical CD players: select some specific songs/tracks or play all songs/tracks after randomly shuffling them. You could also use the program to combine tracks from different CDs and compute the total playing time, part of making your own CD of your favorite songs.

We'll use the program to explore the implementation of overloaded operators. We have used overloaded operators in many programs.

Overloaded operators are used when we add `BigInt` values using a plus sign, compare them using a less-than sign, and read and write them using extraction and insertion operators. These operators are defined for built-in types, but C++ allows programmers to define the operators for programmer-constructed types. Operator overloading is covered in detail in How to E, but we'll give basic guidelines and details here on how to overload operators with minimal programmer effort without sacrificing performance.

The input to the program is a file in the format shown here. Each line of the file consists of the duration of a track followed by the name of the track. For example, for the CD *The Best of Van Morrison* (1990, Mercury Records) the input follows:

```
3:46    Bright Side Of The Road
2:36    Gloria
4:31    Moondance
2:40    Baby Please Don't Go
4:19    Have I Told You Lately
3:04    Brown Eyed Girl
4:21    Sweet Thing
3:22    Warm Love
3:57    Wonderful Remark
2:57    Jackie Wilson Said
3:14    Full Force Gale
4:28    And It Stoned Me
2:46    Here Comes The Night
3:04    Domino
4:05    Did Ye Get Healed
3:32    Wild Night
4:40    Cleaning Windows
4:54    Whenever God Shines His Light
4:54    Queen Of The Slipstream
4:44    Dweller On The Threshold
```

For Handel's *Water Music (Suite in F Major, Suite in D Major)* (Deutsche Grammophon, 1992, Orpheus Chamber Orchestra) the input is

```
3:12    Ouverture
1:49    Adagio e staccato
2:23    Allegro
2:11    Andante
2:25    da capo
3:22    Presto
3:26    Air.Presto
2:33    Minuet
1:38    Bourree.Presto
2:17    Hornpipe
2:53    (without indication)
1:52    Allegro
2:42    Alla Hornpipe
1:01    Minuet
```

```
1:37     Lentement
1:10     Bourree
```

To determine the total playing time of a CD, the following pseudocode provides a good outline:

```
total = 0;
while (getline(input,line))
{   parse track_time and title from line
    total += track_time;
}
cout << "total playing time = " << total;
```

There are several details that must be handled to translate the pseudocode into a working program. Most of these details involve getting the data from a file into the computer for a program to manipulate. Although algorithmically this is a simple problem, the details make it hard to get right.[11] There are enough sticky details in the I/O that developing the program takes patience, even if it seems easy at first.

9.4.1   Throw-Away Code vs. Class Design

We'll be able to read the input using the string and stream functions we've covered in this chapter. In previous programs we used the functions `atoi` and `atof` from *strutils.h*, Program G.8 in How to G, to convert strings to `int`s or `double`s. We can use `atoi` here to transform strings into `int` values for minutes and seconds.

At this point we face a decision as developers of the program. We could develop code specifically for this program that correctly accumulates the total time for a CD. The program would work well for the task at hand, but the code would not be very general. At another extreme, we could develop a class for manipulating time stored in hours, minutes, and seconds with overloaded arithmetic and I/O operators. The class would provide code that could be reused in other contexts. Code reuse is a goal of object-oriented design and programming, but it takes more effort to develop reusable code than to develop program-specific code. The decision as to which approach to take is not always simple; often a "quick and dirty" programming approach is quite appropriate. We might even implement the quick and dirty solution as a first step in developing a working program.

> **Program Tip 9.4:   A quick and dirty solution is sometimes the best approach in getting a working program to solve a problem.** Even quick and dirty programs should be elegant and should be carefully commented since today's quick and dirty, use it once, and forget it program may be still running 10 years from now.

---

[11]David Chaiken, a computer scientist trained at MIT, uses the acronym SMOP to refer to this kind of problem—it's a *Simple Matter Of Programming.* Usually those who claim it's simple aren't writing the program.

Using the three-parameter getline function, for example, we could write this loop to solve the problem:

```
string minutes, seconds, title;
int secSum = 0, minSum = 0;
while (getline(input,minutes,':') &&
        getline(input,seconds,' ') &&
        getline(input,title))            // reading line ok
{   minSum += atoi(minutes);
    secSum += atoi(seconds);
}
cout << "total time is " << minSum << ": " secSum << endl;
```

This will yield a total like 65:644, not quite as readable as 1:15:44. We'll design a class for manipulating time as stored in the format hours:minutes:seconds. We'll name the class ClockTime and write functions that permit times in this format to be added together, compared using Boolean operators, and output to streams.

9.4.2 Implementing the ClockTime Class

In designing a class, two major decisions influence the development process:

1.   What is the class behavior? This helps in determining appropriate public and private member functions. (See Programming Tip 7.1.)
2.   What is the class state? This helps in determining what instance variables are needed for the class.

We'll concentrate on behavior first. To make the ClockTime class minimally useful we'll need to implement the following:

■   **Constructor(s)**. We should probably include a default constructor so that vectors of ClockTime objects can be defined, along with other constructors that seem useful as we develop scenarios of how the class will be used.

■   **Printing**. This means overloading the stream insertion operator << so that ClockTime objects can be written to cout and other streams. We'll use the same method in this class that we use in other classes developed for this book: we'll implement a converter function ClockTime::tostring() that converts a ClockTime object to a string. This makes it easy to insert onto a stream since we can already output string objects. The ClockTime::tostring() function is useful in other contexts. For example, we use it in the implementation of the class CircleStatusBar (from *statusbar.h*) used in Program 6.16, *maxword3.cpp*.

■   **Relational operators**. We'll need at least operator ==, but as we'll see, the implementation of these operators is relatively straightforward.

■   **Arithmetic**. We need to be able to add ClockTime objects since that's the reason we're exploring the class. We'll implement addition only, but make it possible to implement other operations later.

These functions lead to the interface given in *clockt.h*, Program 9.9. As we'll see when discussing overloaded operators, the functions Less and Equal are helper functions for implementing the relational operators. We'll discuss the prototype for the arithmetic operator += in Section 9.4.8, and the function Normalize when we discuss constructors below.

Program 9.9   clockt.h

```
#ifndef _CLOCKTIME_H
#define _CLOCKTIME_H

#include <iostream>
#include <string>
using namespace std;

// class for manipulating "clock time", time given in hours, minutes, seconds
// class supports only construction, addition, Print() and output <<
//
// Owen Astrachan: written May 25, 1994
//                 modified Aug 4, 1994, July 5, 1996, April 29, 1999
//
// ClockTime(int secs, int mins, int hours)
//       -- normalized to <= 60 secs, <= 60 mins
//
//       access functions
//
//       Hours()    -- returns # of hours in ClockTime object
//       Minutes()  -- returns # of minutes in ClockTime object
//       Seconds()  -- returns # of seconds in ClockTime object
//       tostring() -- time in format h:m:s
//                     (with :, no space, zero padding)
//
//       operators (for addition and output)
//
//       ClockTime & operator +=(const ClockTime & ct)
//       ClockTime operator +(const ClockTime & a, const ClockTime & b)
//
//       ostream & operator <<(ostream & os, const ClockTime & ct)
//            inserts ct into os, returns os, uses Print()

class ClockTime
{
  public:
    ClockTime();
    ClockTime(int secs, int mins, int hours);

    int     Hours()     const;    // returns # hours
    int     Minutes()   const;    // returns # minutes
    int     Seconds()   const;    // returns # seconds
    string  tostring()  const;    // converts to string

    bool    Equals(const ClockTime& ct) const; // true if == ct
```

```
    bool    Less   (const ClockTime& ct) const; // true if < ct

    const ClockTime & operator +=(const ClockTime & ct);

  private:

    void Normalize();          // < 60 secs, < 60 min

    int mySeconds;             // constrained: 0-59
    int myMinutes;             // constrained: 0-59
    int myHours;
};
// free functions, not member functions

ostream &  operator << (ostream & os, const ClockTime & ct);
ClockTime operator + (const ClockTime & lhs, const ClockTime & rhs);

bool operator ==   (const ClockTime& lhs, const ClockTime& rhs);
bool operator !=   (const ClockTime& lhs, const ClockTime& rhs);
bool operator <    (const ClockTime& lhs, const ClockTime& rhs);
bool operator >    (const ClockTime& lhs, const ClockTime& rhs);
bool operator <=   (const ClockTime& lhs, const ClockTime& rhs);
bool operator >=   (const ClockTime& lhs, const ClockTime& rhs);

#endif
```

clockt.h

The ClockTime Constructors. An instance of the class ClockTime might be constructed by specifying just the seconds or just the hours. For the preliminary development of the class we'll provide a default constructor, which will initialize a time to 0 hours, 0 minutes, and 0 seconds, and a three-parameter constructor, which specifies all three quantities. In our final design, the default constructor will construct an object representing the current time when the object is constructed, just as the default Date class constructor yields the current day (see *date.h,* Program G.2, How to G).

The first step in implementing the class requires implementing a constructor and some mechanism for determining the value of a ClockTime object. For example, we could implement accessor functions for obtaining hours, minutes, or seconds. We could also implement a function to print a ClockTime object. We can't develop other operators or member functions until we can define objects and determine what the objects look like.

> **Program Tip 9.5:   The first step in implementing a class should include constructors and some method for determining what an object looks like.**
> The state of an object can be examined by accessor functions or by using a tostring method and then printing the object.

We can't implement a constructor without deciding about the state of the class. For the ClockTime class the state instance variables are straightforward: hours, minutes, and seconds. These are each integer fields, although the minutes and seconds fields are constrained to have values in the range 0 through 59. There are alternatives. Rather than store three values, we could store just seconds and convert to other formats for printing. This would make it very easy to add 1:02:15 and 2:17:24 since these values would be represented as 3,735 and 8,244 seconds, respectively. The sum is simple to compute in C++, but conversion to hours, minutes, and seconds is needed for printing.

9.4.3   Class or Data Invariants

What if the user constructs objects as follows (hours first, seconds last)?

```
ClockTime a;
ClockTime b(2,27,31);
ClockTime c(3,77,91);
```

Object a is 0:0:0, object b is 2:27:31, and object c is 4:18:31, although this isn't immediately obvious from the arguments to the constructor of c. We could ignore values that aren't between 0 and 59 for minutes and seconds, but we'd like our class to be robust in the face of errors, so we'll try to do something that makes sense but leaves an object in a good state (i.e., minutes and seconds between 0 and 59).

Just as the constructor may involve overflow values, the code for operator += will need to check for overflow of minutes and seconds and adjust the other fields accordingly. Alternatively, a **normalizing** function could be written to ensure that all minutes and seconds were within proper range, as a **data invariant** of the class ClockTime. Just as a loop invariant is a statement that is true on every pass through a loop, a class data invariant is a property of class state that is true after each method has executed. In this case the data invariant would be something like this:

> Internal representations of minutes and seconds in a ClockTime object are always between 0 and 59.

All objects must maintain this invariant, but some methods like operator += may invalidate the invariant, so the code must ensure that the invariant is reestablished after each method executes. An object that maintains the invariant is said to be in a **normal form.** We'll include a private, helper member function, Normalize, that ensures that the invariant is maintained. This normalizing function will be called after adding two times and after construction in case a time is constructed with 79 seconds. At this point, we'll implement two constructors and accessors for hours, minutes, and seconds. The constructors are shown below with the accessor function for hours.

```
ClockTime::ClockTime()
  : mySeconds(0), myMinutes(0), myHours(0)
// postcondition: time is 0:0:0
{

}
ClockTime::ClockTime(int secs, int mins, int hours)
  : mySeconds(secs), myMinutes(mins), myHours(hours)
```

```
// postcondition: all data fields initialized
{
    Normalize();
}

int ClockTime::Hours() const
// postcondition: return # cf hours
{
    return myHours;
}
```

With the header file *clockt.h*, constructors, and accessors we're ready to test the preliminary implementation. Once we're sure we can construct valid ClockTime objects, we'll turn to implementing the overloaded operators. We'll test the class first so that we know its minimal implementation works correctly before developing new code.

9.4.4 Overloaded Operators

Only member functions have access to an object's private data. This makes it difficult to overload the stream insertion operator <<, which for technical reasons cannot be a member function of the ClockTime class (see How to E). Instead, we implement a member function tostring() that can be used to print a ClockTime object. We can then overload the insertion operator << using tostring().

9.4.5 Friend Classes

It is not so much our friends' help that helps us as the confident knowledge that they will help us.
                                                                             EPICURUS

Sometimes, however, it is useful for nonmember functions to have access to private data fields. You can design functions (and even other classes) that have access to private data by declaring the functions as **friend** functions (or friend classes). However, granting nonmember functions access to private data violates the principles of encapsulation and information hiding that we've upheld in our programs. You should be very careful if you decide you need to implement a friend function. We'll discuss the syntax for declaring friends in Section 12.3.3. The only use of friends in the code used in this book is to couple a class with its associated iterator; for example, the class StringSetIterator is a friend of the class StringSet (see Section 6.5).

    In the ClockTime class, implementing tostring and an overloaded operator += makes it possible to implement operator << and operator + without making them friend functions. We'll also implement member functions Less and Equal and use these to implement overloaded relational operators. An in-depth discussion of why we overload operators this way instead of using friend functions is found in How to E.

9.4.6 Overloaded operator <<

If we assume, for the moment, that the `ClockTime::tostring` function is implemented, we can easily overload the stream insertion operator as follows:

```
ostream& operator << (ostream & os, const ClockTime & ct)
// postcondition: inserts ct onto os, returns os
{
    os << ct.tostring();
    return os;
}
```

The `ClockTime` object `ct` is inserted onto the stream `os` and the stream is returned. Returning the stream allows insertion operations to be chained together since the insertion operator is left-associative (see Table A.4 in How to A). Using a `tostring` member function to overload insertion has two benefits:

- The same method for overloading insertion can be used for any class, and the `tostring` function may be useful in other contexts, such as in a debugging environment.
- Using `tostring` avoids making the insertion operator a friend function.

The statement below first inserts `ct` onto the stream `cout`, then returns the stream so that the string literal `"is the time for fun"` can be inserted next.

```
ClockTime ct(1,30,59);
cout << ct << " is the time for fun" << endl;
```

Careful coding in the implementation of `ClockTime::tostring()` ensures that five seconds is printed as 05 and that 1:02:03 is printed for one hour, two minutes, and three seconds. Two digits are always printed for each number, and a leading zero is added when necessary. The stream manipulator `setw` specifies a field width of 2, and a fill character '0' is specified using the stream function `fill`.

```
string ClockTime::tostring() const
{
    ostringstream os;
    os.fill('0');
    os << Hours() << ":" << setw(2) << Minutes() << ":"
       << setw(2) << Seconds();
    return os.str();
}
```

Because we use an `ostringstream` variable it's fine to set the fill character to '0'. If we were using `cout`, for example, we couldn't set the fill character to '0' and leave it that way since users won't expect the fill character to change (e.g., from the default fill character space) just by printing a `ClockTime` object. Details on setting and resetting the fill character can be found in How to B.

9.4.7 Overloaded Relational Operators

The relational operators $<$, $<=$, $==$, $!=$, $>$, $>=$ should be overloaded for a class as free functions, not as member functions (see How to E for details). As free functions, these operators do not have access to class data that are private. Instead of making the operators friend functions, we'll use member functions Less and Equal in implementing the relational operators. In fact, only operator $==$ and operator $<$ are implemented in terms of class member functions. The other relational operators are implemented in terms of $==$ and $<$ as follows:

```
bool operator != (const ClockTime& lhs, const ClockTime& rhs)
{    return ! (lhs == rhs);
}

bool operator > (const ClockTime& lhs, const ClockTime& rhs)
{    return rhs < lhs;
}

bool operator <= (const ClockTime& lhs, const ClockTime& rhs)
{    return ! (lhs > rhs);
}

bool operator >= (const ClockTime& lhs, const ClockTime& rhs)
{    return ! (lhs < rhs);
}
```

Using this method to overload operators means we implement only operator $==$ and operator $<$, and these implementations are also the same for any class with member functions Less and Equal (see, for example, BigInt and Date).

```
bool operator == (const ClockTime& lhs, const ClockTime& rhs)
// post: returns true iff lhs == rhs
{    return lhs.Equals(rhs);
}

bool operator < (const ClockTime& lhs, const ClockTime& rhs)
// post: returns true iff lhs < rhs
{    return lhs.Less(rhs);
}
```

9.4.8 Overloaded operator + and +=

When implementing arithmetic operators, it is much simpler to implement operator += first and then call += when implementing operator +. Just as using tostring made it simple to overload operator <<, using operator += makes it simple to overload operator + for any class that has both operators.

```
ClockTime operator + (const ClockTime & lhs,
                          const ClockTime & rhs)
// postcondition: return lhs + rhs
{
    ClockTime result(lhs);
    result += rhs;
    return result;
}
```

To execute the statement `lhs + rhs` using this implementation, a copy of `lhs` is made, the value of `rhs` added to the copy, and the result returned. Compare this implementation, for example, to `operator +` for the `Date` class in *date.cpp* (see How to G) – the bodies of the functions are identical.

The implementation of `operator +=` is straightforward; we add values and normalize.

```
ClockTime & ClockTime::operator += (const ClockTime & ct)
// postcondition: add ct, return result (normalized)
{
    mySeconds += ct.mySeconds;
    myMinutes += ct.myMinutes;
    myHours   += ct.myHours;
    Normalize();

    return *this;
}
```

For now, we'll ignore the return type of `ClockTime&` and the last statement `return *this`. These are explained in detail in How to E. If you overload any of the arithmetic assignment operators you should have the same statement to return a value: `return *this;`. The return type should be a `const` reference to the class, such as `const ClockTime&`. The same syntax is used for any of the arithmetic assignment operators, such as `*=`, `-=`, `/=`, and `%=`. The implementation changes, but the format of the overloaded function does not.

Syntax: operator +=

```
const ClassName &
operator += (const ClassName& rhs)
{
    implementation
    return *this;
}
```

9.4.9 Testing the `ClockTime` Class

Before proceeding with the development of the program to manipulate CDs, we must test the `ClockTime` class. In testing the program we'll look for cases that might cause problems, such as adding 59 seconds and 1 second. It may seem like too much work to develop a program just to test a class, but this kind of work pays dividends in the long run. By constructing a simple test program it's possible to debug a class rather than debug a larger application program. This will make the development of the client program easier as well because (we hope) the class will be correct.

In the sample run following this program, a complete set of test data is not used. You should think about developing a set of test data that would test important boundary cases.

Program 9.10   useclock.cpp

```cpp
#include <iostream>
using namespace std;

#include "clockt.h"

// test program for ClockTime class

int main()
{
    int h,m,s;
    cout << "enter two sets of 'h m s' data " << endl
         << "Enter non integers to terminate program." << endl << endl;

    while (cin >> h >> m >> s)
    {   ClockTime a(s,m,h);
        cin >> h >> m >> s;
        ClockTime b(s,m,h);
        ClockTime c = a + b;

        cout << a << " + " << b << " = " << c << endl;
    }
    return 0;
}
```

useclock.cpp

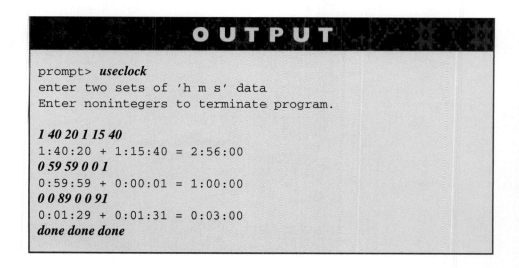

OUTPUT

```
prompt> useclock
enter two sets of 'h m s' data
Enter nonintegers to terminate program.

1 40 20 1 15 40
1:40:20 + 1:15:40 = 2:56:00
0 59 59 0 0 1
0:59:59 + 0:00:01 = 1:00:00
0 0 89 0 0 91
0:01:29 + 0:01:31 = 0:03:00
done done done
```

9.4.10 The Final Program

Each track for a CD is stored in the following format:

```
4:19      Have I Told You Lately
2:46      Here Comes The Night
```

Because white space is used to delimit strings when reading input using the extraction operator >>, we'll need to use getline to read the title of a CD track, since the number of words is different for each track. We'll also use the optional third parameter of getline to signal a sentinel other than newline when we read the minutes and seconds that make up the time of a CD track. We'll read all the characters up to the ':' as the minutes, then all the characters up to a space as the seconds. The remaining characters on a line are the track's title. Since getline reads strings, we'll convert the strings for minutes and seconds to integers using the function atoi from *strutils.h*.[12]

The third parameter for getline has a default value of '\n'. This means that if no value is specified for the third parameter, a **default value** of '\n' is used.

Program 9.11   cdsum.cpp

```cpp
#include <iostream>
#include <fstream>              // for ifstream
#include <cstdlib>             // for exit
#include <string>
using namespace std;

#include "strutils.h"          // for atoi
#include "clockt.h"
#include "prompt.h"

// reads file containing data for a cd in format below (one line/track)
//         min:sec title
// and sums all track times

int main()
{
    ifstream input;
    string filename = PromptString("enter name of data file: ");
    input.open(filename.c_str());

    if (input.fail())
    {   cerr << "could not open file " << filename << endl;
        exit(0);
    }
    string minutes,           // # of minutes of track
           seconds,           // # of seconds of track
           title;             // title of track
    ClockTime total(0,0,0);   // total of all times
```

---

[12]atoi, read as "a two i," stands for "alphabetic to integer."

```
while (getline(input,minutes,':') &&
       getline(input,seconds,' ') &&
       getline(input,title))                   // reading line ok
{   ClockTime track(atoi(seconds.c_str()),atoi(minutes.c_str()),0);
    cout << track << " " << title << endl;
    total += track;
}
cout << "-----------------------------" << endl;
cout << "total = " << total << endl;
return 0;
}
```

cdsum.cpp

```
===================== O U T P U T =====================

prompt> cdsum
enter name of data file vanmor.dat
0:04:31    Moondance
0:02:40    Baby Please Don't Go
0:04:19    Have I Told You Lately
0:03:04    Brown Eyed Girl
0:04:21    Sweet Thing
0:03:22    Warm Love
0:03:57    Wonderful Remark
0:02:57    Jackie Wilson Said
0:03:14    Full Force gail
0:04:28    And It Stoned Me
0:02:46    Here Comes The Night
0:03:04    Domino
0:04:05    Did Ye Get Healed
0:03:32    Wild Night
0:04:40    Cleaning Windows
0:04:54    Whenever God Shines His Light
0:04:54    Queen Of The Slipstream
0:04:44    Dweller On The Threshold
-----------------------------
total = 1:15:54
```

If you review the specification for getline, you'll see that the sentinel is read but is not stored as part of the string minutes. The second getline uses a space to delimit the number of seconds from the title. Finally, the third use of getline relies on the default value of the second parameter: a newline '\n'.

The function atoi converts a string to the corresponding integer. If the string parameter does not represent a valid integer, then zero is returned.

9.18 In *cdsum.cpp*, Program 9.11, the title read includes leading white space if there is more than one space between the track duration and the title. Explain why this is and describe a method for removing the leading white space from the title.

9.19 Provide three sets of data that could be used with *useclock.cpp*, Program 9.10, to test the `ClockTime` implementation.

9.20 Explain why the `ClockTime` parameters for operators <<, +, and += are declared as `const` reference parameters.

9.21 What is output by the statement `cout << ct << endl` after each of the following definitions?

- `ClockTime ct(71,16,1);`
- `ClockTime ct(5,62,1);`
- `ClockTime ct(12);`
- `ClockTime ct(21,5);`
- `ClockTime ct;`

9.22 If operators `-=` and `-` are implemented for subtracting clock times, which one is easiest to implement? Write an implementation for `operator -=`.

9.23 After reading the number of minutes using `getline(input, minutes)`, is it possible to replace the expression `getline(input, seconds)` with `input >> seconds`? What if `seconds` is defined as an `int` rather than as a `string`?

9.5 Chapter Review

In this chapter we discussed details of streams and characters and how these abstractions are implemented in C++. We also discussed operator overloading and how it makes it simpler to use some classes by mirroring how the built-in types work. We saw that a low-level understanding of how strings and streams are implemented is not necessary in order to use them in programs.

The following are some of the important topics covered:

- The type `char` represents characters and is used to construct strings and streams. Most systems use ASCII as a way of encoding characters, but you should try to write code that is independent of any particular character set.
- The library `<cctype>` has prototypes for several functions that can be used to write programs that do not depend on a particular character set such as ASCII.
- Except for output and use in strings, `char` variables can be thought of as `int` variables. In particular, it's possible to add 3 to `'a'` and subtract `'a'` from `'z'`.

- String variables are composed of `char` values. Individual characters of a string are accessible using `[]`, the indexing operator. The standard string class does no range checking for illegal index values.

- The function `getline` is used to read an entire line of text and doesn't use white space to delimit one word from another. The sentinel indicating end of line is an optional third parameter.

- The function `get` reads one character at a time from a stream.

- String streams, variables of type `istringstream` or `ostringstream`, are useful in reading line-oriented data and in writing to a string, respectively.

- State machines can be useful when parsing data one character at a time or even one word at a time.

- Enumerated types, or enums, are useful as symbolic labels. When possible, enums should be declared within a class.

- A friend class (or function) has access to another class's private data members. Friendship must be granted by the class whose private data members will be accessed.

- A class data invariant is a property of class state that is always true after each member function has executed. Using class invariants helps you develop and reason about a class's implementation and use.

- It is possible to overload relational, arithmetic, and I/O operators for classes that you write. A set of guidelines for implementing overloaded operators helps makes coding them a straightforward process.

- Class development and testing should be done together, with testing helping the development process and increasing confidence in the correctness of the class implementation (whether the class works as it should).

9.6 Exercises

9.1 Modify *decomment.cpp*, Program 9.7, so that removed comments are output to a separate file. Use string functions so that the name of the output file has a `.ncm` (for no comments) suffix with the same prefix as the input file. For example, if the comments are removed from *frogwalk.cpp*, the removed comments will be stored in *frogwalk.ncm*. Each comment should be preceded by the line number from which it was removed. For example:

```
3    // author: Naomi Smith
4    // written 4/5/93
10   // update the counter here, watch out for overflow
37   // avoid iterating too many times
```

9.2 Add two new operators to the `ClockTime` class and develop a test program to ensure that the operators work correctly.

■   `operator -` for subtraction of two times. Here it's clear that

```
03:02:05 - 02:01:03 == 01:01:02
```

but you'll have to make a decision about what `0:01:03 - 0:02:05` means.

■   `operator >>` to read from a stream. It's probably easiest to read first into a string, and then convert the string to a `ClockTime` value.

9.3 Modify Program 9.4, *readnums.cpp,* so that all integers on a line are parsed and added to `total` but nonintegers are ignored. You'll need to change the type of the variable `num` to `string`. If you use the function `atoi,` it will be difficult to determine when an integer is read and when a noninteger string such as `"apple"` is read since `atoi("apple")` returns zero. However, all valid integers in C++ begin with either a +, a −, or a digit 0–9.

9.4 Write a program that acts as a spell checker. The program should prompt the user for a filename and check each word in the file. Possible misspellings should be reported for each line with a misspelled word, where the first line in a file is line number one. Print the line number and the entire line, and use the caret symbol to "underline" the word as shown below. Each line should appear only once in the output, with each misspelled word in the line underlined.

```
20:   This is a basic spell chekc program.
                              ^^^^^

31:   There are more thngs in heven and earth,
                      ^^^^^     ^^^^^
```

To tell if a word is misspelled, read a file of words from an on-line list of words (see `words.dat,` which comes with the files for this book). This won't be perfect because of plurals and other endings that typically aren't recorded in word lists, but the program will be a start toward a functioning spell checker. Store the list of words in a `StringSet` object and use the method `StringSet::find()` to search for a match.

For extra credit, when a word ends with `'s'` and is judged as misspelled, look up the word without the `'s'` to see if it's a possible plural.

9.5 Write a program to generate junk mail (or spam, the electronic equivalent of junk mail). The program should read two files:

■   A template file for the junk mail letter; see `spam.dat` below.
■   A data file of names, addresses, and other information used to fill in the template.

For each line of the data file a spam message should be generated. In each message, one line of the template file should generate one line of output, with any entry `<n>` of the template file filled in by the *n*th item in the line of the data file (where the first item in a data file has number zero).

At first you should write the junk letters to `cout`. However, the user should have the option of creating an output file for each entry in the data file. The output files should be named *0.spm*, *1.spm*, and so on. Each output file has a `.spm` suffix, and the name of the file is the number corresponding to the line in the data file that generated the spam output.

A template file looks like `spam.dat` below.

```
Dear <0> <1>,

<0>, as you know, the <1> family name is one
of the few names to be treasured by family name experts.
The branch of the family in <4> is certainly one of
the best of the <1>  families.  <0>, your own family
in <3> is in the unique position to lead the world
of <1> families as we approach the year 2000.

For only $100.00, <0>, you can be one of the
top <1>-family leaders.
```

A corresponding data file for this template follows.

```
John:Doe:26 Main St:Los Alamos:NM:jdoe@aol.com
Susan:Smith:103 Oak St:St. Louis:MO:sues@hotmail.com
Fred:O'Hare:22 Post Rd, #3:Apex:NC:froh@mindspring.com
```

The second line from this data file generates the following message; the linebreaks can change depending on how you write the program:

```
Dear Susan Smith,

Susan, as you know, the Smith family name is one
of the few names to be treasured by family name experts.
The branch of the family in MO is certainly one of
the best of the Smith families.  Susan, your own family
in St. Louis is in the unique position to lead the world
of Smith families as we approach the year 2000.

For only $100.00, Susan, you can be one of the
top Smith-family leaders.
```

9.6 Write a program that reads a text file and creates a pig-latin version of the file. The output (pig latin) file should have the same name as the input file, but with a `.pig` suffix added so that `poe.txt` would be written as `poe.txt.pig` (or, for extra credit, replace any suffix with `.pig`). You can write lines to the output file in one of two ways:

- Each output line corresponds to an input line, but each word on the output line is the pig-latin form of the corresponding word on the input line.
- Write at most 80 characters to each output line (or some other number of characters). Put as many words on a line as possible, without exceeding the 80-character limit, and then start a new line.

The first method is easier, but the lines will be long because each word grows a suffix in its pig-latin form. The lines below could be translated as shown:

```
It was the best of times, it was the worst of times,
it was the age of wisdom, it was the age of fcolishness
```

Here's the translation, with end-of-word punctuation preserved, although the line breaks are not preserved:

```
Itway asway ethay estbay ofway imestay, itway asway ethay
orstway ofway imestay, itway asway ethay ageway ofway
isdomway, itway asway ethay ageway ofway oolishnessfay
```

You'll need to be careful if you want to preserve punctuation. As a first step, don't worry about punctuation at all. See the exercises in Chapter 4 for the definition of pig latin used in the example above.

9.7 Design, implement, and test a class `Rational` for fractions, or rational numbers, like 2/3 and 7/11. Overload operators so that fractions can be added, subtracted, multiplied, and divided. Use `BigInt` values for the (private state) numerator and denominator. You should also write functions so that rational numbers can be printed. You'll need to write a normalizing function to reduce fractions to lowest terms (i.e., so that $\frac{1}{4} + \frac{1}{4} = \frac{1}{2}$). See Euclid's algorithm for finding greatest common divisors in the exercises of Chapter 5 for help with the normalizing function.

You'll want to include at least three different constructors:

```
Rational r(2,3);   // r represents 2/3
Rational t(3);     // t represents 3/1
Rational s;        // s represents 1/1
```

You'll also need to decide what to do if the user uses 0 for the denominator since this isn't a valid fraction.

9.8 Design, implement, and test a class for complex numbers. A complex number has the form $a + b \times i$, where $i = \sqrt{-1}$. Implement constructors from `double` values and from complex values. Overload arithmetic and output operators for complex numbers.

9.9 Design, implement, and test a class `Poly` for polynomials. A polynomial has the form $a_n x^n + a_{n-1} x^{n-1} + \cdots a_1 x + a_0$. For example:

$$(3x^4 + 2x^2 + x - 5) + (2x^4 + 3x^3 - 2x^2 + 5) = (5x^4 + 3x^3 + x)$$

You'll need to use a vector to store exponents and coefficients. You should implement a constructor that takes a coefficient and an exponent as arguments so that you can write

```
Poly c = Poly(3,4) + Poly(2,2) + Poly(7,1) + Poly(-5,0);
```

to get the polynomial $3x^4 + 2x^2 + 7x - 5$. You should overload arithmetic operators `+=`, `-=` and `+`, `-` for addition and subtraction. You should overload `*=` to multiply a polynomial by a constant: $3 \times (2x^3 - 3x) = 6x^3 - 9x$. Finally, you should include a member function `at` that evaluates a polynomial at a specific value for x. For example:

```
Poly c = Poly(4,2)+Poly(3,1)+Poly(5,0); // 4x^2 + 3x + 5

double d = c.at(7); // d = 232 = 4*7^2 + 3*7 + 5
```

9.10 Write a program that reads a file and generates an output file with the same words as the input file, but with a maximum of n characters per line, where n is entered by the user. The first version of the program should read words (white space–delimited characters) and put as many words on a line as possible without exceeding n characters per line. In the output file, each word on a line is separated from other words by one space. The file transforms input as follows:

```
'Well, I'll eat it,' said Alice. 'and if it makes me
grow larger, I can reach the key; and if it makes me
grow smaller, I can creep under the door; so either way
I'll get into the garden, and I don't
care which happens!'
```

This is transformed as shown below for $n = 30$.

```
'Well, I'll eat it,' said
Alice, 'and if it makes me
grow larger, I can reach the
key; and if it makes me grow
smaller, I can creep under the
door; so either way I'll get
into the garden, and I don't
care which happens!'
```

Once this version works, the user should have the option of right-justifying each line. Here the lines are padded with extra white space so that each line contains exactly n characters. Extra spaces should be inserted between words, starting at the left of the line and inserting spaces between each pair of words until the line is justified. If adding one space between each word isn't enough to justify the line, continue adding spaces until the line is justified.

```
'Well,   I'll   eat  it,'  said
Alice,  'and  if   it  makes me
grow  larger,  I can reach the
key;  and  if it makes me grow
smaller, I can creep under the
door;  so  either way I'll get
into  the  garden, and I don't
care       which       happens!'
```

9.11 Write a program to play hangman. In hangman one player thinks of a word and the other tries to guess the word by guessing one letter at a time. The guesser is allowed a fixed number of missed letters, such as 6; if the word is not guessed before 6 misses, the guesser loses. Traditionally each missed letter results in one more part being added to the figure of a person being hanged, as shown in Figure 9.3. When the figure is complete, the guesser loses. Sample output is shown after Figure 9.3.

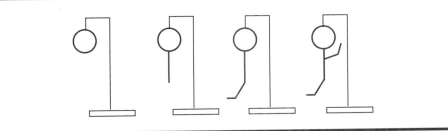

Figure 9.3 Slowly losing at hangman.

```
           O U T P U T

prompt> hangman
# misses left = 6   word =  * * * * * * * * * *
enter a letter: e
# misses left = 6   word =  * * * E * * * * E *
enter a letter: a
# misses left = 5   word =  * * * E * * * * E *
enter a letter: i
# misses left = 4   word =  * * * E * * * * E *
enter a letter: r
# misses left = 4   word =  * * R E * * * * E *
enter a letter: o
# misses left = 3   word =  * * R E * * * * E *
enter a letter: n
# misses left = 3   word =  * * R E N * * * E N
enter a letter: t
# misses left = 3   word =  * T R E N * T * E N
enter a letter: l
# misses left = 2   word =  * T R E N * T * E N
enter a letter: u
# misses left = 1   word =  * T R E N * T * E N
enter a letter: p
YOU LOSE!!! The word is STRENGTHEN
```

Rather than use graphics (although if you have access to a graphics library, you should try to use it), the program should tell the user how many misses are left and should print a schematic representation of what letters have been guessed correctly. You should try to design and implement a program that uses several classes. Some are suggested here, but you're free to develop scenarios, list nouns for classes and verbs for methods, and develop your own classes.

■   Class `WordSource` is the source of the secret word the user tries to guess. This class at first could return the same word every time, but eventually it should read a file (like a file of good hangman words or an on-line dictionary) and return one of the words at random. The same word should not be chosen twice during one run of the program.

- Class `Letters` represents the letters the user has guessed (and the unguessed letters). The user might be shown a list of unguessed letters before each guess, or might request such a list as an option. Guessing an already-guessed letter should not count against the user. The case of a letter should not matter, so that `'e'` and `'E'` are treated as the same letter.

- Class `Word` represents the word the user is trying to guess (it's initialized from `WordSource`). Instead of using the class `string`, this class encapsulates the word being guessed. The class `Word` might have the following methods (and others):

  - `Display` writes the word with spaces or asterisks (or something else) for unguessed letters. See the sample output for an example. This function could write to `cout` or return a string.

  - `ProcessChar` processes a character the user guesses. If the character is in the word, it will be displayed by the next call of `Display`. Perhaps this function should return a Boolean value indicating if the character is in the word.

- Class `Painting` (or `Gallows` for the macabre) is responsible for showing progress in some format as the game progresses. This class might draw a picture, simply display the number of misses and how many remain, or use a completely different approach that's not quite as gruesome as hanging someone (be creative).

Recursion, Lists, and Matrices

10

Art, it seems to me, should simplify. That, indeed, is very nearly the whole of the higher artistic process; finding what conventions of form and what detail one can do without and yet preserve the spirit of the whole—so that all that one has suppressed and cut away is there to the reader's consciousness as much as if it were type on the page.

WILLA CATHER
On the Art of Fiction

In this chapter we focus on **recursion**, a technique for structuring functions and classes that helps solve self-referential problems. We'll also study two classes that structure data: a self-referential structure called a **list** and an extension of the tvector class, called tmatrix, that represents **two-dimensional data**. In studying these structures we'll also explore properties of objects in a program that relate to how and where the objects can be accessed. We'll see two important properties of objects: **scope**, where the object can be accessed, and **lifetime**, the duration of an object during program execution. We'll see that recursive functions seem to "call themselves," but they are better understood as functions that solve problems whose solution can be expressed by combining solutions to problems that are similar, but smaller. Some problems have terse and comprehensible solutions expressed as recursive functions but have convoluted nonrecursive solutions. Other problems seem to be suitable for recursive solution but are better solved nonrecursively.

10.1 Recursive Functions

As a first example of a problem whose solution is elegantly expressed using recursion, we turn to the problem of outputting an English version of an integer by printing each digit's spelled-out English equivalent. For example, 1,053 should be output as "one zero five three." We solved this problem with *digits.cpp*, Program 5.5, using string concatenation. Now we limit ourselves to a solution using only int variables. To make the problem simpler, we'll initially limit the input to four-digit numbers. However, the recursive solution will work for all int values.

10.1.1 Similar and Simpler Functions

When we solved this problem using strings, we concatenated digits to the front of a string as it was built up from each digit in an int. To convert 123, we first concatenated "three" to an empty string called s. Then we concatenated "two" to the front of s, forming "two three". Concatenating "one" to the front of s now yields the desired string (see *digits.cpp*, Program 5.5). Basically, we peeled the number's digits from the right, concatenating them to the string from the left. Since we aren't using `string` functions, we must rewrite the program to print string literals for each digit of an `int`. This is done in *digits2.cpp,* Program 10.1.

Program 10.1   digits2.cpp

```cpp
#include <iostream>
using namespace std;
#include "prompt.h"

// prelude to recursion: print English form of each digit
// in an integer: 123 -> "one two three"

void PrintDigit(int num)
// precondition: 0 <= num < 10
// postcondition: prints English equivalent, e.g., 1->one,...9->nine
{
    if (0 == num)        cout << "zero";
    else if (1 == num)   cout << "one";
    else if (2 == num)   cout << "two";
    else if (3 == num)   cout << "three";
    else if (4 == num)   cout << "four";
    else if (5 == num)   cout << "five";
    else if (6 == num)   cout << "six";
    else if (7 == num)   cout << "seven";
    else if (8 == num)   cout << "eight";
    else if (9 == num)   cout << "nine";
    else cout << "?";
}

void PrintOne(long number)
// precondition: 0 <= number < 10
// postcondition: prints English equivalent of number
{
    if (0 <= number && number < 10)
    {   PrintDigit(number);
    }
}

void PrintTwo(long int number)
// precondition: 10 <= number < 100
// postcondition: prints English equivalent of number
{
    if (10 <= number && number < 100)
    {   PrintOne(number / 10);
        cout << " ";
        PrintDigit(number % 10);
    }
}

void PrintThree(long int number)
// precondition: 100 <= number < 1000
// postcondition: prints English equivalent of number
```

```
{
    if (100 <= number && number < 1000)
    {   PrintTwo(number / 10);
        cout << " ";
        PrintDigit(number % 10);
    }
}

void PrintFour(long int number)
// precondition: 1000 <= number < 10,000
// postcondition: prints English equivalent of number
{
    if (1000 <= number && number < 10000)
    {   PrintThree(number / 10);
        cout << " ";
        PrintDigit(number % 10);
    }
}

int main()
{
    int number = PromptRange("enter an integer",1000,9999);
    PrintFour(number);
    cout << endl;

    return 0;
}
```

digits2.cpp

O U T P U T

```
prompt> digits2
enter an integer between 1000 and 9999: 8732
eight seven three two
prompt> digits2
enter an integer between 1000 and 9999: 7003
seven zero zero three
prompt> digits2
enter an integer between 1000 and 9999: 1000
one zero zero zero
```

The function `PrintFour` prints a four-digit number. We know how to peel the last digit from a number using the modulus and division operators, `%` and `/`. In *digits2.cpp,* a four-digit number is printed by printing the first three digits using the function `PrintThree`, then printing the final digit using the function `PrintDigit`. For example, to print 1,357 we first print 135, which is `1357/10`, by calling `PrintThree` and then print `"seven"`, the last digit of 1,357 obtained using `1357%10`. Printing a three-digit number is a similar process: first print a two-digit number by calling `PrintTwo`, and then print the last digit. For example, to print 135 we first print 13, which is 135/10, and then print "five", which is 135%10. Continuing with this pattern we call PrintOne and PrintDigit to print a two-digit number. Finally, to print a one-digit number we simply print the only digit.

The code in *digits2.cpp* should offend your emerging sense of programming style. Each of the functions PrintFour, PrintThree, and PrintTwo is virtually identical except for the name of the function, PrintXXXX, that each one calls (e.g., PrintThree calls PrintTwo). We can combine the similar code in all the PrintXXXX functions. Rather than using four separate functions, each one processing a certain range of numbers, we can rewrite the nearly identical functions as a single function Print. This is shown in *digits3.cpp*, Program 10.2.

Program 10.2 digits3.cpp

```cpp
#include <iostream>
using namespace std;
#include "prompt.h"

// recursion: print English form of each digit
// in an integer: 123 -> "one two three"

void PrintDigit(int num)
// precondition: 0 <= num < 10
// postcondition: prints English equivalent, e.g., 1->one,...9->nine
{
    if (0 == num)         cout << "zero";
    else if (1 == num)    cout << "one";
    else if (2 == num)    cout << "two";
    else if (3 == num)    cout << "three";
    else if (4 == num)    cout << "four";
    else if (5 == num)    cout << "five";
    else if (6 == num)    cout << "six";
    else if (7 == num)    cout << "seven";
    else if (8 == num)    cout << "eight";
    else if (9 == num)    cout << "nine";
    else cout << "?";
}

void Print(long int number)
// precondition: 0 <= number
// postcondition: prints English equivalent of number
{
    if (0 <= number && number < 10)
    {   PrintDigit(int(number));
    }
    else
    {   Print(number / 10);
        cout << " ";
        PrintDigit(int(number % 10));
    }
}
```

```
int main()
{
    long number = PromptRange("enter an integer",0L,1000000L);
    Print(number);
    cout << endl;

    return 0;
}
```

digits3.cpp

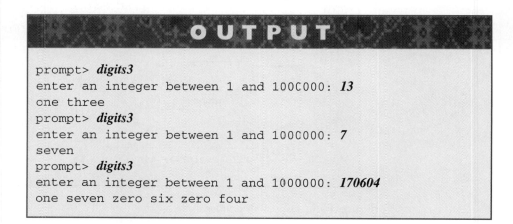

The `if` statement in `Print` from *digits3.cpp* corresponds to the equivalent `if` in the function `PrintOne` from the previous program, *digits2.cpp*. A number in the range 0–9 is simply printed by calling `PrintDigit`. In all other cases, the code in the body of the `else` statement in `Print` from *digits3.cpp*, Program 10.2, is the same code in the functions from *digits2.cpp*, Program 10.1.

Although you may think that the function `Print` is calling itself in *digits3.cpp*, it is not. As shown in Figure 10.1, four separate functions named `Print` are called when the user enters 1478. These functions are identical except for the value of the parameter `number` stored in each function. The first `Print`, shown in the upper-left corner of Figure 10.1, receives the argument 1478 and stores this value in `number`. Since the value of `number` is greater than 10, the `else` statements are executed. A function `Print` is called with the argument 1478 / 10, which is 147. This is not the same function as in the upper left, but another version of the function `Print`, in essence a **clone function** of `Print`, except that the value of `number` is different. Altogether there are four clones of the `Print` function, each with its own parameter `number`. The last clone called (lower-right corner of Figure 10.1) does not generate another `Print` call because the value of `number` is between 0 and 9. The `if` statement is executed, and the function `PrintDigit` is called with the argument 1. It's important to realize that this is the first call of `PrintDigit`, so the first digit printed is "one." Although each clone executes the statement `PrintDigit(number % 10)`, this statement is executed only after the recursive clone function call to `Print`. Each clone waits for control to return from the recursive call, except for the last function, which doesn't make

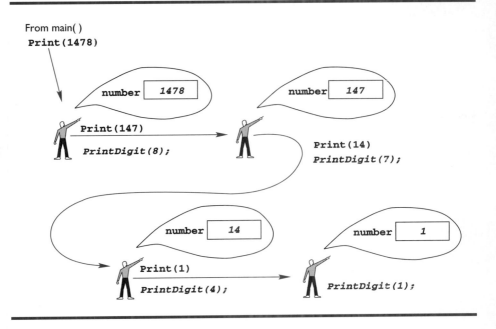

Figure 10.1   Recursively printing digits.

a recursive call. The first clone called is the last clone to print a digit, so the last digit printed is 1478 % 10, which is 8. This means the last word printed is "eight."

You'll need to develop two skills to understand recursive functions:

1. The ability to reason about a recursive function so that you can determine what the function does.
2. The ability to think recursively so that you can write recursive functions to solve problems.

Developing the second skill is more difficult than the first, but practice with reasoning about recursive functions will help with both skills.

10.1.2   General Rules for Recursion

When you write a loop, you reason about when the loop will stop executing so that you don't write an infinite loop. You must take the same care when writing recursive functions to avoid an infinite succession of recursively called clones. Each clone uses space, so you won't be able to actually generate an infinite number of clones, but you can easily use up all the memory in your computing environment if you're not careful. To avoid an infinite chain of recursive calls, each recursive function must include a **base case** that does not make a recursive call. The base case in Print of *digits3.cpp*, Program 10.2, is a single-digit number identified by this test:

```
if (0 <= number && number < 10)
```

A function's base case is usually determined by finding a value, or a set of values, that does not require much work to compute. We'll look at a recursive version of the function to raise a number to a power that we studied in Section 5.1.7.

If you're asked to calculate 3^8, you could multiply $3 \times 3 \times 3 \times 3 \times 3 \times 3 \times 3 \times 3$. You could also calculate $3^4 = 81$ and then calculate $81 \times 81 = 6,561$, since $3^8 = 3^4 \times 3^4$. The second method uses far fewer multiplications to calculate a^n than the first. The method is summarized in the following (repeated from Section 5.1.7):

$$a^n = \begin{cases} 1 & \text{if } n = 0 \\ a^{n/2} \times a^{n/2} & \text{if } n \text{ is even} \\ a \times a^{n/2} \times a^{n/2} & \text{if } n \text{ is odd (note that } n/2 \text{ truncates to an integer)} \end{cases} \qquad (10.1)$$

For example, to calculate 4^{11} using this method, we first calculate $4^{11/2} = 4^5 = 1024$ and then multiply $4 \times 1024 \times 1024 = 4,194,304$. The base case requires no power calculation and no recursion. The base case in the formula corresponds to an exponent of zero. For nonzero exponents, the recursion comes from the calculation of $a^{n/2}$ in the formula. We'll write a function Power with two parameters: one for the base a and one for the exponent n in calculating a^n. Note that there is one recursive call, and the value returned by the call is stored in a local variable semi:

```
double Power(double base, int expo)
// precondition: expo >= 0
// postcondition: returns base^expo
{
    if (0 == expo)
    {   return 1.0;                 // correct for zeroth power
    }
    else
    {   double semi = Power(base,expo/2);
        if (expo % 2 == 0)     // even exponent
        {   return semi*semi;
        }
        else                       // odd exponent
        {   return base*semi*semi;
        }
    }
}
```

The calculation of 2^{35} using Power(2,35) generates seven clone Power functions with expo values 35, 17, 8, 4, 2, 1, 0. Since the recursive call uses expo/2 as the value of the second argument, the total number of recursive calls is limited by how many times the original argument can be divided in half.

The seven clones are shown in Figure 10.2, where the value of expo can be used to determine the sequence of recursive calls. The result of each clone's one recursive call is stored in the calling function's local variable semi. The value of semi is used to calculate the returned result. Just as each iteration of a loop body changes values

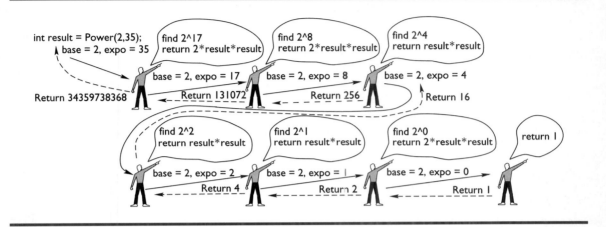

Figure 10.2   Recursively calculating 2^{35}.

so that the loop test eventually becomes false and the loop terminates, each recursive call should get closer to the base case. This ensures that the chain of recursively called clones will eventually stop. In general, recursive functions are built from calling similar, but simpler, functions. The similarity yields recursion; the simplicity moves toward the base case.

Program Tip 10.1:   Recursive functions must make recursive calls that are similar to the original call, but simpler than the original call.

1.   Identify a base case that does not make any recursive calls. Each call should make progress toward reaching the base case; this ensures termination since the function will end.

2.   Solve the problem by making recursive calls that are similar but simpler (i.e., that move toward the base case). The similarity ensures that the recursion works: you'll be solving a similar problem.

10.1.3   Infinite Recursion

You must guard against writing functions that result in infinite recursion, that is, functions that generate a potentially endless number of recursive calls. When you forget a base case, infinite recursion results, as shown in *recdepth.cpp,* Program 10.3. The output for Program 10.3 came from a Pentium PC with 256 megabytes of memory using Metrowerks Codewarrior; it shows that 36,977 recursive calls are made before memory is exhausted.

Program 10.3 recdepth.cpp

```cpp
#include<iostream>
using namespace std;

// Owen Astrachan
// illustrates problems with "infinite" recursion

void
Recur(int depth)
{
    cout << depth << endl;
    Recur(depth+1);
}

int main()
{
    Recur(0);
    return 0;
}
```

recdepth.cpp

OUTPUT

```
prompt> recdepth
0
1

some output removed

36977
36977
Unhandled exception: c00000fd
```

The maximum number of clones, or recursive calls, is limited by the memory of the computer used and depends on certain settings of the programming environment. For example, when I used g++ on a Linux machine with 32 megabytes of memory, the program crashed with a segmentation fault after 698,911 calls.[1] Using Visual C++ 6.0 yields an exception, with the program halting, after 11,740 calls. As a programmer you must be careful when writing recursive functions. You should always identify a base case that does not make any recursive calls.

---

[1]The recursive call in Recur is an example of **tail recursion**. In a tail recursive function the last statement executed is a recursive call. Smart compilers can turn tail recursive functions into looping functions automatically, thus saving memory.

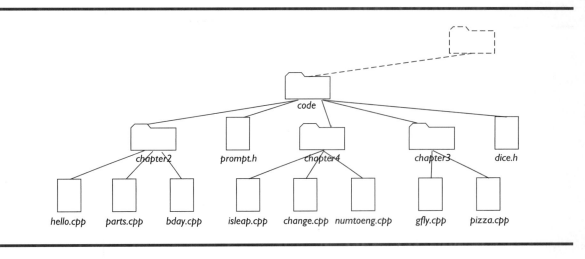

Figure 10.3   Hierarchy of directories and files.

You may study methods in more advanced courses that involve changing a recursive function to a nonrecursive function. This is often a difficult task. Sometimes, however, it is possible to write a simple nonrecursive version of a recursive function. Nevertheless, some functions are much more easily written using recursion; we'll study examples of these functions in the next section.

10.2   Recursion and Directories

In this section we'll use recursion to solve problems that cannot be solved without recursion unless auxiliary data structures are used. The recursive functions find information about files and directories stored on disk. Almost all computers have an operating system in which directories help organize the many files you create and use. For example, you may have a directory for each of the computer courses you have taken, a directory for the electronic mail you receive, and a directory for your home page on the World Wide Web. Using directories to organize files makes it easier for you to find a specific file. Directories contain files as well as **subdirectories,** which can also contain files and subdirectories. For example, the hierarchical arrangement of directories enables you to have a `courses` directory in which you have subdirectories for English, computer science, biology, and political science courses. A diagram of some of my directories and files for this book is shown in Figure 10.3. Directories are shown as file folders, and files are shown as rectangles.

In this section we investigate classes that use recursion to process directory hierarchies. For example, we will develop a program that mimics what some operating systems do (and some don't) in determining how much space files use on disk. We will also develop a program that scans a hierarchy of directories to find a file whose name you remember but whose location you have forgotten.

10.2.1   Classes for Traversing Directories

Program 10.4, *files.cpp*, prompts the user for the name of a directory and then prints all the files in that directory. This kind of listing is often needed when opening files from within a word processor; you must be able to type or click on the name of the file you want to edit. The variable dir is a class DirStream object. The DirStream class supports iteration using Init, HasMore, Next, and Current similarly to other classes (e.g., the class WordStreamIterator from *maxword.cpp*, Program 6.11, and the class StringSetIterator from *setdemo.cpp*, Program 6.14).

Program 10.4   files.cpp

```cpp
#include <iostream>
#include <iomanip>
#include <string>
using namespace std;
#include "directory.h"
#include "prompt.h"

// illustrates use of the DirStream and DirEntry classes

int main()
{
    DirStream dir;              // directory information
    DirEntry entry;            // one entry from a directory
    int num = 0;               // each file is numbered in output

    string name = PromptString("enter name of directory: ");
    dir.open(name);

    if (dir.fail())
    {   cerr << "could not open directory " << name << endl;
        exit(1);
    }
    for(dir.Init(); dir.HasMore(); dir.Next())
    {   entry = dir.Current();
        num++;
        cout << "(" << setw(3) << num << ") " << setw(12) << entry.Name() << "\t";
        if (! entry.IsDir() )
        {   cout << entry.Size();
        }
        cout << endl;
    }
    return 0;
}
```

files.cpp

```
                      O U T P U T

 prompt> files
 enter name of directory: c:\book\mcgraw
 (  1)           .
 (  2)           ..
 (  3)     design.pdf      246489
 (  4) designspecs.pdf     60876
 (  5)      fixreview       24481
 (  6)     hromcik.doc      41472
 (  7)     hsreviews        59797
 (  8)         notes        305
 (  9)         photo        1488
 ( 10) schedule.xls         17403
 ( 11)      tapestry        420692
 ( 12)     tapsurv.SIT      15836
 prompt> files
 enter name of ..\chap22
 could not open directory ..\chap22
```

The member function `DirStream::Current()` returns a `DirEntry` object. Repeated calls of `Current`, in conjunction with the iterating functions `HasMore` and `Next`, return each entry in the directory. These directory entries are either files or subdirectories. In *files.cpp,* the member function `DirEntry::IsDir()` differentiates files from directories, returning true when the `DirEntry` object is a directory and false otherwise. `DirEntry::Size()` returns the size, in bytes, of a file. On Windows machines this is zero for directories; on Linux/Unix machines directories have nonzero sizes. The filename `.` (a single period) represents the current directory. The filename `..` (a double period) represents the parent directory. This convention is followed by many operating systems. The member functions for the class `DirEntry` and the class `DirStream` are given in *directory.h*, Program G.11 in How to G.

The header file, *directory.h,*[2] which contains declarations for the classes `DirEntry` and `DirStream`, is provided on-line with the code for this book.

10.2.2   Recursion and Directory Traversal

Program 10.4, *files.cpp,* prints all the files in a given directory. Some applications require lists of subdirectories, and the files within the subdirectories, as well. For example, to calculate the total amount of disk space used by all files and directories, a program must accumulate the sum of file sizes in all subdirectories. We'll modify *files.cpp,* Program 10.4, so that it prints both files and subdirectories (and files and subdirectories of the subdirectories, and so on). As a first step, we'll move the `for` loop that iterates

---

[2]On some 16-bit systems the file may be named *directry.h.*

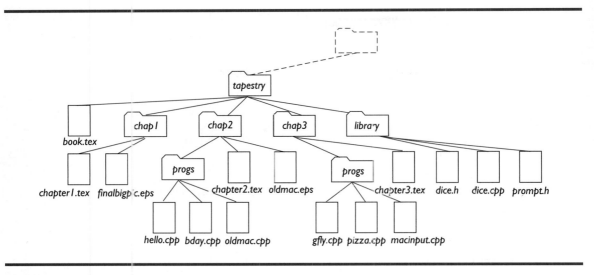

Figure 10.4 Files and subdirectories used in run of *subdir.cpp*, Program 10.5.

over all the files in a directory into a function `ProcessDir`. The final program is *subdir.cpp*, Program 10.5. Figure 10.4 contains a diagram of the files and subdirectories that generate the sample run.[3]

Program 10.5 subdir.cpp

```
#include <iostream>
#include <iomanip>
#include <string>
using namespace std;

#include "directory.h"
#include "prompt.h"


// print all entries in a directory (uses recursion)

void Tab(int count)
// postcondition: count tabs printed to cout
{
    int k;
    for(k=0; k < count; k++)
    {cout << "\t";
    }
}

void ProcessDir(const string & path, int tabCount)
```

---

[3]The suffixes in Figure 10.4 represent different kinds of files: `.cpp` for C++ source code, `.tex` for LaTeX files (a document-processing system), `.eps` for PostScript files, and so on.

```
// precondition: path specifies pathname to a directory
//                tabCount specifies how many tabs for printing
// postcondition: all files and subdirectories in directory 'path'
//                printed, subdirectories tabbed over 1 more than parent
{
    DirStream indir(path);
    DirEntry entry;
    int num = 0;                  // number of files in this directory

    for(indir.Init();  indir.HasMore(); indir.Next())
    {   entry = indir.Current();   // either file or subdirectory

        // don't process self: ".", or parent directory: ".."
        if (entry.Name() != "." && entry.Name() != "..")
        {   num++;
            Tab(tabCount);
            cout << "(" << setw(3)<< num << ")" << "\t" << entry.Name() << endl;
            if (entry.IsDir() )                 // process subdir
            {   ProcessDir(entry.Path(),tabCount+1);
            }
        }
    }
}


int main()
{
    string dirname = PromptString("enter directory name ");
    ProcessDir(dirname,0);
    return 0;
}
```

subdir.cpp

The files in a subdirectory are indented and numbered after the name of the subdirectory is printed. For example, the subdirectory named chap2 contains one subdirectory, progs, and two files, chapter2.tex and oldmac.eps. The subdirectory progs of chap2 contains three files: hello.cpp, bday.cpp, and oldmac.cpp. The directory tapestry, whose name is entered when the program is run, contains four subdirectories: chap1, chap2, chap3, and library, and one file: book.tex. Notice that the files in a subdirectory are numbered starting from one. We cannot control the order in which files and subdirectories are processed using the DirStream iterating functions Init, Next, and Current. For example, the operating system may scan the files alphabetically, ordered by date of creation, or in some random order. However, you can print the files in any order by storing them in a vector and sorting by different criteria.

OUTPUT

```
prompt> subdir
enter directory name tapestry
(   1)     book.tex
(   2)     chap1
    (   1)     chapter1.tex
    (   2)     finalbigpic.eps
(   3)     chap2
    (   1)     chapter2.tex
    (   2)     oldmac.eps
    (   3)     progs
        (   1)     bday.cpp
        (   2)     hello.cpp
        (   3)     oldmac.cpp
(   4)     chap3
    (   1)     chapter3.tex
    (   2)     progs
        (   1)     gfly.cpp
        (   2)     macinput.cpp
        (   3)     pizza.cpp
(   5)     library
    (   1)     prompt.h
    (   2)     dice.cpp
    (   3)     dice.h
```

We'll investigate the function ProcessDir from *subdir.cpp* in detail. One key to the recursion is an understanding of how a complete filename is specified in hierarchical file systems. Most systems specify a complete filename by including the directories and subdirectories that lead to the file. This sequence of subdirectories is called the file's **pathname.** The subdirectories that are pathname components are separated by different delimiters in different operating systems. For example, in UNIX the separator is a forward slash, so the pathname to gfly.cpp shown in the output run of *subdir.cpp* is tapestry/chap3/progs/gfly.cpp. On Windows computers the separator is a backslash, so the pathname is tapestry\chap3\progs\gfly.cpp. The string used as a separator is specified by the constant DIR_SEPARATOR in *directory.h*. The last component in a path is a file's name; it's returned by DirEntry::Name. The entire path, including the name, is returned by DirEntry::Path. Both of these member functions are used in *subdir.cpp*: one to print the name, and one to recurse on a subdirectory because the entire path is needed to specify a directory.

The for loop that iterates over directory entries in the function ProcessDir is similar to the loop used in *files.cpp*, Program 10.4. However, when the information stored in the DirEntry object entry represents a directory, the function ProcessDir makes a recursive call using the pathname for the subdirectory. For example, the call `ProcessDir("tapestry",0)` directly generates four recursive calls for the subdirectories `chap2`, `chap1`, `chap3`, and `library`, as diagrammed in Figure 10.5. The pathname for the subdirectory `chap3` is obtained directly from the `DirEntry` object `entry`, but it can also be formed from the expression

```
path + DIR_SEPARATOR + entry.Name()
```

where, for example, `path` is `"tapestry"` and `entry.Name()` is `"chap3"`. The value of `tabCount` is calculated from the expression `tabCount+1` so that the arguments for the recursive call are

```
ProcessDir("tapestry/chap3",1);
```

This recursive call will, in turn, generate a recursive call for the subdirectory `progs`.

Examine the output run of *subdir.cpp* on the directory `tapestry`, diagrammed in Figure 10.5. Each clone of the function `ProcessDir` is shown as a figure. The call `ProcessDir(dirname,0)` from `main` is shown in the upper-left corner of Figure 10.5 as `ProcessDir("tapestry",0)`; `dirname` has the value `"tapestry"`. Each clone of `ProcessDir` has its own formal parameters `path` and `tabCount` and its own local variables `indir`, `entry`, and `num`. Each recursive clone will print all the files in the subdirectory specified by the clone's `path` parameter. For example, the four clones generated by calls from the upper-left clone of `ProcessDir` are shown with `num` values 1, 2, 3, and 5. When `num` is 4, the file `book.tex` is printed as shown in the output from *subdir.cpp*.

As shown in the output of the program, the files and subdirectories in `tapestry` are processed by `Next` and `Current` in the following order:

1. chap2
2. chap1
3. chap3
4. book.tex
5. library

The first file/subdirectory printed and processed is (1) `chap2`. The number 1 is the value of local variable `num` shown in the stick figure in the upper-left corner. The files/subdirectories of `chap2` are shown indented one level. The indentation level is determined by the value of parameter `tabCount`, which is 1 because of the recursive call of `ProcessDir`:

```
ProcessDir(entry.Path(),tabCount+1);
```

The value passed as the second parameter is `tabCount+1`, which in this case is `0+1=1`. Because the value passed is always one more than the current value, each recursive call results in one more level of indentation. The output of *subdir.cpp* shows that the `progs` subdirectory is the second entry printed in the `chap2` directory. The first entry printed is `chapter2.tex`. The recursive call generated by `progs`, shown in Figure 10.5 as

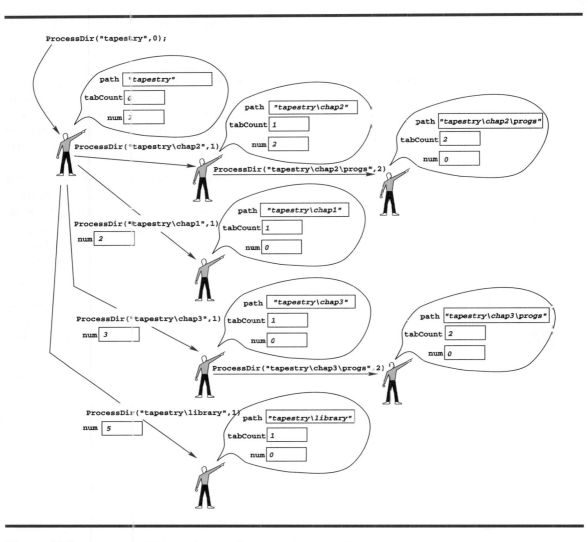

Figure 10.5 Recursive calls/clones for run of *subdir.cpp*, Program 10.5.

the call `ProcessDir("tapestry\chap2\progs",2)`, shows that num has the value 2 when the call is made, reflecting that `progs` is printed as the second entry under chap2: `(2) progs`.

Like all functions, the recursively called functions communicate only via passed parameters. There is nothing magic or different in the case of recursively called functions; each function just happens to have the same name as the function that calls it.

10.2.3 Properties of Recursive Functions

At most, three clones of function `ProcessDir` exist at one time, as shown in Figure 10.5. The three clones at the top of the figure exist at the same time (with `path` values of `"tapestry"`, `"tapestry\chap2"`, and `"tapestry\chap2\progs"`). When the recursive call that processes the `chap2\progs` subdirectory finishes executing, the clone with `path` parameter `"tapestry\chap2"` still has one more entry to process: `oldmac.eps` (see the output). Then this clone finishes executing, and only the first version of `ProcessDir`, invoked by the call `ProcessDir("tapestry",0)`, exists.

A recursive call for the `chap1` subdirectory is then made. When the clone invoked by the call `ProcessDir("tapestry\chap1",1)` finishes executing, a recursive call is made for the `chap3` subdirectory. This, in turn, makes a recursive call for the `chap3\progs` subdirectory. Note that at this point the value of num for the original `ProcessDir` is 3, as shown in Figure 10.5. Finally, after printing (4) `book.tex`, the subdirectory `library` generates the final recursive call; the value of num is 5 as shown.

Pause to Reflect

10.1 Write a function based on `Print` in *digits3.cpp*, Program 10.2, that prints the base 2 representation of a number. The number 17 in base 2 is 10,001 since $17 = 2^4 + 2^0$. Just as 5,467 in base 10 means $5 \times 10^4 + 4 \times 10^3 + 6 \times 10^1 + 7 \times 10^0$, so does 10,110 in base 2 mean $1 \times 2^4 + 0 \times 2^3 + 1 \times 2^2 + 1 \times 2^1 + 0 \times 2^0$.

10.2 The recursive `Power` function makes the recursive call as follows and squares the return value:

```
double semi = Power(base,expo/2);
..
return semi*semi;
```

It's possible to square `base` in the argument to the recursive call and just return the result as follows:

```
double semi = Power(base*base,expo/2);
...
return semi;
```

Explain why these are equivalent. Which do you think is better? Does your answer change if `BigInt` values are used instead of `double` values? How can you test your answers?

10.3 Based on the output generated by *subdir.cpp,* Program 10.5, for the directory `tapestry`, what would be the output of the program *files.cpp,* Program 10.4, if run on `tapestry`? (Make up numbers for file size; it's the names of the files that are important in this question.)

10.4 Why is the `if` statement

```
if (entry.Name() != "." \&\& entry.Name() != "..")
```

used in *subdir.cpp* necessary? Describe what would happen if the comparison with " . " were removed, but the other comparison remained. What would happen if the comparison with " . . " were removed (but the other remained)?

10.5 How can you modify *subdir.cpp* to print a list of every file (starting from a directory whose name the user enters) whose size is larger than a number the user enters?

10.6 How can you modify *subdir.cpp* to print the name of every file containing a word, in either upper- or lowercase, that the user enters?

10.7 Describe how the output of *subdir.cpp* will change if the expression `tabCount+1` in the recursive call is replaced with `tabCount+2`.

10.8 If the call of `Tab` and the `cout << ...` statement in function `ProcessDir` of *subdir.cpp* are moved *after* the `if (entry.IsDir())` statement, how will the output change (e.g., if the directory `tapestry` is used for input)?

10.3 Comparing Recursion and Iteration

As an apprentice software engineer and computer scientist you must learn to judge when recursion is the right tool for a programming task. We've already seen that recursion is indispensable when traversing directories. As an apprentice, you should learn part of the programming folklore of recursion. We'll use two common examples to investigate tradeoffs in implementing functions recursively and iteratively.

10.3.1 The Factorial Function

In *fact.cpp,* Program 5.2, the function `Factorial` computes the **factorial** of a number where $n! = 1 \times 2 \times \cdots \times n$. A loop accumulates the product of the first n numbers. An alternative version of the factorial function is defined mathematically using this definition:

$$n! = \begin{cases} 1 & \text{if } n = 0 \\ n \times (n-1)! & \text{otherwise} \end{cases} \tag{10.2}$$

According to the definition, $6! = 6 \times 5!$. What, then, is to be done about $5!$? According to the definition, it is $5 \times 4!$. This process continues until $1! = 1 \times 0!$ and $0! = 1$ by definition. The method of defining a function in terms of itself is called an **inductive** definition in mathematics and leads naturally to a recursive implementation. The base case of $0! = 1$ is essential since it stops a potentially infinite chain of recursive calls. As we noted in the first section of this chapter, the base case is often a case that requires little or no computation, such as the calculation of zero factorial, which, by definition, is one. Recursive and iterative versions of the factorial function are included and tested in *facttest.cpp,* Program 10.6. Statements are included to check if the values returned by the recursive and iterative functions are different, but the values returned are always the same when I run the program.

Program 10.6 facttest.cpp

```
#include <iostream>
using namespace std;
#include "ctimer.h"
#include "prompt.h"
#include "bigint.h"

BigInt RecFactorial(int num)
// precondition: 0 <= num
// postcondition: returns num! (num factorial)
{
    if (0 == num)
    {   return 1;
    }
    else
    {   return num * RecFactorial(num-1);
    }
}

BigInt Factorial(int num)
// precondition: 0 <= num
// postcondition: returns num! (num factorial)
{
    BigInt product = 1;
    int count;
    for(count=1; count <= num; count++)
    {   product *= count;
    }
    return product;
}

int main()
{
    CTimer rtimer,itimer;
    long j,k;
    BigInt rval,ival;
    long iters = PromptRange("enter # of iterations",1L,1000000L);
    int  limit = PromptRange("upper limit on factorial",10,100);

    for(k=0; k < iters; k++)     // compute factorials specified # of times
    {   for(j=0; j <= limit; j++)
        {   rtimer.Start();                    // time recursive version
```

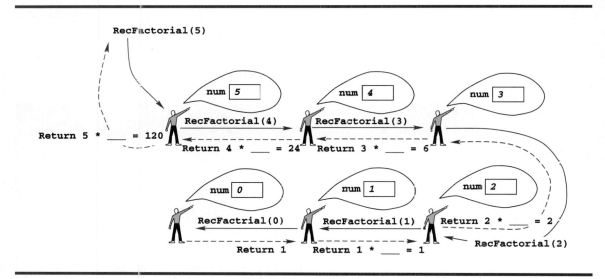

Figure 10.6 Recursive calls of `RecFactorial(6)`.

```
        rval = RecFactorial(j);
        rtimer.Stop();
        itimer.Start();                        // time iterative version
        ival = Factorial(j);
        itimer.Stop();
        if (rval != ival)                      // note any differences
        {   cout << "calls differ for " << j << endl;
            cout << "recursive = " << rval << " iterative = " << ival << endl;
        }
      }
    }
    cout << iters << " recursive trials " << rtimer.CumulativeTime() << endl;
    cout << iters << " iterative trials " << itimer.CumulativeTime() << endl;
    return 0;
}
```

facttest.cpp

The recursive function `RecFactorial` is similar to the inductive definition of factorial given earlier. (See *ctimer.h*, Program G.5 in How to G, for information on the class `CTimer` used to time execution of program segments.)

To compute 5!, six clones of the factorial function are needed as shown in Figure 10.6. The first call, from `main`, is shown in the upper left as `RecFactorial(5)`. The recursive calls are shown as solid arrows. The value passed to parameter `num` is shown in each clone. The return value is calculated by the expression `num * RecFactorial(num-1)`; this is shown by the dashed lines. For example, the last clone called generates no recursive calls and returns 1. This value is used to calculate 1×1 so that 1 is returned from the clone with parameter `num == 1`. Each returned value is plugged into the expression num * RecFactorial(num-1) as the value of the recursive call, finally yielding $5 \times 24 == 120$, which is returned to main.

OUTPUT

Runs on a Pentium II 300Mhz running Windows NT
```
prompt> facttest
enter # of iterations between 1 and 1000000: 1000
upper limit on factorial between 10 and 100: 20
1000 recursive trials 6.2
1000 iterative trials 4.816
 prompt> facttest
enter # of iterations between 1 and 1000000: 1000
upper limit on factorial between 10 and 100: 30
1000 recursive trials 24.807
1000 iterative trials 22.581
```

using int rather than BigInt

```
prompt> facttest
enter # of iterations between 1 and 1000000: 10000
upper limit on factorial between 10 and 100: 20
10000 recursive trials 0.791
10000 iterative trials 0.691
```

Runs on a Sparc Ultra 30 with 384 megabytes of memory
```
prompt> facttest
enter # of iterations between 1 and 1000000: 10000
upper limit on factorial between 10 and 100: 20
10000 recursive trials 4.28
10000 iterative trials 1.9
```

Two things will help you understand recursion, but practice in thinking recursively is the best way to gain understanding.

- Believe the recursion works and verify that the returned value is used correctly.
- Trace each recursive call by drawing clones or other diagrams that show each recursive function call, the function's variables and parameters, and the value returned.

Program Tip 10.2:   Believe the recursion works. This means that you *assume* that the recursive call works correctly, and you examine the code to see that the result of the recursive call is *used* correctly. For example, in calculating 4!, you assume that the call to calculate 3! yields the correct result: 6. The statement that uses this result

```
 return  num * RecFactorial(num-1);
```

will then return 4 × 6, the value of num times the result of the recursive call. This is the correct answer for 4!.

Program Tip 10.3:   Trace the recursive calls to see that the clones produce the correct results. This can be a tedious task, but some people like the assurance of understanding precisely how the recursively called functions work together. (A trace is shown in Figure 10.6 for the computation of 5!). In many examples of recursion that you'll see, tracing all the calls will be difficult to impossible because there will be so many of them. It's often helpful to trace the last call *before* the base case is reached, and to verify that the base case return value works with the last call.

Based on the sample runs, which of the recursive and iterative functions is best? The answer is—as it is so often—*"it depends."* It depends on (at least) how many times the factorial function will be called, what kind of computer is used, and what compiler is used. When run on a Pentium computer, the difference between the two versions is 0.1 seconds for 200,000 calls with int values as shown in the output. The difference is greater for BigInt values. The differences on a Sun UltraSparc computer are much more pronounced since that computer doesn't process recursion very well.

10.3.2   Fibonacci Numbers

Fibonacci numbers are integral in many areas of mathematics and computer science. These numbers occur in nature as well [PL90]. For example, the scales on pineapples are grouped in Fibonacci numbers. In [Emm93], Fibonacci numbers are cited as the conscious basis of works by the composers Bartok and Stockhausen. Knuth [Knu97] describes the mathematical constant $\phi = \frac{1}{2}(1 + \sqrt{5})$ as "intimately connected with the Fibonacci numbers," and the ratio of ϕ to 1 is "said to be the most pleasing proportion aesthetically, and this opinion is confirmed from the standpoint of computer programming aesthetics as well." The first 16 Fibonacci numbers are given below; this sequence originated in 1202 with Leonardo Fibonacci, whom Knuth calls "by far the greatest European mathematician before the Renaissance."

```
1 1 2 3 5 8 13 21 34 55 89 144 233 377 610 987
```

In general, each number in this sequence is the sum of the two numbers before it; the first two Fibonacci numbers are the exception to this rule. In keeping with tradition in C++

numbering schemes, the first Fibonacci number is $F(0)$; that is, we start numbering from zero rather than one. This leads to the inductive or recursive definition of the Fibonacci numbers:

$$F(n) = \begin{cases} 1 & \text{if } n = 0 \text{ or } n = 1 \\ F(n-1) + F(n-2) & \text{otherwise} \end{cases} \qquad (10.3)$$

As is the case with the recursive definition of factorial, the recursive definition of the Fibonacci numbers can be translated almost verbatim into a C++ function. The function RecFib is shown in *fibtest.cpp*, Program 10.7. The function Fib computes Fibonacci numbers iteratively. The difference in this case between the recursive and iterative functions is much more pronounced than it was for the factorial function. Note that $F(30) = 1,346,269$.

Program 10.7   fibtest.cpp

```cpp
#include <iostream>
using namespace std;
#include "ctimer.h"
#include "prompt.h"

// Illustrates "bad" recursion for computing Fibonacci numbers

const int FIB_LIMIT = 20;            // largest fib # calculated

long RecFib(int n)
// precondition: 0 <= n
// postcondition: returns the n-th Fibonacci number
{
    if (0 == n || 1 == n)
    {   return 1;
    }
    else
    {   return RecFib(n-1) + RecFib(n-2);
    }
}

long Fib(int n)
// precondition: 0 <= n
// postcondition: returns the n-th Fibonacci number
{
    long first=1, second=1, temp;
    int k;
    for(k=0; k < n; k++)
    {   temp = first;
        first = second;
        second = temp + second;
    }
    return first;
}

int main()
```

```
{
    CTimer rtimer,itimer;
    int j;
    long  k;
    long ival,rval;
    long iters = PromptRange("enter # of iterations",1L,100000L);
    int limit =  PromptRange("n, for n-th Fibonacci ",1,30);

    for(k = 0; k < iters; k++)
    {   for(j=0; j <= limit; j++)
        {   rtimer.Start();
            rval = RecFib(j);
            rtimer.Stop();
            itimer.Start();
            ival = Fib(j);
            itimer.Stop();
            if (ival != rval)
            {   cout << "calls differ for " << j << endl;
                cout << "recursive = " << ival << " iterative = " << rval << endl;
            }
        }
    }
    cout << iters << " recursive trials " << rtimer.CumulativeTime() << endl;
    cout << iters << " iterative trials " << itimer.CumulativeTime() << endl;
    return 0;
}
```

                                                                    fibtest.cpp

```
                        O U T P U T

Run on a Pentium II 300Mhz running Windows NT
prompt> fibtest
enter # of iterations between 1 and 100000: 100
n, for n-th Fibonacci  between 1 and 30: 30
100 recursive trials 49.932
100 iterative trials 0.02

Run on a Pentium 100Mhz running Linux
prompt> fibtest
enter # of iterations between 1 and 100000: 100
n, for n-th Fibonacci  between 1 and 30: 30
100 recursive trials 205.5
100 iterative trials 0.0
```

    The granularity of the timing doesn't accurately reflect the iterative function; 10,000 calls of the iterative function take about 1.1 seconds to compute $F(30)$. Extrapolating the result of 49.932 seconds for 100 trials of the recursive function shows that 100,000 iterations would take 49,932 seconds, or nearly 13 hours, for what is done in about 10

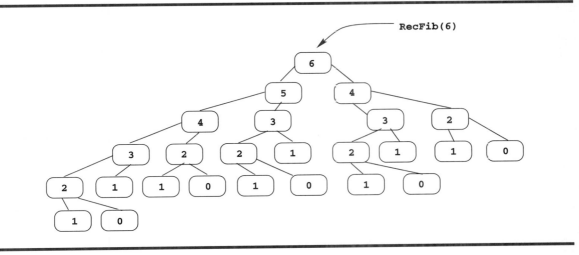

Figure 10.7 Recursive calls of `RecFib(6)`; the number in each box is the value of the parameter `num`.

seconds using the iterative function. What are the differences between calculating $n!$ and $F(n)$ that cause such a disparity in the timings of the recursive and iterative versions? For example, is the time due to the recursive depth (number of clones)? As we will see, the depth of recursive calls is not what causes problems here. Only 30 clones exist at one time to calculate $F(30)$. However, the total number of clones (or recursive calls) is 2,692,637. This huge number of calls is illustrated in Figure 10.7 for the calculation of $F(6)$, which requires a total of 25 recursive calls.

If you examine Figure 10.7 carefully, you'll see that the same recursive call is made many times. For example, $F(1)$ is calculated eight times. Since the computer is not programmed to remember a number previously calculated, when the call $F(6)$ generates calls $F(5)$ and $F(4)$, the result of $F(4)$ is not stored anywhere. When the calculation of $F(5)$ generates $F(4)$ and $F(3)$, the entire sequence of calls for $F(4)$ is made again. The iterative function `Fib` in *fibtest.cpp* is fast because it makes roughly n additions to calculate $F(n)$; the number of additions is **linear**. In contrast, the recursive function makes an **exponential** number of additions. In this case the speed of the machine is not so important, and the recursive function is *much* slower than the iterative function.

In later courses you may study methods that will permit you to determine when a recursive function should be used. For now, you should know that recursion is often very useful, as with the directory searching functions, and sometimes is very bad, as with the recursive Fibonacci function.

10.3.3 Permutation Generation

A **permutation** is a rearrangement. In mathematics, a permutation of a list of n numbers like $(1, 2, 3)$ is any one of the $n!$ different orderings of the numbers. For example, all orderings of the numbers 1–3 follow:

```
1 2 3
1 3 2
2 1 3
2 3 1
3 1 2
3 2 1
```

Permutations are used in a branch of computer science called **combinatorics**, and also in statistics, social sciences, and mathematics. As we'll see, generating permutations recursively uses a technique called **backtracking** that can be applied to solve many different problems.

We'll develop a recursive function for generating all the permutations of the elements in a vector. The function will print all permutations, but we'll discuss how to process the permutations in other ways. We'll follow the two guidelines from Program Tip 10.1 in developing our recursive function. First we'll identify a base case, a case that is easy to compute and that won't make any recursive calls. We also have to identify why it's the base case and use that to focus on the second guideline: what part of the problem will get smaller with each recursive call, thus eventually getting to the base case? Most recursive problems are parameterized by some notion of size. In each recursive call the size decreases, eventually reaching the base case. In *digits3.cpp*, Program 10.2, the size of the problem is the number of digits in the number being converted to English. In traversing directories the size is the the number of subdirectories in a directory; eventually a directory with no subdirectories must be found. In computing factorial, the number n for which $n!$ is computed is the size of the problem.

The permutation problem is parameterized by the size of the vector being permuted. A vector with no elements, or with only one element, is very easy to permute in all ways. If this is the base case, we'll need to work on transforming the problem of permuting an n-element vector into a problem that permutes a smaller vector. If you look at the list of the six different permutations of (1,2,3) you may see that the permutations can be divided into three groups of two permutations. In each group the first number stays the same and the other elements are permuted in all ways. This will work for a four-element list too. The first element can take one of four values. For each of the four values, permute the remaining three in all possible ways. The first six of 24 permutations of (1,2,3,4) are shown below. The 4 is fixed, and the rest of the vector is permuted in all ways as a three-element vector.

```
4 1 2 3
4 1 3 2
4 2 1 3
4 2 3 1
4 3 1 2
4 3 2 1
```

It's actually tricky to develop a recursive solution thinking about the problem this way because the simpler problem, one of permuting the rest of the vector, isn't the same kind of problem as what we start with. We start with a vector of n elements, and the subproblem is to permute everything except the first element. But this subproblem doesn't involve a vector, it involves a part of the vector. We'll adopt an approach that is often useful in recursive problems: we'll think of the problem in a different way that is more easily reducible to a simpler case. Note that in permuting $(1,2,3,4)$ when the first two elements are fixed, say $(4,1)$, the rest of the elements are permuted in all possible ways. We'll use the idea of fixing the first k elements in a vector, those with indexes $0 \ldots k-1$ in a vector. We'll permute the other elements, with indexes $k \ldots n-1$, in all possible ways. The base case that's easily solved is when all n elements are fixed, there are no more elements to permute. Initially no elements are fixed. This leads to the two functions whose headers follow:

```
void PermuteHelper(tvector<int>& list, int n);
// pre: first n elements of list are fixed, don't change
// post: elements n..list.size()-1 are permuted in
//       all possible ways, list is in original order

void Permute(tvector<int>& list)
// post: elements of list permuted in all possible ways
{
    PermuteHelper(list,0);
}
```

Users will call `Permute`; the function `PermuteHelper` exists only to make the recursion simple to code. In a class, `PermuteHelper` would be a private helper function, not accessible to the user.

Developing `PermuteHelper`. We've already decided that the base case, in which all elements are fixed so that `n == list.size()`, results in printing the vector. What about the recursive calls? The vector element with index n is the leftmost element that changes because elements with indexes $0 \ldots n-1$ are fixed. Element `list[n]` must take on all values from the remaining, unfixed elements, and then all permutations should be generated. For example, to permute $(5,3,1,4,2)$, with one element fixed (index zero), we'll let the index one element take on each of the unfixed values. This is shown below, where the x indicates where the 3, originally with index one, is swapped to bring each unfixed element into the index one slot. The 3 originally in the index one slot is swapped into slots with indexes two, three, and four to generate each recursive call. It's swapped back after the recursive call to restore the vector as it was, satisfying the postcondition.

```
5 ___ ___ ___ ___
5 _3_ ___ ___ ___
5 _1_ _x_ ___ ___
5 _4_ ___ _x_ ___
5 _2_ ___ ___ _x_
```

This leads to the function below:

```
void PermuteHelper(tvector<int>& list, int n)
// pre: first n elements of list are fixed, don't change
// post: elements n..list.size()-1 are permuted in
//       all possible ways, list is in original order
{
    int k, len = list.size();
    if (n == len)        // all elements fixed, print
    {   Print(list);
    }
    else
    {   for(k=n; k < len; k++)
        {   Swap(list[n],list[k]);
            PermuteHelper(list,n+1);
            Swap(list[n],list[k]);
        }
    }
}
```

This prints all the permutations. If instead of printing, you wanted to pass the permuted vector to a function for processing, you'd have to change the call of `Print` in `PermuteHelper`. Alternatively, you could develop a method for iterating over the permutations, one at a time. The class `Permuter` does this (see How to G for details). A `Permuter` object is constructed from a vector, and then iterates over the vector returning permutations in alphabetic or lexicographic order. If a `Permuter` is initialized with the vector $(4,3,2,1)$, then the first two vectors returned by `Current` will be $(4,3,2,1)$ and $(1,2,3,4)$ since a `Permuter` wraps to the first vector alphabetically after the list one. A `Permuter` uses only `int` vectors, but as Program 10.8 shows, an `int` vector can be used to index any other vector, effectively permuting any kind of vector.

Program 10.8 usepermuter.cpp

```
#include <iostream>
#include <string>
using namespace std;

#include "tvector.h"
#include "permuter.h"

int main()
{
    tvector<int> list;
    tvector<string> slist;
    string names[] = {"first", "second", "third"};
    int k;
    for(k=0; k < 3; k++)
    {   list.push_back(k);
        slist.push_back(names[k]);
```

```
        }
    Permuter p(list);
    for(p.Init(); p.HasMore(); p.Next())
    {    p.Current(list);
        for(k=0; k < list.size(); k++)
        {    cout << list[k] << " ";
        }
        cout << endl;
    }
    for(p.Init(); p.HasMore(); p.Next())
    {    p.Current(list);
        for(k=0; k < list.size(); k++)
        {    cout << slist[list[k]] << " ";
        }
        cout << endl;
    }
    return 0;
}
```

usepermuter.cpp

OUTPUT

```
prompt> usepermuter
0 1 2
0 2 1
1 0 2
1 2 0
2 0 1
2 1 0
first second third
first third second
second first third
second third first
third first second
third second first
```

10.4 Scope and Lifetime

In this section we'll discuss methods that are used to alter the lifetime of a variable in a class or program and the scope of declaration. We'll use two simple examples that extend the computation of Fibonacci numbers from *fibtest.cpp*, Program 10.7, and then use these examples as a springboard to explore general principles of lifetime and scope. We touched on scope in Section 5.3; the scope of a declaration determines where in a function, class, or program the declaration can be used. *Lifetime* refers to the duration of storage associated with a variable. To be precise, scope is a property of a name or identifier (e.g., of a variable, function, or class) that determines where in a program the identifier can be used. Lifetime is a property of the storage or memory associated with an object.

10.4.1   Global Variables

Suppose we want to calculate exactly how many times the function RecFib is called to compute RecFib(30) in *fibtest.cpp,* Program 10.7. We can increment a counter in the body of RecFib, but we need to print the value of the counter in main when the initial call of RecFib returns. The **global variable** gFibCalls in *recfib.cpp,* Program 10.9, keeps this count. The scope of a global variable is an entire program as opposed to a local variable that can be accessed only within the function in which the variable is defined. In C++ a global variable has **file scope** since it is accessible in all functions defined in the file in which the global variable appears.

Program 10.9   recfib.cpp

```cpp
#include <iostream>
using namespace std;
#include "prompt.h"

// Illustrates "bad" recursion for computing  Fibonacci numbers
// and a global variable to count # function calls

int gFibCalls = 0;

long RecFib(int n)
// precondition: 0 <= n
// postcondition: returns the n-th Fibonacci number
{
    gFibCalls++;
    if (0 == n || 1 == n)
    {   return 1;
    }
    else
    {   return RecFib(n-1) + RecFib(n-2);
    }
}

int main()
{
    int num = PromptRange("compute Fibonacci #",1,40);
    cout << "Fibonacci # " << num << " = " << RecFib(num) << endl;
    cout << "total # function calls = " << gFibCalls << endl;
    return 0;
}
```

recfib.cpp

O U T P U T

```
prompt> recfib
compute Fibonacci # between 1 and 40: 10
Fibonacci # 10 = 89
total # function calls = 177
prompt> recfib
compute Fibonacci # between 1 and 40: 20
Fibonacci # 20 = 10946
total # function calls = 21891
prompt> recfib
compute Fibonacci # between 1 and 40: 30
Fibonacci # 30 = 1346269
total # function calls = 2692537
```

I use the prefix g to differentiate global variables from other variables. Global variables are declared outside of any function, usually at the beginning of a file. Unlike local variables, global variables are automatically initialized to zero unless a different initialization is specified when the variable is defined. There are rare occasions when global variables must be used, as with gFibCalls in *recfib.cpp*. However, using many global variables in a large program quickly leads to maintenance headaches because it is difficult to keep track of what identifiers have been used. In particular, it's possible for a global declaration to be hidden or **shadowed** by a local declaration. For example, suppose you want to implement the member function Point::tostring. The class Point has two private instance variables x and y; both are doubles.

The functions tostring in *strutils.h*, Program G.8 (see How to G), convert ints and doubles to strings, so you might write

```
string Point::tostring() const
{
    return "("+ tostring(x) + ", " + tostring(y) +")";
}
```

Unfortunately, this will not compile. The compiler treats the calls of tostring—which are intended as calls of the free, or global, functions in *strutils.h*—as recursive calls with arguments that do not match the formal parameter list. The member function Point::tostring shadows the global, free functions.

We can fix this problem using the scope resolution operator ::. Applied to an identifier, :: references a global object (or function) so we can write the function as follows:

```
string Point::tostring() const
{
    return "("+ ::tostring(x) + ", " + ::tostring(y) +")";
}
```

10.4.2   Hidden Identifiers

Even nonglobal identifiers can be shadowed, as illustrated in *scope.cpp*, Program 10.10. Because the braces, {}, that delimit function bodies and compound statements cannot overlap, there is always a scope "closest" to an identifier's declaration. It is possible for an identifier to be reused within a **nested scope.** A scope is nested in another when the braces that define the scope occur within another set of braces. When a variable is used, it may seem unclear in which scope the variable is declared, but the "nearest" definition is the one used.

The variable `first` defined within the scope of the `if` statement is accessible only within the `if` statement. Assignments to `first` within the statement do not affect the variable `first` defined at the beginning of `main`, as shown in the output, where `first` is printed as 4, 8, 16, and 32 except for the indented values, which show `first` within the `if` statement. It is also apparent from the output that the value of `second` defined in `main` is not affected by assignments to `second` in the `while` loop since these assignments are made to a variable defined within the loop. Schematically the scopes are illustrated in Figure 10.8, in which a variable is known within the innermost box in which it appears. The variable `second` defined within the `while` loop shadows the variable defined at the top of the function `main`. In general, shadowing leads to unexpected, although well-defined, behavior.

> **Program Tip 10.4:   Avoid using identifiers with the same name in nested scopes.** Hidden and shadowed identifiers lead to programs that are difficult to understand and ultimately lead to errors.

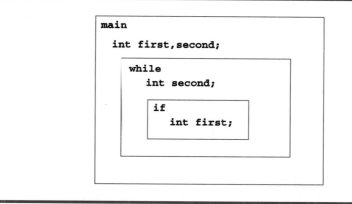

Figure 10.8 Boxing to illustrate scope in Program 10.10.

Program 10.10 scope.cpp

```cpp
#include <iostream>
using namespace std;

// illustrates scope

int main()
{
    int first = 2;
    int second = 0;

    while (first < 20)
    {   int second = first * 2;                 // shadows previous second
        cout << "\tsecond = " << second << endl;
        first *= 2;
        if (first > 10)
        {   int first = second;                 // shadows previous first
            first = first/10;
            cout << "\tfirst = " << first << endl;
        }
        cout << "first = " << first << endl;
    }
    cout << "second = " << second << endl;
    return 0;
}
```

scope.cpp

```
         O U T P U T

prompt> scope
        second = 4
first = 4
        second = 8
first = 8
        second = 16
        first = 1
first = 16
        second = 32
        first = 3
first = 32
second = 0
```

10.4.3 Static Definitions

Global variables maintain their value throughout the execution of a program; they exist for the duration of the program. In contrast, a local variable defined in a function is constructed anew each time the function is called. We can change the lifetime of a local variable so that the variable maintains its value throughout a program's execution by using the word **static** as a modifier when the variable is defined. This is illustrated in *recfib2.cpp*, Program 10.11. A static tvector is defined to keep track of recursive calls so that the same recursive call is never made more than once. For example, the first call of RecFib(4) results in recursive calls of RecFib(3) and RecFib(2). When these values are calculated, the values are stored in the tvector storage so that the values can be retrieved, for example, when RecFib(2) is called again. The key idea is that a recursive call is made once. All subsequent recursive calls with the same argument are evaluated by retrieving the stored value from storage rather than by making a recursive call. Notice how many fewer calls are made compared to the calculations of *recfib.cpp*, Program 10.9.

Program 10.11 recfib2.cpp

```cpp
#include <iostream>
using namespace std;
#include "tvector.h"
#include "prompt.h"

// Illustrates "bad" recursion for computing  Fibonacci numbers
// but made better using a static vector for storing values

int gFibCalls = 0;
const int FIB_LIMIT = 40;

long RecFib(int n)
// precondition: 0 <= n
// postcondition: returns the n-th Fibonacci number
{
    static tvector<int> storage(FIB_LIMIT+1,0);

    gFibCalls++;
    if (0 == n || 1 == n)
    {   return 1;
    }
    else if (storage[n] == 0)
    {   storage[n] = RecFib(n-1) + RecFib(n-2);
        return storage[n];
    }
    else
    {   return storage[n];
    }
}

int main()
{
```

```
int num = PromptRange("compute Fibonacci #",1,FIB_LIMIT);

cout << "Fibonacci # " << num << " = " << RecFib(num) << endl;

cout << "total # function calls = " << gFibCalls << endl;

return 0;
}
```

recfib2.cpp

Like global variables, static local variables are automatically initialized to zero. However, it is a good idea to make initializations explicit. Static variables are constructed and initialized when a program first executes, *not* when a function is first called. The variable `storage` must be static in *recfib2.cpp*, or the values stored will not be maintained over all recursive calls. For recursive functions like `RecFib`, only one static variable is defined for all the recursive clones. The variable `storage` is local to `RecFib` but maintains its values for the duration of the program *recfib2.cpp*.

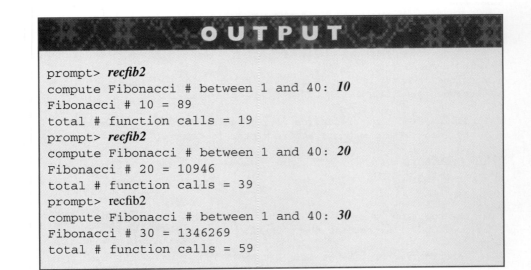

```
OUTPUT

prompt> recfib2
compute Fibonacci # between 1 and 40: 10
Fibonacci # 10 = 89
total # function calls = 19
prompt> recfib2
compute Fibonacci # between 1 and 40: 20
Fibonacci # 20 = 10946
total # function calls = 39
prompt> recfib2
compute Fibonacci # between 1 and 40: 30
Fibonacci # 30 = 1346269
total # function calls = 59
```

10.4.4 Static or Class Variables and Functions

Just as it's possible for a static variable to have a lifetime for the duration of a program, maintaining its value over many function calls, a **static class variable** maintains its value over many object definitions. A static class variable actually exists outside of any object; it's part of a class rather than an object. In *staticdemo.cpp*, Program 10.12, the static variable `ourCount` is incremented each time a `Pair` object is constructed. Its value is the number of `Pair` objects constructed in an entire program execution.

Program 10.12   staticdemo.cpp

```cpp
#include <iostream>
using namespace std;
#include "prompt.h"

struct Pair
{
  int x, y;
  Pair(int a, int b)
    : x(a), y(b)
  { ourCount++; }

  static int ourCount;
};

int Pair::ourCount = 0;

int main()
{
    Pair p(0,0);
    int k,limit = PromptRange("number of pairs? ",1,20000);
    for(k=0; k < limit; k++)
    {   Pair p(k,2*k);
    }
    cout << "# pairs created = " << Pair::ourCount << endl;
    return 0;
}
```

staticdemo.cpp

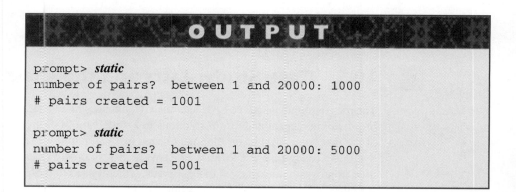

```
prompt> static
number of pairs?  between 1 and 20000: 1000
# pairs created = 1001

prompt> static
number of pairs?  between 1 and 20000: 5000
# pairs created = 5001
```

As shown, static class variables must be initialized outside the class declaration. Static variables are defined before main begins to execute. A static variable or function can be accessed using dot notation as though it were an instance variable or member function. In *staticdemo.cpp* the last output line could print p.ourCount. However, since static variables belong to a class rather than an object, it's possible to access them using the class name and the scope resolution operator as shown. The prefix `our` signifies that the variable belongs to all objects, not to any particular object.

Pause to Reflect

10.9 The code segment shown below illustrates shadowing. Describe an input sequence that causes the words `Banana yellow Banana red Apple` to be printed (one per line).

```
string last = "Apple";
string word;
while (cin >> word && word != last)
{   string last = "Banana";
    cout << last << " " << word << endl;
}
cout << last << endl;
```

Describe an input sequence that causes the single word `Apple` to be printed. If the definition of `last` within the `while` loop is removed, what input sequence generates `Banana yellow Banana red Apple`?

10.10 In the code fragment in the previous problem, if the definition of `last` before the `while` loop is removed, will the segment compile? Why?

10.11 Describe how to use a static vector in a function to compute factorial to avoid computing $n!$ if it has been computed before.

10.12 In *staticdemo.cpp*, if `p.ourCount` is used instead of `Pair::ourCount`, what variable p is accessed? If two `Pair` variables p and q are defined before the loop, and the only statement in the loop is

```
p = q;
```

what will the output of the program be?

10.5   Case Study: Lists and the Class `CList`

The programming language Lisp, and related languages like Scheme, have a long history of providing elegant and useful solutions to a wide variety of problems. Lisp was one of the first languages; its development began in 1958, and it was running on computers by 1960. Today Lisp is still used extensively, has an object-oriented extension, and is used in programming the text editor Emacs, which I used to write this book. The basic structure in Lisp is a **list**. In this section we'll use a Lisp-like list class[4] called **CList** to explore recursion and an elegant solution to representing polynomials.

---

[4]It's Lisp-like in that programmers don't worry about memory management and cannot change a list once the list is created. It's not Lisp-like in that in this chapter list elements must be the same type.

10.5.1   What Is a CList Object?

The class CList is similar to the class tvector in that it's a homogeneous aggregate: each element of a list has the same type. It differs in two ways:

- CList collections do not support random access; accessing the first element takes less time than accessing the second, and accessing the nth element takes n times longer than accessing the first element.
- A CList collection is **immutable**. Once a list is created, it cannot be changed. You can't change an element of a list, and you can't add an element to an existing list. Instead, you can create new lists. The C in CList stands for constant since lists cannot change once created.

There are two ways to create a CList object. Defining a CList object creates an empty list, one with no elements. The function cons is used to create a new list from a first element and an existing list. The program *listdemo.cpp*, Program 10.13, shows how cons is used to create lists from old lists.[5]

Program 10.13   listdemo.cpp

```cpp
#include <iostream>
#include <string>
using namespace std;
#include "clist.h'

void Display(const CList<string>& list)
// post: list displayed on one line, comma separated
{
    cout << "size = " << list.Size() << ": " << list.Printer(",") << endl;
}
int main()
{
    CList<string> s1, s2, s3, s4, s5;  // create empty lists
    s2 = cons(string("tomato"),s1);
    s3 = cons(string("carrot"),s2);
    s4 = cons(string("celery"),s3);
    s5 = cons(string("peapod"),s3);

    Display(s1); Display(s1.Tail()); cout << "---" << endl;
    Display(s2); Display(s2.Tail()); cout << "---" << endl;
    Display(s3); Display(s3.Tail()); cout << "---" << endl;
    Display(s4); Display(s4.Tail()); cout << "---" << endl;
    Display(s5); Display(s5.Tail()); cout << "---" << endl;
    return 0;
}
```

listdemo.cpp

---

[5]The explicit use of string as a constructor for the literal "carrot", for example, is required in some compilers because of how templates are instantiated.

A CList is divided into two parts: the **Head**, which is a string in a list of strings, an int in a list of ints, and so on; and the **Tail**, which is another CList, but without the first element (the Head). The function cons makes a new list by creating a new head and using an existing tail.

```
OUTPUT

prompt> listdemo
size = 0:
size = 0:
---
size = 1:  tomato
size = 0:
---
size = 2:  carrot,tomato
size = 1:  tomato
---
size = 3:  celery,carrot,tomato
size = 2:  carrot,tomato
---
size = 3:  peapod,carrot,tomato
size = 2:  carrot,tomato
---
```

Figure 10.9 is a diagram of the five lists from *listdemo.cpp*. The lists s4 and s5 share the same tail. All the lists except for the empty s1 share the list value "tomato", which is at the head of s2, is the tail of s3, and is part of s4 and s5 as well.

The method CList::Printer acts like an I/O manipulator. The delimiter argument to Printer separates each item in the list being inserted onto the stream, so commas appear between each list element as shown. If no parameter is used, that is, list.Printer(), then each list item appears on a separate line; the separator is the newline character '\n'. It's possible to insert a list directly on a stream. For the list s4 in *listdemo.cpp*, the call below generates the output shown with parentheses at the beginning and end of the output and commas separating each list element:

```
cout << "list = " << s4 << " size = " << s4.Size() << endl;
```

```
OUTPUT

list = (celery, carrot, tomato) size = 3
```

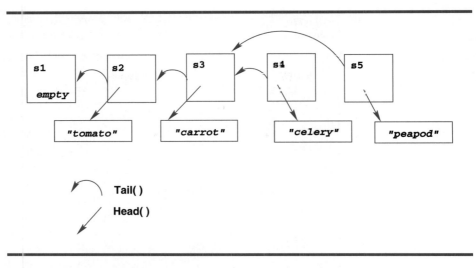

Figure 10.9 Diagram of five CList objects showing structure sharing.

10.5.2 Tail-ing Down a List

We can easily write a free function version of CList::Size as shown in Program 10.14. The first, recursive version is emblematic of many CList functions. The empty list is the base case, and the simpler recursive call results from using a list's tail, which has one fewer element than the list. The iterative version uses the associated CListIterator class; it's slightly more cumbersome than the recursive version.

Program 10.14 listsize.cpp

```
int Size(const CList<string> & list)
// post: returns # elements in list
{
  if (list.IsEmpty()) return 0;
  return 1 + Size(list.Tail());
}
int Size(const CList<string> & list)
// post: returns # elements in list
{
  CListIterator<string> iter(list);
  int count = 0;
  for(iter.Init(); iter.HasMore(); iter.Next())
  {  count++;
  }
  return count;
}
```

listsize.cpp

Maurice Wilkes (b. 1913)

Maurice Wilkes is one of the elder statesmen of computer science. He was a peer of Alan Turing and worked in England on the EDSAC computer. Wilkes was

awarded the second Turing award in 1967.

In work written in 1955 and published in 1956 [Wil56], Wilkes offers advice for team programming projects. It is interesting that the advice still seems to hold 40 years later. "It is very desirable that all the programmers in the group should make use of the same, or substantially the same, methods. Not only does this facilitate communication and cooperation between the members of the group, but it also enables their individual experience more readily to be absorbed into the accumulated experience of the group as a whole . . . the group should be organized to produce, on a common plan, the input routines, basic library subroutines, and error-diagnosis subroutines . . .it will be much easier, once they are prepared, for an individual programmer to make use of them rather than to set about designing a system of his own." Wilkes wonders where computer science fits—whether it is more closely tied to mathematics or to engineering [Wil95]:

> *Many students who are attracted to a practical career find mathematics uncongenial and difficult; certainly it is not the most popular part of an engineering course for the majority of students. Admittedly, mathematics trains people to reason, but reasoning in real life is not of a mathematical kind. Physics is a far better training in this respect. The truth may be that computer science does not by itself constitute a sufficiently broad education, and that it is better studied in combination with one of the physical sciences or with one of the older branches of engineering.*

Wilkes pioneered many of the ideas in current computer architectures, including microprogramming and cache memories. In 1951 he published the first book on computer programming. About object-oriented programming he says,

> *[Object-oriented programming is] in my view, the most important development in programming languages that has taken place for a long time. Object-oriented programming languages may still be described as being in a state of evolution. No completely satisfactory language in this category is yet available.*

For more information see [Wil87, Wil95, Wil56].

10.5.3 cons-ing Up a List

To see the benefits of recursion, we'll look at *readlist.cpp*, Program 10.15. The program reads words from a file and uses a standard list technique of **cons-ing up** a list by assigning the cons return value to the list that's the argument to cons. Since the last word read is the last word cons-ed to the front. the list is in reverse order.

We'd like to have a version of Read that returns a list of words in the same order in which they're read. To do this efficiently (using cons) we'll need to think recursively. We'll recursively read from a stream using the following ideas:

1. If there are no words in the stream we'll return an empty list; this is the base case of the recursion.
2. Otherwise, we'll make a recursive call. We must decide what the arguments in the call are and how to process the returned result. To get closer to the base case of no words in the stream, we'll read a word. The resulting stream will be "shorter" and closer to the base case because it contains fewer words. What do we do with the result returned from the recursion?

Program 10.15 readlist.cpp

```cpp
#include <iostream>
#include <string>
#include <fstream>
using namespace std;

#include "clist.h"
#include "prompt.h"

CList<string> Read(istream& input)
// post: returns list, order of words reversed from input
{
    CList<string> result;
    string word;
    while (input >> word)
    {   result = cons(word,result);
    }
    return result;
}
int main()
{
    string filename= PromptString("filename ");
    ifstream input(filename.c_str());
    StringList list = Read(input);
    cout << "# words = " << list.Size() << endl;
    cout << "words: first = " << list.Head()
         << ",  last = " << list.Last() << endl;
    return 0;
}
```

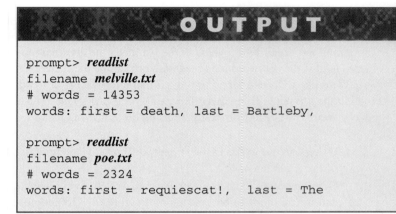

```
prompt> readlist
filename melville.txt
# words = 14353
words: first = death, last = Bartleby,

prompt> readlist
filename poe.txt
# words = 2324
words: first = requiescat!, last = The
```

In developing the recursive function, think about what the postcondition must be. We want the words to be in the same order in which they're read. Combined with the base case, this is what we have so far:

```
CList<string> Read(istream& input)
// post: returns list, order of words same as in input
{
    string word;
    if (input >> word)
    {
        // ??? must develop this code
    }
    else
    {   return Clist<string>();   // an empty list
    }
```

Note that a temporary, or anonymous, variable (see Section 7.4.1) is returned by constructing a CList<string> object. The following code is equivalent but uses a named variable:

```
    ...
    else
    {   CList<string> temp;
        return temp;
    }
```

In the recursive case, the recursive call will satisfy the postcondition. Remember that you must believe the recursion will work (see Program Tip 10.2). What can you do with the returned result? What does it represent? The returned result represents a list of words except for the word just read, and *the order in list is the same as the order in input* according to the postcondition. This means you simply cons the word read to what's returned by the recursive call. If we use this function, the output of *readlist.cpp* changes:

```
CList<string> Read(istream& input)
// post: returns list, order of words same as in input
{
    string word;
    if (input >> word)
    {    return cons(word,Read(input));
    }
    return CList<string>();
}
```

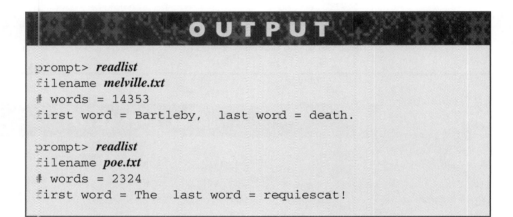

```
OUTPUT

prompt> readlist
filename melville.txt
# words = 14353
first word = Bartleby,  last word = death.

prompt> readlist
filename poe.txt
# words = 2324
first word = The  last word = requiescat!
```

10.5.4 Append, Reverse, and Auxiliary Functions

In this section we'll look at one more list function, **append**, which adds a new element to the end of a list. Since we cannot change a list, a new element isn't really added. Instead, appending an element to a list creates a new list that's a copy of the old list, but with a new element added to the end. This is fundamentally different than cons. When cons creates a new list by adding an element to the front of a list, all the list storage, except that used by the new element at the front, is shared between the lists as diagrammed in Figure 10.9. When append is used, no storage can be shared. Program 10.16 illustrates the differences. The class, or static, function ConsCalls reports how much memory has been allocated by the CList class.

Program 10.16 listappend.cpp

```
#include <iostream>
using namespace std;
#include "clist.h"
```

```
int main()
{
    CList<int> list,list2;
    int k;
    for(k=7; k >=0; k--)
    {   list = cons(k,list);
    }
    cout << list.Printer(",") << endl;
    cout << "memory = " << CList<int>::ConsCalls() << endl;

    for(k=0; k < 8; k++)
    {   list2 = append(k,list2);
    }
    cout << list.Printer(",") << endl;
    cout << "memory = " << CList<int>::ConsCalls() << endl;

    return 0;
}
```

listappend.cpp

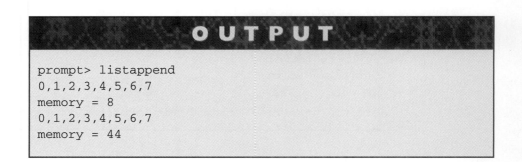

```
prompt> listappend
0,1,2,3,4,5,6,7
memory = 8
0,1,2,3,4,5,6,7
memory = 44
```

To create a list of eight elements using cons requires only eight list elements. However, using append requires 36 elements ($44 - 8 = 36$; note that $1 + \ldots + 8 = 36$). Essentially, creating an eight-element list using append requires creating a one-element list, a two-element list, a three-element list, and so on until the eight-element list is created. So although append is a useful function, it's an expensive function to use.

> **Program Tip 10.5:   Don't worry about efficiency until you know that you need to.** If you can easily solve a list problem using append, then it's the right tool to use until you determine that its inefficiencies make a difference.

Suppose, for example, that you need to reverse a list. A natural recursive solution using append can be derived as follows:

1. The base case, as it is with many list functions, is an empty list. The reverse of an empty list is an empty list, so no recursion is needed.

Table 10.1 Reversing a list using an auxiliary reversed-so-far list.

List Being Reversed	List Reversed-so-far
(1,2,3,4)	()
(2,3,4)	(1)
(3,4)	(2,1)
(4)	(3,2,1)
()	(4,3,2,1)

2. Most recursive list functions recurse on a list's tail. If we've successfully reversed the tail (remember, believe in the recursion), how can we reverse the entire list? Appending the head of the list to the reversed tail yields the reverse of the entire list.

This reasoning leads to the following function:

```
CList<string> Reverse(const CList<string>& list)
{
    if (list.IsEmpty()) return list;
    return append(list.Head(),Reverse(list.Tail()));
}
```

This solution is terse and elegant, but it's expensive in time and memory. Reversing an n-element list requires calling append n times and a total of $1+2+\cdots+n = n(n+1)/2$ allocated list elements. We'd like to develop a reversing algorithm using cons, but if you think about the recursion for a while, you'll see that it's not straightforward to develop.

We'll use a common technique of accumulating the reversed result in another list variable. We'll use two parameters in the reversing function:

- The list being reversed. The function recurses on this list, using the standard technique of using the list's tail as the recursive argument.
- The list that's the reversed list so far. Initially this list is empty since nothing has been reversed. When there's one element left in the list being reversed, all the other elements from the original list will be in this reversed-so-far list in reverse order.

Table 10.1 shows what we want the relationship between these two lists to be if we start with a list (1,2,3,4).

The insight of using the auxiliary reversed-so-far list enables us to use cons to build the reversed list. We can add the head/first element from the list being reversed to the front of the reversed-so-far list, making progress toward the base case. We'll call the auxiliary, two-parameter reversing function from a single parameter function so that client code can create a reversed list without knowing about the second parameter. Two reversing functions, Reverse and Reverse2, are shown in Program 10.17.

Reverse2 uses the auxiliary function. The output shows the number of list elements allocated when both functions are called. In this program we use an alias StringList for CList<string>. We'll discuss the syntax for the alias after the program.

Program 10.17 listreverse.cpp

```cpp
#include <iostream>
#include <string>
using namespace std;
#include "clist.h"

StringList RevAux(StringList list, StringList sofar)
// pre: list = (a_0, a_1, ..., a_(n-1))
// post: returns (a_(n-1), ..., a_1, a_0, sofar)
{
    if (list.IsEmpty()) return sofar;
    return RevAux(list.Tail(), cons(list.Head(),sofar));
}
StringList Reverse2(StringList list)
// pre: list = (a_0, a-1, ..., a_(n-1))
// post: return  (a_(n-1), ... a_1, a_0)
{
    return RevAux(list,StringList());
}
StringList Reverse(StringList list)
// pre: list = (a_0, a-1, ..., a_(n-1))
// post: return  (a_(n-1), ... a_1, a_0)
{
   if (list.IsEmpty()) return list;
   return append(list.Head(),Reverse(list.Tail()));
}
void Print(StringList list)
{
    cout << list.Printer(",") << endl;
    cout << "# cons calls = " << StringList::ConsCalls() << endl << endl;
}


int main()
{
    StringList spices,spices2;

    spices = cons(string("paprika"), cons(string("cayenne"),
                cons(string("chili"), cons(string("turmeric"),
                    cons(string("pepper"), StringList()))))));
    spices2 = cons(string("curry"), cons(string("coriander"),
                cons(string("cumin"), spices)));
    Print(spices);
    Print(spices2);
    Print(Reverse(spices));
    Print(Reverse2(spices));
    return 0;
}
```

listreverse.cpp

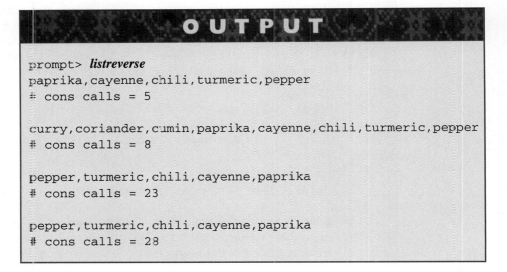

```
                        O U T P U T

prompt> listreverse
paprika,cayenne,chili,turmeric,pepper
# cons calls = 5

curry,coriander,cumin,paprika,cayenne,chili,turmeric,pepper
# cons calls = 8

pepper,turmeric,chili,cayenne,paprika
# cons calls = 23

pepper,turmeric,chili,cayenne,paprika
# cons calls = 28
```

Using the name CList<string> each time we want to define a variable or declare a parameter leads to lots of typing and code that's hard to read. Using an alias, implemented in C++ using a **typedef**, makes code simpler to read and can make some modifications easier. The header file *clist.h*, Program G.12 in How to G, introduces the typedefs StringList and StringListIterator. A typedef is a

convenience, but the alias introduced often helps in reading and understanding code. For example, you might use the new name Integer,

---
Syntax: typedef

```
typedef CList<string> StringList;
typedef BigInt Integer;
```
---

as shown in the syntax diagram. You can use the name Integer as a type, but change it later to int and recompile your program to update all uses of Integer. Complicated declarations are often easier to understand with a typedef. For example, the definition CList<CList<string>> list will not compile because the compiler misinterprets the >> as the insertion operator; you must include a space, as in CList<CList<string> > list. Using a typedef can make this simpler: CList<StringList> list.

Pause to Reflect

10.13 In *listdemo.cpp*, Program 10.13, how will the output change if the call below (where X is 1,2,3,4)

```
Display(sX.Tail());
```

is changed in all five places it occurs to the following?

```
Display(sX.Tail().Tail());
```

10.14 In the initialization of `spices` in Program 10.17, *listreverse.cpp*, the final argument in the constructor is `StringList()`. Why is this argument used? Can it be replaced by `spices`? Can it be replaced by `StringList::EMPTY`?

10.15 If the following statement is added as the last statement in `main` in *readlist.cpp*, Program 10.15, what values are printed for each of the runs shown in the output box?

```
cout << "# cons calls = "
     << CList<string>::ConsCalls() << endl;
```

Suppose the call to `cons` in the `while` loop of the function `Read` is replaced by a call to `append`. What values are printed by the `ConsCalls()` statement?

10.16 Write a nonrecursive function that reverses a list using a `CListIterator` and `cons`. Using the same idea that's used in the recursive function, define a variable *sofar* and maintain the invariant: *sofar is the reverse of all the elements already processed.* The loop test should be

```
while (! list.IsEmpty())
```

10.17 Write a function `append` that appends one list to another. Conceptually, the call below yields the list `(1,2,3,4,5,6)`:

```
append( (1,2,3), (4,5,6) )
```

The function should `cons` as many elements as there are in parameter `lhs`.

```
CList<int> append(const CList<int>& lhs,
                  const CList<int>& rhs)
// pre: lhs = (a1,a2,...,an), rhs = (b1,b2,...bm)
// post: returns list (a1,a2,...,an,b1,b2,..,bm)
```

10.18 Write a function `Flatten` that creates one list from a list of lists. For example, the first list below is flattened into the second.

```
( ("apple", "cherry"),
  ("big", "little", "tiny"),
  ("november") )

("apple", "cherry", "big", "little", "tiny", "november")

StringList Flatten(CList<StringList> list)
// post: return a flattened form of list
```

10.19 Consider the function Create that follows. What's printed by the statement calling Create?

```
cout << Create(5).Printer(" ") << endl;
```

You'll need to think carefully about what's going on here and review what happens when a list is inserted onto an output stream (see *listdemo.cpp*, Program 10.13):

```
typedef CList<int> IntList;
CList<IntList> Create(int n)
{
    CList<IntList> result;
    int j,k;
    for(j=0; j < n; j++)
    {   IntList nlist;
        for(k=j; k >= 0; k--)
        {   nlist = cons(k,nlist);
        }
        result = cons(nlist,result);
    }
    return result;
}
```

10.5.5 Polynomials Implemented with Lists

The class CList is simple to use and motivates recursion since many list functions are more easily implemented recursively than iteratively. But what good is the class other than as something to study? In general, when should we think about using a CList object rather than a tvector object? A tvector can grow to accommodate more elements, supports random access, and allows its elements to change. A CList cannot be changed, is grown by creating new lists, and provides sequential access. Lists efficiently represent **sparse structures**. For example, consider the polynomial $2x^7 + 4x^3 + 6x^2 + 3$. For the moment we'll consider just the exponents and ignore the coefficients. Conceptually the polynomial's exponents are (7, 3, 2, 0). Should these be stored as a list or a vector? As with many questions, the answer is "it depends."

It depends on what operations we'll perform on polynomials. Suppose that we want to add $5x^4 + 3x^3 + x$ to the polynomial. Again, using exponents we have (7, 3, 2, 0) + (4, 3, 1). The result (again without coefficients) is (7, 4, 3, 2, 1, 0) since the resulting polynomial is $2x^7 + 5x^4 + 7x^3 + 6x^2 + x + 8$. To add a term like $5x^4$ to a polynomial requires shifting the terms of the polynomial to make room for the new term if we keep the terms in order, sorted by exponent. Keeping terms in order is a good idea because it will make arithmetic on polynomials much simpler. However, shifting vector elements is expensive. If we use vectors, we might choose to represent $2x^7 + 4x^3 + 6x^2 + 8$ with coefficients as (2, 0, 0, 0, 4, 6, 0, 8) giving the coefficient for every term, where the position in the vector determines the exponent. This structure makes addition very simple. For example, $(2x^7 + 4x^3 + 6x^2 + 8) + (5x^4 + 3x^3 + x)$ is realized with vectors as follows:

```
    (2,  0,  0,  0,  4,  6,  0,  8)
+               (5,  3,  0,  1,  0)
    ------------------------------
    (2,  0,  0,  5,  7,  6,  1,  8)
```

which is the result $2x^7 + 5x^4 + 7x^3 + 6x^2 + x + 8$. This representation is very inefficient in its use of storage for the polynomial $7x^{100} + 2x + 1$. In general, polynomials are sparse because not every exponent between zero and the degree of the polynomial is typically represented by a nonzero coefficient.[6]

10.5.6   CList and Sparse, Sequential Structures

Using CList objects to represent polynomials lets us represent sparse polynomials simply. Since most polynomials are accessed sequentially, processing each term of the polynomial in order, vectors don't supply an advantage because their principal strength is random access. As we'll see, CList representations of polynomials are efficient and easy to use in programs.

Program 10.18   polydemo.cpp

```cpp
#include <iostream>
using namespace std;

#include "poly.h"

// simple demo of polynomials

int main()
{
    Poly p1, p2, p3;

    p1 = Poly(5,7) + Poly(4,2) + Poly(3,1) + Poly(2,0);
    p2 = Poly(3,5) + Poly(2,4) + Poly(3,2);

    cout << "p1 = "   << p1 << endl;
    cout << "p2 = "   << p2 << endl;
    cout << "sum = " << p1+p2 << endl;
    cout << "p3 = "   << p3 << endl;
    return 0;
}
```

polydemo.cpp

---

[6]The degree of a polynomial is the largest exponent.

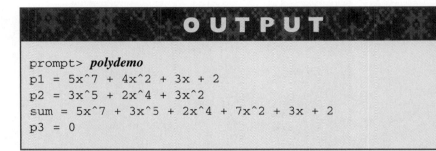

```
prompt> polydemo
p1 = 5x^7 + 4x^2 + 3x + 2
p2 = 3x^5 + 2x^4 + 3x^2
sum = 5x^7 + 3x^5 + 2x^4 + 7x^2 + 3x + 2
p3 = 0
```

Polynomials are created in four ways:

1. The default constructor creates the constant zero.
2. A single-term polynomial ax^n is created by `Poly p(a,n);`
3. Polynomials can be added together to create new polynomials.
4. A polynomial can be multiplied by a constant to create a new polynomial.

The polynomial class is largely a **wrapper** class around a `CList<Pair>` object, where a `Pair` is simply a `struct` with a coefficient and an exponent. For details on the implementation see *poly.h*, Program G.13 in How to G. A `Poly` object has a leading term, obtained via `Poly::Head`, and all the other terms, obtained via `Poly::Tail`. Accessor functions supply the degree and leading coefficient of a polynomial, as shown in the function `MonoMult` of *polymult.cpp*, Program 10.19. The program also shows how to evaluate a polynomial at a point; how to multiply by a constant; the static function `Poly::TermsAllocated`, which reports memory usage for polynomials; and the static constant `Poly::ZERO`, which represents the constant 0.

Program 10.19 polymult.cpp

```cpp
#include <iostream>
using namespace std;

#include "poly.h"

Poly MonoMult(const Poly& mono, const Poly& rhs)
// pre: mono is a single term (monomial)
// post: return mono*rhs
//       if mono is a polynomial, returns mono.Head()*rhs
{
    if (rhs.IsPoly())
    {   return Poly(mono.leadingCoeff()*rhs.leadingCoeff(),
                mono.degree() + rhs.degree()) + MonoMult(mono,rhs.Tail());
    }
    return Poly::ZERO;  // base case accumulated properly
}

int main()
{
```

```
Poly p1,p2,p3,p4;
double x;
cout << "value of x ";
cin >> x;

p1 = Poly(3,2) + Poly(4,1) + Poly(-3,0);
p2 = Poly(4,2) + Poly(3,1) + Poly(2,0);
p3 = Poly(5,3);

cout << "p1 at " << x << ", " << p1.at(x) << "\t : " << p1 << endl;
cout << "p2 at " << x << ", " << p2.at(x) << "\t : " << p2<< endl;
cout << "p3 at " << x << ", " << p3.at(x) << "\t : " << p3 << endl;
p4 = MonoMult(p3,p1);
cout << "p4 at " << x << ", " << p4.at(x) << "\t : " << p4 << endl;
cout << "5p4 at " << x << ", " << (5*p4).at(x) << "\t : " << 5*p4 << endl;

cout << "total # terms used = " << Poly::TermsAllocated() << endl;
return 0;
}
```

polymult.cpp

OUTPUT

```
prompt> polymult
value of x 3
p1 at 3, 36       : 3x^2 + 4x + -3
p2 at 3, 47       : 4x^2 + 3x + 2
p3 at 3, 135      : 5x^3
p4 at 3, 4860     : 15x^5 + 20x^4 + -15x^3
5p4 at 3, 24300   : 75x^5 + 100x^4 + -75x^3
total # terms used = 25
```

More details of the implementation are provided in How to G, but we'll reproduce the private section of the class `Poly` and mention three important points of the implementation.

```
class Poly
{
    ...

    private:
      struct Pair         // this is the (a,b) in ax^b
      {   double coeff;
          int expo;
          Pair() : coeff(0.0), expo(0) { }
          Pair(double c, int e) : coeff(c), expo(e) { }
      };
```

```
    typedef CList<Pair> Polist;
    typedef CListIterator<Pair> PolistIterator;
    static bool ourInitialized;

    Poly(Polist p);   // poly from list of terms, helper
    Polist myPoly;    // the list of terms
};
```

- The struct Pair that represents a coefficient and an exponent is declared in the private section of Poly. It's used only in the implementation of polynomials. In general, it's possible to declare structs and classes inside other classes.
- A private constructor is declared for creating a polynomial from a CList<Pair> object, though the alias Polist is used for the CList<Pair> object. Client programs don't need to know that a list is being used, so the constructor should not be accessible to clients, but it's useful in implementing other member functions.
- (*This is advanced; it's fine to ignore it.*) The static variable ourInitialized will be false until the program is run. Then Poly::ZERO will be constructed, creating a zero polynomial and making the value of ourInitialized true. Then, every time a client calls the default Poly constructor, the object Poly::ZERO will be used. This means if 10,000 zero polynomials are created, only one cons call is actually made—see Program 10.20, *polycount.cpp*.

Program 10.20 polycount.cpp

```
#include <iostream>
using namespace std;
#include "poly.h"

int main()
{
    int k;
    for(k=0; k < 1000; k++)
    {   Poly p;
    }
    cout << "# terms created = " << Poly::TermsAllocated() << endl;

    for(k=0; k < 1000; k++)
    {   Poly p(3,4);
    }
    cout << "# terms created = " << Poly::TermsAllocated() << endl;

    return 0;
}
```

OUTPUT

```
prompt> polycount
# terms created = 1
# terms created = 1001
```

10.6   The Class `tmatrix`

A vector is a one-dimensional structure; an index accesses an element of the array by ranging from zero to one less than the number of elements stored. In some applications two-dimensional arrays are necessary. For example, the pixels on a computer screen are usually identified by a row and column position. Mileage tables that provide distances between cities on a road map also use two dimensions. Positions of pieces in a chess game are usually given by specifying a row and a column.

10.6.1   A Simple `tmatrix` Program

A two-dimensional array is sometimes called a **matrix** (the plural is matrices). The Cartesian (x, y) coordinate system uses two dimensions to specify a point in the plane. The system of latitude and longitude uses two dimensions to specify a location on the earth. Two-dimensional vectors, as we will implement them using the class `tmatrix`, use row and column indexes to specify an entry of the matrix. The program *matdemo.cpp,* Program 10.21, defines a matrix, fills it with the equivalent of a multiplication table, and prints the matrix.

As with `tvector` variables, the type used to define the element stored in each matrix cell can be any built-in type or any programmer-defined type that has a default (parameterless) constructor. If a `tmatrix` is defined with the default constructor, the matrix has zero rows and columns. In that case the member function `resize` should be used to set the number of rows and columns. The first parameter in a constructor or with `resize` is the number of rows; the second parameter is the number of columns. Rows and columns are numbered starting with zero as with `tvector` variables. A third parameter can be used to provide initial values for all the cells of a matrix just as a second parameter provides values for `charCounts` in *letters.cpp,* Program 8.3. For example, the definition `tmatrix<double> chart(3,5,1.0);` defines a three-by-five matrix of 15 `doubles`, all initialized to 1.0.

> **Syntax: `tmatrix` definition**
>
> `tmatrix<`*Type*`> mat;`
> `tmatrix<`*Type*`> mat(`*row, col*`);`
> `tmatrix<`*Type*`> mat(`*row, col, fillvalue*`);`

Complete documentation for the `tmatrix` class is found in the header file *tmatrix.h*; see How to G for details.

```cpp
#include <iostream>
#include <string>
#include <iomanip>        // for setw
using namespace std;
#include "tmatrix.h"

// demonstrate class tmatrix

template <class T>
void Print(const tmatrix<T>& mat)
{
    int j,k;
    int rows = mat.numrows(), cols = mat.numcols();
    for(j=0; j < rows; j++)
    {   for(k=0; k < cols; k++)
        {   cout << setw(4) << mat[j][k];
        }
        cout << endl;
    }
}

int main()
{
    int rows, cols,j,k;
    cout << "row col dimensions: ";
    cin >> rows >> cols;

    tmatrix<int> mat(rows,cols);
    for(j=0; j < rows; j++)                 // fill matrix
    {   for(k=0; k < cols; k++)
        {   mat[j][k] = (j+1)*(k+1);
        }
    }
    Print(mat);
    return 0;
}
```

```
                        O U T P U T

   prompt> matdemo
   row col dimensions: 3 5
          1    2    3    4    5
          2    4    6    8   10
          3    6    9   12   15

   prompt> matdemo
   row col dimensions: 7 4
          1    2    3    4
          2    4    6    8
          3    6    9   12
          4    8   12   16
          5   10   15   20
          6   12   18   24
          7   14   21   28
```

10.6.2   Case Study: Finding Blobs

In this section we'll use the `tmatrix` class to assist in looking for organisms on the kinds of slides used under microscopes. Of course we'll be using a simulated slide, but the algorithm and design techniques could be used if we were guiding a digital microscope, a radiological CT scan or MRI, or a graphics-painting program. We'll use a character-based picture, but a similar class based on the graphics library documented in How to H is included in the exercises for this chapter. Slides will be represented by a character **bitmap**, using the class `CharBitMap` declared in *charbitmap.h*. Program 10.22 illustrates most of the bitmap class.

Program 10.22   bitmapdemo.cpp

```cpp
#include <iostream>
using namespace std;
#include "charbitmap.h"
#include "prompt.h"
#include "randgen.h"

int main()
{
    int rows, cols;
    cout << "enter row col size ";
    cin >> rows >> cols;
    CharBitMap bmap(rows,cols);
    int pixelCount = PromptRange("# pixels on ",1,rows*cols);
```

```
int k;
RandGen gen;
for(k=0; k < pixelCount; k++)
{    bmap.SetPixel(gen.RandInt(0,rows-1),gen.RandInt(0,cols-1),CharBitMap::black);
}
bmap.Display(cout);
return 0;
}
```

bitmapdemo.cpp

The pixels in a CharBitMap object can have values CharBitMap::white and
CharBitMap::black; the identifiers black and white are class enum values.
CharBitMap pixel coordinates are the same as tmatrix coordinates, ranging from
zero to one less than the number of rows or columns.

```
                    O U T P U T

prompt> bitmapdemo
enter row col size 10 50
# pixels on  between 1 and 750: 200
+----------------------------------------------------+
| *** **       *  ***     **      * *    ***    *  * |
|     * *      *  **    *        *   *** **   ** * * |
|     *       * **  *   *      * *  ***     *  * ** ** |
|*      * *   ***    *        *   * *  *    *** **   * |
|*  *  * * * **      *            ****        *    * |
|*       *  *    *    *** **           * *  *       |
|***  * *   *  *  *      ** *      *  *****    ***   |
|   *   * *     *         ** ***   *      * * ***    |
|   * *  ***   *  *  ***     *  *     ** *   * * ** |
|   *   * *       *      *           *      *** * * |
+----------------------------------------------------+
```

We want to identify organisms on the slide. We'll define an organism to be a group
of adjacent black pixels, where adjacent means connected horizontally or vertically. In
the diagram below, there is a 14-pixel organism on the left, a 2-pixel organism in the
middle, and a 5-pixel organism on the right.

```
    ***           *        *    *
    *****         *        *  * *
      **          *        *  *
    ****          *        **
```

The other asterisks in the diagram can be considered one-pixel organisms or random
noise. The middle organism is only a two-pixel organism because diagonally adjacent
pixels are not considered to be part of the same organism.

We want to design a class that counts the organisms in a `CharBitMap` object. The minimal size of an organism will be specified by the user; organisms smaller than this size will be considered noise. In the exercises we'll explore changing the definition of an organism to include diagonally adjacent cells, so we'll design the program to make extensions or modifications as simple as possible. In our initial design we'll need only two member functions other than a constructor in the class `Blobs`:[7]

1.   A function `Blobs::Display` to display blobs.
2.   A function `Blobs::FindBlobs` to which we pass a bitmap and a minimal size.

The `FindBlobs` function does all the work of finding the organisms/blobs, setting up for a subsequent call of `Display`, and returning the number of organisms found. We'll need some private helper functions that do most of the work needed to implement `FindBlobs`. Helper functions are useful in general but are particularly helpful in recursion. Often, the method called by the client does not have the correct prototype for a recursive call or requires some initializing bookkeeping that's not appropriate in every recursive call. The method called by the client code can perform the initialization and then call the recursive helping function.

> **Program Tip 10.6: Many member functions that use a recursive algorithm are most easily implemented by calling a recursive, private helper function.** The public method can set up bookkeeping and sometimes pass private data as an argument to the initial call of the recursive helper method. The bookkeeping should be done only once, and the private data are not available for clients to pass as arguments.

The recursive algorithm for finding an organism can be visualized by thinking of the recursive clones as scouts, sent out by an initial blob counter to report on adjacent pixels and whether the adjacent pixels are part of the blob being counted.

Find a blob containing pixel (*x,y*); return size of blob.

- If (x, y) isn't black, it's not part of a blob; stop and return zero.
- Otherwise, (x, y) is part of a blob; send out blob-counting scouts/clones, and accumulate results reported back.
  - Four clones are sent, one in each direction.
  - Each clone reports how many pixels it found that are part of the blob.
  - Each clone covers its tracks so that its work won't be duplicated by other clones.

Each call that finds a black pixel accumulates the results of the four clones and returns this result plus one for the found black pixel. If you believe that the clones work correctly (see Program Tip 10.2), then the correct result will be returned assuming each clone can cover its tracks.

---

[7]We'll use "blobs" rather than "organisms" because it's more fun to say "blobs."

It's essential that each clone marks where it has been so that clones sent out later don't count pixels that have already been counted. We'll implement this marking mechanism by using an int matrix. Initially we'll use values for black and white that won't be used as blob-marking values. When we mark blobs, we'll use a different int value for each blob that's found. The recursive helper function BlobFill in *blobs.cpp*, Program 10.23, does all the work. Before looking at the implementation, we'll discuss the interface and how BlobFill is called. In the calls below, the instance variable myBlobCount is the value of how many blobs have been found so far. The int constants PIXEL_ON and PIXEL_OFF are used to initialize the Blob grid based on values from the CharBitMap parameter passed to FindBlob.

```
int Blobs::BlobFill(int row, int col,
                    int lookFor, int fillWith)
// spec: look for blob with pixel-value 'lookFor',
//       color in this blob using 'fillWith' value,
//       return size of blob
// post: returns size of blob at (row,col) and ``colors''
//       blob so that it won't be counted again
//
```

Keeping this specification in mind, BlobFill is called as follows. If BlobFill reports a blob whose size is more than the minimal value being searched for, the number of blobs is incremented; otherwise, the blob doesn't count. If the blob doesn't count, it must be erased since the BlobFill call and its clones may have marked the too-small blob.

```
// j and k range over all row, column values
if (BlobFill(j,k, PIXEL_ON, myBlobCount+1)) > minSize)
{ myBlobCount++;
}
else    // too small, erase
{ BlobFill(j,k, myBlobCount+1, PIXEL_OFF);
}
```

When a too-small blob is erased, the lookFor value is the same as the fillWith value from the call to BlobFill that just reported the too-small value.

Program 10.23 blobs.cpp

```
#include <iostream>
#include <iomanip>
using namespace std;
#include "tmatrix.h"
#include "randgen.h"
#include "prompt.h"
#include "charbitmap.h"

// find blobs in a two-dimensional grid/bitmap
```

```
class Blobs
{
  public:

    Blobs();
    int FindBlobs(const CharBitMap& cbm, int minSize);
    void Display(ostream& out) const;

  private:

    tmatrix<int> myGrid;
    int          myBlobCount;

    int BlobFill(int row, int col,int lookFor, int fillWith);
    void Initialize(const CharBitMap& cbm);

    static int PIXEL_OFF, PIXEL_ON;
};

int Blobs::PIXEL_OFF = 0;
int Blobs::PIXEL_ON = -1;

Blobs::Blobs()
  : myBlobCount(0)
{
  // grid is empty
}

void Blobs::Display(ostream& out) const
// post: display the blobs
{
    int j,k;
    int rows = myGrid.numrows();
    int cols = myGrid.numcols();
    for(j=0; j < rows; j++)
    {   for(k=0; k < cols; k++)
        {   char ch = '.';
            if (myGrid[j][k] > PIXEL_OFF)
            {   ch = char ('0' + myGrid[j][k]);
            }
            out << ch;;
        }
        out << endl;
    }
}

int Blobs::FindBlobs(const CharBitMap& cbm, int minSize)
// post: return # blobs whose size > minSize
{
    int j,k;
    myGrid.resize(cbm.Rows(), cbm.Cols());
    Initialize(cbm);
    int rows = myGrid.numrows();
    int cols = myGrid.numcols();
    for(j=0; j < rows; j++)
```

```
        {   for(k=0; k < cols; k++)
            {   if (myGrid[j][k] == PIXEL_ON)
                {   if (BlobFill(j,k,PIXEL_ON,myBlobCount+1) > minSize)
                    {   myBlobCount++;
                    }
                    else
                    {   BlobFill(j,k,myBlobCount+1,PIXEL_OFF); // erase it
                    }
                }
            }
        }
        return myBlobCount;
}

void Blobs::Initialize(const CharBitMap& cbm)
// post: myGrid initialized from cbm
{
    int j,k;
    int rows = myGrid.numrows();
    int cols = myGrid.numcols();
    for(j=0; j < rows; j++)
    {   for(k=0; k < cols; k++)
        {   if (cbm.GetPixel(j,k) == CharBitMap::black)
            {   myGrid[j][k] = PIXEL_ON;
            }
            else
            {   myGrid[j][k] = PIXEL_OFF;
            }
        }
    }
    myBlobCount = 0;    // no blobs yet
}

int Blobs::BlobFill(int row, int col, int lookFor, int fillWith)
// spec: look for blob with pixel-value 'lookFor', color in this
//       blob using 'fillWith' value and return size of blob
// post: returns size of blob at (row,col) and ''colors''
//       blob so that it won't be counted again
{
    static int rowoffset[] = { -1,+1,0,0 }; // north,south,east,west
    static int coloffset[] = { 0,0,+1,-1 };
    const int  NBR_COUNT = 4;

    if (0 <= row && row < myGrid.numrows() &&
        0 <= col && col < myGrid.numcols())
    {
        if (myGrid[row][col] != lookFor)  // not part of this blob
        {   return 0;
        }

        // we found a blob element, color it and its neighbors
        myGrid[row][col] = fillWith;
        int k,r,c;
        int size = 1;  // count this pixel, add connected counts
        for(k=0; k < NBR_COUNT; k++)
```

```
        {   r = row + rowoffset[k];
            c = col + coloffset[k];
            size += BlobFill(r,c,lookFor,fillWith);
        }
        return size;
    }
    return 0;    // not on grid, not part of blob
}


int main()
{
    int rows, cols;
    cout << "enter row col size ";
    cin >> rows >> cols;
    CharBitMap bmap(rows,cols);
    int k;
    RandGen gen;
    Blobs blobber;
    int pixelCount = PromptRange("# pixels on: ",1,rows*cols);
    for(k=0; k < pixelCount; k++)
    {   bmap.SetPixel(gen.RandInt(0,rows-1),gen.RandInt(0,cols-1),
                      CharBitMap::black);
    }
    bmap.Display(cout);
    int bsize;
    int blobCount;
    do
    {   bsize = PromptRange("blob size (0 to exit) ",0,50);
        if (bsize != 0)
        {   blobCount = blobber.FindBlobs(bmap,bsize);
            blobber.Display(cout);
            cout << endl << "# blobs = " << blobCount << endl;
        }
    } while (bsize > 0);
    return 0;
}
```

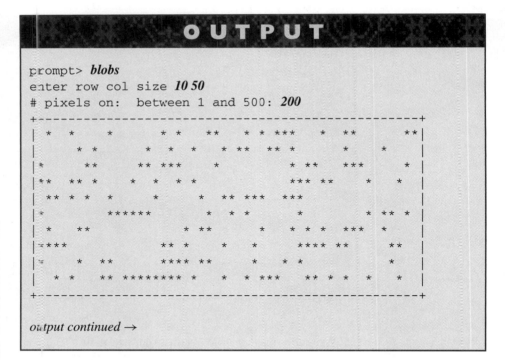

```
prompt> blobs
enter row col size 10 50
# pixels on:  between 1 and 500: 200
+-----------------------------------------------------------+
|  *    *     *       * *   **    * * ***    *   **       ** |
|     * *       *   *   *    * **  **  *        *      *     |
| *       **    ** ***     *          *  **    ***        * |
| **  **  *    *   *   *    *              *** **     *    * |
| **  *  *    *       *       *   ** ***   ***              |
| *        ******       *    *  *          *         *  ** *|
|   *    **           *  **       *    *  *  *   ***    *   |
| ****           ** *      *     *        **** **      **   |
| *      *   **       **** **       *    *  *          *    |
|   *  *     **  ******** *    *    * ***    ** * *    *   * |
+-----------------------------------------------------------+
```

output continued →
```
blob size (0 to exit)  between 0 and 50: 10
...............................111................
...............................11.1..............
...............................1.11...........
...............................111............
...............................111..............
................................1.............
.............2................................
...........22.2...............................
..........2222................................
.......22222222...............................
```

`# blobs = 2`

output continued →

```
                          OUTPUT

blob size (0 to exit)  between 0 and 50: 5
..............................111......22........
............................11.1......2.........
..........................1.11...222.......
.........................111..............
.........3...............111..............
.........333333.................1...............
.4...............5..............6.6..........
4444..........55.5............6666..........
4.............5555............6.............
..........55555555.............................

# blobs = 6
blob size (0 to exit)  between 0 and 50: 0
```

Pause to Reflect

10.20 Write the function RowSum that returns the sum of the entries in one row of a matrix and the function ColSum that returns the sum of the entries in one column of a matrix.

```
int RowSum(const tmatrix<int>& m, int r)
// pre: 0 <= r < m.numrows()
// post: returns sum of numbers in row r

int ColSum(const tmatrix<int>& m, int c)
// pre: 0 <= c < m.numcols()
// post: returns sum of numbers in column c
```

10.21 A *magic square* is a square matrix whose rows, columns, and main diagonals all sum to the same number. A 3 × 3 magic square follows:

```
6   1   8
7   5   3
2   9   4
```

Write a Boolean-valued function IsMagic that returns true if its square matrix parameter is magic and false otherwise. Call the functions RowSum and ColSum from the previous exercise.

10.22 The code in *bitmapdemo.cpp*, Program 10.22, prompts the user for the number of pixels to turn on. In fact, fewer than this number will be on in almost every run of the program. Why, and how can you change the code to ensure that exactly pixelCount pixels are on?

10.23 It's possible to change three lines in `Blobs::BlobFill` so that diagonally adjacent pixels are considered part of an organism. What are the three lines and how should they be changed?

10.24 In an $N \times N$ bitmap, what is the approximate number of pixels examined by `Blobs::FindBlobs`?

10.25 Suppose you want to add the capability of reading in a bitmap from data stored in a file. Where's the right place to add this capability and why? Consider additions to `CharBitMap`, to `Blobs`, or writing another class or function.

10.26 The class `Blobs` counts blobs and prints them, but there's no way for clients to access the blobs either individually or collectively. Develop two ways to allow client programs to access individual blobs [i.e., to get a collection of (x, y) pairs that make up a blob by calling appropriate `Blob` member functions]. Consider using vectors or lists. The class `Point` from *point.h*, Program G.10, may help.

10.27 Discuss how to add features to the class `Blob` so that client code can find the size of the largest blob (an `int` value). Develop two methods, one that examines approximately N^2 pixels in an $N \times N$ bitmap and one that examines the total number of blob pixels.

10.7 Chapter Review

In this chapter we discussed recursion, a useful programming technique that can be misused. A recursive function does not "call itself" but calls a clone function, an identical copy of itself. Each recursively called function has its own parameters and its own local variables. We also covered variable scope and lifetime. A variable's scope is the part of the program in which the variable can be accessed. A variable's lifetime is how long the variable exists. The class `CList` is useful for representing sparse structures and lists of objects. The class `tmatrix` is like a two-dimensional vector.

Important topics covered include the following:

■   Recursion is an alternative to iteration using loops. Recursive functions iterate by making recursive calls.

■   Recursively called functions use memory; there is a limit on the number of recursive calls or recursively called functions. This limit depends on the amount of memory in the computer.

■   Some problems are naturally solved with recursive functions and would be difficult to solve using loops.

■   Some functions should not be coded recursively. One example is computing Fibonacci numbers.

■   Recursive functions are often divided into two cases: a base case that does not involve a recursive call and a recursive case that makes a recursive call. The recursive call should get closer to the base case so that there are a finite number of recursive calls.

- A variable's scope determines in which part of the program the variable can be accessed. Variables can be defined globally, accessible in all functions, or locally, accessible in the function in which the variable is defined.

- Variables can be defined within the braces, { and }; this means a variable's scope can be restricted to any compound statement (e.g., accessible only within a loop).

- The scope resolution operator, : :, is used to access global variables when the variable identifier is shadowed by a local variable.

- Static variables maintain values throughout program execution, unlike nonstatic variables, whose lifetime is for the duration of the function in which the variable is defined.

- Static class variables belong to a class rather than to an object. Class variables are useful for keeping track of statistics involving all objects (e.g., counting the number of objects created).

- The class CList represents immutable lists. A list is homogeneous: all elements are the same type. Lists are created using cons and processed, usually recursively, using Head and Tail.

- The class CList represents sparse structures efficiently. Representing polynomials provides one example.

- Two-dimensional vectors, or matrices, are useful for representing and manipulating data. We use a tmatrix class for two-dimensional arrays.

- Member functions that call for recursion are often most easily implemented using a private helper function.

10.8 Exercises

10.1 An integer is printed with commas inserted in the proper positions similarly to the way in which digits in English are printed in *digits3.cpp*, Program 10.2. That is, to print the number 12345678 as 12,345,678, the 678 cannot be printed until *after* the preceding part of the number is printed. Write a recursive function PrintWithCommas that will print its BigInt parameter with commas inserted properly. The outline of the function is

```
if (number < 1000)
   print normally, no commas needed
else
    recursively print the number
               without the last three digits
    print a comma and the last three digits
```

You'll need to be careful with leading zeroes to ensure, for example, that the number 12,003 is printed properly. Write the function nonrecursively also by creating a string from the BigInt value and then printing the string appropriately with commas.

Modify the recursive function to return a string equivalent to the BigInt but with commas properly inserted.

10.2 Modify Program 10.5, *subdir.cpp*, so that instead of printing the names of all files and subdirectories, the size of each subdirectory is calculated, returned, and printed. Use the member function `DirEntry::Size()` to calculate the size (usually expressed in bytes) of each file. Print the size of each subdirectory in a format that makes it easy to determine where large files might be found. Do *not* print the names of every file; just print the names of the subdirectories and the size of all the files within the subdirectory.

10.3 Pascal's triangle can be used to calculate the number of different ways of choosing k items from n different items. The first seven rows of Pascal's triangle are

$$
\begin{array}{ccccccccccccc}
 & & & & & & 1 & & & & & & \\
 & & & & & 1 & & 1 & & & & & \\
 & & & & 1 & & 2 & & 1 & & & & \\
 & & & 1 & & 3 & & 3 & & 1 & & & \\
 & & 1 & & 4 & & 6 & & 4 & & 1 & & \\
 & 1 & & 5 & & 10 & & 10 & & 5 & & 1 & \\
1 & & 6 & & 15 & & 20 & & 15 & & 6 & & 1
\end{array}
$$

If we use C_k^n to represent the number of ways of choosing k items from n, then $C_0^n = 1$ and $C_n^n = 1$ as shown in the outside edges of the triangle. For values of k other than 0 and n, the following relationship holds:

$$C_k^n = C_{k-1}^{n-1} + C_k^{n-1} \tag{10.4}$$

Viewed in the triangle, each entry other than the outside 1's is equal to the two entries in the row above it diagonally up and to the left and right. For example,

$$C_2^5 = 10 = (C_1^4 + C_2^4) = (4 + 6)$$

Write a function *Choose*, with two parameters n and k, that returns the number of ways that k items can be chosen from n. Use this function to print the first 15 rows of Pascal's triangle.

10.4 Repeat the previous exercise, but try to develop a mechanism for storing the results of each recursive call using a static local variable so that no calculation is made more than once. This is tricky using `tvector` variables, but it is possible if you can develop a method for calculating a unique index for each pair of values used in the recursive calls. Alternatively, you can also use a `tmatrix`.

10.5 The value C_k^n can also be computed using the factorial function and this equation:

$$C_k^n = \frac{n!}{k! \cdot (n-k)!} \tag{10.5}$$

Write two versions of a function to compute the value of C_k^n, one based on the factorial function (where factorial is computed iteratively, *not* recursively) and one based on the recursive definition in the previous exercise. Time how long it takes to compute different values of C_k^n. Use `BigInt` values and compute C_k^n for large values of k and n.

10.6 Implement multiplication of polynomials. For example,

$$(x^3 + 2x^2 + 3) \times (2x^2 + x - 2) = 2x^5 + 5x^4 + 2x^2 + 3x - 6$$

You should use the function `MonoMult` from *polymult.cpp*, Program 10.19, as a helper function. Use this function to implement polynomial exponentation so that you can calculate $(x^2 + 3x + 4)^3$ efficiently.

10.7 The function `Poly::at` for evaluating polynomials is implemented inefficiently. Evaluating $x^{100} + 3x^{99} + 5$ is done by raising x^{100}, then adding the result of $3x^{99}$, then adding 5. It would be more efficiently calculated using $(x^{99} + 3)x + 5$. In general this method of evaluating a polynomial is called *Horner's Rule*:

$$a_n x^n + a_{n-1} x^{n-1} - \cdots + a_1 x + a + 0 =$$
$$(\ldots((a_n x + a_{n-1})x + \cdots + a_1)x + a_0$$

The coefficient of the largest exponent, a_n, is multiplied by x. Then a_{n-1} is added and the result multiplied by x; then a_{n-2} is added and the result multiplied by x, and so on. The simplest way to implement Horner's rule for evaluating polynomials requires a nonsparse representation (i.e., all coefficients, including zero coefficients, are needed). Write a function to produce a nonsparse representation of a polynomial. You won't be able to use a polynomial itself since the addition of polynomials with zero coefficients is ignored by `operator +=` for polynomials. Instead, you'll need to create a `CList<int>` object storing exponents and a `CList<double>` object storing coefficients; or you can create a list storing exponents and coefficients by declaring a `struct` like `Pair` used in the implementation of `Poly`. Use this to evaluate a polynomial using Horner's rule and see if this method is more efficient in practice.

10.8 The towers of Hanoi puzzle is traditionally studied in computer science courses. The roots of the puzzle are apparently found in the Far East, where a tower of golden disks is said to be used by monks. The puzzle consists of three pegs and a set of disks that fit over the pegs. Each disk is a different size. Initially the disks are on one peg, with the smallest disk on top, the largest on the bottom, and the disks arranged in increasing order. The object is to move the disks, one at a time, to another peg. No disk can be placed on a smaller disk.

  If four disks are used and all disks are initially on the leftmost peg, numbered **1** in Figure 10.10, the following sequence of disk moves shows how to reach the configuration of disks shown. A move is indicated by the pegs involved since the topmost disk is always moved.

```
Move 1 to 3
Move 1 to 2
Move 3 to 2
```

To finish moving all the disks from the left peg to the middle peg, the top disk is moved from 1 to 3, then (recursively) the disks are moved from peg 2 to peg 3. The largest disk is then moved from peg 1 to peg 2. Finally (and recursively), the disks from peg 3 are moved to peg 2. Pegs are numbered 1, 2, and 3. To move seven disks from peg 1 to peg 2, the function call `Hanoi(1,2,3,7)` is used. To move these seven disks, two recursive calls are necessary: `Hanoi(1,3,2,6)`, which moves six disks from peg 1 to peg 3, with peg 2 as the auxiliary peg; followed by a nonrecursive move of the largest disk from peg 1 to peg 2; followed by a recursive `Hanoi(3,2,1,6)` to move the six disks from peg 3 to peg 2, with the now empty peg 1 as the auxiliary peg.

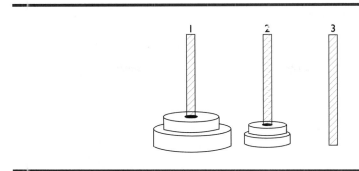

Figure 10.10 The Towers of Hanoi.

Write the function `Hanoi`. The base case, and the single-disk case, should print the peg moves. For example, the output for a four-disk tower follows:

```
                          O U T P U T

prompt> hanoi
number of disks:  between 0 and 30: 4
move from 1 to 3
move from 1 to 2
move from 3 to 2
move from 1 to 3
move from 2 to 1
move from 2 to 3
move from 1 to 3
move from 1 to 2
move from 3 to 2
move from 3 to 1
move from 2 to 1
move from 3 to 2
move from 1 to 3
move from 1 to 2
move from 3 to 2
```

Consider a function `Hanoi` using the following prototype:

```
void Hanoi(int from, int to, int aux, int numDisks)
// pre:  top numDisks-1 disks on 'from' peg
//           are all smaller than top disk on
//           'aux' peg
// post: top numDisks disks moved from
//        'from' peg to 'to' peg
```

10.9 Modify the *hanoi.cpp* program from the previous exercise to time how long it takes for different numbers of disks from 1 to 25. Comment out (put // before each statement) the statements that print disk moves so that the number of recursive calls is timed. Use a global variable that is incremented each time `Hanoi` executes. Print the value of this variable for each number of disks so that the total number of disk moves is printed, along with the time it takes to move the disks. This can lead to a new measure of computer performance: **DIPS,** for "disks per second."

10.10 A square matrix `a` is symmetric if `a[j][k] == a[k][j]` for all values of `j` and `k`; that is, the matrix is symmetric with respect to the main diagonal from (0,0) to $(n-1, n-1)$ for an $n \times n$ matrix. Write a `bool`-valued function that returns true if its matrix parameter is symmetric and false otherwise.

10.11 The *N*-queens problem has a long history in mathematics and computer science. The problem is posed in two ways:

- Can *N* queens be placed on an $N \times N$ chess board so that no two queens attack each other?
- How many ways can *N* queens be placed on an $N \times N$ board so that no two queens attack each other?

In chess, queens attack each other if they're on the same row, the same column, or the same diagonal. The sample output below shows one way to place eight queens so that no two attack each other.

```
                         O U T P U T

prompt> nqueens
size of board:   between 2 and 12: 8
X.......
......X.
....X...
.......X
.X......
...X....
.....X..
..X.....
```

Solving the *N*-queens problem uses an algorithmic technique called **backtracking** that's related to the method used for generating permutations recursively in Section 10.3.3. The general idea of backtracking is to make a tentative attempt to solve a problem and then proceed recursively. If the tentative attempt fails, it is undone or *backtracked*, and the next way of solving the problem is tried.

In the *N*-queens problem, we try to place a queen in each column. When the backtracking function is called, queens are successfully placed in columns 0 through `col`, and the function tries to place a queen in column `col+1`. There are *N* possible ways to place a queen, one for each row, and each one is tried in succession. If a queen can be placed in the row, it is placed and a recursive call for the next column tries to complete the solution. If the recursive call fails, the just-placed queen is "unplaced," or removed, and the next row tried for a placement. If all rows fail, the function fails. The *backtracking* comes when the function undoes an attempt that doesn't yield a solution. A partial class declaration for solving the *N*-queens problem is given below. Complete the class and then modify it to return the total number of solutions rather than just printing the first solution found.

Program 10.24 nqueenpartial.cpp

```
class Queens
{
  public:
    Queens(int size);
    bool Solve();                    // return true if solvable
    void Print(ostream& out) const;  // print the last board
  private:
    // helper functions
    bool NoQueensAttackingAt(int r, int c) const;
    bool SolveAtCol(int col);

    tmatrix<bool> myBoard;           // the board
};

bool Queens::NoQueensAttackingAt(int r, int c) const
// post: return true if row clear and diagonals crossing at
//       (row,col) clear

bool Queens::Solve()
// post: return true if n queens can be placed
{
    return SolveAtCol(0);
}

bool Queens::SolveAtCol(int col)
// pre: queens placed at columns 0,1,...,col-1
// post: returns true if queen can be placed in column col
//       if col == size of board, then n queens are placed
{
    int k;
    int rows = myBoard.numrows();
    if (col == rows) return true;   // N queens placed
    for(k=0; k < rows; k++)
    {   if (NoQueensAttackingAt(k,col))  // can place here?
        {   myBoard[k][col] = true;       // try it
            if (SolveAtCol(col+1))        // recurse
            {    return true;
            }
            myBoard[k][col] = false;      // backtrack
        }
    }
    return false;
}
```

```
int main()
{
    int size = PromptRange("size of board: ",2,12);
    Queens nq(size);
    if (nq.Solve())
    {   nq.Print(cout);
    }
    else
    {   cout << "no solution found" << endl;
    }
    return 0;
}
```
nqueenpartial.cpp

10.12 An image can be represented as a two-dimensional matrix of pixels, each of which can be off (white) or on (black). Color and gray-scale images can be represented using multivalued pixels; for example, numbers from 0 to 255 can represent different shades of gray. A **bitmap** is a two-dimensional matrix of 0s and 1s, where 0 corresponds to an off pixel and 1 corresponds to an on pixel. Instead of using the class `CharBitMap`, for example, the following matrix of `int`s represents a bitmap that represents a 9×8 picture of a < sign:

```
0 0 0 0 0 1 1 0
0 0 0 0 1 1 0 0
0 0 0 1 1 0 0 0
0 0 1 1 0 0 0 0
0 1 1 0 0 0 0 0
0 0 1 1 0 0 0 0
0 0 0 1 1 0 0 0
0 0 0 0 1 1 0 0
0 0 0 0 0 1 1 0
```

You can use the class `CharBitMap` used in Program 10.22, *bitmapdemo.cpp*, or you can create a new version of the class for use with the graphics package in How to H. Write a client program that provides the user with a menu of choices for manipulating an image:

- Read an image from a file.
- Write an image to a file.
- Invert the current image (change black to white and vice versa).
- Enlarge an image.
- Enhance the image using median filtering (described below).

Enlarging an Image. A bitmap image can be enlarged by expanding it horizontally, vertically, or in both directions. Expanding an image in place (i.e., without using an auxiliary array) requires some planning. In Figure 10.11 an image is shown partially expanded by three vertically and by two horizontally. By beginning the expansion in the lower-right corner as shown, the image can be expanded in place—that is, *without* the use of an auxiliary array or bitmap.

Enhancing an Image. Sometimes an image can be "noisy" because of the way in which it is transmitted; for example, a TV picture may have static or "snow." Image

Figure 10.11 Enlarging a bitmap image.

enhancement is a method that takes out noise by changing pixel values according to the values of the neighboring pixels. You should use a method of enhancement based on setting a pixel to the median value of those in its "neighborhood." Figure 10.12 shows a 3-neighborhood and a 5-neighborhood of the middle pixel, whose value is 28. Using **median filtering,** the 28 in the middle is replaced by the median of the values in its neighborhood. The nine values in the 3-neighborhood are (10 10 12 25 25 28 28 32 32). The median, or middle, value is 25—there are four values above 25 and four values below 25. The values in the 5-neighborhood are (10 10 10 10 10 10 12 12 12 18 18 18 25 25 25 25 25 25 32 32 32 32 32 32 32), and again the median value is 25 because there are 12 values above and 12 values below 25. The easiest way to find the median of a list of values is to sort them and take the middle element.

Pixels near the border of an image don't have "complete" neighborhoods. These pixels are replaced by the median of the partial neighborhood that is completely on the grid of pixels. One way of thinking about this is to take, for example, a 3 × 3 grid and slide it over an image so that every pixel is centered in the grid. Each pixel is replaced by the median of the pixels of the image that are contained in the sliding grid. This requires using an extra array to store the median values, which are then copied back to the original image when the median filtering has finished. This is necessary so that the

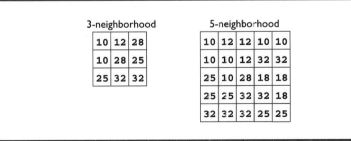

Figure 10.12 Neighborhoods for median filtering.

Figure 10.13   Median filtering of a noisy image.

pixels are replaced by median values from the original image, not from the partially reconstructed and filtered image.

Applying a 3×3 median filter to the image on the left in Figure 10.13 results in the image on the right (these images look better on the screen than they do on paper).

Sorting, Templates, and Generic Programming 11

No transcendent ability is required in order to make useful discoveries in science; the edifice of
science needs its masons, bricklayers, and common labourers as well as its foremen,
master-builders, and architects. In art nothing worth doing can be done without genius; in
science even a very moderate capacity can contribute to a supreme achievement.

BERTRAND RUSSELL
Mysticism and Logic

Many human activities require collections of items to be put into some particular order.
The post office sorts mail by ZIP code for efficient delivery; telephone books are sorted
by name to facilitate finding phone numbers; and hands of cards are sorted by suit to
make it easier to go fish. **Sorting** is a task performed well by computers; the study of
different methods of sorting is also intrinsically interesting from a theoretical standpoint.
In Chapter 8 we saw how fast binary search is, but binary search requires a sorted list
as well as random access. In this chapter we'll study different sorting algorithms and
methods for comparing these algorithms. We'll extend the idea of conforming interfaces
we studied in Chapter 7 (see Section 7.2) and see how conforming interfaces are used in
template classes and functions. We'll study sorting from a theoretical perspective, but
we'll also emphasize techniques for making sorting and other algorithmic programming
more efficient in practice using **generic programming** and **function objects**.

11.1 Sorting an Array

There are several elementary sorting algorithms, details of which can be found in books
on algorithms; Knuth [Knu98b] is an encyclopedic reference. Some of the elementary
algorithms are much better than others, both in terms of performance and in terms of
ease of coding. Contrary to what some books on computer programming claim, there are
large differences between these elementary algorithms. In addition, these elementary
algorithms are more than good enough for sorting reasonably large vectors,[1] *provided
that the good elementary algorithms are used.*

In particular, there are three "classic" simple sorting algorithms. Each of these sorts
is a **quadratic** algorithm. We'll define quadratic more carefully later, but quadratic
algorithms behave like a quadratic curve $y = x^2$ in mathematics: if a vector of 1,000
elements is sorted in 4 seconds, a vector of 2,000 elements will be sorted in 16 seconds
using a quadratic algorithm. We'll study sorting algorithms that are more efficient than
these quadratic sorts, but the quadratic sorts are a good place to start.

The three basic sorting algorithms are

---

[1]What is "reasonably large"? The answer, as it often is, is "It depends"—on the kind of element sorted,
the kind of computer being used, and on how fast "pretty fast" is.

■   Selection sort.

■   Insertion sort.

■   Bubble sort.

We'll develop selection sort in this section. You've already seen insertion sort in Section 8.3.4, where an element is inserted into an already-sorted vector and the vector is kept in sorted order. However, a few words are needed about bubble sort.

> **Program Tip 11.1:   Under *no* circumstances should you use bubble sort.**
> Bubble sort is the slowest of the elementary sorts, for reasons we'll explore as an exercise. Bubble sort is worth knowing about only so that you can tell your friends what a poor sort it is. Although interesting from a theoretical perspective, bubble sort has no practical use in programming on a computer with a single processor.

11.1.1   Selection Sort

The basic algorithm behind selection sort is quite simple and is similar to the method used in shuffling tracks of a CD explored and programmed in *shuffle.cpp,* Program 8.4. To sort from smallest to largest in a vector named A, the following method is used:

1.   Find the smallest entry in A. Swap it with the first element A[0]. Now the smallest entry is in the first location of the vector.

2.   Considering only vector locations A[1], A[2], A[3], ...; find the smallest of these and swap it with A[1]. Now the first two entries of A are in order.

3.   Continue this process by finding the smallest element of the remaining vector elements and swapping it appropriately.

This algorithm is outlined in code in the function SelectSort of Program 11.1, which sorts an int vector. Each time through the loop in the function SelectSort, the index of the smallest entry of those not yet in place (from k to the end of the vector) is determined by calling the function MinIndex. This function (which will be shown shortly) returns the index, or location, of the smallest element, which is then stored/swapped into location k. This process is diagrammed in Figure 11.1. The shaded boxes represent vector elements that are in their final position. Although only five elements are shaded in the last "snapshot," if five out of six elements are in the correct position, the sixth element must be in the correct position as well.

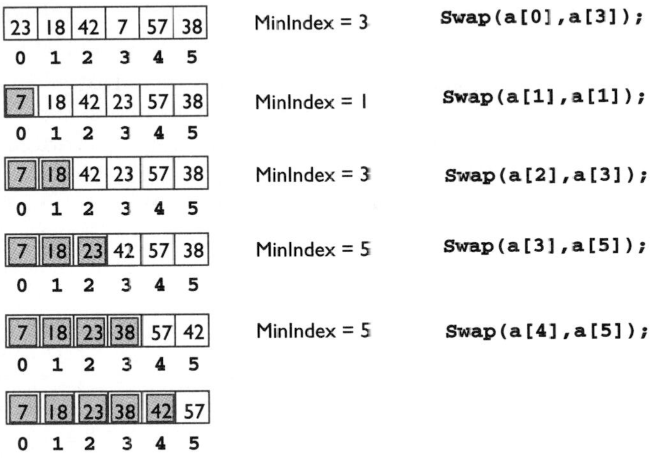

23	18	42	7	57	38		MinIndex = 3	`Swap(a[0],a[3]);`
0	1	2	3	4	5			

| 7 | 18 | 42 | 23 | 57 | 38 | | MinIndex = 1 | `Swap(a[1],a[1]);` |
| 0 | 1 | 2 | 3 | 4 | 5 | | | |

| 7 | 18 | 42 | 23 | 57 | 38 | | MinIndex = 3 | `Swap(a[2],a[3]);` |
| 0 | 1 | 2 | 3 | 4 | 5 | | | |

| 7 | 18 | 23 | 42 | 57 | 38 | | MinIndex = 5 | `Swap(a[3],a[5]);` |
| 0 | 1 | 2 | 3 | 4 | 5 | | | |

| 7 | 18 | 23 | 38 | 57 | 42 | | MinIndex = 5 | `Swap(a[4],a[5]);` |
| 0 | 1 | 2 | 3 | 4 | 5 | | | |

| 7 | 18 | 23 | 38 | 42 | 57 | |
| 0 | 1 | 2 | 3 | 4 | 5 | |

Figure 11.1 Selection sort.

Program 11.1 selectsort1.cpp

```
#include "tvector.h"
int MinIndex(tvector<int> & a, int first, int last);
// precondition: 0 <= first, first <= last
// postcondition: returns k such that a[k] <= a[j], j in [first..last]
//                i.e., index of minimal element in a

void Swap(int & a, int & b);
// postcondition: a and b interchanged/swapped

void SelectSort(tvector<int> & a)
// precondition: a contains a.size() elements
// postcondition: elements of a are sorted in nondecreasing order
{
    int k, index, numElts = a.size();

    // invariant: a[0]..a[k-1] in final position
    for(k=0; k < numElts - 1; k+=1)
    {   index = MinIndex(a,k,numElts - 1);   // find min element
        Swap(a[k],a[index]);
    }
}
```

selectsort1.cpp

Each time the loop test `k < numElts - 1` is evaluated, the statement "elements `a[0]..a[k-1]` are in their final position" is true. Recall that any statement that is true each time a loop test is evaluated is called a **loop invariant.** In this case the statement is true because the first time the loop test is evaluated, the range $0 \ldots k-1$ is $[0 \ldots -1]$, which is an empty range, consisting of no vector elements. As shown in Figure 11.1, the shaded vector elements indicate that the statement holds after each iteration of the loop. The final time the loop test is evaluated, the value of k will be numElts - 1, the last valid vector index. Since the statement holds (it holds each time the test is evaluated), the vector must be sorted. The function MinIndex is straightforward to write:

```
int MinIndex(const tvector<int> & a, int first, int last)
// pre: 0 <= first, first <= last
// post: returns index of minimal element in a[first..last]
{
    int smallIndex = first;
    int k;
    for(k=first+1; k <= last; k++)
    {   if (a[k] < a[smallIndex] )
        {   smallIndex = k;
        }
    }
    return smallIndex;
}
```

MinIndex finds the minimal element in an array; it's similar to code discussed in Section 6.4 for finding largest and smallest values. The first location of the vector a is the initial value of smallIndex, then all other locations are examined. If a smaller entry is found, the value of smallIndex is changed to record the location of the new smallest item.

Program 11.2 selectsort2.cpp

```
void SelectSort(tvector<int> & a)
// pre: a contains a.size() elements
// post: elements of a are sorted in nondecreasing order
{
    int j,k,temp,minIndex,numElts = a.size();

    // invariant: a[0]..a[k-1] in final position
    for(k=0; k < numElts - 1; k++)
    {   minIndex = k;                  // minimal element index
        for(j=k+1; j < numElts; j++)
        {   if (a[j] < a[minIndex])
            {   minIndex = j;          // new min, store index
            }
        }
        temp = a[k];                   // swap min and k-th elements
        a[k] = a[minIndex];
        a[minIndex] = temp;
    }
}
```

selectsort2.cpp

The function `MinIndex`, combined with `Swap` and `SelectSort`, yields a complete implementation of selection sort. Sometimes it's convenient to have all the code in one function rather than spread over three functions. This is certainly possible and leads to the code shown in *selectsort2.cpp,* Program 11.2. However, as you develop code, it's often easier to test and debug when separate functions are used. This allows each piece of code to be tested separately.

The code in Program 11.2 works well for sorting a vector of numbers, but what about sorting vectors of strings or some other kind of element? If two vector elements can be compared, then the vector can be sorted based on such comparisons. A vector of strings can be sorted using the same code provided in the function `SelectSort`; the only difference in the functions is the type of the first parameter and the type of the local variable `temp`, as follows:

```
void SelectSort(tvector<string> & a)
// pre: a contains a.size() elements
// post: elements of a are sorted in nondecreasing order
{
    int j, k, minIndex, numElts = a.size();
    string temp;
    // code here doesn't change
}
```

Both this function and `SelectSort` in *selectsort2.cpp* could be used in the same program since the parameter lists are different. In previous chapters we overloaded the + operator so that we could use it both to add numbers and to concatenate strings. We've also used the function `tostring` from *strutils.h* (see How to G) to convert both doubles and ints to strings; there are two functions with the same name but different parameters. In the same way, we can overload function names. Different functions with the same name can be used in the same program provided that the parameter lists of the functions are different. In these examples the function `Sort` is overloaded using three different

kinds of vectors. `DoStuff` is overloaded because there are two versions with different parameter lists. The names of the parameters do not matter; only the types of the parameters are important in resolving which overloaded function is actually called. It is *not* possible, for example, to use the two versions of

---

Syntax: Function overloading

```
void Sort(tvector<string>& a);
void Sort(tvector<double>& a);
void Sort(tvector<int>& a);
int DoStuff(int a, int b);
int DoStuff(int a, int b, int c);
```

`FindRoots` below in the same program because the parameter lists are the same. The different return types are not sufficient to distinguish the functions:

```
int    FindRoots(double one, double two);
double FindRoots(double first, double second);
```

Shafi Goldwasser *(b. 1958)*

Shafi Goldwasser is Professor of Computer Science at MIT. She works in the area of computer science known as **theory,** but her work has practical implications in the area of secure cryptographic protocols—methods that ensure that information can be reliably transmitted between two parties without electronic eavesdropping. In particular, she is interested in using randomness in designing algorithms. She was awarded the first Gödel prize in theoretical computer science for her work.

So-called **randomized algorithms** involve (simulated) coin flips in making decisions. In [Wei94] a randomized method of giving quizzes is described. Suppose a teacher wants to ensure that students do a take-home quiz, but does not want to grade quizzes every day. A teacher can give out quizzes in one class, then in the next class flip a coin to determine whether the quizzes are handed in. In the long run, this results in quizzes being graded 50 percent of the time, but students will need to do all the quizzes. Goldwasser is a coinventor of **zero-knowledge interactive proof protocols.** This mouthful is described in [Har92] as follows:

> *Suppose Alice wants to convince Bob that she knows a certain secret, but she does not want Bob to end up knowing the secret himself. This sounds impossible: How do you convince someone that you know, say, what color tie the president of the United States is wearing right now, without somehow divulging that priceless piece of information to the other person or to some third party?*

Using zero-knowledge interactive proofs it is possible to do this. The same concepts make it possible to develop smart cards that would let people be admitted to a secure environment without letting anyone know exactly who has entered. In some colleges, cards are used to gain admittance to dormitories. Smart cards could be used to gain admittance without allowing student movement to be tracked.

Goldwasser has this to say about choosing what area to work in:

> *Choosing a research area, like most things in life, is not the same as solving an optimization problem. Work on what you like, what feels right. I know of no other way to end up doing creative work.*

For more information see [EL94].

11.1.2   Insertion Sort

We've already discussed the code for insertion sort and used it in *stocks2.cpp*, a program discussed in Section 8.3.4; the code is shown in that section. The invariant for selection sort states that elements with indexes $0 \ldots k - 1$ are in their final position. In contrast, the insertion sort invariant states that elements with indexes $0 \ldots k - 1$ are sorted relative to each other but are not (necessarily) in their final position. Program 11.3 shows the code for insertion sort, and Figure 11.2 shows a vector being sorted during each iteration of the outer `for` loop.

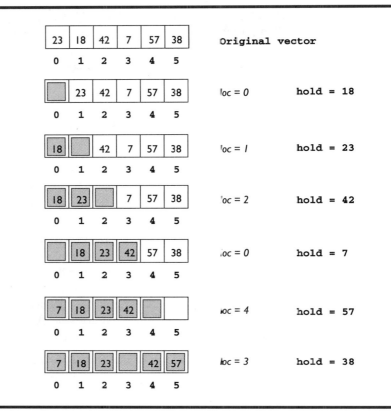

Figure 11.2 Insertion sort.

To reestablish the invariant, the inner `while` loop shifts elements until the location where `hold` (originally `a[k]`) belongs is determined. If `hold` is already in its correct position relative to the elements that precede it, that is, it's larger than the element to its left, then the inner `while` loop doesn't iterate at all. This is illustrated in Figure 11.2 when `hold` has the values 23, 42, and 57. In those cases no vector elements are shifted. When `hold` has the value 7, all the elements that precede it in the vector are larger, so all are shifted and the element 7 is stored in the first (index zero) vector location. Although the outer loops in Program 11.2 and Program 11.3 iterate the same number of times, it's possible for the inner loop of the insertion sort (Program 11.3) to iterate fewer times than the corresponding inner loop of the selection sort (Program 11.2).

Program 11.3 insertsort.cpp

```cpp
void InsertSort(tvector<string> & a)
// precondition: a contains a.size() elements
// postcondition: elements of a are sorted in nondecreasing order
```

```
{
    int k,loc, numElts = a.size();

    // invariant: a[0]..a[k-1] sorted
    for(k=1; k < numElts; k++)
    {   string hold = a[k];      // insert this element
        loc = k;                 // location for insertion

        // shift elements to make room for hold/a[k]
        while (0 < loc  && hold < a[loc-1])
        {   a[loc] = a[loc-1];
            loc--;
        }
        a[loc] = hold;
    }
}
```

insertsort.cpp

We'll discuss why both insertion sort and selection sort are called quadratic sorts in more detail in Section 11.4. However, the graph of execution times for the quadratic sorts given in Figure 11.3 provides a clue; the shape of each curve is quadratic. These timings are from a single run of *timequadsorts.cpp*, Program 11.4, shown below. For more accurate empirical results you would need to run the program with different vectors, that is, for more than one trial at each vector size. A more thorough empirical analysis of sorts is explored in the exercises for this chapter.

Program 11.4 timequadsorts.cpp

```
#include <iostream>
#include <string>
using namespace std;
#include "ctimer.h"
#include "tvector.h"
#include "sortall.h"
#include "randgen.h"
#include "prompt.h"

// compare running times of quadratic sorts

void Shuffle(tvector<int> & a, int count)
// precondition: a has space for count elements
// postcondition: a contains 0..count-1 randomly shuffled
{
    RandGen gen;     // for random # generator
    int randIndex,k;

    // fill with values1 0..count-1
    for(k=0; k < count; k++)
    {   a[k] = k;
    }
    // choose random index from k..count-1 and interchange with k
    for(k=0; k < count - 1; k++)
    {   randIndex = gen.RandInt(k,count-1);   // random index
        Swap(a,k,randIndex);                  // swap in sortall.h
```

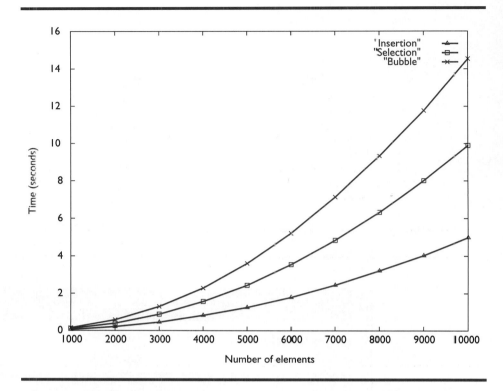

Figure 11.3 Execution times for quadratic sorts of `int` vectors on a Pentium II/300 running Windows NT.

```
    }
}

int main()
{
    int size,minSize,maxSize,incr; // sort minSize, minSize+incr, ... maxSize
    CTimer timer;

    cout << "min and max size of vector: ";
    cin >> minSize >> maxSize;
    incr =  PromptRange("increment in vector size",1,1000);

    cout << endl << "n\tinsert\tselect\tbubble" << endl << endl;
    for(size=minSize; size <= maxSize; size += incr)
    {   tvector<int> copy(size), original(size);
        cout << size << "\t";
        Shuffle(original,size);

        copy = original;     // sort using insertion sort
        timer.Start();
        InsertSort(copy,copy.size());
        timer.Stop();
```

```
        cout << timer.ElapsedTime() << "\t";

        copy = original;      // sort using selection sort
        timer.Start();
        SelectSort(copy,copy.size());
        timer.Stop();
        cout << timer.ElapsedTime() << "\t";

        copy = original;      // sort using bubble sort
        timer.Start();
        BubbleSort(copy,copy.size());
        timer.Stop();
        cout << timer.ElapsedTime() << endl;
    }
    return 0;
}
```
                                                                    timequadsorts.cpp

OUTPUT

```
prompt> timequadsorts
min and max size of vector: 1000 10000
increment in vector size between 1 and 1000: 1000

n       insert  select  bubble

1000    0.04    0.1     0.14
2000    0.2     0.381   0.571
3000    0.44    0.871   1.282
4000    0.811   1.553   2.273
5000    1.232   2.423   3.585
6000    1.773   3.525   5.183
7000    2.433   4.817   7.12
8000    3.195   6.299   9.313
9000    4.006   7.982   11.736
10000   4.958   9.864   14.501
```

Pause to Reflect

11.1 What changes are necessary in Program 11.2, *selectsort2.cpp*, so that the vector a is sorted into decreasing order rather than into increasing order? For example, why is it a good idea to change the name of the identifier minIndex, although the names of variables don't influence how a program executes?

11.2 Why is k < numElts - 1 the test of the outer for loop in the selection sort code instead of k < numElts? Could the test be changed to the latter?

11.3 How many swaps are made when selection sort is used to sort an *n*-element vector? How many times is the statement `if (a[j] < a[minIndex])` executed when selection sort is used to sort a 5-element vector, a 10-element vector, and an *n*-element vector?

11.4 How can you use the sorting functions to "sort" a number so that its digits are in increasing order? For example, 7,216 becomes 1,267 when sorted. Describe what to do and then write a function that sorts a number (you can call one of the sorting functions from this section if that helps).

11.5 If insertion sort is used to sort a vector that's already sorted, how many times is the statement `a[loc] = a[loc-1];` executed?

11.6 If the vector `counts` from Program 8.3, *letters.cpp*, is passed to the function `SelectSort`, why won't the output of the program be correct?

11.7 In the output from *timequadsorts.cpp*, Program 11.4, the ratio of the timings when the size of the vector doubles from 4,000 elements to 8,000 is given in Table 11.1.

Table 11.1 Timing quadratic sorts.

Sort	4,000 elts.	8,000 elts.	Ratio
insertion	0.811	3.195	3.939
select	1.553	6.299	4.056
bubble	3.585	9.313	4.097

Assuming the ratio holds consistently (rounded to 4), how long will it take each quadratic algorithm to sort a vector of 16,000 elements? 32,000 elements? 1,000,000 elements?

11.2 Function Templates

Although it is possible to overload a function name, the sorting functions in the previous sections are not ideal candidates for function overloading. If we write a separate function to use selection sort with a vector of `ints`, a vector of `strings`, and a vector of `doubles` the code that would appear in each function is nearly identical. The only differences in the code would be in the definition of the variable `temp` and in the kind of `tvector` passed to the function. Consider what might happen if a more efficient sorting algorithm is required. The code in each of the three functions must be removed, and the code for the more efficient algorithm inserted. Maintaining three versions of the function makes it much more likely that errors will eventually creep into the code because it is difficult to ensure that whenever a modification is made to one sorting function, it is made to all of the sorting functions (see Program Tip. 4.1).

Fortunately, a mechanism exists in C++ that allows code to be reused rather than replicated. We have already used this mechanism behind the scenes in the implementation of the `tvector` class and the `CList` class.

A **function template**, sometimes called a **templated function,** can be used when different types are part of the parameter list and the types conform to an interface used in the function body. For example, to sort a vector of a type T using selection sort we must be able to compare values of type T using the relational operator < since that's how elements are compared. We wouldn't expect to be able to sort Dice objects since they're not comparable using relational operators. We should be able to sort ClockTime objects (see *clockt.h*, Program 9.9) since they're comparable using operator <. The sorting functions require objects that conform to an interface of being comparable using operator <. A templated function allows us to capture this interface in code so that we can write one function that works with any type that can be compared. We'll study templates in detail, building toward them with a series of examples.

11.2.1   Printing a `tvector` with a Function Template

Program 11.5, *sortwlen.cpp*, reads a file and tracks all words and word lengths. Both words and lengths are sorted using the templated function SelectSort from *sortall.h*. A templated function Print that prints both string and int vectors is shown in *sortwlen.cpp*.

Program 11.5   sortwlen.cpp

```cpp
#include <icstream>
#include <fstream>
#include <string>
using namespace std;
#include "tvector.h"
#include "prompt.h"
#include "sortall.h"

// illustrates templates, read words, sort words, print words

template <class Type>
void Print(const tvector<Type>& list, int first, int last)
// post: list[first]...list[last] printed, one per line
{
    int k;
    for(k=first; k <= last; k++)
    {   cout << list[k] << endl;
    }
}

int main()
{
    tvector<string> wordList;
    tvector<int>    lengthList;
    string filename = PromptString("filename: ");
    string word;
    ifstream input(filename.c_str());

    while (input >> word)
```

```
{    wordList.push_back(word);
     lengthList.push_back(word.length());
}
SelectSort(wordList,wordList.size());
SelectSort(lengthList,lengthList.size());

Print(wordList,wordList.size()-5,wordList.size()-1);
Print(lengthList,lengthList.size()-5,lengthList.size()-1);

return 0;
}
```

sortwlen.cpp

```
                    O U T P U T

prompt > sortwlen
filename: poe.txt
your
your
your
your
your
16
16
18
18
19
```

Just as not all types of vectors can be sorted, not all types of vectors can be printed. The function Print in *sortwlen.cpp* expects a vector whose type conforms to the interface of being insertable onto a stream using operator <<. Consider an attempt to print a vector of vectors.

```
tvector<tvector<int> > ivlist;
ivlist.push_back(lengthList);
Print(ivlist,0,1);
```

The first two lines compile without trouble, but the attempt to pass ivlist to Print fails because the type tvector<int> does not conform to the expected interface: there is no overloaded operator << for tvector<int> objects. The error messages generated by different compilers vary from informative to incomprehensible.

The error message from Visual C++ 6.0 is very informative:

```
sortwlen.cpp(17) : error C2679: binary '<<' : no operator
defined which takes a right-hand operand of type
'const class tvector<int>'
```

The error message from the Metrowerks Codewarrior compiler is less informative:

```
Error    : illegal operand                    __
sortwlen.cpp line 17   {   cout << list[k] << endl;
```

The error message from the Linux g++ compiler is informative, though difficult to comprehend:

```
'void Print<tvector<int>>(const class
  tvector<tvector<int> >&)': sortwlen.cpp:17:
  no match for '_IO_ostream_withassign
  & << const tvector<int> &'
```

In general, a call of a templated function fails if the type of argument passed can't be used in the function because the expected conforming interface doesn't apply. What that means in the example of Print is spelled out clearly by the error messages: the type const tvector<int> can't be inserted onto a stream, and stream insertion using operator << is the interface expected of vector elements when Print is called.

One reason the error messages can be hard to understand is that the compiler *catches* the error and indicates its source in the templated function: line 17 in the example of Print above (see the error message). However, the error *is caused* by a call of the templated function, what's termed the template function **instantiation**, and you must determine what call or instantiation causes the error. In a small program this can be straightforward, but in a large program you may not even be aware that a function (or class) is templated. Since the error messages don't show the call, finding the real source can be difficult.

> **Program Tip 11.2:** If the compiler indicates an error in a templated function or class, look carefully at the error message and try to find the template instantiation that causes the problem. The instantiation that causes the problem may be difficult to find, but searching for the name of the class or function in which the error occurs using automated Find/Search capabilities may help.

A function is declared as a templated function when it is preceded by the word **template** followed by an angle bracket–delimited list of class identifiers that serve as type parameters. At least one of the type parameters must be used in the function's parameter list. Any name can be the template parameter, such as Type, T, and U as shown in the syntax diagram. This name can be used for the return type, as the type (or part of a type) in the parameter list, or as the type of a local variable in the function body. It is possible to have more than one template class parameter. The function doThat in the syntax box has two template parameters, T and U. DoThat could be called as follows:

> **Syntax: Function template**
>
> ```
> template <class T> void doIt(T& t);
>
> template <class Type>
> Type minElt(const tvector<Type>);
>
> template <class T, class U>
> void doThat(CList<T> t, CList<U> u);
> ```

```
doThat(cons(3,CList<int>()),
       cons(string("help"),CList<string>()));
```

Here the template parameter T is **bound to** or **unified with** the type int, and the template type U is bound to string. If the template instantiation succeeds, all uses of T and U in the body of the function doThat will be supported by the types int and string, respectively.

11.2.2 Function Templates and Iterators

We've seen many different iterator classes: WordStreamIterator for iterating over each word in a file, CListIterator for iterating over the contents of a list, RandomWalk for iterating over a simulated random walk, and even Permuter for generating permutations of an int vector. Because all these classes adhere to the same naming convention for the iterating methods, namely Init, HasMore, Next, and Current, we can use the iterators in a general way in templated functions.

We'll use a simple example to illustrate how a templated function can count the number of elements in any iterator. We're using this example not because it's powerful but because it's the first step toward a very powerful technique of writing and using templated functions.

The function CountIter in Program 11.6, *countiter.cpp*, counts the number of elements in an iterator. We'll call the function in two ways: to count the number of words in a file and to calculate *n*! by generating every permutation of an *n*-element vector and counting the number of permutations. Counting words in a file this way is reasonably efficient; calculating *n*! is not efficient at all.

Program 11.6 countiter.cpp

```
#include <iostream>
#include <string>
```

```
using namespace std;

#include "permuter.h"
#include "worditer.h"
#include "tvector.h"
#include "prompt.h"

template <class Type>
int CountIter(Type& it)
{
    int count = 0;
    for(it.Init(); it.HasMore(); it.Next())
    {   count++;
    }
    return count;
}

int main()
{
    string filename = PromptString("filename: ");
    int k,num = PromptRange("factorial: ",1,8);
    tvector<int> vec;
    WordStreamIterator witer;

    for(k=0; k < num; k++)
    {   vec.push_back(k);
    }
    witer.Open(filename);

    cout << "# words = " << CountIter(witer) << endl;
    cout << num << " factorial = " << CountIter(Permuter(vec)) << endl;

    return 0;
}
```

countiter.cpp

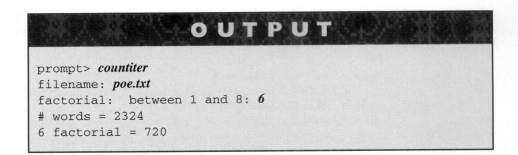

```
prompt> counter
filename: poe.txt
factorial:  between 1 and 8: 6
# words = 2324
6 factorial = 720
```

The parameter `it` used in the function `CountIter` must conform to the iterator interface we use in this book. The variable `it` is used as an object that supports methods `Init`, `HasMore`, and `Next`. Since the function `Current` isn't used in `CountIter`, we could pass an object to `CountIter` that has a method named `GetCurrent` instead of `Current`. Since there is no call `it.Current()`, `Current` is not part of the interface that the compiler expects to find when processing an argument passed in a call to CountIter.[2]

The method Current is used in UniqueStrings in Program 11.7 to count the number of unique strings in an iterator. We use it to determine the number of different strings in a file and in a list constructed from the words in the file.

Program 11.7   uniqueiter.cpp

```cpp
#include <iostream>
#include <string>
using namespace std;

#include "clist.h"
#include "worditer.h"
#include "stringset.h"
#include "prompt.h"

template <class Type>
int UniqueStrings(Type& iter)
// post: return # unique strings in iter
{
    StringSet uni;
    for(iter.Init(); iter.HasMore(); iter.Next())
    {    uni.insert(iter.Current());
    }
    return uni.size();
}

int main()
{
    string filename = PromptString("filename: ");
    WordStreamIterator witer;
    witer.Open(filename);
    CList<string> slist;

    for(witer.Init(); witer.HasMore(); witer.Next())
    {    slist = cons(witer.Current(),slist);
    }

    cout << "unique from WordIterator = "
         << UniqueStrings(witer) << endl;
    cout << "unique from CList = "
         << UniqueStrings(CListIterator<string>(slist)) << endl;
    return 0;
}
```

uniqueiter.cpp

---

[2] The function Permuter::Current is a void function; it returns a vector as a reference parameter. It doesn't have the same interface as other Current functions, which aren't void but return a value.

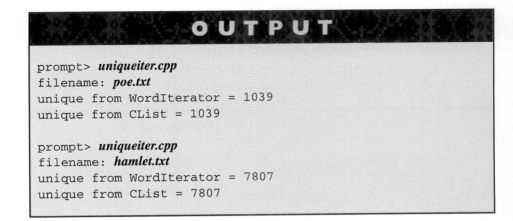

```
prompt> uniqueiter.cpp
filename: poe.txt
unique from WordIterator = 1039
unique from CList = 1039

prompt> uniqueiter.cpp
filename: hamlet.txt
unique from WordIterator = 7807
unique from CList = 7807
```

Although only standard iterator methods are used with parameter `iter`, the object returned by `iter.Current()` is inserted into a `StringSet`. This means that any iterator passed to `UniqueStrings` must conform to the expected interface of returning a `string` value from `Current`. For example, if we try to pass an iterator in which `Current` returns an `int`, as in the call below that uses a `CListIterator` for an `int` list, an error message will be generated by the compiler when it tries to instantiate the templated function.

```
cout << UniqueStrings(
              CListIterator<int>(CList<int>::EMPTY)
                    ) << endl;
```

The error message generated by Visual C++ 6.0 is reasonably informative in telling us where to look for a problem:

```
itertempdemo.cpp(16) : error C2664: 'insert' :
cannot convert parameter 1 from 'int' to
'const class std::basic_string<char,struct
std::char_traits<char>,class std::allocator<char> > &'
```

The call to `insert` fails, and the error message says something about converting an `int` to something related to a "basic_string". The `basic_string` class is used to implement the standard class `string`; the class `basic_string` is templated to make it simpler to change from an underlying use of `char` to a type that uses Unicode, for example. This is a great idea in practice, but leads to error messages that are very difficult to understand if you don't know that identifier `string` is actually a `typedef` for a complicated templated class.[3]

---

[3]The actual typedef for string is `typedef basic_string<char, char_traits<char>, allocator<char> > string;`, which isn't worth trying to understand completely.

> **Program Tip 11.3:** **The name `string` is actually a typedef for a templated class called `basic_string`, and the template instantiation is somewhat complicated.** If you see an error message that you can't understand, generated by either the compiler or a debugger, look carefully to see if the error is about the class `basic_string`; such errors are almost always caused by a problem with `string` objects or functions.

The function templates we've seen for sorting, printing, and iterating are powerful because they generalize an interface. Using function templates we can write functions that use an interface without knowing what class will actually be used to satisfy the interface. We'll explore an important use of templated functions in Section 11.3, where we'll see how it's possible to sort by different criteria with one function.

11.2.3 Function Templates, Reuse, and Code Bloat

Function templates help avoid duplicated code because a templated function is written once but can be instantiated many times. The template function `Print` in *sortwlen.cpp*, Program 11.5, is not compiled into object code as other functions and classes are when the program is compiled. Instead, when `Print` is instantiated, the compiler generates object code for the specific instantiation. If a templated function is never called/instantiated in a program, then it doesn't generate any code. A nontemplated function is always compiled into code regardless of whether it's called. The word *template* makes sense here; a templated function works as a function generator, generating different versions of the function when the template is instantiated. However, different code is generated each time the function is instantiated with a different type. For example, if the templated `Print` function is called from three different statements using `int` vectors, two statements using `string` vectors, and one statement using `Date` vectors, then three different functions will be instantiated and emit compiled object code: one each for `int`, `string`, and `Date`.

> **Program Tip 11.4:** **Function templates can generate larger-than-expected object files when they're instantiated with several types in the same program.** A function template saves programmer resources and time because one function is written and maintained rather than several. However, a function template can lead to **code bloat**, where a program is very large because of the number of template instantiations. Smart compilers may be able to do some code sharing, but code bloat can be a real problem.

11.3 Function Objects

In the program *sortwlen.cpp*, Program 11.5, we used a templated function `SelectSort` to sort vectors of `strings` and `ints`. The vector of `strings` was sorted alphabetically.

Suppose we need to generate a list of words in order by length of word, with shortest words like "a" coming first, and longer words like "acknowledgment" coming last. We can certainly do this by changing the comparison of vector elements to use a string's length. In the function `SelectSort`, for example, we would change the comparison

```
if (a[j] < a[minIndex])
```

to a comparison using string lengths:

```
if (a[j].length() < a[minIndex].length())
```

This solution does not generalize to other sorting methods. We may want to sort in reverse order, "zebra" before "aardvark"; or to ignore case when sorting so that "Zebra" comes after "aardvark" instead of before it as it does when ASCII values are used to compare letters. We can, of course, implement any of these sorts by modifying the code, but in general we don't want to modify existing code—we want to reuse and extend it.

> **Program Tip 11.5: Classes, functions, and code should be open for extension but closed to modification. This is called the *open-closed principle*.**
> This design heuristic will be easier to realize when we've studied templates and inheritance (see Chapter 13). Ideally we want to adapt programs without breaking existing applications, so modifying code isn't a good idea if it can be avoided.

In all these different sorts, we want to change the method used for comparing vector elements. Ideally we'd like to make the comparison method a parameter to the sort functions so that we can pass different comparisons to sort by different criteria. We've already discussed how vector elements must conform to the expected interface of being comparable using the relational `operator <` if the sorting functions in `sortall.h` are used. We need to extend the conforming interface in some way so that in addition to using `operator <`, a parameter is used to compare elements. Since all objects we've passed are instances of classes or built-in types, we need to encapsulate a comparison function in a class and pass an object that's an instance of a class. A class that encapsulates a function is called a **function object** or a **functor**. We'll use functors to sort on several criteria.[4]

11.3.1 The Function Object `Comparer`

In the language C, there is no class `string`. Instead, special arrays of characters are used to represent strings. We won't study these kinds of strings, but we'll use the same convention in creating a class to compare objects that's used in C to compare strings. Just as certain method names are expected with any iterators used in this book (by convention)

---

[4]In this section we'll use classes with a function named `compare` to sort. In more advanced uses of C++, functors use an overloaded `operator()` so that an object can be used syntactically like a function, (e.g., `foo(x)` might be an object named `foo` with an overloaded `operator()` applied to x). My experience is that using an overloaded function application operator is hard for beginning programmers to understand, so I'll use named functions like `compare` instead.

and with iterators used by templated functions like UniqueStrings in Program 11.7, *uniqueiter.cpp* (enforced by the compiler), we'll expect any class that encapsulates a comparison function to use the name compare for the function. We'll use this name in writing sorting functions, and we'll expect functions with the name to conform to specific behavior. If a client uses a class with a name other than compare, the program will not compile because the templated sorting function will fail to be instantiated. However, if a client uses the name compare but doesn't adhere to the behavior convention we'll discuss, the program will compile and run, but the vector that results from calling a sort with such a function object will most likely not be in the order the client expects. Using a conforming interface is an example of **generic programming**, which [Aus98] says is a "set of requirements on data types."

The sorting functions expect the conforming interface of StrLenComp::compare below. The method is const since no state is modified — there is no state.

```
class StrLenComp
{
  public:
    int compare(const string& a, const string& b) const
    // post: return -1/+1/0 as a.length() < b.length()
    {
        if (a.length() < b.length()) return -1;
        if (a.length() > b.length()) return  1;
        return 0;
    }
};
```

The conforming interface is illustrated by the function prototype: it is a const function, returns an int, and expects two const-reference parameters that have the same type (which is string in the example above). The expected behavior is based on determining how a compares to b. Any function object used with the sorts in this book must have the following behavior:

- If a is less than b then −1 is returned.
- If a is greater than b then +1 is returned.
- Otherwise, a == b and 0 is returned.

As shown in StrLenComp::compare, the meaning of "less than" is completely determined by returning −1, similarly for "greater than" and a return value of +1. Program 11.8 shows how this function object sorts by word length.

Program 11.8 strlensort.cpp

```
#include <iostream>
#include <string>
#include <fstream>
using namespace std;
```

```
#include "tvector.h"
#include "sortall.h"
#include "prompt.h"

class StrLenComp
{
  public:
      int compare(const string& a, const string& b) const
      // post: return -1/+1/0 as a.length() < b.length()
      {
          if (a.length() < b.length()) return -1;
          if (a.length() > b.length()) return  1;
          return 0;
      }
};
int main()
{
    string word, filename = PromptString("filename: ");
    tvector<string> wvec;
    StrLenComp slencomp;
    int k;
    ifstream input(filename.c_str());

    while (input >> word)
    {   wvec.push_back(word);
    }
    InsertSort(wvec, wvec.size(), slencomp);

    for(k=0; k < 5; k++)
    {   cout << wvec[k] << endl;
    }
    cout << "-------" << endl << "last words" << endl;
    cout << "-------" << endl;
    for(k=wvec.size()-5; k < wvec.size(); k++)
    {   cout << wvec[k] << endl;
    }
    return 0;
}
```

strlensort.cpp

The sorts declared in *sortall.h* and implemented in *sortall.cpp* have two forms: one that expects a comparison function object as the third parameter and one that uses `operator <` and so doesn't require the third parameter. The headers for the two versions of `InsertSort` are reproduced below:

```
template <class Type>
void InsertSort(tvector<Type> & a, int size);
// post: a[0] <= a[1] <= ... <= a[size-1]

template <class Type, class Comparer>
void InsertSort(tvector<Type> & a, int size,
                const Comparer & comp);
// post: first size entries sorted by criteria in comp
```

The third parameter to the function has a type specified by the second template parameter `Comparer`. Any object can be passed as the third parameter if it has a method named `compare`. In the code from Program 11.8 the type `StrLenComp` is bound to the type `Comparer` when the templated function `InsertSort` is instantiated.

```
                              O U T P U T

prompt> strlensort
filename: twain.txt
a
I
I
I
a
-------
last words
-------
shoulder--so--at
discouraged-like,
indifferent-like,
shoulders--so--like
"One--two--three-git!"
```

As another example, suppose we want to sort a vector of stocks, where the `struct` `Stock` from *stocks.cpp*, Program 8.6, is used to store stock information (see *stock.h* in the on-line materials or Program 8.6 for details, or Program 11.9 below). We might want to sort by the symbol of the stock, the price of the stock, or the volume of shares traded. If we were the implementers of the class we could overload the relational `operator < ` for `Stock` objects, but not in three different ways. In many cases, we'll be client programmers, using classes we purchase "off-the-shelf" for creating software. We won't have access to implementations, so using function objects provides a good solution to the problem of sorting a class whose implementation we cannot access, and sorting by multiple criteria. In *sortstocks.cpp*, Program 11.9, we sort a vector of stocks by two different criteria: price and shares traded. We've used a `struct` for the comparer objects, but a class in which the `compare` function is public works just as well.

Program 11.9   sortstocks.cpp

```cpp
#include <iostream>
#include <fstream>
#include <string>
#include <iomanip>
using namespace std;
```

```cpp
#include "tvector.h"
#include "strutils.h"   // for atoi and atof
#include "prompt.h"
#include "sortall.h"
#include "stock.h"

struct PriceComparer    // compares using price
{
    int compare(const Stock& lhs, const Stock& rhs) const
    {   if (lhs.price < rhs.price) return -1;
        if (lhs.price > rhs.price) return +1;
        return 0;
    }
};
struct VolumeComparer   // compares using volume of shares traded
{
    int compare(const Stock& lhs, const Stock& rhs) const
    {   if (lhs.shares < rhs.shares) return -1;
        if (lhs.shares > rhs.shares) return +1;
        return 0;
    }
};

void Read(tvector<Stock>& list, const string& filename)
// post: stocks from filename read into list
{
    ifstream input(filename.c_str());
    string symbol, exchange, price, shares;
    while (input >> symbol >> exchange >> price >> shares)
    {   list.push_back(Stock(symbol,exchange,atof(price),atoi(shares)));
    }
}

Print(const tvector<Stock>& list, ostream& out)
// post: stocks in list printed to out, one per line
{
    int k,len = list.size();
    out.precision(3);          // show 3 decimal places
    out.setf(ios::fixed);
    for(k=0; k < len; k++)
    {   out << list[k].symbol << "\t" << list[k].exchange << "\t"
            << setw(8) << list[k].price << "\t" << setw(12)
            << list[k].shares << endl;
    }
}
int main()
{
    string filesymbol = PromptString("stock file ");
    tvector<Stock> stocks;
    Read(stocks,filesymbol);
    Print(stocks,cout);
    cout << endl << "----" << endl << "# stocks: " << stocks.size() << endl;
    cout << "----sorted by price----" << endl;
    InsertSort(stocks,stocks.size(), PriceComparer());
    Print(stocks,cout);
```

```
cout << "----sorted by volume----" << endl;
InsertSort(stocks,stocks.size(), VolumeComparer());
Print(stocks,cout);
return 0;
}
```

sortstocks.cpp

```
                    O U T P U T

prompt> sortstocks
filename: stocksmall.dat
KO          N           50.500              735000
DIS         N           64.125              282200
ABPCA       T            5.688               49700
NSCP        T           42.813              385900
F           N           32.125              798900


----
# stocks: 5
----sorted by price----
ABPCA       T            5.688               49700
F           N           32.125              798900
NSCP        T           42.813              385900
KO          N           50.500              735000
DIS         N           64.125              282200
----sorted by volume----
ABPCA       T            5.688               49700
DIS         N           64.125              282200
NSCP        T           42.813              385900
KO          N           50.500              735000
F           N           32.125              798900
```

11.3.2 Predicate Function Objects

As a final example, we'll consider the problem of finding all the files in a directory that are larger than a size specified by the user or that were last modified recently (e.g., within three days of today). We'll use a function templated on three different arguments: every entry (one template parameter) in an iterator (another template parameter) is checked, and those entries that satisfy a criterion (the last template parameter) are stored in a vector.

```
template <class Iter, class Pred, class Kind>
void IterToVectorIf(Iter& it, const Pred& p,
tvector<Kind>& list)
// post: items in Iter that satisfy Pred are added to list
{
    for(it.Init(); it.HasMore(); it.Next())
    {   if (p.Satisfies(it.Current()))
        {   list.push_back(it.Current());
        }
    }
}
```

The parameter it is used as an iterator in the function body, so we could pass a DirStream object or a CListIterator object among the many kinds of iterators we've studied. Since it has type Iter, when the function is instantiated/called, the first argument should be an iterator type. The second parameter of the function, p, has type Pred. If you look at the function body, you'll see that the only use of p is in the if statement. The object passed as a second parameter to p must have a member function named Satisfies that returns a bool value for the template instantiation to work correctly. Finally, the third parameter to the function is a vector that stores Kind elements. Elements are stored in the vector by calling push_back with it.Current() as an argument. The vector passed as the third argument to IterToVectorIf must store the same type of object returned by the iterator passed as the first argument. I ran the program on May 16, 1999, which should help explain the output.

Program 11.10   dirvecfun.cpp

```
#include <iostream>
#include <fstream>
#include <string>
#include <iomanip>
using namespace std;
#include "directory.h"
#include "prompt.h"
#include "tvector.h"

// illustrates templated functions, function objects

// find large files
struct SizePred     // satisfies if DirEntry::Size() >= size
{
    SizePred(int size)
        : mySize(size)
    {}
    bool Satisfies(const DirEntry& de) const
    {
        return de.Size() >= mySize;
    }
    int mySize;
```

```
};

// find recent files
struct DatePred      // satisfies if DirEntry::GetDate() >= date
{
  DatePred(const Date& d)
    : myDate(d)
  { }
  bool Satisfies(const DirEntry& de) const
  {
      return !de.IsDir() && de.GetDate() >= myDate;
  }
  Date myDate;
};

void Print(const tvector<DirEntry>& list)
// post: all entries in list printed, one per line
{
    int k;
    DirEntry de;
    for(k=0; k < list.size(); k++)
    {   de = list[k];
        cout << setw(10) << de.Size() << "\t" << setw(12)
             << de.Name() << "\t"  << de.GetDate() << endl;
    }
    cout << "---\n# entries = " << list.size() << endl;
};

template <class Iter, class Pred, class Kind>
void IterToVectorIf(Iter& it, const Pred& p, tvector<Kind>& list)
// post: all items in Iter that satisfy Pred are added to list
{
    for(it.Init(); it.HasMore(); it.Next())
    {   if (p.Satisfies(it.Current()))
        {   list.push_back(it.Current());
        }
    }
}

int main()
{
    Date today;
    string dirname = PromptString("directory ");
    int size =      PromptRange("min file size",1,300000);
    int before =    PromptRange("# days before today",0,300);

    DatePred datePred(today-before);  // find files within before days of today
    SizePred sizePred(size);          // find files larger than size
    DirStream dirs(dirname);          // iterate over directory entries
    tvector<DirEntry> dirvec;         // store satisfying entries here

    IterToVectorIf(dirs,datePred,dirvec);
    cout << "date satisfying" << endl << "---" << endl;
    Print(dirvec);
```

```
dirvec.resize(0);    // remove old entries
cout << endl << "size satisfying"<< endl << "---" << endl;
IterToVectorIf(dirs,sizePred,dirvec);
Print(dirvec);
return 0;
}
```

dirvecfun.cpp

OUTPUT

```
prompt> dirvecfun
directory  c:\book\ed2\code
min file size between 1 and 300000: 50000
# days before today between 0 and 300: 0
date satisfying
---
        4267       directory.cpp    May 16 1999
        4814        directory.h     May 16 1999
        2251       dirvecfun.cpp    May 16 1999
        2316        nqueens.cpp     May 16 1999
---
# entries = 4


size satisfying
---
       99991           foot.exe     April 14 1999
       64408           mult.exe     March 10 1999
       53760           mult.opt     March 31 1999
      165658            tap.zip     April 21 1999
      111163         tcwdef.csm     April 14 1999
---
# entries = 5
```

The structs `SizePred` and `DatePred` are called **predicates** because they're used as Boolean function objects. We use the method name `Satisfies` from a term from mathematical logic, but it makes sense that the predicate function object returns true for each `DirEntry` object satisfying the criteria specified by the class.

Program Tip 11.6: A function object specifies a parameterized policy.
Functions that implement algorithms like sorting, but allow function object parameters to specify *policy*, such as how to compare elements, are more general than functions that hardwire the policy in code.

Pause to Reflect

11.8 If the function `Print` from *sortwlen.cpp*, Program 11.5, is passed a vector of `DirEntry` objects as follows, the call to `Print` will fail:

```
tvector<DirEntry> dirvec;
 // store values in dirvec
 Print(dirvec,0,dirvec.size()-1);
```

Why does this template instantiation fail? What can you do to make it succeed?

11.9 Show how to prompt the user for the name of a directory and call `CountIter` from *countiter.cpp*, Program 11.6, to count the number of files and subdirectories in the directory whose name the user enters.

11.10 Write a function object that can be used to sort strings without being sensitive to case, so that `"ZeBrA" == "zebra"` and so that `"Zebra" > "aardvark"`.

11.11 Write three function objects that could be used in sorting a vector of `DirEntry` objects ordered by three criteria: alphabetically, by name of file, in order of increasing size, or in order by the date the files were last modified (use `GetDate`).

11.12 Suppose you want to use `IterToVectorIf` to store every file and subdirectory accessed by a `DirStream` object into a vector. Write a predicate function object that always returns true so that every `DirEntry` object will be stored in the vector. (See Program 11.10, *dirvecfun.cpp*.)

11.13 Write a templated function that reverses the elements stored in a vector so that the first element is swapped with the last, the second element is swapped with the second to last, and so on (make sure you don't undo the swaps; stop when the vector is reversed). Do not use extra storage; swap the elements in place.

11.14 Write a function modeled after `IterToVecIf` but with a different name: `IterToVecFilter`. The function stores every element accessed by an iterator in a vector, but the elements are filtered or changed first. The function could be used to read strings from a file and convert the strings to lowercase. The code below could do this with the right class and function implementations:

```
string filename = PromptString("filename: ");
WordStreamIterator wstream;
tvector<string> words;
wstream.Open(filename);
LowerCaseConverter lcConverter;
IterToVecFilter(wstream,lcConverter,words);
// all entries in words are in lowercase
```

11.4 Analyzing Sorts

Using function objects we can sort by different criteria, but what sorting algorithms should we use? In this section we'll discuss techniques for classifying algorithms in general, and sorting algorithms in particular, as to how much time and memory the algorithms require.

We discussed several quadratic sorts in Section 11.1 and discussed selection sort and insertion sort in some detail. Which of these is the best sort? As with many questions about algorithms and programming decisions, the answer is "It depends"[5]—on the size of the vector being sorted, on the type of each vector element, on how critical a fast sort is in a given program, and many other characteristics of the application in which sorting is used. You might, for example, compare different sorting algorithms by timing the sorts using a computer. The program *timequadsorts.cpp,* Program 11.4, uses the templated sorting functions from *sortall.h,* Program G.14 (see How to G), to time three sorting algorithms. The graph in Figure 11.3 provides times for these sorts.

Although the timings are different, the curves have the same shape. The timings might also be different if selection sort were implemented differently, as by another programmer. However, the general shapes of the curves would not be different because the shape is a fundamental property of the algorithm rather than of the computer being used, the compiler, or the coding details. The shape of the curve is called **quadratic** because it is generated by curves of the family $y = ax^2$ (where a is a constant). To see (informally) why the shape is quadratic, we will count the number of comparisons between vector elements needed to sort an N-element vector. Vector elements are compared by the `if` statement in the inner `for` loop of function `SelectSort` (see Program 11.2).

```
if (a[j] < a[minIndex])
{   minIndex = j;   // new smallest item, remember where
}
```

We'll first consider a 10-element vector, then use these results to generalize to an N-element vector. The outer `for` loop (with `k` as the loop index) iterates nine times for a 10-element vector because `k` has the values $0, 1, 2, \ldots, 8$. When $k = 0$, the inner loop iterates from $j = 1$ to $j < 10$, so the `if` statement is executed nine times. Since `k` is incremented by 1 each time, the `if` statement will be executed 45 times because the inner loop iterates nine times, then eight times, and so on:

$$9 + 8 + 7 + 6 + 5 + 4 + 3 + 2 + 1 = \frac{9(10)}{2} = 45 \qquad (11.1)$$

The sum is computed from a formula for the sum of the first N integers; the sum is $N(N + 1)/2$. To sort a 100-element vector, the number of comparisons needed is $99(100)/2 = 4,950$. Generalizing, to sort an N-element vector, the number of comparisons is calculated by summing the first $N - 1$ integers:

$$\frac{(N - 1)(N)}{2} = \frac{N^2 - N}{2} = \frac{N^2}{2} - \frac{N}{2} \qquad (11.2)$$

This is a quadratic, which at least partially explains the shape of the curves in Figure 11.3. We can verify this analysis experimentally using a a templated class `SortWrapper` (accessible in *sortbench.h*) that keeps track of how many times sorted elements are

---

[5]Note that the right answer is *never* bubble sort.

compared and assigned. We've discussed comparisons; assignments arise when vector elements are swapped. The class `SortWrapper` is used in Program 11.11.

Program 11.11 checkselect.cpp

```cpp
#include <iostream>
#include <string>
#include <fstream>
using namespace std;
#include "sortbench.h"
#include "sortall.h"
#include "prompt.h"

int main()
{
    typedef SortWrapper<string> Wstring;
    string word, filename = PromptString("filename:");
    ifstream input(filename.c_str());

    tvector<Wstring>list;
    while (input >> word)
    {   list.push_back(Wstring(word));
    }
    cout << "# words read =\t " << list.size() << endl;

    Wstring::clear(); // clear push_back assigns
    SelectSort(list,list.size());
    cout << "# compares\t = " << Wstring::compareCount() << endl;
    cout << "# assigns\t = " << Wstring::assignCount() << endl;
    return 0;
}
```

checkselect.cpp

```
                    O U T P U T

prompt> checkselect
filename: poe.txt
# words read =    2324
# compares        = 2699326
# assigns         = 4646
```

The number of comparisons is $2{,}323 \times 2{,}324/2$, which matches the formula in Equation 11.2 exactly. The number of assignments is exactly $2(N-1)$ for an N-element vector because a swap requires two assignments and one construction, for example, for strings:

```
void Swap(string& x, string& y)
{
    string temp = x;    // construction, not assignment
    x = y;              // assignment
    y = temp;           // assignment
}
```

In general, when there are N elements there will be $N - 1$ swaps and $3(N - 1)$ data movements (assignments and constructions). Before analyzing other sorts, we need to develop some terminology to make the discussion simpler.

11.4.1   O Notation

When the execution time of an algorithm can be described by a family of curves, computer scientists use *O* **notation** to describe the general shape of the curves. For a quadratic family, the expression used is $O(N^2)$. It is useful to think of the O as standing for **order** because the general shape of a curve provides an approximation *on the order of* the expression rather than an exact analysis. For example, the number of comparisons used by selection sort is $O(N^2)$, but more precisely is $(N^2/2) - (N/2)$. Since we are interested in the general shape rather than the precise curve, coefficients like 13.5 and lower-order terms with smaller exponents like N, which don't affect the general shape of a quadratic curve, are not used in O notation.

In later courses you may learn a formal definition that involves calculating limits, but the idea of a family of curves defined by the general shape of a curve is enough for our purposes. To differentiate between other notations for analyzing algorithms, the term **big-Oh** is used for O notation (to differentiate from little-oh, for example).

Algorithms like sequential search (Table 8.1) that are linear are described as $O(N)$ algorithms using big-Oh notation. This indicates, for example, that to search a vector of N elements requires examining nearly all the elements. Again, this describes the shape of the curve, not the precise timing, which will differ depending on the compiler, the computer, and the coding. Binary search, which requires far fewer comparisons than sequential search, is an $O(\log N)$ algorithm, as discussed in Section 8.3.7.

Table 11.2 provides data for comparing the running times of algorithms whose running times or **complexities** are given by different big-Oh expressions. The data are for a (hypothetical) computer that executes one million operations per second.

11.4.2   Worst Case and Average Case

When we use O notation, we're trying to classify an algorithm's running time, or sometimes the amount of memory it uses. Some algorithms behave differently depending on the input. For example, when searching sequentially for an element in a vector, we might find the element in the first location or in the middle location, or we might not find it after examining all locations. How can we classify sequential search when the behavior is different depending on the item searched for? Typically, computer scientists use two methods to analyze an algorithm: **worst case** and **average case**. The worst-case analysis is based on inputs to an algorithm that take the most time or use the most memory. In

Table 11.2 Comparing big-Oh expressions on a computer that executes one million instructions per second.

N	Running time (seconds)			
	$O(\log N)$	$O(N)$	$O(N \log N)$	$O(N^2)$
10	0.000003	0.00001	0.000033	0.0001
100	0.000007	0.00010	0.000664	0.1000
1,000	0.000010	0.00100	0.010000	1.0
10,000	0.000013	0.01000	0.132900	1.7 min
100,000	0.000017	0.10000	1.661000	2.78 hours
1,000,000	0.000020	1.0	19.9	11.6 days
1,000,000,000	0.000030	16.7 min	8.3 hours	318 centuries

sequential search, for example, the worst case occurs when the element searched for isn't found; every vector element is examined. It's more difficult to define average case, and if you continue your studies of computer science you'll encounter different ways of defining average. In this book I'll use average case very informally to mean what happens with most kinds of input, not the worst and not the best. To get an idea of what average case means we'll consider sequential search again. In an N-element vector there are $N + 1$ different ways for a sequential search algorithm to terminate:

■ The item searched for is found in one of N different locations.
■ The item searched for is not found.

If we look at the total number of vector items examined for every possible case when the search is successful, we'll be able to apply Equation 11.2 again to get the total number of comparisons as $N(N+1)/2$. Since there are N different ways to terminate successfully, we can argue that the average number of elements examined is

$$\frac{N(N+1)/2}{N} = \frac{(N+1)}{2} \tag{11.3}$$

This is still $O(N)$, so sequential search is $O(N)$ in both the worst and average cases.

11.4.3   Analyzing Insertion Sort

The code for insertion sort in *insertsort.cpp*, Program 11.3, shows that the outer for loop executes $N - 1$ times for an N-element vector since k varies from 1 to $N - 1$. The number of times the inner while loop executes depends on the order of the elements and the value of loc after the while loop, as shown in Figure 11.2. In the worst case, the vector is in reverse order and the inner loop will execute k times. The total number of times the body of the inner while loop executes is $(N - 1)N/2$ using Equation 11.2 since we're summing the first $N - 1$ numbers. There is one assignment each time the inner loop executes, and one assignment after the loop. The total number of assignments is $(N - 1)N/2 + N$, which is $O(N^2)$ and exactly $N(N + 1)/2$. There is one vector comparison each time the inner loop executes and one comparison of $0 < \text{loc}$. We'll count only the vector comparison since although the comparison to see that the index loc is valid affects the execution time, it is independent of the kind of element being sorted. There are a total, then, of $(N - 1)N/2$ comparisons in the worst case.

In the best case, when the vector is already sorted, the inner loop body is never executed. There will be $O(N)$ comparisons and $O(N)$ assignments, which is about as good as we can expect since we have to examine every vector element simply to determine if the vector is sorted.

We can argue informally that on average the inner loop executes $k/2$ times since the worst case is k and the best case is zero. The algorithm is still an $O(N^2)$ algorithm, but the number of comparisons will be fewer than with selection sort. This is why the timings in Figure 11.3 show insertion sort as faster than selection sort—it won't be faster always, but on average it is. We can verify some of these results experimentally with Program 11.12, *checkinsert.cpp*.

Program 11.12   checkinsert.cpp
<hr style="width:40%">

```cpp
#include <iostream>
#include <string>
#include <fstream>
using namespace std;

#include "sortbench.h"
#include "sortall.h"
#include "prompt.h"
#include "tvector.h"

typedef SortWrapper<string> Wstring;

struct ReverseComparer   // for sorting in reverse alphabetical order
{
    int compare(const Wstring& lhs, const Wstring& rhs) const
    {   if (lhs < rhs) return +1;
        if (rhs < lhs) return −1;
        return 0;
    }
};

int main()
{
    string word, filename = PromptString("filename:");
    ifstream input(filename.c_str());
    tvector<Wstring>list;

    while (input >> word)
    {   list.push_back(Wstring(word));
    }
    cout << "# words read =\t " << list.size() << endl;

    Wstring::clear(); // clear push_back assigns
```

```
InsertSort(list,list.size());
cout << "# compares\t = " << Wstring::compareCount() << endl;
cout << "# assigns\t = " << Wstring::assignCount() << endl;

Wstring::clear();
cout << endl << "sorting a sorted vector" << endl;
InsertSort(list,list.size());
cout << "# compares\t = " << Wstring::compareCount() << endl;
cout << "# assigns\t = " << Wstring::assignCount() << endl;

InsertSort(list,list.size(),ReverseComparer());
Wstring::clear();
cout << endl << "sorting a reverse-sorted vector" << endl;
InsertSort(list,list.size());
cout << "# compares\t = " << Wstring::compareCount() << endl;
cout << "# assigns\t = " << Wstring::assignCount() << endl;

return 0;
}
```

checkinsert.cpp

OUTPUT

```
prompt> checkinsert
filename: poe.txt
# words read =    2324
# compares       = 1339264
# assigns        = 1339269

sorting a sorted vector
# compares       = 2323
# assigns        = 2323

sorting a reverse-sorted vector
# compares       = 2673287
# assigns        = 2674325
```

11.5 Quicksort

The graph in Figure 11.3 suggests that selection sort and bubble sort are both $O(N^2)$ sorts.[6] In this section we'll study a more efficient sort called **quicksort**. Quicksort is a recursive, three-step process:

---

[6] To be precise, the graph does not prove that bubble sort is an $O(N^2)$ sort; it provides evidence of this. To prove it more formally would require analyzing the number of comparisons.

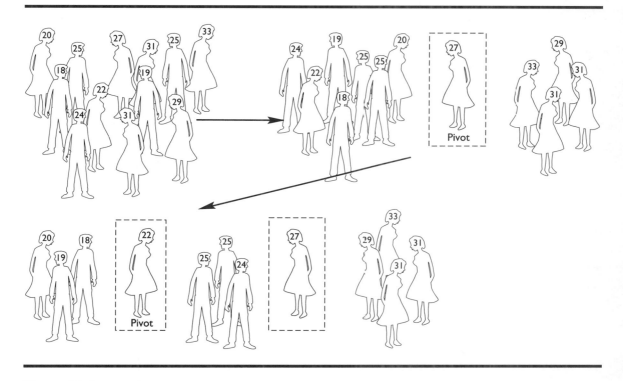

Figure 11.4 Quicksort.

1. A pivot element of the vector being sorted is chosen. Elements of the vector are rearranged so that elements less than or equal to the pivot are moved before the pivot. Elements greater than the pivot are moved after the pivot. This is called the **partition** step.

2. Quicksort (recursively) the elements before the pivot.

3. Quicksort (recursively) the elements after the pivot.

The partition step could use an explanation; we'll discuss the algorithm pictured in Figure 11.4.

Suppose a group of people must arrange themselves in order by age so that the people are lined up with the youngest person to the left and the oldest person to the right. One person is designated as the pivot person. All people younger than the pivot person stand to left of the pivot person, and all people older than the pivot person stand to the right of the pivot. In the first step, the 27-year-old woman is designated as the pivot. All younger people move to the pivot's left (from our point of view); all older people move to the pivot's right. It is imperative to note at this point that the 27-year-old woman *will not move again*! In general, after the rearrangement takes place, the pivot person (or vector element) is in the correct order relative to the other people (elements). Also, people to the left of the pivot always stay to the left.

After this rearrangement, a recursive step takes place. The people to the left of the 27-year-old pivot must now sort themselves. Once again, the first step is to partition the group of seven people. A pivot is chosen—in this case, the 22-year-old woman. All people younger move to the pivot's left, and all people older move to the pivot's right. The group that moves to the right (two 25-year-olds and a 24-year-old) are now located between the two people who are in their final positions. To continue the process, the group of three (20, 18, and 19 years old) would sort themselves. When this group is done, the group of 25- and 24-year-olds would sort themselves. At this point, the entire group to the left of the original 27-year-old pivot is sorted. Now the group to the right of this pivot must be recursively sorted.

The code for quicksort is very short and reflects the three steps outlined above: partition and recurse twice. Since the recursive calls specify a range in the original vector, we'll use a function with parameters for the left and right indexes of the part of the vector being sorted. For example, to sort an n-element `int` vector a, the call `Quick(a,0,n-1)` works, where `Quick` is

```
void Quick(tvector<int>& a,int first,int last)
// postcondition: a[first] <= ... <= a[last]
{
    int piv;
    if (first < last)
    {   piv = Pivot(a,first,last);
        Quick(a,first,piv-1);
        Quick(a,piv+1,last);
    }
}
```

The three statements in the `if` block correspond to the three parts of quicksort. The function `Pivot` rearranges the elements of a between positions `first` and `last` and returns the index of the pivot element. This index is then used recursively to sort the elements to the left of the pivot (in the range `[first … piv-1]`) and the elements to the right of the pivot (in the range `[piv+1 … last]`).

11.5.1   The Partition/Pivot Function

There are many different ways to implement the partition function. All these methods are linear, or $O(N)$, where N is the number of elements rearranged. We'll use a partition method described in [Ben86] that is simple to remember and that can be developed using invariants.

The diagrams in Figure 11.5 show the sequence of steps used in partitioning the elements of a vector between (and including) locations `first` and `last`. Understanding the second diagram in the sequence is the key to being able to reproduce the code. The second diagram describes an invariant of the `for` loop that partitions the `tvector`.

The `for` loop examines each vector element between locations `first` and `last` once; this ensures that the loop is linear, or $O(N)$, for partitioning N elements. The loop has the following form, where the element with index `first` is chosen as the pivot element:

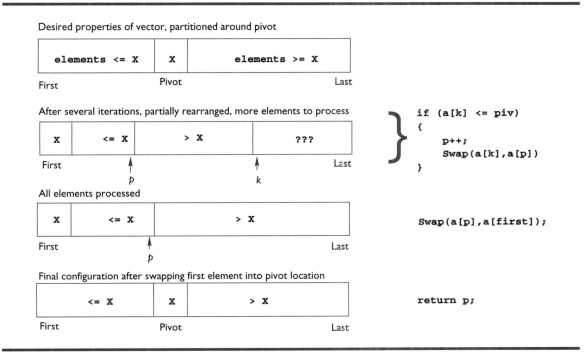

Figure 11.5   Partitioning for quicksort.

```
for(k=first+1; k <= last; k++)
{   if (a[k] <= a[first])
    {   p++;
        swap(a[k], a[p])
    }
}
```

As indicated by the question marks "???" in Figure 11.5, the value of a[k] relative to the pivot is not known. If a[k] is less than or equal to the pivot, it belongs in the first part of the vector. If a[k] is greater than the pivot, it belongs in the second part of the vector (where it already is!). The if statement in Figure 11.5 compares a[k] to the pivot and then reestablishes the picture as true, so that the picture represents an invariant (true each time the loop test is evaluated).

   This works because when p is incremented, it becomes the index of an element larger than the pivot, as shown in the diagram. The statement Swap(a[k],a[p]) interchanges an element less than or equal to the pivot, a[k], and an element greater than the pivot, a[p]. This informal reasoning should help convince you that the picture shown is an invariant and that it leads to a correct partition function. One more step is necessary, however; the invariant needs to be established as true the first time the loop test is evaluated. In this situation, the part of the vector labeled ??? represents the entire vector because none of the elements has been examined.

The first element is arbitrarily chosen as the pivot element. Setting k = first+1 makes k the index of the leftmost unknown element, the ??? section, as shown in the diagram. Setting p = first makes p the index of the rightmost element that is known to be less than or equal to the pivot because in this case only the element with index first is known to be less than or equal to the pivot—it is equal to the pivot because it *is* the pivot.

The last step is to swap the pivot element, which is a[first], into the location indexed by the variable p. This is shown in the final stage of the diagram in Figure 11.5.

The partition function, combined with the three-step recursive function for quicksort just outlined, yields a complete sorting routine that is included as part of *sortall.h*, Program G.14. We can change the call of SelectSort to QuickSort in *timequadsorts.cpp*, Program 11.4, and remove the call to BubbleSort to compare quicksort and insertion sort. We'll call the renamed program *timequicksort.cpp*, and we won't show a listing since it doesn't change much from the original program.

O U T P U T

```
prompt> timequicksort
min and max size of vector: 6000 20000
increment in vector size between 1 and 10000: 2000

n        insert  quick

6000     1.792   0.03
8000     3.185   0.04
10000    5.177   0.05
12000    7.331   0.06
14000    10.075  0.07
16000    13.009  0.09
18000    16.604  0.101
20000    20.52   0.11
```

You can see from the sample runs that quicksort is *much* faster than insertion sort. If we extrapolate the data for insertion sort to a 300,000-element vector, we can approximate the time as 4,660 seconds. The ratio 300,000/10,000 = 30 shows that the execution time jumps by a factor of 900 from 10,000 to 300,000 since insertion sort is an $O(N^2)$ sort. Multiplying $5.177 \times 900 = 4,659.3$, we determine that insertion sort takes a little more than 1 hour and 17 minutes to sort a 300,000-element vector. Removing the call to InsertSort so the program executes more quickly, we find that QuickSort takes 2.16 seconds to sort a 300,000-element vector. That's quick.

11.5.2 Analysis of Quicksort

With the limited analysis tools we have, a formal analysis of quicksort that provides a big-Oh expression of its running time is difficult. The choice of the pivot element in the partition step plays a crucial role in how well the method works. Suppose, for example, that in Figure 11.4 the first person chosen for the pivot is the 18-year-old person. All the people younger than this person move to the person's left; all the older people move to the person's right. In this case there are no younger people. This means that the two subgroups that would be sorted recursively are not the same size. If a "bad" partition continues to be chosen in the recursively sorted groups, quicksort degenerates into a slower, quadratic sort. On the other hand, if the pivot is chosen so that each subgroup is roughly the same size (i.e., half the size of the group being partitioned), then quicksort works very quickly.[7]

Since the partition algorithm is linear, or $O(N)$, for an N-element vector, the **computational complexity,** or running time, of quicksort depends on how many partitions are needed. In the best case the pivot element divides the vector being sorted into two equal parts. A more sophisticated analysis than we have the tools for shows that in the average case the vector is still divided approximately in half. If you examine the code for Quick below carefully, and assume that the value of piv is roughly in the middle, then you can reason about the sizes of the vector segments sorted with each pair of recursive calls.

```
void Quick(tvector<int>& a,int first,int last)
// postcondition: a[first] <= ... <= a[last]
{
    int piv;
    if (first < last)
    {   piv = Pivot(a,first,last);
        Quick(a,first,piv-1);
        Quick(a,piv+1,last);
    }
}
```

If Quick is first called with a 1,000-element vector, a "good" pivot generates two recursive calls on 500-element vectors.[8] The number of elements being sorted is $2 \times 500 = 1,000$. Each of the 500-element vectors generates two recursive calls on 250-element vectors. Since there are two 500-element vectors, each generating two recursive calls, the number of elements being sorted is $4 \times 250 = 1,000$. This continues with four 250-element vectors each generating two calls on 125-element vectors, but the total number of elements being sorted is still $8 \times 125 = 1,000$. Every group of recursive calls yields a total of 1,000 elements to sort, but the size of the vectors being sorted decreases. Eventually there will be 500 two-element vectors. Each of these will generate two recursive calls, but these recursive calls are the base case of a one- or zero-element vector. With each group of recursive calls, there are 1,000 elements to sort. For an

---

[7]It's not an accident that C.A.R. Hoare named the sort *quicksort.*

[8]A perfect partition will yield one 499-element vector and one 500-element vector since the pivot element doesn't move. We'll ignore this difference and treat each vector as a 500-element vector.

N-element vector there will be N elements to partition and sort. Since we know that the partition code is $O(N)$, there is $O(N)$ work done at each recursive stage.

How many recursive stages are there? As we saw in Section 8.3.7, the number N can be divided in half approximately $log_2 N$ times. Each group of recursive calls requires $O(N)$ work, and there are $log_2 N$ groups of calls. This makes quicksort an $O(NlogN)$ algorithm. We ignore the base 2 on the log because $log_b N / log_2 N$ is a constant for any value of b. Since we ignore constants in O notation, we ignore the base of the log. However, in computer science nearly all uses of a logarithm function can be assumed to use a base 2 log. Quicksort is an $O(NlogN)$ algorithm in the average case but not in the worst case, where we've noted that it's an $O(N^2)$ algorithm. If we choose the first element as the pivot, then a sorted vector generates the worst case. It's possible to choose the partition in such a way that the worst case becomes extremely unlikely, but there are other sorts that are always $O(N \log N)$ even in the worst case. Nevertheless, quicksort is not hard to code, and its performance is extremely good in general. In the implementation of QuickSort in *sortall.cpp*, the median (or middle) of the first, middle, and last vector elements is chosen as the pivot. This makes QuickSort very fast except in degenerate cases that are unlikely in practice, though still possible. Implementations of two other $O(NlogN)$ sorts, MergeSort and HeapSort, are accessible from *sortall.h* (Program G.14). These sorts have good $O(NlogN)$ worst-case behavior, so if you must guarantee good performance, use one of them. Merge sort is particularly simple to implement for lists, and we'll explore this in an exercise.

Pause to Reflect

11.15 Why are the average and worst cases of selection sort the same, whereas these cases are different for insertion sort?

11.16 In the output of *checkinsert.cpp*, Program 11.12, the worst case for insertion sort, sorting a vector that's in reverse order, yields 2,673,287 comparisons for a vector with 2,324 elements. However, $(2,323 \times 2,324)/2 = 2,699,326$. Explain this discrepancy. (Hint: Are all the words in the vector unique?)

11.17 The timings for insertion sort are better than for selection sort in Figure 11.3. Selection sort will likely be better if strings are sorted rather than ints (int vectors were used in Figure 11.3). If DirEntry objects are sorted the difference will be more pronounced; selection sort timings will not change much between ints, strings, and DirEntry objects, but insertion sort timings will get worse. What properties of the sorts and the objects being sorted could account for these observations?

11.18 If we sort a 100,000-element int vector using quicksort, where all the ints are in the range [0 . . . 100], the sort will take a very long time. This is true because the partition diagrammed in Figure 11.5 cannot result in two equal parts of the vectors; the execution will be similar to what happens with quicksort when a bad pivot is chosen. If the range of numbers is changed to [0 . . . 50,000] the performance gets better. Why?

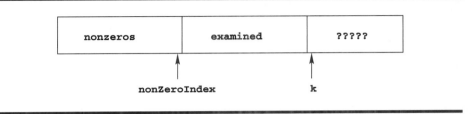

Figure 11.6 Removing zeroes from an array/vector.

11.19 The implementation of quicksort in *sortall.cpp* uses a different stopping criterion than the one described in Section 11.5. The code presented there made recursive calls until the size of the vector being sorted was one or zero; that is, the base case was determined by if (first < last). Instead, the function below is used, where CUTOFF is 30:

```
void Quick(tvector<int>& a,int first,int last)
// postcondition: a[first] <= ... <= a[last]
{
    if (last - first > CUTOFF)
    {   int piv = Pivot(a,first,last);
        Quick(a,first,piv-1);
        Quick(a,piv+1,last);
    }
    else
    {   Insert(a,first,last);   // call insertion sort
    }
}
```

This speeds up the execution of quicksort. Why?

11.20 Write a function that removes all the zeros from a vector of integers, leaving the relative order of the nonzero elements unchanged, without using an extra vector. The function should run in linear time, or have complexity $O(N)$ for an N-element vector.

```
void RemoveZeros(tvector<int> & list, int & numElts)
// postcondition: zeros removed from list,
//                numElts = # elts in list
```

If you're having trouble, use the picture in Figure 11.6 as an invariant. The idea is that the elements in the first part of the vector are nonzero elements. The elements in the section "???" have yet to be examined (the other elements have been examined and are either zeros or copies of elements moved into the first section). If the kth element is zero, it is left alone. If it is nonzero, it must be moved into the first section.

11.21 After a vector of words read from a file is sorted, identical words are adjacent to each other. Write a function to remove copies of identical words, leaving only one occurrence of the words that occur more than once. The function should have complexity $O(N)$, where N is the number of words in the original vector (stored in the file). Don't use two loops. Use one loop and think carefully about the right invariant. Try to draw a picture similar to the one used in the previous exercise.

11.22 Binary search requires a sorted vector. The most efficient sorts are $O(N \log N)$; binary search is $O(\log N)$, and sequential search is $O(N)$. If you have to search an N-element vector that's unsorted, when does it make sense to sort the vector and use binary search rather than to use sequential search?

11.6 Chapter Review

We discussed sorting, generic programming, templated functions, function objects, and algorithm analysis, including O notation. Two quadratic sorts—insertion sort and selection sort—are fast enough to use for moderately sized data. For larger data sets an $O(N \log N)$ sort like quicksort may be more appropriate. Functions that implement sorts are often implemented as templated functions so they can be used with vectors of any type, such as int, string, double, Date, and so on. A second template parameter can be used to specify a sorting policy (e.g., to sort in reverse order or to ignore the case of words). This parameter is usually a function object: an object used like a function in code. Using big-Oh expressions allows us to discuss algorithm efficiency without referring to specific computers. O notation also lets us hide some details by ignoring low-order terms and constants so that $3N^2, 4N^2+2N$, and N^2 are all $O(N^2)$ algorithms.

Topics covered include the following:

- Selection sort is an $O(n^2)$ sort that works fast on small vectors (where small is relative).
- Insertion sort is another $O(n^2)$ sort that works well on nearly sorted data.
- Bubble sort is an $O(n^2)$ sort that should rarely be used. Its performance is much worse, in almost all situations, than that of selection sort or insertion sort.
- Overloaded functions permit the same name to be used for different functions if the parameter lists of the functions differ.
- Templated functions are used for functions that represent a pattern, or template, for constructing other functions. Templated functions are often used instead of overloading to minimize code duplication.
- Function objects encapsulate functions so that the functions can be passed as policy arguments—that is, so that clients can specify how to compare elements being sorted.
- O notation, or big-Oh, is used to analyze and compare different algorithms. O notation provides a convenient way of comparing algorithms, as opposed to implementations of algorithms on particular computers.
- The sum of the first n numbers, $1 + 2 + \cdots + n$, is $n(n + 1)/2$.

■   Quicksort is a very fast sort, $O(n \log n)$ in the average case. In the worst case, quicksort is $O(n^2)$.

11.7   Exercises

11.1   Implement *bogosort* from Chapter 1 using a function that shuffles the elements of a vector until they're sorted. Test the function on *n*-element vectors (for small *n*) and graph the results showing average time to sort over several runs.

11.2   You may have seen the word game Jumble in your newspaper. In Jumble the letters in a word are mixed up, and the reader must try to guess what the word is (there are actually four words in a Jumble game, and a short phrase whose letters have to be obtained from the four words after they are solved). For example, *neicma* is *iceman*, and *cignah* is *aching*.

Jumbles are easy for computers to solve with access to a list of words. Two words are anagrams of each other if they contain the same letters. For example, *horse* and *shore* are anagrams.

Write a program that reads a file of words and finds all anagrams. You can modify this program to facilitate Jumble solving. Use the declaration below to store a "Jumble word":

```
struct Jumble
{
    string word;            // regular word, "horse"
    string normal;          // sorted/normalized, "ehors"
    Jumble(const string& s); // constructor(s)
};
```

Each English word read from a file is stored along with a sorted version of the letters in the word in a Jumble struct. For example, store *horse* together with *ehors*. To find the English word corresponding to a jumbled word like cignah, sort the letters in the jumbled word yielding acghin, then look up the sorted word by comparing it to every Jumble word's normal field. It's easiest to overload operator == to compare normal fields; then you can write code like this:

```
string word;
cout << "enter word to de-jumble";
cin >> word;
Jumble jword(word);
// look up jword in a vector<Jumble>
```

A word with anagrams will have more than one Jumble solution. You should sort a vector of words by using the sorted word as the key, then use binary search when looking up the jumbled word. You can overload operator < for the struct Jumble, or pass a function object that compares the normal field of two Jumble objects when sorting.

You should write two programs, one to find all the anagrams in a file of words and one to allow a user to interactively search for Jumble solutions.

11.3   Write a program based on *dirvecfun.cpp*, Program 11.10. Replace IterToVectorIf with a function `IterToListIf` that returns a `CList` object rather than a vector object.

11.4 Write a program based on *dirvecfun.cpp*, Program 11.10, specifically on the function `IterToVectorIf`, but specialized to the class `DirStream`. The program should allow the client to implement predicate function objects and apply them to an entire directory hierarchy, not just to a top-level directory (see the run of the Program 11.10).

The client should be able to specify a directory in a `DirStream` object and get back a vector of every file that matches some predicate function object's `Satisfies` criteria that's contained in the specified directory or in any subdirectory reachable from the specified directory.

Users of the program should have the option of printing the returned files sorted by several criteria: date last modified, alphabetically, or size of file.

11.5 In Exercise 7 of Chapter 6 an algorithm was given for calculating the variance and standard deviation of a set of numbers. Other statistical measures include the **mean** or average, the **mode** or most frequently occurring value, and the **median** or middle value.

Write a class or function that finds these three statistical values for a `tvector` of `double` values. The median can be calculated by sorting the values and finding the middle value. If the number of values is even, the median value can be defined as either the average of the two values in the middle or the smaller of the two. Sorting the values can also help determine the mode, but you may decide to calculate the mode in some other manner.

11.6 The bubble sort algorithm sorts the elements in a vector by making *N* passes over a vector of *N* items. On each pass, adjacent elements are compared, and if the element on the left (smaller index) is greater it is swapped with its neighbor. In this manner the largest element "bubbles" to the end of the vector. On the next pass, adjacent elements are compared again, but the pass stops one short of the end. On each pass, bubbling stops one position earlier than the pass before until all the elements are sorted. The following code implements this idea:

```
template <class Type>
void BubbleSort(tvector<Type> & a, int n)
// precondition: n = # of elements in a
// postcondition: a is sorted
//                note: this is a dog of a sort
{
    int j,k;
    for(j=n-1; j > 0; j--)
    {   // find largest element in 0..k, move to a[j]
        for(k=0; k < j; k++)
        {   if (a[k+1] < a[k])
            {   Swap(a[k],a[k+1]);
            }
        }
    }
}
```

Bubble sort can be "improved" by stopping if no values are swapped on some pass,[9] meaning that the elements are in order. Add a `bool` flag variable to the preceding code so that the loops stop when no bubbling is necessary. Then time this function and compare it to the other $O(n^2)$ sorts: selection sort and insertion sort.

11.7   Write a function that implements insertion sort on `CList` objects. First test the function on lists of strings. When you've verified that it works, template the function and try it with lists of other types, such as `int`. Since a `CList` object cannot change, you'll have to create a new sorted list from the original. The general idea is to insert one element at a time from the original list into a new list that's kept sorted. The new list contains those elements moved from the original list processed so far. It's easiest to implement the function recursively. You may also find it helpful to implement a helper function:

```
CList<string> addInOrder(const string& s,
                         CList<string>& list)
// pre: list is sorted
// post: return a new list, original with s added,
//        and the new list is sorted
```

Implement the sort in a test program that prints the results from `CList::ConsCalls`. Graph the number of calls as a function of the size of the list being sorted.

11.8   Merge sort is another $O(N \log N)$ sort (like quicksort), although unlike quicksort, merge sort is $O(N \log N)$ in the worst case. The general algorithm for merge sort consists of two steps to sort a `CList` list of N items:

- Recursively sort the first half and the second half of the list. To do this you'll need to create two half-lists: one that's a copy of the first half of a `CList` and the other which is the second half of the `CList`. This means you'll have to `cons` up a list of $N/2$ elements given an N element list. The other $N/2$ element list is just the second half of the original list.
- Merge the two sorted halves together. The key idea is that merging two sorted lists together, creating a sorted list, can be done efficiently in $O(N)$ time if both sorted lists have $O(N)$ elements. The two sorted lists are scanned from left to right, and the smaller element is copied into the list that's the merge of the two.

Write two functions that together implement merge sort for `CList` lists.

```
CList<string>
merge(const CList<string>& a, const CList<string>& b);
// pre: a and b are sorted
// post: return a new list that's sorted,
//        containing all elements from a and b

CList<string> mergesort(CList<string> list);
// post: return a sorted version of list
```

---

[9]This improvement can make a difference for almost-sorted data, but it does not mitigate the generally atrocious performance of this sort.

Dynamic Data, Lists, and Class Templates

Something deeply hidden had to be behind things.
ALBERT EINSTEIN
autobiographical handwritten note
"The Einstein Letter That Started It All"
NY Times Magazine, *August 2, 1964, Ralph E. Lapp*

Although `tvector` variables can be resized and increase (or decrease) in capacity, excess storage is often allocated when vectors are used. Since vectors typically double in size when grown, memory will be wasted unless all vector cells are used. For example, consider a program that counts how many times each of the 3,124 unique words in the file `melville.txt` (*Bartleby, the Scrivener*) occurs by storing the words in a vector using `push_back`. The vector grows in size from 0 to 2, to 4, 8, 16, ... 4,096 elements. Since the automatic resizing operation throws out the old vector after copying elements into a new vector, a total of $2 + 4 + \cdots + 2,048 = 4,094$ elements are thrown out while $4,096 - 3,124 = 972$ elements in the final vector are unused. Although the `tvector` class takes the necessary step to reclaim the storage thrown away, some applications require more precise memory allocation. We've also studied an example of a sparse polynomial class (see Programs 10.18 and 10.19) that was more efficiently implemented using a `CList` collection of terms than a `tvector` collection. In this chapter we'll study a data structure called a **linked list**, which provides an alternative to using vectors. We'll also study how **pointers**, which are used in implementing linked lists and trees, expand the kinds of programs we can write. Pointers are essential in working with large object-oriented programs in C++ and in exploiting inheritance, which we'll cover in Chapter 13. However, once we use pointers, we have to be careful in designing classes to avoid problems we haven't faced before.

12.1 Pointers as Indirect References

12.1.1 What Is a Pointer?

We'll cover three basic uses of pointers in this chapter:

1. Pointers are indirect references that permit resources to be shared among different objects. For example, several random walkers could share an object that records all their positions or shows the positions graphically. Without pointers it's not possible to share an object and to change which object is shared among all the walkers.

2. Pointers let code allocate memory **dynamically**, on an as-needed basis during program execution rather than when the program is compiled. The programmer

controls the lifetime of dynamically allocated memory, unlike the **statically** allocated memory we've used so far. Here static is used as the opposite of dynamic, not to mean allocating static variables as discussed in Section 10.4.3. The variables we've used so far have a lifetime determined by the variable's scope.[1]

3.   Pointers are the basis for implementing linked data structures, which are used in many applications. We'll see how linked lists are the basis for the implementation of the class `CList` and how they are used to implement a set class similar to `StringSet`.

At a basic level, a pointer stores an **address** in computer memory. More abstractly, a pointer refers to something indirectly. If you look up *pointer* in the index of this book, you'll see a reference, or "pointer," to this page. Forwarding addresses also serve as indirect references. Suppose someone named Dave Reed lives at 104 Oak Street. If Dave moves, he'll leave a forwarding address with the post office. If he moves to 351 Coot Lane, then mail addressed to him at 104 Oak Street will be delivered, with some delay, using the forwarding address. The forwarding address is a pointer, or indirect reference, to Dave's new address.

Program 12.1, *pointerdemo.cpp*, shows how pointers are defined and **dereferenced**. A pointer variable is defined when an asterisk ` * ` appears between a type/class name and a variable name. A pointer is an address, but it's an address of a specific type of object, such as `Dice`, `Date`, `int`, or any other built-in or class type. Just as `int x;` defines variable x with no value, a pointer has no value unless one is assigned.

We'll allow pointers to point to (or reference) objects in two ways: allocating an object using **new** or sharing objects between pointers. The new operator returns a pointer to an object created on the **heap**; we'll say more about this later. We can also assign one pointer value to another as shown with d and d2. To access

---

Syntax: Pointers

```
Date * d; // points to garbage
Date * d = new Date();
Date * d2 = d;
Date next = *d + 1;
int month = d->Month();
```

---

the object pointed to by a pointer p, the expression `*p` is used, where `*` is the **dereference** operator. To select a member function in an object pointed to by p we'll use the **selector** operator `->` and write `p->Function()`. The selector operator is shorthand for writing `(*p).Function()`, where dereferencing p yields an object on which the method `Function` is invoked.

Program 12.1 pointerdemo.cpp

```
#include <iostream>
using namespace std;
#include "tvector.h"
#include "date.h"
```

---

[1]For example, the lifetime of a variable declared locally in a function is the duration of the function. See Section 10.4 for details.

```
#include "dice.h"

// basic pointer demo

int main()
{
    Date today;
    Date * nextDay = new Date(today+1);
    Date * prevDay = new Date(today-1);

    cout << "today\t\t tomorrow\t\yesterday" << endl;
    cout << today << "\t" << nextDay << "\t" << prevDay << endl;
    cout << today << "\t" << *nextDay << "\t" << *prevDay << endl;

    nextDay = prevDay;
    cout << today << "\t" << *nextDay << "\t" << *prevDay << endl;
    *prevDay += 2;
    cout << today << "\t" << *nextDay << "\t" << *prevDay << endl;
    cout << today << "\t" << nextDay << "\t" << prevDay << endl;

    cout << endl << "k\tsides\troll\tcount" << endl <<endl;
    const int DICE_COUNT = 6;
    tvector<Dice *> dice(DICE_COUNT);
    int k;
    for(k=0; k < DICE_COUNT; k++)
    {   dice[k] = new Dice(2*k+1);
    }
    for(k=0; k < DICE_COUNT; k++)
    {   cout << k << "\t" << dice[k]->NumSides() << "\t"
             << dice[k]->Roll() << "\t";
        cout << dice[k]->NumRolls() << endl;
    }
    return 0;
}
```

pointerdemo.cpp

Memory addresses in C++ are typically shown using the base 16, or **hexadecimal**, number system, where the letter a corresponds to 10, b to 11, and so forth, with f corresponding to 15. Don't worry about trying to understand hexadecimal notation; you can think of addresses as having values like "101 Main Street." The important relationship is that the value of a pointer is an address. In the output from Program 12.1, the printed values of the pointers nextDay and prevDay are the addresses of what each points to in memory. When the pointers are dereferenced, for example, in the expression *nextDay, the object being pointed to, a Date, is printed.

I ran Program 12.1 on May 18, 1999. The first line of output shows that nextDay and prevDay point to different objects since the addresses printed are different. The last line of Date output shows that these pointers refer to the same object since the addresses are the same. Since the two pointers refer to the same object, when that object is incremented by two in the statement *prevDay += 2, what happens to the value of *nextDay? Since *nextDay is "the object pointed to by nextDay",[2] and this

---

[2]I pronounce *nextDay as "star nextDay." Sometimes I say "the object pointed to by nextDay" to be precise.

object is the same object as `*prevDay`, the statement `*prevDay += 2` affects what `nextDay` points to as well.

```
                          OUTPUT

prompt> pointerdemo
today                    tomorrow           yesterday
May 18 1999              0x00142a10         0x00142a20
May 18 1999              May 19 1999        May 17 1999
May 18 1999              May 17 1999        May 17 1999
May 18 1999              May 19 1999        May 19 1999
May 18 1999              0x00142a20         0x00142a20


k          sides      roll      count

0          1          1         1
1          3          2         1
2          5          3         1
3          7          4         1
4          9          3         1
5          11         5         1
```

The second part of the program creates a vector of `Dice` pointers and rolls each of the `Dice` objects once. Recall that it's not possible to create a `tvector<Dice>` variable because there is no default `Dice` constructor. However, a vector of `Dice` *pointers* can be created as shown in Figure 12.1.

When the vector is defined, the six pointers do not have specific values; they point at "garbage." The word "garbage" means the value of a pointer may be something like 6 or it may be something like 0xffde2000: we don't know if the value is a valid memory location. We create a separate `Dice` object on the heap for each vector pointer to

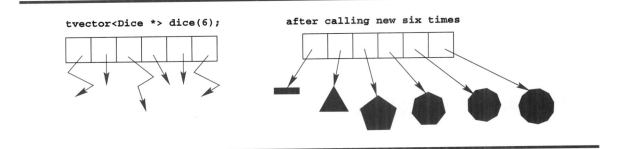

Figure 12.1 A vector of pointers to `Dice` objects.

reference, each Dice object with a different number of sides as shown in the code and the output. The selector operator -> accesses the member functions of each pointed-to Dice object. I pronounce d->NumRolls() as "d arrow NumRolls," but sometimes I say "the NumRolls method of the object pointed to by d." The latter pronunciation makes the pointer/pointed-to difference very clear. A few programmers prefer to write (*d).NumRolls(). The dot operator '.' has higher precedence than the dereference operator '*', so parentheses are needed in the expression (*d).Roll(). Otherwise, the expression *d.Roll() results in an attempt to dereference the Roll() function of d. This would fail for two reasons:

- d is not a class object, so a dot can't follow it.
- Roll() is not a pointer, so it can't be dereferenced (assuming that d.Roll() made syntactic sense).

Most programmers prefer ->, the selector operator, which is typed using the minus sign followed by the greater-than sign. It's easier to read and type p->foo() than (*p).foo().

12.1.2   Heap Objects

The variables today, nextDay, and prevDay are defined in the function main of Program 12.1. The memory for these variables is associated with the function. In general, variables defined in a function are constructed when the function is called and cease to exist when the function exits. These variables are called **automatic** variables since the memory for them is automatically allocated when the function is called and de-allocated when the function exits. Sometimes the term **stack** variable is used, and memory is said to be "allocated on the runtime stack" for variables defined in a function.

In contrast, memory allocated by calling **new** is obtained dynamically when the new statement executes, not automatically. The memory initialized by new is allocated from the **heap**, sometimes called the **freestore**. Objects constructed on the heap last until the program specifically de-allocates them (using **delete**, which we'll discuss in Section 12.1.7), unlike automatic variables, which are de-allocated automatically when they go out of scope. If the class/type allocated by new uses a constructor, then arguments must be provided if the constructor requires them as shown in the vector of Dice pointers of Program 12.1. A constructor with no parameters does not require parentheses, so that Date * d = new Date; creates an object represent-

```
Syntax: The new operator

Thing * t = new Thing;
Thing * t = new Thing();
Thing * t = new Thing(parameters);
```

ing today that's pointed to by d. Parentheses may be used; the statement Date * d = new Date(); creates the same kind of object. I'll use parentheses even when no parameters are passed to the constructor.

In this book I'll use pointers only to point to objects on the heap. In C++ it's possible for objects to point to memory on the stack as well. Invariably this leads to problems because memory on the stack "goes away" when a scope ends. A pointer to stack memory that is out-of-scope will eventually cause problems if the pointer is dereferenced. To help you read programs written by others, I'll show how the **address-of** operator **&** is used to get the address of stack variables, but it's a good idea to stay away from the address-of operator until you're a reasonably accomplished programmer.

```
int main()
{
    Date * d = new Date();        // d points to today
    Date * d2 = new Date(*d+1);   // d2 points to tomorrow
    Date * d3;                    // d3 points to garbage
    if (*d < *d2)
    {   Date yday(*d-1);     // yesterday, all my troubles ...
        d3 = &yday;          // d3 points to yesterday
        cout << "yesterday " << *d3 << endl;
    }
    cout << *d3 << " " << *d << " " << *d2 << endl;
    return 0;
}
```

If I run this program on May 15, 1999, the output will be unpredictable:

```
yesterday May 14 1999
?????  May 15 1999   May 16 1999
```

The code is problematic: d3 points to an object that doesn't exist. The address-of operator & applied to yday returns the address of yday. This works as intended in the body of the if statement, but the variable yday doesn't exist after the body of the if statement executes. This means that d3 points to a nonexistent object; what's printed depends on a number of unknown factors, including how the compiler works and how the operating system behaves. The program may produce what's expected the first time it runs, but not the second.

> **Program Tip 12.1:** **Memory referenced by a pointer should be allocated from the heap.** Using the address-of operator to obtain the address of memory allocated on the stack will eventually lead to problems if that memory goes out of scope. Tracking down this kind of error is difficult because the error often manifests itself differently on different runs of the program and sometimes occurs in code unrelated to where the address-of operator is used.

Pause to Reflect

12.1 Write code that defines two `Dice` pointers, allocates one eight-sided `Dice` object using new that both point to, and then rolls the `Dice` twice, once with each pointer.

12.2 Write a code fragment that defines a vector `dicevec` of 30 pointers to `Dice` objects, initializes `dicevec[k]` to point to a $(k+1)$-sided die (so that `dicevec[0]` is a one-sided die and `dicevec[29]` is a 30-sided die), and then rolls the dice object pointed to by `dicevec[k]` k times.

12.3 Write a code fragment that creates a vector `datevec` of pointers to `Date` objects. There should be as many pointers as there are days in the month the code is executed (e.g., if run in April there should be 30 pointers, if run in May there should be 31 pointers). Initialize `datevec[k]` to point to an object representing the $(k+1)$ day of the month, so `datevec[0]` is the first day of the month. Print each day by looping over all the vector elements.

12.4 Write a function that returns a pointer to a `Date` object that represents exactly one year from the date the function is executed.

12.5 Consider the following function `MakeDie`, which returns a pointer to a `Dice` object:

```
Dice * MakeDie(int n)
// post: return pointer to n-sided Dice object
{
    Dice nSided(n);
    return &nSided;
}
```

Explain why this function can cause problems in code. In particular, the code below may print 6, 4, or some unknown value:

```
Dice * cube  = MakeDie(6);
Dice * tetra = MakeDie(4);
cout << cube->NumSides() << endl;
```

When compiled under Linux/g++, the code generates the warning "*address of local variable 'nSided' returned.*"

12.6 In the worst case, selection sort makes $O(N^2)$ comparisons and $O(N)$ swaps and assignments to sort an N-element vector of strings. Insertion sort makes $O(N^2)$ comparisons and $O(N^2)$ object assignments. If vectors of pointers to strings are sorted rather than vectors of strings, insertion sort may speed up, while selection sort slows down. Explain these observations; think about how comparisons are made (how does the code change) and how objects are swapped/assigned. The change in execution time is less noticeable if int vectors are sorted (compared to int * vectors) and more noticeable if vectors of large `BigInt` objects are sorted (compared to `BigInt` * vectors).

12.7 Suppose that the following definition is made:

```
tvector<tvector<int> *> v(10);
```

so that `v[0]` is a pointer to a vector of integers. The following code fragment makes `v[0]` point to a vector of 100 integers, all equal to 2:

```
v[0] = new tvector<int>(100,2);
```

Since `v[0]` points to a vector of 100 integers, how is an element of this 100-integer vector indexed? Write a loop to print all elements of the 100-element vector.

12.8 What do you think happens if the `new` operator is called, but there is no memory on the heap? How could this happen in a program?

12.9 If a vector of pointers to strings is sorted using `operator < ` to compare the pointers, the output will be based on the addresses of the strings (i.e., `a[0]` will be the string with the lowest numerical address in memory). Complete the function object `StrPtrCompare` to sort `vector<string *>` a so that the strings pointed to will be in alphabetical order.

```
struct StrPtrCompare
{
    int compare(string * lhs, string * rhs)
    {
        // fill in code here
    }
};
```

12.1.3 Sharing Objects

In this section we'll see how pointers make it possible to share an object. In all the classes we've used so far, the instance variables in one object are independent from the instance variables in any other object. Suppose that we want to create several random walk objects (see Programs 7.10 and 7.12), but keep in one vector a record of the positions visited by all the walkers. We'd like to share the vector among all the random walkers, but without pointers we cannot do this. We'll illustrate the problem with a simpler toy example before developing a solution for the posed problem with random walkers.

Program 12.2 shows what happens when two `Kid` objects try to share a `Toy`. The situation we'd like to have is illustrated in Figure 12.2. The figure and the program output show what actually happens.

Program 12.2 sharetoy.cpp

```
#include <iostream>
#include <string>
```

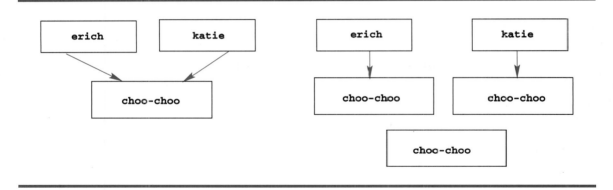

Figure 12.2 Sharing without pointers. On the left is what we want: objects `erich` and `katie` share a toy. On the right is what we have: three copies of a toy, no sharing.

```
using namespace std;

// references and pointers for sharing, a prelude

class Toy    // kids play with toys
{
  public:
    Toy(const string& name);
    void Play();           // prints a message
    void BecomeBroken();   // the toy becomes broken
  private:
    string myName;
    bool   myIsWorking;
};

class Kid
{
  public:
    Kid(const string& name, Toy& toy);
    void   Play();          // plays with own toy
  private:
    string myName;
    Toy    myToy;
};

Toy::Toy(const string& name)
 : myName(name), myIsWorking(true)
{ }

void Toy::Play()
// post: toy is played with, message printed
{
    if (myIsWorking)
    {   cout << "this " << myName << " is so fun :-)" << endl;
    }
```

```
        else
        {   cout << "this " << myName << " is broken :-(" << endl;
        }
}

void Toy::BecomeBroken()
// post: toy is broken
{
        myIsWorking = false;
        cout << endl << "oops, this " << myName << " just broke" << endl << endl;
}

Kid::Kid(const string& name,Toy& toy)
 : myName(name), myToy(toy)
{ }

void Kid::Play()
// post: kid plays and talks about it
{
        cout << "My name is " << myName << ", ";
        myToy.Play();
}

int main()
{
        Toy plaything("choo-choo train");
        Kid erich("erich", plaything);
        Kid katie("katie", plaything);

        erich.Play(); katie.Play();
        plaything.BecomeBroken();        // the toy is now broken
        erich.Play(); katie.Play();
        return 0;
}
```

sharetoy.cpp

Although the Toy object plaything is broken in main, the kids continue to enjoy a working toy. The problem is that the instance variable myToy in each kid is a **copy** of the toy defined in main. When we assign one variable to another, we don't expect the variables to share anything. In other words, we expect the output of the following statements to be "hello world," not "hello hello."

```
string a = "world";
string b = a;
a = "hello ";
cout << a << b << endl;
```

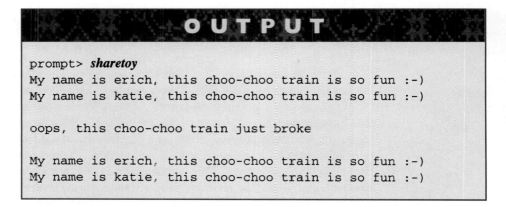

If we want the instance variable myToy to reference memory (a toy) allocated elsewhere, such as in main, we have two choices: use a reference variable or use a pointer.

12.1.4   Reference Variables

We can achieve the desired behavior by adding one character to the code in Program 12.2. If we change the declaration of Toy myToy to Toy& myToy the output changes as follows:

```
                          OUTPUT

prompt> sharetoy
My name is erich, this choo-choo train is so fun :-)
My name is katie, this choo-choo train is so fun :-)

oops, this choo-choo train just broke

My name is erich, this choo-choo train is broken :-(
My name is katie, this choo-choo train is broken :-(
```

Just as a reference parameter is an alias for memory allocated elsewhere, a reference variable refers to memory allocated elsewhere. In Program 12.2, making myToy a reference variable avoids creating a copy when myToy is initialized in the Kid initializer list. Instance variables that are references *must* be constructed and initialized using an initializer list, not in the body of the class constructor. Once a reference variable is constructed, it cannot be reassigned to. In Program 12.2, *sharetoy.cpp*, this means that a Kid object cannot change toys; it's impossible to add new member functions that change the toy a kid uses for play.

12.1.5   Pointers for Sharing

In some situations we'd like to change the object being shared, that is, change the toy shared in Program 12.2. Furthermore, it's not possible to have vectors of references in C++, so we must turn to pointers. Using pointers for sharing allows a shared object to be changed and makes it possible to use a vector to share many objects.

We'll develop a program for several walkers to record their movements with a `WalkRecorder` object shared among the walkers. We'll keep the example simple to illustrate the concept and to highlight a problem that arises frequently when several interdependent classes are used in the same program. The problem arises when class A uses class B and vice versa. This interdependency can create compilation problems if you don't design the class interfaces properly and write the header files with care. We'll discuss the design of the walker program, then the problems with interdependencies; then we'll show the program implementation that addresses the interdependency problems.

We'll use two classes in the program:

■   The class `Walker` simulates a one-dimensional walker, recording the walk with a `WalkRecorder` object.

■   The class `WalkRecorder` records a walker's position. A walker is passed to the recorder, and the recorder then queries the walker to get its position to record it.

To record a walk, each walker must know about a `WalkRecorder` object. We'll design the `Walker` class so that each walker object maintains a pointer to the recorder that's recording the walker's movements. It will be possible to share a recorder among several walkers or to give each walker a separate recorder object. In designing the classes and programs we must consider at least three questions:

■   A `WalkRecorder` records a walker. Who is responsible for passing the walker? How is the walker passed to the `WalkRecorder`?

■   Where are `Walker` and `WalkRecorder` objects created? In `main`? Does a walker create its own recorder?

■   How is the data recorded by a `WalkRecorder` displayed?

To keep the program simple we'll create all the objects in `main`. In a more complex program you might create a class in charge of object creation. We'll create a recorder, then pass the recorder to each `Walker` object when the `Walker` is created; but we'll also design a method for changing a walker's recorder.

Since a walker knows its recorder, we'd like the walker to ask the recorder to make a record of the walker itself. Each walker can pass itself to its recorder using the reserved word **this**, which every object has as a pointer to itself. A variable named `foo` in `main` might be known as the parameter `firstFoo` in a function to which it's passed as an argument. In general, objects have different names in different places in a program. However, in C++ every object uses the identifier `this` as its own name. Because `this` is a pointer, `*this` is the way an object identifies itself since "star this" is also "the object pointed to by this," which is itself!

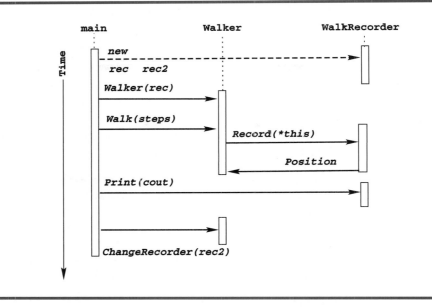

Figure 12.3 Interaction diagram for the classes Walker and WalkRecorder showing a recorder being shared and changed.

Finally, the code in main will ask a recorder to print the data the recorder has kept track of. Again, in a more complex program we might provide member functions for retrieving the data, but for now we'll be content with printing the recorded data.

A first draft of the two classes is shown in Program 12.3. The interactions between these classes and the main of Program 12.4, *frogwalk3.cpp*, are shown in the **interaction diagram** in Figure 12.3. As a program executes, time increases from the top of the diagram to the bottom. Arrows indicate when one class (or program segment) calls another, and the method used to make the call. The dashed line at the top of the diagram indicates an indirect call of a constructor via new.

12.1.6 Interdependencies, Class Declarations, and Header Files

We're ready to start implementing the classes. Although the final program *frogwalk3.cpp* shows everything in one file, we'll discuss the class declarations and definitions assuming that separate .h and .cpp files are used. A high-level first pass yields Walker on the right and WalkRecorder on the left.

Program 12.3 walkdesign.cpp

```
#infdef _WALKRECCRDER_H          #ifndef _WALKER_H
#define _WALKRECCRDER_H          #define _WALKER_H
```

```
#include "walker.h"                    #include "walkrecorder.h"
class WalkRecorder                     class Walker
{                                      {
  public:                                public:
    WalkRecorder();                        Walker(WalkRecorder* wrec);
    void Record(const Walker& walker);     void Walk(int steps);
    void Print(ostream& out) const;        int  Position() const;
  private:                                 void ChangeRecorder(WalkRecorder* wrec);
    tmatrix<int> myRecord                private:
};                                         int  myPosition;
                                           WalkRecorder * myRecorder;
                                       };
```

walkdesign.cpp

This design won't compile when we create the main program that includes both header files. Remember that the preprocessor (see Section 7.2.3) literally cuts and pastes a .h file when a #include is processed, and that include files that are included by an include file are also cut-and-pasted (and include files that they include and so on). This is why the #ifndef _CLASSNAME_H appears at the top of each include file. Without this, consider the following main program that includes both classes:

```
#include "walker.h"
#include "walkrecorder.h"
int main()
{
    // ...
    return 0;
}
```

Since walker includes walkrecorder, which includes walker, which includes ..., there would be an infinite chain of cut-and-paste includes without the protecting #ifndef statements. These protecting statements do stop an infinite chain of includes, but there's a different problem.

The line #include"walker.h" appears in *walkrecorder.h* (as simulated and shown in *walkdesign.cpp*, Program 12.3) because the class Walker is used as a parameter in WalkRecorder::Record. Similarly the class WalkRecorder is a parameter in two Walker methods. However, if the main program above is used, where the first include is #include "walker.h", then the preprocessor creates the following compilation unit:

```
class WalkRecorder
{
    ...
};
class Walker
{
    ...
};
// more code here
```

The classes appear in the order shown, with WalkRecorder first, because the preprocessor first processes *walker.h*. The first line in this header file is another #include so
this include for *walkrecorder.h* is processed before the declaration of the class Walker
is read by the preprocessor. The include file in *walkrecorder.h* isn't a problem—it's not
preprocessed because of the #ifndef protection—but the class WalkRecorder does
appear first when the compiler is called after the preprocessor finishes.

The compiler stops at the declaration of the method WalkRecorder::Record
because the compiler hasn't yet seen the class Walker, so it doesn't know anything
about the parameter! How can this problem be fixed? This problem is fixable, but only
because the classes make reference to each other in the class declarations using only
references or pointers to the other class. The compiler doesn't need to know the names
of Walker member functions or how big a Walker object is to compile the header file
for WalkRecorder. Similarly, the header file for Walker can be compiled without
knowing the details of WalkRecorder. Suppose, however, that the instance variable
myRecorder isn't a pointer, but is declared as follows:

```
WalkRecorder myRecorder;
```

With this declaration we won't be able to share recorders since a Walker object's
recorder will be a copy (see Program 12.2). In addition, the compiler must know how
much memory a WalkRecorder requires (the sum of the sizes of its instance variables)
to compile this declaration. Because all pointers and references are basically aliases or
indirect references to memory allocated elsewhere, all pointers and references use the
same amount of memory, regardless of the type of object being pointed to or referenced. If
the class declaration in a header file uses another class with only pointers or references,
it's possible to create a **forward reference** to the class being used. For *walker.h* the
forward reference of WalkRecorder looks like this:

```
class WalkRecorder;
class Walker
{
  public:
    Walker(WalkRecorder* wrec);

    void Walk(int steps);
    int  Position() const;
    void ChangeRecorder(WalkRecorder* wrec);

  private:
    int  myPosition;
    WalkRecorder * myRecorder;
};
```

Now the preprocessor won't have any problems. The compiler parses the forward reference of WalkRecorder as a class whose declaration will be supplied later. Later is
good enough since the compiler doesn't need to know the names of WalkRecorder
methods nor how big a WalkRecorder object is to compile the Walker declaration.

In the implementation file, *walker.cpp*, you'll need to write

```
#include "walkrecorder.h"
```

since the implementation of `Walker::Walk` calls `myRecorder->Record` as shown in the interaction diagram Figure 12.3. This isn't a problem, though, because the header files don't include each other; they're simply included in a .cpp file as needed. The complete Program 12.4 shows forward declarations, class declarations, and implementations. A run follows the program listing.

> **Program Tip 12.2:   Use forward references rather than #includes whenever possible in a header file.** If a class Foo uses a class Thing and Thing objects appear only as pointers or references in parameters and instance variables, then the header file *foo.h* should use `class Thing;` as a forward reference rather than `#include "thing.h"`.

Program 12.4 frogwalk3.cpp

```
#include <iostream>
#include <fstream>
#include <string>
using namespace std;

#include "prompt.h"
#include "tvector.h"
#include "randgen.h"
#include "dice.h"

class Walker;
class WalkRecorder
{
  public:
    WalkRecorder();
    void Record(const Walker& walker);
    void Print(ostream& out) const;

  private:
    static int MAX;
    tvector<int> myRecord;
    int          myBeyondCount;
};

class Walker
{
  public:
    Walker(WalkRecorder* wrec);

    void Walk(int steps);
```

```
    int  Position() const;
    void ChangeRecorder(WalkRecorder* wrec);

  private:
    int  myPosition;
    WalkRecorder * myRecorder;
};

int WalkRecorder::MAX = 100;

WalkRecorder::WalkRecorder()
    : myRecord(2*MAX+1,0), myBeyondCount(0)
{
    // record -MAX..MAX, all zero
}

void WalkRecorder::Record(const Walker& walker)
{
    int pos = walker.Position();
    if (fabs(pos) > MAX)
    {   myBeyondCount++;
    }
    else
    {   myRecord[pos+MAX]++;
    }
}

void WalkRecorder::Print(ostream& out) const
{
    int lowIndex=-1,highIndex=0,k;
    for(k=0; k < 2*MAX+1; k++)
    {   if (myRecord[k] != 0)
        {   if (lowIndex == -1) lowIndex = k;
            highIndex = k;
        }
    }
    if (lowIndex == -1)
    {   out << " no steps taken" << endl;
        return;
    }
    for(k=lowIndex; k <= highIndex; k++)
    {   cout << k-MAX << "\t" << myRecord[k] << endl;
    }
    cout << endl << "beyond boundaries = " << myBeyondCount << endl;
}

Walker::Walker(WalkRecorder * wrec)
    : myPosition(0), myRecorder(wrec)
{

}

void Walker::Walk(int steps)
{
    Dice d(2);
```

```
    int k;
    for(k=0; k < steps; k++)
    {   if (d.Roll() == 1)
        {   myPosition++;
        }
        else
        {   myPosition--;
        }
        myRecorder->Record(*this);
    }
}


int Walker::Position() const
{
    return myPosition;
}


void Walker::ChangeRecorder(WalkRecorder* wrec)
{
    myRecorder = wrec;
}


int main()
{
    WalkRecorder * rec =  new WalkRecorder();
    WalkRecorder * rec2 = new WalkRecorder();
    Walker w1(rec);
    Walker w2(rec);
    int steps = PromptRange("how many steps ",1,10000);
    w1.Walk(steps);
    w2.Walk(steps);
    rec->Print(cout);

    cout << endl << "another walk" << endl << endl;

    w1.ChangeRecorder(rec2);
    w2.ChangeRecorder(rec2);
    w1.Walk(steps);
    w2.Walk(steps);
    rec2->Print(cout);
    return 0;
}
```

frogwalk3.cpp

```
          O U T P U T
```

prompt> *frogwalk3*

how many steps between 1 and 10000: *20*
```
-6      1
-5      2
-4      3
-3      5
-2      7
-1      7
 0      5
 1      6
 2      4
```

beyond boundaries = 0

another walk

```
-1      1
 0      2
 1      5
 2      7
 3      6
 4      6
 5      5
 6      4
 7      3
 8      1
```

beyond boundaries = 0

12.1.7 delete and Destructors

Whenever a program allocates memory from the freestore (heap) using new, the memory should eventually be returned to the freestore using **delete** when the memory is no longer needed. For example, at the end of main in Program 12.4 we could add the lines shown here:

```
int main()
{
    WalkRecorder * rec =  new WalkRecorder();
    WalkRecorder * rec2 = new WalkRecorder();
```

```
   . . .
   delete rec;
   delete rec2;
   return 0;
}
```

Returning the `WalkRecorder` objects referenced by pointers `rec` and `rec2` to the heap isn't really necessary here since all memory used by a program is reclaimed by the system when the program terminates. The `delete` operator returns memory allocated by `new`; it takes a pointer as an argument. Although the argument to delete is a pointer,

> **Syntax: The `delete` operator**
>
> ```
> delete ptr;
> ```

an object is returned to the heap, not the pointer used in the statement when `delete` is called. The pointer must point to an object allocated by `new` or an error will occur. If you delete a stack object, for example, the system may think the object came from the heap and will be reused in a subsequent call of `new`. This almost always causes trouble in a program. Similarly, you should not delete an object twice since the system's bookkeeping may think the object is free twice, but there is only one object, not two.

```
Date * dptr = new Date();   // today
delete dptr;                // ok, reclaim memory
delete dptr;                // trouble, reclaimed twice
```

Deleting an object *does not* change the value of the pointer to the object, but the pointer is now referencing memory that is no longer valid having been returned to the freestore. It is also an error to dereference a pointer immediately after the object it points to has been deleted:

```
Date * dptr = new Date();       // today
delete dptr;                    // ok, reclaim memory
Date tomorrow(*dptr + 1);       // trouble, *dptr doesn't exist
```

The code above may seem to work when you run it, but this style of programming will eventually lead to an error that's very difficult to track down. Some programmers assign the special pointer value zero to a pointer after deleting the object it points to.

```
Date * dptr = new Date();       // today
delete dptr;                    // ok, reclaim memory
dptr = 0;                       // errors easier to find
delete dptr;                    // ok, no memory
Date tomorrow(*dptr + 1);       // immediate error caused
```

A pointer with the value zero is called a **null pointer**. In C++ you can write `p = NULL` where `p` is a pointer, but the identifier `NULL` is not a reserved word; it's a preprocessor macro defined in the standard header file `<cstddef>`, which is almost always included by some other standard header file. It's better to use zero since no header files are needed. Dereferencing a null pointer causes an immediate error: a segmentation fault on Unix/Linux systems, a general protection fault or unhandled exception on other systems.

Immediate errors are good because you can almost always find the cause of the error using a symbolic debugger. It is not an error to delete a null pointer, so assigning zero to a pointer after deleting the object it points to is a reasonable defensive programming strategy.

In general you should try to return memory no longer needed to the heap, or it's possible your program will eventually use up all the memory available. Consider the following code:

```
Date today;
Date * dptr;
while (true)
{
   int month = PromptString("enter month (0 to exit)", 0.12);
   if (month == 0) break;
   dptr = new Date(1,month,today.Year());
   MakeCalendar(*dptr);
   // should call delete dptr here, but forgot
}
```

Each time the loop iterates a `Date` object is allocated from the heap. The next time the loop iterates, the previous `Date` object is lost; there is no pointer referencing it, so it has become inaccessible. If the loop executes 10,000 times then 10,000 `Date` objects will have been allocated and remain unusable. In some languages, like Java, memory that is no longer accessible is automatically reclaimed using a technique called **garbage collection**. In standard C++ environments there is no automatic garbage collection; programmers are responsible for it.

> **Program Tip 12.3: Deleting objects is a good idea, but deleting improperly will cause problems in your program.** You can't, for example, delete an object twice without eventually causing problems. Nor can you delete an object that wasn't allocated using `new` without causing problems. When you're developing a program, add `delete` code only when you know your program is working correctly so that any error due to improper deletes can be found without looking at other code.

The Destructor Member Function. Just as a constructor is called automatically when an object is defined, a special member function called the **destructor** is called automatically when an object goes out of scope.[3] When an class object allocates memory, the object should be responsible for deleting the memory. If the memory is referenced by an instance variable it cannot be deleted until the object is no longer needed. The destructor will be called either when the program deletes the object using `delete` or when the object goes out of scope and isn't accessible. For any class named `Thing`, a member

---

[3] You can think of *going out of scope* as becoming undefined to contrast with definition and the constructor.

function named ˜Thing is the class **destructor**. We'll discuss destructors in more
detail in Section 12.3.5.

Pause to Reflect

12.10 Assume that a reference instance variable Toy& myToy is used in the class Kid
as described in Section 12.1.4. The function MakeKid returns a pointer to a Kid
object as follows:

```
Kid * MakeKid()
{
    Toy block("wooden block");
    Kid * kptr = new Kid("alex",block);
    return kptr;
}
```

Explain why the object pointed to and returned by MakeKid will cause problems.

12.11 If the instance variable myToy is changed to a pointer, how do the member
functions of the class Kid change?

```
class Kid
{
   ...
   private:

       Toy * myToy;
};
```

12.12 Write declarations and implementations of all methods of a modified Kid class.
Each Kid creates his/her own toy allocated from the heap and stores a pointer to
the toy. Three methods are added: GetToy, ShareFrom, and Unshare. The
functions are used as follows:

```
Kid robert("robert");   // creates his own toy
Kid laura("laura");     // creates her own toy
laura.Play();           // play with own toy
robert.Play();

robert.ShareFrom(laura); // robert shares laura's toy
robert.Play();           // with laura's toy
robert.Unshare();
robert.Play();           // with robert's original toy
```

The function GetToy is called in the implementation of ShareFrom. Can
GetToy be private?

12.13 Using forward references (see Program Tip 12.2) rather than #include statements can save on preprocessor time and make it less necessary to recompile a client program when classes the client uses are changed. Consider the program fragment in the previous exercise that shows two Kid objects playing. Explain why it is necessary to have #include "kid.h" in the program above, but it is *not* necessary to have #include"toy.h". Explain why class Toy can be a forward reference in *kid.h* but why #include "toy.h" is needed in *kid.cpp*. Finally, explain why the client code above does *not* need to be recompiled if the implementation of Toy changes, but why *kid.cpp* will need to be recompiled, and why the program must be relinked.

12.14 Create an interaction diagram for the code fragment above in which two Kid objects play and share a toy. Show main, Kid, and Toy. Include details about when/where objects are created and when/where all member functions are called.

12.15 Design a class ToyChest that holds several pointers to toy objects. Kids should be able to get toys from the chest and put toys back in the chest. Consider at least two ways to have toys added to the chest: when constructed the chest creates its own toys; and a Kid can add a toy to a chest that originated in a different toy chest. You'll need to think carefully about the design so that a toy can be shared among kids playing with it, but reside in only one toy chest.

12.16 If a Kid allocates his/her own toy from the heap, who is responsible for deleting the toy?

12.17 In *frogwalk3.cpp*, Program 12.4, a new recorder is attached to the Walker objects in main. Write a new member function WalkRecorder::Clear() that clears a recorder's memory. Show how to use this new function to achieve the same effect of *frogwalk3.cpp*, but using only one recorder that's cleared rather than using two recorders.

12.18 When should the WalkRecorder objects in *frogwalk3.cpp* be deleted?

12.19 How can the class WalkRecorder be changed to track every position, not just those between −MAX and MAX?

12.20 What is the purpose of the loop in WalkRecorder::Print? Why is the value of lowIndex compared to −1?

12.21 Write code to create a vector of 100 pointers to Dice objects, making a[k] point to a $(2k + 1)$-sided Dice. Roll each Dice 1,000 times, then delete all the objects.

Alan Perlis *(1922–1990)*

In 1966 Alan Perlis became the first recipient of the Turing award. The award was given for his work in programming language design. In 1965 he established the

first graduate program in computer science at what was then the Carnegie Institute of Technology and is now Carnegie-Mellon University.

In [AS96], Perlis is quoted with some important advice to novices and experts in computer science: *"I think that it's extraordinarily important*

that we in computer science keep fun in computing. . . . I hope the field of computer science never loses its sense of fun. . . . What's in your hands, I think and hope, is intelligence: the ability to see the machine as more than when you were first led up to it, that you can make it more."

In his Turing award address, Perlis looked ahead to parallel and distributed computation, a field that has been growing steadily and receiving increased attention in recent years. He also talked of the intellectual foundation of programming, from Turing's work to the languages Lisp and ALGOL, which have had a profound impact on programming language design.

In [AS96] he writes about programming:

To appreciate programming as an intellectual activity in its own right you must turn to computer programming; you must read and write computer programs—many of them. It doesn't matter much what the programs are about or what applications they serve. What does matter is how well they perform and how smoothly they fit with other programs in the creation of still greater programs.

A list of Perlis epigrams has been gathered, including these:

- Most people find the concept of programming obvious, but the doing impossible.
- Once you understand how to write a program, get someone else to write it.
- The best book on programming for the layman is *Alice in Wonderland*; but that's because it's the best book on anything for the layman.

For more information see [Per87].

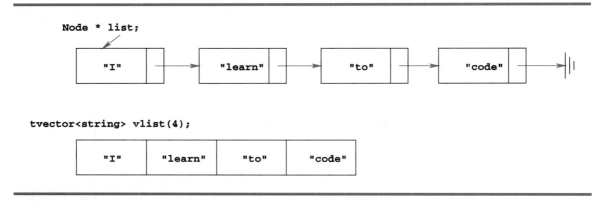

Figure 12.4 Comparing vectors and linked lists.

12.2 Linked Lists

A **linked list** stores a sequence of items, as does a vector. However, vectors support random access to any element: the time needed to access a[5] is the same as the time needed to access a[100] when a is a tvector. In contrast, items that are stored near the front of a linked list are accessed more quickly than items near the end of a linked list. This is analogous to how the songs, or tracks, on a cassette tape are arranged. Accessing the fifth song requires skipping over the first four, and songs near the end of the tape take longer to access than songs near the front. Arrays are more like compact discs: it's as easy to play the last track of a CD as it is the first because CD players provide random access to the tracks.

Like any recording tape, linked lists permit new items to be "spliced" into the middle of a list. In the same way that tapes can become longer by splicing in new segments of tape and can be made shorter by cutting out segments of tape, linked lists can have items added and deleted from any location in the list without shifting other items in the list. In some sense, pointers link together the different items of a list in the same way that glue or tape is used to splice segments of magnetic tape.

If a vector contains 100 items, the items must be allocated contiguously in memory. When linked lists are used, the different items (these items are usually called **nodes** in contrast with the cells of a vector) do *not* need to be allocated contiguously. Each node of a linked list has a pointer to the node that follows it; these pointers are the "tape" used to splice nodes together. Figure 12.4 shows a linked list and an array that store the same values. The last node of a list usually points to 0 (NULL) so that a program can determine when the last node has been reached. This is diagrammed in Figure 12.4 with the symbol for an electrical ground, three vertical bars.

Abstractly, a linked list is very similar to a CList object, and in fact linked lists are used to implement the CList class. A linked list has a first node, like the head of a CList. The first node points to all the other nodes in the linked list, specifically to the first of these other nodes. The other nodes are like the tail of a CList object. More concretely, a node in a linked list contains the information stored in the node, and a pointer to the next node in the list. In C++ a node storing a string is declared like this:

```
struct Node
{
    string info;
    Node * next;
};
```

The info field of the struct stores information, in this case a string. The next field stores a pointer to the next node in the list. This declaration is self-referential: the declaration for Node includes a pointer to a node. This is fine because a pointer can be declared without knowing completely how much memory the thing it points to uses, as we saw in Section 12.1.6. It would be illegal, for example, to declare Node as

```
struct Node
{
    string info;
    Node next;
};
```

Here the next field isn't a pointer, but a Node. This declaration is circular and will be rejected by the compiler. The g++ compiler generates an error message (in a program named *foo.cpp*):

```
foo.cpp:4: field 'next' has incomplete type
```

When the compiler parses the declaration for next, the declaration for the struct Node is not yet complete. The declaration can be incomplete for a pointer to a Node to be used, but not for a Node.

Program 12.5, *strlink.cpp*, shows how a tvector and a linked list are initialized to contain the four strings "I," "learn," "to," "code." A tvector of strings is stored in the variable vec, and a linked list based on the struct Node is pointed to by a pointer variable first. When you write code that uses linked lists you'll need to maintain a pointer to the first node in the list. Often you'll need to maintain a pointer to the last node to make it easier to add a node at the end of the list. You could write code to find the last node by starting at the beginning and traversing the list until the last node is found (the next field of the last node points to 0). It's much faster, however, to maintain pointers to both the first and last nodes. Only one pointer, to the first node of a list, is maintained in *strlink.cpp*.

Program 12.5 strlink.cpp

```
#include <iostream>
#include <string>
using namespace std;
#include "tvector.h"

// compare linked list construction to vector construction
```

```
struct Node
{
    string info;
    Node * next;
    Node(const string& s, Node * link)
      : info(s),
        next(link)
    { }
};

void Print(Node * list);
void Print(const tvector<string> & list);

int main()
{
    Node * first=0;     // initially no nodes in list
    Node * temp=0;      // initialize to 0 for defensive programming
    int k;
    tvector<string> vec;
    string storage[] = {"I", "learn", "to", "code"};

    for(k=0; k < 4; k++)
    {   vec.push_back(storage[k]);
        temp = new Node(storage[k],first);   // new node before first
        first = temp;                        // make first point at new node
    }
    cout << "vector:\t\t";
    Print(vec);
    cout << "linked list:\t";
    Print(first);
    return 0;
}

void Print(Node * list)
// pre: list is 0-terminated (last node's next field is 0)
// post: all info fields of list printed on one line
{
    Node * temp;
    for(temp = list; temp != 0; temp = temp->next)
    {   cout << temp->info << " ";
    }
    cout << endl;
}

void Print(const tvector<string> & list)
// pre: list contains list.size() entries
// post: all elements printed on one line
{
    int k;
    for(k=0; k < list.size(); k++)
    {   cout << list[k] << " ";
    }
    cout << endl;
}
```

strlink.cpp

```
prompt> strlink
vector:          I learn to code
linked list:     code to learn I
```

12.2.1 Creating Nodes with Linked Lists

The values stored in the built-in array `storage` are used to initialize the vector `vec` and the linked list pointed to by `first`. Since new values are added to the front of the list, the values are in reverse order from those stored in the vector as the output shows. To add new nodes at the end of the list requires maintaining a pointer to the last node. This is straightforward except for a fencepost problem of creating the first node. As we'll see, it's easy to add or splice in a new node after another node. Initially there are no nodes, so there's no last node to add a new node after. We'll need special-case code to deal with this fencepost problem, or we'll need to use a header node as discussed in Section 12.2.6.

> **Program Tip 12.4: Creating a linked list often requires special-case code to manage the creation of the first node since this node is the only node that doesn't follow another node.** Sometimes creating a dummy first node (called a header node) avoids lots of special-case code.

Since there's a constructor for the `struct Node`, it's simple to create a new node and initialize its fields. If there were no constructor we'd need three statements to allocate and initialize a node:

```
temp = new Node();        // create new node
temp->info = storage[k];  // store info
temp->next = first;       // point at first node of list
```

The two statements creating the node and ensuring that `first` points at the new node can be combined into a single statement:

```
first = new Node(storage[k],first);  // new first node
```

The "old" value of `first` is used to construct the node, so the new node points at the old first node. The pointer to the newly created node is returned by `new`, and the pointer value is assigned to first creating a new first node. This statement mirrors exactly the use of `cons` with a `CList` object for adding a new node to the front of a list.

```
CList<string> list;
list = cons(string("apple"), list);
```

12.2.2 Iterating over a Linked List

The `for` loop that prints all the nodes of the linked list in the function `Print` of Program 12.5, *strlink.cpp*, is the standard method for looping over all nodes of a linked list. If `list` points at the first node, we write:

```
Node * temp;
for(temp = list; temp != 0; temp = temp->next)
{
    // process *temp
}
```

The statement `temp = temp->next` advances the pointer `temp` so that it points at the next node (e.g., at the second node if it used to point to the first node). When the loop finishes, `temp` is zero, or NULL. Because `list` is passed by value to `Print`, changes to `list` don't affect the argument passed. Since the parameter is a copy, we don't need the temporary pointer and could write the following loop instead:

```
for( ;  list != 0; list=list->next)
{   cout << list->info << " ";
}
```

There's no initialization in the `for` loop because `list` points at the first node.

Many programmers prefer to use a `while` loop for iterating over a list.

```
while (list != 0)
{   // process *list
    list = list->next;
};
```

There's nothing inherently wrong with using the temporary pointer, and we'll see that a temporary pointer is often required in a class-based use of linked lists.

Of course `Print` can be written recursively, too:

```
void Print(Node * list)
{
    if (list != 0)
    {   cout << list->info << " ";
        Print(list->next);
    }
}
```

The recursive function doesn't insert an `endl` onto the stream. This would be done in the client code that calls the recursive `Print`.

> **Program Tip 12.5:** **When a node pointer is passed by value, changes to the pointer cannot affect the pointer passed as an argument, but changes *can* be made to the object pointed to; these changes have an effect on the node.** The distinction here is between the pointer, which is passed by value, and the node, which isn't really passed; but the pointer to the node can be used to change the node. In other words, list = NULL doesn't affect a pointer parameter list passed by value, but *list = ... does affect the object pointed to.

12.2.3 Adding a Last Node to a Linked List

We'll discuss modifications to *strlink.cpp* that add new nodes to the end of the list instead of the front. We'll use a pointer named last that always points to the last node of the list being constructed, so the statement "last points to last node in linked list" is a loop invariant. Since the invariant must be true the first time the for loop test is evaluated, we must create a last node before the loop. Initializing last = 0 does *not* create a node, so we must create a node before the loop. We have two choices in creating an initial node:

- Store data in the node so that the initial last node is also the initial first node storing "I" in Program 12.5. This is the approach used in the program fragment below. Since we use the same loop for creating nodes and vector elements, we would need to add a value to the vector before the loop, too.
- Create a dummy, also called a header, node that does not store data but is used so that even the first node in a list has a node before it. With a header node, every node in the list has a predecessor node (the header node isn't considered part of the list).

The formation of the linked list at each iteration of the loop is diagrammed in Figure 12.5. Note that after each loop iteration the variable last points to the last node of the linked list. The variable first, initialized before the loop because of the fencepost problem, never moves and always points to the first node of the linked list.

```
Node * first = 0;
Node * last = 0;
last = first = new Node(storage[0],0);  // last is first
for(k=1; k < 4; k++)
{   last->next = new Node(storage[k],0); // new last node
    last = last->next;                   // update last
}
```

12.2.4 Deleting Nodes in a Linked List

The nodes allocated in Program 12.5, *strlink.cpp*, are not deleted. We'll write a function DeleteNodes to delete all the nodes in a linked list whose first node is passed to the

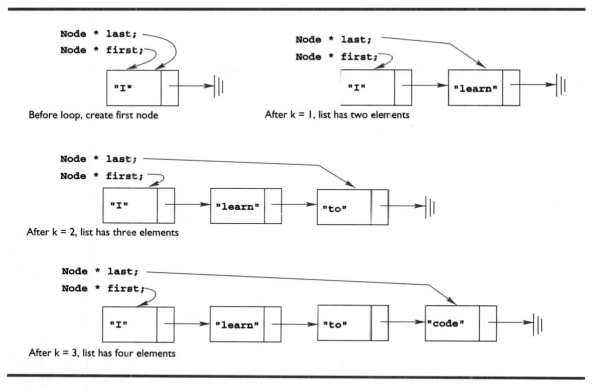

Figure 12.5 Building a linked list by adding a last node.

function. Deleting nodes in a linked list requires careful coding. We'll use recursion in DeleteNodes because it's much easier than writing a loop. As with all recursive functions, some base case must be identified. When linked lists are used, the base case is usually the empty list (typically a NULL/zero pointer) although sometimes a one-node list can be used as a base case.

```
void DeleteNodes(Node * list)
// post: all nodes in list are deleted
{
    if (list != 0)
    {   DeleteNodes(list->next);   // delete after me
        delete list;               // delete first node
    }
}
```

If you believe that the recursion handles all nodes after the first node, then the function works as intended since after deleting all the other nodes, the first node is returned to the freestore. Writing an iterative version of this function requires a temporary pointer, as illustrated in Figure 12.6.

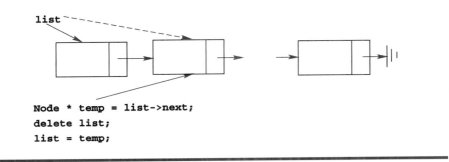

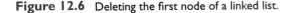

```
Node * temp = list->next;
delete list;
list = temp;
```

Figure 12.6   Deleting the first node of a linked list.

Since the first node will be deleted, we must initialize a temporary pointer `temp` to point to the second node. After deleting the first node, the pointer `list` can be reassigned to point to the second node, whose value was saved in `temp`.

```
void DeleteNodes(Node * list)
// post: all nodes in list are deleted
{
    Node * temp;
    while (list != 0)
    {   temp = list->next;   // remember next node in list
        delete list;         // first node gone
        list = temp;         // new first node
    }
}
```

At first, you might think that a temporary pointer isn't necessary and that the following code can be used to delete the first node pointed to by `list`:

```
delete list;
list = list->next;
```

There is a problem with this code: you can't be sure what happens to the node pointed to by `list` after the deletion. Once deleted, the node is garbage and may be reclaimed by some other program or some other part of the system. Some programming environments may explicitly fill all deleted storage with garbage. In these cases, dereferencing `list` using `list->next` can result in a bad dereference, causing the program to abort. Although your code has not done anything with the storage that `list` used to point to, which was just deleted, you cannot be sure that the node still exists or that the `next` field has the same value. You must use a temporary variable.

12.2.5   Splicing Nodes into a Linked List

One of the primary advantages of using a linked list instead of a vector is the ability to add new nodes to the middle of a list without shifting the other nodes. To add a new value to a sorted vector we must shift the vector elements to make room for the new element. No shifting is required to add a new node to a sorted linked list so that the list remains sorted. Program 12.6 shows a function `AddInOrder` that inserts a new string into a sorted linked list of strings, keeping the list sorted. We'll discuss several different implementations of `AddInOrder`.

Program 12.6   orderedlist.cpp

```cpp
#include <iostream>
#include <fstream>
#include <string>
using namespace std;
#include "prompt.h"

// read words in a file, store in order in a linked list

struct Node
{
    string info;
    Node * next;
    Node(const string& s, Node * link)
      : info(s), next(link)
    { }
};

Node* AddInOrder(Node* list, const string& s)
// pre: list is sorted
// post: add s to list, keep list sorted, return new list with s in it
{
    Node * first = list;    // hang onto first node

    // if new node is first, handle this case and return
    if (first == 0 || s < first->info)
    {   return new Node(s,first);
    }

    // assert: s >= list->info
    while (list->next != 0 && list->next->info < s)
    {   list = list->next;
    }
    // assert: s >= list->info and s < list->next->info (conceptually)

    list->next = new Node(s,list->next);
    return first;
}

void Print(Node * list)
{
    for(; list != 0; list=list->next)
    {   cout << list->info << endl;
    }
}
```

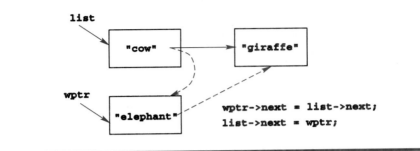

Figure 12.7 Adding a new node to a sorted linked list.

```cpp
int main()
{
    Node * list = 0;   // empty
    string word, filename = PromptString("filename: ");
    ifstream input(filename.c_str());
    while (input >> word)
    {   list = AddInOrder(list,word);
    }
    Print(list);
    return 0;
}
```

orderedlist.cpp

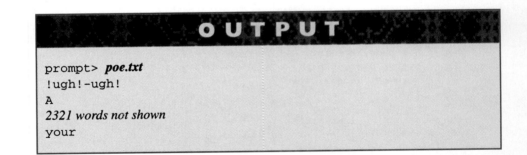

To add a new node in order using iteration we must maintain a pointer to the node before where the new node goes. In Figure 12.7 a new node containing `"elephant"` is added to a sorted linked list. In the diagram, the new node is pointed to by `wptr`, and the node is added after the `"cow"` node pointed to by `list`. To search for the location to add the new node we must look one node ahead. For example, we don't know that `"elephant"` goes after `"cow"` until we know `"giraffe"` follows `"cow"`. If `"dog"` follows `"cow"`, we need to keep searching.

A recursive version of the function `AddInOrder` from Program 12.6 is simpler than the iterative version. Note that the base case is also handled in the original version of `AddInOrder`.

```
Node* AddInOrder(Node* list, const string& s)
// pre: list is sorted
// post: add s to list, keep list sorted, return new list
{
    if (list == 0 || s < list->info)  // new node first
    {   return new Node(s,list);
    }
    list->next = AddInOrder(list->next,s);
    return list;
}
```

The base case handles an empty list or a list in which all strings are greater than the string being added. The order of the Boolean tests is important. If the test for s < list->info is made first, the test will cause an error when list == 0 since a NULL/zero pointer will be dereferenced.

> **Program Tip 12.6: Every pointer dereference should be guarded either explicitly by a check that the pointer is not NULL/zero or implicitly by documenting and reasoning that the pointer cannot be zero.** Each time you write code of the form list->data_member you should either check list != 0 before the dereference or be able to show with formal reasoning that list cannot be NULL/zero.

We can change the function AddInOrder so that list is passed by reference. It may be harder to see that this function is correct.

```
void AddInOrder(Node* & list, const string& s)
// pre: list is sorted
// post: add s to list, keep list sorted
{
    if (list == 0 || s < list->info)  // new node first
    {   list = new Node(s,list);
    }
    else
    {   AddInOrder(list->next,s);
    }
}
```

Two observations may help you see that this version of AddInOrder works correctly:

1. The base case correctly changes list when the list is empty or when the new node belongs before all other nodes. The base case creates a node that points to the old first node and makes list point to the new node. Since list is passed by reference, the change is propagated back to the calling statement.

2. In each recursive call, the argument list->next is passed by reference. This

means that each clone called recursively uses the name `list` as an alias for some `next` field of the linked list being processed.

You may need to think carefully about the second observation, but it brings up a key point about creating new nodes and adding them to a linked list.

> **Program Tip 12.7: Code that adds a new node to a list must assign a value to some `next` field or the new node will not be linked into the list. Similarly, removing a node from a list also requires an assignment to some `next` field.** When recursion is used, the `next` field can be an argument passed recursively. The required assignment to a `next` field can be implemented by a recursive assignment to a parameter that is a reference to a `next` field.

12.2.6   Doubly and Circularly Linked Lists, Header Nodes

Header Nodes. The special-case code for adding a new node to the end of a list we saw in Sect. 12.2.3 can be avoided if we use a **dummy** or **header** node. Using a header node also makes it simpler to remove nodes from a list. A header node ensures that every node in the list has a predecessor. The first node in the linked list is preceded by the header node, which isn't considered part of the list.

```
Node * list = 0;                // traditional empty list
Node * header = new Node(); // dummy/header node
```

Program 12.7 listremove.cpp

```cpp
void Remove(Node * header, const string& key)
// post: all nodes containing key removed from list/header
{
   Node * before = header;
   Node * list = header->next;  // first "real node"

   // invariant: list = before->next, key doesn't appear in header->..->before
   while (list != 0)
   {   if (list->info == key)
       {   before->next = list->next;  // link around
           delete list;
           list = before->next;        // invariant maintained
       }
       else                            // invariant maintained
       {   before = list;
           list = list->next;
       }
   }
}
```

listremove.cpp

Since the header node is never changed, and all list accesses go through the header, list functions can change the contents in a list without passing the list by reference. You'll need to think carefully about this code to see that it's correct; the invariant should help. Initially no nodes have been examined and the invariant is true. Each time through the loop one of two cases occurs:

- The node being examined, `list`, doesn't contain `key`. In this case both `before` and `list` are advanced.

- We need to remove a node containing `key`. The node before the `key` node is linked around the `key` node. We can't advance `before` since the code hasn't examined the node that now comes after `before`.

Writing `Remove` iteratively without a header node is difficult to do correctly. It's much simpler to implement `Remove` recursively. In the following function we assume there is no header node; note that `list` is passed by reference since it changes:

```
void Remove(Node * & list, const string& key)
// post: all nodes containing key removed from list
{
    if (list != 0)
    {   Remove(list->next,key);
        if (list->info == key)
        {   Node * temp = list;
            list = list->next;
            delete temp;
        }
    }
}
```

Doubly and Circularly Linked Lists. Linked lists are sequential structures; most operations traverse the list from front to back. Some applications require traversal in two directions: from back to front as well as front to back. For example, a text editor normally allows the user to move the cursor forward and backward. Implementing a simple editor using a linked list is not difficult if we use a **doubly linked list**. In a doubly linked list each node maintains pointers to the node before it in the list as well as to the node after it. This requires one additional data member in the node `struct`. A diagram of a doubly linked list is shown in Figure 12.8. We'll explore code for manipulating doubly linked lists in the exercises.

In the modified version of Program 12.5, *strlink.cpp*, which we studied in Section 12.2.3, we maintained pointers to both the first and last nodes of a linked list. When both pointers are needed, it's a common convention to use a **circularly linked list**. In a circularly linked list the last node of the list points back to the first node instead of pointing to NULL/zero. By keeping only a pointer to the last node of a circularly linked list we can find the first node very simply: `last->next` is the first node. In a circularly linked list with only one node, the last node points to itself since the first node is the last node. The following function counts the nodes in a circularly linked list:

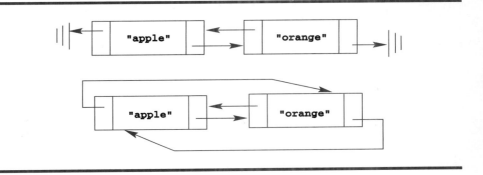

Figure 12.8   Doubly linked list and circular doubly linked list.

```
int Count(Node * list)
// pre: list is circularly linked, list points to last node
// post: return # nodes in list
{
    if (list == 0) return 0;     // special case
    int count = 0;               // # nodes
    Node * first = list->next;
    while (first != list)
    {   count++;
        first = first->next;
    }
    return count + 1;            // count the last node too
}
```

Figure 12.8 shows a doubly linked list that's also a circularly linked list. The last node points back at the first node, and the first node points at the last node.

Pause to Reflect

12.22 Write a function Count that counts the number of nodes in a linked list. Write the function recursively and with a while loop.

12.23 Write a function Clone that returns a copy of its list parameter (assume it's a linked list of strings).

```
Node * Clone(Node * list)
// post: return copy of list
```

It's easiest to write this function recursively, especially if you take advantage of the Node constructor.

12.24 Write a function that returns a pointer to the node of a linked list that has the minimal value in the list (assume a list of strings and that minimal means first alphabetically).

```
Node * FindMin(Node * list)
// post: return pointer to minimal node,
//       return 0 if list is empty
```

12.25 Describe the effects of the function Change that follows:

```
void Change(Node * list)
{
    while (list && list->next)
    {   Node * temp = list->next;
        list->next = list->next->next;
        list = list->next;
        delete temp;
    }
}
```

12.26 Describe the effects of the function Chop, where list is a linked list storing int values:

```
void Chop(Node * & list)
{
    if (list != 0)
    {   Chop(list->next);
        if (list->info % 2 == 0)
        {   list = list->next;
        }
    }
}
```

12.27 Write the function CreateList with header as shown. CreateList creates a linked list of *n* integers where the first node contains 1 and the last node contains *n*. The call Print(CreateList(5)) should print 1 2 3 4 5, where Print is from *strlink.cpp*, Program 12.5.

```
Node * CreateList(int n)
// pre: 0 < n
// post: creates list 1->2->...->n
//       a list in which node k contains the int k
```

12.28 Write the function `GaussList` with header as shown. The function calls `Print(GaussList(4))` should print 1 2 2 3 3 3 4 4 4 4.

```
Node * GaussList(int n)
// pre: 0 < n
// post: returns sorted list, in which
//       k occurs k times, 1 <= k <= n
```

12.29 Write a function `Reverse` that reverses the order of the nodes in a linked list. Reverse the list by changing pointers, not by swapping `info` fields.

```
void Reverse(Node * & list)
// precondition: list =  (a b c ... d)
// postcondition: list = (d ... c b a), list is reversed.
```

12.30 Write a nonrecursive version of the function `Remove` from Section 12.2.6 where the list doesn't have a header node.

12.31 Write either an iterative or recursive version of `Remove` that works with doubly linked lists. Assume the list has a header and a tail node where the tail is an extra node at the end of the list serving as sentinel node so that every node has a successor node.

12.32 Write functions `AddAtFront` and `AddAtBack` that add new nodes to the front and back, respectively, of a circularly linked list.

12.33 Write a function that doubles a linked list by duplicating each node; that is, the list (*a b c d*) is changed to (*a a b b c c d d*). Use the header shown, where `list` is *not* passed by reference. (*Hint:* It's probably easier to write this recursively.)

```
void DoubleList(Node * list)
// precondition:  list = (a b c d)
// postcondition: list = (a a b b c c d d)
```

12.3   A Templated Class for Sets

To show how linked lists are used in implementing classes we'll develop a class implementing sets similar to `StringSet` (see Section 6.5), but capable of storing elements of any kind, not just strings. Like classes `tvector` and `CList`, the class we design will be templated so that it can represent sets of any type, not just sets of strings. We'll develop a testing program that illustrates how pointers used as instance variables in objects do not always behave as expected.

> **Program Tip 12.8:   When developing a templated class, develop a non-templated version of the class first. Test and debug the nontemplated version first, then implement the templated class.** Develop, test, and debug simple programs whose inevitable errors may be easier to find than those in more complex programs.

A set class based on linked lists will not be very efficient, but it will eventually lead to a very efficient class when you study another kind of linked structure called a tree.

12.3.1   Sets of Strings with Linked Lists

We'll implement a class for representing sets of strings, test and debug the class, then use the tested class as the basis for a templated set class. We'll implement the same methods used in the class `StringSet` (see Program G.7 in How to G), which makes the analysis phase of development simple.

Since we know that searching in a linked list of N elements is an $O(N)$ operation, most of the set functions will be $O(N)$ since they require determining if a string is in the set. The functions we'll implement, their descriptions, and their complexities are given in Table 12.1.

Table 12.1   Operations for sets of strings implemented using linked lists. Complexities are for a set with $O(N)$ elements.

Operation	Description	Complexity
Construct	Make an empty set	$O(1)$
Insert	Add s to set	$O(N)$
Erase	Remove s from set	$O(N)$
Clear	Make set empty	$O(1)$
Contains	Search for s in set	$O(N)$
Size	Number of elements in set	$O(1)$

All the $O(N)$ operations require searching for an element in the set. For example, we'll add a new element at the front of a linked list, which is a **constant time** or $O(1)$ operation. However, we must first determine that the element is not already in the set before adding it. The expression $O(1)$ is used for an operation whose complexity does not depend on the size of the problem being measured, in this case on the number of elements in the set. Our `clear` function will actually be $O(N)$, but we'll explore a constant time version in the exercises.

We'll create a singly linked list with a header node and add new nodes to the front of the list. We'll use the same declarations for member function found in *stringset.h*, Program G.7. Keeping in mind the advice from Programming Tip 9.5, we'll implement a constructor, a method to add elements to a set, and a method for printing the contents of a set. Eventually we'll want to implement an associated iterator class, but at first we'll simply write a set to `cout`, the standard output stream. Our first cut is shown below.

```
class LinkStringSet
{
  public:
    LinkStringSet();
    int  size() const;
    void print()const;
    void insert(const string& s);
  private:
    struct Node
    {   string info;
        Node * next;
        Node(const string& s, Node * link)
          : info(s), next(link)
        { }
    };
    Node * myFirst;   // header node
    int    mySize;    // # elements in set
};
```

We've already developed code for inserting an element at the front of a linked list and for printing a linked list. We'll need to search for a string before inserting it, but sequential search in a list is nearly identical to sequential search in a vector, so we don't anticipate any difficulties. We'll implement all these methods, test them, and then turn to implementing other methods. We won't show the complete test program for these functions, but after testing them thoroughly we can add new methods, knowing any bugs will be in the new methods or in the interactions between the new methods and the already debugged methods.

12.3.2 Searching, Clearing, Helper Functions

We've already written the code for `LinkStringSet::contains` since we searched the linked list before inserting a new node at the front. We'd like to reuse this code since we know duplicating code will inevitably lead to a maintenance headache (see Program Tip 4.1). Thinking ahead to the member function `erase` we see that we'll need to search the list to implement that function as well. We'd like to write a private helper function (see Program Tip 7.14), but what should be the interface of the helper function?

■   `contains` returns a Boolean value; we need to know if the element is in the set.
■   `insert` can use `contains` directly; the location of the element isn't needed since we're adding a new node to the front.
■   `erase` removes a node; we need a pointer to the node before the removed node to erase and link around the removed node.

If we used a doubly linked list, the private searching function could return a pointer to the node containing the string being searched for. To remove a node from a singly linked list a pointer to the node being removed won't help; we need a pointer to the node *before* the node being removed to unsplice the removed node and link around it. We'll write a helper function findNode as follows:

```
Node * LinkStringSet::findNode(const string& s) const
// post: returns pointer to node before s
//       returns NULL/0 if !contains(s)
```

We can use findNode to implement contains and insert very easily. Recall that myFirst points to a header node so a new node is added *after* the header node.

```
bool LinkStringSet::contains(const string& s) const
// post: return true iff s in set
{
    return findNode(s) != 0;
}
void LinkStringSet::insert(const string& s)
// post: if ! contains(s) then s is added to set
{
    if (! contains(s))
    {   myFirst->next = new Node(s,myFirst->next);
        mySize++;
    }
}
```

We'll leave the implementation of findNode as an exercise, but the header we use above fails to compile when we use it in *linkstringset.cpp*. Visual C++ generates the following error message:

```
linkstringset.cpp(56):error C2501:
'Node':missing decl-specifiers (more errors here)
```

The problem is that the declaration Node is known only within the LinkStringSet declaration. We can use Node in parameter lists of member functions, and as the type for a local variable in a member function, because member functions "know" about all the class declarations including Node. However, the return type of a function is not part of the function's prototype (see the explanation on function overloading in Section 11.1.1), so we must qualify Node as follows:

```
LinkStringSet::Node *
LinkStringSet::findNode(const string& s) const
// post: returns pointer to node before s
//       return NULL/0 if !contains(s)
```

If we use this helper function to implement contains, and call contains from insert, we'll need to test insert again since its implementation has changed. Once we've tested these functions we'll implement erase.

```
void LinkStringSet::erase(const string& s)
// post: ! contains(s), s is removed from set
{
   Node * temp = findNode(s);
   if (temp != 0)
   {  Node * removal = temp->next;   // remove this node
      temp->next = removal->next;    // link around
      delete removal;                // delete
      mySize--;
   }
}
```

After testing all the member functions we'll turn to the problem of designing, implementing, and testing an associated iterator class. We'll see that the iterator class methods are very simple to implement, but we'll need to have the iterator access the linked list that's used to implement the LinkStringSet class.

12.3.3 Iterators and Friend Functions

We'd like to implement a class LinkStringSetIterator to access set elements one at a time. The version of Print below shows the class used just like any of the iterator classes we've studied so far since all the iterators we develop conform to the same interface. We could easily make this a templated function to work with any iterator as discussed in Section 11.2.2, but we're concerned here with iterating over a LinkStringSet.

```
void Print(const LinkStringSet& set)
{
   LinkStringSetIterator it(set);
   for(it.Init(); it.HasMore(); it.Next())
   {  cout << it.Current() << endl;
   }
   cout << "size = " << set.size() << endl;
}
```

To access elements one at a time we have two choices:

■   Provide methods in the class LinkStringSet for accessing individual set elements (i.e., strings stored in the underlying linked list).

■   Permit the associated iterator class to access the linked list, but not allow client code to access individual elements.

We'll adopt the second of these options. In general, a **container** class is a **collection** of elements and should have an associated iterator class; the container class provides access exclusively via the associated iterator. The container class and its iterator are tightly coupled (see Program Tip 6.8), and the iterator class will need to access the private instance variables of the container class. Access to a class private section can be granted by the class by declaring another class to be a **friend**. The class Foo grants friend status to the class FooFriend, whose methods can access private data and helper functions of a Foo object. A declaration of friend status is made by the class whose private data will be accessed. It's not possible for a class to request friend status, only for a class to grant friend status. In the iterator class that follows, all the methods are implemented inline within the class declaration to make it simpler to read the code.

> **Syntax: Declaring friends**
>
> ```
> class Foo
> {
>   public:
>     friend class FooFriend;
>   private:
> };
> ```

Program 12.8 linkstringsetiterator.h

```
class LinkStringSetIterator
{
  public:
    LinkStringSetIterator(const LinkStringSet& lset)
      : mySet(lset), myCurrent(0)
    { }
    void Init()
    {   myCurrent = mySet.myFirst->next;  // first node
    }
    bool HasMore() const
    {   return myCurrent != 0;
    }
    string Current() const
    {   return myCurrent->info;
    }
    void Next()
    {   myCurrent = myCurrent->next;
    }
  private:
    typedef LinkStringSet::Node Node;
    const LinkStringSet& mySet;
    Node *              myCurrent;
};
```

linkstringset terator.h

Each function consists of a single statement that is part of a typical linked list traversal (e.g., initialization, test, update, and process-element). An iterator is bound to a particular set when the iterator is constructed. As shown, the set is stored as a reference instance variable. We use a const reference so that we can iterate over constant sets, for example, in the function Print we showed above to demonstrate the LinkStringSetIterator class. More information on const-ness and iterators is found in How to D.

12.3.4   Interactive Testing

We now have both a set class and a friend iterator class. To test the classes we'll use an **interactive** testing program. The program is interactive because the user is given a menu of choices, and each choice tests one of the `LinkStringSet` member functions or uses an iterator. The interactive nature allows us to test different cases that we anticipate might cause problems. These include the following:

- Adding the same element more than once.
- Deleting an element more than once.
- Deleting an element not in the set.
- Deleting all the elements then adding new elements.
- Clearing the set, adding elements, and clearing again.

The interactive program can stress the relationships between the member functions, but it's not designed to insert thousands of elements. Stressing the class with large input sets is best done with an **automatic** test program. We'll use the interactive test program *testlinkset.cpp*, Program 12.9. In a larger program, we would use one function for each test case rather than incorporate the code within the `switch` statement. In other words, we would replace

```
case 'i' :
   word = PromptlnString("enter word : ");
   set.insert(word);
   break;
```

with a function call that handles the set insertion:

```
case 'i':
   DoInsert(set);
   break;
```

The interactive test program shown here stresses only one set. After we've verified that the set member functions work as expected, or after finding bugs in the functions and fixing them, we'll need to develop a program that uses more than one set to see if problems arise when more than one set is used in the same program. Testing one class is a difficult, time-consuming, but necessary process. Testing a larger program with interacting classes is made simpler if each class is tested separately so that any bugs found are more likely to be from the class interactions rather than from bugs within a class.

> **Program Tip 12.9:   Every class you develop should be developed with a test suite of programs.** You may want to include both automatic and interactive programs in the test suite. More complex programs with interacting classes will be developed with fewer errors if each individual class is tested separately.

Program 12.9 testlinkset.cpp

```cpp
#include <iostream>
#include <string>
#include <cctype>      // for tolower
using namespace std;

#include "linkstringset.h"
#include "prompt.h"

void Print(const LinkStringSet& set)
{
    LinkStringSetIterator it(set);
    cout << "----------" << endl;
    for(it.Init(); it.HasMore(); it.Next())
    {   cout << it.Current() << endl;
    }
    cout << "----------  size = " << set.size() << endl;
}

void Help()
{
    cout << "(h)elp      print help"        << endl;
    cout << "(i)insert  word into set"      << endl;
    cout << "(c)lear     set"               << endl;
    cout << "(e)rase    word from set"      << endl;
    cout << "(p)rint    the set and size"   << endl;
    cout << "(s)earch   for word in set"    << endl;
    cout << "(q)uit      program"           << endl;
    cout << "---" << endl;
}

void TestSet()
{
    string word, commandLine;
    LinkStringSet set;
    char command = 'h';
    while (command != 'q')
    {   commandLine = PromptlnString("enter command : ");
        if (commandLine == "")
        {   command = 'h';
        }
        else
        {   command = tolower(commandLine[0]);
        }
        switch (command)
        {
            case 'h' :
                Help();
                break;
            case 'i' :
                word = PromptlnString("enter word : ");
```

```cpp
                    set.insert(word);
                    break;
            case 'c':
                    set.clear();
                    break;
            case 'e':
                    word =PromptlnString("enter word : ");
                    set.erase(word);
                    break;
            case 'p':
                    Print(set);
                    break;
            case 's':
                    word = PromptlnString("enter word : ");
                    if (set.contains(word))
                    {   cout << word << " was found" << endl;
                    }
                    else
                    {   cout << word << " was NOT found" << endl;
                    }
            case 'q':
                    break;
            default:
                    cout << "unrecognized command" << endl;
                    break;
        }
    }
}


int main()
{
    TestSet();
    return 0;
}
```

testlinkset.cpp

OUTPUT

```
prompt> testlinkset
enter command : h
(h)elp     print help
(i)insert  word into set
(c)lear    set
(e)rase    word from set
(p)rint    the set and size
(s)earch   for word in set
(q)uit     program
---
enter command : i
enter word : apple
enter command : i
enter word : cherry
enter command : p
----------
cherry
apple
----------  size = 2
enter command : i
enter word : apple
enter command : i
enter word : watermelon
enter command : p
----------
watermelon
cherry
apple
----------  size = 3
enter command : s
enter word : cherry
cherry was found
enter command : s
enter word : grapefruit
grapefruit was NOT found
enter command : e
enter word : apple
enter command : p
----------
watermelon
cherry
----------  size = 2
```

output continued

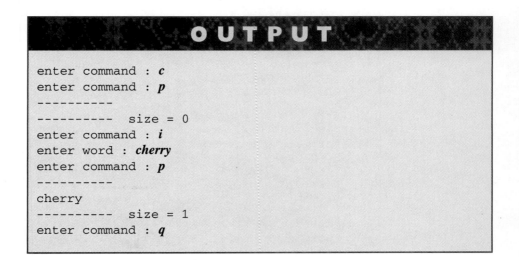

```
enter command : c
enter command : p
----------
----------  size = 0
enter command : i
enter word : cherry
enter command : p
----------
cherry
----------  size = 1
enter command : q
```

12.3.5 Deep Copy, Assignment, and Destruction

After thorough testing with an interactive test program we turn to testing more than one class in the same program. Since we're developing a set class we might think about operations we'd like to have that aren't available in the simple StringSet class we used as the original model for this class. Typical set operations include union, intersection, and set difference. Before turning to these operations we find a serious flaw in the implementation revealed by the simple Program 12.10, *linksetdemo.cpp*. The program shows that assigning one set to another results in what at first is unexpected behavior. However, thinking back to Program 12.1, *pointerdemo.cpp*, the first program we studied that uses pointers, we see that the results make sense.

Program 12.10   linksetdemo.cpp

```cpp
#include <iostream>
using namespace std;
#include "linkstringset.h"

// demo of string sets implemented with linked lists

void Print(const LinkStringSet& set)
{
    LinkStringSetIterator it(set);
    for(it.Init(); it.HasMore(); it.Next())
    {   cout << "\t" << it.Current() << endl;
    }
    cout << "---------- size = " << set.size() << endl;
}
```

```
int main()
{
    LinkStringSet a,b;

    a.insert("apple");
    a.insert("cherry");
    cout << "a : "; Print(a);
    b = a;
    cout << "b : "; Print(b);
    a.clear();
    cout << "a : "; Print(a);
    cout << "b : "; Print(b);
    return 0;
}
```

linksetdemo.cpp

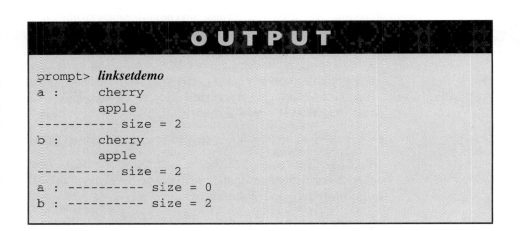

```
OUTPUT

prompt> linksetdemo
a :       cherry
          apple
---------- size = 2
b :       cherry
          apple
---------- size = 2
a : ---------- size = 0
b : ---------- size = 2
```

The first printed output for sets a and b is what we expect. However, after set a is cleared, there is nothing in set b either, although its size is still two. The problem is that executing the statement b = a results in copying the value of the pointer a.myFirst to b.myFirst. The value of the instance variable mySize is copied too, but that doesn't cause a problem. Each set has its own pointer, but both pointers reference the same linked list as shown in Figure 12.9.

Since assignment of one class object to another simply copies the values of each instance variable, the pointers are copied, but the linked lists they point to are not copied. The call a.clear() removes all the nodes from a's linked list, which are also the nodes in b's linked list. There's nothing in the set b, though the value of b.mySize is still two since it's not changed by calling a.clear(). When an instance variable points to an object, we may want to copy the object pointed to, not just the pointer, when assigning the class containing the pointer. Copying the object pointed to, and all the objects it may point to, is called a **deep copy**. The default assignment in C++ simply copies pointers, not objects, which is called a **shallow copy**. Before we used pointers we didn't need to worry about these differences because every class we've used behaves properly. Classes that require deep copies, like the tvector class, implement the required deep copy

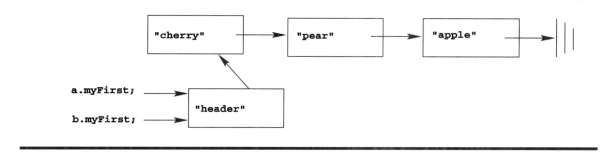

Figure 12.9 Assignment without copying, shared lists.

functions. There are three member functions that must be implemented to generate a deep copy properly: the **copy constructor**, the **assignment operator**, and the **destructor**.

When you design a class, you should aim for the behavior of the class to meet user expectations. For classes like `LinkStringSet` and `tvector` this means that users should be able to assign objects to each other and pass parameters by value if necessary, since the built-in types support these operations. We didn't need to worry about deep copies and shallow copies with the `CList` class because there are no operations that change a `CList` object. Shared storage is only a problem when what's stored changes.

The Copy Constructor. The copy constructor is a special constructor called when an object is first defined and initialized from another object of the same type. For example, consider defining several `Date` objects.

```
Date today;
Date tomorrow(today+1);    // calls copy constructor
Date yesterday(today-1);   // calls copy constructor

yesterday = tomorrow;      // calls assignment operator
Date weekago = today-7;    // calls copy constructor
```

The objects `tomorrow`, `yesterday`, and `weekago` are each constructed and initialized from another `Date` object. The assignment `yesterday = tomorrow` doesn't call a copy constructor because the variable `yesterday` has already been defined. The class copy constructor is called only when an object is first defined, not when it's assigned to or reinitialized in some other way.

Whenever an object is constructed from another object of the same type, a copy constructor is used for the construction and initialization. If you examine the `Date` class you won't see a special constructor because none is needed.

Every class has a **default copy constructor** that simply copies the value of each instance variable from one object to another. If a shallow copy is acceptable, the default copy constructor is sufficient. Since shallow copies are fine except when there is shared storage, we need to worry about a copy constructor only when there's a shared resource like an object

```
Syntax: Copy constructor

Foo::Foo(const Foo& f);
Foo::Foo(Foo& f);
```

pointed to by an instance variable. Normally only the copy constructor from a const object is needed (the top one in the syntax diagram). On rare occasions the behavior of copying from a nonconst object is different, and both copy constructors are required.

To copy a LinkStringSet object we must initialize both instance variables myFirst and mySize. In the copy constructor that follows, a header node is created in the initializer list. The next field of the header node points to a copy of the linked list that stores the elements of the parameter set. The copy is created by the private helper function clone. Since a copy of a list will be needed in both the assignment operator and the copy constructor, the code to create the copy is factored out into a helper function.

```
LinkStringSet::LinkStringSet(const LinkStringSet& set)
  : myFirst(new Node("header",set.clone())),
    mySize(set.size())
{
    //initializer list makes deep copy
}
```

If you think carefully about the list copy, you'll realize that the private function clone is being called by a different object than is making the clone. Private variables and functions can be accessed by any object of the same class.

The Assignment Operator. The assignment operator is similar to the copy constructor in making a deep copy, but the assignment operator is called to reinitialize an object that has already been constructed. Because the object being assigned to already exists, some extra bookkeeping is required that wasn't necessary in the copy constructor.

After the assignment b = a, b will represent a different set than it did before the assignment. The nodes that were part of the old value of b should be reclaimed (e.g., returned to the freestore). Two additional requirements should be met by every implementation of an assignment operator. Assignments can be chained together (e.g.,

```
Syntax: Assignment operator

const Foo&
Foo::operator = (const Foo& f);
```

a = b = c) so the assignment operator must return a value. Since assignment is right associative (e.g., a = (b = c);) the value of the object after assignment is returned. Users may inadvertently write a = a. This can cause problems if not checked, so self-assignment should be explicitly guarded in each assignment operator implementation.

The return statement of every assignment operator should be

```
return *this;
```

since an object returns itself after assignment. We don't want to return a copy, we want to return the object itself, so the return type should be a reference, such as Foo&. Finally, the reference should be const to avoid allowing code like (a = b).clear() to compile:

```
const LinkStringSet&
LinkStringSet::operator = (const LinkStringSet& set)
{
    if (this != &set)
    {   reclaimNodes(myFirst->next);
        myFirst->next = set.clone();
        mySize = set.size();
    }
    return *this;
}
```

To protect against self-assignment, an object checks that the object being assigned to, itself, is different from the object being assigned, set in the operator above. We check addresses because we want to guard against assigning the same object, not objects with the same value.

```
string s = "hello";
string t = "hello";
s = t;    // this is fine
s = s;    // guard against weird behavior
```

The Destructor. A local variable defined in a function is not accessible outside the function. The variable is constructed when the function begins execution and may accumulate resources as the function executes. Ideally the resources will be reclaimed when they're not needed, which happens when the function returns in the case of a local variable. Consider the variable set in the following code:

```
int CountUnique(ifstream& input)
//post: return # unique words in input
{
    string word;
    LinkStringSet set;
    while (input >> word)
    {   set.insert(word);
    }
    return set.size();
}
```

Function CountUnique correctly counts and returns the number of different or unique words in the stream input. What happens to the nodes allocated by set after the function returns the size? Although set is no longer accessible after CountUnique returns, the linked list referenced by set.myFirst just before the function returns will continue to exist after the function returns because the nodes are allocated from the heap; their lifetime is the duration of the program unless the nodes are explicitly deleted.

The destructor member function is called automatically when an object goes out of scope (e.g., for the local variable `set` when the function above returns). The destructor should take care of reclaiming any resource, particularly storage allocated by new.

Syntax: Class destructor

`Foo::~Foo();`

The destructor has the same name as the class it belongs to, but is preceded by a tilde: ` ` ~ ` `.[4] When you first implement a class, the destructor should be a stub function. After you've debugged other member functions, implement the destructor to reclaim storage (or other resources). The advice in Program Tip 12.3 makes particular sense when you're implementing a destructor.

```
LinkStringSet::~LinkStringSet()
{
    reclaimNodes(myFirst);
    myFirst = 0;
}
```

We can call the helper function `reclaimNodes` that we used in the assignment operator. Since nodes are reclaimed in both places it makes sense to factor out the code into a helper function. In the implementation of `LinkStringSet` we would make `reclaimNodes` a stub function and implement it after debugging other member functions.

Program Tip 12.10: When you implement one of the following three member functions, it is normally an indication that you should implement all three functions.

1. Copy constructor, for initializing an object based on another object of the same type.

2. Assignment operator =, for assigning a new value of the same type to an existing object.

3. Destructor, for reclaiming resources allocated by an object during its lifetime (e.g., memory allocated by new).

12.3.6   A Templated Version of `LinkStringSet`

With the string set class debugged, we'll turn to creating a templated version of the class. We'll call the class `LinkSet`, and we'll define variables of type `LinkSet<string>` and `LinkSet<int>` among the many kinds of sets we can create. Most of the changes in creating a templated class are syntactic in nature. I copied the header file *linkstringset.h*

---

[4]The tilde ~ is sometimes pronounced "twiddle," but tilde is an acceptable pronunciation.

(accessible with the code that comes with this book) to the file *linkset.h*. I automatically replaced every occurrence of string with T, the identifier I used for the template parameter. I replaced all occurrences of LinkStringSet with LinkSet, too. To indicate the class is templated, I added the following line, whose syntax is the same as the declaration for creating a templated function as shown, for example, in Section 11.2:

```
template <class T>
```

The only other changes needed in the header file were for the iterator class. The name had been changed to LinkSetIterator when I changed all occurrences of LinkStringSet to LinkSet. I added the same template declaration before the class that I used to indicate that LinkSet was a templated class. Finally, I changed the friend declaration in LinkSet as follows to indicate that the iterator class is templated:

```
friend class LinkSetIterator<T>;
```

The compiler needs information that LinkSetIterator is a templated class to parse this friend declaration, so I added the following forward declaration just before the class LinkSet (see Program Tip 12.2 for reasons to use forward references):

```
template <class T> class LinkSetIterator;
```

In the iterator class declaration, all occurrences of LinkSet must be replaced with LinkSet<T> to indicate that the class LinkSet is templated. This yields the complete declaration *linkset.h*.

Program 12.11   lirkset.h

```
#ifndef _LINKSET_H
#define _LINKSET_H

template <class T> class LinkSetIterator;

template <class T>
class LinkSet
{
  public:
    LinkSet();

    // methods for deep copy
    LinkSet(const LinkSet& set);
    const LinkSet& operator =(const LinkSet& set);
    ~LinkSet();

    // accessors
    bool contains(const T& s) const;  // true iff s in set
    int  size()               const;  // # elements in set

    // mutators
    void insert(const T& s);  // add to set
    void erase(const T& s);   // remove from set
```

```cpp
    void clear();              // delete all elements

    friend class LinkSetIterator<T>;

  private:

    struct Node
    {   T info;
        Node * next;
        Node(const T& s, Node * link)
          : info(s), next(link)
        { }
    };
    Node * findNode(const T& s) const;   // helper
    void   reclaimNodes(Node * ptr);     // delete/reclaim
    Node * clone() const;                // copy list

    Node * myFirst;
    int    mySize;
};

template <class T>
class LinkSetIterator
{
  public:
    LinkSetIterator(const LinkSet<T>& lset)
      : mySet(lset),
        myCurrent(0)
    { }

    void Init()
    {   myCurrent = mySet.myFirst->next;  // first node
    }
    bool HasMore() const
    {   return myCurrent != 0;
    }
    T Current() const
    {   return myCurrent->info;
    }
    void Next()
    {   myCurrent = myCurrent->next;
    }
  private:
    typedef LinkSet<T>::Node Node;
    const LinkSet<T>& mySet;
    Node *         myCurrent;
};

#include "linkset.cpp"

#endif
```

linkset.h

Notice that the last line of the header file (before the `#endif`) is an include directive:

```cpp
#include "linkset.cpp"
```

Templated classes, like templated functions, are used to instantiate class code rather than being class code (see Section 11.2.3). When client code instantiates a templated class by defining objects, the template class declarations are used to generate code for the specific type used in the instantiation.

```
ListSet<string>  sset;
ListSet<int>     iset;
ListSet<Date>    dset;
ListSet<int>     iset2;
```

The four set definitions here generate code for three different `ListSet` instantiations: one for `int` sets, one for `Date` sets, and one for `string` sets. The compiler is smart enough to instantiate the `int` set code only once even though two objects are defined — only the first instantiation of a templated class actually creates code.

The compiler must be able to find definitions for the member functions of a templated class *when the class is instantiated*. This is a different process than is used for nontemplated classes. When we create nontemplated class definitions, such as in *linkstringset.cpp* or *date.cpp*, the definitions can be compiled into object code that is linked with client code to create an executable program. It's not possible to compile the definitions in *linkset.cpp* because these definitions are not code; they're used to generate code when a `ListSet` is instantiated. Because client programs typically include .h files that specify interfaces, a templated-class interface file usually includes the corresponding implementation or .cpp file as it does in *linkset.h*, Program 12.11. The compiler then has access to the template definitions so that they can be compiled into object code when they're instantiated by the client program.

> **Program Tip 12.11:   The compiler must access both interface and implementation when instantiating a templated class. Typically templated classes are defined inline, within the class declaration, or separately in a .cpp file that is included by the corresponding .h file.** In either case the compiler has access to the template definitions when client code instantiates a templated class. The C++ standard specifies that only those member functions that are called by a client program are instantiated.

If a client program that uses `ListSet<int>` objects calls only `insert` and `size`, but never `contains`, `clear`, or `erase`, then code for the functions not called in the client program will *not* be instantiated by the compiler. The compiler tries to minimize the code created so that the programmer is freed from that worry.

The `LinkSet` Implementation: linkset.cpp.   The code in *linkset.cpp*, Program 12.12, highlights the massive syntactic ugliness of template-class member function definitions. When you first read these definitions, try to ignore the `template <class T>` that precedes each method definition. This is the same syntax for declaring templated functions we saw in Section 11.2, but reproduced once for each method. Since `LinkSet` is a templated class, the class name that qualifies each method must somehow indicate the template parameter. Instead of writing

```
int LinkSet::size() const
```

we must write

```
template <class T>
int LinkSet<T>::size() const
```

to indicate that the definition is for the class LinkSet templated on a type argument T.

I created *linkset.cpp* by copying the implementation file *linkstringset.cpp*. I first replaced every occurrence of LinkStringSet with LinkSet<T>.[5] I then replaced every occurrence of string with T. Finally, I added template <class T> before each member function.

Program 12.12 linkset.cpp

```
#include "linkset.h"

template <class T>
LinkSet<T>::LinkSet()
  : myFirst(new Node(T(),0)),
    mySize(0)
{
    // header node created
}

template <class T>
bool LinkSet<T>::contains(const T& s) const
{
    Node * temp = findNode(s);
    return temp != 0;
}
template <class T>
int LinkSet<T>::size() const
{
    return mySize;
}
template <class T>
void LinkSet<T>::insert(const T& s)
{
    if (! contains(s))
    {   myFirst->next = new Node(s,myFirst->next);
        mySize++;
    }
}
template <class T>
void LinkSet<T>::erase(const T& s)
```

---

[5]This caused two problems with constructors since LinkSet<T>::LinkSet() is the default constructor, not LinkSet<T>::LinkSet<T>(); and a similar problem with the destructor name.

```
{
    Node * temp = findNode(s);
    if (temp != 0)
    {   Node * removal = temp->next;
        temp->next = removal->next;
        delete removal;    // can we reuse this?
        mySize--;
    }
}

template <class T>
void LinkSet<T>::reclaimNodes(Node * ptr)
{
    if (ptr != 0)
    {   reclaimNodes(ptr->next);
        delete ptr;
    }
}
template <class T>
void LinkSet<T>::clear()
{
    reclaimNodes(myFirst->next);
    myFirst->next = 0;            // nothing in the set
    mySize = 0;
}

template <class T>
LinkSet<T>::Node * LinkSet<T>::findNode(const T& s) const
// post: returns pointer to node before s or NULL/0 if !contains(s)
{
    Node * list = myFirst; // list nonzero

    while (list->next != 0 && list->next->info != s)
    {   list = list->next;
    }
    if (list->next == 0) return 0;
    return list;
}

template <class T>
LinkSet<T>::LinkSet(const LinkSet<T>& set)
  : myFirst(new Node(T(),set.clone())),
    mySize(set.size())
{
    // initializer list made deep copy
}
template <class T> const LinkSet<T>&
LinkSet<T>::operator = (const LinkSet<T>& set)
{
    if (this != &set)
    {   reclaimNodes(myFirst->next);
        myFirst->next = set.clone();
        mySize = set.size();
    }
    return *this;
```

```
}

template <class T>
LinkSet<T>::~LinkSet()
{
    reclaimNodes(myFirst);
    myFirst = 0;
}
template <class T>
LinkSet<T>::Node * LinkSet<T>::clone() const
{
    Node front(T(),0);    // node, not pointer, anchors copy
    Node * last = &front;    // be wary of using address of operator!

    Node * temp = myFirst->next;
    while (temp != 0)
    {   last->next = new Node(temp->info,0);
        last = last->next;
        temp = temp->next;
    }
    return front.next;
}
```

linkset.cpp

When I first tested the templated class, I created `LinkSet<string>` objects and used the same testing programs that helped test the original nontemplated `LinkStringSet` class. Then I added `LinkSet<int>` definitions and discovered two small problems that were simple to fix. The constructor definition for the nontemplated class `LinkStringSet` follows:

```
LinkStringSet::LinkStringSet()
  : myFirst(new Node("header",0)),
    mySize(0)
{
    // header node created
}
```

Using the cut-paste-and-change technique for creating a templated version generated this constructor:

```
template <class T>
LinkSet<T>::LinkSet()
  : myFirst(new Node("header",0)),
    mySize(0)
{
    // header node created
}
```

This definition works fine with a `string` set but fails with an `int` set. Can you see why? The problem is in the construction of the header node. The private `struct Node` is now templated, so it cannot be initialized with a string. Instead, we use the default constructor for the template type T, written as T() as shown in each Node construction in *linkset.cpp*, Program 12.12.

Following the advice outlined in Program Tip 12.8 made it very easy to create the templated class once the nontemplated class had been designed, implemented, debugged, and tested. Because the syntax of templated classes is daunting at first, following this advice is a good idea. It remains a good idea even after you have considerable experience programming using C++.

Pause to Reflect

12.34 In the implementation of linkset.cpp, Program 12.12, the function clone is a const function. Is this necessary? Is the function called somewhere on a const set?

12.35 Why is the declaration of Node in the set classes in the private section and not in the public section?

12.36 Why is the LinkSet<T>::clear() function $O(N)$ as implemented? Can you think of a modification to the class that results in a constant time $O(1)$ implementation of clear? (Hint: Put off deletion as long as possible.)

12.37 Suppose you're forming the union of two LinkStringSet objects a and b. The union is a new set containing all the elements in both a and b. If a has 10 elements and b has 100 elements, does the order in which elements from the sets are inserted into the new set being constructed make a difference (i.e., should elements from the small set be inserted before elements from the big set, or vice versa)?

12.38 If sets are implemented using a sorted vector instead of a linked list so that contains is an $O(\log N)$ operation using binary search, does the order in which the union of two sets is done (see the previous question) make more of a difference? Why?

12.39 The assignment operator returns a reference to the object just assigned to. If the return type is a copy instead of a reference (e.g., LinkStringSet instead of const LinkStringSet&), the copy constructor must be called to create the copy. Why is a copy less than ideal?

12.40 In the final version of clone in *linkset.cpp*, Program 12.12, a local Node named front is defined, and the address of front is assigned to last. What's the purpose of the assignment and definition? What's an alternative that avoids using &, the address-of operator?

12.4   Chapter Review

In this chapter we discussed pointers. Pointers are indirect references, useful when data need to be accessed in more than one way and when data must be allocated dynamically. We discussed sharing objects between classes using reference variables and pointers. We also discussed self-referential data structures called linked lists that have many applications. It's possible to insert new elements into a linked list without shifting the existing elements, making linked lists the method of choice for many sparse structures. We studied copy constructors, assignment operators, and destructors, three member functions often required when instance variables point to objects on the heap. We also saw an example of designing, implementing, and testing a templated class by starting with a nontemplated class.

Topics covered include these:

- Variables have names, values, and addresses. The address of a variable can be assigned to a pointer.

- As part of defensive programming, make pointers point to objects allocated on the heap using `new`, not to objects allocated on the stack.

- Several operators are used to manipulate pointers: `->`, `*`, `&`, and operators `new` and `delete`.

- Pointers can be used for efficiency since a `tvector` of pointers to strings requires less space than a `tvector` of strings, especially if the `tvector` is not full.

- The `new` operator is used to allocate memory dynamically from the heap. Memory can be allocated using `new` in conjunction with a constructor with arguments.

- Pointers are dereferenced to find what they point to. Pointers can be assigned values in four ways: using `new`, using `&` to take the address of existing storage (not a good idea, in general), assigning the value of another pointer, and assigning 0 or `NULL`.

- A destructor member function is called automatically when an object goes out of scope. Any memory allocated using `new` during the lifetime of the object should be freed using `delete` in the destructor.

- Reference instance variables can be used to share an object among more than one object. Reference instance variables must be initialized at construction; once constructed and bound to an object, a reference variable cannot be bound to a different object (unlike a pointer, for example).

- Pointers can be used to change the values of parameters indirectly. This is how parameters are changed in C: addresses are passed rather than values. The indirect addresses are used to change values.

- Linked lists support splicing, or fast insertions and deletions (in contrast to vectors, in which items are often shifted during insertion and deletion). However, items near the end of a linked list take more time to access than items near the front.

- Recursive linked list functions (sometimes with pointers passed by reference) are often shorter than an equivalent iterative version of the function.

- A header node can be used when implementing linked lists to avoid lots of special-case code, especially when deleting and inserting elements.

- Doubly and circularly linked lists are alternatives to singly linked lists.

- Classes can be templated so that they can be used to generate literally thousands of different classes, just as templated functions represent thousands of functions.

12.5   Exercises

12.1   Implement quicksort for linked lists. The partition function should divide a list into two sublists, one containing values less than or equal to the pivot, the other containing values greater than the pivot. Conceptually the partition function returns three things:

- The pivot element (a node).
- The list of items less than or equal to the pivot element.
- The list of items greater than or equal to the pivot element.

Since you'll need to join lists together after recursively sorting, you'll need to think carefully about how to develop the program. You might, for example, maintain pointers to the first and last nodes of each list returned from the partition function. Alternatively, you could maintain a pointer to the last node and make these lists circular.

When you've implemented the sort, develop a test program to verify that the original list is sorted. Then time the sort using either randomly constructed large lists or by reading words from a text file and sorting them. Consider writing a templated version of the sort as well.

12.2   Develop an implementation of merge sort for linked lists. Merge sort is described in the exercises of Chapter 11. Write two functions, one to merge two sorted lists and one to implement the merge sort.

```
Node * merge(Node * lhs, Node * rhs)
// pre: lhs is sorted, rhs is sorted
// post: returns sorted list containing all nodes
//       from lhs and rhs no new nodes are created,
//       nodes are relinked, complexity is O(a + b),
//       where a = # nodes in lhs, b = # nodes in rhs

void mergesort(Node * & list)
// post: list is sorted
//       (rearranging pointers, not copying values)
```

Write a program to test the sort on linked lists of strings. Then compare the runtime of your sort with the time to copy the values from a list into a vector, sort the vector using the merge sort code from *sortall.h*, then copy the values back into the linked list.

12.3   The *Josephus problem* (see [Knu98b]) is based on a "fair" method for designating one person from a group of *N* people. Assume that the people are arranged in a circle and are numbered from 1 to *N*. If we count off every fourth person, removing a person as we count them off, then the first person removed is number 4. The second person removed is number 8, the third person removed is 5 (because the fourth person is no longer in the circle), and so on. Write a program to print the order in which people are removed from the circle given *N*, the number of people, and *M*, the number used to count off. The problem originates from a group determined to commit suicide rather than surrender or be killed by the enemy. Consider using a doubly linked or a circularly linked list as appropriate.

12.4   Write a program to automatically stress/test the class `LinkStringSet` or its templated equivalent `LinkSet`. The program should insert thousands of items, delete thousands, and in general exercise each set method. For each test, develop a rationale for why you've chosen the test as a way of stressing the implementation.

When you've developed the program, change the set implementation in the manner described below and see if the change results in improved running times. You'll need to instrument your test program using `CTimer` objects (see *ctimer.h*, Program G.5, in How to G) to judge if the implementation is more efficient.

The current set implementations "reclaims" nodes by deleting them when one set is assigned to another or when a set object's destructor is called. Instead of deleting nodes, add the reclaimed nodes to a **static class** linked list of free nodes.

```
// in linkset.h
template <class T>
class LinkSet
{
    ...

    private:

        static Node * ourFreeList;
};

// in linkset.cpp
template <class T> LinkSet<T>::Node *
LinkSet<T>::ourFreeList = 0;    // initially empty
```

The idea is that there is one linked list shared by all `LinkSet<T>` objects — recall that a static class variable is shared by all objects (see Section 10.4.3). When nodes are reclaimed, they are added to the front of the static, shared linked list. When nodes are needed (i.e., during insertion), the shared linked list of free nodes is used as a source of nodes before `new` is called. Nodes are allocated using `new` only if there are no nodes on the list pointed to by `ourFreeList`.

Implement this change and time the program to see if it's more efficient to maintain a free list of nodes than to use the system freestore.

12.5   In Section 10.5.5 a class for representing polynomials was developed. The class used a `CList` list to store terms. Reimplement the class using linked lists. You'll need to implement a copy constructor, an assignment operator, and a destructor that were not needed in the original implementation of the class `Poly`. Shallow copies were fine in that implementation because it's not possible to change a `CList` object, only to create a new object. The new implementation should create copies of polynomials as needed, but change a polynomial, for example, when `operator +=` is used to add a term to a polynomial.

Test the program and compare its performance to the original implementation. You'll need to develop automated testing functions that stress the polynomial class by creating huge polynomials, adding them, multiplying them, and so on.

12.6   Implement free functions for creating the union and intersection of two `LinkSet<T>` objects. The union of two sets is denoted $a \cup b$; it is a set containing all the elements in either *a* or *b*. The intersection of two sets is denoted *a* ∩ *b*; it is a set containing those elements that are common to both *a* and to *b*.

```
LinkSet<string> a, b, c, d;
// fill a and b with values

c = union(a,b);    // c is the union of a and b
d = intersect(a,b); // d is the intersection of a and b
```

When you've tested these functions, overload operator + for union and operator * for intersection. This means you should also implement overloaded operators += and *= (see the guidelines for overloading operators in Section 9.4 or How to E).

12.7 Write a program to implement a *kid/toy* simulation. A file stores information about available toys in a format specific to this problem.

```
wooden blocks     : sturdy
choo-choo train   : sturdy
bucket and shovel : durable
talking doll  : sturdy
hothot wheels : durable
wickets, mallets, and croquet balls  : durable
nose glasses : flimsy
mr. zucchini head : flimsy
```

There are least three categories of toy: sturdy, durable, and flimsy. These categories indicate how long a toy can be played with before it breaks and must be fixed. Toys don't wear out in this model; they can be fixed many times and last forever. All discussions are in "play units," which can be thought of as hours. A sturdy toy breaks 2% of the time it's played with, a durable toy breaks 15% of the time, and a flimsy toy breaks 45% of the time. We'll interpret this as a probability, so each hour (play unit) a sturdy toy is played with, there's a 2 in 100 chance it will break. Broken toys require time to repair: sturdy toys can be fixed in one hour, durable toys in two hours, and flimsy toys in four hours.

The program should read a data file and construct a *toy chest* from which toys are borrowed to be played with. Kids use toys. The number of kids in a simulation is specified when the simulation begins. During one step of the simulation, each kid takes a turn playing with his/her toy. At the next step, the order in which kids take turns changes; the order should be shuffled using a shuffling function like the one in *shuffle.cpp*, Program 8.4. The number of steps in the simulation is specified when the simulation begins.

When a toy breaks, it must be placed back in the toy chest and remain there until it is fixed. A kid putting a toy in the chest takes a new toy out of the chest. If there are no toys in the chest, the kid picks another kid at random and shares that kid's toy. The toy is shared until it breaks or until one of the kids gets bored with the toy. A toy can be shared among everyone, there's no limit; but each time a kid plays with a toy counts as a "play unit." Kids like flimsy toys, so they get bored less often with flimsy toys than they do with sturdy toys. After playing with a toy, a kid trades the toy in for a new toy (or for sharing someone's toy) if bored. A kid gets bored after playing with the same toy for *n* play units/hours, where *n* = 2 for sturdy toys, *n* = 3 for durable toys, and *n* = 4 for flimsy toys.

12.8 Boggle is a game of finding words by connecting letters on a two-dimensional grid. Design and implement a program to find all the words on a grid based on structuring data using sets as described in this exercise. The output of some of the words that begin with "a" found on a randomly generated board is shown below. For each word, a list of the positions in which the letters of the word appear on the board is shown (positions give row and column indexes using matrix coordinates: (0,0) is the upper-left corner).

```
                      O U T P U T

prompt> wordgame
board size  between 3 and 8: 7
    g   n   t   b   s   h   z
    d   s   w   u   u   d   r
    e   n   u   a   a   i   a
    z   z   m   e   b   e   a
    u   a   t   y   r   i   y
    i   y   n   e   v   p   a
    d   s   o   s   r   t   o
file of words: gamewords
abet      (2, 4)  (3, 4)  (3, 3)  (4, 2)
aid       (4, 1)  (5, 0)  (6, 0)
air       (5, 6)  (4, 5)  (4, 4)
airy      (5, 6)  (4, 5)  (4, 4)  (4, 3)
amaze     (2, 3)  (3, 2)  (4, 1)  (3, 1)  (2, 0)
amuse     (4, 1)  (3, 2)  (2, 2)  (1, 1)  (2, 0)
more words found ...
```

Letters are considered adjacent if they touch horizontally, vertically, or diagonally (see the output for examples). Once a grid position is used in forming a word, the position cannot be used again in the same word.

There are many ways to find all the words; the method suggested here uses sets and is relatively straightforward to implement, though certainly not trivial. Part of a class WordGame declaration is shown as *wordgame.h*.

Program 12.13 wordgame.h

```
#ifndef _WORDGAME_H
#define _WORDGAME_H

#include <string>
using namespace std;
#include "point.h"
#include "tvector.h"
#include "linkset.h"

class WordGame
```

```
{
public:
   WordGame(int size);   // max grid size
   void MakeBoard();     // create a grid of letters

   // is a word on the board?  one version returns locations
   bool OnBoard(const string& s);
   bool OnBoard(const string& s, tvector<Point>& locations);

   // other functions

private:
   typedef LinkSet<Point>        PointSet;
   typedef LinkSetIterator<Point> PointSetIterator;

   tmatrix<char>     myBoard;
   tvector<PointSet> myLetterLocs;
   PointSet          myVisited;

   bool IsAdjacent(const Point& p, const Point& q);
   bool OnBoardAt(const string& s, const Point& p,
              tvector<Point>& locs);
};
```
_____

wordgame.h
_____

The instance variable myLetterLocs is the key to the program. It's a vector of 26 sets; each set stores positions (positions are recorded using the struct Point from *point.h*, Program G.10). The value of myLetterLocs[0] is the set of locations at which the letter 'a' appears on the board. Similarly, myLetterLocs[1] records all locations of the letter 'b,' and so on. These sets are initialized when the board is constructed. The private helper function OnBoardAt works using **backtracking**, discussed in the exercises from Chapter 11. You must determine how this function works and implement the other functions to find all words in a file of words.

_____

Program 12.14 wordgame.cpp
_____

```
bool Boggle::OnBoardAt(const string& s, const Point& p, tvector<Point>& locs)
// post: return true iff string s can be found on the board
//       beginning at location p (s[0] found at p, s[1] at a location
//       adjacent to p, and so on). If found, locs stores the locations
//       of the word, locations are added using push_back
{
    if (s.length() == 0) return true;  // all letters done, found the word

    PointSet ps = myLetterLocs['z' - s[0]];  // set of eligible letters
    PointSetIterator psi(ps);                // try all locations
    for(psi.Init(); psi.HasMore(); psi.Next())
    {   Point nextp = psi.Current();
        if (IsAdjacent(p,nextp) && ! myVisited.contains(nextp))
        {    myVisited.insert(nextp);
             locs.push_back(nextp);
             if (OnBoardAt(s.substr(1,s.length()-1),nextp,locs))
             {    return true;
```

```
            }
            locs.pop_back();
            myVisited.erase(nextp);
        }
    }
    return false;    // tried all locations, word not on board
}
```

12.9 A **stack** is a data structure sometimes called a **LIFO** structure, for "last in, first out." A stack is modeled by cars pulling into a driveway: the last car in is the first car out. In a stack, only the last element stored in the stack is accessible. Rather than use insert, remove, append, or delete, the vocabulary associated with stack operations is

- **push**—add an item to the stack; the last item added is the only item accessible by the top operation.
- **top**—return the topmost, or most recent, item pushed onto the stack; it's an error to request the top item of an empty stack.
- **pop**—delete the topmost item from the stack; it's an error to pop an empty stack.

For example, the sequence push(3), push(4), pop, push(7), push(8) yields the stack (3,7,8) with 8 as the topmost element on the stack.

Stacks are commonly used to implement recursion because the last function called is the first function that finishes when a chain of recursive clones is called.

Write a (templated) class to implement stacks (or just implement stacks of integers). In addition to member functions push, pop, and top, you should implement size (returns number of elements in stack), clear (makes a stack empty), and isEmpty (determines if the stack is empty). Use either a vector or a linked list to store the values in the stack. Write a test program to test your stack implementation.

After you've tested the Stack class, use it to evaluate **postfix** expressions. A postfix expression consists of two values followed by an operator. For example: 3 5 + is equal to 8. However, the values can also be postfix expressions, so the following expression is legal:

```
3  5 + 4  8 * + 6 *
```

This expression can be thought of as parenthesized, where each parenthesized subexpression is a postfix expression.

```
( ( (3 5 +) (4 8 *) +) 6 * )
```

However, it's easy to evaluate a postfix expression from left to right by pushing values onto a stack. Whenever an operator (+, *, etc.) is read, two values are popped from the stack, the operation computed on these values, and the result pushed back onto the stack. A legal postfix expression always leaves one number, the answer, on the stack. Postfix expressions do not require parentheses; $(6 + 3) \times 2$ is written in postfix as $6\ 3\ +2\ \times$. Write a function to read a postfix expression and evaluate it using a stack.

Inheritance for Object-Oriented Design 13

Instead of teaching people that O-O is a type of design, and giving them design principles, people have taught that O-O is the use of a particular tool. We can write good or bad programs with any tool. Unless we teach people how to design, the languages matter very little. The result is that people do bad designs with these languages and get very little value from them.

DAVID PARNAS
personal note to Fred Brooks, in The Mythical Man Month, *Anniversary Edition*

In this chapter we'll explore **inheritance**, one of the cornerstones of object-oriented programming. Many experts in programming languages differentiate between *object-based* programming, in which inheritance is not used, and *object-oriented* programming, in which inheritance is used. As you'll see, inheritance makes it possible to reuse classes in a completely different way from what we've seen to this point. The key aspect of inheritance that we'll explore is essentially changing class behavior without having access to the class implementation. This kind of reuse allows companies to design class tool kits for different applications (e.g., for graphics, networking, or games) and for clients to specialize these classes for their own purposes. The companies designing the tool kits do *not* need to release their implementations, which can be an attractive feature for those who do not want to release proprietary designs or code.

13.1 Essential Aspects of Inheritance

In Chapter 7 we designed and implemented Program 7.8, *quiz.cpp*, for giving students different kinds of quizzes. We developed classes for two different kinds of quiz questions: an arithmetic quiz question about simple addition problems (see Program 7.6, *mathquest.h*) and a geography quiz question about U.S. states and their capitals (see *capquest.h*.) By using the same class name, Question, for both different kinds of quiz question, we made it possible to reuse the same quiz program as well as the classes Quiz and Student defined in the quiz program.

However, to have different quizzes we had to change the preprocessor include directive from #include "mathquest.h" to #include "capquest.h" and recompile the program. In this chapter we'll study **inheritance**, a programming technique that permits a common interface to be *inherited* or reused by many classes. Client programs written to conform to the interface can be used with any of the interface-inheriting classes. Programs do not, necessarily, need to be recompiled to use more than one of the conforming classes. As we'll see, several different quiz questions can be used in the same program when we use inheritance.

13.1.1   The Inheritance Hierarchy for Streams

You've already used inheritance in many of the C++ programs you've written, although you probably haven't been explicitly aware of doing so. The stream hierarchy of classes uses inheritance so that you can write a function with an `istream` parameter but pass as arguments `cin`, an `ifstream` variable, or an `istringstream` variable. This use of streams is shown in *streaminherit.cpp*, Program 13.1.

Program 13.1 streaminherit.cpp

```cpp
#include <iostream>
#include <fstream>
#include <sstream>
#include <string>
using namespace std;
#include "prompt.h"

// show stream inheritance

void doInput(istream& input)
// precondition: there are three strings to read in input
{
    string s;
    int k;
    for(k=0; k < 3; k++)
    {   input >> s;
        cout << k << ".\t" << s << endl;
    }
    cout << endl;
}

int main()
{
    string filename = PromptString("filename: ");
    ifstream input(filename.c_str());
    string firstline;
    getline(input,firstline);              // first line of input file
    istringstream linestream(firstline); // stream bound to first line

    cout << "first three words on first line are\n-----" << endl;
    doInput(linestream);

    cout << "first three words on second line are\n---" << endl;
    doInput(input);

    cout << "first three words from keyboard are\n---" << endl;
    doInput(cin);
    return 0;
}
```

```
                         O U T P U T

prompt> poe.txt
first three words on first line are
-----
0.      The
1.      Cask
2.      of

first three words on second line are
---
0.      Edgar
1.      Allan
2.      Poe

first three words from keyboard are
---
this is a test of reading from the keyboard
0.      this
1.      is
2.      a
```

The code in the function doInput from *streaminherit.cpp* uses only stream behavior that is common to all input streams (i.e., extraction using operator >>). Other common stream behavior includes input using get or getline and functions clear, fail, and ignore. By conforming to the common input stream interface, the code is more general since it can be used with any input stream. This includes input stream classes that aren't yet written, but that when written will conform to the common stream interface by using the inheritance mechanism discussed in this chapter. If the function doInput used the stream function seekg (see How to B) to reset the stream to the beginning, then unexpected behavior will result when cin is passed since the standard input stream cin is not a *seekable input stream* as are ifstream and istringstream streams.[1] If doInput uses seekg the code is not conforming to the common interface associated with all streams (the seekg function can be applied to cin, but the application doesn't do anything).

---

[1] A seekable input stream can be reread by moving or *seeking* the location of input to the beginning (or end, or sometimes middle). The standard input stream isn't seekable in the same way a file bound to a text file is seekable.

13.1.2   An Inheritance Hierarchy: Math Quiz Questions

We'll return to the example of giving a computer-based quiz to students. We discussed the development of a program to give quizzes to two students sharing a keyboard in Section 6.2. In this chapter we'll use a simpler quiz program to show the power of inheritance. Because the syntactic details of using inheritance in C++ are somewhat cumbersome, rather than discussing the syntax in detail at first, we'll look at the program, make a modification to it to show what inheritance can do, and then look more at the implementation details.

Program 13.2, *inheritquiz.cpp*, gives an arithmetic quiz to a student. Only one chance is given to get each question correct, and no score is kept. Three different kinds of questions are used in the program, ranging in difficulty from easy to hard (depending, of course, on your point of view). The program is a **prototype** to show what can be done, but it is not a finished product (this program tip repeats Tip 6.6).

> **Program Tip 13.1:   A prototype is a good way to start the implementation phase of program development and to help in the design process.** A prototype is a "realistic model of a system's key functions" [McC93]. Booch says that "prototypes are by their very nature incomplete and only marginally engineered." [Boo94] A prototype is an aid to help find some of the important issues before design and implementation are viewed as frozen, or unchanging. For those developing commercial software, prototypes can help clients articulate their needs better than a description in English.

As we'll see when we explore implementation details of using inheritance in C++, pointers to objects are often used rather than objects themselves. All our uses of inheritance will use pointers or references; both are used in *inheritquiz.cpp*.[2]

Program 13.2   inheritquiz.cpp

```
#include <iostream>
#include <string>
using namespace std;

#include "tvector.h"
#include "prompt.h"
#include "randgen.h"
#include "mathquestface.h"

// prototype quiz program for demonstrating inheritance

void GiveQuestion(MathQuestion& quest)
// post: quest is asked once, correct response is given
{
    string answer;
```

---

[2]All our examples of inheritance use **polymorphism**, which we'll define later. Polymorphism requires either a pointer or a reference.

```
    cout << endl << quest.Description() << endl;
    cout << "type answer after the question" << endl;
    quest.Create();
    quest.Ask();
    cin >> answer;
    if (quest.IsCorrect(answer))
    {   cout << 'Excellent!, well done" << endl;
    }
    else
    {   cout << 'I'm sorry, the answer is " << quest.Answer() << endl;
    }
}

int main()
{
    tvector<MathQuestion *> questions;       // fill with questions

    questions.push_back(new MathQuestion());
    questions.push_back(new CarryMathQuestion());
    questions.push_back(new HardMathQuestion());

    int qCount = PromptRange("how many questions",1,10);
    RandGen gen;
    int k;
    for(k=0; k < qCount; k++)
    {   int index = gen.RandInt(0,questions.size()-1);
        GiveQuestion(*questions[index]);
    }
    for(k=0; k < questions.size(); k++)
    {   delete questions[k];
    }
    return 0;
}
```

inheritquiz.cpp

The parameter to the function GiveQuestion is a MathQuestion passed by reference. Based on the declaration and initialization of the vector questions, it appears that each vector element holds a pointer to a MathQuestion, but that the pointers actually point to a MathQuestion, a CarryMathQuestion, and a HardMathQuestion, respectively, for indexes 0, 1, and 2.

Examining the sample output that follows shows that three different kinds of question are, in fact, asked during one run of the program. Looking at the program carefully will help us develop some questions that will guide the discussion of inheritance, how it works, and how it is implemented in C++.

1. How can a pointer to MathQuestion actually point to some other type of object (the other kinds of questions)?

2. How can different objects (dereferenced by the * in the GiveQuestion call) be passed to GiveQuestion, which expects a MathQuestion by reference?

3. How are different questions actually created by the call quest.Create() in GiveQuestion?

4. How can we develop another kind of question and add it to the program?

```
                        O U T P U T

prompt> inheritquiz
how many questions between 1 and 10: 4

addition of three-digit numbers
type answer after the question
     134
+    122
-------
     256
Excellent!, well done

addition of three-digit numbers
type answer after the question
     175
+    192
-------
     267
I'm sorry, the answer is 367

addition of two-digit numbers with NO carry
type answer after the question
      11
+     18
-------
      29
Excellent!, well done

addition of two-digit numbers with a carry
type answer after the question
      38
+     39
-------
      77
Excellent!, well done
```

To answer the four questions raised above, we'll look at inheritance conceptually, and how it is implemented in C++. The example of stream inheritance in Program 13.1, *streaminherit.cpp*, showed that a common interface allows objects with different types to be used in the same way, by the same code. The math quiz program, *inheritquiz.cpp*, leverages a common interface in the same way. Each of the three question types stored

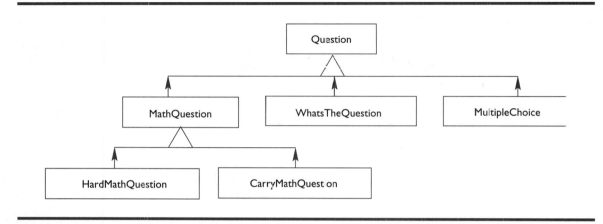

Figure 13.1 Hierarchy of math and other quiz questions.

in the vector `question` **is a kind of** `MathQuestion`. This **is-a** relationship is conceptual and realized in code. Conceptually, clients write quiz programs with code that conforms to the `MathQuestion` class interface and expect to use `MathQuestion` objects. For example, the function `GiveQuestion` has a `MathQuestion` parameter. Objects that are instances of other classes that inherit from `MathQuestion`, like `CarryMathQuestion`, can be used as though they were `MathQuestion` objects (e.g., they can be elements of a vector like `question` in `main`).

An inheritance hierarchy, like the one illustrated in Figure 13.1, models an is-a relationship, where is-a means "has the same behavior" and "can be used in place of-a or as-a." This kind of hierarchy is realized in C++ by declaring **subclasses**, also called **derived classes**, to inherit from a **base class**, also called a **super class**. In Figure 13.1 the classes `CarryMathQuestion` and `HardMathQuestion` derive from the super class `MathQuestion`. However, `MathQuestion` itself is a derived class or subclass of the super/base class `Question`. Derived classes have functions with the same names as functions in the super class (e.g., the functions `Create`, `Ask`, and `Answer` for the `Question` hierarchy). These functions can have different behavior in each subclass, which is what makes the different kinds of quiz question in the same program possible.

13.1.3 Implementing Inheritance

The interfaces for the three different kinds of `MathQuestion` classes are declared in *mathquestface.h*, Program 13.3. We'll use four new syntactic constructs in C++ to implement an inheritance hierarchy. Three of the new syntactic constructs are shown in *mathquestface.h*:

- Public inheritance.
- Virtual functions.
- Protected data members (and functions).

The fourth syntactic construct, the abstract base class, is discussed in Section 13.2.

Program 13.3 mathquestface.h

```cpp
#ifndef _MATHQUESTFACE_H
#define _MATHQUESTFACE_H

// quiz questions involving arithmetic (addition)
// see comments in questface.h for the naming conventions
// used in quiz classes
//
// MathQuestion()      -- no carry involved, two-digit numbers
// CarryMathQuestion() -- does have carry, two-digit numbers
// HardMathQuestion()  -- three-digit addition
//
// these classes add method Description() to the question hierarchy

#include "questface.h"

class MathQuestion : public Question
{
  public:
    MathQuestion();
    virtual bool    IsCorrect(const string& answer) const;
    virtual string Answer()                         const;
    virtual void    Ask()                           const;
    virtual string Description()                     const;

    virtual void Create();  // create a new question

  protected:
    string myAnswer;  // store the answer as a string here
    int myNum1;       // numbers used in question
    int myNum2;
};

class CarryMathQuestion : public MathQuestion
{
  public:
    CarryMathQuestion();
    virtual string Description()  const;
    virtual void   Create();
};

class HardMathQuestion : public MathQuestion
{
  public:
    HardMathQuestion();
    virtual string Description()  const;
    virtual void   Create();
};

#endif
```

mathquestface.h

13.1.4   Public Inheritance

In *mathquestface.h*, the subclasses CarryMathQuestion and HardMathQuestion each express their dependence on the superclass from which they're derived. This dependency is shown on the first line of each class declaration.

```
class CarryMathQuestion : public MathQuestion
{...
};
class HardMathQuestion : public MathQuestion
{...
};
```

In general, each subclass expresses a dependency relationship to a superclass by using the keyword **public** and the name of the superclass. This is called **public inheritance** (we will not use private inheritance, virtual inheritance, or any of the other kinds of inheritance that are possible in C++.) As we'll see, a subclass inherits an interface from its superclass, and can inherit behavior (member functions) too. Inheritance is a chained, or transitive, relationship so that if subclass C inherits from superclass B, but B is itself a subclass of superclass A, then C inherits from A as well, although this is not shown explicitly in the declaration of C. In Figure 13.1, the class HardMathQuestion is a subclass of both MathQuestion and Question.

> **Syntax: Public inheritance**
>
> class *Subclass* : public *Superclass*
> {
>   *methods and instance variables*
> };

As we mentioned earlier, inheritance models an is-a relationship. When a subclass B inherits from a superclass A, any object of type B can be used where an object of type A is expected. This makes it possible, for example, to pass a HardMathQuestion object to the function GiveQuestion, which has a parameter of type MathQuestion. However, as we use inheritance, the is-a relationship captured by public inheritance will *not* work correctly in a C++ program unless references or pointers are used. An object, say hmq, that's an instance of the HardMathQuestion class can be passed as a parameter to a function expecting a MathQuestion object *only* if hmq is passed by reference or as a pointer. Similarly, hmq can be assigned as a MathQuestion object only if the assignment of hmq uses a pointer to hmq. In *inheritquiz.cpp* objects are passed by reference to GiveQuestion, and the vector question holds pointers to MathQuestion objects so that inheritance will work as intended. We'll study why this restriction is necessary in Section 13.1.5.

> **Program Tip 13.2:   Public inheritance should model an is-a relationship.**
> For is-a to work as expected, objects in an inheritance hierarchy should be passed by reference or as pointers and assigned using pointers whenever a subclass object is used as a superclass object.

13.1.5   Virtual Functions

Inheritance is exploited in *inheritquiz.cpp* since we can pass any kind of math quiz question to the function `GiveQuestion` and create different questions depending on the type of the object passed. From the compiler's perspective, the parameter to `GiveQuestion` is a reference to a `MathQuestion` object. How does the compiler know to call `HardMathQuestion::Create` when a hard question object is passed and to call `CarryMathQuestion::Create` when a carry question object is passed?

The compiler does not determine which function to call at **compile time** (when the program is compiled) but delays choosing which function to call until **run time** (when the program is executing or running). At run time different objects can be passed to `GiveQuestion`. Although the compiler thinks of the parameter as having type `MathQuestion`, the actual type may be different because of inheritance. The compiler calls the "right" version of `Create` because the function `Create` is a **virtual function**. Virtual functions are called **polymorphic** functions because they can take many forms[3] depending on the run-time type of an object rather than the compile-time type of an object.

What does all that really mean? It means that if you put the key word *virtual* before a member function in a superclass, then the member function that's called will be the subclass version of the member function if a subclass is what's actually used when the program is running. In *inheritquiz.cpp*, Program 13.2, different kinds of question are created because the member functions `Create` in each of the three classes in the math question hierarchy are different, as you can see in *mathquestface.cpp*, Program 13.4. We'll discuss when to make functions virtual in Section 13.2.2.

> **Program Tip 13.3:   The keyword `virtual` is not required in subclasses, but it's good practice to include it as needed in each subclass.** Any member function that is virtual in a superclass is also virtual in a derived class. Since a subclass may be a superclass at some point (e.g., as `MathQuestion` is a subclass of `Question` but a superclass of `HardMathQuestion`), including `virtual` every time a member function is declared is part of safe programming.

As you can see in the definitions of each member function in *mathquestface.cpp*, the word `virtual` appears only in the interface, or .h file, not in the implementation or .cpp file. Note that the constructors for `CarryMathQuestion` and `HardMathQuestion` each explicitly call the superclass constructor `MathQuestion()`. A superclass constructor will always be called from a subclass, even if the compiler must generate an implicit call. As we'll see in Section 13.2, some classes cannot be constructed, which is why `MathQuestion` does not call the constructor for `Question`, its superclass.

---

[3]The word polymorphic is derived from the Greek words *polus* (many) and *morphe* (shape).

> **Program Tip 13.4: Each subclass should explicitly call the constructor of its superclass.** The constructor will be called automatically if you don't include an explicit call, and sometimes parameters should be included in the superclass constructor. Superclass constructors must be called from an initializer list, not from the body of the subclass constructor. If the superclass is an *abstract base class* (see Section 13.2) no superclass constructor can be called.

Program 13.4 mathquestface.cpp

```cpp
#include <iostream>
#include <iomanip>
using namespace std;
#include "mathquestface.h"
#include "randgen.h"
#include "strutils.h"

MathQuestion::MathQuestion()
    : myAnswer("*** error ***"),
      myNum1(0),
      myNum2(0)
{
    // nothing to initialize
}

void MathQuestion::Create()
{
    RandGen gen;
    // generate random numbers until there is no carry
    do
    {
        myNum1 = gen.RandInt(10,49);
        myNum2 = gen.RandInt(10,49);
    } while ( (myNum1 % 10) + (myNum2 % 10) >= 10);

    myAnswer = tostring(myNum1 + myNum2);
}

void MathQuestion::Ask() const
{
    const int WIDTH = 7;
    cout << setw(WIDTH) << myNum1 << endl;
    cout << "+" << setw(WIDTH-1) << myNum2 << endl;
    cout << "-------" << endl;
    cout << setw(WIDTH-myAnswer.length()) << " ";
}

bool MathQuestion::IsCorrect(const string& answer) const
{
    return myAnswer == answer;
}
```

```
string MathQuestion::Answer() const
{
    return myAnswer;
}

string MathQuestion::Description() const
{
    return "addition of two-digit numbers with NO carry";
}

CarryMathQuestion::CarryMathQuestion()
  : MathQuestion()
{
  // all done in base class constructor
}

void CarryMathQuestion::Create()
{
    RandGen gen;
    // generate random numbers until there IS a carry
    do
    {
        myNum1 = gen.RandInt(10,49);
        myNum2 = gen.RandInt(10,49);
    } while ( (myNum1 % 10) + (myNum2 % 10) < 10);

    myAnswer = tostring(myNum1 + myNum2);
}

string CarryMathQuestion::Description() const
{
    return "addition of two-digit numbers with a carry";
}

HardMathQuestion::HardMathQuestion()
  : MathQuestion()
{
  // all done in base class constructor
}

void HardMathQuestion::Create()
{
    RandGen gen;
    myNum1 = gen.RandInt(100,200);
    myNum2 = gen.RandInt(100,200);
    myAnswer = tostring(myNum1 + myNum2);
}

string HardMathQuestion::Description() const
{
    return "addition of three-digit numbers";
}
```

mathquestface.cpp

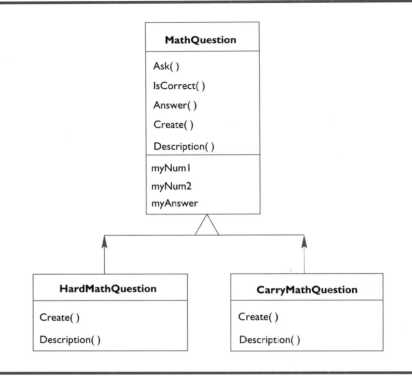

Figure 13.2 Overriding functions in the MathQuestion hierarchy.

Overriding Inherited Functions. In *mathquestface.h*, Program 13.3, the declarations for CarryMathQuestion and HardMathQuestion include only a constructor and prototypes for Create and Description. Declarations for the other inherited, virtual functions IsCorrect, Ask, and Answer are *not included*. This relationship is diagrammed in Figure 13.2.

Nevertheless, it's possible to call CarryMathQuestion::Ask() and have an addition question that requires the user to carry. The functions Create and Description are included in the interfaces of the derived classes and implemented in *mathquestface.cpp* because their behavior is different from what's inherited from the superclass versions of these functions. When a subclass implements an inherited function, it is called **overriding** the inherited function. When a method is overridden in a subclass, the subclass uses its own version of the method rather than the inherited version. Sometimes an inherited function works well even in subclasses. This is the case with the inherited functions Ask, Answer, and IsCorrect. The behavior, or implementation, of each of these functions does not need to be changed or **specialized** in the subclasses, so these inherited functions are not overridden. Since they're inherited unchanged, the functions do not appear in the declarations of the derived classes.

13.1.6 Protected Data Members

A subclass inherits more than behavior from its superclass: it also inherits state. This means that in addition to inheriting member function interfaces and, sometimes, implementations, a subclass inherits instance variables. Private instance variables are accessible only within member functions of the class in which the variables are declared; private data of a superclass are *not* accessible in any derived class. The private data are present in the derived classes. If there are accessor functions or mutator functions inherited from the superclass, these inherited functions can be used to access the private data; but no derived class member functions can access the private data directly.

In some inheritance hierarchies it makes sense for derived classes to access the instance variables that make up the state. In the math question hierarchy, for example, the functions Create assign values to myNum1 and myNum2, and these values are used in the functions Ask (although Ask is not overridden by the derived classes). Any variables and functions that are declared as **protected** are accessible not only to the member functions of the class in which they're declared as protected, but also to the member functions of all derived classes. The instance variables myNum1, myNum2, and myAnswer are all declared as protected, so they are accessible in MathQuestion methods and also in the derived classes HardMathQuestion and CarryMathQuestion. This is diagrammed in Figure 13.2.

It's often a good idea to avoid inheriting state and to inherit only interface and behavior. The problems that arise from inheriting state invariably stem from trying to inherit from more than one class, so-called **multiple inheritance**. We won't use multiple inheritance in this chapter, although we do use it in conjunction with the graphics package discussed in How to H.

> **Program Tip 13.5: When possible, inherit only interface and behavior, not state.** Minimize the inheritance of state if you think you'll eventually need to inherit behavior or interfaces from more than one class. When you're designing an inheritance hierarchy, protected data are accessible in derived classes, but private data are not, although the private data are present.

Pause to Reflect

13.1 If the call to *new* is not included in each call to push_back in Program 13.2, *inheritquiz.cpp*, will the program compile? Why?

13.2 Suppose the dereferencing operator isn't used in the call to GiveQuestion from main in *inheritquiz.cpp*. Explain how GiveQuestion should be modified so that it works with this call: GiveQuestion(questions[index]).

13.3 Suppose you create a new class named `MultMathProblem` for quiz questions based on multiplying a one-digit number by a two-digit number. Explain why the method `Ask` should be overridden in this class although it wasn't necessary to override it in the addition quiz questions.

13.4 Arguably, the behavior of the `Description` function in each of the classes in the math question hierarchy is exactly the same, but the string returned differs. The behavior is the same because each function returns a string but doesn't do anything else different. Explain modifications to the three classes that make up the math question hierarchy so that the description is an argument when the class is constructed and the method `Description` is not overridden in each subclass. The constructor calls in `main` might look like this (arguments are abbreviated):

```
questions.push_back(
    new MathQuestion("+, 2-digits, no carry"));
questions.push_back(
    new CarryMathQuestion("+. 2-digits, carry"));
questions.push_back(
    new HardMathQuestion("+, 3-digits"));
```

Why is this approach (arguably) not as good as the approach taken in the code (where `Description` is overridden)? Think about what client code should be responsible for and what classes used in client code should be responsible for.

13.5 If `protected` in `MathQuestion` is changed to `private`, the `Create` functions in each subclass will not compile. Why?

13.6 Design a new class for addition of three two-digit numbers with no carry. What inherited methods must you override? Why will you need to add a new data member in the new class? Why is it better to include the data member, say `myNum3`, in the new class rather than in the class `MathQuestion`?

13.7 Suppose you add state and behavior to the math question hierarchy so that each question tracks how many times its `Create` method is called. This number should be tracked and updated by the question classes but readable by client code. In what class(es) should the data and methods go?

13.2 Using an Abstract Base Class

The question hierarchy shown in Figure 13.1 shows other kinds of questions than math questions. The class `WhatsTheQuestion` is designed to encapsulate and generalize the state-capital question generator declared in *capquest.h*, discussed in Section 7.2.6, and implemented in *capquest.cpp*, Program 7.9. The class is generalized because it permits questions like "What's the capital of Texas?" and "What artist recorded *Slowhand*?" (the answers, respectively, are Austin and Eric Clapton). We'd like to incorporate all these kinds of questions in the same quiz program: "what-the" questions, math questions, and other kinds of questions we haven't yet designed or implemented.

The new class `WhatsTheQuestion` should not derive from `MathQuestion` if the new class doesn't have anything to do with mathematics. Since inheritance models *is-a* relationships, it would be a mistake to derive a question about state capitals from `MathQuestion` because the state-capital question cannot be used as a math question, and `is-a` means "can be used in a program as a" in our use of inheritance. Instead, we'll create a new abstraction, one that captures the idea of any kind of question. We'll call this new class `Question`; both `MathQuestion` and `WhatsTheQuestion` will derive from `Question` as shown in Figure 13.1.

The class `Question` is an **interface class**. The class exists as a superclass, but primarily as an interface for client programs. Clients write code to the specifications described in prose and code in *questface.h*, Program 13.5. As we'll see, it is not possible to create `Question` objects. Instead, we can create objects that are instances of classes that derive from `Question` and that inherit its interface. Since client programs are written to the interface, the new classes can be used in any client code that uses `Question` objects by reference or as pointers. For example, if we use `Question` instead of `MathQuestion` in the prototype of `GiveQuestion` in Program 13.2, *inheritquiz.cpp*, we'll be able to use the quiz prototype program for all kinds of questions. A new version of the function `GiveQuestion` is shown below. The call to `quest.Description` is commented out and the extraction `operator >>` is replaced by `getline` to allow the user to enter several words in response to a question.

```
void GiveQuestion(Question& quest)
// post: quest is asked once, correct response is given
{
  string answer;
  // cout << endl << quest.Description() << endl;
  cout << "type answer after the question" << endl;
  quest.Create();
  quest.Ask();
  getline(cin,answer);
  if (quest.IsCorrect(answer))
  { cout << "Excellent!, well done" << endl;
  }
  else
  { cout << "I'm sorry, the answer is "
         << quest.Answer() << endl;
  }
}
```

The call of `Description` is commented out because it's a method from the `MathQuestion` hierarchy, but not in our current version of the `Question` hierarchy declared in *questface.h*, Program 13.5.

The declaration for `Question` is like other class declarations, but all the member functions, except the destructor, are declared with = 0 after the function prototype. As we'll see, these make `Question` an **abstract base class**.

Program 13.5   questface.h

```
#ifndef _QUESTIONTERFACE_H
#define _QUESTIONTERFACE_H

// abstract base class for quiz questions
// derived classes MUST implement four functions:
//
// void Ask()         to ask the question
// string Answer()    to return the answer
// bool IsCorrect(s) to tell if an answer s is correct
// void Create()      to create a new question
//
// This class conforms to the naming conventions
// of quiz questions in "A Computer Science Tapestry" 2e

#include <string>
using namespace std;

class Question
{
  public:
    virtual ~Question() { }   // must implement destructor, here inline

    // accessor functions

    virtual bool    IsCorrect(const string& answer)  const = 0;
    virtual string  Answer()                         const = 0;
    virtual void    Ask()                            const = 0;

    // mutator functions

    virtual void Create() = 0;
};

#endif
```

questface.h

13.2.1   Abstract Classes and Pure Virtual Functions

A function with = 0 as part of its prototype in a class declaration *must* be overridden in subclasses; such functions are called **pure virtual functions**. The syntax and naming convention are ugly; it's better to think of these functions as **abstract interfaces**. They're abstract because implementations are not provided,[4] and they're interfaces because subclasses must implement a member function with the same prototype, thus conforming to the interface declared in the base class.

---

[4]The "must be overridden" rule is correct, but it's possible to supply an implementation of a pure virtual function that can be called from the overriding function in the subclass. However, any class that contains a pure virtual function cannot be instantiated/constructed. For our purposes, pure virtual functions will not have implementations; they're interfaces only.

A class that contains one pure virtual function is called an **abstract base class**, sometimes abbreviated as an **abc** (or, redundantly, an abc class[5]). I'll refer to these as abstract classes. It's not possible to define variables of a type that's an abstract class. Instead, subclasses of the abstract class are designed and implemented. Variables that are instances of these **concrete subclasses** can be defined. A concrete class is one for which variables can be constructed. Concrete is, in general, the opposite of abstract.

Why Use Abstract Classes? Designing an inheritance hierarchy can be tricky. One reason it's tricky is that to be robust, a hierarchy must permit new subclasses to be designed and implemented. Often, the original designer of the hierarchy cannot foresee everything clients will do with the hierarchy. Nevertheless, a well-designed hierarchy will be flexible in both use and modification through subclassing.

One design heuristic that helps make a class hierarchy flexible is to derive only from abstract classes. Clients are forced to implement each pure virtual function and are thus less likely to forget to implement one, thus getting inherited but unexpected behavior. The hierarchies we show in this book won't cause trouble *as we're using them.* But what about how other programmers will use our hierarchies? In general, you cannot expect all programmers to use your code wisely and not make mistakes. I certainly don't. A lengthy description of why it's a good idea to use abstract classes as superclasses is found in [Mey96] as item 33. This is one of several items that appear in a section called *Programming in the Future Tense.*

Program Tip 13.6: Good software is flexible, robust, and reliable. It meets current needs but adapts well to future needs, ideally to ideas not completely anticipated when the software is designed and implemented. Good programmers anticipate that things will change and design code to be adaptable in the face of inevitable change and maintenance.

Program 13.6 whatsthequizmain.cpp

```
int main()
{
    tvector<Question *> questions;
    questions.push_back(new HardMathQuestion());
    questions.push_back(new WhatsTheQuestion("what's the capital of ","statequiz.dat"));
    questions.push_back(new WhatsTheQuestion("what artist made ","cdquiz.dat"));

    int qCount = PromptInRange("how many questions",1,10);
    RandGen gen;
    for(int k=0; k < qCount; k++)
    {   int index = gen.RandInt(0,questions.size()-1);
        GiveQuestion(*questions[index]);
```

---

[5]What does PIN stand for — the thing you type as a password when you use an ATM? There is no such thing as a PIN number, nor an ATM machine. Well, there are such things, but there shouldn't be.

```
    }
    for(int k=0; k < questions.size(); k++)
    { delete questions[k];
    }
    return 0;
}
```

We'll pass different objects to the modified function `GiveQuestion` that uses the `Question` interface. The `main` that's shown is part of *whatsthequiz.cpp*.[6]

```
O U T P U T

prompt> whatsthequiz
how many questions between 1 and 10: 5

type answer after the question
what's the capital of  South Dakota : pierre
Excellent!, well done

type answer after the question
    191
+   102
-------
    293
Excellent!, well done

type answer after the question
what artist made  No Jacket Required : who knows
I'm sorry, the answer is Phil Collins

type answer after the question
    157
+   146
-------
    303
Excellent!, well done

type answer after the question
what artist made  Terrapin Station : grateful dead
Excellent!, well done
```

We use `PromptInRange` instead of `PromptRange` because we're using `getline` in `GiveQuestion` instead of `operator >>` (see Program Tip 9.3). The

---

[6]The entire program is not shown here but is available with the code that comes with this book.

vector `question` is now a vector of pointers to `Question` objects instead of `MathQuestion` objects. Class `WhatsTheQuestion` is declared in *whatstheface.h*.

Program 13.7   whatstheface.h

```
#ifndef _WHATSTHEQUESTION_H
#define _WHATSTHEQUESTION_H

#include <string>
using namespace std;

// see "questface.h" for details on member functions
//
// A class for generating quiz questions like
// "What's the capital of Arkansas"
// "Who wrote Neuromancer"
// "What artist recorded 'Are You Gonna Go My Way'"
//
// A file of questions is read, one is used at random each time Create
// is called.  The file is in the format
//
// question
// answer
// question
// answer
//
// i.e., a question uses two lines, the answer is the second line, the
// question is the first line:
//
// Terrapin Station
// Grateful Dead
// Hoist
// Phish
// It's A Shame About Ray
// Lemonheads
// -------------------
//
// The constructor and method Open take a prompt and a file of questions
// as parameters, e.g.,
// WhatsTheQuestion capitals("What's the capital of", "capitals.dat");

#include "questface.h"
#include "tvector.h"

class WhatsTheQuestion : public Question
{
  public:
    WhatsTheQuestion();
    WhatsTheQuestion(const string& prompt,
                     const string& filename);

    virtual bool   IsCorrect(const string& answer) const;
    virtual string Answer()                        const;
```

```
      virtual void    Ask()                                    const;

      virtual void    Create();
      virtual void    Open(const string& prompt,
                          const string& filename);

  protected:
    struct Quest
    {
        string first;
        string second;
        Quest() {}      // need vector of Quests
        Quest(const string& f, const string& s)
          : first(f),
            second(s)
        {}
    };
    tvector<Quest> myQuestions; // list of questions read
    string         myPrompt;    // prompt the user, "what's the ..."
    int            myQIndex;    // current question (index in myQuestions)
};

#endif
```

13.2.2 When Is a Method `virtual`?

We've discussed the advantages of using an inheritance hierarchy and saw how few modifications were needed in a client program like *inheritquiz.cpp*, Program 13.2, to use completely different kinds of questions. A case has been made to design inheritance hierarchies by deriving from abstract classes, but when should functions be virtual and when should they be pure virtual? One easy answer is that if you're designing an inheritance hierarchy, you should make every member function virtual.

> **Program Tip 13.7: Make all methods in a superclass virtual methods.** The superclass may be an abstract class in which at least some of the methods are pure virtual. It's an easy decision to make all methods in a superclass virtual. The cost is a possible mild performance penalty since virtual functions are slightly more expensive to call than nonvirtual functions. However, until you know where your code needs performance tuning, do not try to anticipate performance problems by making methods in a superclass nonvirtual.

Three classes in *inheritdemo.cpp*, Program 13.8, form a small inheritance hierarchy. We'll use the superclass `Person` and subclasses `Simpleton` and `Thinker` to demonstrate what can happen when functions in a superclass aren't virtual. In the listing and first run of the program, all classes are virtual. The class `Person` is abstract since `Person::ThinkAloud` is a pure virtual method. Implementations are provided for the other methods in `Person`, but all methods are virtual, so they can be overridden in derived classes.

Program 13.8 inheritdemo.cpp

```cpp
#include <iostream>
#include <string>
using namespace std;

#include "dice.h"

class Person      // abstract base class for every Person
{
  public:
    virtual ~Person() {}

    virtual void ThinkAloud() = 0;     // makes class abstract

    virtual void   Reflect()  const
    {   cout << "...As I see it, ...";
    }
    virtual string Name()  const
    {   return "Ethan";
    }
};

class Simpleton : public Person        // a simple thinker
{
  public:
    Simpleton(const string& name);
    virtual void ThinkAloud();

    virtual void   Reflect() const;
    virtual string Name()     const;

  private:
    string myName;
};

class Thinker : public Person          // a cogent person
{
  public:
    Thinker(const string& name);
    virtual void ThinkAloud();

    virtual void   Reflect() const;
    virtual string Name()     const;

  private:
    string myName;
    int    myThoughtCount;
};
```

```
Simpleton::Simpleton(const string& name)
  : myName(name)
// postcondition: ready to think
{  }

void Simpleton::ThinkAloud()
// postcondition: has thought
{
    cout << "I don't think a lot" << endl;
}

void Simpleton::Reflect() const
// postcondition: has reflected
{
    Person::Reflect();
    cout << "I'm happy" << endl;
}

string Simpleton::Name() const
// postcondition: returns name
{
    return myName + ", a simpleton";
}

Thinker::Thinker(const string& name)
  : myName(name),
    myThoughtCount(0)
// postcondition: ready to think
{ }

void Thinker::ThinkAloud()
// postcondition: has thought
{
    if (myThoughtCount < 1)
    {   cout << "I'm thinking about thinking" << endl;
    }
    else
    {   cout << "Aha! I have found the answer!" << endl;
    }
    myThoughtCount++;
}

void Thinker::Reflect() const
// postcondition: has reflected
{
    cout << "I'm worried about thinking too much" << endl;
}

string Thinker::Name() const
// postcondition: returns name
{
    return myName + ", a thinker";
}

void Think(Person & p)
```

```
// postcondition: p has thought and reflected once
{
    cout << "I am " << p.Name() << endl;
    p.ThinkAloud();
    p.Reflect();
}

int main()
{
    Simpleton s ("Sam");
    Thinker   t ("Terry");
    int k;
    for(k=0;  k < 2;  k++)
    {   Think(s);
        cout << "----" << endl << endl;
        Think(t);
        cout << "----" << endl << endl;
    }
    return 0;
}
```

inheritdemo.cpp

Note that `Simpleton::Reflect` calls the superclass `Reflect` method by qualifying the call with the name of the superclass. All superclass methods are inherited and can be called even when the methods are overridden in a subclass.

```
                      O U T P U T

prompt> inheritdemo
I am Sam, a simpleton
I don't think a lot
...As I see it, ...I'm happy
----

I am Terry, a thinker
I'm thinking about thinking
I'm worried about thinking too much
----

I am Sam, a simpleton
I don't think a lot
...As I see it, ...I'm happy
----

I am Terry, a thinker
Aha! I have found the answer!
I'm worried about thinking too much
----
```

If we make Person::Name *nonvirtual*, the behavior of the program changes. Each subclass inherits the nonvirtual Name, but any call to Name through a pointer or reference to the superclass Person cannot be overridden. What this means is that in the function Think, where the parameter is a Person reference, the call p.Name() will call Person::Name *regardless* of the type of the argument passed to Think. Recall that nonvirtual functions are resolved at compile time. This means that the determination of what function is called by p.Name() is made when the program is compiled, not when the program is run. The determination of what function is actually called by p.ThinkAloud() and p.Reflect() is made at run time because these functions are virtual. Because of this **late binding** of the virtual function actually called, the execution reflects arguments passed to the function at run time rather than what the compiler can determine when the program is compiled. In the sample run that follows only one round of thinking and reflecting is shown since this is enough to see the effects of the nonvirtual function Person::Name: every person in the program prints the name Ethan although that's not really any person's name!

OUTPUT

```
prompt> inheritdemo
I am Ethan
I don't think a lot
...As I see it, ...I'm happy
----

I am Ethan
I'm thinking about thinking
I'm worried about thinking too much
----
```

Virtual Destructors. Although it hasn't mattered in the examples we've studied so far, the destructor in any class with virtual methods *must* be virtual. Many compilers issue warnings if the destructor in a class is not virtual when some other method is virtual. As we noted in Program Tip 13.4, each subclass automatically calls the superclass constructor. The same holds for subclass destructors. Whenever a subclass destructor is called, the superclass destructors will be called as well. Superclass destructor calls, like all destructor calls, are automatic. This means you must implement a superclass destructor, even for abstract classes! Although abstract classes cannot be constructed, it's very likely that you'll call a destructor through a superclass pointer. The last loop in main of *inheritquiz.cpp*, Program 13.2, calls a destructor through a pointer to the superclass MathQuestion. The destructor should be virtual to ensure that the real destructor, the one associated with the actual object being destroyed, is called. This is illustrated in Figure 13.3 where the Subclass destructor is called through s, a

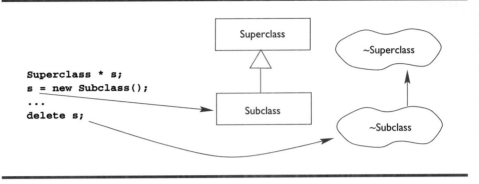

```
Superclass * s;
s = new Subclass();
...
delete s;
```

Figure 13.3 The subclass destructor automatically calls the superclass destructor, even when the superclass is abstract. The superclass must provide a destructor implementation even when the destructor is pure virtual.

`Superclass` pointer. The destructor `~Superclass()` is automatically called by `~Subclass()`.

When to Make a Virtual Function Pure. Any class with one pure virtual method is abstract. Every method that's an intrinsic part of a superclass interface, and that must be implemented in every subclass, should be pure virtual in the superclass. If you can decide at design time that a default implementation of a method in the superclass is a good idea, then the method can be virtual rather than pure virtual. A pure virtual method doesn't have a reasonable default implementation but is clearly part of the interface in an inheritance hierarchy.

It's possible that you'll want default implementations for every method but still want an abstract class. You can do this by making the destructor pure virtual and still provide an empty-body implementation. This is a two-step process:

■ Declare the destructor pure virtual, that is,

```
virtual ~Superclass() = 0;
```

■ Provide an empty-body implementation in a .cpp file that must be linked in creating the final program.

```
Superclass::~Superclass()
{
}
```

You'll get a link error if you fail to provide an implementation. Remember that a pure virtual function must be overridden, but you can provide an implementation (that can be called by subclass implementations).

Pause to Reflect

13.8 In the run of *whatsthequiz.cpp* in Section 13.2.1, the user types `pierre` as the capital of South Dakota, and the answer is acknowledged as correct. However, the entry for South Dakota in the data file `statequiz.dat` is `Pierre`, with a capital 'P.' What method judges the lowercase version `pierre` as correct? Given the declaration *whatstheface.h*, Program 13.7, write the method.

13.9 If the user had typed `Bismark` for the capital of South Dakota, what would have been printed as the correct answer? In particular, what case would be used for the first letter of the answer?

13.10 Suggest an alternative design to `WhatsTheQuestion` that would enable the user to construct an instance of the class by giving the filename, but without giving the prompt used for the question. (Hint: What information is stored in the file?)

13.11 There is no destructor `~WhatsTheQuestion()` declared in *whatstheface.h*, Program 13.7, nor is there a destructor declared in *mathquestface.h*, Program 13.3. However, the final loop that deletes objects through pointers in *inheritquiz.cpp* and its modification that uses class `Question` doesn't generate errors. Why?

13.12 If `Question` is modified to have a `Description` function similar to the function used by `MathQuestion` classes, but so that subclasses *must* override `Description`, then what does the declaration look like in *questface.h*, Program 13.5?

13.13 Should the function `Person::Name()` in Program 13.8 have a default implementation, or would it be better to make the function pure virtual? Why?

13.14 Suppose an implementation of `Person::ThinkAloud()` is defined as follows (in-line in the class declaration):

```
virtual void ThinkAloud()
{
    cout << "My brain says...";
}
```

Show how this function can be called by `Thinker::ThinkAloud()` only in the case that `Thinker` prints the message below:

```
Aha! I have found the answer!
```

13.15 If the default implementation from the previous problem is provided, and the word `virtual` removed from the declaration of `Person::ThinkAloud`, how does the output of the program change? (Show your answer by modifying the full run of the program.)

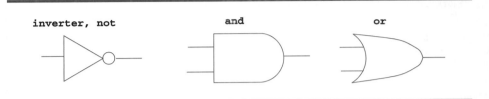

Figure 13.4 Three basic gates for building circuits.

13.3 Advanced Case Study: Gates, Circuits, and Design Patterns

In this section we'll study the design and implementation of a class hierarchy and set of programs for simulating **logic gates** and circuits.[7] We'll see how a well-designed class hierarchy enables us to model in software the same modular, component-based circuit construction that hardware designers use. We'll use the heuristics for programming with inheritance discussed earlier in the chapter as well as some of the **design patterns** from [GHJ95] that have become part of the standard tool kit for object-oriented programmers.

13.3.1 An Introduction to Gates and Circuits

In both an abstract and concrete sense, current computers are built from gates and chips, sometimes called **digital logic**. Although computers now have specially designed chips for tasks like playing sound, doing graphics, and reading disks, at some low level everything can be built from gates that regulate when and how electricity flows through a circuit. We'll use a standard set of three gates to construct different circuits and then use these circuits to construct other circuits. Eventually this process can lead to a working computer. Instead of physically building the gates we'll model them in software. The relationship between mathematical logic and digital logic was first recognized by Claude Shannon (see his biography in Section 4.4.2).

The three gates we'll use are shown in Figure 13.4. They are the **and-gate**, the **or-gate**, and the **inverter** or **not-gate**. Each of these gates corresponds to a Boolean operator with the same name in C++. Traditionally, the behavior of these gates is shown with truth tables identical to those in Table 4.3 for the logical operators. Program 13.9 simply creates one of each gate and tests it with all possible inputs to show how gate behavior is the same as the behavior of the logical operators shown in Table 4.3.

---

[7]This example was motivated by a related example in [AS96]. If you read only one (other) book in computer science, that should be the one. It is simply the best introductory book on computer science and programming, though it's not easy reading.

Program 13.9 gatetester.cpp

```cpp
#include <iostream>
using namespace std;

#include "gates.h"
#include "wires.h"

// show truth tables for each digital logic gate

int main()
{
    Gate * andg = new AndGate();
    Gate * org  = new OrGate();
    Gate * inv  = new Inverter();

    GateTester::Test(andg);
    GateTester::Test(org);
    GateTester::Test(inv);

    return 0;
}
```

gatetester.cpp

```
                        O U T P U T

prompt> gatetester
testing and (0)
-----
0 0        :        0
1 0        :        0
0 1        :        0
1 1        :        1
------
testing or (0)
-----
0 0        :        0
1 0        :        1
0 1        :        1
1 1        :        1
------
testing inv (0)
-----
0          :        1
1          :        0
------
```

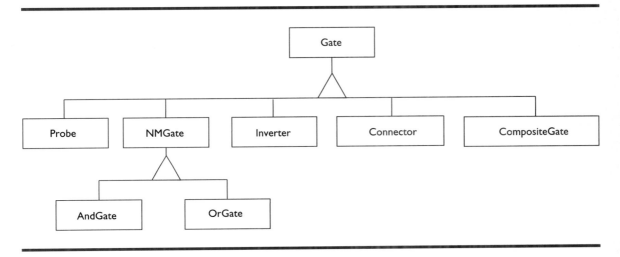

Figure 13.5   Hierarchy of components for building circuits.

The output is displayed using ones and zeros instead of true and false, but one corresponds to true and zero corresponds to false. If you look at *gatetester.cpp* carefully, you'll notice that new is called for three different types, but the returned pointer is assigned to variables of the same type: Gate. The inheritance hierarchy that enables this assignment is shown in Figure 13.5. The class GateTester, included via #include"gates.h", contains a static method Test. We could have made Test a free function, but by making it a static function in the GateTester class we avoid possible name clashes with other functions named Test.[8] Gates by themselves aren't very interesting; to build circuits we need to connect the gates together using wires. Complex circuits are built by combining gates and wires together. Once a circuit is built, it can become a component in other circuits, acting essentially like a more complex gate.

13.3.2   Wires, Gates, and Probes

Program 13.10, *gatewiredemo.cpp*, shows another method of gate construction. Wires are created, and then gates are constructed with wires attached to each gate's input(s) and output(s). The gates in Program 13.9 were constructed without wires attached to the inputs and outputs, but as we'll see later, it's possible to attach wires after a gate has been constructed as well as to construct a gate from wires as shown in Program 13.10. All three of the principal logic gates (and, or, inverter) can be given names when constructed, as shown for the andg gate pointer.

The gates in *gatewiredemo.cpp* are wired together as shown in Figure 13.6. An and-gate and an or-gate are attached so that the output of the and-gate feeds into the or-gate. In addition, Probe objects are attached to the output wires of the gates. As

---

[8]The C++ **namespace** feature (see Section A.2.3) could also be used to avoid name conflicts, but several compilers still don't support namespaces.

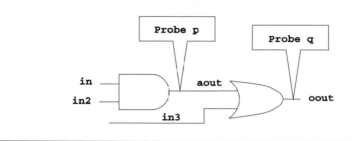

Figure 13.6 A simple example using gates, wires, and probes.

shown in Figure 13.5, a `Probe` *is-a* `Gate`. Abstractly, gates are attached to wires (and vice versa), so a probe is similar to an and-gate in this respect. A `Probe` object prints a message whenever the current on the wire it's monitoring changes, but also prints a message when it's first attached to a wire.

When a wire is constructed, the current on the wire is set to zero/false. The current changes either when it's explicitly changed using `Wire::SetCurrent`, or when a change in current propagates from an input wire to an output wire through a gate. A careful reading of the program and output shows that wires can be printed, and that each wire is numbered in the order in which it's created (a static counter in *wires.h*, Program G.15, keeps track of how many wires have been created). After the circuit is constructed, the probes detect and print changes caused by changes in the circuit.

Program 13.10 gatewiredemo.cpp

```cpp
#include <iostream>
using namespace std;

#include "gates.h"
#include "wires.h"

int main()
{
    Wire * in  =  new Wire();   // and-gate in
    Wire * in2 =  new Wire();   // and-gate in
    Wire * in3 =  new Wire();   // cr-gate in
    Wire * aout = new Wire();   // and-gate out
    Wire * oout = new Wire();   // or-gate out

    Gate * andg = new AndGate(in,in2,aout,"andgate");
    Gate * org  = new OrGate(in3,andg->OutWire(0),oout);
    cout << "attaching probes" << endl;
    Probe * p = new Probe(aout);       // attach to the and-out wire
    Probe * q = new Probe(oout);       // attach to the or-out wire

    cout << "set " << *in << " on" << endl;
    in->SetSignal(true);
```

```
cout << "set " << *in2 << " on" << endl;
in2->SetSignal(true);
cout << "set " << *in << " off" << endl;
in->SetSignal(false);
cout << "set " << *in3 << " on" << endl;
in3->SetSignal(true);
return 0;
}
```

gatewiredemo.cpp

After the probes are attached, the current on wire 0, one of the and-gate inputs, is turned on (or set). Since the other and-gate input has no current, no current flows out of the and-gate. When the current to wire 1 is set, the and-gate output (wire 3) becomes set and the probe detects this. Since the and-gate output is one of the or-gate inputs, the or-gate output (wire4) is also set and the other probe detects this change. The probes continue to detect changes as current is turned off and on as illustrated in the program and output.

OUTPUT

```
prompt> gatewiredemo
attaching probes
  (wire 3)          signal= 0
  (wire 4)          signal= 0
set  (wire 0) on
set  (wire 1) on
  (wire 4)          signal= 1
  (wire 3)          signal= 1
set  (wire 0) off
  (wire 4)          signal= 0
  (wire 3)          signal= 0
set  (wire 2) on
  (wire 4)          signal= 1
```

13.3.3 Composite Gates and Connectors

Program 13.12 shows two ways of constructing the **xor-gate** illustrated in Figure 13.7. The output of an xor-gate is set when one of its inputs is set, but not when both are set. The truth table generated by GateTester::Test for an xor-gate is shown in the output. Both methods create a CompositeGate object, another of the gates in the hierarchy shown in Figure 13.5. A CompositeGate is-a gate as shown in the diagram, but it's a gate made up of other gates. In particular, a composite gate can be formed from the basic gate building blocks, but also from other composite gates. A collection of connected gates is also known as a **circuit**, so a CompositeGate object represents a circuit. The key idea here is that a circuit is also a gate for building other circuits.

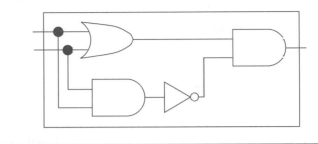

Figure 13.7 Building an xor circuit.

> **Program Tip 13.8: The class CompositeGate is a concrete example of the *Composite* design pattern [GHJ95].** There, the pattern is a solution to a problem stated as "you want clients to be able to ignore the difference between compositions of objects and individual objects. Clients will treat all objects ... uniformly."

A linked list can also be viewed as a composite. A node is an individual item in a list, but it also represents a complete list since the node provides access to the rest of the list. Just as a node contains information and a pointer to another node, a CompositeGate contains information about the gate and many pointers to other gates, the gates that make up the circuit. Rather than dwell on the implementation of the class, we'll see how it's used to create complex circuits.

It's almost simpler to create a new class XorGate than to build a composite gate that works like an xor-gate. However, creating a new class requires writing code and recompiling a program. As we'll see in the final program from this chapter, it's possible to create a gate-construction language or program that can build new gates while a program is running. The only member function of a class XorGate that differs in a substantive way from either AndGate or OrGate is XorGate::Act, the method that determines how a signal propagates through the gate.

Program 13.11   xorgate.cpp

```
class XorGate : public Gate
{
 public:
    virtual void Act()
    {
       myOuts[0]->SetSignal(
             (myIns[0]->GetSignal() || myIns[1]->GetSignal()) &&
           !(myIns[0]->GetSignal() && myIns[1]->GetSignal())
       )
    }
};
```

xorgate.cpp

The partial class declaration and definition shown above captures in Boolean logic and code exactly the relationship shown in digital logic in Figure 13.7. The output is set when either input is set, but not when both inputs are set.

Constructing `CompositeGate` Objects. Three `CompositeGate` methods allow a complex gate to be constructed from other gates:

■ `AddGate` adds a gate to a composite gate. Presumably the added gates will be connected in some way (otherwise the composite gate won't be very useful).

■ `AddIn` adds an input wire to a composite gate. Presumably each input wire is connected to a gate that's part of the composite object. Each call of `AddIn` adds a new input wire.

■ `AddOut` adds an output wire to a composite gate. As with `AddIn`, presumably each added output wire is connected to one of the gates added to the composite.

Each of these methods is shown in `MakeXOR` of Program 13.12. Note that each call of `AddIn` and `AddOut` adds a wire that is an input (respectively output) of a gate already added to the composite. The input and output wires could be specified first, then the gates added; the net effect is the same.

Using the Method `Gate::clone`. The `MakeXOR` function also shows the method `Gate::clone` applied to the `AndGate` object `ag`. The method `clone` is abstract[9] in `Gate`, so every concrete subclass must provide an implementation. Client programs typically define objects and reference them through pointers of type `Gate *` more often than by pointers of a specific subclass like `AndGate *` or `CompositeGate *`. Since `clone` is virtual, the object actually `cloned` returns a copy of itself.

```
void DoStuff(Gate * g)
// post: do something with a copy of g
{
  Gate * copy = g->clone();
  // what kind of gate is copy?  we can't tell but
  // we can apply any generic Gate method to copy
}
```

In this example, the object referenced by `copy` is some kind of gate, and if `clone` works as expected, `copy` is a duplicate of the gate `g` passed to the function `DoStuff`. The `Gate::clone` method is an example of what's often called a **virtual constructor**. The `clone` method is used to create objects, like a constructor, but the `clone` method is virtual, so it creates an object whose type isn't known at compile time.

---

[9]Recall that I use *abstract* rather than the more C++ specific term *pure virtual*.

Program Tip 13.9: **The `clone` method is a concrete example of what's called the *Factory Method* design pattern in [GHJ95].** There the pattern is a solution to a problem paraphrased as "client code can't anticipate what kind of objects it must create or wants to delegate responsibility of creation to subclasses in a class hierarchy."

Using Connectors. The functions `MakeXOR` and `MakeXOR2` illustrate the differences between calling `Connect` to connect wires to gate inputs and output (in `MakeXOR`) and constructing gates from existing wires (`MakeXOR2`). When gates are constructed without wires attached as they are in `MakeXOR`, the gate functions `InWire` and `OutWire` are used to access input wires and output wires, respectively, for attaching these wires to other wires using connectors. A connector is a gate that simply transfers current from one wire to another as though the wires are joined or soldered together.

As the output shows, the circuit created by `MakeXOR` uses more wires than the circuit created by `MakeXOR2`. When gates are constructed without wires in client code, each gate creates its own wires for input and output. Counting the input and output wires for each gate in Figure 13.7 shows that there are 11 wires: $3 \times (2$ and-gates$) + 3 \times (1$ or-gate$) + 1 \times (2$ inverters$)$. The wires for the gate created by `MakeXOR2` are explicitly created in the client program. There are fewer wires since, for example, the connections between the inputs of the rightmost and-gate (whose output is the circuit's output) and their sources (the outputs of the or-gate and inverter) require only two wires, whereas four wires are used by `MakeXOR`.

Program 13.12 xordemo.cpp

```
#include <iostream>
using namespace std;

#include "gates.h"
#include "wires.h"
#include "tvector.h"

// illustrate connecting wires to gates using Connect

CompositeGate * MakeXOR()
// post: return an xor-gate
{
    CompositeGate * xorg = new CompositeGate(); // holds xor-gate
    Gate * ag = new AndGate();                  // build components
    Gate * ag2= ag->clone();                    // and gate a different way
    Gate * og  = new OrGate();
    Gate * inv = new Inverter();

    Connect(og->InWire(0),   ag->InWire(1) );   // wire components
    Connect(og->InWire(1),   ag->InWire(0) );
    Connect(ag->OutWire(0),  inv->InWire(0));
```

```
    Connect(inv->OutWire(0), ag2->InWire(1));
    Connect(og->OutWire(0),  ag2->InWire(0));

    xorg->AddGate(ag);  xorg->AddGate(ag2);      // add gates to xor-circuit
    xorg->AddGate(inv); xorg->AddGate(og);

    xorg->AddOut(ag2->OutWire(0));                    // add inputs/outputs
    xorg->AddIn(og->InWire(0)); xorg->AddIn(og->InWire(1));

    return xorg;
}

CompositeGate * MakeXOR2()
// post: returns an xor-gate
{
    CompositeGate * xorg = new CompositeGate();
    tvector<Wire *> w(6);     // need 6 wires to make circuit
    tvector<Gate *> gates;    // holds the gates in the xor-circuit
    int k;
    for(k=0; k < 6; k++)
    {   w[k] = new Wire();
    }
    gates.push_back(new OrGate( w[0], w[1], w[2]) ); // create wired gates
    gates.push_back(new AndGate(w[0], w[1], w[3]) ); // share inputs
    gates.push_back(new Inverter(w[3], w[4]) );       // and out->inv in
    gates.push_back(new AndGate(w[2], w[4], w[5]) ); // combine or, inv

    for(k=0; k < gates.size();k++)                    // add gates to xor
    {   xorg->AddGate(gates[k]);
    }
    xorg->AddIn(w[0]); xorg->AddIn(w[1]);            // add inputs/outputs
    xorg->AddOut(w[5]);

    return xorg;
}

int main()
{
    CompositeGate * g = MakeXOR();
    CompositeGate *g2 = MakeXOR2();
    cout << "circuit has " << g->CountWires() << ' wires" << endl;
    GateTester::Test(g);
    cout << "circuit has " << g2->CountWires() << " wires" << endl;
    GateTester::Test(g2);

    return 0;
}
```

xordemo.cpp

The code in MakeXOR2 exploits the Gate class hierarchy by creating a vector of pointers to Gate * objects but creating different kinds of gates for each pointer to reference. A vector of Gate * pointers is also used in the private section of the CompositeGate class to store the gates used in constructing the composite object. Although the functions MakeXOR and MakeXOR2 create different digital circuits, the circuits are identical from a logical viewpoint: they compute the same logical operator as shown by the truth tables. The different functions create a `CompositeGate` using the same process:

1. Create an initially empty composite.
2. Construct gates, wire them together, and add the gates to the composite.
3. Specify input wires and output wires for the composite.
4. The composite object is finished.

As we've noted, steps two and three can be interchanged; the relative order in which these steps are executed does not affect the final composite gate.

```
O U T P U T

prompt> xordemo
circuit has 11 wires
testing composite: 4 gates, 2 in wires, 1 out wires
-----
0 0        :        0
1 0        :        1
0 1        :        1
1 1        :        0
------
circuit has 6 wires
testing composite: 4 gates, 2 in wires, 1 out wires
-----
0 0        :        0
1 0        :        1
0 1        :        1
1 1        :        0
------
```

Pause to Reflect

13.16 Suppose a probe `pin` is added to the input wire `in` as part of Program 13.10:

```
Probe * q =   new Probe(oout); // in original program
Probe * pin = new Probe(in)    // added here
```

As a result of adding this probe three lines of output are added. What are the lines and where do they appear in the output? (Hint: One line is printed when the probe is attached.)

13.17 If the `AndGate` instance `andg` in Program 13.10 is tested at the end of main, the truth table printed is the standard truth table for an and-gate.

This happens even though the output of `andg` is connected to the input of the or-gate `org`. Why? (Hint: Is the circuit consisting of the and-gate and or-gate combined into a `Gate` object?)

```
GateTester::Test(andg);
```

13.18 The probe `p` can be removed from the wire `aout` at the end of Program 13.10 using a `Wire` member function. What's the function, and what call uses it to remove the probe? (See *wires.h*, Program G.15, for `Wire` methods.)

13.19 Write the function `RemoveProbe` whose header follows. (See *wires.h* and *gates.h* in How to G.)

```
void RemoveProbe(Probe * p)
// post: p is removed from the wire it monitors/probes
```

13.20 The return type of the function `MakeXOR` is `CompositeGate *` in Program 13.12, *xordemo.cpp*. If the return type is changed to `Gate *` an xor-gate is still returned, but the call of `MakeXOR` below fails to compile.

```
CompositeGate * g = MakeXOR();
```

If `g`'s type is changed to `Gate *` the definition of `g` compiles, but then the output statement below fails to compile.

```
cout << "circuit has " << g->CountWires()
     << " wires" << endl;
```

What's the cause of this behavior? (Hint: `CountWires` is not a `Gate` method.)

13.21 The circuit diagrammed in Figure 13.8 shows a circuit that is logically equivalent to an or-gate but that is constructed from an and-gate and three inverters. Write a function `MakeOR` that returns a `CompositeGate` representing the circuit diagrammed in Figure 13.8. Draw a similar circuit that's logically equivalent to an and-gate using only inverters and or-gates.

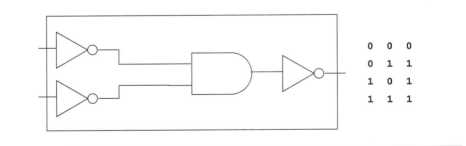

Figure 13.8 Building an or-gate from other basic gates.

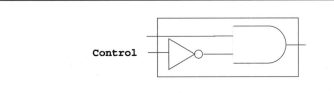

Figure 13.9 A disabler circuit.

13.22 The circuit diagrammed in Figure 13.9 is a **disabler** circuit. The signal on the wire labeled *Control* determines if the signal on the (other) input wire is passed through to the output wire of the disabler. When the control signal is zero (off), the input signal goes through to the output (i.e., the input and the output are the same). When the control signal is set (i.e., true/one), the input signal is stopped, or disabled, and the output wire is false/zero regardless of the value on the input wire.

Write a function `MakeDisabler` that returns a disabler circuit. Construct both gates without wires so that you must use `Connect` to wire the circuit together. How many wires are used in the circuit? (Do this exercise on paper, not necessarily by writing and testing a function.) Implement an alternative version called `MakeDisabler2` that does not use `Connect` so that both gates in the circuit are constructed with wires. How many wires are used in the circuit?

13.23 Write the method `Disabler::Act` that represents the logic of a disabler circuit. Model the function on the version of `XorGate::Act` shown in Section 13.3.3.

13.24 The **comparator** circuit shown in Figure 13.10 determines whether the signal on the wire labeled R is less than the signal on the wire labeled C, where one/zero are used for true/false. Write a truth table for the circuit by tracing all four possible

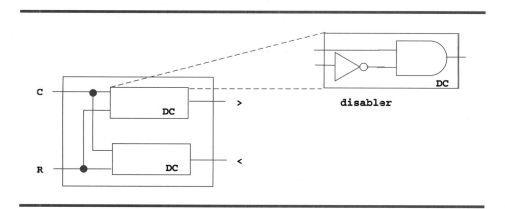

Figure 13.10 A comparator circuit for selecting the larger of two values.

combinations of zero/one for inputs and labeling the corresponding outputs. Verify that if the signals are the same, the outputs are both zero. If $R < C$ then the lower output wire labeled < is one/true and the upper wire is zero/false. If $R > C$ then the upper output labeled > is one/true and the lower wire is zero/false.

13.25 Assume a function `MakeDisabler` is written that returns a disabler-gate/circuit. Use this function to write a `MakeComparator` function that returns a `CompositeGate` encapsulating a comparator circuit.

13.26 Do you expect the truth tables printed by the two calls of `GateTester::Test` that follow to be the same? Why?

```
void TruthTwice(Gate * g)
{
   Gate * copy = g->clone();
   GateTester::Test(g);
   GateTester::Test(copy);
}
```

13.3.4   Implementation of the `Wire` and `Gate` Classes

The interactions between classes in the `Gate` hierarchy and the class `Wire` are fairly complex. It's not essential to understand these interactions to write simple programs like the ones we studied in previous sections, but a solid understanding of the interactions is needed before you write your own `Gate` subclasses or write more involved programs.

Once we've looked at the classes and their implementations in more detail, we'll be able to make judgments about the overall design of the `Gate`/`Wire` framework. We'll see that there are some problems in the `Gate` class hierarchy that make it more difficult to add an `XorGate` subclass than it should be. It's not difficult to add such a class, but the process would be considerably more simple with the introduction of a new class encapsulating behavior common to `AndGate`, `OrGate`, and what would be `XorGate`. As we've stressed, software should be grown: the design process does not finish when you have a working program or prototype. Since programs and classes evolve, it makes sense to step back and examine a design and implementation after the initial kinks have been ironed out.

> **Program Tip 13.10:**   **Class methods sometimes need to be *refactored* into other classes, or into new classes that weren't part of an initial design.** Refactoring means you don't add new functionality, but you redistribute (to existing classes) or reassign (to new classes) existing behavior and functionality to make classes and code more reusable.

As a start toward understanding the design we'll consider the simple code in Program 13.13 that creates an or-gate, attaches a probe to the output of the gate, and sets one of the input gates to true. The interactions and method calls made by all classes for the three lines of code in *gwinteraction.cpp* are shown in Figure 13.11.

Program 13.13 gwinteraction.cpp

```
#include <iostream>
using namespace std;

#include "gates.h"
#include "wires.h"

int main()
{
    Gate * org = new OrGate();
    Probe * p  = new Probe(org->OutWire(0));
    org->InWire(0)->SetSignal(true);

    return 0;
}
```

gwinteraction.cpp

OUTPUT

```
prompt> gwinteraction
  (wire 2)          signal= 0
  (wire 2)          signal= 1
```

Two separate concepts generate almost all the interactions shown in Figure 13.11. We'll give an overview of each concept, discuss why they're used in the Wire/Gate frame-work, and then provide a more in-depth look at each of them.

1. A Wire object can have any number of gates attached to it. Every time the signal on a wire changes, the wire notifies all the attached gates that the signal has changed using the method Gate::Act. Each gate responds differently when it's acted on; for example, probes print a value, or-gates propagate a true value to their output wires if one of their input wires is set, and so on.

2. When a Gate is constructed without wires, such as in *gwinteraction.cpp* or in MakeXOR as opposed to MakeXOR2 of Program 13.12, *xordemo.cpp*, the gate creates its own wires. Rather than calling new Wire directly, a gate requests a wire from a WireFactory associated with the entire Gate hierarchy by a static instance variable of the Gate class.

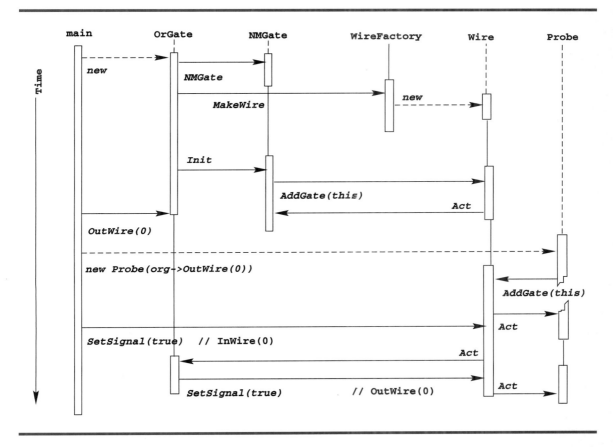

Figure 13.11 Interaction diagram: creating an or-gate with no connected wires, attaching a probe to the output of the gate, and setting the signal on the first of the gate's two inputs.

13.3.5 Gates and Wires: Observers and Observables

Look carefully at the inputs to the xor-gate diagrammed in Figure 13.7 and the comparator diagrammed in Figure 13.10. In both cases one wire is attached to the inputs of two different gates. Any change in the wire must propagate a signal through both gates. Suppose a probe is attached to one of the input wires that feeds into more than one gate. Then a change in the wire must notify two gates and a probe, which is really three gates since a probe is-a gate. How are changes in a circuit propagated? In the framework discussed here, a gate attaches itself to a wire, or can be attached by another object to a wire using the method Wire::AddGate. For example, a Probe instance adds itself during construction to the wire it probes.

```
Probe::Probe(Wire * w)
  : myWire(w)
// post: probe is attached to w
{
```

```
        myWire->AddGate(this);
}
```

It's almost as though each attached gate listens to the wire, waiting for a change. However, a gate doesn't actively listen; it is notified by the wire when the wire's signal changes. The wire notifies all the gates that have been attached to it using the following code:

```
void Wire::SetSignal(bool signal)
// post: notify attached/listening gates if signal changes
{
    if (signal != mySignal)
    {   mySignal = signal;
        int k;
        for(k=0; k < myGates.size(); k++)
        {    myGates[k]->Act( );
        }
    }
}
```

You can look at the code in *wires.h* for details (see How to G), but the code above is mostly self-explanatory from the names of the instance variables and the syntax of how they're used — for example, myGates seems to be a tvector object from how it's used. Gates that have been attached using AddGate can subsequently be removed using Wire::RemoveGate. Gate identity for removal is based on pointer values, so any object added can be removed since the address of an object doesn't change.

> **Program Tip 13.11:** In [GHJ95] the *Observer* pattern is a solution to a problem "when a change to one object requires changing others, and you don't know how many objects need to be changed." The Observer pattern is sometimes called Observer/Observable or Publish/Subscribe.

In the code above you can see that a wire's gates are notified in the same order in which they are added to the wire. Suppose Wire object w2 notifies the first of the two gates that are (hypothetically) attached to w2. Since a gate's Act method may set other wires, that will in turn call other Act methods; the second gate attached to w2 may have its Act method invoked well after other gates have acted. In one of the modifications in the exercises you'll be asked to introduce time into the Wire/Gate framework to account for these anomalies.

The Observer pattern is common outside of programming. Volunteer firefighters are notified when there's an event they must respond to, but the firefighters do not actively phone the fire department to find fires. The firefighters correspond to gates in our framework; the fire department is the wire notifying the firefighters. Auctions sometimes model the pattern: bidders are notified when a new, higher bid has been made. A bidder actively monitoring new bids doesn't quite fit the model, but a bidder that responds only when notified of a new bid does.

Bjarne Stroustrup

Bjarne Stroustrup is truly the "father" of C++. He began its design in 1979 and is still involved with both design and implementation of the language. His interests span computer science, history, and literature. In his own words:

C++ owes as much to novelists and essayists such as Martin A. Hansen, Albert Camus, and George Orwell, who never saw a computer, as it does to computer scientists such as David Gries, Don Knuth, and Roger Needham. Often, when I was tempted to outlaw a feature I personally disliked, I refrained from doing so because I did not think I had the right to force my views on others.

In writing about creating software, Stroustrup (p. 693) [Str97] mentions several things to keep in mind. Three are ideas we've emphasized in this book: (1) there are no "cookbook" methods that can replace intelligence, experience, and good taste in design and programming; (2) experimentation is essential for all nontrivial software development; and (3) design and programming are iterative activities.

Stroustrup notes that it is as difficult to define what a programming language is as to define computer science:

Is a programming language a tool for instructing machines? A means of communicating between programmers? A vehicle for expressing high-level designs? A notation for algorithms? A way of expressing relationships between concepts? A tool for experimentation? A means of controlling computerized devices? My view is that a general-purpose programming language must be all of those to serve its diverse set of users.

For his work in the design of C++, Stroustrup was awarded the 1994 ACM Grace Murray Hopper award, given for fundamental contributions made to computer science by work done before the age of 30. Most of this material is taken from [Str94].

13.3.6 Encapsulating Construction in `WireFactory`

The simple three-line program in Program 13.13 constructs an or-gate without providing wires when the or-gate is constructed. The or-gate makes its own wires, and the program connects a probe to the created output wire. As we saw in the two different functions

MakeXOR and MakeXOR2 of Program 13.12, a gate can be created by attaching existing wires to the gate when the gate is constructed, or by creating a gate and then connecting wires to the input/output wires the gate constructs itself. Where do these self-constructed wires come from? The simplest method is to create new wires using new Wire() — sample code for the Inverter constructor shows this (this isn't the real constructor, which uses a different technique discussed later). An Inverter has an input, an output, a name, and a number.

```
Inverter::Inverter(const string& name)
  : myIn(new Wire(name)), myOut(new Wire(name))
    myName(name), myNumber(ourCount)
{
    ourCount++;
    myIn->AddGate(this);
}
```

Since an Inverter creates the wires using the new operator. the class is responsible for deleting the wires in its destructor. This approach tightly couples the Gate and Wire classes. If a better wire class is designed, or we want to run a circuit simulation using a LowEnergyWire class representing a new kind of wire that's a subclass of Wire, we'll have to rewrite every gate's constructor to use the new kind of wire. We can't reduce the coupling inherent in the circuit framework because wires and gates do depend on each other, but we can reduce the coupling in how gates create wires. To do this we design a WireFactory class. When a client wants a wire, the wire is "ordered" from the factory rather than constructed using new. If a new wire class is created, we order wires from a new factory that makes the new kind of wires. Because we use inheritance to model is-a relationships, the new kind of wires can be used in place of the original wires since, for example, a LowEnergyWire is-a Wire. By isolating wire creation in a WireFactory, changing the kinds of wires used by all gates means simply changing the factory, and the factory is created in one place so it can be changed easily. The Inverter constructor actually used in *gates.cpp* illustrates how a factory isolates wire construction in one place:

```
Inverter::Inverter(const string& name)
  : myIn(ourWireFactory->MakeWire(name)),
    myOut(ourWireFactory->MakeWire(name)),
    myName(name), myNumber(ourCount)
{
    ourCount++;
    myIn->AddGate(this);
}
```

The my/our naming convention tells us that ourWireFactory is a static instance variable. The factory is shared by every Gate object since it's defined as a protected static data member in the abstract Gate superclass. This means every Inverter, every AndGate, and every gate subclass not yet implemented can share the factory.

> **Program Tip 13.12:** **Using a factory class to isolate object creation decreases the coupling between the created objects and their collaborating classes. This design pattern is called *Abstract Factory* in [GHJ95].** A factory class is used when "a system should be independent of how its products are created, composed, and represented" or when "a system should be configured with one of multiple families of products."

Our `WireFactory` class is not abstract, but we'll explore how to create more than one kind of factory in the exercises by creating an abstract base class from which `WireFactory` derives. The `Gate::clone` method outlined in Program Tip 13.9 as a realization of a factory *method* shares characteristics with the `WireFactory` class, which is a factory *class*: both isolate object creation so that clients can use objects without knowing how to create them.

13.3.7 Refactoring: Creating a `BinaryGate` Class

When I first designed the `Gate` hierarchy in Figure 13.5 I anticipated creating classes like `And3Gate`, an and-gate with three inputs that sets its output only when all three inputs are set. I considered an `And3Gate` to be a 3-1-gate, a gate with three inputs and one output. The existing `AndGate` class represents a 2-1-gate while the comparator circuit diagrammed in Figure 13.10 is a 2-2-gate with two inputs and two outputs. Similarly, the full-adder diagrammed in Figure 13.13 is a 3-2-gate. Thinking there would be some common behavior in these gates, I created a class `NMGate` to model an n-m-gate as I've just described. Since a subclass is responsible for calling its superclass constructor, this leads to the constructor below for an `AndGate` instance constructed without wires.

```
AndGate::AndGate(const string& name)
  : NMGate(ourCount,name)
// post: this and-gate is constructed
{
    tvector<Wire *> ins(2), outs(1);
    ins[0] = ourWireFactory->MakeWire(myName);
    ins[1] = ourWireFactory->MakeWire(myName);
    outs[0] = ourWireFactory->MakeWire(myName);
    NMGate::Init(ins,outs);
    ourCount++;
}
```

The `AndGate` constructor creates two input wires and one output wire and puts these wires into vectors for initializing the parent `NMGate` class. The general class `NMGate` is initialized with vectors of wires for input and output so that it can be used for a 3-2-gate as well as an 8-8-gate. The `OrGate` constructor shows striking similarities to the `AndGate`.

```
OrGate::OrGate(const string& name)
  : NMGate(ourCount,name)
```

```
    {
        tvector<Wire *> ins(2), outs(1);
        ins[0] = ourWireFactory->MakeWire(myName);
        ins[1] = ourWireFactory->MakeWire(myName);
        outs[0] = ourWireFactory->MakeWire(myName);
        NMGate::Init(ins,outs);
        ourCount++;
    }
```

This duplicated code will be replicated in any new 2-1-gate (e.g., if we implement an XorGate class). The Act methods of these classes differ because the gates model different logic, and the clone methods differ since each gate must return a copy of itself; but the other AndGate and OrGate methods are the same. Since 2-1-gates are quite common, and we may be implementing more "basic" 2-1-gates in the future, it's probably a good idea to refactor the behavior in common to the 2-1-gates into a new class BinaryGate. The new class derives from NMGate and is a parent class to AndGate and OrGate. The AndGate constructor will change as follows:

```
AndGate::AndGate(const string& name)
    : BinaryGate(ourCount,name)
// post: this and-gate is constructed
{
    ourCount++;
}
```

The behavior common to the AndGate and OrGate constructors has been factored out into the BinaryGate constructor. Similarly, all the methods whose behavior is the same in the binary gate subclasses are factored into the new BinaryGate superclass.

Pause to Reflect

13.27 The method Wire::AddGate is implemented as follows:

```
void Wire::AddGate(Gate * g)
// post: g added to gate collection, g->Act() called
{
    myGates.push_back(g);
    g->Act();
}
```

Identify each call of g->Act() whose source is AddGate that appears in the interaction diagram of Figure 13.11. Which of the calls generate(s) output?

13.28 Constructing an Inverter and connecting a probe to its output generates the output shown: (*continued*)

```
Gate * inv = new Inverter();
Probe * p   = new Probe(inv->OutWire(0));
```

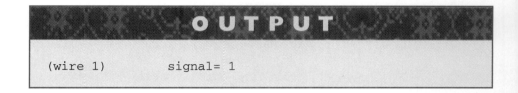

```
(wire 1)          signal= 1
```

Why is the wire labeled `(wire 1)`? Where is wire 0? Draw an interaction diagram like Figure 13.11 for these two statements. Trace all method calls, particularly the `Gate::Act` calls, and show why the call of `g->Act()` in `Wire::AddGate` shown in the previous exercise is necessary to get the behavior shown in the output. What would the output of the probe be if the call `g->Act()` wasn't included in the method `AddGate`? Why?

13.29 The statements below construct a disabler circuit as diagrammed in Figure 13.9. The circuit isn't formed as a composite, but the gates and wires together make a disabler circuit with a probe attached to the circuit's output wire.

```
Wire * controller= new Wire();
Gate * ag=       new AndGate();
Gate * inv=      new Inverter(controller, ag->InWire(1));
Probe * p=       new Probe(ag->OutWire(0));
ag->InWire(0)->SetSignal(true); // send a signal
```

Since the `controller` is false/zero when constructed, the signal set should propagate through the disabler. Draw an interaction diagram like Figure 13.11 for these five statements.

13.30 As implemented, the `WireFactory` class cannot recycle used wires (i.e., if a `Gate` is destroyed, the wires it may have ordered from the factory are not reused). The factory does keep track of all the wires ever allocated/ordered, and cleans the wires up when the factory ceases to exist.

In what function does the current `WireFactory` destroy all the wires allocated during the factory's lifetime? Sketch a design that would allow the factory to recycle wires no longer needed. You'll need to identify how the factory stores recycled wires and how the factory collaborates with the `Gate` classes to get wires back when a gate no longer needs them.

13.31 The class `NMGate` is an abstract class because it has at least one abstract/pure virtual function (e.g., `Act`). However, there is an `NMGate` constructor, and an `NMGate` class has state: the input and output wires. Why is the class an abstract class, which means it's not possible to create an `NMGate` object, but the class still has a constructor and state? Note that the statement below will not compile for two reasons: the constructor is protected and the class is abstract.

```
Gate * g = new NMGate(); // won't compile
```

13.32 Why is ourCount++ used in the body of the refactored AndGate constructor at the end of Section 13.3.7? Why isn't the increment factored into the BinaryGate constructor?

13.33 The following statement, added as the last statement in main of Program 13.12, *xordemo.cpp*, produces the output shown:

```
cout << g2->deepString() << endl;
```

The output shows the components of the composite gate g2 created by MakeXOR2. The method deepString is implemented in each Gate subclass, although it often defaults to the same function as tostring. Why are the and-gates numbered 2 and 3? Where are and-gates numbered 0 and 1? Draw the circuit for this composite and label every gate and wire with its number.

```
            O U T P U T

composite: 4 gates, 2 in wires, 1 out wires
all-in   (wire 11)   (wire 12)
all-out  (wire 16)
        or (1)
        in  (wire 11)   (wire 12)        out   (wire 13)
----

        and (2)
        in  (wire 11)   (wire 12)        out   (wire 14)
----

        inv (1)
        in (wire 14)     out (wire 15)
----

        and (3)
        in  (wire 13)   (wire 15)        out   (wire 16)
----

------
```

13.34 Instead of refactoring AndGate and OrGate into a new BinaryGate class, suppose a new constructor is added to the NMGate class in which the number of inputs and outputs is specified as shown in the following. Is this a better solution than introducing a new class `BinaryGate`? Why? Write the constructor that takes the number of inputs and outputs as parameters.

```
AndGate::AndGate(const string& name)
  : NMGate(2,1,ourCount,name)
// post: this and-gate is constructed
{
    ourCount++;
}
```

13.3.8 Interactive Circuit Building

Program 13.12, *xordemo.cpp*, shows how a composite circuit can be built by creating gates and wires, then wiring them together. In Section 13.3.3 we described how to create new class declarations and definitions using an `XorGate` class as an example. Both these methods for creating circuits require writing, compiling, testing, and debugging programs. A different approach is outlined in the run of *circuitbuilder.cpp*. A complete version of this program is not provided; you'll be asked to write it as an exercise. We'll discuss why it's a useful program and some of the design issues that arise in developing it.

A graphical circuit-building program in which the user creates new gates by choosing from a palette of standard gates, uses the mouse to wire gates together, and tests the circuits built might be the best way of designing and building new circuits. However, a text-based interactive circuit builder is easier to design and implement. Many of the classes and ideas in a text-based program may transfer to a graphics-based program, so we'll view the text-based program as a useful prototype.

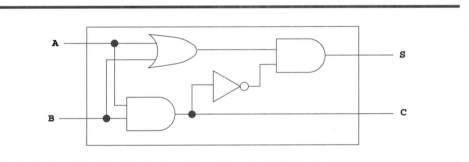

Figure 13.12 Building a half-adder circuit.

We'll use the interactive circuit building program to build a *half-adder*, a circuit for adding two one-digit binary numbers diagrammed in Figure 13.12.[10] We'll use the half-adder to build a *full-adder*, a circuit that basically adds three one-bit numbers, though we'll view the inputs as two numbers and a carry from a previous addition, diagrammed

---

[10]A binary digit is usually called a **bit**, which is almost an acronym for **binary dig**it.

in Figure 13.13. Full-adders can be wired together easily to form an *n-bit ripple-carry adder* for adding two *n*-bit binary numbers that we'll explore in an exercise.

Binary, or base 2, numbers are added just like base 10 numbers, but since the only values of a binary digit (or bit) are zero and one, we get Table 13.1 as a description of the half-adder.

Table 13.1 Adding two one-bit numbers.

A	B	S	C
0	0	0	0
0	1	1	0
1	0	1	0
1	1	0	1

The output labeled S in Figure 13.12 and Table 13.1 is the sum of two bits. The output labeled C is the carry. Since we have $1 + 1 = 10$ in base 2, the last line of the table shows the sum is zero and the carry is one, where the sum is the rightmost or least significant digit. Similarly, in Figure 13.13 the sum and carry represent adding the three input bits. A table for the full-adder is shown in the output of *circuitbuilder.cpp*.

Before looking at a run of the program we'll outline a list of requirements for an interactive circuit builder. The program doesn't meet all these requirements in the run shown, but you can add features as explored in chapter exercises.

1. The program should allow the user to choose standard gates for building circuits, but the list of gates should grow to include circuits built during the program. In other words, the program may start with only three gates (and, or, inverter), but any circuits built with the program become gates used in building other circuits.

2. The program should be simple to use; commands should correspond to user expectations. First-time users should be able to use the program without much help, but experienced users should be able to use their experience to build circuits quickly.

3. The program should be able to load circuits built by the program. This means the user should be able to save newly constructed circuits and load these circuits in a later run.

4. Connecting gates and wires should not require an in-depth knowledge of the Gate and Wire classes we've studied. Circuit designers shouldn't need to be experts in object-oriented programming and design to use the program.

5. The program should be flexible enough to adapt to new requirements we expect to receive from users once the program has been reviewed and tested. For example, users make mistakes in building circuits; it would be nice to support *undo* features to change gates and connections already created.

In the run below there is no facility for saving and loading circuits and there is no *undo* command, but attempts are made to meet the other requirements. The program shows an initial collection of the three standard gates available for creating circuits. In the run,

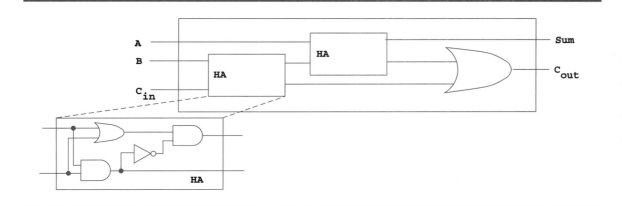

Figure 13.13 Building a full-adder from half-adders and an or-gate.

the user builds the half-adder diagrammed in Figure 13.12 by creating gates, printing the composite made from the gates in order to find the name of each wire, then connecting the gates and specifying inputs and outputs for the composite gate constructed. After the new circuit is finished, the user types *stop*, the circuit is tested, and the new circuit is added to the list of available gates.

The full-adder diagrammed in Figure 13.13 is built next using the same process:

■ Gates are added to the composite: two half-adders and an or-gate.
■ The composite is printed (the half-adders show up as composites), the wires between the gates are connected, and the inputs and outputs are specified.
■ The circuit is finished, tested, and added to the tool kit of available circuits.

Designing for Both Novice and Expert Users. The command *add*, which adds gates to the composite being constructed, comes in three forms, each illustrated in the run.

■ *add and*: The user specifies the gate to add.
■ *add*: The user doesn't specify a gate, and is prompted for one.
■ The user presses enter/return when prompted for a gate, and a list of available gates is printed (see the end of the output).

Minimal Knowledge of Gate *and* Wire *Classes.* Every gate displayed is shown with inputs and outputs. The input and output wires are numbered, and users connect wires by using a wire's number rather than typing and(1)->InWire(0); this might be used in a program but shouldn't be demanded from a user.[11]

---

[11] Implementation aside: wire numbers can be used to find wires only because a WireFactory supports wire lookup by number.

OUTPUT

```
prompt> circuitbuilder
0.      and
1.      or
2.      inverter
command: add and
command: add and
command: add or
command: add inverter
command: show
current circuit
composite: 4 gates, 0 in wires, 0 out wires
all-in
all-out
        and (1)
        in  (wire 8)  (wire 9)      out  (wire 10)
----
        and (2)
        in  (wire 11)  (wire 12)      out  (wire 13)
----
        or (1)
        in  (wire 14)  (wire 15)      out  (wire 16)
----
        inv (1)
        in (wire 17)      out (wire 18)
-----
connections: none

command: connect 10 17
command: connect 18 12
command: connect 16 11
command: connect 14 8
command: connect 9 15
command: in 14
command: in 9
command: out 13
command: out 10
command: test
output continued →
```

OUTPUT

```
testing composite: 4 gates, 2 in wires, 2 out wires
-----
0 0     :       0 0
1 0     :       1 0
0 1     :       1 0
1 1     :       0 1
------
command: stop
name for circuit: half
command: add half
command: add half
command: add or
command: show
current circuit
composite: 3 gates, 0 in wires, 0 out wires
all-in
all-out
        composite: 4 gates, 2 in wires, 2 out wires
all-in  (wire 25)  (wire 20)
all-out (wire 24)  (wire 21)
```
output elided/removed
```
------
        composite: 4 gates, 2 in wires, 2 out wires
all-in  (wire 36)  (wire 31)
all-out (wire 35)  (wire 32)
```
output elided/removed
```
------
        or (4)
        in  (wire 41)  (wire 42)      out  (wire 43)
connections: none
command: connect 24 31
command: connect 21 42
command: connect 32 41
command: in 36
command: in 25
command: in 20
command: out 35
command: out 43
command: test
```

output continued →

```
        O U T P U T

testing composite: 3 gates, 3 in wires, 2 out wires
-----
0 0 0     :        0 0
1 0 0     :        1 0
0 1 0     :        1 0
1 1 0     :        0 1
0 0 1     :        1 0
1 0 1     :        0 1
0 1 1     :        0 1
1 1 1     :        1 1
------
command: stop
name for circuit: full
command: add
gate name:
0.        and
1.        or
2.        inverter
3.        half
4.        full
```

13.3.9 `SimpleMap`: Mapping Names to Gates

In my prototype for the interactive builder program I used a structure called a *map*. I'll show the simple version I used in this prototype, which is good enough for the prototype, easy to understand, and not fully functional. You don't need the class `SimpleMap` to write the interactive circuit builder, but you'll need to implement something just like it. (See *simplemap.h*, Program G.17.)

A `SimpleMap` is templated on two classes: one class is the **value** stored in the map, and the other is the **key** used to look up a value. In *simplemapdemo.cpp*, `Gate *` values are stored in the map and `int` values are keys to retrieve gate pointers. The same kind of map is used in *circuitbuilder.cpp*, but strings are used to look up a gate rather than integers. Users are more comfortable typing `add  and` than typing `add  0`, where 0 is the index of the and-gate stored in a map.

Program 13.14 simplemapdemo.cpp

```cpp
#include <iostream>
using namespace std;
```

```
#include "simplemap.h"
#include "gates.h"

int main()
{
   SimpleMap<int,Gate *> gatemap;
   gatemap.insert(0, new AndGate("map-and-gate"));
   gatemap.insert(1, new OrGate("map-or-gate"));
   gatemap.insert(2, new Inverter("map-not-gate"));

   Gate * g = 0;                                    // get g from map
   SimpleMapIterator<int,Gate*> git(gatemap);
   for(git.Init(); git.HasMore(); git.Next())
   {   int index = git.Current();
      g = gatemap.getValue(index);
      cout << index << "\t" << *g << "\t" << *(g->clone()) << endl;
   }
   return 0;
}
```

simplemapdemo.cpp

The program shows how a map works as a gate tool kit. The program retrieves a gate and makes a copy of it using `clone`. The copy could be added to a composite being constructed by the user. When a new circuit is finished it can be easily added to the tool kit using the method `SimpleMap::insert`.

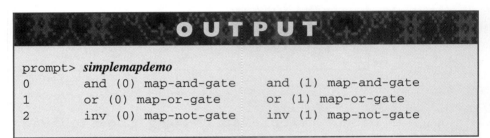

```
prompt> simplemapdemo
0       and (0) map-and-gate       and (1) map-and-gate
1       or (0) map-or-gate         or (1) map-or-gate
2       inv (0) map-not-gate       inv (1) map-not-gate
```

13.4 Chapter Review

We discussed inheritance, a powerful technique used in object-oriented programming for reusing a common interface. We saw several examples of inheritance hierarchies in which superclasses specified an interface, and subclasses implemented the interface with different behavior, but using a common naming convention. Inheritance allows an object that's an instance of a subclass to be substituted for, or used as an instance of, the corresponding superclass. In this book inheritance always models an "is-a" relationship, which ensures that objects can be substituted for other objects up an inheritance hierarchy.

Topics covered include these:

■   Streams form an inheritance hierarchy. A function with an `istream` parameter can receive many kinds of streams as arguments, including `cin`, `ifstream`, and `istringstream` objects.

- Prototypes are first attempts at designing and implementing a program or classes that allow the programmer and the client to get a better idea of where a project is headed.

- Inheritance in C++ requires superclass functions to be declared as *virtual* so that subclasses can change or specialize behavior. We use *public* inheritance, which models an is-a relationship. Virtual functions are also called polymorphic functions. (Other uses of inheritance are possible in C++, but we use inheritance only with virtual functions and only with public inheritance.)

- Virtual superclass functions are always virtual in subclasses, but the word `virtual` isn't required. It's a good idea to continue to identify functions as virtual even in subclasses because a subclass may evolve into a superclass.

- Subclasses should call superclass constructors explicitly; otherwise an implicit call will be generated by the compiler.

- An inherited virtual function can be used directly, overridden completely, or overridden while still calling the inherited function using `Super::function` syntax.

- Data and functions declared as *protected* are accessible in subclasses, but not to client programs. Data and functions declared as *private* are not accessible to subclasses except using accessor and mutator functions that might be provided by the superclass. Nevertheless, a subclass contains the private data, but the data aren't directly accessible.

- Abstract base classes contain one pure virtual function, a function identified with the ugly syntax of `= 0`. An abstract base class is an interface; it's not possible to define an object whose type is an abstract base class. It's very common, however, to define objects whose type is `ABC *` where ABC is an abstract base class. An abstract base/superclass pointer can reference any object derived from the superclass.

- Flexible software should be extendable; programming in the future tense is a good idea. Using abstract classes that can have some default function definitions, but should have little state, is part of good programming practice.

- Several design patterns were used in designing and implementing a `Gate/Wire` framework for modeling digital circuits. The patterns used include *Composite*, *Factory*, *Abstract Factory*, and *Observer*.

- Programs should be grown rather than built; refactoring classes and functions is part of growing good software.

- A class `SimpleMap` is a usable prototype of the map classes you'll study as you continue with computer science and programming. The map class facilitates the implementation of an interactive circuit-building program.

 ## 13.5 Exercises

13.1 Design a hierarchy of math quiz questions that covers the operations of addition, subtraction, multiplication, and division. You might also consider questions involving ratios, fractions, or other parts of basic mathematics. Each kind of question should have both easy and hard versions (e.g., addition might require carrying in the hard version). Keep the classes simple to make it possible to write a complete program; assume the user is in fourth or fifth grade.

Design and implement a quiz class that uses the questions you've just designed (and tested). The quiz should use different questions, and the questions should get more difficult if the user does well. If a user isn't doing well, the questions should get simpler. The quiz class should give a quiz to one student, not to two or more students at the same time. Ideally, the quiz class should record a student's scores in a file so that the student's progress can be tracked over several runs of the program.

13.2 Implement the class MultipleChoice shown in Figure 13.1. You'll need to decide on some format for storing multiple-choice questions in a file, and specify a file when a MultipleChoice question object is created. Incorporate the new question into *inheritquiz.cpp*, Program 13.2, or design a new quiz program that uses several different quiz questions.

13.3 We studied a templated class LinkSet designed and implemented in Section 12.3.6 (see Programs 12.11 and 12.12, the interface and implementation, respectively). New elements were added to the front of the linked list representing the set elements. Design a class like the untemplated version of the set class, LinkStringSet, that was developed first. The new class supports only the operations Add and Size. Call the class WordList; it can be used to track the unique words in a text file as follows:

```
void ReadStream(WordStreamIterator& input,
                WordList * list)
// post: list contains one copy of each word in input
{
    string word;
    for(input.Init(); input.HasMore(); input.Next())
    {   word = input.Current();
        ToLower(word);
        StripPunc(word);
        list->Add(word);
    }
    cout << list->Size() << " different words" << endl;
}
```

Make the function Add a pure virtual function, and make the helper function FindNode from LinkStringSet virtual and protected rather than private. Then implement three subclasses, each of which uses a different technique for maintaining the linked list (you may decide to use doubly linked lists, which make the third subclass slightly simpler to implement):

■   A class AddAtFront that adds new words to the front of the linked list. This is similar to the class LinkStringSet.

■   A class AddAtBack that adds new words to the end of the linked list (keep a pointer to the last node, or use a circularly linked list).

■   A class SelfOrg that adds new nodes at the back, but when a node is found using the virtual, protected FindNode, the node is moved closer to the front by one position. The idea is that words that occur many times move closer to the front of the list so that they'll be found sooner.

Test each subclass using the function ReadStream shown above. Time the implementations on several text files. Try to provide reasons for the timings you observe.

As a challenge, make two additions to the classes once they work. (1) Add an iterator class to access the elements. The iterator class will need to be a friend of the superclass WordList, but friendship is *not* inherited by subclasses. You'll need to be careful in designing the hierarchy and iterator so the iterator works with any subclass. (2) Make the classes templated.

13.4   Program 12.4, *frogwalk3.cpp* in Section 12.1.6, shows how to attach an object that monitors two random walkers to each of the walkers. The class Walker is being observed by the class WalkRecorder, though we didn't use the term *Observer* when we discussed the example in Chapter 12.

Create an inheritance hierarchy for WalkRecorder objects that monitors a random walker in different ways. Walkers should accept any number of WalkRecorders, rather than just one, by storing a vector of pointers rather than a single pointer to a WalkRecorder. Implement at least two different recorders, but try to come up with other recorders that you think are interesting or useful.

■   Implement a recorder that works like the original WalkRecorder in tracking every location of all the walkers it's recording.

■   Implement an ExtremeRecorder class that tracks just the locations that are furthest left (lowest) and right (highest) reached by any walker being monitored by the ExtremeRecorder. Alternatively, have the recorder keep track of one pair of extremes per walker rather than one pair of extremes for all walkers (this is tricky).

■   Use the graphics package in How to E and create a class that displays a walker as a moving square on a canvas. Each walker monitored should appear as a different color. Walkers can supply their own colors, or the recorder can associate a color with a walker (it could do this using a SimpleMap object or in several other ways).

13.5   Design a hierarchy of walkers, each of which behaves differently. The walkers should wander in two dimensions, so a walker's location is given by a Point object (see *point.h*, Program G.10). The superclass for all walkers should be named Walker.

Design a WalkerWorld class that holds all the walkers. WalkerWorld::Step asks the world to ask each of its walkers to take one step; taking a step is a virtual function with different implementations by different Walker subclasses. You can consider implementing a hierarchy of WalkerWorld classes too, but at first the dimensions of the world in which the walkers roam should be fixed when the world is created. The lower-left corner of the world has location (0,0); the upper-right corner has location (maxX,maxY). In a world of size 50 × 100 the upper-right corner has coordinates (49,99).

Consider the following different behaviors for step taking, but you should be imaginative in coming up with new behaviors. A walker should always start in the middle of the world.

■ A random walker that steps left, right, up, and down with equal probability. A walker at the edge of the world, for example, whose location is $(0,x)$, can't move off the edge, but may have only three directions to move. A walker in the corner of the world has only two choices.

■ A walker that walks immediately to the north edge of the world and then hugs the wall circling the world in a clockwise direction.

■ A walker that wraps around the edge of the world; for example, if it chooses to walk left/west from location $(0,y)$, its location becomes $(maxX,y)$.

You'll probably want to add at least one `WalkRecorder` class to monitor the walkers; a graphics class makes for enjoyable viewing.

13.6 Function objects were used to pass comparison functions encapsulated as objects to sorting functions; see Section 11.3 for details. It's possible to use inheritance rather than templates to enforce the common interface used by the comparison function objects described in Section 11.3. Show how the function header below can be used to sort using function objects, although the function is templated on only one parameter. (Contrast it to the declaration for `InsertSort` in *sortall.h*, Program G.14.)

```
template <class Type>
void InsertSort(tvector<Type> & a,
int size, const Comparer & comp);
```

You should show how to define an abstract `Comparer` class and how to derive sub-classes that are used to sort by different criteria.

13.7 The circuit constructed by the statements below is self-referential. Draw the circuit and trace the calls of `Gate::Act` through the or-gate, inverter, and probe. What happens if the circuit is programmed? What happens if the or-gate is changed to an and-gate?

```
Gate * org = new OrGate("trouble");
Gate * inv = new Inverter();
Probe * p =  new Probe(inv->OutWire(0));

Connect(org->OutWire(0),inv->InWire(0));
Connect(inv->OutWire(0), org->InWire(1));
```

13.8 Implement a complete program for interactively building circuits. Invent a circuit description language you can use to write circuits to files and read them back. You should try to use a factory for creating the gates and circuits used in the program, but you'll need a factory to which you can add new circuits created while the program is running. Using a `SimpleMap` can make the factory implementation easier, but you'll need to think very carefully about how to design the program.

13.9 Implement a class `GateFactory` that encapsulates creation of the four standard gate classes (`AndGate`, `OrGate`, `Inverter`, `CompositeGate`) as well as a class

XorGate. The factory class is used like the `WireFactory` class, but for creating gates rather than wires; see the code on the next page. For example, the code below creates a disabler circuit (see Figure 13.9):

```
GateFactory gf;
Gate * cg = gf.MakeComposite();
Gate * ig = gf.MakeInverter();
Gate * ag = gf.MakeAndGate();
// connect wires, add gates, input/output wires, to cg
```

This class enables gates to be created using a factory, but it doesn't force client programs to use the factory. Nor does it stop clients from creating hundreds of factories. The second concern can be addressed using a design pattern called *singleton*. A singleton class allows only one object to be created. Clients can have multiple pointers to the object, but there's only one object. The class `Singleton` in *singleton.h* illustrates how to do this.

Program 13.15 singleton.h

```
#ifndef _SINGLETON_H
#define _SINGLETON_H

// demo code for a singleton implementation

class Singleton
{
  public:
    static Singleton * GetInstance();
    // methods here for Singleton behavior
  private:
    static Singleton * ourSingleton;
    Singleton();   // constructor
};

Singleton * Singleton::ourSingleton = 0;

Singleton * Singleton::GetInstance()
{   if (ourSingleton == 0)
    {   ourSingleton = new Singleton();  // ok to construct
    }
    return ourSingleton;
}

Singleton::Singleton()
{   // nothing to construct in this simple example
}
```

```
#endif
```
singleton.h

Show by example how client code uses a singleton object. Assume there's a void method `Singleton::DoIt()`, and write code to call it. Explain how client programs are prevented from creating `Singleton` objects and how the class limits

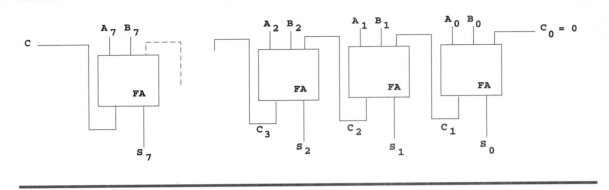

Figure 13.14 A ripple-carry adder for 8-bit numbers.

itself to creating one object. Then modify either your `GateFactory` or the existing `WireFactory` class to be singletons.

13.10 The circuit in Figure 13.14 is an eight-bit ripple-carry adder, a concrete version of the more general n-bit ripple-carry adder. The circuit adds two eight-bit numbers represented by A and B, where $A = A_7 A_6 A_5 A_4 A_3 A_2 A_1 A_0$, and A_0 is the least significant bit. The largest eight-bit value is 1111111, which is 255_{10} (base 10). Each box labeled FA is a full-adder; see Figure 13.13 for details. This ripple-adder is a 17-9-gate circuit, with 17 inputs: eight bits for A, eight bits for B, and the initial carry-in value; and nine outputs: eight bits for the sum and a final carry-out.

Write an English description for how the ripple-carry adder works. Note that the initial carry-in C_0 is set to zero. Other carries ripple through the circuit, hence the name. Then write a function `RippleAdder` to create and return a composite gate representing an n-bit ripple-carry adder, where n is a parameter to the function. Assume you have a function `FullAdder`. To test the function you'll need to implement the `FullAdder` function, which in turn will require implementing a `HalfAdder` function.

13.11 In real circuits, electricity does not travel through a circuit instantaneously, but is delayed by the gates encountered. Different gates have different built-in delays, and the delays of the built-in gates affect circuits built up from these gates.

For example, we'll assume a delay of three time-units for an and-gate, five units for an or-gate, and two units for an inverter (you'll be able to change these values in the program you write). Assume a disabler circuit as diagrammed in Figure 13.9 has the input to the and-gate from the outside on, the input to the inverter off, so that the output signal is on. If the inverter input signal is set to true, the circuit's output will change to false five time-units later. There will be a two-unit delay for the inverter followed by a three-unit delay for the and-gate.

Develop a new class called `TimedGate` that acts like a gate but delays acting for a set amount of time. This is a nontrivial design, so you'll need to think very carefully about how to incorporate delays into the circuit system. Assume you'll be using only `TimedGates`, not mixing them with regular gates. One way to start is shown in the following:

```
class TimedGate : public Gate
{
  public:
    // substitute me for g
    TimedGate(Gate * g, int delay);

    virtual int InCount()              const
        {return myGate->InCount();}
    virtual int OutCount()             const
        {return myGate->OutCount();}
    virtual Wire * InWire(int n)       const
        {return myGate->InWire(n);}
    virtual Wire * OutWire(int n)      const
        {return myGate->OutWire(n);}
    virtual string tostring()          const;
        // can use g's tostring

    virtual Gate * clone()
    {
      return new TimedGate(myGate->clone(), myDelay);
    }
    virtual void Act();  // act with delay

  protected:
    Gate * myGate;
    int    myDelay;
};
```

This class can be used as-a gate. It forwards most requests directly to the gate it encapsulates as shown. The constructor and the `TimedGate::Act` function require careful thought.

A `TimedGate` object must remove the `Gate` g it encapsulates from the wires connected to g's inputs. Then the `TimedGate` object substitutes itself for the the inputs. All this happens at construction.

In addition, you'll need to define some kind of structure that stores timed events so that they happen in the correct order. In my program I used a static `EventSimulator` object that all `TimedGates` can access. Events are put into the simulator and arranged to occur in the proper order. Again, you'll need to think very carefully about how to do this.

13.12 The circuit in Figure 13.15 is designed to control an elevator. It's a simple circuit designed to direct the elevator up or down, which are the circuit's outputs. The inputs are the current floor and the requested floor. The diagram shows a circuit for an elevator in a four-story building. The current floor is specified by the binary number C_1C_0, so that 00 is the first floor,[12] 01 is the second floor, 10 is the third floor, and 11 is the fourth floor. The digit C_1 is the most significant digit. Similarly, R_1R_0 is a binary representation of the requested floor.

---

[12]This is a book on C++, so floors are numbered beginning with zero.

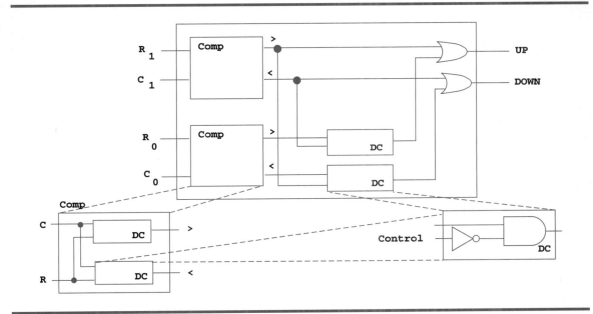

Figure 13.15 A circuit for choosing which direction an elevator travels. The inputs labeled C are the current floor (2 bits), and the R inputs are for the requesting floor.

The purpose of the circuit is to direct the elevator up when the requested floor is greater than the current floor, and down when the requested floor is less than the current floor.

Write an English description of why the circuit works. Be attentive to the order of inputs to the comparator gates, and see Figure 13.10 and Figure 13.9 and the associated descriptions.

Write a truth table by hand for a four-input two-output circuit, or build the circuit with a program and have GateTester::Test print the truth table for the circuit. Try to generalize the circuit to a building with 2^N floors rather than four floors.

How to: Use Basic C++ Syntax and Operators

A

In this How to we summarize the basic syntax of C++ and the rules and operators that are used in C++ expressions. This is a brief language reference for C++ as used in this book, not the entire language. We don't cover the use of dynamic memory in this How to.

A.1 Syntax

A.1.1 The Function `main`

C++ programs begin execution with a function `main`. The smallest C++ program is shown below. It doesn't do anything, but it's syntactically legal C++.

```cpp
int main()
{
    return 0;
}
```

The return value is passed back to the "system"; a nonzero value indicates some kind of failure. Although not used in this book, the function `main` can have parameters; these are so-called **command-line parameters**, passed to the program when the function is run. A brief synopsis of command-line parameters is given in Section A.2.6.

A.1.2 Built-in and Other Types

The built-in types in C++ used in this book are `int`, `double`, `bool`, and `char`. A type `void` is used as a built-in "empty-type," but we don't treat `void` as an explicit type. A function declared as `void` does not return a value of type `void`, but returns no value. In addition to `double`, the type `float` can be used to represent floating point values; but `float` is less precise and we do not use it. We also don't use the modifiers `short`, `long`, and `unsigned`. The most useful of these is `unsigned`, which effectively doubles the range of positive values (e.g., on many systems a `char` value is signed and ranges from -128 to 128, but an `unsigned char` value ranges from 0 to 255).

The range of values represented by `int` and `char` expressions is accessible using values given in the header file `<climits>` (or `<limits.h>`). The range for floating point values is found in `<cfloat>` (or `<float.h>`). See How to F for information about these standard header files.

Types other than built-in types in C++ are called programmer-defined types. Many programmer-defined types are implemented for use in this book. Information about these types can be found in How to G. Standard C++ programmer-defined types used in this book include `string` and `vector`. We use a class `tvector` with error-checking rather than the standard vector class, but we use the standard C++ string class declared in `<string>`. For programmers without access to this class we provide a class `tstring` that can be used in place of `string` for all the programs in this book. The class `tstring` is accessible via the header file *tstring.h*.

A.1.3 Variable Definition and Assignment

Variables are **defined** when storage is allocated. Variable definitions include a type and a name for the variable. An initial value may optionally be supplied. The C++ statements below define an `int` variable without an initial value, a `double` variable with an initial value, two `string` variables with initial values, and one without.

```
int minimum;
double xcoord = 0.0;
string first = "hello", second, third="goodbye";
```

In this book we usually define only one variable per statement, but as the string definitions above show, any number of variables can be defined for one type in a definition statement. One good reason to define only one variable in a statement is to avoid problems with pointer variables. The statement below makes `foop` a pointer to a `Foo`, but `foop2` is a `Foo`, not a pointer:

```
Foo * foop, foop2;
```

To make both variables pointers requires the following:

```
Foo * foop, * foop2;
```

Variables that are instances of a class, as opposed to built-in types like `int` or `bool`, are constructed when they are defined. Typically the syntax used for construction looks like a function call, but the assignment operator can be used when variables are defined as in the second line below. This statement constructs a variable only; it does not construct then assign, although the syntax looks like this is what happens:

```
Dice cube(6);        // construct a 6-sided Dice
Dice dodo = 12;      // construct a 12-sided Dice
Date usb(1,1,2000);  // construct Jan 1, 2000
```

It's legal to use constructor syntax for built-in types too:

```
int x(0);
int y = 0;   // both define ints with value zero
```

Table A.I Arithmetic assignment operators.

Symbol	Example	Equivalent
+=	x += 1;	x = x + 1;
*=	doub *= 2;	doub = doub * 2;
-=	n -= 5;	n = n - 5;
/=	third /= 3;	third = third / 3;
%=	odd %= 2;	odd = odd % 2;

The Assignment Operator. The assignment operator, operator =, assigns new values to variables that have *already been defined*. The assignment operator assigns values to tomorrow and baker below:

```
Date today;
Date tomorrow = today + 1;  // definition, not assignment
int  dozen = 12, baker = 0; // definition, not assignment
tomorrow = today - 1;    // make tomorrow yesterday
baker    = dozen + 1;    // a triskaidekaphobe's nightmare
```

Assignments can be chained together. The first statement using operator = below shows a single assignment; the second shows chained assignment:

```
double average;
int min,max;

average = 0.0;
min = max = ReadFirstValue();
```

The assignment of 0.0 to average could have been done when average is defined, but the assignments to min and max cannot be done when the variables are defined since, presumably, the function ReadFirstValue is to be called only once to read a first value, which will then be assigned to be both min and max.

In addition to the assignment operator, several arithmetic assignment operators alter the value of existing variables using arithmetic operations as shown in Table A.1.

The expectation in C++ is that an assignment results in a copy. For classes that contain pointers as data members, this usually requires implementing/overloading an assignment operator and a copy constructor. You don't need to worry about these unless you're using pointers or classes that use pointers. See How to E for details on overloading the assignment operator.

Table A.2   C++ keywords.

asm	default	for	private	struct	unsigned
auto	delete	friend	protected	switch	using
bool	do	goto	public	template	virtual
break	double	if	register	this	void
case	dynamic_cast	inline	reinterpret_cast	throw	volatile
catch	else	int	return	true	wchar_t
char	enum	long	short	try	while
class	explicit	mutable	signed	typedef	
const	extern	namespace	sizeof	typeid	
const_cast	false	new	static	typename	
continue	float	operator	static_cast	union	

A.1.4   C++ Keywords

The keywords (or reserved words) in C++ are given in Table A.2. Not all the keywords are used in this book. We either discuss or use in code all keywords except for the following:

> asm, auto, goto, register, throw, volatile, catch, wchar_t, short, try, extern, typeid, typename, union

A.1.5   Control Flow

We use most of the C++ statements that change execution flow in a program, but not all of them. We use the statements listed in Table A.3.

Table A.3   Control flow statements in C++.

if (*condition*) *statement*
if (*condition*) *statement* **else** *statement*
switch (*condition*) *case/default statements*

while (*condition*) *statement*
do *statement* **while** (*condition*)
for (*init statement* ; *condition* ; *update expression*)

case *constant expression* : *statement*
default **:** *statement*
break;
continue;
return *expression* (expression is optional)

There are few control statements we do not use; these are the ones:

- ■ **try** and **catch** for handling exceptions. We do not use exceptions in the code in this book, so we do not need `try` and `catch`.
- ■ **goto** for jumping to a labeled statement. Although controversial, there are occasions where using a `goto` is very useful. However, we do not encounter any of these occasions in the code used in this book.

Selection Statements. The `if` statement by itself guards a block of statements so that they're executed only when a condition is true.

```
if (a < b)
{  // statements executed only when a < b
}
```

The `if/else` statement selects one of two blocks of statements to execute:

```
if (a < b)
{ // executed when a < b
}
else
{ // executed when a >= b
}
```

It's possible to chain `if/else` statements together to select between multiple conditions (see Section 4.4.2). Alternatively, the `switch` statement selects between many *constant* values. The values must be integer/ordinal values; that is, `ints`, `chars`, and `enums` can be used, but `doubles` and `strings` cannot.

```
switch (expression)
{
  case 1 :
     // do this
     break;
  case 2 :
     // do that
     return;
  case 20:
  case 30:
     // do the other
     break;
  default:
     // if no case selected
}
```

Conditional Expressions: The `?:` Operator. Although not a control statement, the question-mark/colon operator used in a **conditional expression** replaces an `if/else` statement that distinguishes one of two values. For example, consider the statement below:

```
if (a < b)     // assign to min the smallest of a and b
{   min = a;
}
else
{   min = b;
}
```

This can be expressed more tersely by using a conditional:

```
// assign to min the smallest of a and b
  min = (a < b) ? a : b;
```

A conditional expression consists of three parts: a condition whose truth determines which of two values are selected, and two expressions for the values. When evaluated, the conditional takes on one of the two values. The expression that comes before the question mark is interpreted as Boolean-valued. If it is true (nonzero), then *expression a* is used as the value of the conditional; otherwise *expression b* is used as the value of the conditional.

> **Syntax: Conditional statement (the ?: operator)**
>
> *condition expression* ? *expression a* : *expression b*

We do not use `operator ?:` in the code shown in the book although it is used in some of the libraries provided with the book (e.g., it is used in the implementation of the `tvector` class accessible in *tvector.h*).

Repetition. There are three loop constructs in C++; they're shown in Table A.3. Each looping construct repeatedly executes a block of statements while a guard or test expression is true. The `while` loop may never execute—for example, when a > b before the first loop test in the following:

```
while (a < b)
{   // do this while a < b
}
```

A `do-while` loop always executes at least once.

```
do
{   // do that while a < b
} while (a < b);
```

A `for` statement combines loop initialization, test, and update in one place. It's convenient to use `for` loops for definite loops, but none of the loop statements generates code that's more efficient than the others.

```
int k;
for(k = 0; k < 20; k++)
{ // do that 20 times
}
```

It's possible to write infinite loops. The `break` statement branches to the first statement after the innermost loop in which the `break` occurs.

```
while (true)       for(;;)            while (true)
{ // do forever    { // do forever    { if (a < b) break;
}                  }                  }
```

Occasionally the `continue` statement is useful to jump immediately back to the loop test.

```
while (expression)
{  if (something)
   { // do that
     continue;  // test expression
   }
   // when something isn't true
}
```

Function Returns. The `return` statement causes control to return immediately from a function to the statement following the function call. Functions can have multiple `return` statements. A `void` function cannot return a value, but `return` can be used to leave the function other than by falling through to the end of the function.

```
void dothis()            int getvalue()
{  if (test) return;     {  if (test) return 3;
   // do this               // do that

}  // function returns   } // error, no value returned
```

A.2 Functions and Classes

A.2.1 Defining and Declaring Functions and Classes

A function is *declared* when its prototype is given and *defined* when the body of the function is written. A function's header must appear before the function is called, either as part of a function definition or as a prototype. Two prototypes follow:

```
int doThat(int x, int y);     void readIt(const string& s);
```

The return type of a function is part of the prototype but isn't used to distinguish one function from another when the function is overloaded. Overloaded functions have the same names but different parameter lists:

```
void check(int x);            void check(string s);
void check(bool a, bool b);   int check(int x);  // conflict
```

A class is *declared* when member function prototypes and instance variables are provided, typically in a header file. The bodies of the member functions aren't typically included as part of their declaration.

```
class Bug;      // forward declaration
class Doodle    // Doodle declaration only, not definition
{
  public:
    Doodle();
    Doodle(int x);
    int     getDoo() const;
    void    setDoo(int x) ;
  private:
    int     myDoo;
    Bug * myBug;
};
```

Functions that don't alter class state should be declared as const. See How to D for details. The class *definition* occurs in an implementation file, typically with a .cpp suffix.

```
int Doodle::getDoo() const     // method definition
{
    return myDoo;
}
```

It's possible to define member functions **inline** as part of the class declaration:

```
class Simple  // declaration and inline definitions
{
  public:
    Simple(const string& s) : myString(s) { }
    void Set(const string& s)
    {  myString = s;
    }
    int Get() const { return myString; }
  private:
    string myString;
};
```

The class Simple shows an initializer list used to construct private instance variables. Initializer lists are the preferred form of giving values to instance variables/data members when an object is constructed.

Initializer Lists. A class can have more than one constructor; each constructor should give initial values to all private data members. All data members will be constructed before the body of the constructor executes. Initializer lists permit parameters to be passed to data member constructors. Data members are initialized in the order in which they appear in the class declaration, so the initializer list should use the same order.

In C++ it's not possible for one constructor to call another of the same class. When there's code in common to several constructors it should be factored into a private Init function that's called from the constructors. However, each constructor must have its own initializer list.

A.2.2 Importing Classes and Functions: `#include`

Class and function libraries are typically compiled separately and linked with client code to create an executable program. The client code must import the class and function declarations so the compiler can determine if classes and functions are used correctly. Declarations are typically imported using the preprocessor directive `#include`, which literally copies the specified file into the program being compiled.

The C++ standard specifies that standard include files are specified without a .h suffix, that is, `<iostream>` and `<string>`. For the most part, these header files import declarations that are in the *std* **namespace** (see Section A.2.3). Using a file with the .h suffix, for example `<iostream.h>`, imports the file in the global namespace. This means that the directives below on the left are the same as that on the right:

```
#include <iostream>                 #include <iostream.h>
using namespace std;
```

Although most systems support both `<iostream>` and `<iostream.h>`, the namespace version is what's called for in the C++ standard. In addition, some files do not have equivalents with a .h suffix—the primary example is `<string>`.

A.2.3 Namespaces

Large programs may use classes and functions created by hundreds of software developers. In large programs it is likely that two classes or functions with the same name will be created, causing a conflict since names must be unique within a program. The namespace mechanism permits functions and classes that are logically related to be grouped together. Just as member functions are specified by qualifying the function name with the class name, as in `Dice::Roll` or `string::substr`, functions and classes that are part of a namespace must specify the namespace. Examples are shown in Program A.1 for a user-defined namespace *Math* and the standard namespace *std*. Note that `using namespace std` is not part of the program.

Program A.1 namespacedemo.cpp

```
#include <iostream>

// illustrates using namespaces

namespace Math
{
  int factorial(int n);
  int fibonacci(int n);
}

int Math::factorial(int n)
// post: return n!
{
    int product = 1;
    // invariant: product = (k-1)!
```

```
    for(int k=1; k <= n; k++)
    {    product *= k;
    }
    return product;
}

int Math::fibonacci(int n)
// post: return n-th Fibonacci number
{
    int f = 1;
    int f2= 1;
    // invariant: f = F_(k-1)
    for(int k=1; k <= n; k++)
    {    int newf = f + f2;
        f = f2;
        f2 = newf;
    }
    return f;
}

int main()
{
    int n;
    std::cout << "enter n ";
    std::cin >> n;

    std::cout << n << "! = "          << Math::factorial(n) << std::endl;
    std::cout << "F_(" << n << ")= " << Math::fibonacci(n) << std::endl;

    return 0;
}
```

namespacedemo.cpp

```
prompt> namespacedemo
enter n 12
12 = 479001600!
F_(12) = 233
```

Writing std::cout and std::endl each time these stream names are used would be cumbersome. The **using** declaration permits all function and class names that are part of a namespace to be used without specifying the namespace. Hence all the programs in this book begin with using namespace std;, which means function and class names in the standard namespace *std* do not need to be explicitly qualified with std::. When you write functions or classes that are not part of a namespace, they're said to be in the **global namespace**.

Table A.4 C++ operator precedence and associativity.

Operator symbol	Name/description	Associativity
::	Scope resolution	Left
()	Function call	Left
[]	Subscript/index	Left
.	Member selection	Left
->	Member selection (indirect)	Left
++ --	Post increment/decrement	Right
dynamic_cast<type>		Right
static_cast<type>		Right
const_cast<type>		Right
sizeof	Size of type/object	Right
++ --	Pre-increment	Right
new	Create/allocate	Right
delete	Destroy/de-allocate	Right
!	Logical not	Right
- +	Unary minus/plus	Right
&	Address of	Right
*	Dereference	Right
(type)	Cast	Right
.* ->*	Member selection	Left
* / %	Multiply, divide, modulus	Left
+	Plus (binary addition)	Left
-	Minus (binary subtraction)	Left
<<	Shift-left/stream insert	Left
>>	Shift-right/stream extract	Left
< <= > >=	Relational comparisons	Left
== !=	Equal, not equal	Left
&	Bitwise and	Left
^	Bitwise exclusive or	Left
|	Bitwise or	Left
&&	Logical and	Left
||	Logical or	Left
=	Assignment	Right
+= -= *= /= %=	Arithmetic assignment	Right
<<= >>=	Shift assign	Right
? :	Conditional	Right
throw	Throw exception	Right
,	Sequencing	Left

A.2.4   Operators

The many operators in C++ all appear in Table A.4 [Str97]. An operator's precedence determines the order in which it is evaluated in a complex statement that doesn't use parentheses. An operator's associativity determines whether a sequence of connected operators is evaluated left-to-right or right-to-left. The lines in the table group operators of the same precedence.

A.2.5   Characters

Characters in C++ typically use an ASCII encoding, but it's possible that some implementations use UNICODE or another encoding. Table F.3 in How to F provides ASCII values for all characters. Regardless of the underlying character set, the escape sequences in Table A.5 are part of C++.

    The newline character \n and the carriage return character \r are used to indicate end-of-line in text in a platform-specific way. In Unix systems, text files have a single end-of-line character, \n. In Windows environments two characters are used, \n\r. This can cause problems transferring text files from one operating system to another.

A.2.6   Command-Line Parameters

Command-line parameters are not covered in this book, but Program A.2, *mainargs.cpp*, shows how command-line parameters are processed by printing each parameter. Parameters are passed in an array of C-style strings conventionally named argv (argument vector). The number of strings is passed in an int parameter named argc (argument count). Every program has one parameter, the name of the program that is stored in argv[0].

Table A.5   Escape sequences in C++.

Escape sequence	Name	ASCII
\n	Newline	NL (LF)
\t	Horizontal tab	HT
\v	Vertical tab	VT
\b	Backspace	BS
\r	Carriage return	CR
\f	Form feed	FF
\a	Alert (bell)	BEL
\\	Backslash	\
\?	Question mark	?
\'	Single quote (apostrophe)	'
\"	Double quote	"

Program A.2 mainargs.cpp

```cpp
#include <iostream>
using namespace std;

int main(int argc, char * argv[])
{
    int k;
    cout << "program name = " << argv[0] << endl;
    cout << "# arguments passed = " << argc << endl;

    for(k=1; k < argc; k++)
    {   cout << k << "\t" << argv[k] << endl;
    }
    return 0;
}
```

mainargs.cpp

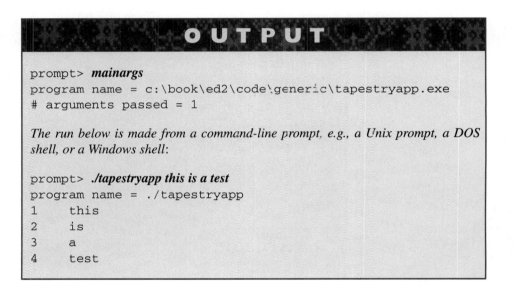

```
prompt> mainargs
program name = c:\book\ed2\code\generic\tapestryapp.exe
# arguments passed = 1
```

The run below is made from a command-line prompt, e.g., a Unix prompt, a DOS shell, or a Windows shell:

```
prompt> ./tapestryapp this is a test
program name = ./tapestryapp
1     this
2     is
3     a
4     test
```

As you can see if you look carefully at the output, the name of the program is actually `tapestryapp`, although we've used the convention of using the filename of the program, in this case `mainargs`, when illustrating output.

How to: Format Output and Use Streams

B

 ## B.1 Formatting Output

Most of the programs we've shown have generated unformatted output. We used the stream **manipulator** setw in *windchill.cpp,* Program 5.8, (and some other programs) to force column-aligned output, but we have concentrated more on program design and development than on making output look good.

In addition to using well-formatted code, good programs generate well-formatted output. The arrangement of the output aids the program user in interpreting data. However, it is altogether too easy for a programmer to spend an inordinate amount of time formatting output trying to make it "pretty." The objective of this book is to present broad programming concepts, which include documenting code and formatting output. You should strike a balance between the objectives of producing working programs and writing programs so that users can understand both the program and the output.

There are two methods for altering an output stream to change the format of values that are inserted into the stream: using stream member functions and using an object called a manipulator, accessible via the include file <iomanip> (or <iomanip.h>). Formatting functions and manipulators are summarized in Tables B.1 and B.2. In general, it's much easier to use a manipulator than the corresponding stream-formatting member function. Three programs illustrate how the output functions and manipulators change a stream so that strings and numbers are formatted according to several criteria.

Using Flags. Stroustrup [Str97] calls using flags "a time-honored if somewhat old-fashioned technique." Sticking to manipulators, which don't use flags, will make your life simpler than using the flag-based member functions of the ostream hierarchy. A flag is conceptually either on or off. Rather than using several bool variables, flags are normally packed as individual bits in one int. For example, since eight flags can be stored in an eight-bit number, one eight-bit number, represents 256 different combinations of flags being on or off.

B.1.1 General and Floating-Point Formatting

Table B.1 shows the stream member functions that take parameters and their corresponding manipulators. All stream-formatting functions except for width are *persistent*; once applied to the stream they stay in effect until they're removed. The width function,

Table B.1 Parameterized stream-formatting functions and manipulators.

Stream function	Manipulator	Brief description
`width(int w)`	`setw(int w)`	Output field width
`precision(int p)`	`setprecision(int p)`	# of digits
`fill(), fill(int)`	`setfill(int)`	Pad/fill character
`setf(int )`	`setiosflags`	Add flags
`unsetf(int)`	`resetiosflags`	Remove flags
`flags(), flags(int)`		Read, set flags

and its corresponding manipulator `setw`, affect only the next string or number output. The functions in Table B.1 are used in Program B.1 as part of Section B.1.1. They're summarized below.

- `width(int n)` sets the field width of the next string or numeric output to the specified width. Output is padded with blanks (see `fill`) as needed. Output that requires a width larger than n isn't truncated; it overflows the specified width.

- `precision(int n)` sets the number of digits that appear in floating-point output. This is the number of digits to the right of the decimal point in either `fixed` or `scientific` format, and the total number of digits otherwise (see Program B.1 for examples). Values are rounded, not truncated.

- `fill(int n)` sets the fill character to n and returns the old fill value. Without a parameter `fill()` returns the current fill value.

- `setf(int n)` sets the flag(s) specified by n without affecting other flag values. Similarly, `unsetf` unsets one or more flags. More than one flag can be specified by using bitwise-or as shown in Program B.3.

- `flags(int n)` sets the flags to n (the only flags set are those in n) and returns the old flags. In contrast, `setf` leaves other flags unaffected. Without a parameter `flags` returns the current flags. These functions are demonstrated in Program B.3.

B.1.2 Manipulators

Most of the flags that can be set using the stream member functions `setf`, `flags`, and `unsetf` are given in Table B.2. These flags are very cumbersome to use since some require specifying an additional parameter when using `setf`. For example, the following statements set left justification (the default justification is right) and then generate as output '1.23 ' with two spaces of padding/fill:

```
cout.setf(ios_base::left,  ios_base::adjustfield);
cout << "'"; cout.width(6);
cout << 1.23 << "'" << endl;
```

It's much simpler to use a manipulator; the statement below has the same effect:

```
cout << left << "'" << setw(6) << 1.23 << "'" << endl;
```

Table B.2 Stream-formatting flags and corresponding manipulators. The flags are used with the `setf` stream member function; all flags are static constants in the class `ios_base`, called `ios` in earlier versions of C++. See Program B.2.

Stream flags	Flag option	Manipulator
`hex, oct, dec`	`io_base::basefield`	`hex, oct, dec`
`left, right`	`ios_base::adjustfield`	`left, right`
`fixed, scientific`	`ios_base::floatfield`	`fixed, scientific`
`showbase`	*none*	`showbase, noshowbase`
`showpoint`	*none*	`showpoint, noshowpoint`
`boolalpha`	*none*	`boolalpha, noboolalpha`
`showpos`	*none*	`showpos, noshowpos`

The flags and manipulators in Table B.2 are summarized here. They are used in the programs that follow.

- `hex`, `oct`, and `dec` set the base of numeric output to 16, 8, and 10, respectively. The default base is 10. If `showbase` is specified octal numbers are preceded by a zero and hexadecimal numbers are preceded by `0x`; see Program B.3.

- `left` and `right` set the justification of string and numeric output. These don't have a visible effect unless the output requires a width smaller than the default width, six, or than the width specified by using `setw/width`; then fill characters are added to the right and left, respectively (left justification means adding fill characters to the right).

- `showbase`, `showpoint`, and `showpos`, respectively, show what base is in effect, show a decimal point, and show a leading plus sign. Without `showpoint`, the value 70.0 is displayed as 70, regardless of the precision value. With `showpoint` as many zeros are shown as are set by `precision`.

- `boolalpha` makes `true` and `false` display as those strings rather than 1 and 0. See Program B.3 for an example.

Precision and Justification for Floating-Point Values Using Manipulators. Formatted output for floating-point numbers is shown in Program B.1, *formatdemo.cpp*.

Program B.1 formatdemo.cpp

```cpp
#include <iostream>
#include <iomanip>
#include <cmath>
using namespace std;

// formatting using manipulators
```

```cpp
int main()
{
    const double CENTIPI = 100 * acos(-1); // arccos(-1) = PI
    const int MAX = 10;
    const int TAB = 15;
    int k;

    cout << "default setting " << CENTIPI << ", with setprecision(4), "
        << setprecision(4) << CENTIPI << endl;

    cout << "\nfixed floating-point, precision varies, fixed/scientific\n" << endl;
    for(k=0; k < MAX; k++)
    {   cout << left << "pre. " << k << "\t" << setprecision(k) << setw(TAB)
            << fixed << CENTIPI <<  scientific  << '\t" << CENTIPI << endl;
    }

    cout << endl << "width and justification vary, fixed, precision 2\n" << endl;
    cout << setprecision(2) << fixed;
    for(k=3; k < MAX+3; k++)
    {   cout << "wid. " << k << "\t+" << left << setw(k) << CENTIPI << right
            << "+\t\t-" << setw(k) << CENTIPI << "-" << endl;
    }

    cout << endl << "repeated, fill char = @\n" << endl;
    cout << setfill('@');
    for(k=3; k < MAX+3; k++)
    {   cout << "wid. " << k << "\t+" << left << setw(k) << CENTIPI << right
            << "+\t\t-" << setw(k) << CENTIPI << "-" << endl;
    }


    return 0;
}
```

formatdemo.cpp

The manipulator setw affects the next numeric output only; other manipulators (such as precision, left, and right) are persistent and last until changed. See Table B.2 for descriptions of manipulators. The manipulator precision rounds floating-point values rather than truncating them. When floating-point values are printed using either fixed or scientific, the precision is the number of decimal digits, otherwise (see the first line of output) the precision is the total number of digits. The default precision is six, as shown on the first line of output. The justification is set to left in the first loop, but varies in the subsequent output.

```
                    O U T P U T

prompt> formatdemo
default setting 314.159, with setprecision(4), 314.2

fixed floating-point, precision varies, fixed/scientific

pre. 0   314              3.141593e+002
pre. 1   314.2            3.1e+002
pre. 2   314.16           3.14e+002
pre. 3   314.159          3.142e+002
pre. 4   314.1593         3.1416e+002
pre. 5   314.15927        3.14159e+002
pre. 6   314.159265       3.141593e+002
pre. 7   314.1592654      3.1415927e+002
pre. 8   314.15926536     3.14159265e+002
pre. 9   314.159265359    3.141592654e+002


width and justification vary, fixed, precision 2

wid. 3   +314.16+                 -314.16-
wid. 4   +314.16+                 -314.16-
wid. 5   +314.16+                 -314.16-
wid. 6   +314.16+                 -314.16-
wid. 7   +314.16 +                - 314.16-
wid. 8   +314.16  +               -  314.16-
wid. 9   +314.16   +              -   314.16-
wid. 10  +314.16    +             -    314.16-
wid. 11  +314.16     +            -     314.16-
wid. 12  +314.16      +           -      314.16-


repeated, fill char = @

wid. 3   +314.16+                 -314.16-
wid. 4   +314.16+                 -314.16-
wid. 5   +314.16+                 -314.16-
wid. 6   +314.16+                 -314.16-
wid. 7   +314.16@+                -@314.16-
wid. 8   +314.16@@+               -@@314.16-
wid. 9   +314.16@@@+              -@@@314.16-
wid. 10  +314.16@@@@+             -@@@@314.16-
wid. 11  +314.16@@@@@+            -@@@@@314.16-
wid. 12  +314.16@@@@@@+           -@@@@@@314.16-
```

Formatting Using Stream Member Functions. Program B.2 demonstrates some of the same formatting features shown in Program B.1, but using stream member functions instead of manipulators. As you can see, using manipulators is much simpler.

Program B.2   streamflags.cpp

```cpp
#include <iostream>
#include <cmath>
using namespace std;

int main()
{
    const double PI = acos(-1);  // arccos(-1) = PI radians
    const int MAX = 10;          // max precision used in demo
    int k;
    // set right justified, fixed floating format

    cout.setf(ios_base::right, ios_base::adjustfield);
    cout.setf(ios_base::fixed, ios_base::floatfield);

        cout << "fixed, right justified, width 10, precision varies\n" << endl;

    for(k=0; k < MAX; k++)
    {   cout.precision(k);
        cout << k << "\t+";
        cout.width(MAX);
        cout << PI << "+" << endl;
    }


    // use different fill characters

    int fillc = cout.fill();
    cout.precision(2);
    cout << "\nshow fill char, precision is 2\n" << endl;
    for(k='a'; k <= 'd'; k++)
    {   cout << "old fill = '" << char(fillc) << "' +";
        cout.width(MAX);
        cout.fill(k);
        cout << PI << "+" << endl;
        fillc = cout.fill();
    }


    return 0;
}
```

streamflags.cpp

```
                          O U T P U T

    prompt> streamflags
    fixed, right justified, width 10, precision varies

    0          +           3+
    1          +         3.1+
    2          +        3.14+
    3          +       3.142+
    4          +      3.1416+
    5          +     3.14159+
    6          +    3.141593+
    7          +  3.1415927+
    8          +3.14159265+
    9          +3.141592654+

    show fill char, precision is 2

    old fill = ' '  -aaaaaa3.14+
    old fill = 'a'  -bbbbbb3.14+
    old fill = 'b'  +cccccc3.14+
    old fill = 'c'  +dddddd3.14+
```

Using Flags as Parameters. Program B.3 shows how to pass format flags as parameters. The stream member function `flags` returns the current flags, but also sets the flags to the value of its parameter as shown in the function `output`. Flags can be combined using the bitwise-or operator, `operator |`, as shown in `main`. Each flag as a bit is one or zero. The bitwise-or operation corresponds to a Boolean or but uses bits instead. In Program B.3, the result of combining the bits with or is a single number in which both flags are set.

Program B.3 formatparams.cpp

```cpp
#include <iostream>
#include <iomanip>
using namespace std;

void output(ostream& out, ios_base::fmtflags flags)
// post: print using flags, restore old flags
{
    ios_base::fmtflags oldflags = out.flags(flags);

    out << "oldflags: " << oldflags << "\tnew: "
        << out.flags() << "\t";
```

```
    out << 12.47 << "\t" << true << "\t"
        << 99.0  << "\t" << 255 << endl;

    out.flags(oldflags);  // restore as before
}

int main()
{
    output(cout, cout.flags());         // default
    output(cout, ios_base::showpos);    // leading +
    output(cout, ios_base::boolalpha);  // print true
    output(cout, ios_base::showpoint);  // show .0

    output(cout, ios_base::boolalpha|ios_base::hex);     // bool on, base 16
    output(cout, ios_base::hex|ios_base::showbase);      // show 0x in front
    return 0;
}
```

formatparams.cpp

```
O U T P U T

prompt> formatparams
oldflags: 513   new: 513   12.47   1     99      255
oldflags: +513  new: +32   +12.47  1     +99     +255
oldflags: 513   new: 16384 12.47   true  99      255
oldflags: 513   new: 16    12.4700 1     99.0000 255
oldflags: 201   new: 4800  12.47   true  99      ff
oldflags: 0x201 new: 0x808 12.47   1     99      0xff
```

B.1.3   Stream Functions

We've used stream functions `fail` and `open` and mentioned `close` in Chapter 6. We summarize these and a few other stream functions here:

■   `open(const char *)` opens an `ifstream` bound to the text file whose name is an argument. We use `string::c_str()` to obtain the C-style string pointer needed as an argument. It's possible to `open` an output file for appending rather than writing. In general `open` takes an optional second argument we haven't used:

  ▪ `ios_base::app`: open output for appending.
  ▪ `ios_base::out`: open a stream for output.
  ▪ `ios_base::in`: open a stream for input.
  ▪ `ios_base::binary`: open for binary I/O.
  ▪ `ios_base::trunc`: truncate to zero length.

- `fail()` returns true if an I/O operation has failed but characters have not been lost. You may be able to continue reading after calling `clear`.

- `clear()` clears the error state of the stream. After a stream has failed it must be cleared before I/O will succeed.

- `good()` returns true if a stream is in a good state. This is a nearly useless function; "good" isn't well defined. You shouldn't need to ever call `good`.

- `close()` flushes any pending output and manages all system resources associated with a stream. Many operating systems have a limit on the number of files that can be opened at one time. You don't often need to call `close` explicitly; it's called by the appropriate destructor.

- `eof()` returns true if the end-of-file condition of a stream is detected. This is another worthless function (see `good`). If `fail` is true, this function may be able to tell you if `fail` is true because end-of-file is reached.

- `ignore(int n, int sentinel)` skips as many as n characters. It stops skipping when the `sentinel` character is read or when n characters are read, whichever comes first.

- `seekg(streampos p)` seeks an input stream to a position p. We use `seekg(0)` to reset a stream in the class `WordStreamIterator`; other uses are illustrated in the next section.

B.2   Random Access Files

We've used `ifstream` and `ofstream` streams as character-based streams; all the input and output is done a character at a time. Although operators `operator <<` and `operator >>` make it possible to insert and extract values of many types without reading one character at a time, underneath the streams are still character-based.

Occasionally files are written as raw binary data rather than as character-based text. If you think you must write binary files, you may be correct, but you'll give up a great deal:

- Binary files aren't readable (as text) in a text editor, so you can't examine them without writing a program to help, and you can't fix mistakes without writing a program.

- If you're writing objects whose size isn't fixed, such as strings, or objects containing pointers, you'll need to do lots of work to use files of raw binary data.

Seeking to a Fixed Position in a File. The file methods `seekg` and `tellg` shown in Program B.4 can be applied to text files as well as to binary files. Since text files are character-based, seeking is based on the size of a character. Input files have a **get position**, which can be moved using `seekg` and whose position can be obtained using `tellg`, where the "g" is for *get*. Similarly, output files use `seekp` and `tellp` for the **put position**. Using the seek and tell functions makes it possible to randomly access data in a file, as opposed to the sequential access we've used so far. Here random access means that it's possible to jump to location p without reading locations 0 through $p-1$, just as vectors have random access and linked lists do not.

You'll need to consult a more advanced book on C++ for more information. A careful reading of *binaryfiles.cpp*, Program B.4, will show how to work with binary files. Program B.4 writes two files of Dates, one in text format, one as raw binary data. The low-level stream functions read and write manage a chunk of memory for reading or writing. The functions assume the memory is a C-style array of characters; to interpret the memory as something else it must be cast to the appropriate type as shown by using the reinterpret_cast operator.

Program B.4   binaryfiles.cpp

```cpp
#include <iostream>
#include <string>
#include <fstream>
using namespace std;
#include "prompt.h"
#include "date.h"

// illustrates reading/writing raw bits, binary files

int main()
{
    string filename = PromptString("file for storing Dates: ");
    int limit =        PromptRange("# of Dates ",10,10000);
    Date today;
    int start = today.Absolute();
    string text = filename + ".txt";
    string binary = filename + ".bin";
    cout << "testing program on " << today << endl;

    ofstream toutput(text.c_str());      // open text file
    int k;
    for(k=start; k < start+limit; k++)  // write text form of dates
    {   toutput << Date(k) << endl;
    }
    toutput.close();

    // open binary file, write raw dates
    ofstream boutput(binary.c_str(),ios_base::binary);
    for(k=start; k < start+limit; k++)
    {   Date d(k);
        boutput.write(reinterpret_cast<const char *>(&d),sizeof(d));
    }
    boutput.close();

    // open input file to read raw dates from
    ifstream input(binary.c_str(),ios_base::binary);
    input.seekg(0,ios_base::beg);        // to the beginning
    streampos startp= input.tellg();     // position of start
    input.seekg(0,ios_base::end);        // seek to end of stream
    streampos endp = input.tellg();      // position of end
```

```
    int size = endp-startp;              // number of entries

    cout << "size of file: "  << size << ", # dates = "
        << size/sizeof(Date) << endl;

    // read alldates in file, start at front
    input.seekg(0, ios_base::beg);
    for(k=0; k < size/sizeof(Date); k++)
    {   input.read(reinterpret_cast<char *>(&today),sizeof(today));
        cout << today << endl;
    }
    return 0;
}
```

binaryfiles.cpp

To show why you don't want to use binary files, the first three lines of bindate.txt follow:

```
May 27 1999
May 28 1999
May 29 1999
```

Here are the first few characters in bindate.bin:

```
^[^@^@^@^E^@^@^@\317^G^@^@^\
```

```
                        O U T P U T

prompt> binaryfiles
file for storing Dates: bindate
# of Dates  between 10 and 10000: 10
testing program on May 27 1999
size of file: 120, # dates = 10
May 27 1999
May 28 1999
May 29 1999
May 30 1999
May 31 1999
June 1 1999
June 2 1999
June 3 1999
June 4 1999
June 5 1999
```

B.3   I/O Redirection

UNIX and MS-DOS/Windows machines provide a useful facility for permitting programs that read from the standard input stream, `cin`, to read from files. As we've seen, it's possible to use the class `ifstream` to do this. However, we often use programs written to read from the keyboard and use the stream `cin` to read from files instead. You can use **input redirection** to do this. When you run a program that reads from `cin`, the input can be specified to come from a text file using the symbol < and the name of the text file. Running Program 6.7, *countw.cpp,* as shown in the following, indicates how input redirection works.

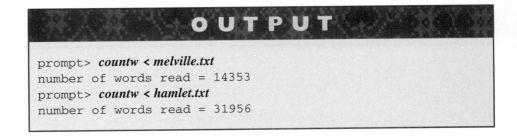

```
prompt> countw < melville.txt
number of words read = 14353
prompt> countw < hamlet.txt
number of words read = 31956
```

The less-than sign, <, causes the program on the left of the sign (in this case, *countw*) to take its `cin` input from the text file specified on the right of the < sign. The operating system that runs the program recognizes when the text file has "ended" and signals end of file to the program *countw.* This means that no special end-of-file character is stored in the files. Rather, end of file is a state detected by the system running the program.

It is possible to run the word-counting program on its own source code.

```
prompt> countw < countw.cpp
number of words read = 54
```

Among the *words* of Program 6.7, *countw.cpp,* are `"main()"`, `"{"`, `"(cin"`, and `"endl;"`. You should examine the program to see if you can determine why these are considered words.

How to: Use the Class string

C

> Experience shows that it is impossible to design the perfect **string**. People's taste, expectations, and needs differ too much for that. So, the standard library string isn't ideal. I would have made some design decisions differently, and so would you.
>
> BJARNE STROUSTRUP
> The C++ Programming Language, *Third Edition, p. 579*

> "I'm a frayed knot."
> A STRING GOING INTO A BAR FOR THE THIRD TIME
> *An old string joke*

C.1   The Class string

The standard C++ string class is imported into client programs using

```
#include<string>
```

It's possible you'll be programming in C++ using an older compiler that doesn't support the standard class, or that you'll be using a different string class, that is, the class apstring that is part of the Advanced Placement Computer Science C++ classes. A class tstring is provided with this book as a replacement for the standard class. It is identical to the class apstring except that the constant identifying an illegal position is tstring::npos instead of the global constant npos used in apstring.

The standard class string is better than a simple encapsulation of the C-style string, which is a zero-terminated array of characters. The class string is actually a typedef for a templated class. The template makes it possible to change more easily to an alphabet with more characters than can be represented by a char value. The type char typically limits an alphabet to 128 or 256 different characters. I won't discuss the templated class basic_string. See one of the more advanced books on C++ for details, such as [Str97]. I will outline some of the member functions that you may find useful in writing programs. For information on all the string functions consult the header file <string> or a C++ reference.

C.1.1   Basic Operations

Strings can be read, written, assigned, copied, and compared using relational operators. The relational operators compare using **lexicographical** order, which is alphabetical order except that the underlying character set's ordinal values are used. This means that in an ASCII environment the string `"Zebra"` comes *before* the string `"aardvark"` because the ASCII value of the character "Z" is 90 while the value of "a" is 97.

Some string implementations may use efficient implementation techniques such as reference counting to share storage, but you can think of strings as working like the built-in types: assignment works as you should expect it to.

```
string a = "hello";
string b = a;        // b constructed as copy of a
b[0] = 'j';          // a still represents "hello"
```

As this example shows, individual characters are accessed using the indexing bracket operator `[]`. There is no range-checking; an index that is greater than `s.length()-1`, the largest valid index, or less than zero, the smallest valid index, will be processed silently and almost certainly lead to an error later. The class `tstring`, like `apstring`, does do range-checking for the indexing operator. The standard class supports `at`, which does do range-checking:

```
string s = "hello";
s[30] = 'x';         // problem eventually, bad index
s.at(30) = 'x';      // error, exception thrown
```

Characters are indexing beginning with zero; the last valid index is `s.length()-1` as we've noted. The function `length` returns the number of characters in the string, which is one larger than the largest valid index because the first character has index zero.

C.1.2 Conversion to/from C-Style Strings

Many C++ functions predate the C++ standard; other functions are written to be used with C-style strings. The method `string::c_str()` returns a C-style string equivalent to a string. We use this method extensively in opening text files.

```
string filename = "c:\\data\\hamlet.txt";
ifstream input(filename.c_str());            // open file
```

A string can also be constructed from a C-style string. This is how strings are constructed from string literals since a string literal is treated as a C-style string.

```
string s = "hello world"; // construct string(const char *)
```

Some of the useful C-style functions such as `atoi` and `atof` have equivalents in the library of string free functions from *strutils.h*, Program G.8. See How to G for details.

C.2 String Member Functions

C.2.1 Adding Characters or Strings

In this book we use overloaded `operator +=` and `operator +` extensively for appending characters to a string and concatenating strings, respectively.

```
string c = 'a';       // no good, cannot construct from char
string s = "hello";
string t = " world";
string u = "el";
u += "ephant";        // ok, u = "elephant"
u += 's';             // ok to append char, u = "elephants"
string v = s + t;     // ok, v = "hello world"
v = 't' + s;          // no good, can't concatenate to a char
v = string("") + 't' + s; // ok. join char to string
```

As shown, it's not possible to concatenate a string to a char, but it is possible
to concatenate a char to a string. To guard against errors, there is no string
constructor from one char; this is why concatenation of strings to chars doesn't
work. It is possible, however, to concatenate a char to a string as shown in the
examples above.

It's also possible to add a string (or a string literal/C-style string) at a given
position/index using the method string::insert. The local copy below is needed
because the parameters are const:

```
string Fullname(const string& first, const string& last)
// post: returns fullname, e.g., first + last
{
    // return first + " " + last;
    string copy(last);
    copy.insert(0," ");     // copy is now " " + last
    copy.insert(0,first);   // copy is now first + " " + last
    return copy;
}
```

C.2.2 Using Substrings

A substring can be extracted from a string using the method string::substr().
Substrings are specified using a starting index/position and the number of characters in
the substring. The number of characters is optional.

```
string string::substr(int index = 0, int n = npos) const;
// post: return substring of n characters starting at index
```

The method substr "does the right thing" when too many characters are specified—
only as many as are available are returned. On the other hand, if the starting position is
out of range an error occurs. Program C.1 shows the substr method used together with
other string methods we discuss in the next section. The function prototype above shows
default values for both parameters, but the first argument is almost always provided.

The method string::replace, also shown in Program C.1, uses a position and
a length to replace a substring of characters in a string.

```
string& string::replace(int index, int n, const string& s);
// post: replace n chars beginning at index with s,
//        return result
```

Thus `substr` reads (a copy of) part of a string and `replace` writes a part of a string. Both functions use as many characters as specified by the optional second parameter, but don't generate an error if there are fewer characters in the string than specified.

<hr>

Program C.1   stringdemo.cpp

```cpp
#include <iostream>
#include <string>
using namespace std;

int main()
{
    string s = "I sing the body electric";

    cout << s << endl;
    cout << s.substr(2,4) << endl;
    cout << s.substr(s.find("electric")-5) << endl << endl;

    string copy(s);
    int bodyPos = copy.find("body");
    copy.replace(bodyPos,copy.length(),"blues");
    cout << copy << endl << endl;

    cout << "search for chars/strings" << endl;
    cout << "first e at " << s.find('e')  << endl;
    cout << "last e at "  << s.rfind('e') << endl;
    cout << "first z at " << s.find('z')  << endl;
    cout << "space after body "   << s.find(" ", bodyPos) << endl;
    return 0;
}
```

stringdemo.cpp

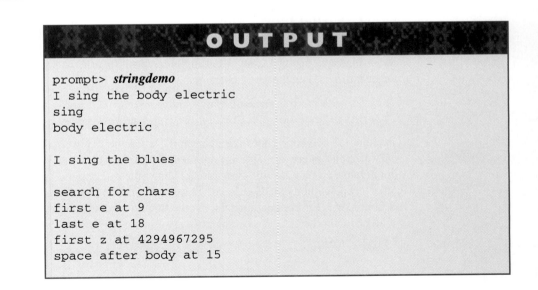

```
prompt> stringdemo
I sing the body electric
sing
body electric

I sing the blues

search for chars
first e at 9
last e at 18
first z at 4294967295
space after body at 15
```

C.2.3 Finding (Sub)strings and Characters

The string member functions `find` and `rfind` return the index in a string at which another string or character begins. If the searched-for value isn't found, the functions return `string::npos`. As the output shows, this is the largest positive value for an index. Your programs should not rely on `string::npos` having any particular value.

The functions `find` and `rfind` come in many flavors. We'll use only the basic versions, though these have an optional second argument indicating at what index the search begins as shown in Program C.1.

```
int string::find(const string& s, int loc = 0) const;
// post: return position/index of first location of s
//       starting search at index loc,
//       return npos if not found

int string::find(char ch, int loc = 0) const;
// post: as above, search for character ch

int string::rfind(const string& s, int loc = 0) const;
// post: return position/index of first location of s
//       starting search at index loc, searching backward
//       return npos if not found

int string::rfind(char ch, int loc = 0) const;
// post: as above, search for character ch backward
```

Although we've used the type `int` for all indexes, the type `size_type` is actually used in all `string` member functions. In nearly every implementation this will be the same as `size_t`, an `unsigned int` or some other unsigned integer type, such as `long`.

How to: Understand and Use const

D

An important factor, both for and against C++, was the willingness
of the C++ community to acknowledge C++'s many imperfections.

BJARNE STROUSTRUP
The Design and Evolution of C++, p. 178

The keyword **const** in C++ is used in many contexts. Using classes that support object "const-ness" is straightforward, but developing classes that support const-ness requires some care in design and implementation and some knowledge of often overlooked C++ features that facilitate designing with const.

D.1 Why const?

Many C++ programmers rely on object const-ness to combine efficiency and safety. For example, passing parameters by value (the default mechanism in C++ and the only parameter-passing mechanism in C and Java) creates a copy of the passed argument.[1] Consider passing a copy of a string:

```
void verse(int bottleCount, string beverage)
{
    cout << bottleCount << " bottles of "
        << beverage << " on the wall" << endl;
    cout << bottleCount << " bottles of "
        << beverage << endl;
    // and so on
}
```

This function might be called several times in a loop as shown here:

```
// illustration of function call and argument/parameter copy
string bev;
cout << "enter a beverage ";
cin >> bev;
for(int k = 100; k > 0; k--)
{
    verse(k,bev);
}
```

---

[1]In Java everything is a pointer (or a reference, depending on your viewpoint), so making copies isn't expensive. In C nearly everything is a pointer, so making copies isn't expensive. In C++ value semantics mean "make a copy," so copies are expensive.

737

In this example, the 100 function calls create 100 copies of the variable `bev`: one per call.[2] If the prototype of the function `verse` is changed to use a `const` reference parameter as shown below, then no copies are made:

```
void verse(int bottleCount, const string & beverage)
{
    // function here
}
```

The pass-by-reference (indicated by the & in the parameter) means that no copy is made in passing an argument. The `const` modifier means that the parameter `beverage` cannot be modified within the body of `verse`. The reference is for efficiency, and the `const` is for safety. Since many C++ programmers rely on passing `const` reference parameters, class designers should know how to support this style of programming.

D.1.1 Literal Arguments

In the example above, it's possible to use pass-by-reference without the `const` modifier to achieve efficiency without regard to safety.[3] However, in C++ if the parameter `beverage` is a reference parameter, but *not* a `const` reference parameter, then the function call below will not compile:

```
verse(99,"orange juice");
```

Here the second parameter is the string literal `"orange juice"`. Literals must be passed by value or by `const` reference. In the latter case a temporary object will be constructed to hold the literal. The C++ standard requires a `const` reference parameter in this case; a reference parameter without the `const` modifier won't support literal (constant) arguments.

D.2 `const` Member Functions

How does the compiler determine what functions are safe to call when a parameter is defined as `const`? For example, in the `verse` function above, suppose the programmer adds the line below to convert the first character of the beverage to its uppercase equivalent (`toupper` is accessible via the header file `<cctype>`; see How to F).

```
void verse(int bottleCount, const string & beverage)
{
    beverage[0] = toupper(beverage[0]);
    // verse output here
}
```

---

[2]The compiler might be able to reuse the same copy, but not necessarily.

[3]This is typical, for example, in Pascal programs where arrays are passed as `var` parameters to avoid the overhead of copying the array (e.g., consider a binary search function that searches in $O(\log n)$ time but takes $O(n)$ time to copy the array: not the paradigm of efficiency we'd like).

Compiling this code under Visual C++ 5.0 yields the error message

```
error C2106: left operand must be l-value
```

That's an "ell," where an l-value (for left-hand side of an assignment value) is a value that can be assigned to. In the code above, it is not possible to assign to beverage[0] since the parameter beverage is const. How does the compiler determine this?

In the example above, the compiler knows the prototype/signature of all string member functions. These member functions include two indexing operators: one operator [] for const strings and one operator [] for non-const strings. Both prototypes are shown below:

```
char   operator[ ]( int k )   const; // const strings
char & operator[ ]( int k );         // non-const strings
```

Note that the const indexing operator returns a char, which will be a copy of the k-th character in the string. The non-const function returns a char&, a reference to a character in the string. Returning a reference means that the actual character in the string can be modified (e.g., the code below turns "hello" into "jello" since string fruit is not const).

```
string fruit = "hello";
fruit[0] = 'j';
```

This code works because the value returned by the indexing operator is a reference (note the return type: char &) to a character in the string. Sometimes it helps to realize that the two statements below are equivalent:

```
fruit[0] = 'j';
fruit.operator[](0) = 'j';
```

At first it may seem strange to see a function call used as an l-value (i.e., the result returned by the call is assigned to). This is an essential part of how reference return types are used in C++.

As shown in the example above, some member functions have the word const as part of their prototype/signature—the word const appears after the parameter list. To see another example, part of the header file for the class Date is reproduced below (see *date.h*, Program G.2) with some of the const methods shown.

```
class Date
{
  public:
    Date(int m,int d,int y);
    // accessor functions

    int Month()   const;  // return month
    int Day()     const;  // return day
    int Year()    const;  // return year
    ...
};
```

As shown in the comment in the code above, the terminology often used for const member functions is **accessor**, indicating that (private) data are accessed only, not modified. In contrast, non-const member functions are often called **mutators**.

> **Program Tip D.1:   A const member function is a member function that can be applied to a const object.** The compiler ensures that const member functions do not modify private data. The compiler also ensures that only const member functions are called for const objects — const objects most often occur in programs as const reference parameters.

const member functions can also be applied to non-const objects. As we saw with operator [] earlier, and as explained in the next section, it's possible to have two versions of a function: one for const and one for non-const objects.

The key here is that any member function that doesn't modify data should be declared const in both the .h file and in the .cpp file (prototypes of member functions must match declaration and definition—declaration is the .h file, definition is the .cpp file). Only const functions are called on const objects; non-const objects can call both const and non-const functions.

D.2.1   Overloading on const

Two functions are **overloaded** when they have the same name. Overloaded functions must have different parameter lists so that the compiler can determine which function to call. For example, typically a class has several constructors, all with the same name (the name of the class) but with different parameters. In the Date class there are three overloaded constructors.

It's possible to have two member functions with the same name, where one is const and the other non-const. We saw this in the example of the overloaded indexing operators for the string class, which are reproduced below.

```
char    operator[ ]( int k )    const; // const strings
char&   operator[ ]( int k );          // non-const strings
```

At first glance these functions may appear to have the same parameter list and thus violate the rule requiring parameter lists of overloaded functions to be different. However, the const modifier for a member function really is part of the parameter list—it modifies the parameter this that is implicit in every member function and that refers to the object actually passed to the member function. In some sense you can think of all member functions having an implicit first parameter, a parameter of the type of the class to which the member function belongs. The string indexing functions would then be rewritten as follows as *non*member functions (using *self* for *this*):

```
char    operator[ ](const string&  self, int k );
char&   operator[ ](string&  self, int k );
```

If we actually developed the code like this, instead of using `s.operator[](k)` we would write `operator[](s,k)`, where `operator[]` is now a free function with two parameters instead of a member function of the `string` class with one parameter.

D.3 mutable Data

Sometimes a class is logically `const` but not physically `const`. This means that from a user viewpoint a function doesn't appear to change the class, but internally a change is needed to implement the function. One prototypical instance of this is a group of member functions that iterate over data in a collection. Not all of our iterator classes have been developed in a `const`-friendly way because we didn't want to discuss the issues raised here, but in more advanced applications you'll want `const` and non-`const` iterators. The class `CListIterator` is `const`-friendly, but first we'll discuss another iterator class. Consider a `WordStreamIterator` counting the words in a file:

```
WordStreamIterator ws;
ws.Open("hamlet.txt");
int count = 0;
for(ws.Init(); ws.HasMore(); ws.Next())
{ count++;
}
```

Is the variable `ws` const? It doesn't seem to be since it's reading data from the `ifstream` object it encapsulates. So we don't expect the `WordStreamIterator` methods to be `const`, although `HasMore` is clearly an accessor and should be `const`.

In a different context, what about iterating over a `CList` object? (See *clist.h*, Program G.12; recall that `CList` objects cannot change.)

```
void print(const StringList& list)
{
   StringList iter(list);
   for(iter.Init(); iter.HasMore(); iter.Next())
   { cout << iter.current() << endl;
   }
}
```

The problem here is that parameter `list` is const, as it should be, since the print function doesn't modify `list`. However, the iterating member functions will need to keep a pointer to the current node of the `CList` list and advance the pointer as needed. For example, here's the code from *clist.cpp* for the `Next` iterator function:

```
template <class Type>
void CListIterator<Type>::Next() const
{
   if (HasMore())
   {   myCurrent= myCurrent->next;
   }
}
```

Here the iterator function `Next` is labeled as a `const` function, meaning that it cannot modify any of the object's state/instance variables. As a result, if `myCurrent` is declared as a `Node *` pointer, the definition of `Next` above will not compile. If we make `Next` non-const, then we cannot support the concept of a `const` iterator: an iterator over a `const` collection. We'd like to differentiate between `const` collections and non-`const` collections, and have iterators that support both types.

There are two solutions. One is to cast away the `const`-ness in the function `Next`. The other is to declare the private variable `myCurrent` as **mutable**. The keyword `mutable` is a relatively new addition to C++ but is supported by most recent compilers. A `mutable` data member can be modified by a `const` function. It's a good idea to keep `mutable` data to a minimum. However, in some situations where logical `const`-ness (the iterator doesn't change the list) and physical `const`-ness (the iterator updates a pointer) don't coincide, `mutable` is a nice feature. The declaration for the `CListIterator` class is reproduced below; again, see Program G.12 for full details.

```
template <class Type>
class CListIterator
{
  public:
    CListIterator(const CList<Type>& list);

    void Init()      const;
    bool HasMore()   const;
    void Next()      const;
    Type Current()   const;

  private:
      typedef CList<Type>::TNode Node;
      Node * myFirst;              // front of list
      mutable Node * myCurrent; // current node
};
```

If your compiler doesn't support `mutable` you can cast away `const`-ness using either the `const_cast` operator or an old-style cast. Both lead to incredibly ugly code. Since the iterator is `const`, the object `*this` must have its `const`-ness cast away as shown. Since `this` is a pointer to a `const` object (see Section D.4) we must cast so that `*this` isn't `const`; we want to change the object referenced by `this`.

```
template <class Type>
void CListIterator<Type>::Next() const
// post: iterator advanced to next item
{
  if (HasMore())
  { const_cast<CListIterator<Type> *>(this)->myCurrent
      = myCurrent->next;
  }
}
```

For compilers that don't support const_cast the following alternative will work:

```
// use an old-style cast
(CListIterator<Type> *)(this)->myCurrent = myCurrent->next;
}
```

In both cases, before the cast the pointer this has type

```
const CListIterator<Type> *
```

The cast changes this to point to a non-const object, so that the object's state can be changed. This non-const reference can be modified since it is an l-value.

> **Program Tip D.2:** It's *not* a good idea to cast away const-ness. C++ allows this, but you should try to minimize throwing away const since the use of const is for safety (a good thing). Using the keyword mutable marks logical const-ness in a way that is easy to see and easier syntactically than using casts.

D.4   Pointers and const

Many functions have pointer parameters modified by const. Consider, for example, the string constructor from a C-style string:

```
string::string(const char * p)
// post: initialized to C-style string p
```

Since the asterisk follows the type it makes a pointer to, p is a *pointer to a constant character*. This means that the object pointed to by p cannot be changed: it's constant. You cannot change an object through a pointer declared in this way. Pointers can be modified by const in other ways:

```
Date * tptr        = new Date(); // points to today
Date * const cptr  = new Date(); // constant pointer
const Date * coptr = new Date(); // constant object

*tptr += 1;        // ok, tomorrow
*cptr += 1;        // ok, object isn't const
cptr = tptr;       // no, cptr is a constant pointer
*coptr += 1;       // no, *coptr is a const object
coptr = tptr;      // ok, pointer isn't const, object is
```

These examples illustrate the differences between a pointer to a constant object (coptr in the code above) and a const pointer (cptr in the same code).

D.5 Summary

Programming with `const` can be painful. It's easy to miss the appearance of `const` in compiler error messages — be sure that you look for it when you get a "member function XXX not implemented" error. You'll usually be told the function signature/prototype causing the error; look for `const` to see if you put a `const` in the header file but forgot to add the `const` when defining the function.

Some people decide `const` is too painful and never program with `const` reference parameters. However, it's easy to use `const` when you don't have to write the classes, assuming that the class designer and implementer liked `const` too.

So use `const` for safety, and learn to design and implement classes that support use of `const` by others.

How to: Overload Operators

E

Just as most people want government benefits without having to pay for them, most C++
programmers want implicit type conversions without incurring any cost for temporaries.

SCOTT MEYERS

More Effective C++, p. 105

E.1 Overloading Overview

C++ allows you to overload operators. This means, for example, that you can write
expressions that are natural, such as

```
BigInteger a,b;
cout << "enter two integer values ";
cin >> a >> b;
cout << "a + b = " << (a+b) << endl;
```

Here operators <<, >>, and + are overloaded for BigInteger values. Of course it's
possible to run amok with operator overloading and use + to mean multiply just because
you can. Rather than dwell on when to overload operators, this How to will explain how
to overload operators. Many books show the syntax for declaring overloaded operators,
but few offer guidelines for keeping the amount of code you write to a minimum and for
avoiding code duplication. The guidelines in this How to do not necessarily result in the
most efficient code from an execution standpoint, but development efforts are minimized
while efficiency and maintainability from a coding standpoint are emphasized. Of course
once you succeed in implementing overloaded operators you can then concentrate on
making things efficient. To quote Donald Knuth (as cited in [McC93]):

Premature optimization is the root of all evil

E.2 Arithmetic Operators

Arithmetic operators include +=, -=, *=, /=, %=, and their binary cousins +, -, *,
/, %. The easiest way to implement these operators is to implement the arithmetic
assignment operators as member functions, and then to implement the binary operators
using the arithmetic assignment functions. The binary operators are implemented as
free, non-member functions.

E.2.1   **Binary Operators**

Here we assume that all arithmetic assignment operators have been implemented, and we discuss how to implement the binary arithmetic operators. We'll use + as an example, assuming we're implementing addition for a class BigInt, but the example applies to all the binary arithmetic operators for any class.

```
BigInt operator + (const BigInt & lhs, const BigInt & rhs)
// postcondition: returns lhs + rhs
{
    BigInt copy(lhs);
    copy += rhs;
    return copy;
}
```

The code here is straightforward. A copy of the parameter lhs (left-hand side) is made and the sum accumulated in this copy, which is then returned. Assuming that += is implemented properly, it's possible to shorten the body of the function:

```
BigInt operator + (const BigInt & lhs, const BigInt & rhs)
// postcondition: returns lhs + rhs
{
    return BigInt(lhs) += rhs;
}
```

This implementation actually uses the return value of operator += (see Section E.2.2) and is potentially more efficient though less clear to read at first. The efficiency gains are spelled out in some detail in [Mey96]; we'll mention them briefly later in this section.

Symmetry Is Good: Why operator + *Is Not a Member Function.* In some textbooks, operator + is implemented as a member function. In the example above operator + is a *free function*, not a member of any class. The problem with making it a member function is that it must have an object that it can be applied to. For example, consider operator + as a member function:

```
BigInt BigInt::operator +(const BigInt & rhs)
  // postcondition: returns (*this) + rhs
  {
      BigInt copy(*this);
      // code here to add rhs to copy, and return result
  }
```

The copy of *this is required since evaluating a + b should not result in changing the value of a. Note that a + b is the same as a.operator +(b) when operator + is a member function. The real drawback here is that the following statements are legal when operator + is a member function:

```
BigInt a = Factorial(50); // a large number
BigInt b = a + 1;          // one more than a large number
```

However, the following statements are **not** legal:

```
BigInt a = Factorial(50);    // a large number
BigInt b = 1 + a;            // one more than a large number
```

The expression a + 1 compiles and executes because (we're assuming) there is a BigInt constructor that will create a BigInt from an int (i.e., the constructor below is implemented). We'll have more to say on constructors that act as implicit converters later.

```
BigInt::BigInt(int num);
// postcondition: *this has the value num
```

This constructor creates an *anonymous* BigInt variable for the int value 1. This anonymous variable is passed to the function operator +. However, the symmetric expression 1 + a cannot be evaluated if operator + is a member function because the translation to 1.operator +(a) is syntactic nonsense — 1 is a literal, so it cannot have a member function applied to it, nor will C++ create an anonymous variable so that a member function can be applied.

> **Program Tip E.1: Overloaded operators for classes should behave like operators for built-in types.** The binary arithmetic operators are commutative. When they're overloaded they should behave as users expect them to. So for symmetry and commutativity, binary arithmetic operators should not be member functions.

The alternative is to make operator + a friend function; then it has access to the private instance variables of the class for which it is overloaded. However, the approach outlined above where operator + is implemented in terms of operator += avoids declaring friend functions. Since friend status should be granted sparingly, and since clients of a class cannot grant friendship after the class declaration is fixed, the approach outlined here should be used.

Consequences. The approach here uses a local variable that is a copy of one of the parameters. A copy is also made when the value is returned from the function. Since the function must return by value, the copy on return cannot be avoided. Since we don't want a + b to have the side effect of altering the value of a, a copy of a cannot be avoided. Furthermore, compiler optimization should be able to avoid the copy in many situations, particularly if the one-line implementation of the operator shown above is used. This implementation, reproduced here,

```
return BigInt(lhs) += rhs;
```

facilitates what's called the *return value optimization* [Mey96]. Smart compilers can generate efficient code so that the cost of temporaries is negligible or nothing in evaluating statements like the following:

```
x = a + b;
```

If you've benchmarked a program and determined that the line below is executed millions of times and is using temporaries and time:

```
x = a + b + c + d + e;
```

then you can recode the line using the corresponding arithmetic assignment operator:

```
x += a; x += b; x += c; x += d; x += e;
```

This code won't create any temporaries. This code should be as efficient as you can get it to be, and you have two benefits: ease of developing overloaded operators and efficiency when you need it.

E.2.2 Arithmetic Assignment Operators

Again we'll use operator += for a class BigInt as an exemplar of the syntax and semantics for overloading arithmetic assignment operators.

```
const BigInt& BigInt::operator += (const BigInt & rhs)
// postcondition: rhs has been added to *this,
//                *this returned
```

Using this prototype the code below compiles:

```
BigInt a = Factorial(25);
BigInt b = Factorial(30);

a += b;
BigInt c = (b += b);
```

Note that operator += returns a value (a constant reference) that is assigned to c. This isn't typical, but it's legal C++ for the built-in arithmetic operators, so it should be legal for overloaded arithmetic operators. As we saw in the implementation of operator +, it's possible to make good use of the return value of operator +=.

> **Program Tip E.2: Overloaded operators should have the same semantics as their built-in counterparts.** This means that arithmetic assignment operators should return values. The return type must be a reference to avoid a copy, and it should be const.

Return Values from Overloaded Operators. A reference is returned since there is no reason to make a copy. A const reference is returned so that the returned value is not an lvalue, that is, so that it cannot be assigned to

```
BigInt a = Factorial(25);
BigInt b = Factorial(30);

(a += b) = b;                    // this is NOT legal C++ !!!
```

The expression (a += b) is not an lvalue since the value returned is const reference. The const modifier is the essential piece of preventing the return value from being an lvalue.

The expression returned from an overloaded arithmetic operator should be *this, the value of the object being operated on:

```
const BigInt& BigInt::operator += (const BigInt & rhs)
// postcondition: rhs has been added to *this,
//                *this returned
{
    // code here
    return *this;
}
```

Aliasing. In one of the examples above the expression b += b is used. In this case the parameter rhs will be an alias for the object on which operator += is invoked. This can cause problems in some situations since the value of rhs may change during the computation of intermediate results. (rhs doesn't change, it's const; but it's an alias for *this, whose instance variables may be changing as the function operator += executes.)

When aliasing could cause a problem, this needs to be checked as a special case just as it is for overloaded assignment operators (of which the arithmetic assignment operators are a special case).

```
    if (this == &rhs)   // special case
```

In some situations it may be possible to use other overloaded operators to handle the special cases. For example, the code below is from the implementation of the BigInt class operator +=:

```
    if (this == &rhs)       // to add self, multiply by 2
    {   *this *= 2;
        return *this;
    }
```

This will not always be possible because operator *= will not always be overloaded for int values.

Special Cases. Sometimes, often for efficiency (but make it right before making it fast), arithmetic operators are overloaded more than once for a given class. For example, the class BigInt has the following overloaded member functions and free functions:

```
    // member functions

    const BigInt & operator *= (const BigInt &);
    const BigInt & operator *= (int num);

    // free functions
```

```
BigInt operator *(const BigInt & lhs, const BigInt & rhs);
BigInt operator *(const BigInt & lhs, int num);
BigInt operator *(int num, const BigInt & rhs);
```

Here it's possible to evaluate b * 5 for a BigInt b variable without converting the 5 to an anonymous variable. This may be done for efficiency or because the specialized versions of operator += and operator + are used in implementing the nonspecialized versions. Note that for symmetry operator + is overloaded twice for adding BigInt and int values.

E.3   Relational Operators

Implementing the Boolean relational operators <, >, <=, >=, ==, and != requires a technique similar to the method discussed in Section E.2.1 for binary arithmetic operators. This is because we want to be able to write the code below (all three comparison expressions involving <):

```
BigInt x;
// code giving x a value

if (x < y)    // do something

if (x < 128) // do something

if (1024 < x) // do something
```

For reasons similar to those outlined in Section E.2.1, the creation of anonymous variables for either left- or right-hand sides of a relational expression (e.g., involving < or = =) requires that these operators not be member functions. If they're implemented as free functions, then they'll need to be friend functions unless the approach outlined here is used.

Although relational operators can be implemented as friend functions, there is an easy method for implementing them that is similar to the method using arithmetic assignment operators such as += to implement the corresponding relational operator, in this case +, that avoids declaring any friend functions.

For example, consider a class Date for representing calendar dates, such as January 23, 1999. Determining if two dates are equal, or if one comes before another, can be done simply if == and < (and the other relational operators) are overloaded for Date objects. The approach I use is illustrated by the partial declaration of the Date class that follows:

```
class Date
{
  public:
    // constructors and other member functions elided
    // functions for implementing relational operators

    bool equal(const Date & rhs) const;
    bool less(const Date & rhs)  const;

  private:
    // stuff here
};
```

Here the functions `equal` and `less` determine if one date is equal to or less than another, respectively. These functions are implemented to facilitate overloading the relational operators, although these functions can be useful in debuggers. The code below shows `equal` in use:

```
Date a(1,1,1998), b(12,31, 1997);

if (a.equal(b+1)) // just checking
```

Using functions `equal` and `less` is the Java method for comparisons, so using this approach in C++ has the added benefit of easing a transition to Java. But this method is useful on its own, especially with inheritance as we'll see later. Once the functions are implemented, implementing the overloaded relational operators is straightforward. For the class `Date` we have Program E.1.

Program E.1   datecomps.cpp

```
// relational operators for Date class

bool operator == (const Date & lhs, const Date & rhs)
// post: return true iff lhs == rhs
{
    return lhs.equal(rhs);
}

bool operator != (const Date & lhs, const Date & rhs)
// post: return true iff lhs != rhs
{
    return ! (lhs == rhs);
}

bool operator <  (const Date & lhs, const Date & rhs)
// post: return true iff lhs < rhs
{
    return lhs.less(rhs);
}
```

```
bool operator >  (const Date & lhs, const Date & rhs)
// post: return true iff lhs > rhs
{
    return rhs < lhs;
}

bool operator <= (const Date & lhs, const Date & rhs)
// post: return true iff lhs <= rhs
{
    return ! (lhs > rhs);
}

bool operator >= (const Date & lhs, const Date & rhs)
// post: return true iff lhs >= rhs
{
    return rhs <= lhs;
}
```

———————
datecomps.cpp

In these examples only == and < use the member functions equal and less directly; the other overloaded operators are implemented in terms of == and <. However, it's clearly possible to use equal and less only for implementing all the overloaded operators.

When using the STL (Standard Template Library) the header file <function> is typically included. Templated function declarations in this file implement all relational operators in terms of < and ==, so typically only these operators are overloaded for classes that are used in environments in which STL is available. For example, part of the SGI implementation of the header file function.h is shown below:

```
template <class T>
inline bool operator!=(const T& x, const T& y)
{
    return !(x == y);
}

template <class T>
inline bool operator>(const T& x, const T& y)
{
    return y < x;
}
```

If you use STL, you typically will overload only operator < and operator ==; by including the header file <function>, you'll include templated functions that will implement the other relational operators in terms of < and ==. Note that these templated functions are defined as **inline** functions for efficiency. Functions defined as inline *may* be implemented without calling the function by literally substituting the code in the body of the function where the call is made, with parameters instantiated appropriately. The *inline* declaration is a request to the compiler, not a requirement.

E.4   I/O Operators

We'll look first at overloading the insertion operator, `operator <<`, for stream output. Here it's absolutely not possible to make the operator a member function of the class for which output is being defined. The statement

```
cout << x;
```

could be interpreted by the compiler as `cout.operator <<(x)`, where the insertion operator is a member function of the `ostream` class of which `cout` is an instance. The insertion operator could also be a free function with two parameters, much like `operator +` as discussed above. Since programmers don't typically have access to redefining the standard I/O classes, the I/O operators are typically implemented as free functions. The header for the insertion operator for `BigInt` is shown below:

```
ostream& operator <<(ostream & out, const BigInt & big
// postcondition: big inserted onto stream out
```

The return type must be a reference type because the stream on which the object is inserted is returned for subsequent insertion operations. This is what allows insertions to be chained together:

```
BigInt b = factorial(val);
string s = " factorial = ";

cout << s << b;
```

The last statement could be written more cumbersomely as follows since `operator <<` is overloaded as a free function for both `string` and `BigInt` objects:

```
operator << (operator << (cout,s), b);
```

However, it's essential that `operator <<` be an operator and not a function since the order in which arguments are evaluated in C−+ is not defined. In the statement `x = min(sqrt(x),sqrt(y))`, compilers are not required to evaluate `sqrt(x)` before evaluating `sqrt(y)` (this is a C legacy; it's too bad that the order in which arguments are evaluated isn't prescribed). However, the associativity of `operator <<` is defined; it's left-associative, which means that

```
cout << x << y << z;
```

requires that x be inserted before y and that y be inserted before z.

Now that we know the prototype for the overloaded `operator <<`, how do we implement the operator? As with overloaded arithmetic operators there are two choices:

- Make `operator <<` a friend of the class whose output is being overloaded, for example, of `BigInt` in the examples above.
- Create a member function that can be used in implementing `operator <<` as a free, nonfriend function.

We'll adopt the second approach, since it avoids the coupling entailed by creating friend classes; the solution we'll use is easily extensible to other, nonstream output, such as on a graphics display.

E.4.1   The Function `tostring()`

One very simple way to provide output is to create a member function `tostring()` that converts an object to a string form. Assuming that `tostring()` returns a string and that `operator <<` is overloaded for strings, we can write

```
ostream& cperator <<(ostream & out, const BigInt & big)
// postcondition: big inserted onto stream out
{
    out << big.tostring();
    return out;
}
```

Note that in the code above you cannot determine just by reading if `tostring()` returns a standard `string`, an `apstring`, a `tstring`, or some other type—it must return a type for which stream insertion is overloaded.

The implementation above works for any class for which a member function `tostring()` exists (this is how Java overloads + to work as a string catenator with any object, which is then used for output in Java).

Inheritance and `tostring()`. In an inheritance hierarchy, requiring all subclasses to implement `tostring` by making it (pure) virtual in superclasses makes it possible to write one overloaded `operator <<` that works with every class in the hierarchy. In Chapter 13 we explored a hierarchy of classes for implementing digital logic. Part of the abstract superclass `Gate` and an appropriately overloaded operator are shown below.

```
// from gates.h
class Gate
{
  public:
    virtual ~Gate() {}
    virtual string tostring() const = 0;
    ..
};
// from gates.cpp
ostream& operator << (ostream& out, const Gate& g)
{
    out << g.tostring();
    return out;
}
```

All `Gate` subclasses—`AndGate`, `Inverter`, `OrGate`, and `CompositeGate`—are "printable" since these concrete classes must supply an implementation of `tostring` and the overloaded `operator <<` uses the polymorphic `tostring`. Clients designing new `Gate` subclasses get output for free as well.

The Function `print()`. A member function `print()` is like using `tostring()`. Typically, `print` takes a stream parameter.

```
ostream& operator <<(ostream & out, const BigInt & big)
// postcondition: big inserted onto stream out
{
    big.print(out);
    return out;
}
```

This works without using a `string` class but is restricted to stream output. To write an object on a graphics screen, conversion to `string` is usually simpler since most graphics screens have functions to facilitate text display.

Overloading for Input. You can overload `operator >>` for input as `operator <<` is overloaded for output. It's also possible to implement an overloaded `getline` function that reads a line at a time rather than using white space–delimited input, which is expected with `operator >>`. By far the easiest way to do input is to convert from a string. This is easy, but not always completely general since string input is required to be white space–delimited. For example, if you're implementing an overloaded input operator for the `BigInt` class, what value is read by the line of text that follows?

```
12345678912345678890is a large number
```

Ideally the characters `is a number` will remain on the stream, and input of the `BigInt` will stop with the zero. However, this requires reading one character at a time rather than a string at a time. You'll need to decide what method is best: converting from a string or parsing input one character at a time, based on the constraints of the problem you're solving.

E.5 Constructors and Conversions

The techniques we describe for overloading binary arithmetic and relational operators were motivated in part by concerns for symmetry. For example, we wanted to write both `a + 2` and `2 + a` when using `BigInt` variables. As we noted, symmetry in this case is made possible by a constructor that creates a `BigInt` from an `int`. Because constructors permit this kind of implicit conversion, unexpected behavior can occur when conversions happen that the programmer doesn't expect. The second statement below may be a typo, or the programmer may mean to assign to `u` a vector of one element.

```
tvector<int>  u(10); // vector of 10 elements
u = 1;               // we mean u[0] = 1
```

We know there's a vector constructor that takes an `int` argument since it's used in the first statement. This means it's possible that the second statement does two things:

■   Creates an anonymous/temporary `int` vector with one element.

■   Assigns/copies this temporary vector to `u`.

However, in the `tvector` class the second statement doesn't compile. To limit implicit conversions with the vector class, the keyword **explicit** is used with the constructor:

```
explicit tvector(int size); // size and capacity = size
```

A constructor modified by `explicit` cannot act as an implicit converter; an explicit use of the class name is required. The two statements that follow make an explicit use of the constructor:

```
tvector<int>  u(10); // vector of 10 elements
u = tvector<int>(1); // copy one-element vector to u
```

By using `explicit`, it's harder for unanticipated conversions to take place in client code—it's unlikely a programmer would type the second line above by mistake.

How to: Understand and Use Standard Libraries F

By its very nature, the library provided with a programming language is a mixed bag.
P.J. Plauger
The Standard C Library, p. x

F.1 Functions

C++ inherits many free (nonclass) functions from C. A **function library** is a collection of cohesive functions that have a common domain. For example, the header file `<cmath>` imports mathematical functions, the file `<cctype>` imports character functions, and the library `<cstdlib>` imports "standard" algorithms like the C-based functions `atoi` and `atof`. In addition to the function libraries inherited from C, C++ includes several standard class libraries. In particular, the *Standard Template Library*, or STL, provides implementations of functions, algorithms, and container classes like vector. We use some of the ideas from STL, for example in the class `tvector` and in the sorting functions of *sortall.h*, but a complete discussion of STL is beyond the scope of this book. Complete though terse information on STL is available in [Str97]; a description of why the library works as it does and a wonderful book on generic programming is [Aus98].

The function libraries imported using header files of the form `<cXXX>` are in the *std* namespace. For a brief introduction to namespaces see Section A.2.3 in How to A. Functions in the global namespace are imported using `<XXX.h>`. For example, use `<cmath>` for functions in the *std* namespace, but `<math.h>` for functions in the global namespace. Older libraries/environments typically support only the `.h` versions of the function libraries.

F.1.1 The Library `<cmath>`

Functions in the standard math library, `<cmath>`, are given in Table F.1. On older systems this library is called `<math.h>`. All trigonometric functions use radian measure. See the functions in *mathutils.h*, Program G.9, for functions to convert between degrees and radians.

Most of the functions in `<cmath>` are described sufficiently in Table F.1. The arguments to `atan2` are presumed to be x- and y-coordinates, so that `atan2(1,1)` is the same as `atan2(3,3)` or `atan(π/4)`.

Table F.1   Some functions in `<cmath>`.

Function name	Prototype	Returns
double fabs	(double x)	Absolute value of x
double abs	(double x)	Absolute value of x (C++ only)
double log	(double x)	Natural log of x
double log10	(double x)	Base-10 log of x
double sin	(double x)	Sine of x (x in radians)
double cos	(double x)	Cosine of x (x in radians)
double tan	(double x)	Tangent of x (x in radians)
double asin	(double x)	Arc sine of x $[-\pi/2, \pi/2]$
double acos	(double x)	Arc cosine of x $[0, \pi]$
double atan	(double x)	Arc tangent of x $[-\pi/2, \pi/2]$
double atan2	(double x, double y)	Atan(x/y)
double sinh	(double x)	Hyperbolic sine of x
double cosh	(double x)	Hyperbolic cosine of x
double tanh	(double x)	Hyperbolic tangent of x
double pow	(double x, double y)	x^y
double sqrt	(double x)	$\sqrt{x}$, square root of x
double fmod	(double d, double m)	Floating-point remainder d/m
double ldexp	(double d, int i)	d*pow(2,i)
double floor	(double x)	Largest integer value $\leq x$
double ceil	(double x)	Smallest integer value $\geq x$

F.1.2   The Library `<cctype>`

The functions in `<cctype>` operate on `char` values; they're summarized in Table F.2. On older systems this library is called `<ctype.h>`. You would expect functions with the prefix `is`, such as `islower` and `isalnum`, to have return type `bool`. However, to ensure compatibility with both C and C++ code, many libraries use integer values for the return type of these predicates in `<cctype>`. These Boolean-valued functions return some nonzero value for true, but this value is not necessarily one. All the functions use `int` parameters, but arguments are expected to be in the range of legal `char` values.

F.2   Constants and Limits

Several header files import constants and functions that encapsulate platform-specific limits on the maximum and minimum values of different built-in types. Unfortunately, the C++ standard does not require an `int` to be represented by 32 bits, nor a `double`

Table F.2 Some functions in `<cctype>`.

Function prototype	Returns true when
`int isalpha(int c)`	c is alphabetic (upper- or lowercase)
`int isalnum(int c)`	c is alphabetic or a digit
`int islower(int c)`	c is a lowercase letter
`int isdigit(int c)`	c is a digit character "0"–"9"
`int iscntrl(int c)`	c is a control character
`int isprint(int c)`	c is a printable character including space
`int ispunct(int c)`	c is a punctuation character (printable, not space, not alnum)
`int isspace(int c)`	c is any white-space character: `' ','\t','\n','\v', '\r','\f'`
`int isupper(int c)`	c is an uppercase letter

	Returns
`int tolower(int c)`	Lowercase equivalent of c
`int toupper(int c)`	Uppercase equivalent of c

to be represented by 64 bits, although these are the standard sizes on 32-bit computers and are the standard sizes used in languages like Java.

F.2.1 Limits in `<climits>`

The header file `<climits>` (or `<limits.h>`) imports the constants shown in *oldlimits.cpp*, Program F.1. However, the value `INT_MIN`, for example, is almost certainly a preprocessor #define rather than a C++ constant. Although these constants are simple to use, consider using the constants and classes defined in `<limits>`, whose use is shown in Program F.2.

Program F.1 oldlimits.cpp

```
#include <iostream>
#include <iomanip>              // for setw
#include <climits>
#include <string>
using namespace std;

// illustrates range of values for integral types

const int FIELD_SIZE = 13;            // size of field for output chunk

void Print(const string& type, long low, unsigned long high);
```

```
int main()
{
    cout << setw(FIELD_SIZE) << "type"
         << setw(FIELD_SIZE) << "low"
         << setw(FIELD_SIZE) << "high" << endl << endl;

    Print("char",  CHAR_MIN, CHAR_MAX);
    Print("uchar", 0,        UCHAR_MAX);
    Print("short", SHRT_MIN, SHRT_MAX);
    Print("ushort",0,        USHRT_MAX);
    Print("int",   INT_MIN,  INT_MAX);
    Print("uint",  0,        UINT_MAX);
    Print("long",  LONG_MIN, LONG_MAX);
    Print("ulong", 0,        ULONG_MAX);
    return 0;
}

void Print(const string& type, long int low, unsigned long int high)
// postcondition: values printed in field width FIELD_SIZE
{
    cout << setw(FIELD_SIZE) << type
         << setw(FIELD_SIZE) << low
         << setw(FIELD_SIZE) << high << endl;
}
```

oldlimits.cpp

O U T P U T

```
prompt> oldlimits
        type          low         high

        char         -128          127
       uchar            0          255
       short       -32768        32767
      ushort            0        65535
         int  -2147483648   2147483647
        uint            0   4294967295
        long  -2147483648   2147483647
       ulong            0   4294967295
```

F.2.2   double Limits in <cfloat>

The header file <cfloat> (or <float.h>) imports several constants, including DBL_MIN and DBL_MAX, which specify the minimum and maximum double values, respectively.

F.2.3 Limits in `<limits>`

The header file `<limits>` imports a templated class `numeric_limits` that provides values related to all the built-in types. Clients can create versions of `numeric_limits` for programmer-defined classes. For example, we could create a version for the class `BigInt`. All the methods and constants in `numeric_limits` are static, so no variables of type `numeric_limits` are created.

We use only four of the methods available in the class `numeric_limits`. There are many more, for example, in the class `numeric_limits<double>` specifically for floating-point values. In the function `printLimits` we use the standard C++ operator `typeid`, imported from `<typeinfo>`. Basically, `typeid` allows types to be compared for equality and provides access to a string form of a type's name. For more information on `numeric_limits` and `typeid` see [Str97].

Program F.2 limits.cpp

```cpp
#include <iostream>
#include <limits>
#include <typeinfo>
#include <iomanip>
using namespace std;

// print class-specific limits using numeric_limits from <limits>

template <class Type>
void printLimits(const Type& t)
// post: print max,min values and # bits used by t
{
    cout << "\ninformation for " << typeid(t).name() << endl;
    cout << "min =\t"   << numeric_limits<Type>::min()  << endl;
    cout << "max =\t"   << numeric_limits<Type>::max()  << endl;
    cout << "#bits\t" << numeric_limits<Type>::digits << endl;
    cout << "is integral? "
         << boolalpha << numeric_limits<Type>::is_integer << endl;
}

int main()
{

    printLimits(0);
    printLimits(0u);
    printLimits(0L);
    printLimits('a');
    printLimits(static_cast<unsigned char>('a'));
    printLimits(0.0);
    printLimits(static_cast<float>(0.0));
    return 0;
}
```

limits.cpp

```
O U T P U T
```

```
prompt> limits
information for int
min =    -2147483648
max =    2147483647
#bits=  31
is integral? true

information for unsigned int
min =    0
max =    4294967295
#bits=  32
is integral? true

information for long
min =    -2147483648
max =    2147483647
#bits=  31
is integral? true

information for char
min =    -128          actually prints a char, not an int
max =    128           actually prints a char, not an int
#bits=  7
is integral? true

information for unsigned char
min =    0
max =    255
#bits=  8
is integral? true

information for double
min =    2.22507e-308
max =    1.79769e+308
#bits=  53             # bits in mantissa
is integral? false

information for float
min =    1.17549e-38
max =    3.40282e+38
#bits=  24             # bits in mantissa
is integral? false
```

F.2.4 ASCII Values

Since most C++ environments use ASCII coding for characters, Table F.3 provides ASCII values for all the standard characters.

Table F.3 ASCII values.

ASCII character set							
Decimal	Char.	Decimal	Char.	Decimal	Char.	Decimal	Char.
0	^@	32	space	64	@	96	`
1	^A	33	!	65	A	97	a
2	^B	34	"	66	B	98	b
3	^C	35	#	67	C	99	c
4	^D	36	$	68	D	100	d
5	^E	37	%	69	E	101	e
6	^F	38	&	70	F	102	f
7	^G	39	'	71	G	103	g
8	^H	40	(	72	H	104	h
9	^I	41	)	73	I	105	i
10	^J	42	*	74	J	106	j
11	^K	43	+	75	K	107	k
12	^L	44	,	76	L	108	l
13	^M	45	–	77	M	109	m
14	^N	46	.	78	N	110	n
15	^O	47	/	79	O	111	o
16	^P	48	0	80	P	112	p
17	^Q	49	1	81	Q	113	q
18	^R	50	2	82	R	114	r
19	^S	51	3	83	S	115	s
20	^T	52	4	84	T	116	t
21	^U	53	5	85	U	117	u
22	^V	54	6	86	V	118	v
23	^W	55	7	87	W	119	w
24	^X	56	8	88	X	120	x
25	^Y	57	9	89	Y	121	y
26	^Z	58	:	90	Z	122	z
27	escape	59	;	91	[	123	{
28	fs	60	<	92	\	124		
29	gs	61	=	93	]	125	}
30	rs	62	>	94	^	126	~
31	us	63	?	95	_	127	del

How to: Understand and Use Tapestry Classes

◼ G.1 A Library of Useful Classes

This book supplies many classes for you to use in programming and exploring computer science. These classes extend what's available in the base C++ language by supplying off-the-shelf components that you can use to solve more problems than if you had to design and implement the classes from scratch. If someone tells you that you're not really using C++ if you use these supplied classes because the classes are not part of the C++ language, these people are narrow-minded and without a clue as to how people write software today. However, it may be prudent not to tell them this. The classes introduced in this book have been designed to be powerful but simple so that they are easy for beginning programmers to use. This means the classes may not be as powerful as similar classes that are designed to serve a larger audience of professional programmers. However, the classes are designed to be understandable by novice programmers while still being powerful enough to be used in large, real programs. Sometimes an industrial-strength class that covers 95% of all applications is not as powerful as a class that covers 65% of all applications if the industrial-strength class is much harder to learn and use. The Tapestry classes are used by people programming for a living and programming for fun. Sometimes this is the same group of people.

G.1.1 Summary of Classes and Functions

I refer to the core classes and function libraries introduced in this book as **libtapestry**. The easiest way to use these classes is to create a library, which is then linked automatically with every program you write. With Unix you do this with a makefile; with Windows or Macs you do this with a project as part of an IDE (Integrated Development Environment). Information on creating libraries is available in How to I. Only the nontemplated classes and functions are part of the library.

There are many other programs used in the book, but the core classes and functions are summarized in Table G.1. The header files for most of these classes are reproduced in the following sections as documentation for each class.

Table G.1 The classes and function libraries introduced in this book that make up
`libtapestry`.

Class	Header file	Description
BigInt	*bigint.h*	Unbounded integers
CList	*clist.h*	Immutable lists
ClockTime	*clockt.h*	Clock times (e.g., 13:24:09)
CTimer	*ctimer.h*	Stopwatch timing for code
Date	*date.h*	Dates (e.g., July 16, 2007)
Dice	*dice.h*	Simulate N-sided dice
DirStream and DirEntry	*directory.h*	Access directories
Permuter	*permuter.h*	Permutes int vectors
Point	*point.h*	Two-dimensional points
RandGen	*randgen.h*	Random numbers
SimpleMap	*simplemap.h*	Rudimentary map class
StringSet	*stringset.h*	Sets of strings
tvector	*tvector.h*	Range-checked vector class
tmatrix	*tmatrix.h*	Range-checked 2D matrix
WordStreamIterator	*worditer.h*	Reading files of words

Free Functions	Header file	Description
deg2rad, PI, ...	*mathutils.h*	Math utilities
PromptRange, ...	*prompt.h*	Prompt for values
QuickSort, bsearch, ...	*sortall.h*	Sorting and searching
ToLower, atoi, ...	*strutils.h*	String functions
WaitForReturn	*utils.h*	Wait for user to press return

The classes `CList`, `tvector`, `tmatrix`, and `SimpleMap` are templated, as are
the functions in *sortall.h*. The classes in *directory.h* are implemented differently for Unix
and Windows platforms. All other classes should be platform independent, although it
is possible there are some differences I have not encountered.

G.1.2 Implementations of Tapestry Classes

I have designed the classes and functions in Table G.1 to be used from the beginning of
an introductory course, though some stress topics not typically covered in the first weeks,
such as vectors, matrices, and maps. Although the classes are designed to be used by
client programs, most of them can be studied as examples of class design. However, some
implementations depend on topics not covered in this book, or rely on platform-specific
libraries that aren't of general interest. These include the following:

- Classes in *directory.cpp* use low-level operating system specific functions.
- Classes in *tvector.h* allocate built-in arrays using `operator new []`, not covered in this text.

■ Classes in *date.cpp*, *randgen.cpp*, and *clockt.cpp* use C functions for accessing time to determine the current time of the day or the current day of the week.

All other classes have been documented so that their implementations can be studied.

G.2 Header Files for Tapestry Classes

G.2.1 Prompting Functions in `prompt.h`

Each prompting function comes in two forms, one using `operator >>` for input, the other using `getline`. For example, functions `PromptRange` and `PromptInRange` both request integer input in a specific range, though the latter reads an entire line of text while the former reads only the first string. All the functions read strings and convert to the type requested, such as `int` or `double`.

Program G.1 prompt.h

```
#ifndef _PROMPT_H
#define _PROMPT_H

#include <string>
using namespace std;

// facilitates prompting for int, double or string
//
// each function has a PromptInXXX equivalent that reads a line of
// text
//
// PromptRange: used for int or double entry
//
// int PromptRange(const string & prompt,int low, int high)
//                           -- returns int in range [low..high]
// Example:
//   int x = PromptRange("enter weekday",1,7);
//
// generates prompt: enter weekday between 1 and 7
//
// double PromptRange(const string & prompt,double low, double high)
//                           -- returns int in range [low..high]
// Example:
//   double d = PromptRange("enter value",0.5,1.5);
//
// generates prompt: enter value between 0.5 and 1.5
//
// const string & promptString(const string & prompt)
//                           -- returns a string
// Example:
//   string filename = PromptString("enter file name");
//
// bool PromptYesNo(const string & prompt)
```

```
//                                   -- returns true iff user enter yes
// (or any string beginning with y, only strings beginning with y or
//   n are accepted)
//
// Example:
//    if (PromptYesNo("continue?"))
//        DoStuff();
//    else
//        Quit();

long int PromptRange(const string & prompt,long int low, long int high);
// precondition: low <= high
// postcondition: returns a value between low and high (inclusive)

long int PromptlnRange(const string & prompt,long int low, long int high);
// precondition: low <= high
// postcondition: returns a value between low and high (inclusive)
//                reads an entire line

int PromptRange(const string & prompt,int low, int high);
// precondition: low <= high
// postcondition: returns a value between low and high (inclusive)

int PromptlnRange(const string & prompt,int low, int high);
// precondition: low <= high
// postcondition: returns a value between low and high (inclusive)
//                reads an entire line

double PromptRange(const string & prompt,double low, double high);
// precondition: low <= high
// postcondition: returns a value between low and high (inclusive)

double PromptlnRange(const string & prompt,double low, double high);
// precondition: low <= high
// postcondition: returns a value between low and high (inclusive)
//                reads an entire line

string PromptString(const string & prompt);
// postcondition: returns string entered by user

string PromptlnString(const string & prompt);
// postcondition: returns string entered by user, reads entire line

bool PromptYesNo(const string & prompt);
// postcondition: returns true iff user enters "yes" (any string with
//                'y' as first letter, only 'y' and 'n' strings accepted)

bool PromptlnYesNo(const string & prompt);
// postcondition: returns true iff user enters "yes" (any string with
//                'y' as first letter, only 'y' and 'n' strings accepted)
//                reads entire line
#endif
```

G.2.2 The Class Date

Program G.2 date.h

```
#ifndef _DATE_H
#define _DATE_H

/***********************************************************************
This code is freely distributable and modifiable providing you
leave this notice in it.
Copyright @ Owen Astrachan
***********************************************************************/
#include <iostream>
#include <string>
using namespace std;

// a class for manipulating dates
//
// Date class represents a date in the Gregorian calendar
// works only for dates after October, 1752
//
// attempts to construct invalid dates, e.g., 15 month,
// or 38th day result in month == 1, day == 1.  years aren't checked
// for validity
//
// Date()                --- construct default date (today)
// Date(long days)       --- construct date given absolute # of days from
//                           1 A.D., e.g., 710,347 = November 12, 1945
//
// Date(int m,int d,int y) --- constructor requires three parameters:
//                           month, day, year, e.g.,
//                           Date d(4,8,1956); initializes d to represent
//                           the date April 8, 1956.  Full year is required
//
//
// int Month()           --- return, respectively, month, day, and year
// int Day()                 corresponding to date with 1 = january,
// int Year()                2 = february, ... 12 = december
//
//
// string DayName()      --- return string corresponding to day of week
//                           either "Monday", "Tuesday", ... "Sunday"
// string MonthName()    --- return string corresponding to month
//                           either "January", "February",..."December"
//
// int DaysIn()          --- return number of days in month
//
//
// long Absolute() --- returns absolute # of date assuming
//                           that Jan 1, 1 AD is day 1.  Has property
//                           that Absolute() % 7 = k, where k = 0 is sunday
//                           k = 1 is monday, ... k = 6 is saturday
//
```

```
// string ToString()  -- returns string version of date, e.g.,
//                     -- d.SetDate(11,23,1963); then d.ToString()
//                        returns string "November 23 1963"
// *************************************************
//        arithmetic operators for dates
// *************************************************
//
// dates support some addition and subtraction operations
//
// Date d(1,1,1960);         // 1960 is a leap year
// d++;                      // d represents January 2, 1960
// d--;                      // d is back to January 1, 1960
// d += 31;                  // d is February 1, 1960
// d -= 32;                  // d is December 31, 1959
// Date d2 = d + 1;          // d2 is January 1, 1960
// Date d3 = 365 + d2;       // d3 is December 31, 1961
// Date d4 = d - 1;          // d4 is December 30, 1959
//
// *************************************************
class Date
{
  public:
              // constructors
    Date();                         // construct date with default value
    Date(long days);        // construct date from absolute #
    Date(int m,int d,int y);       // construct date with specified values

              // accessor functions

    int Month()           const;    // return month corresponding to date
    int Day()             const;    // return day corresponding to date
    int Year()            const;    // return year corresponding to date
    int DaysIn()          const;    // return # of days in month
    string DayName()      const;    // "monday", "tuesday", ... or "sunday"
    string MonthName()    const;    // "january","february",... or "december"
    long Absolute()       const;    // number of days since 1 A.D. for date
    string ToString()     const;    // returns string for date in ascii

    bool Equal(const Date & rhs) const;  // for implementing <, >, etc
    bool Less(const Date & rhs) const;

    // mutator functions

    Date operator ++(int);          // add one day, postfix operator
    Date operator --(int);          // subtract one day, postfix operator
    Date& operator +=(long dx);     // add dx, e.g., jan 1 + 31 = feb 1
    Date& operator -=(long dx);     // subtract dx, e.g., jan 1 - 1 = dec 31

  private:

    int myDay;                      // day of week, 0-6
    int myMonth;                    // month, 0-11
    int myYear;                     // year in four digits, e.g., 1899

    void CheckDate(int m, int d, int y); // make sure that date is valid
```

```
};

Date operator + (const Date & d, long dx);    // add dx to date d
Date operator + (long dx, const Date & d);    // add dx to date d
Date operator - (const Date & d, long dx);    // subtract dx from date d
long operator - (const Date & lhs, const Date & rhs);

ostream & operator << (ostream & os, const Date & d);
bool operator == (const Date & lhs, const Date & rhs);
bool operator != (const Date & lhs, const Date & rhs);
bool operator <  (const Date & lhs, const Date & rhs);
bool operator >  (const Date & lhs, const Date & rhs);
bool operator <= (const Date & lhs, const Date & rhs);
bool operator >= (const Date & lhs, const Date & rhs);

#endif
```
date.h

G.2.3　The Class Dice

Changes from the first-edition code include making accessor functions const and moving the random number generator from *dice.h* to *dice.cpp*.

<hr>

Program G.3　dice.h

```
#ifndef _DICE_H
#define _DICE_H

//   class for simulating a die (object "rolled" to generate
//                             a random number)
//
//   Dice(int sides) -- constructor, sides specifies number of "sides"
//                 for the die, e.g., 2 is a coin, 6 is a 'regular' die
//
//   int Roll() -- returns the random "roll" of the die, a uniformly
//                 distributed random number between 1 and # sides
//
//   int NumSides() -- access function, returns # of sides
//
//   int NumRolls() -- access function, returns # of times Roll called
//                    for an instance of the class

class Dice
{
  public:
    Dice(int sides);          // constructor
    int Roll();               // return the random roll
    int NumSides() const;     // how many sides this die has
    int NumRolls() const;     // # times this die rolled

  private:
    int myRollCount;          // # times die rolled
    int mySides;              // # sides on die
```

```
};

#endif    /* _DICE_H not defined */
```

G.2.4 The Class RandGen

Program G.4   randgen.h

```
#ifndef _RANDGEN_H
#define _RANDGEN_H

#include <limits.h>                    // for INT_MAX

// designed for implementation-independent randomization
// if all system-dependent calls included in this class, then
// other classes can make use of this class in independent manner
// all random numbers are uniformly distributed in given range
//
// RandGen() ---       constructor sets seed of random # generator
//                     once per program, not per class/object
//
// RandInt(int max)
// RandInt(int low,int max) - return random integer in range [0..max)
//                     when one parameter used, [low..max] when
//                     two parameters used
//
//        examples:    rnd.RandInt(6) is random integer [0..5] or [0..6]
//                     rnd.RandInt(3,10) is random integer [3..10]
//                     rnd.RandInt()  is random integer [0..INT_MAX)
//
// RandReal()       -- returns random double in range [0..1)
// RandReal(double low, double max) -- random double in range [low..max)

class RandGen
{
  public:
    RandGen();                          // set seed for all instances
    int RandInt(int max = INT_MAX);    // returns int in [0..max)
    int RandInt(int low, int max);     // returns int in [low..max]
    double RandReal();                  // returns double in [0..1)
    double RandReal(double low, double max); // range [low..max]

    static void SetSeed(int seed);      // static (per class) seed set
private:
    static int ourInitialized;          // for 'per-class' initialization
};
```

```
#endif
```

G.2.5 The Class `CTimer`

Program G.5 ctimer.h

```
#ifndef _CTIMER_H
#define _CTIMER_H

// a class that can be used to "time" parts of programs
// or as a general timer
//
// operations are:
//
//      Start() : starts the timer
//      Stop()  : stops the timer
//      ElapsedTime() : returns the elapsed time between
//                      start and the last stop
//      CumulativeTime(): returns cumulative total of all
//                        "laps" (timed intervals), i.e., sum of
//                        calls to ElapsedTime
//      Reset()      : resets cumulative time to 0
//                     so "removes" history of timer
//
//

class CTimer{
  public:
    CTimer();                        // constructor
    void Reset();                    // reset timer to 0
    void Start();                    // begin timing
    void Stop();                     // stop timing
    double ElapsedTime();            // between last start/stop
    double CumulativeTime();         // total of all times since reset
  private:
    long myStartTime,myEndTime;
    double myElapsed;                // time since start and last stop
    double myCumulative;             // cumulative of all "lap" times
};

#endif      // _CTIMER_H not defined
```

ctimer.h

G.2.6 The Class `WordStreamIterator`

Changes from the first edition include renaming the iterator functions.

Program G.6 worditer.h

```
#ifndef _WORDSTREAMITERATOR_H
#define _WORDSTREAMITERATOR_H

// Owen Astrachan 7/3/95, modified 4/9/99
```

```
//
// class WordStreamIterator
//
// void Open(string name)
//          -- initializes iterator to file specified by name
//
// void Init(), void Next(), bool HasMore()
//          -- "standard" iterating functions (see below)
//
// usage: call Init(), before accessing Current()
//          call Next() to move to  the next word in the stream
//          call Current() to access the current word
//          call HasMore() to determine if Current() is valid
//
// string Current()
//          -- returns current string (see below)
//
// WordStreamIterator iter;
// iter.Open("testfile.dat");
// for(iter.Init(); iter.HasMore(); iter.Next())
//     cout << iter.Current() << endl;
//
//

#include <string>
#include <fstream>
using namespace std;

class WordStreamIterator
{
  public:
    WordStreamIterator();
    void Open(const string & name);   // bind stream to specific text file
    void Init();                      // initialize iterator
    string Current();                 // returns current word
    bool HasMore();                   // true if more words
    void Next();                      // advance to next word

  private:
    string myWord;                    // the current word
    bool myMore;                      // true if more words
    ifstream myInput;                 // the stream to read from
};

#endif
```

G.2.7 The Class `StringSet`

Program G.7 stringset.h

```cpp
#ifndef _STRINGSET_H
#define _STRINGSET_H

#include <string>
#include "tvector.h"
using namespace std;

class StringSet
{
  public:
    StringSet();
    StringSet(int isize);  // initialize size -- for efficiency

    // accessors
    bool contains(const string& s) const;
    int  size()                const;

    // mutators
    void insert(const string& s);
    void erase (const string& s);
    void clear();

    friend class StringSetIterator;
  private:

    int     myCount;         // # of entries stored in myList
    tvector<string> myList;  // storage for each string

    int search(const string & key) const; // returns index in myList of key
};

class StringSetIterator
{
  public:
    StringSetIterator(const StringSet& s);

    void Init()       const;
    bool HasMore()    const;
    void Next()       const;
    string Current() const;
  private:
    const StringSet&  mySet;
    mutable int myIndex;
};

#endif
```

stringset.h

G.2.8 The String Functions in `strutils.h`

Program G.8 strutils.h

```
#ifndef _STRUTILS_H
#define _STRUTILS_H

#include <iostream>
#include <string>
using namespace std;

void ToLower(string & s);
// postcondition: all alphabetic characters in s changed to lowercase
//                (only uppercase letters changed)

void ToUpper(string & s);
// postcondition: all alphabetic characters in s changed to uppercase
//                (only uppercase letters changed)

void StripPunc(string & s);
// postcondition: s has no leading/trailing punctuation

void StripWhite(string & s);
// postcondition: s has no leading/trailing white space

string LowerString(const string & s);
// postcondition: return lowercase equivalent of s

string UpperString(const string & s);
// postcondition: return uppercase equivalent of s


int atoi(const string & s);        // returns int equivalent
double atof(const string & s);     // returns double equivalent
string itoa(int n);                // returns string equivalent
string tostring(int n);            // like itoa, convert int to string
string tostring(double d);         // convert double to string

#endif
```
strutils.h

G.2.9 The Math Helper Functions in `mathutils.h`

Program G.9 mathutils.h

```
#ifndef _MATHUTIL_H
#define _MATHUTIL_H

bool FloatEqual(double lhs, double rhs);
// post: returns true iff lhs == rhs
```

```
//       where == is determined by using relative error, i.e.
//       |lhs-rhs| / min(|lhs|,|rhs|)


// convert degrees to radians and vice versa

double deg2rad(double deg);
double rad2deg(double rad);

const double PI = 3.1415926535897;

// returns smaller of lhs and rhs, operator < must
// be overloaded for the type T

template <class T>
T min(const T& lhs, const T& rhs)
{
    return lhs < rhs ? lhs : rhs;
}

// returns larger of lhs and rhs, operator < must
// be overloaded for the type T

template <class T>
T max(const T& lhs, const T& rhs)
{
    return lhs < rhs ? rhs : lhs;
}

#endif
```

mathutils.h

G.2.10 The struct Point

Program G.10 point.h

```
#ifndef _POINT_H
#define _POINT_H

#include <string>
using namespace std;

struct Point
{
  Point();
  Point(double px, double py);

  string tostring()                 const;
  double distanceFrom(const Point& p) const;
  double x;
  double y;
};
```

```
bool operator == (const Point& lhs, const Point& rhs);
bool operator != (const Point& lhs, const Point& rhs);
bool operator  < (const Point& lhs, const Point& rhs);
bool operator  > (const Point& lhs, const Point& rhs);
bool operator <= (const Point& lhs, const Point& rhs);
bool operator >= (const Point& lhs, const Point& rhs);


ostream& operator << (ostream& os, const Point& p);

#endif
```
point.h

G.2.11   The Classes in `directory.h`

Program G.11   directory.h

```
#ifndef _DIRECTORY_H
#define _DIRECTORY_H


//
// author: Owen Astrachan
// date:   9/21/93
//
// modified 11/28/94
// modified  4/5/95
// modified 1/18/96
// modified 5/10/99, ported to 32-bit windows
//
// classes for manipulating directories
// provide a standard interface for directory
// queries from C++ programs that can, in theory, be implemented
// on several platforms
//
// currently supported: Unix, DOS, Windows
//
// the class DirEntry provides directory information
// accessible via methods Name, Size, and IsDir
//
// the class DirStream does I/O on directories
// it supports "standard" (for the Tapestry book)
// iterator methods/member functions
//

// ********  DirEntry member functions:
//
// string Name() -- returns name of file
// int Size()    -- returns size of file (in bytes)
// bool IsDir()  -- returns false if NOT directory, else true
// string Path() -- returns full path to file
```

```
// DirEntry()      -- constructor, directory entry undefined attributes

// ********  DirStream member functions:
//
// DirStream(string name) -- constructor (pass name of directory)
// DirStream()            -- default constructor (use current directory)
// void open(string name) -- opens directory stream with given name
// bool fail()            -- returns true if directory operations has
//                           failed, else returns false
// void close()           -- close stream
//
//
// void Init()            -- set DirStream so first entry is accessible
// bool HasMore()         -- returns true if current ok, else false
// void Next()            -- advance to next entry
// DirEntry Current()     -- return current directory entry
//                           call only when HasMore = true

#include <string>
using namespace std;

const string DIR_SEPARATOR = "\\";  // platform specific

class DirStream;      // need forward reference for friendship
class WIN32_DATA;     // defined in .cpp file (avoid parsing huge <windows.h>

#include "date.h"
#include "clockt.h"

class DirEntry
{
  public:
    DirEntry();                      // constructor
    ~DirEntry();                     // destructor

    string Name() const;        // return name (not full path) of file
    string Path() const;        // return canonicalized path of file
    long  Size()  const;        // return size (bytes) of file
    bool IsDir()  const;        // return false if file, true if directory
    Date GetDate() const;
    ClockTime GetTime() const;
    friend DirStream;      // class has access to internals

  private:

    // this is the private directory entry information
    // it is platform specific, probably should be a 'handle'
    // to a class PrivateDirEntry defined in directory.cc

    DirEntry(WIN32_DATA* dat); // from platform-specific constructor

    string myName;               // NOT full path, just 'file' name
    string myPath;               // full, canonicalized path
    Date   myDate;               // creation date
    ClockTime myTime;            // creation time
```

```cpp
    long mySize;                // in bytes
    bool myIsDirectory;         // true if directory, else false
};

class HHandle;  // forward, really a HANDLE, but avoid parsing <windows.h>

class DirStream
{

  public:
    DirStream(const string & name);  // name is path to directory
    DirStream();                     // current directory
    ~DirStream();                    // destructor
    void open(const string & name);  // open, bind to file with name
    void close();                    // close the stream
    bool fail();                     // return true if failed, else false

    void Init();                        // standard iterator functions
    void Next();
    bool HasMore();
    DirEntry Current();

    // stuff below is 'esoteric' C++
    //
    // the () method returning void * is what allows
    // the expression: while (dirstream)
    // to work [see Teale, The I/O Stream Handbook]

    operator void *() const
    {
        return myStatus ? (void *) this : (void *) 0;
    };

    // allow the expression if (!dirstream)

    int operator !() const
    {
        return !myStatus;
    }

  private:

    HHandle  *   myStream;  // for Windows
    WIN32_DATA * myData;    // for Windows
    bool      myStatus;     // if true, everything ok, else all done
    string    myPath;       // full path to this directory
    DirEntry  myEntry;      // cached, current entry
    bool      myIsClosed;   // already closed myStream?

    void Initialize(const string & s);  // private init commonality
    void SetEntry();                     // common code (Init/Next)

  // disable assignment and copy

    DirStream operator = (const DirStream & dir);
```

```
    DirStream(const DirStream & dir);
};

#endif /* _DIRECTORY_H not defined */
```

G.2.12 The Class CList

Program G.12 clist.h

```
#ifndef _LIST_H
#define _LIST_H

#include <iostream>
#include <string>
using namespace std;

template <class Type> class CListIterator;
template <class Type> class CListPrinter;

// CList is a constant, or immutable list.  Once a
// list is created, neither the list nor its contents
// can be changed.  This means new lists can safely
// share storage with existing lists since none will be
// changed during program execution.
//
// Head(), First()
//     return the first element of a list, error if IsEmpty()
// Tail()
//     returns a listi with all but first element
//     list.Tail() is empty if list is empty
// Last()
//     returns last element in list, constant time access
// Size()
//     returns # elements in list, constant time
// IsEmpty()
//     returns true if list is empty, else returns false
// Contains(Type t)
//     returns true iff list contains t
// Find(Type t)
//     returns a (sub)list with Head() == t, or EMPTY if !Contains(t)
// Address()
//     returns a string-ized form of the hex address of the first element
// Printer(), Printer(const string& delimiter)
//     effectively returns a stream manipulator, inserts the list
//     onto a stream with delimiter between elements, the
//     default/no-parameter function inserts newlines between elements
//
//     usage: cout << list.Printer(",") << end;
//
// static ConsCalls() -- returns # times cons called
// static EMPTY  -- effectively a constant for the empty list
```

```
//
// CListIterator is the standard tapestry iterator, constructed from
// a list

template <class Type>
class CList
{
  public:

    CList();                                 // make an empty list

    // accessors, determine properties of list, get first/last values

    Type    Head()           const;       // abbreviation for First()
    Type    First()          const;       // return copy of first element
    Type    Last()           const;       // return copy of last element
    CList   Tail()           const;

    bool Contains(const Type & t) const;   // true if t in list
    int  Size()                   const;   // # of items in list
    bool IsEmpty()                const;   // true if Size() == 0
    CList<Type> Find(const Type& t) const; // return l with l.Head() == t

    string Address()                const;

    CListPrinter<Type> Printer() const;
    CListPrinter<Type> Printer(const string& delimiter) const;

    static

    CList<Type> cons(const Type & s, const CList<Type>& slist);

    static CList<Type> EMPTY;

    static int ConsCalls();

    friend class CListIterator<Type>;

  private:
    CList(const Type& t, const CList<Type>& lst);  // make a new list

    struct TNode
    {
        // data members
        Type info;               // value stored
        TNode * next;            // link to next TNode

        // constructors
        TNode()
            : next(0)
        { }
        TNode(const Type & val, TNode * link=0)
            : info(val),
              next(link)
        { }
```

```cpp
    };

    TNode * myFirst;           // first node of list
    TNode * myLast;            // last node of list
    int myCount;               // # of items in list

    static int ourConsCount;   // # calls of cons
};


template <class Type> inline
CList<Type> cons(const Type& t, const CList<Type>& slist)
{
    return slist.cons(t,slist);
}

template <class Type>
CList<Type> append(const Type& t, const CList<Type>& slist);

template <class Type>
class CListPrinter
{
  public:
    CListPrinter(const CList<Type>& list);
    CListPrinter(const CList<Type>& list, const string& delimiter);
    CList<Type> myList;
    string      myDelimiter;
};

template <class Type>
ostream& operator << (ostream& output, const CListPrinter<Type>& p);

template <class Type>
ostream& operator << (ostream& output, const CList<Type>& list);

template <class Type>
class CListIterator
{

  public:

    CListIterator(const CList<Type>& list);

    void Init()      const;
    bool HasMore()   const;
    void Next()      const;
    Type Current()   const;

  private:
      typedef CList<Type>::TNode Node;
    Node * myFirst;
    mutable  Node * myCurrent;
};

#include "clist.cpp"
```

```
typedef CList<string> StringList;
typedef CListIterator<string> StringListIterator;

#endif
```

G.2.13   The Class Poly

Program G.13   poly.h

```
#ifndef _POLY_H
#define _POLY_H

#include <string>
using namespace std;
#include "clist.h"

// polynomials in 'x' (can be easily modified for
// polys in any variable, and templated for polys of ..)
//
// coefficients are doubles
// Poly() or Poly::ZERO represent 0, otherwise
// Poly(a,b) represents ax^b
//
// polynomials of more than one term are constructed using +=, e.g.,
// Poly a = Poly(5,3) + Poly(4,2) + Poly(3,1) + Poly(2,0)
// then a = 5x^3 + 4x^2 + 3x + 2
//
// Head() returns the leading term, Tail() returns all but Head()
// both return Poly objects [and return non-poly on error]
// IsPoly() returns true if object is a "good" polynomial, e.g.,
// Poly().Tail().IsPoly() == false
//
// accessors include
// leadingCoeff(), degree() for first term
// at(double x) to evaulate a polynomial at x
// tostring() -- standard helper function
//

class Poly
{
  public:
    Poly();
    Poly(double coeff, int exp);

    const Poly& operator += (const Poly& rhs);
    const Poly& operator *= (double c);

    string tostring()      const;
    double at(double x)    const;
    int    degree()        const;
```

```
      double leadingCoeff()  const;

      Poly Tail()            const;
      Poly Head()            const;
      bool IsPoly()          const;

      static Poly ZERO;
      static int TermsAllocated();

   private:
      struct Pair            // this is the (a,b) in ax^b
      {   double coeff;
          int expo;
          Pair()
            : coeff(0.0),expo(0) { }
          Pair(double c, int e) : coeff(c), expo(e) { }
      };
      typedef CList<Pair> Polist;
      typedef CListIterator<Pair> PolistIterator;
      static bool ourInitialized;

      Poly(Polist p);        // make poly from list of terms, helper
      Polist myPoly;         // the list of terms
};

Poly operator + (const Poly& lhs, const Poly& rhs);
Poly operator * (double c, const Poly& p);
Poly operator * (const Poly& p, double c);
ostream& operator << (ostream& out, const Poly& p);
#endif
```

poly.h

G.2.14   The Sorting Functions in `sortall.h`

Program G.14   sortall.h

```
#ifndef _SORTALL_H
#define _SORTALL_H


#include "tvector.h"
#include "comparer.h"

// *****************
// prototypes for sort functions and search functions
// author: Owen Astrachan
//
// see also: comparer.h, sortall.cpp
//
// for "plain" sorts, the type being sorted
// must be comparable with < and for Merge and Quick also with <=
// for sorts with the Comparer template parameter the type
```

```
// for Comparer (see comparer.h) must have a member function
// named compare that takes two const Type arguments: lhs, rhs,
// and that returns -1, 0, or +1 if lhs <, ==, > rhs, respectively
//
// search functions take a Comparer object also
//
// ******************

template <class Type>
void InsertSort(tvector<Type> & a, int size);

template <class Type, class Comparer>
void InsertSort(tvector<Type> & a, int size, const Comparer & comp);

template <class Type>
void SelectSort(tvector<Type> & a, int size);

template <class Type, class Comparer>
void SelectSort(tvector<Type> & a, int size, const Comparer & comp);

template <class Type>
void BubbleSort(tvector<Type> & a, int size);

template <class Type>
void MergeSort(tvector<Type> & a,int n);

template <class Type, class Comparer>
void MergeSort(tvector<Type> & a, int n, const Comparer & comp);

template <class Type>
void QuickSort(tvector<Type> & a, int size);

template <class Type, class Compare>
void QuickSort(tvector<Type> & a, int size,const Compare& comp);

template <class Type>
void HeapSort(tvector<Type>& a, int size);

template <class Type>
void Swap(tvector<Type>& v, int j, int k);
// post: v[k] and v[j] swapped


// searching functions

template <class Type>
int bsearch(const tvector<Type>& list, const Type& key);

template <class Type, class Comparer>
int bsearch(const tvector<Type>& list, const Type& key, const Comparer& c);


template <class Type, class Comparer>
int search(const tvector<Type>& list, const Type& key, const Comparer& c);
```

```
template <class Type>
int search(const tvector<Type>& list, const Type& key);

#include "sortall.cpp"

#endif
```

G.2.15   Header Files from Circuit Simulation

Program G.15   wires.h

```
#ifndef _WIRES_H
#define _WIRES_H

#include <iostream>
#include <string>
using namespace std;
#include "tvector.h"

// A wire has current flowing through it.
// When the current changes, a wire notifies
// all the gates listening on the wire that the current
// has changed.  The gates act accordingly (see gates.h).
//
// Some of the "gates" are really connectors to other wires.
// A connector allows gates to be strung together, but connectors
// are more like solder than real gates.  As such, connectors aren't
// part of a CompositeGate.  To facilitate finding a wire's
// connectors, a ConnectorIterator can be used to access all a wire's
// connectors.

class Gate;
class Connector;

class Wire
{
  public:
    Wire(const string& name="");
    virtual ~Wire();
    virtual bool   GetSignal() const;       // true/false, on/off
    virtual string tostring()  const;       // for I/O

    virtual void   SetSignal(bool signal);  // set signal, propagate
    virtual void   AddGate(Gate * g);       // g monitors this wire
    virtual void   RemoveGate(Gate * g);    // g stops monitoring
    virtual int    Number() const;          // which wire is this?

    friend class ConnectorIterator;         // access myGates

  private:
```

```
      tvector<Gate *>       myGates;
      bool                  mySignal;
      string                myName;
      int                   myNumber;
      static int            ourCount;           // class wide, keeps count
};

ostream& operator << (ostream& out, const Wire& w);

// A WireFactory is used to encapsulate wire creation.
// If wires are "ordered" from the factory, the factory takes
// care of cleaning up the wires when the factory ceases to exist.
// This is a rudimentary factory, there's no facility for clients
// to recycle wires and the factory doesn't clean up the gates
// attached to the wires it destroys.
//
// MakeWire -- creates a new wire
// GetWire  -- retrieves an already created wire by the wire's number

class WireFactory
{
  public:
    WireFactory();
    virtual ~WireFactory();
    virtual Wire * MakeWire(const string& name="wire"); // create anew
    virtual Wire * GetWire(int num) const;              // get by number
  private:
    tvector<Wire *> myWires;
};

// standard tapestry iterator for iterating over all
// connectors attached to a wire

class ConnectorIterator
{
  public:
    ConnectorIterator(Wire* w);
    void Init();
    bool HasMore();
    void Next();
    Connector * Current();
  private:
    Wire *      myWire;
    Connector * myConnector;
    int         myIndex;
};

#endif
```

Program G.16 gates.h

```cpp
#ifndef _GATES_H
#define _GATES_H

#include <iostream>
#include <string>
using namespace std;
#include "tvector.h"

class Wire;
class WireFactory;
class Gate
{
  public:
    virtual ~Gate() {}
    virtual void Act() = 0;
    virtual string tostring() const = 0;
    virtual int    InCount()  const = 0;
    virtual int    OutCount() const = 0;
    virtual Wire * InWire(int n)  const = 0;
    virtual Wire * OutWire(int n) const = 0;
    virtual Gate * clone() = 0;

    virtual string deepString() const { return tostring();}

    static Wire * WireByNumber(int num);

  protected:
    static WireFactory * ourWireFactory;
};

ostream& operator << (ostream& out, const Gate& g);

class Connector : public Gate
{
  public:
    Connector(Wire * in, Wire * out);
    virtual void Act();
    virtual string tostring() const;
    int InCount()   const {return 1;}
    int OutCount()  const {return 1;}
    Wire * InWire(int n)   const {return myIn;}
    Wire * OutWire(int n)  const {return myOut;}
    Gate * clone();
  private:
    Wire * myIn;
    Wire * myOut;
};

class Inverter : public Gate
{
  public:
```

```
      Inverter(Wire * in, Wire * out, const string& name="");
      Inverter(const string& name="");
      virtual void Act( );
      virtual string tostring() const;

      int InCount()  const {return 1;}
      int OutCount() const {return 1;}
      Wire * InWire(int n)  const {return myIn;}
      Wire * OutWire(int n) const {return myOut;}
      Gate * clone();

      virtual string deepString() const;

   private:
      Wire * myIn;
      Wire * myOut;
      string myName;
      int     myNumber;
      static int ourCount;
};

class NMGate : public Gate
{
   public:

      virtual void Act( ) = 0;
      virtual string tostring() const = 0;

      int InCount()  const {return myIns.size();}
      int OutCount() const {return myOuts.size();}

      Wire * InWire(int n)  const {return myIns[n];}
      Wire * OutWire(int n) const {return myOuts[n];}

      virtual string deepString() const;

   protected :

      NMGate(int number=0, const string& name="generic");

      void Init(const tvector<Wire *>& in, const tvector<Wire *>& out);
      tvector<Wire *> myIns;
      tvector<Wire *> myOuts;
      int     myNumber;
      string myName;
};

class AndGate : public NMGate
{
   public:
      AndGate(Wire * in, Wire * in2, Wire * out, const string& name ="");
      AndGate(const string& name="");
      virtual void Act( );
      virtual string tostring() const;
      Gate * clone();
```

```
    private:
      static int ourCount;
};

class OrGate : public NMGate
{
  public:
    OrGate(Wire * in, Wire * in2, Wire * out, const string& name ="");
    OrGate(const string& name = "");
    virtual void Act( );
    virtual string tostring() const;
    Gate * clone();
  private:
    static int ourCount;
};

class CompositeGate : public NMGate
{
  public:
    CompositeGate();
    virtual string tostring() const;
    virtual void Act();

    virtual void AddIn(Wire * w);
    virtual void AddOut(Wire * w);
    virtual void AddGate(Gate * g);


    virtual Gate * clone();
    virtual string deepString() const;
    virtual int    CountWires() const;

  private:
    tvector<Gate *> myGates;

};

class Probe : public Gate
{
  public:
    Probe (Wire * w);
    virtual void Act( );
    virtual string tostring() const;

    int InCount() const {return 1;}
    int OutCount() const {return 1;}
    Wire * InWire(int n) const {return myWire;}
    Wire * OutWire(int n) const {return myWire;}
    Gate * clone() {return this;}

  protected:
    Wire * myWire;

};
```

```
class GateTester
{
  public:
    static void Test(Gate * gate);
};

void Connect(Wire * w1, Wire * w2);

#endif                                                          gates.h
```

G.2.16 The Map Class SimpleMap

Program G.17 simplemap.h

```
#ifndef _SIMPLEMAP_H
#define _SIMPLEMAP_H

#include "tvector.h"

// simple map, supports (for map m):
//    m.insert(Key,Value);
//    v = m.getValue(k);    // returns default Value() if k not found


template <class Key,class Value> class SimpleMapIterator;

template <class Key, class Value>
class SimpleMap
{
  public:
    SimpleMap()
    { }
    void insert(const Key& k, const Value& v)
    {
        myKeys.push_back(k);
        myValues.push_back(v);
    }
    Value getValue(const Key& key) const
    {   for(int k=0; k < myKeys.size(); k++)
        {   if (myKeys[k] == key) return myValues[k];
        }
        return Value();
    }
    };


    friend class SimpleMapIterator<Key,Value>;

  private:
    tvector<Key>   myKeys;
    tvector<Value> myValues;
};
```

```
template <class Key,class Value>
class SimpleMapIterator
{
  public:
    SimpleMapIterator(const SimpleMap<Key,Value>& map)
      : myMap(map),
        myIndex(-1)
    { }
    void Init()
    {    myIndex = 0;
    }
    bool HasMore()
    {    return myIndex < myMap.myKeys.size();
    }
    bool Next()
    {    myIndex++;
    }
    Key Current()
    {    return myMap.myKeys[myIndex];
    }
  private:
    const SimpleMap<Key,Value>& myMap;
    int                myIndex;
};

#endif
```

simplemap.h

How to: Use the Graphics Classes in `canvas.h`

H

 ## H.1 The Graphics Library: TOOGL 1.0

The documentation in this section describes version 1.0 of TOOGL, the Tapestry Object-Oriented Graphics Library (for Exploring and Experimenting).[1]

The graphics library consists of several classes for drawing and animating shapes. These classes provide support for client programs to create and manipulate shapes and images, and for the shapes to interact with the program and the user via the keyboard and mouse. The classes are built on a graphics engine underneath them doing the drawing and event processing; the engine is not part of the library. The current implementation uses an engine created by a group at Carnegie Mellon University. The principal author of the CMU graphics engine is Geoff Washburn; the package is accessible from the *Tapestry* Web page (given below).

The current TOOGL classes are fully functional but may evolve as they're more extensively used. In particular, the origin is currently fixed in the upper-left corner, with x-coordinates increasing to the right and y-coordinates increasing down the screen. Coordinates are expressed in pixels rather than in an absolute measure like centimeters. In the future the ability to choose the coordinate system will become part of the TOOGL classes, and coordinates will be specified in centimeters or inches.

If you're reading this as part of *A Computer Science Tapestry*, the pictures of the screen images created by the graphics classes will be in black and white. For full-color pictures and a much more extensive set of examples, including animations rather than still screen captures, see the supporting Web pages at the following URL:

```
http://www.cs.duke.edu/csed/tapestry
```

The programs and examples in this How to show the functionality of the graphics classes by using language features like arrays/vectors and inheritance. It's possible, however, to introduce every C++ concept with a graphical example, so that the first graphics programs might have no control statements, just shapes drawn on a canvas. Again, for a fuller treatment see the Web site for the book.

---

[1]TOOGL is pronounced too-gull, not too-gee-ell.

H.2 Using the `Canvas` Class

The basic window for drawing with TOOGL is an instance of the class `Canvas`, accessible by using `#include"canvas.h"`. A `Canvas` object is not double buffered, and is intended for drawing shapes or figures once rather than as part of an animation. For drawing, redrawing, and animation, use the class `AnimatedCanvas` described in Section H.3.

H.2.1 Canvas Basics

You construct a `Canvas` object by specifying its width, height, and distance in the x- and y-direction of the upper-left corner of the canvas from the upper-left corner of the screen; constructor parameters are integers. Any number of `Canvas` objects can be created in the same program. When a `Canvas` object is used, the standard console window is still visible, and all standard output streams are functional, so text and graphical output can be easily mixed. However, if the console window covers part of a `Canvas`

> **Syntax: Canvas constructor**
>
> `Canvas can(width, height, x, y);`

window, the `Canvas` window may be erased when the console window is moved. To ensure that all windows in a program are visible, the first `Canvas` created in a program displays the message "click with mouse to begin." Before clicking, you should move windows so that they don't overlap, ensuring that the console window won't erase any part of a `Canvas` window.

H.2.2 Drawing Styles, and Colors

Program H.1, *circles.cpp*, draws seven circles, each in a different color. Circles are drawn in a filled style, in which the entire circle is filled with a color, and a frame style, in which just the outline of the circle is drawn. As the output of *circles.cpp* in Figure H.1 shows, the default style of drawing uses filled figures, as though `Canvas::SetFilled()` had been explicitly called. The circles on the left of Figure H.1 are filled, while the circles on the right are framed, because the method `Canvas::SetFrame()` changes the drawing style just before the circles on the right are drawn. The largest-radius circle must be drawn first when the filled style is used or else each drawn circle would completely obscure the circles drawn previously. To ensure that the graphics window remains visible after drawing has finished, the method `Canvas::runUntilEscape` keeps the graphics window showing until the escape key is pressed when the graphics window has the focus.[2] It's also possible to use the free function `WaitForReturn()` in *utils.h*, which pauses until the user presses the return (or enter) key.[3]

---

[2] A window *has the focus* when it is the active window. In most windowing systems you make a window active by clicking in the title bar of the window or in the window itself.

[3] On many systems the return key must be pressed twice.

Program H.1   circles.cpp

```cpp
#include "canvas.h"

// show simple Canvas functions, change style and color of drawing

void circles(Canvas& c, const Point& p, double size)
// post: series of circles drawn on c. centered at p
//       initial size = size (decreased by 20% for each one
{
    color spectrum[] = {CanvasColor::RED,    CanvasColor::ORANGE, CanvasColor::YELLOW,
                        CanvasColor::GREEN,  CanvasColor::BLUE.   CanvasColor::INDIGO,
                        CanvasColor::VIOLET};
    int k;
    for(k=0; k < 7; k++)
    {   c.SetColor(spectrum[k]);
        c.DrawCircle(p,size);
        size *= 0.80;
    }
}

int main()
{
    const int WIDTH = 250, HEIGHT = 150;
    Canvas c(WIDTH, HEIGHT, 20,20);
    circles(c, Point(WIDTH/4, HEIGHT/2),   WIDTH/4);
    c.SetFrame();
    circles(c, Point(3*WIDTH/4, HEIGHT/2), WIDTH/4);
    c.runUntilEscape();
    return 0;
}
```

circles cpp

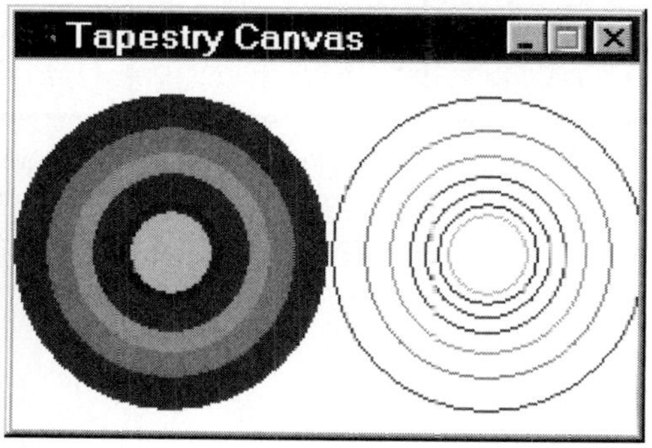

Figure H.1 Circles drawn in different colors and styles using *circles.cpp*, Program H.1.

Table H.1   `DrawXXX` methods for the `Canvas` class. All methods are `void`.

Method	Prototype
`DrawPixel`	`(const Point& p);`
`DrawRectangle`	`(const Point& p1, const Point& p2);`
`DrawCircle`	`(const Point& center, int radius);`
`DrawEllipse`	`(const Point& p1, const Point& p2);`
`DrawTriangle`	`(const Point& p1, const Point& p2,`
	`const Point& p3);`
`DrawPolygon`	`(const tvector<Point>& a, int numPoints);`
`DrawString`	`(const string& s, const Point& p,`
	`int fontsize=14);`
`DrawPieWedge`	`(const Point& p, int radius,`
	`double startRad, double endRad);`

H.2.3   Drawing Shapes and Text

The `DrawXXX` methods described in Table H.1 make lines, curves, and other shapes appear on a `Canvas` object. Once set, the color and the style (filled/frame) in a canvas apply to all drawings, though both the color and style can be changed between invocations of `DrawXXX` methods using `SetColor(..)`, `SetFramed()`, and `SetFilled()` as shown in Program H.1. Colors are described in Section H.3.8.

The `DrawPieWedge`[4] method draws a segment of a circle whose center and radius are specified. Parameters `startRad` and `endRad` specify the angles (in radians) of the segment. For example, the call below draws a quarter-circle centered at point p with radius 100.[5]

```
c.DrawPieWedge(p, 100, 0.0, PI/2);
```

Many of the `Canvas` methods are shown in *drawshapes.cpp*, Program H.2, which draws randomly sized different shapes at random locations. Two runs are shown in Figure H.2. The screen capture on the right uses the default filled drawing mode; the capture on the left uses the code shown in *drawshapes.cpp*, where the call `c.SetFrame()` uses the framed, outline style for each figure.

Program H.2   drawshapes.cpp

```
#include "canvas.h"
#include "prompt.h"
#include "randgen.h"
#include "dice.h"
```

---

[4]The `DrawPieWedge` method is called by the `StatusCircle` class declared in *statusbar.h* and used in Program 6.16.

[5]The constant `PI` and functions to convert degrees to radians can be found in *mathutils.h*; see How to G.

```cpp
// fill screen with random shapes

Point getPoint(Canvas& c)
// postcondition: return a random point in Canvas c
{
    RandGen gen;
    return Point(gen.RandReal(0,c.width()), gen.RandReal(0,c.height()));
}

void drawShape(Canvas & c)
// postcondition: random shape/random size drawn on c
{
    const int NUM_SHAPES = 4;    // # different shapes
    const int MAX_SIZE = 30;     // max size of a shape
    Dice shapeDie(NUM_SHAPES);   // for randomizing selections
    Dice sizeDie(MAX_SIZE);      // for randomizing size

    Point p1(getPoint(c));
    Point p2(p1.x + sizeDie.Roll(), p1.y + sizeDie.Roll());

    switch (shapeDie.Roll())
    {
        case 1 :
          c.DrawRectangle(p1,p2);
          break;
        case 2 :
          c.DrawEllipse(p1,p2);
          break;
        case 3 :
          c.DrawCircle(p1, sizeDie.Roll());
          break;
        case 4 :
          c.DrawTriangle(p1,p2,getPoint(c));
          break;
    }
}

int main()
{
    const int WIDTH=  200, HEIGHT= 200;
    RandGen rnd;
    Canvas c(WIDTH,HEIGHT,20,20);
    int numSquares = PromptRange("# of shapes: ",1,1000);
    int k;
    for(k=0; k < numSquares; k++)
    {   // c.SetFrame();
        c.SetColor(CanvasColor(rnd.RandInt(0,255), rnd.RandInt(0,255),
                               rnd.RandInt(0,255)));
        drawShape(c);
    }
    c.runUntilEscape();
    return 0;
}
```

drawshapes.cpp

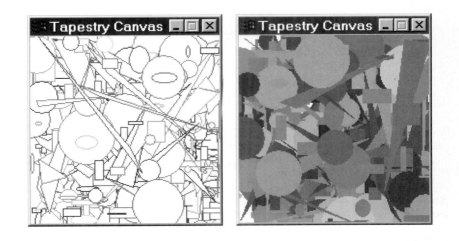

Figure H.2 Many shapes of random size and random color.

Using `DrawText`. As shown in Table H.1, the `DrawText` method has an optional parameter that specifies the font size. Program H.3, *grid.cpp*, shows the `DrawLine` and `DrawText` methods used to create the labeled grids in Figure H.3.

Program H.3 grid.cpp

```
#include "canvas.h"      // for Canvas
#include "strutils.h"    // for tostring(int)
// illustrates line and text drawing in Canvas class
int main()
{
    const int GRID_SIZE = 200;
    const int SIZE=  20;    // fudge dimensions to make room for text
    Canvas c(GRID_SIZE+SIZE, GRID_SIZE+SIZE,100,100);
    int j;
    for(j=0; j <= GRID_SIZE; j+= SIZE)
    {   c.SetColor(BLACK);
        c.DrawString(tostring(j), Point(0,j));   // draw text labels
        c.DrawString(tostring(j), Point(j,0));
    }
    c.SetColor(BLUE);
    for(j=0; j <= GRID_SIZE; j+= SIZE)
    {   c.DrawLine(Point(j,0), Point(j,GRID_SIZE));   // horizontal line
        c.DrawLine(Point(0,j), Point(GRID_SIZE,j));   // vertical line
    }
    c.runUntilEscape();
    return 0;
}
```

grid.cpp

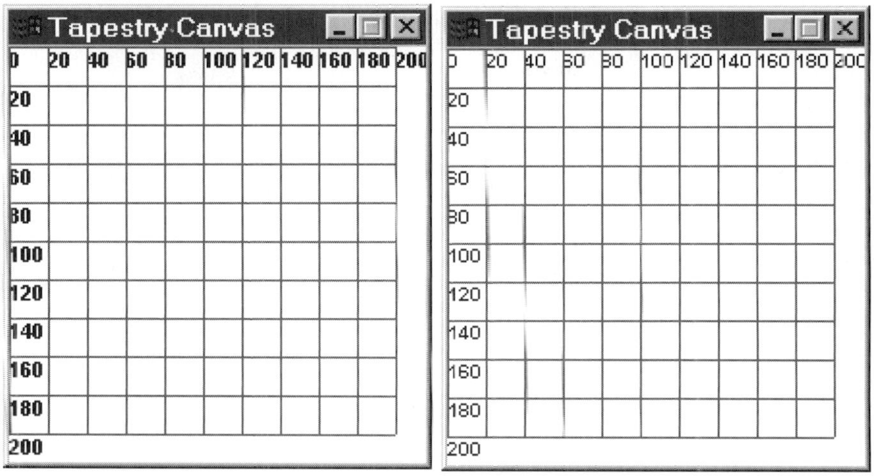

Figure H.3 Grids drawn with *grid.cpp*, on the left with default font size of 14, on the right with a font size of 12.

H.3 Using the `AnimatedCanvas` Class

The class `AnimatedCanvas` supports the same methods that `Canvas` supports[6] but is double buffered so it can be used for animations. Although both classes support the notion of `Shape` objects that draw themselves, these shapes don't work very well without double buffering.

Double buffering is a technique that uses two canvases, one for displaying and one for drawing, to make flicker-free animations possible. All drawing takes place on an off-screen drawing buffer, which acts just like a canvas but isn't visible. When drawing on the off-screen buffer is complete, the buffer is displayed on the visible canvas very quickly using an operation called **bitblt**, pronounced "bit blit."

H.3.1 The `Shape` Hierarchy

Client code draws directly on a `Canvas` object using one of the `DrawXXX` methods from Table H.1. In contrast, shapes are added to an `AnimatedCanvas`, and each shape knows how to draw itself on the canvas (using one or more of the `DrawXXX` methods). Client programs don't normally draw on an `AnimatedCanvas`, although it's possible to do so. It doesn't make sense to draw directly because each time the off-screen buffer is copied on-screen, any drawings made directly on the canvas will be erased.

---

[6]The class `Canvas` is actually a subclass of `AnimatedCanvas` without double buffering. This means `Canvas` doesn't support animations. Both classes are subclasses of a class `BaseCanvas` that communicates with the underlying graphics engine.

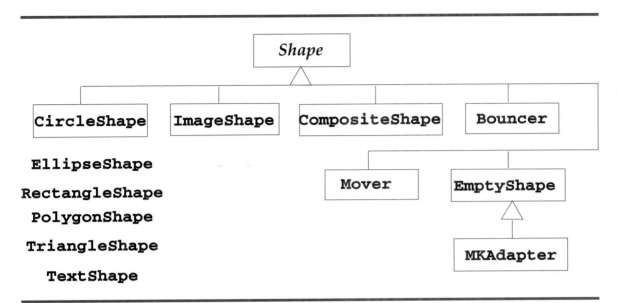

Figure H.4 The hierarchy of shapes in *shapes.h* used with the `AnimatedCanvas` class. The shapes on the left encapsulate a method of the corresponding name.

Instead, shapes are added to an `AnimatedCanvas`, which then cycles through all the shapes asking each shape to draw itself. Animations are possible because a shape can draw itself at different locations. The double buffering makes it seem as though the shapes are moving, although what's actually happening is that all the shapes are erased, redrawn at new locations, and then displayed again.

The different shapes are accessible in *shapes.h*, which is included as part of *canvas.h*. The shape inheritance hierarchy is shown in Figure H.4. The classes on the left correspond to a `DrawXXX` method; the other classes extend the kind of shape objects and the behavior of shape objects.

H.3.2 Properties of Shape Objects

Every shape has a current position, a color, and a **bounding box**. The abstract base class `Shape`, from which all classes in the hierarchy in Figure H.4 derive, is shown as Program H.4, which shows just the superclass. As the declaration shows, all derived classes must implement the following methods (they're abstract, or pure virtual, in `Shape`):

- `draw(AnimatedCanvas& c)` is the method that an `AnimatedCanvas` object calls, passing itself (the canvas), so that a shape object can draw itself.
- `setLocation(const Point& p)` sets the location of a shape object; see the related `bbox` method.
- `getLocation()` returns the current location of a shape object.
- `bbox()` returns the bounding box of a shape object. The bounding box is a

(minimal) rectangle that surrounds the shape. The bounding box is used to draw and detect overlap with other shapes.

■   clone() returns a copy of a shape. The superclass Shape implements clone to return a NULL/0 pointer, which will cause immediate problems in most cases so subclasses should override clone.

In most cases you'll first be using the classes in Figure H.4 rather than creating your own classes.

Program H.4   abcshape.h

```
class Shape
{
    public:
      Shape();
      virtual ~Shape() {}

      virtual void draw(AnimatedCanvas& c)    = 0;
      virtual void setLocation(const Point& p) = 0;
      virtual Shape * clone();

      int         id  ()        const {return myCount;}
      virtual Point  getLocation() const = 0;
      bool        contains(const Point& p) const;
      bool        overlaps(const Shape& s) const;

      virtual Box    bbox()      const = 0;
      virtual string tostring()  const;

    protected:

      static int ourCount;
      int        myCount;
};
```

abcshape.h

H.3.3   Using Shapes: addShape and clone

Program H.5 shows how simple it is to create shapes with interesting behavior. A five-line program creates a bouncing ball; snapshots are shown in Figure H.5.[7] The program creates a CircleShape, adds bouncing behavior to the circle by creating a Bouncer object from the circle, then adds the bouncer to the canvas and runs the program until the user presses the escape key. We'll discuss the Bouncer class in more detail in Section H.3.6, but the parameters are a shape, a direction in radians, and a velocity. One radian is approximately 57 degrees.

---

[7]See the Web site whose URL is given at the beginning of this How to for access to an animation, or run the program.

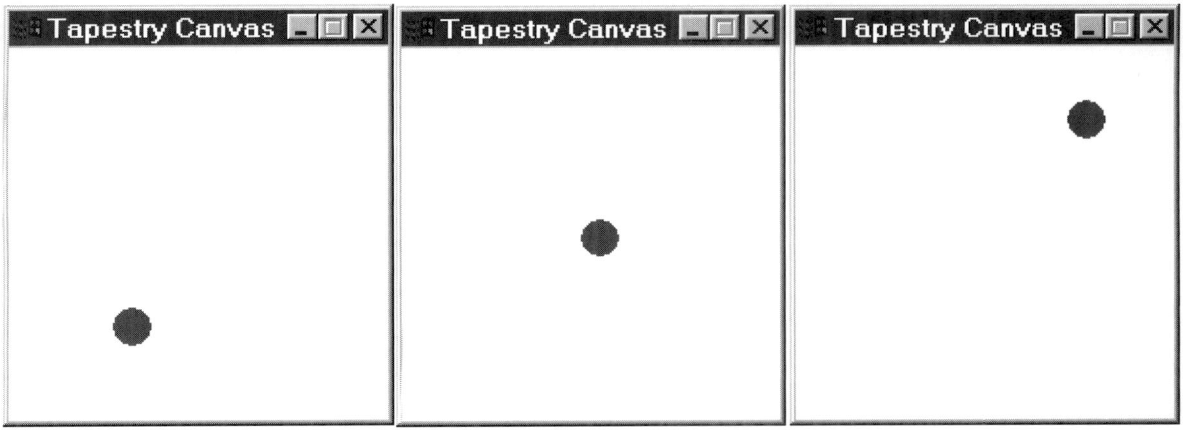

Figure H.5   Three snapshots of a bouncing ball in an `AnimatedCanvas`.

Program H.5   bouncedemo.cpp

```cpp
#include "canvas.h"

// simple bouncer, one circle bouncing

int main()
{
    AnimatedCanvas canvas(200,200,20,20);
    CircleShape circle(Point(100,100), 10.0, CanvasColor::RED);
    Bouncer b(circle,1,2);
    canvas.addShape(b);
    canvas.runUntilEscape(10);
    return 0;
}
```

bouncedemo.cpp

An `AnimatedCanvas` object stores pointers to all the shapes it contains. Client code can create shapes on the heap by calling `new`, or can construct shapes as local (stack) variables as shown in Program H.5. Objects added to an `AnimatedCanvas` are cloned if they're not added as pointers.[8] In Program H.5, for example, the bouncer object b will be cloned by the `addShape` method. Normally client programs don't need to be concerned about cloning, but it's difficult to remove cloned shapes from a canvas. New shape classes may implement cloning improperly, so fewer bugs are usually encountered when shapes are allocated on the heap and not cloned.

---

[8]To be precise, `clone` is called when an object is passed by reference rather than by a pointer. Cloning can be circumvented using the address-of operator, but this is almost always a very bad idea.

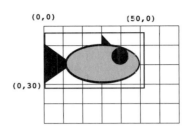

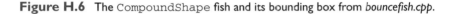

Figure H.6 The CompoundShape fish and its bounding box from *bouncefish.cpp*.

H.3.4 The CompositeShape Class

The class CompositeShape allows you to construct a new shape by combining several shapes together. Program H.6, *bouncefish.cpp*, shows how one fish is made from several shapes, then cloned to create an aquarium. Just as the addShape method clones shapes added to a canvas when the shapes aren't allocated on the heap, the CompositeShape::add method clones shapes not allocated on the heap. The CompositeShape fish that's part of *bouncefish.cpp*, Program H.6, is shown in Figure H.6 with its bounding box; a snapshot of the bouncing fish is shown in Figure H.7.

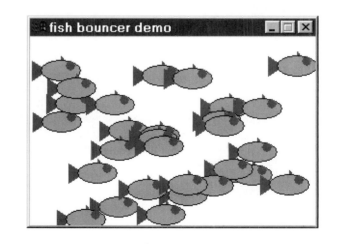

Figure H.7 An aquarium of 40 bouncing fish from *bouncefish.cpp*.

```cpp
#include <iostream>
using namespace std;
#include "canvas.h"
#include "randgen.h"
#include "prompt.h"
#include "mathutils.h"

int main()
{
    const int WIDTH=  300;
    const int HEIGHT= 200;
    AnimatedCanvas display(WIDTH,HEIGHT,20,20);
    RandGen rgen;

    display.SetTitle("fish bouncer demo");

    EllipseShape    body (Point(10,10), Point(50,30), CanvasColor::YELLOW);
    EllipseShape    bodyb(Point(9,9),   Point(51,31), CanvasColor::BLACK);
    CircleShape     eye  (Point(40,15), 5, CanvasColor::RED);
    TriangleShape   fin  (Point(30,5), Point(30,11), Point(35,11), CanvasColor::BLUE);
    TriangleShape   tail (Point(0,10), Point(0,30),  Point(15,20), CanvasColor::GREEN);
    CompositeShape fish;
    fish.add(fin);
    fish.add(tail);
    fish.add(bodyb);
    fish.add(body);
    fish.add(eye);

    // fish should start on grid, not bouncing

    const int MAX_FISH_X = WIDTH  — fish.bbox().width();
    const int MAX_FISH_Y = HEIGHT — fish.bbox().height();

    int numFish = PromptRange("how many fish: ",1,100);
    int k;
    for(k=0; k < numFish; k++)
    {   fish.setLocation(Point(rgen.RandInt(0,MAX_FISH_X),
                              rgen.RandInt(0,MAX_FISH_Y)));
        Bouncer fishb(fish, deg2rad(rgen.RandInt(0,360)), rgen.RandInt(2,7));
        display.addShape(fishb);
    }
    display.runUntilEscape(10);

    return 0;

}
```

H.3.5 Processing Mouse and Key Events

An AnimatedCanvas object cycles through all the shapes that have been added, calling Shape::draw on each one. It's possible to have individual shapes respond to mouse clicks and key presses, but it's more often useful to add click/key behavior to an entire canvas. We'll discuss methods for doing this with TOOGL.

The simplest way to incorporate functions that respond to mouse presses and key clicks is to create a class that derives from MKAdapter (Mouse and Key Adapter) and add an instance of the new class to a canvas. In *circlefun.cpp* a simple class MakeCircle is created that responds to mouse clicks by creating a circle at the point of the click and labeling the center. The radius of the circle is chosen randomly as a multiple of 5 between 5 and 30. Output from one run is shown in Figure H.8.

Program H.7   circlefun.cpp

```
#include <iostream>
using namespace std;

#include "canvas.h"
#include "dice.h"

// illustrate MKAdapter, make a circle where mouse is clicked

class MakeCircle : public MKAdapter  // stateless, make a circle where clicked
{
  public:
    MakeCircle()
    { }
    void processClick(const Point& p, AnimatedCanvas& ac)
    // post: circle of random radius created at mouse click point
    //       center labeled withcoordinates
    {
        Dice d(6);

        CircleShape circ(p,d.Roll()*5, CanvasColor::MAGENTA);
        ac.addShape(circ);
        TextShape label(p,p.tostring(),CanvasColor::BLACK);
        ac.addShape(label);
    }
};

int main()
{
    AnimatedCanvas ac(200,200,20,20);
    MakeCircle mc;
    ac.addShape(mc);
    ac.runUntilEscape(10);

    return 0;
}
```

circlefun.cpp

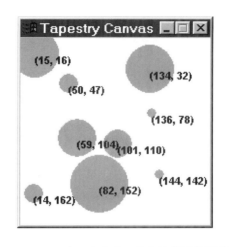

Figure H.8 Responding to mouse clicks by creating circles in Program H.7, *circlefun.cpp.*

It's possible for a new class derived from `MKAdapter` to have a `processClick` method for responding to mouse clicks and a `processKey` method for responding to keys. Both methods are called by an `AnimatedCanvas` object, which passes itself (the canvas) and either the point of the mouse click or the key press. An `MKAdapter` is also a `Shape` so that it can be added to a canvas via the `addShape` method. However, `MKAdapter` derives from `EmptyShape`, a shape with size zero and no drawing behavior. The `EmptyShape` class is often used to add behavior to a canvas via an invisible shape.

As a simple illustration of responding to key presses, Program H.8 implements a version of the toy *Etch-a-Sketch*. By pressing arrow keys, the user can create pictures by moving a drawing pen around the screen. This program uses a `Canvas` rather than an `AnimatedCanvas` because lines are drawn rather than shapes, and we don't want to erase the lines via double buffering. A rudimentary drawing using the program is shown in Figure H.9.

Program H.8 sketchpad.cpp

```
#include "canvas.h"

// illustrates MKAdapter with SketchAnEtch (stealing shamelessly
// from EtchASketch, a trademarked product)

class SketchPad : public MKAdapter
{
  public:

    SketchPad(const Point& start);   // begin to draw at start
```

```cpp
      void processKey(const Key& key, AnimatedCanvas& c);

  private:
      static const int DELTA;          // each key click moves this amount
      Point myPoint;                   // current point in drawing
};

const int SketchPad::DELTA = 2;
SketchPad::SketchPad(const Point& start)
  : myPoint(start)
{

}

void SketchPad::processKey(const Key& key, AnimatedCanvas& c)
// post: line drawn from oldpoint to newpoint in given direction
//       specified by key (arrow key)
{
    Point newPoint = myPoint;

    if (key.isuparrow())
    {   newPoint.y -= DELTA;
    }
    else if (key.isdownarrow())
    {   newPoint.y += DELTA;
    }
    else if (key.isleftarrow())
    {   newPoint.x -= DELTA;
    }
    else if (key.isrightarrow())
    {   newPoint.x += DELTA;
    }
    c.DrawLine(myPoint,newPoint);
    myPoint = newPoint;
}

int main()
{
    const int WIDTH=200, HEIGHT=200;
    Canvas c(WIDTH,HEIGHT,20,20);       // double buffering off
    c.SetColor(CanvasColor::BLACK);
    c.SetTitle("Tapestry SketchAnEtch");

    SketchPad sp = SketchPad(Point(WIDTH/2,HEIGHT/2)); // start in middle
    c.addShape(sp);
    c.runUntilEscape(10);

    return 0;
}
```

sketchpad.cpp

Figure H.9   Creative drawing using *sketchpad.cpp*.

H.3.6   Animations with `Bouncer` and `Mover`

The classes `Bouncer` and `Mover` make it relatively simple to write programs with animated shapes, either by using the classes directly or by creating new classes derived from them, but with motion behavior specific to a problem. A `Bouncer` object controls its own movement; a `Mover` object has its movement controlled by client code outside the class.

Bouncer Basics.   When `Bouncer` objects are used, typically the objects are created and added to an `AnimatedCanvas`, and then the canvas is "run" for a set number of steps or until the user presses escape using, respectively, `AnimatedCanvas:``:run(int)` or `AnimatedCanvas::runUntilEscape()`. Both functions take an optional second `int` parameter that specifies a millisecond delay between drawing cycles.

```
void AnimatedCanvas::run(int steps,int pause)
// post: all objects in canvas drawn for steps cycles
//       with pause millisecond delay (pause is optional)

void AnimatedCanvas::runUntilEscape(int pause)
// post: all objects drawn until user presses Escape
//       with pause millisecond delay (pause is optional)
```

A `Bouncer` object bounces off the borders of the window it's in, bouncing off so that the angle of impact equals the angle of reflection. Clients can subclass `Bouncer` to create different behavior when a border is hit. For example, objects could disappear from the left and reappear on the right with the same y-coordinate, could change color, or could do nearly anything when hitting a border. There are two ways to change behavior: by overriding `Bouncer::update` or one of the methods it calls. The update function is called just before any `Bouncer` object draws itself, as shown in the code for `Bouncer::draw`:

```
void Bouncer::draw(AnimatedCanvas& c)
// post: bouncer updated and drawn
{
    update(c);
    myShape->draw(c);
}
```

As this example shows, a `Bouncer` object is a wrapper around an existing `Shape` object, stored in the `Bouncer` as the instance variable `myShape`. The `Bouncer` class is an example of the design pattern **Decorator** [GHJ95].

> **Program Tip H.1:** **(From [GHJ95]) Use** `Decorator` **to add responsibilities to individual objects dynamically and transparently and when extension by subclassing is impractical.** For example, it would be impractical to create classes `BouncingCircle`, `BouncingRectangle`, `BouncingText`, and so on.

The word "transparent" here means that a shape object can be turned into a bouncing shape without affecting other shapes and it can still be used as a shape.

Client programs can override `update` or one of the four methods `update` calls each time a bouncing object hits a border.

```
void Bouncer::updatetop    (AnimatedCanvas& c, Point& p)
void Bouncer::updatebottom (AnimatedCanvas& c, Point& p)
void Bouncer::updateleft   (AnimatedCanvas& c, Point& p)
void Bouncer::updateright  (AnimatedCanvas& c, Point& p)
```

A Bouncer subclass could, for example, override just `updatebottom` to change behavior when an object reaches the bottom of a canvas. It's also possible to add behavior, as shown in the example below, from *backandforth.cpp* (this program is on-line and is shown only partially in Program H.9). A subclass of `Bouncer`, called `BackAndForthBouncer`, constructs objects that change appearance when they hit the left or right border. For example, by creating a left-facing fish that mirrors the fish from *bouncefish.cpp*, Program H.6, we can make the fish appear to swim back and forth as shown in Figure H.10. We do this by simply storing two shapes and alternating between which one is displayed depending on the direction the object is moving. We override only two of the `updateXXX` methods as shown in the code that follows. Since we're creating a new shape, we need to override `clone` as well or else the new class will have the same behavior as the `Bouncer` class because it inherits `Bouncer::clone`. All other inherited methods can be used as is.

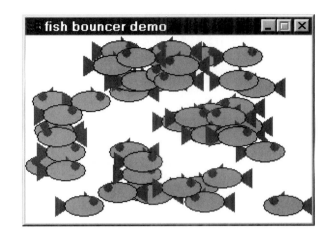

Figure H.10   Bouncing by creating a subclass as shown in *backandforth.cpp*.

Program H.9   fishforth.cpp

```cpp
// from backandforth.cpp
class BackForthBouncer : public Bouncer
{
  public:
    BackForthBouncer(Shape * left, Shape * right,
                     double angle, double velocity);
    virtual void updateright (AnimatedCanvas& c, Point& p);
    virtual void updateleft  (AnimatedCanvas& c, Point& p);
    virtual Shape* clone();
  protected:
    Shape * myLeft;
    Shape * myRight;
};

void BackForthBouncer::updateright(AnimatedCanvas& c, Point& p)
{
    myShape = myLeft;          // use left-facing shape
    myShape->setLocation(p);   // update location
    Bouncer::updateright(c,p); // bounce
}

void BackForthBouncer::updateleft(AnimatedCanvas& c, Point& p)
{
    myShape = myRight;         // use right-facing shape
    myShape->setLocation(p);   // update location
    Bouncer::updateleft(c,p);  // bounce
}
```

```
Shape* BackForthBouncer::clone()
{
  return
    new BackForthBouncer(myLeft,myRight,myAngle,myVelocity);
}
```

H.3.7 Canvas Iterator

As a final example of extending the class `Bouncer` by subclassing, we'll show how to process collisions using the `Canvas` iterator class. Part of the class `MoleBouncer` from *bouncefun.cpp* shows how to determine if a shape collides with another shape. The overridden `update` function is shown in Program H.10. The complete program isn't shown, but it's nearly identical to *circlefun.cpp*, Program H.7, except it creates MoleBouncer objects where the mouse is clicked instead of drawing circles. Two snapshots are shown in Figure H.11.

Program H.10 molebouncer.cpp

```
class MoleBouncer : public Bouncer
{
  public:
    MoleBouncer(Shape& s, double angle, double v)
      : Bouncer(s,angle,v)
    {  }
    virtual void update(AnimatedCanvas& ac)
    {
        RandGen rgen;
        Iterator<Shape> it(ac.makeIterator());
        bool collided = false;              // collision or still bouncing?
        Point p = getLocation();
        double angle = getAngle();
        for(it.Init(); it.HasMore(); it.Next())
        {   // check for collision, but not with myself
            if (it.Current().id() != this->id() && it.Current().overlaps(*this))
            {   ac.removeShape(this);
                ac.addShape(
                  new MoleBouncer(
                      CircleShape(Point(rgen.RandReal(0,ac.width()/10),
                                        rgen.RandReal(0,ac.height()/10)),
                      RADIUS, CanvasColor::BLUE), 2*PI - angle, 4));
                collided = true;
                break;
            }
        }
        if (!collided)            // no collision, update
        {   Bouncer::update(ac);
        }
    }
};
```

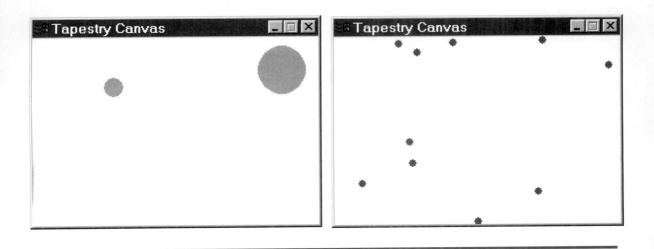

Figure H.11   Molecules bouncing in *bouncefun.cpp*.

Collisions are detected using the method `Shape::overlaps`, which is implemented in the abstract class `Shape` using bounding boxes. When a `MoleBouncer` object detects a collision, it removes itself and creates a new object that is placed initially in the upper-left corner of the canvas. Mouse clicks create larger, magenta objects; collisions create smaller, blue objects.

If no collision is detected, an object updates itself as a normal `Bouncer` by calling the parent method `Bouncer::update`. It's essential that objects avoid checking themselves for collisions since every object will collide with itself. All `Canvas` objects support the `makeIterator` method used in *molebouncer.cpp*. The method `Current` in the class `CanvasIterator` (see *canvasiterator.h*) returns a reference to a shape, so the shapes can be modified via the iterator.

Mover Basics. Shapes can be wrapped (or decorated) by the `Mover` class and controlled by client programs rather than by the objects themselves, as when `Bouncer` objects are used. Client programs must call `moveTo` or `moveBy` and then explicitly ask an `AnimatedCanvas` to redraw its shapes. This differs from how `Bouncer` objects are moved, since `Bouncers` are typically part of a canvas cycling through its shapes using `run` or `runUntilEscape`. In contrast, when `Mover` objects are used client programs usually call `AnimatedCanvas::run(1)` to redraw all shapes once.

```
void Mover::moveTo(const Point& p)
// post: mover is at location p
{
    myShape->setLocation(p);
}

void Mover::moveBy(double dx, double dy)
```

```
// post: mover moved by dx,dy from current point
{
    Point p = myShape->getLocation();
    p.x += dx;
    p.y += dy;
    myShape->setLocation(p);
}
```

H.3.8 Specifying Color with Class CanvasColor

The class CanvasColor supplies over 130 named constants for identifying and using colors. Each constant is specified using *RGB* values, supplying a value between 0 and 255 for red, green, and blue that contributes to the color. See the header file *canvascolor.h* for details, and note that the CanvasColor class encapsulates the colors used by the CMU graphic engine that runs underneath TOOGL. Part of the header file is shown below.

```
class CanvasColor
{
  public:
    CanvasColor(unsigned char red = 0,
                unsigned char green = 0,
                unsigned char blue = 0)
      : myRed(red), myGreen(green), myBlue(blue)
    { }
    // see canvascolor.h for details, all data are public

    string tostring( ) const;

    unsigned char myRed;
    unsigned char myGreen;
    unsigned char myBlue;

    static const color SNOW;
    static const color GHOSTWHITE;
    static const color WHITESMOKE;
    static const color GAINSBORO;
    static const color FLORALWHITE;
    static const color OLDLACE;
    // about one hundred more constants
    ..
};
```

H.3.9   The Class Key in *key.h*

The class Key encapsulates key presses when used with TOOGL. Part of the class declaration is shown below; the entire class is accessible in *key.h*. As the declaration shows, a Key object responds to a wide variety of query/predicate methods for determining what key it represents.

```
class Key
{
  public:
    enum Kind{ascii, escape, function, arrow, none};

    Key();
    Key(char ch);
    Key(char ch, Kind k);

    char aschar()       const;    // the key as a character
    bool isnothing()    const;
    bool isasc()        const;
    bool isfunction()   const;
    bool isarrow()      const;
    bool isescape()     const;
    bool iscontrol()    const;
    bool isleftarrow()      const;
    bool isrightarrow()     const;
    bool isuparrow()        const;
    bool isdownarrow()      const;
    bool ishome()           const;
    bool isend()            const;
    // more
};
```

How to: Cope with C++ Environments

I

The tools we use have a profound (and devious!) influence on our thinking habits, and, therefore,
on our thinking abilities.

EDSGER DISJKSTRA

Selected Writings on Computing: A Personal Perspective

I.I Coping with Compilers

Compilers and programming environments are supposed to be our friends. Once mastered, they stay out of the way and let us concentrate on the task at hand: solving problems and writing programs. However, they can be unbelievably frustrating when they don't work as we expect them to (or just plain don't work).

In this How to I'll provide some guidance on using compilers and IDEs (Integrated Development Environments). More complete information can be found at the book's Web site:

```
http://www.cs.duke.edu/csed/tapestry
```

For the purposes of this How to, compilers and IDEs fall into three groups as shown in Table I.1. Most compilers are available at very reasonable prices for educational use. In particular, the Cygwin suite of tools is available for both Linux and Windows NT/95/98, and it's free. See http://www.cygnus.com for details.

The libraries of code and classes discussed in this text are accessible via the book's Web site for each of the compilers listed in Table I.1. I realize that there are other

Table I.I Compilers and IDEs.

Platform	Compiler/IDE
Windows 95, 98, NT	Metrowerks Codewarrior
	Visual C++
	Borland C++ Builder/5.0x
	Cygwin egcs
Linux/Unix	g++
	egcs (preferred)
Macintosh	Metrowerks Codewarrior

compilers. Many people use Borland Turbo 4.5; although it runs all the examples in this book except for the graphical examples, it doesn't track the C++ standard, and it's really a compiler for an older operating system (Windows 3.1). I strongly discourage people from using it.

In theory, all the programs and classes in this book run without change with any compiler and on any platform. In practice, compilers conform to the C++ standard to different degrees. The only differences I've encountered in using the code in this book with different compilers is that as I write this, the egcs compilers still use <strstream> and istrstream instead of <sstream> and istringstream for the string stream classes. Otherwise, except for the classes DirStream and DirEntry from *directory.h*, which are platform specific, the other code is the same on all platforms.

1.1.1   Keeping Current

Once printed, a book lasts for several years before being revised. Compilers and IDEs have major new releases at least once a year. Rather than being out-of-date before publication, I'll keep the book's Web site current with information about the latest releases of common compilers and IDEs. I'll include a general discussion here about the major issues in developing programs that use a library of classes and functions, but detailed instructions on particular compilers and platforms, including step-by-step instructions for the common environments, can be found on the Web.

1.2   Creating a C++ Program

The steps in creating a C++ program are explained in detail in Sections 7.2.3, 7.2.4, and 7.2.5. The steps are summarized here for reference, repeating material from those sections, but augmented with explanations of specific compilers/environments.

1.   The **preprocessing** step handles all #include directives and some others we haven't studied. A **preprocessor** is used for this step.

2.   The **compilation** step takes input from the preprocessor and creates an **object file** (see Section 3.5) for each .cpp file. A **compiler** is used for this step.

3.   One or more object files are combined with libraries of compiled code in the **linking** step. The step creates an executable program by linking together system-dependent libraries as well as client code that has been compiled. A **linker** is used for this step.

1.2.1   The Preprocessor

The preprocessor is a program run on each source file before the source file is compiled. A source file like *hello.cpp*, Program 2.1, is translated into a **translation unit**, which is then passed to the compiler. The source file isn't physically changed by the preprocessor, but the preprocessor does use **directives** like #include in creating the translation unit that the compiler sees. Each preprocessor directive begins with a sharp (or number) sign # that must be the first character on the line.

Where Are `include` Files Located? The preprocessor looks in a specific list of directories to find `include` files; this list is the **include path**. In most environments you can alter the include path so that the preprocessor looks in different directories. In many environments you can specify the order of the directories that are searched by the preprocessor.

> **Program Tip I.1:** **If the preprocessor cannot find a file specified, you'll probably get a warning. In some cases the preprocessor will find a different file than the one you intend—one that has the same name as the file you want to include.** This can lead to compilation errors that are hard to fix. If your system lets you examine the translation unit produced by the preprocessor, you may be able to tell what files were included. You should do this only when you've got real evidence that the wrong header file is being included.

Changing the Include Path.

- In Metrowerks Codewarrior the include path is automatically changed when you add a .cpp file or a library to a project. The path is updated so that the directory in which the added file is located is part of the path. Alternatively, the path can be changed manually using this sequence of menus:

  Edit→ Console-App Settings→ Target → Access Paths

- In Visual C++ the include path must often be changed manually, although projects do automatically generate a list of external dependencies that includes header files. To change the include path use the sequence of menus below; then choose *Include Files* to specify where the preprocessor looks for files:

  Tools → Options → Directories

- In Borland, the include path is not always searched in the order in which files are given. To change the include path choose the sequence of menus below, then change the include path in the *Source Directories* section:

  Options → Project → Directories

- The include path for g++ and egcs is specified with a `-I` argument on the command line to the compiler or in a `Makefile`. Multiple arguments are possible. The line below makes an executable named *prog*, from the source file *prog.cpp*, using the current directory and `/foo/code` as the include path (the current directory is always part of the path):

```
g++ -I. -I/foo/code -o prog prog.cpp
```

I.2.2   The Compiler

The input to the compiler is the translation unit generated by the preprocessor from a source file. The compiler generates an **object file** for each compiled source file. Usually the object file has the same prefix as the source file, but ends in .o or .obj. For example, the source file *hello.cpp* might generate *hello.obj* on some systems. In some programming environments the object files aren't stored on disk, but remain in memory. In other environments the object files are stored on disk. It's also possible for the object files to exist on disk for a short time so that the linker can use them. After the linking step the object files might be automatically erased by the programming environment.

Libraries. Often you'll have several object files that you use in all your programs. For example, the implementations of `iostream` and `string` functions are used in nearly all the programs we've studied. Many programs use the classes declared in *prompt.h*, *dice.h*, *date.h*, and so on. Each of these classes has a corresponding object file generated by compiling the .cpp file. To run a program using all these classes the object files need to be combined in the linking phase. However, nearly all programming environments make it possible to combine object files into a library that can then be linked with your own programs. Using a library is a good idea because you can link with fewer files, and it's usually simple to get an updated library when one becomes available.

I.2.3   The Linker

The linker combines all the necessary object files and libraries together to create an executable program. Libraries are always needed, even if you are not aware of them. Standard libraries are part of every C++ environment and include classes and functions for streams, math, and so on. Often you'll need to use more than one library. For example, I use a library called *tapestry.lib* for all the programs in this book. This library contains the object files for classes `Dice`, `Date`, and `RandGen` and functions from `strutils`, among many others. The suffix .lib is typically used for libraries.

You aren't usually aware of the linker as you begin to program because the libraries are linked automatically. However, as soon as you begin to write programs that use several .cpp files, you'll probably encounter linker errors.

These errors may be hard to understand. The key thing to note is that they are **linker errors**. Programming environments differ in how they identify linker errors, but all environments differentiate between compilation errors and linker errors. If you get a linker error, it's typically because you forgot a .cpp file in the linking step (e.g., you left it out of the project) or because you didn't implement a function the compiler expected to find.

Bibliography

[AA85] Donald J. Albers and G.L. Alexanderson. *Mathematical People*. Birkhäuser, 1985.

[ACM87] ACM. *Turing Award Lectures: The First Twenty Years 1966–1985*. ACM Press, 1987.

[AS96] Harold Abelson and Gerald Jay Sussman. *Structure and Interpretation of Computer Programs*. 2nd. ed. MIT Press and McGraw-Hill, 1996.

[Asp90] William Aspray. *Computing Before Computers*. Iowa State University Press, 1990.

[Aus98] Matthew H. Austern *Generic Programming and the STL*. Addison-Wesley, 1998.

[Ben86] Jon Bentley. *Programming Pearls*. Addison-Wesley, 1986.

[Ben88] Jon Bentley. *More Programming Pearls*. Addison-Wesley, 1988.

[Ble90] Guy E. Blelloch. *Vector Models for Data-Parallel Computing*. MIT Press, 1990.

[Boo91] Grady Booch. *Object-Oriented Design with Applications*. Benjamin Cummings, 1991.

[Boo94] Grady Booch. *Object-Oriented Design and Analysis with Applications*. 2nd. ed. Benjamin Cummings, 1994.

[BRE71] I. Barrodale, F.D. Roberts, and B.L. Ehle. *Elementary Computer Applications in Science Engineering and Business*. John Wiley & Sons Inc., 1971.

[Coo87] Doug Cooper. *Condensed Pascal*. W.W. Norton, 1987.

[Dij82] Edsger W. Dijkstra. *Selected Writings on Computing: A Personal Perspective*. Springer-Verlag, 1982.

[DR90] Nachum Dershowitz and Edward M. Reingold. "Calendrical Calculations." *Software-Practice and Experience* 20, (September 1990), pp. 899–928.

[(ed91] Allen B. Tucker (ed.). *Computing Curricula 1991 Report of the ACM/IEEE-CS Joint Curriculum Task Force*. ACM Press, 1991.

[EL94] Susan Epstein and Joanne Luciano, eds. *Grace Hopper Celebration of Women in Computing*. Computing Research Association, 1994. HopperBook@cra.org.

[Emm93]   Michele Emmer, ed. *The Visual Mind: Art and Mathematics*. MIT Press, 1993.

[Gü95]   Denise W. Gürer. "Pioneering Women in Computer Science." *Communications of the ACM* 38, (January 1995), pp. 45–54.

[Gar95]   Simson Garfinkel. *PGP: Pretty Good Privacy*. O'Reilly & Associates, 1995.

[GHJ95]   Erich Gamma, Richard Helm, Ralph Johnson, and John Vlissides. *Design Patterns: Elements of Reusable Object-Oriented Programming*. Addison-Wesley, 1995

[Gol93]   Herman H. Goldstine. *The Computer from Pascal to von Neumann*. Princeton University Press, 1993.

[Gri74]   David Gries. "On Structured Programming—A Reply to Smoliar." *Communications of the ACM* 17, 11 (1974), pp. 655–657.

[GS93]   David Gries and Fred B. Schneider. *A Logical Approach to Discrete Math*. Springer-Verlag, 1993.

[Har92]   David Harel. *Algorithmics, The Spirit of Computing*. 2nd. ed. Addison-Wesley, 1992.

[Hoa89]   C.A.R. Hoare. *Essays in Computing Science*, ed. C.B. Jones. Prentice-Hall, 1989.

[Hod83]   Andrew Hodges. *Alan Turing: The Enigma*. Simon & Schuster, 1983.

[Hor92]   John Horgan. Claude E. Shannon. *IEEE Spectrum*, April 1992.

[JW89]   William Strunk Jr. and E.B. White. *The Elements of Style*. 3rd. ed. Macmillan Publishing Co., 1989.

[Knu97]   Donald E. Knuth. *The Art of Computer Programming*, vol. 1, Fundamental Algorithms. 3rd ed. Addison-Wesley, 1997.

[Knu98a]   Donald E. Knuth. *The Art of Computer Programming*, vol. 2, Seminumerical Algorithms. 3rd. ed. Addison-Wesley, 1998.

[Knu98b]   Donald E. Knuth. *The Art of Computer Programming*, vol. 3, Sorting and Searching. 3rd ed. Addison-Wesley, 1998.

[KR78]   Brian W. Kernighan and Dennis Ritchie. *The C Programming Language*. Prentice-Hall, 1978.

[KR96]   Samuel N. Kamin and Edward M. Reingold. *Programming with Class: A C++ Introduction to Computer Science*. McGraw-Hill, 1996.

[Mac92]   Norman Macrae. *John von Neumann*. Pantheon Books, 1992.

[McC79]   Pamela McCorduck. *Machines Who Think*. W.H. Freeman and Company, 1979.

[McC93]   Steve McConnell. *Code Complete*. Microsoft Press, 1993.

[MGRS91] Albert R. Meyer, John V. Gutag, Ronald L. Rivest, and Peter Szolovits, eds. *Research Directions in Computer Science: An MIT Perspective*. MIT Press, 1991.

[Neu95]   Peter G. Neumann. *Computer Related Risks*. Addison-Wesley, 1995.

[Pat96]   Richard E. Pattis. *Get A-Life: Advice for the Beginning Object-Oriented Programmer*. Turing TarPit Press, 2000.

[Per87]   Alan Perlis. "The Synthesis of Algorithmic Systems." In *ACM Turing Award Lectures: The First Twenty Years*. ACM Press, 1987.

[PL90]   Przemyslaw Prusinkiewicz and Aristid Lindenmayer. *The Algorithmic Beauty of Plants*. Springer-Verlag, 1990.

[RDC93]   Edward M. Reingold, Nachum Dershowitz, and Stewart M. Clamen. "Calendrical Calculations, II: Three Historical Calendars." *Software-Practice and Experience* 23 (April 1993), pp. 383–404.

[Rie96]   Arthur Riel. *Object-Oriented Design Heuristics*. Addison-Wesley, 1996.

[Rob95]   Eric S. Roberts. "Loop Exits and Structured Programming: Reopening the Debate." In *Papers of the Twenty-Sixth SIGCSE Technical Symposium on Computer Science Education*. ACM Press, March 1995. SIGCSE Bulletin V. 27 N 1, pp. 268–272.

[Rob95]   Eric S. Roberts. *The Art and Science of C*. Addison-Wesley, 1995.

[Sla87]   Robert Slater. *Portraits in Silicon*. MIT Press, 1987.

[Str87]   Bjarne Stroustrup. *The C++ Programming Language*. Addison-Wesley, 1987.

[Str94]   Bjarne Stroustrup. *The Design and Evolution of C++*. Addison-Wesley, 1994.

[Str97]   Bjarne Stroustrup. *The C++ Programming Language*. 3rd. ed. Addison-Wesley, 1997.

[Mey92]   Scott Meyers. *Effective C++*. Addison-Wesley, 1992.

[Mey96]   Scott Meyers. *More Effective C++*. Addison-Wesley, 1996.

[Wei94]   Mark Allen Weiss. *Data Structures and Algorithm Analysis in C++*. Benjamin Cummings, 1994.

[Wil56]   M.V. Wilkes. *Automatic Digital Computers*. John Wiley & Sons, Inc., 1956.

[Wil87]   Maurice V. Wilkes. "Computers Then and Now." In *ACM Turing Award Lectures: The First Twenty Years*. ACM Press, 1987, pp. 197–205.

[Wil95]   Maurice V. Wilkes. *Computing Perspectives*. Morgan Kaufmann, 1995.

[Wir87]   Niklaus Wirth. "From Programming Language Design to Compiler Construction." In *ACM Turing Award Lectures: The First Twenty Years*. ACM Press, 1987.

Photo Credits

Index